MW01622766

Ellsworth Kelly

Ellsworth Kelly

by Tricia Y. Paik

with contributions from
Gavin Delahunty, Gary Garrels,
Richard Shiff and Robert Storr

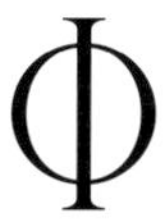

Introduction

"I'm not an inventor," Ellsworth Kelly has often declared.[1] Such a comment might sound humble, naive, or even puzzling coming from an artist whose paintings early in his career proposed an original and inventive approach to abstraction, through both their appearance and method of making. Although one of his main goals as a young American in Paris in the late 1940s was to create an "anonymous" art absent of artistic personality, his abstractions of brilliant color and crisp form are now identifiable as iconically "Kelly." Over the course of almost seven decades, he has remained remarkably single-minded and consistent in his focus, continuing to produce work that still looks new and fresh today.

However, when they debuted in Paris in 1950 and several years later in New York, his works did not immediately register as new and innovative to critics and the public in the way the art of contemporaries such as Jasper Johns, Robert Rauschenberg, and Frank Stella was initially received. While many of these artists burst out of the starting gate, garnering instant critical acclaim, Kelly ran the course slow and steady. While he made a name for himself in the 1960s New York art world, earning praise from critics and curators, he experienced a substantial delay in the critical validation and thorough consideration of his art for many years. The passage of time, aided by his longevity, has allowed his mastery of invention—or non-invention—to be revealed.

With the hindsight offered to us well into the twenty-first century, it is now possible to place Kelly in the pantheon of modernist masters that include such twentieth-century luminaries as Henri Matisse and Pablo Picasso, whose art he admired, especially the latter, and who both remained artistically relevant throughout their long careers. Kelly was among the last of many American artists who flocked to Paris, studying there on the G.I. Bill, where his abstract aesthetic was informed by European art and architecture, not only twentieth-century avant-garde movements such as Dada and Surrealism, but also those from the Byzantine and Romanesque periods in particular. He belongs to a key generation of American artists who emerged in New York City during the mid-1950s, after the Abstract Expressionists, when New York was proclaiming itself the new capital of the artistic avant-garde, stealing such stature from a Paris still recuperating after World War II.

In this regard, Kelly functions as a crucial link and transition between the early twentieth-century European avant-garde in Paris and the mid-twentieth century American avant-garde in New York. When considering the people he met during his French sojourn from 1948 to 1954, meetings engineered through pluck as well as luck, even the shortened list reads as a veritable who's who of modernism: Jean Arp, Constantin Brancusi, Marcel Breuer, John Cage, Alexander Calder, Merce Cunningham, Alberto Giacometti, and Joan Miró. Kelly may lay claim to being one of the last living Americans to have met Alice B. Toklas, the lifelong partner of Gertrude Stein. He is also the last of a rare artistic and historical breed: a master of modernism who belongs to "The Greatest Generation," the term journalist Tom Brokaw coined to define the exceptional generation of Americans who grew up during the Great Depression and then served in World War II. Affirming Brokaw's assessment of this generation, Kelly, like his army peers, has remained humble, not only about his service to his country, but also about his art.

Kelly's career spans a significant period in the development of American art, from the late 1940s to the present day, with the contemporary art scene having expanded its scope to a truly global reach. During this period of almost seventy years, he has produced an extensive and varied body of work—paintings, sculptures, reliefs, drawings, prints, and large-scale commissions—and has shown at countless solo and group exhibitions internationally, including seminal exhibitions such as "Sixteen Americans" at the Museum of Modern Art (MoMA) in 1959 and "Primary Structures" at the Jewish Museum in 1966. He is the recipient of numerous international awards for artistic achievement, such as the Praemium Imperiale for Painting in 2000 and, most recently, the National Medal of Arts bestowed by President Barack Obama in 2013, Kelly's ninetieth birthday year. Throughout that same year, a number of major museums, in the U.S. and abroad, celebrated the artist's nonagenarian status with special exhibitions and installations featuring his work.

This survey will examine Kelly's prolific career, focusing on key phases, works of art, and artistic strategies, as well as meaningful anecdotes and biographical facts. His geographic passages will be our overarching guide as we move chronologically from his childhood days in New Jersey to his service during World War II and his formative years in Boston and France, to his maturing years in New York City and then in upstate New York. My essay, in four chapters, is punctuated with shorter essays written by leading art historians and curators—Robert Storr, Gavin Delahunty, Richard Shiff, and Gary Garrels—all of whom offer additional insight into particular aspects of Kelly's practice. The book also features over 150 full and double-page images of key works by Kelly. Presented in roughly chronological order, in three discrete sections, the selections have been made in close collaboration with the artist, and represent all of his major works and periods, from his key early works to his distinctive paintings featuring monochrome panels and silhouetted shapes, from his floor-based sculptures to his large-scale outdoor works and commissions for architecture.

As we travel along, retracing the artist's own steps, we will see what Kelly meant by his statement "I'm not an inventor." Though it is a short declaration, unpacking such a curious and intriguing admission will take time and prove to be revelatory, allowing us to understand the origins, development, and refinement of his goals, concepts, and methods as the story of his life and career unfolds.

—Tricia Y. Paik

From Newburgh to Normandy and Boston, 1923–48

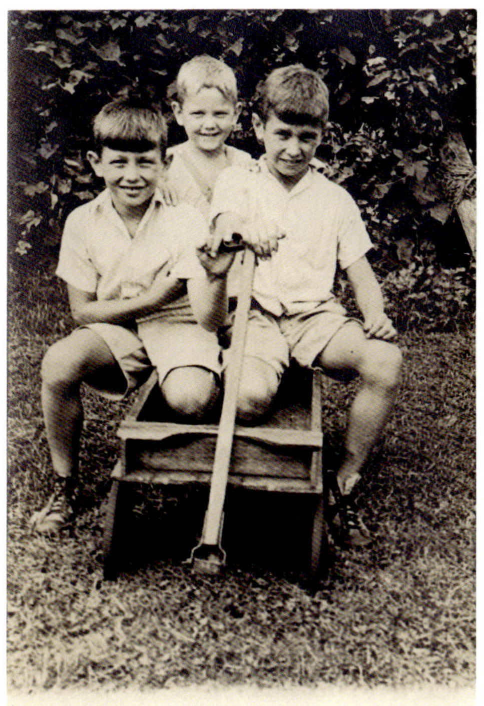

fig. 1: Ellsworth Kelly with his two brothers, 1930

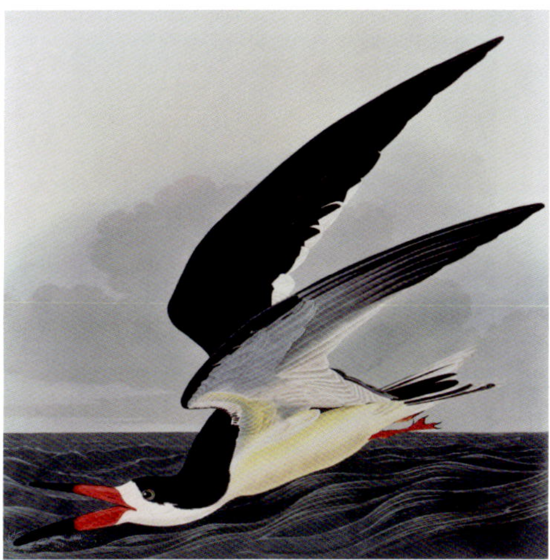

fig. 2: John James Audubon, *Black Skimmer, or Razor-billed Shearwater*, 1827–38, colored engraving, 8⅜ × 8¼ in, 21.3 × 21 cm

Watching Birds

Kelly was born on May 31, 1923, to Allan Howe Kelly and Florence Githens Kelly, in the city of Newburgh, upstate New York, an hour-and-a-half drive from where the artist currently lives. At the time of his birth, his father, of Scottish-Irish and German ancestry, worked for the United States Army at West Point, New York; his mother, of Welsh and Pennsylvania-German descent, was a former grade-school teacher. At six months old, Kelly moved with his parents and older brother Allan, Jr., to Pittsburgh, Pennsylvania, and his younger brother David was born a few years later (fig. 1). In 1929 the family relocated to Oradell, New Jersey, after Kelly's father took a position as an insurance executive. Although the family remained in the Oradell region for many years, they moved quite often, since Kelly's mother was always in search of a better house.[2]

By his own admission, Kelly was a sensitive, quiet boy who drew all the time, displaying an early interest in art. Prone to illness during his childhood years, he would develop a speech impediment later in his teens, making him more reserved. When he was sick at five years old, his mother and grandmother introduced him to bird-watching as an outdoors diversion to improve his health. The young Kelly took to it immediately, an activity that would become a lifelong hobby. Such a willingness revealed an early ability for focused and extended observation, as well as an enthusiasm for finding forms in the natural world. In the woods along the Oradell Reservoir behind his house, Kelly learned to identify local birds from their shapes and colors. During these excursions, Kelly was already honing his naturally keen eye. The artist himself would later credit his bird-watching and time spent in nature as deeply formative: "I remember vividly the first time I saw a Redstart, a small black bird with a few very bright red marks. I believe my early interest in nature taught me how to 'see.'"[3]

At age seven or eight, Kelly went to the local library in Oradell to learn more. There, he came across the work of John James Audubon, both the ornithologist's travel writings and his masterful nineteenth-century engravings of birds.[4] Such a discovery resonated with the young Kelly, and over the years he continued to be drawn to Audubon's painstaking presentation of birds. After thorough observation of each species, Audubon depicted his specimens in their natural habitat, in flight or on branches, an approach that diverged from the then common practice of showing birds in stiff taxidermied poses. Audubon's method resulted in distinctly shaped birds placed against various colored backgrounds. He often enlarged the size of the bird to such a degree that its shape dominated the engraved page, its outline almost bursting out of the edges of the sheet, as in his rendering of a black skimmer, a coastal seabird (fig. 2). It is no coincidence that a similar but abstracted approach to Audubon's amplified silhouettes would later emerge in Kelly's own painting, such as works made while living in France like ***Plant I* (1949)** (fig. 3) and ***Plant II* (1949)** (p. 49) and especially those produced during his years in New York, including ***South Ferry* (1956)** (p. 138), ***42nd* (1958)** (fig. 4), ***Blue Green* (1962)** (p. 155), and ***Green Blue Red* (1963)** (p. 154). Kelly appreciated how Audubon's birds seemed to appear cut out and in relief against their backgrounds. Later on, after practicing collage for many years, he would be intrigued to learn that Audubon, too, in preparation for his engravings, employed the technique of collage to lay out the outlines of his birds.[5]

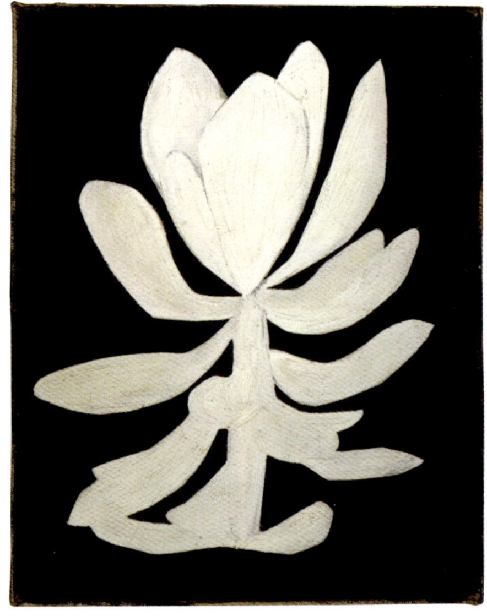

fig. 3: *Plant I*, 1949, oil on canvas, 14 × 11 in, 35.6 × 27.9 cm

Kelly's love of birds fostered an overall love of nature during his childhood. So while he spent time searching the skies for fluttering or soaring birds, he looked to the ground on which he walked, watching crawling beetles and observing how weeds, reeds, and other plant life grew from the earth. As an adult, he carried this appetite for nature wherever he went, on travels to the beaches in Belle-Île, France, summer trips to Bridgehampton, Long Island, and perhaps most significantly, his move when he was forty-six to upstate New York, where he could live among vast sloping hills, far from the congested urban life of Manhattan. This engagement with nature and the outdoors would grow into a career-long practice of drawing plants, from early Parisian renderings (fig. 3) to his iconic linear drawings such as *Orange* (1968) (fig. 5).

"Go Stand in the Corner"

Kelly once said, "My painting is about the memory of things."[6] It is not surprising, then, that besides his recollections of watching birds, there are a number of other childhood stories that he likes to tell, illustrating how his aesthetic inclinations formed early on. There's the anecdote of Kelly as a three year old stomping on a slab of butter in the house in Pittsburgh, compressing its bulk with each stamp of his little shoes in what he describes as "my first artistic gesture—to flatten."[7] There's the memory of fainting when he was about ten or eleven. He remembered actually liking the disorienting sensation of being turned upside down and not being able to recognize what he was seeing:

> when I came to, my head was upside down. I looked at the room ... and for a brief moment I couldn't understand anything until my mind realized that I was upside down and I righted myself. But for the moment that I didn't know where I was, it was fascinating. It was like a wonderful world because I didn't know where I was. And I've always remembered that vision.[8]

In that very instant the world had transformed for him into something he could not understand. The world had become unknowable—that is, abstract. And then there's the story of the nine-year-old Kelly getting into trouble with his teacher while working on a class art project. He and his classmates had been assigned to make "a drawing of springtime" on construction paper. He was trying to draw a purple iris with green leaves, but became dissatisfied with how the paper received his crayon. When he drew lightly, the resulting color was too pale. However, when he pressed down more firmly, he realized he could achieve a solid, more vivid color. But as a young boy still developing his hand-eye coordination skills, he was not able to stay within the lines. So midway through, he decided he would cut out his colored shapes. As the artist has said, he was trying to make his "first collage, building up blocks of solid color" while everyone else was "drawing so palely." The teacher admonished him saying, "Kelly, we're not here to make a mess. Go stand in the corner."[9] The thought of Kelly making something messy, even as a child, is the exact opposite of what we

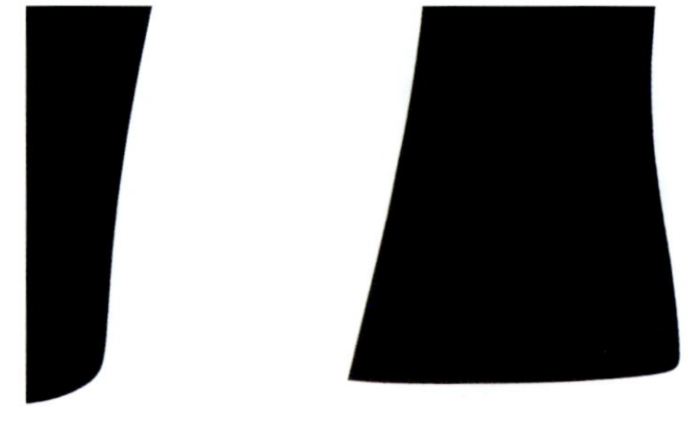

fig. 4: *42nd,* 1958, oil on canvas, 60½ × 80 in, 153.7 × 203.2 cm

would expect from an artist known and admired for sharply painted forms and flat bold color. And that is indeed what the young Kelly was already exploring. He had not really made a mess, but instead had just failed to follow his teacher's directions. As a result, he had to separate himself from the rest of the group and stand in the corner. Facing the wall for the remainder of the class, he felt misunderstood and frustrated, questioning why the teacher did not understand that he had wanted to make a collage instead of a drawing.

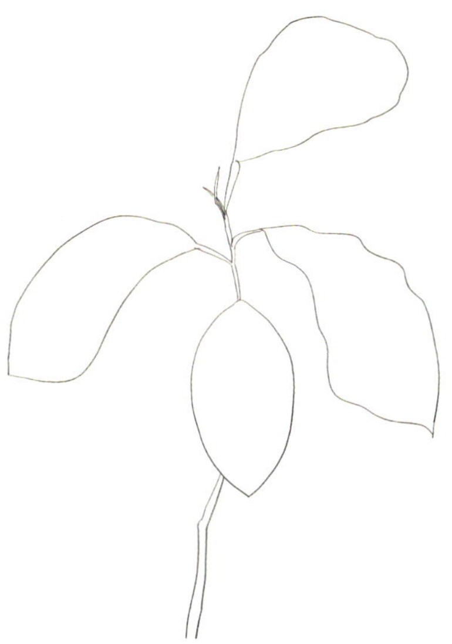

fig. 5: *Orange*, 1968, graphite on paper, 29⅛ × 23⅛ in, 74 × 58.7 cm

This childhood anecdote is prescient of the future Kelly and the formation of his artistic methods, even of the ways in which his art would later be received by the art world and resisted easy categorization. The social dynamic experienced by Kelly in school would play out similarly among his contemporaries in the years to come, as the artist remained focused on his own particular take on abstraction. After showing in Paris in the early 1950s, with works such as *Gate-Board* (1950) (p. 55), *Ormesson*, (1950) (p. 64), and *Colors for a Large Wall* (1951) (p. 69), he was quickly mistaken for a follower of the Dutch De Stijl master Piet Mondrian, a misinterpretation that would follow him for many years. Several years later, after his first solo exhibition in New York at the prestigious Betty Parsons Gallery in 1956, where he presented works made in France and new paintings from the mid-1950s, including *Black Curves* (1954) (p. 129), *White Plaque: Bridge Arch and Reflection* (1955) (p. 131), *Bar* (1955) (p. 132), and *Black Ripe* (1955) (p. 130), his abstract style was considered too European and not American enough, namely not "expressive" or "gestural" like the Abstract Expressionists, whose influence was still being exerted, yet would soon begin to wane. Just as he was misunderstood by his teacher, Kelly was miscategorized for a good part of his career, especially during the 1950s and 1960s, when he was included in a number of group exhibitions that associated him with styles or movements to which he felt he did not belong, such as geometric abstraction, Minimalism, Color Field painting, and Op Art.

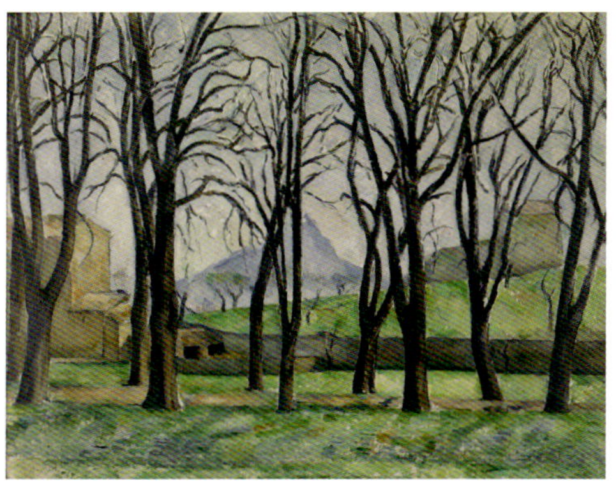

fig. 6: Paul Cézanne, *Chestnut Trees at Jas de Bouffan*, c.1885–86, oil on canvas, 28 × 35½ in, 71 × 90 cm

Though someone who liked to spend time alone, Kelly was still social enough to find a place for himself among artist friends and communities. However, he often felt that his artistic goals did not necessarily match or connect with other ideas developing at the time. Just like the nine-year-old boy standing in the corner of the classroom while the rest of the children continued drawing, the adult Kelly stayed in the same arena of activity, grouped with other fellow artists and shown in the same exhibitions, but still remaining in his own corner. He even left New York City in 1970, in part to free himself from the social pressures of the growing New York art world that he believed was hampering his creative process. And while he received positive notices when he came onto the scene during the mid-1950s and 1960s, he remained several steps behind his key peers in regard to critical recognition.

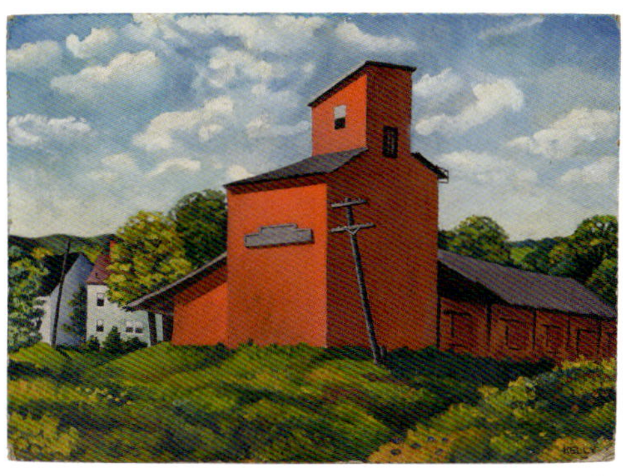

fig. 7: *Grain Elevator, Oradell*, 1940, oil on canvas board, 18 × 24 in, 45.7 × 61 cm

And it was the same way at home for Kelly as a teenager. By his high school years, he had realized he wanted to become an artist. His parents, however, did not approve of this idea, a lack of validation that Kelly would have to face until his father attended one of his solo exhibition openings at Betty Parsons and was impressed by the crowd of people who had gathered there. Yet despite not fully supporting her son's artistic ambitions, his mother did give him a newly published book in 1939 called *World-Famous Paintings*, edited by artist Rockwell Kent with an essay also penned by him. Inside the book, the teenage Kelly admired paintings by Giovanni Bellini and Hans Holbein the Younger, plus a Paul Cézanne, *Chestnut Trees at Jas de Bouffan*, c.1885–86 (fig. 6). So it was at school, except for the "go stand in the corner" incident, where Kelly found support for his artistic talents, from sixth-grade teacher Dorothy Opsut, whom he would continue to visit into his adult years, and then from his teachers at Dwight Morrow High School in Englewood, New Jersey.

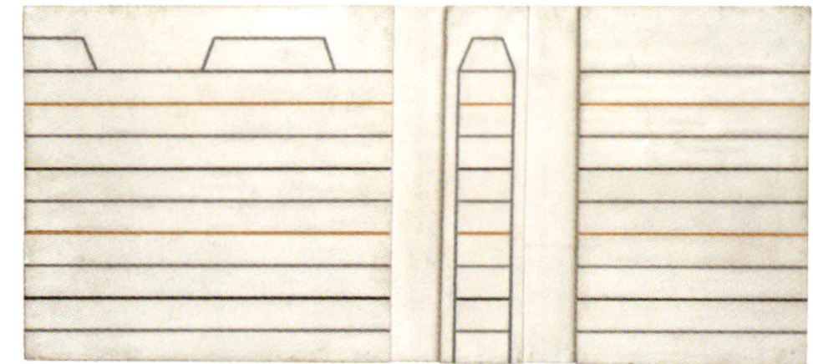

fig. 8: *Saint Louis I*, 1950, oil and gesso on wood, 12½ × 27 × 1 in, 31.8 × 68.6 × 2.5 cm

While in high school, Kelly made his first oil painting, unfortunately no longer extant. After seeing this work, his high-school art teacher Evelyn Robbins recognized Kelly's talent and began to encourage him. His first documented painting, *Grain Elevator, Oradell* (1940) (fig. 7), made when he was seventeen, displays an early confidence in the way he treated color and structure. Dominant at center, the grain elevator building commands attention through its bold red-orange hue. The young Kelly focused on the broad planes of the structure, accurately depicting the architecture in illusionistic perspective and the surrounding landscape in a representational style. Ten years later, while living in France, he would eliminate such illusionistic treatment in his paintings, instead opting to fragment buildings he observed into discrete planes, often conflating the flatness of his chosen architectural plane, such as a wall, with the flatness of the canvas itself, as in *Saint Louis I* (1950) (fig. 8). Although this painting at first appears totally abstract, it is in fact based on the unique surface pattern of an old wall on Île Saint-Louis in Paris. In a retrospective tour of the city in 1967, Kelly photographed this wall as a way to document his early inspirations (fig. 9). *Saint Louis I* displays the beginnings of his singular approach to abstraction: paintings and reliefs inspired by things that he saw and found in the world, subject matter *not invented* by him.

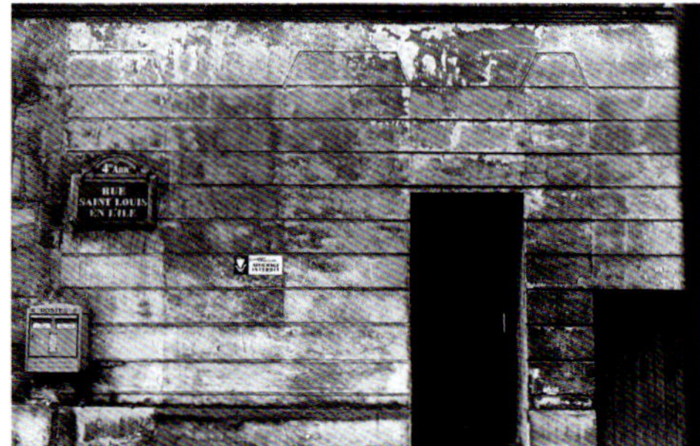

fig. 9: *Wall, rue Saint-Louis-en-l'Île, Paris,* 1967, gelatin silver print

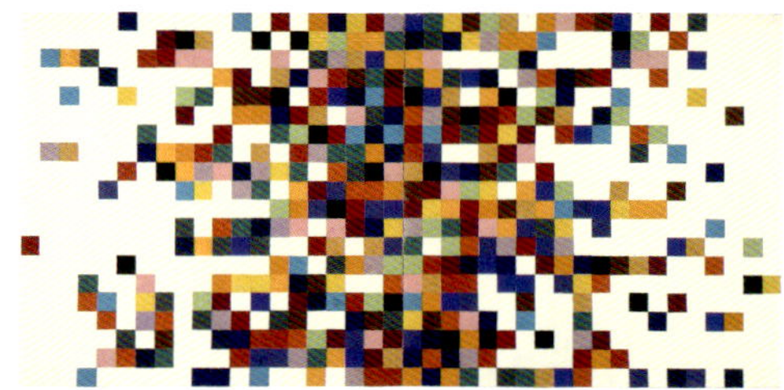

fig. 10: *Spectrum Colors Arranged by Chance I,* 1951, graphite and collage on paper, 19½ × 39 in, 49.5 × 99.1 cm

Also at Dwight Morrow High, Kelly, a handsome shy teenager with thick brown hair, and now with a mild stammer, took to acting under the guidance of his drama teacher, Helen Travolta (the mother of future actor John Travolta). In one class she assigned Kelly and his fellow classmates to memorize a speech from Shakespeare. After Kelly recited his, selected from *Hamlet* and delivered with adrenalin pumping and to his surprise and pride without any pronunciation setbacks, Travolta lauded his performance by claiming, "We have an actor here in our midst." She suggested he attend a performance of *Hamlet* in New York, featuring actor Maurice Evans. Kelly returned home, eager to ask his mother for the two-dollar bus fare into Manhattan, to which she exclaimed, "You want to see *Hamlet*? Shakespeare? FINALLY! ... I've been waiting for this all my life."[10] Yet when Kelly, encouraged by Travolta, asked his parents about attending drama school, they said no. Faced with this dilemma of theater or art, a limited option proposed by their teenage son, perhaps strategically, they finally relented. They agreed that he could attend art school, with the condition that it must offer commercial training. His mother, a habitual reader of the *New York World-Telegram*, decided that she and her son should ask the *Telegram*'s art critic Emily Genauer for advice. Genauer—who would later review Kelly's work, sometimes negatively—agreed to meet with them in her New York office and suggested the Pratt Institute in Brooklyn, New York, advice that the artist and his parents would follow.

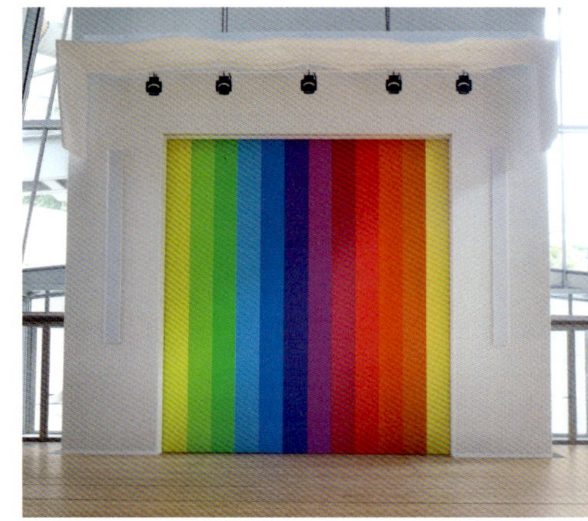

fig. 11: *Spectrum VIII*, 2014, acrylic on canvas, 12 joined panels, 250 × 230 in, 635 × 584.2 cm

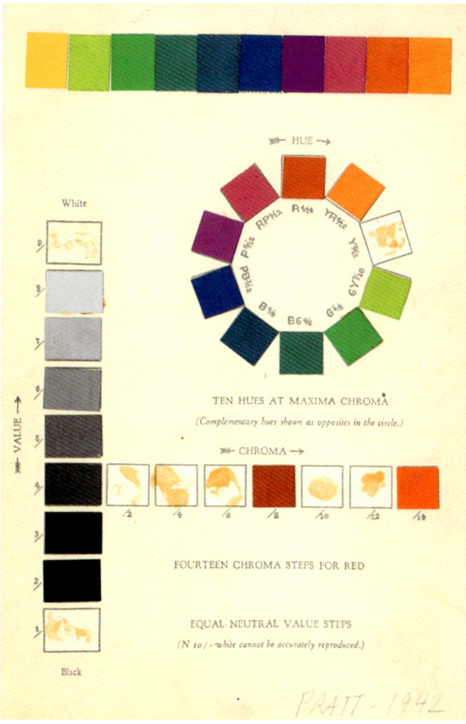

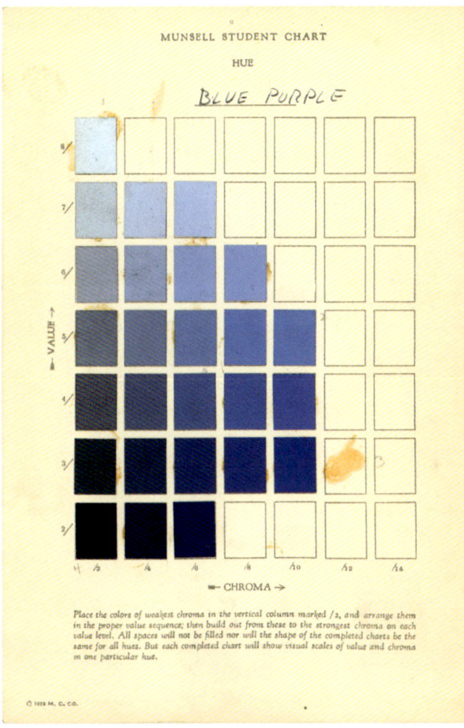

fig. 12: Munsell Student Charts completed by the artist, 1942

After graduating from high school in the spring of 1941, Kelly moved to Brooklyn later that fall to attend Pratt, commencing studies in the applied arts. Overall, he was not content with the technical training he received there, but one particular exercise did capture his interest—learning the concepts behind the Munsell color system, first developed in 1905 by artist and professor Albert H. Munsell. Studying human responses to color, Munsell had identified three dimensions that constitute color: hue (the actual color of something), value (the relative lightness or darkness of the hue), and chroma (the level of purity or saturation of the hue). As he improved and advanced this color theory in the ensuing years, Munsell published books as well as color-chart kits, which are still used by art and design students today. So in 1942, in a Pratt class taught by Maitland E. Graves, one of the few teachers whom Kelly has credited with providing useful lessons in visual design, he and his fellow students were assigned to practice the Munsell color chart, using a kit published in 1929 (fig. 12). After Kelly had executed the assignment, his teacher praised him for doing the best job of getting the colors "right."

Kelly took this assignment a step further, executing one more color study of his own devising on the first card. At the top he pasted ten color chips in a row, beginning with yellow and ending in orange. He chose chips with the maximum chroma while still trying to create an even transition of color with each subsequent chip. About a decade later, he would start his "Spectrum" series with *Spectrum I* (1953) (p. 87), yet it was here, in 1942, when the young artist made his first attempt at creating a spectrum, an act that would grow into a lifelong engagement through collage (fig. 10), painting (pp. 180–81), prints, and even large-scale commissions (fig. 11).

Serving as Camoufleur

Kelly's education at Pratt would soon be cut short by World War II and the patriotic call of duty. After listening to the radio with his family about the attack on Pearl Harbor, he knew he had to volunteer, like the other young men of his generation who felt it inconceivable not to defend their country. Kelly has recalled, "It's hard to capture the emotion we felt—even then, my older brother and I said, 'Ah—we're going into the army.' I had to get into the army. It would have ruined me if I'd been 4-F [not qualified for service]. Isn't that amazing? I just had to get in."[11]

While at Pratt in 1942, he came across an article in the paper about an intriguing army unit, the 603rd Engineers Camouflage Battalion, one of four units that would later comprise the 23rd Headquarters Special Troops formed in early 1944. Known today as the "Ghost Army," the 23rd was a special tactical army of about 1,100 men whose mission was to deceive the German enemy by impersonating real U.S. Army units with inflatable tanks and jeeps, fake radio transmissions, sound trucks, and more, often near the front lines. Greatly contrasting with the common military goal to remain concealed from the enemy, the goal of these non-combatant "secret soldiers" was to be eventually *discovered* in order to falsely tip off German intelligence, to divert their attention away from the true locations of the Americans or to make them think the U.S. had more troops than it really did. During the war, even most American soldiers were not made aware of these Special Troops, and the missions of the Ghost Army were kept secret until 1996, with many files still classified.

For this special operation, the U.S. Army recruited artists, architects, engineers, designers, illustrators, actors, writers, and other creative types. Kelly volunteered for service, requesting assignment to the 603rd. On January 1, 1943, a nineteen-year-old Kelly was inducted into the U.S. Army at Fort Dix, New Jersey. Within less than a month, he was sent to Camp Cooper Hill in Colorado to train with an elite mountain-ski corps, most likely by mistake, since he had never skied before. But he weathered the challenge, learning to ski alongside men quite comfortable on the slopes, even Olympic champions. Surprisingly, Kelly found this time beneficial as he pondered his future: "The army was taking care of me—I didn't have to worry about how I was going to make a living. Being in the army allowed me the freedom of thought without the pressure to earn a living."[12] One sleepless night, he looked out of the window and experienced an "epiphany": he realized that he did not want to become a commercial artist—"I wanted to be an artist just for me."[13] In March 1943 his request to join the unit of camoufleurs was answered, and he was transferred to Fort Meade, Maryland, about twenty-five miles from Washington, DC, allowing him to visit the National Gallery of Art on a regular basis. Assigned to A Company, he met a fellow G.I. assigned to B Company, a young Bill Blass. Kelly introduced himself to the future fashion designer, and Blass, already possessing great style and panache, replied, "Ellsworth—that's a pretty long name. I think I'll call you 'Worth.'"[14]

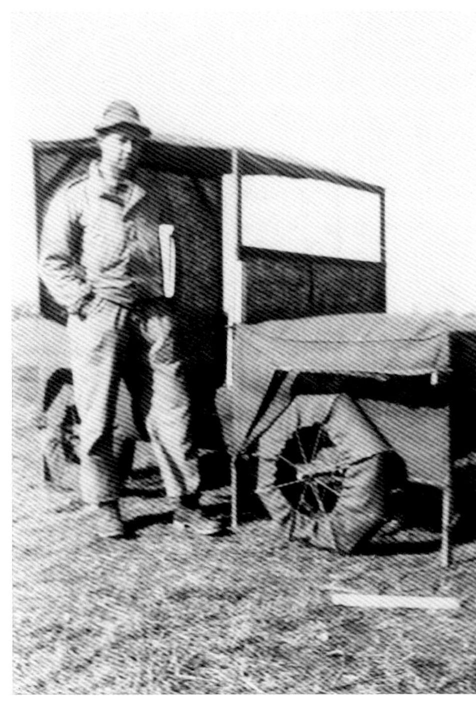

fig. 13: Ellsworth Kelly with first dummy, Fort Meade, MD, 1943

There at Fort Meade the "secret soldiers" learned the principles and techniques of camouflage, dating back to World War I. Kelly and his fellow officers learned how to build decoys of trucks, tanks, and guns out of burlap, plywood, and chicken wire (fig. 13), which were then painted in green and earthen colors, mimicking the look of trees, leaves, and the landscape. Afterwards the G.I.s were taught how to conceal these dummies with the aid of netting and other textiles. Since shadows are a dead giveaway for the presence of hidden equipment or a soldier in hiding, the privates were taught how to construct "fishnet" canopies, using netting woven with thin strips of osnaburg, a cross-weave textile, in order to fracture large shadows into much smaller, less recognizable shapes. The men of the 603rd also underwent standard military training such as drills of combat and physical endurance, including twenty-mile hikes.

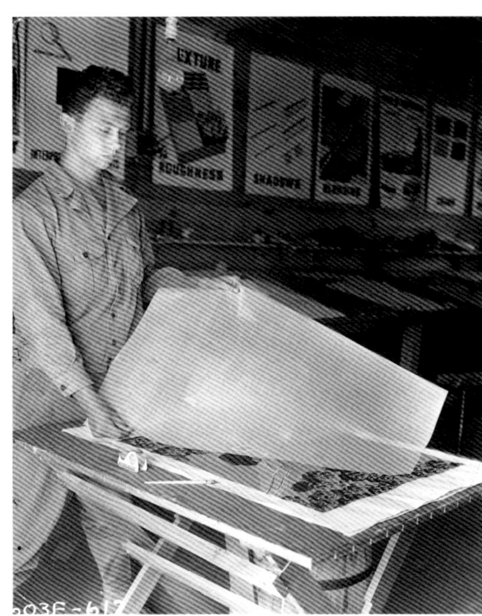

fig. 14: Ellsworth Kelly with screen prints, Fort Meade, MD, 1943

One of Kelly's main tasks at Fort Meade was to produce camouflage propaganda posters, which were distributed to the regular combatant units to teach concealment techniques. As explained by Kelly, "Out of all the guys, they chose me to make posters because I immediately caught on: we were abstracting nature."[15] Documented in a 1943 photograph of Kelly (fig. 14), the specific topics of such educational posters included "texture," "shadows," and "blending." Made using the silkscreen process, these posters featured muted earth colors. Kelly quickly learned the silkscreen technique and also cut stencils in the process. He did not, however, play a role in designing the posters. Private Kelly was, of course, the lowest on the totem pole, so his duties were only to follow orders. It has been speculated that the designs, which Kelly deemed unsuccessful in terms of both communication and aesthetics, came from the camouflage headquarters at Fort

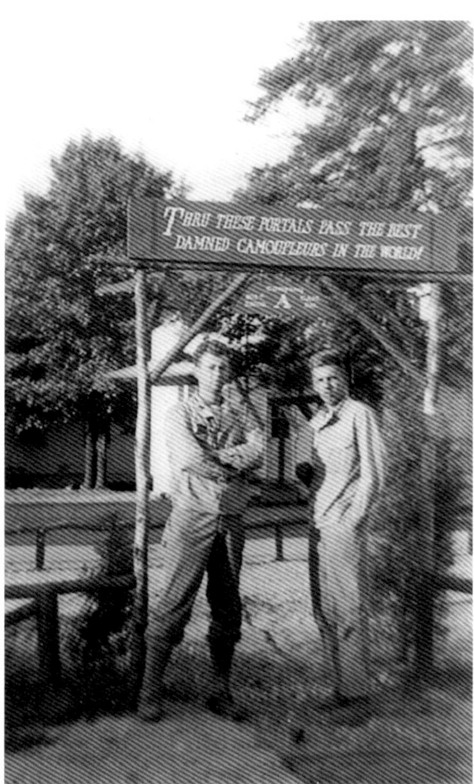

fig. 15: Ellsworth Kelly (left) and Elmer Mellebrand, Camp des Loges, Saint-Germain-en-Laye, 1944

Belvoir, Virginia, commanded by Colonel Homer Saint-Gaudens, the son of renowned sculptor Augustus Saint-Gaudens.

Several months later, in January 1944, the camouflage battalion relocated to Camp Forrest, Tennessee, where it officially joined the newly formed 23rd Headquarters Special Troops, and the battalion's mission shifted, from solely defensive operations to visually deceptive tactical strategies in order to fool the enemy. The camoufleurs learned now to fabricate more detailed and sophisticated decoys of tanks, jeeps, guns, and even airplanes made of rubber and inflated by air compressors. In the end, their imposter equipment was quite convincing. The Ghost Army soldiers learned how to conceal the dummy equipment out in the fields, but intentionally not perfectly, since their goal was for the false camps to be spotted by the Germans from the air or on the ground. While the camoufleurs were officially non-combatant soldiers, they also had to impersonate regular soldiers, functioning as decoys themselves, equipped with fake insignias sewn on their uniforms. Pretending to be on active duty at their fake camps, they were at times even caught in the line of fire. Kelly has recalled an experience in Brittany, revealing the effectiveness of their decoys as well as their own performances, when he and his fellow G.I.s were not able to deflate their dummies in time: "One time, we didn't get the call and our troops went right by us and met the Germans head on. Then they retreated, and they saw our blow-up tanks and thought they were real and said, 'Why didn't you join us?' So, you see, we really did make-believe."[16] With the three other units devoted to sonic deception, "spoof radio," and "atmosphere," incorporating theatrical effects, the 23rd Headquarters Special Troops functioned like a well-choreographed stage set, a theatrical road show, even a temporary art installation. Remarkably, Kelly, the once aspiring actor, was able to merge his interests in art and drama in the theater of war.

In May 1944, Kelly's unit was sent to England, and in June was involved in the Allied invasion of Normandy, landing ten days after D-Day. They set up fields of fake vehicles and armor to flummox the Germans who were photographing them from the air at night, while the Signal Corps, the deceptive sonic unit of the 23rd, broadcasted the sounds of moving tanks. As Kelly has described, "When the enemy forces attacked us, believing we were an authentic army division, we would very quickly deflate our 'dummies' and get out of there. Then our own divisions would successfully attack with a pincer movement. We were active all through France, Luxembourg, and into Germany."[17]

In September 1944, Kelly's unit was stationed for about two weeks at deserted French barracks in Saint-Germain-en-Laye (fig. 15), just ten miles away from Paris. The young artist visited the city for the first time, returning as often as he could. He took to observing and sketching the architecture, churches, and parks, since the museums were closed during the war, and was so impressed by this fascinating city that it was an easy decision to return during the fall of 1948 after his studies in Boston. But even though he did not get to see much art while in Paris, he continued to teach himself about art history. Intriguingly, in 1944 the U.S. Army had published a book, *A Treasure of Art Masterpieces*, which they gave out to soldiers on request. Kelly, of course, put in his request and enjoyed the paintings featured there, from Giotto to Picasso. One particular painting impressed him, the well-known *Portrait of a Lady* by Rogier van der Weyden of c.1460. Kelly admired the upside-down geometric V-shape of her transparent white headdress, how it remained tightly confined within the canvas and contrasted with the blackness of her dress (fig. 16).

When not on missions, Kelly's other main duty during the war was truck detail, ferrying troops or transporting supplies. According to the artist, he logged many hours driving across France and Luxembourg. During breaks, he found time to draw, carrying sketchbooks wherever he went, of which only a few remain. Like other camoufleurs, Kelly bought art supplies whenever he was able. His abstract aesthetic had not yet formed, so he continued to draw realistically, sketches of other G.I.s, self-portraits, children, and civilians on stops along the way. Other sketches, despite being dashed off during quick breaks, provide telling hints about the way in which Kelly was already observing and registering the empirical world.

For one small pencil sketch from 1944 (fig. 17), Kelly drew a quick linear rendering of fields into his pocket-sized spiral notebook, with areas of hatched pencil marks to denote darker areas. Although it might look like a run-of-the-mill sketch, what is distinctive is the way in which Kelly identified the specific colors that he saw in the fields before him, labeling areas throughout the notebook page, such as "ochre," "lite yellow," and "purplish green." Despite his duties as a soldier, he remained attuned to his growing artistic instincts. Here, he was beginning to filter what he saw simply in terms of color. Such a sketch is also distinctive for its historical location, since it was drawn at a location south of Bastogne, the Belgian town where part of the Battle of the Bulge was waged at the tail end of 1944. Kelly's company, as well as the rest of the Special Troops, however, did not serve in this bloodiest of battles; at the start of the siege of Bastogne, the Special Troops were ordered away to Verdun on December 21.

Near the end of the war, during spring 1945, Kelly was on one of his truck assignments. His task was to transport fresh replacements to the German front, for the Battle of the Rhine. Ordered to wait until complete dark, he went to the back of the truck to inspect the troops, all green and fearful. Having the time to do so, he began to draw, noticing how these scared boys were huddled together, visible through the opening of the rear of the truck. In that moment, what he saw transformed into a haunting visual metaphor. The back of the truck looked like a coffin with the frightened boys inside appearing already dead (fig. 18). The order was then called for Kelly to head out. With the drawing left unfinished, he drove them to their destination and watched them march away in line. He would find out later that they were killed in their first fire; he, like his fellow G.I.s, was incensed that the replacements had been ordered to the front without proper training. Though done quickly, this wartime sketch is prophetic of Kelly's future focus on specific shapes in the world, which he singled out in his studies and final paintings, reliefs, and sculptures. The opening of the truck is the dominant shape in this 1945 sketch, emphasized by the shaded areas and the dense rendering of the cramped soldiers inside. This compressed treatment prefigures the way in which Kelly would abut his forms close to the edges of many of his canvases,

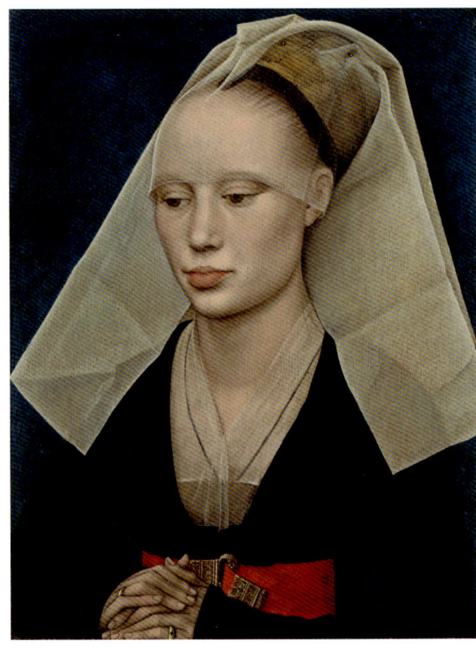

fig. 16: Rogier van der Weyden, *Portrait of a Lady*, c.1460, oil on panel, $13\frac{3}{8} \times 10\frac{1}{16}$ in, 34 × 25.4 cm

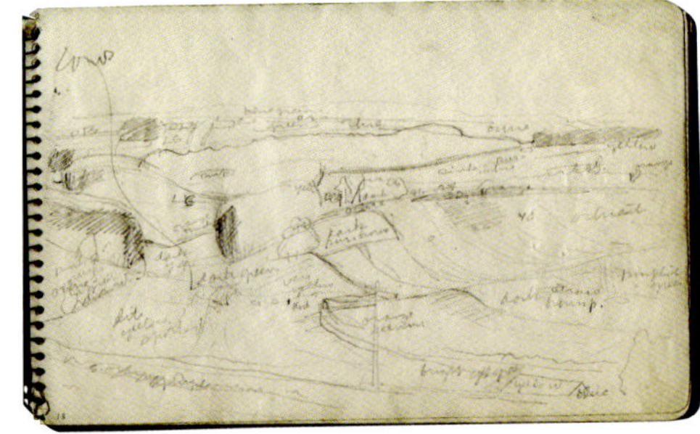

fig. 17: *South of Bastogne* (from sketchbook 1), 1944, graphite on paper, $5\frac{1}{4} \times 8\frac{1}{4}$ in, 13.3 × 21 cm

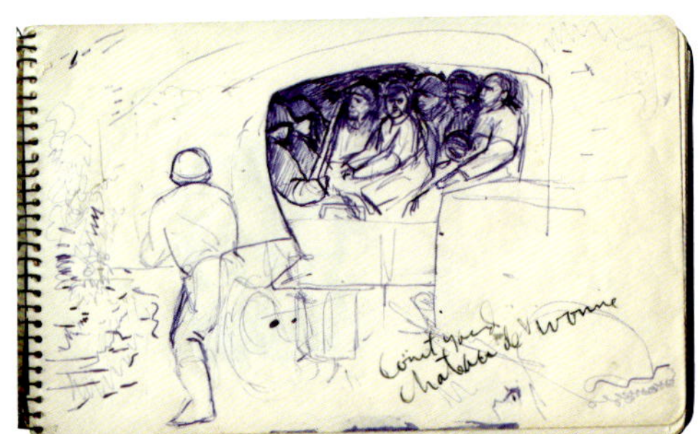

fig. 18: *Young Soldiers Being Transported to the Front, Remagen, Courtyard, Château de Divonne, France* (from sketchbook 2), 1945, ink on paper, $5\frac{1}{4} \times 8\frac{1}{4}$ in, 13.3 × 21 cm

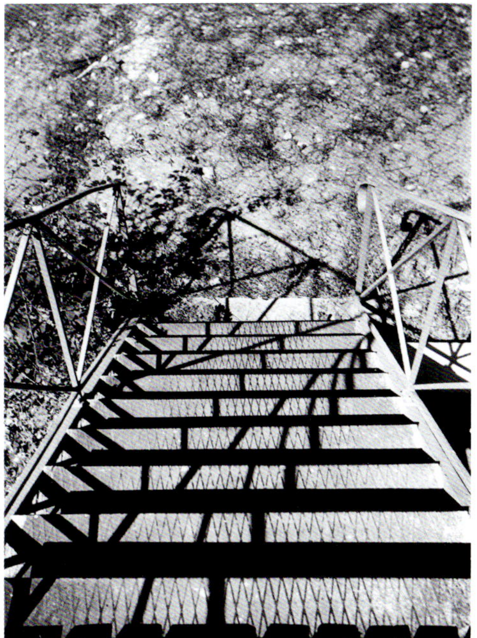

fig. 19: *Shadows on Stairs, Villa La Combe, Meschers,* 1950, gelatin silver print

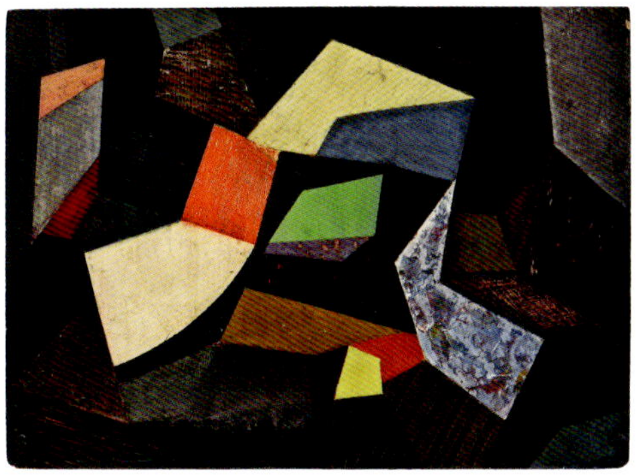

fig. 20: *Untitled (Abstraction)*, 1946, oil on Masonite, 18 × 24 in, 45.7 × 61 cm

as in examples painted in New York such as ***Black Ripe* (1955)** (p. 130) and ***Blue Black Red* (1964)** (p. 166).

Nearing the war's end, with the Allies as the clear victors, the camouflage battalion was no longer needed for missions, and in May 1945 they were sent home. The artist was discharged several months later from Jacksonville, Florida. His two and a half years of wartime service proved to be a greatly formative experience in his life, as it was undoubtedly to every other soldier of his generation. These were crucial years of his maturity into manhood, and it was during this time, as discussed earlier, that he came to his epiphanic realization that he had to be an artist *just for himself,* and not in commercial work for a company or a brand, as his parents had insisted. And so he returned to civilian life even more confident in his decision to become an artist.

Camouflage and Kelly

While it is not clear cut how Kelly's experience of camouflage directly influenced his art, it is inconceivable that his tenure in this unusual military outfit did not shape his artistic approaches in some way, or at least inform how he looked at and took in the empirical world. He had arrived at camouflage training with a sharp eye already fine-tuned by his years of bird-watching, which, of course, requires great patience as one waits for the chance arrival of a particular species—in many ways, akin to being on the lookout for the enemy on the fields of battle. Kelly transferred such modes of looking to his military duties. He continued to learn how to study and identify the distinctions between form and shadow, how to make things look like other things, or disappear into the world (though not perfectly). As the artist has reflected, "Working with camouflage meant working with perception. I've always been interested in perception—as a visualist, a lot of my work is about understanding what I see. It's an investigation of what we see. The camouflage experience heightened it."[18]

Hence, one particular path that can be traced is Kelly's developing interest in light and shadow. It seems quite likely that the experience of learning how to break apart shadows cast by concealed equipment or soldiers made the young artist more attuned to the ways in which shadows form. In the years to come, he would often focus on the contrast of light and dark. As he said in 2001, "I love black and white, day and night, sun and … shadow."[19] In fact, a number of works made during his years in France and those in New York came from the witnessing of light and shadow, such as ***Relief with Blue* (1950)** (p. 58), ***La Combe I* (1950)** (p. 61), ***Seine* (1951)** (p. 66), ***White Plaque: Bridge Arch and Reflection* (1955)** (p. 131), and ***Atlantic* (1956)** (p. 139).

La Combe I, made five years after the end of his military service, displays such an interest in "sun and … shadow." While visiting La Combe, the home of friends in Meschers, France, Kelly noticed how shadows of an intricate patterning occurred on an outdoors metal staircase at a certain time of day. Borrowing a Leica camera from the hostess, he documented this from the top of the stairs, capturing how the diagonal design of the metal balusters cast fractured black lines onto each stair (fig. 19). He also drew a number of sketches of this observation. Back in his Paris studio, he made *La Combe I*, a two-dimensional rendition of this inspiration. By this time he was working in an abstract mode with no interest in depicting exactly what he saw. Instead, what he chose to paint was a stark red version of the geometric patterning of the shadows onto a painted white canvas. He carried over the appearance of the nine steps, as seen in the photograph, to the canvas by dividing it into nine equally spaced sections, yet without any shading to depict volume. Kelly developed this concept even further with *La Combe II*, 1951 (p. 60), a folding screen of nine hinged panels. Here, each of the nine steps is physically represented by its own panel, now painted with an altered fractured patterning in black against white.

Kelly's attraction to these unique shadows draws parallels with the training he received as a camoufleur in making and installing netted canopies to produce plentiful and fractured shadows. In early works such as *La Combe I* and *II*, the artist was learning how to create a new kind of abstraction, though still inspired by the empirical world. Many of his early French paintings and reliefs are the first examples of Kelly choosing *not* to be an inventor. As he has explained, "I would see shadows, [I] would see shapes. I was *not inventing*."[20]

Camouflage is about false appearances, making one thing look like another, such as flat pieces of rubber transformed to appear like a three-dimensional tank. Considered this way, it stems from the illusionistic tradition of mimetic art that began in the Renaissance. As Kelly said about his wartime experience, he learned how to "make-believe." Yet in the years that followed, he would shed this goal of illusionism. He took from his camouflage experience, however, vestiges of what mimetic art entails—looking at the world and finding inspiration in what he saw. But what he saw, what he eventually zeroed in on, was *not* the traditional subject matter found in representational painting, such as the human form depicted in its entirety or landscapes that seem to go on for infinity. Instead, in the years to come, with his trained eye, he would focus on fragments of vision—the perception of a specific color or shape, even things as small and transient as black shadows cast by a metal staircase.

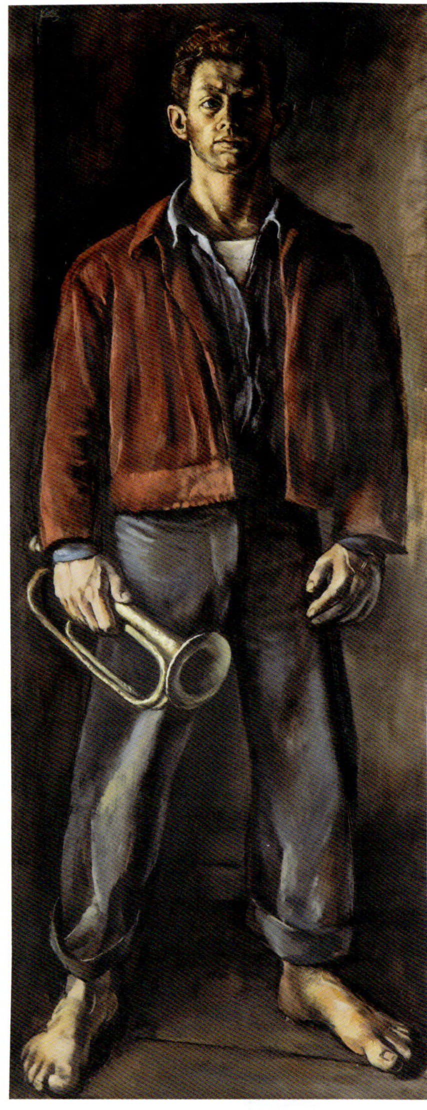

fig. 21: *Self-Portrait with Bugle*, 1947, oil on tar paper mounted on Masonite, 65 × 24⅞ in, 165.1 × 63.2 cm

Boston on the G.I. Bill

Discharged on October 23, 1945 in Jacksonville, Florida, Kelly was a civilian again. Now with the full determination of becoming an artist, the twenty-two year old had to decide his next steps. Unsatisfied with his time at Pratt, he wanted to find other options. While in service, he had heard of Black Mountain College, the progressive school in North Carolina. Founded in 1933 as an experimental alternative to traditional modes of education in all the arts—fine arts, dance, music, theater, poetry—the College had earned a solid reputation as an avant-garde school where leading artistic figures such as Marcel Breuer, Fernand Léger, Walter Gropius, Aldous Huxley, and Thornton Wilder had already made pilgrimages for guest lectures.

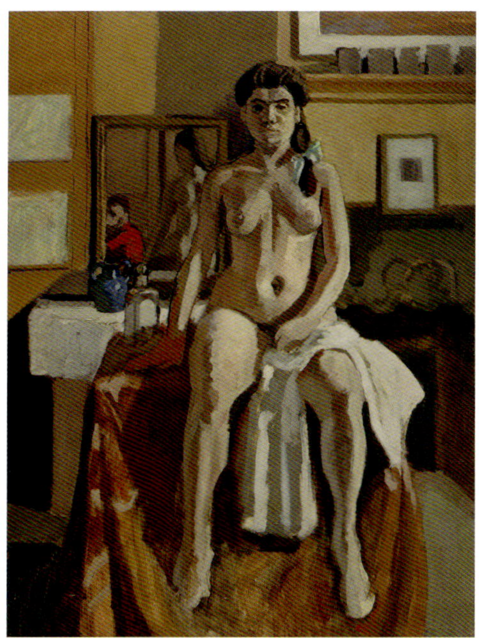

fig. 22: Henri Matisse, *Carmelina*, 1903, oil on canvas, 32 × 23¼ in, 81.3 × 59.1 cm

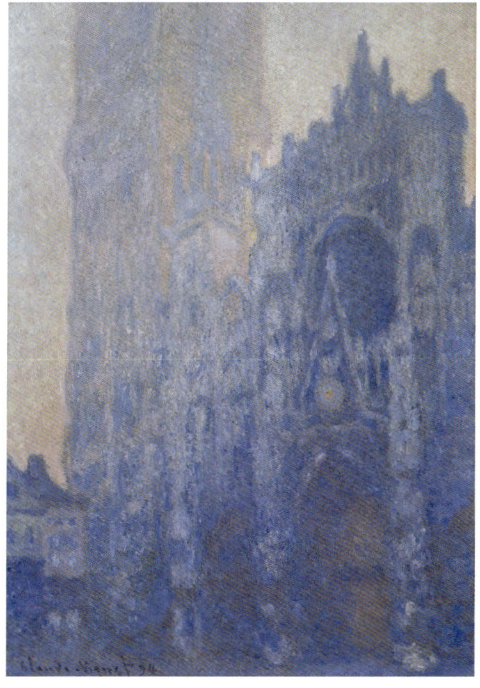

fig. 23: Claude Monet, *Rouen Cathedral Façade and Tour d'Albane (Morning Effect)*, 1894, oil on canvas, 41¾ × 29⅛ in, 106.1 × 73.9 cm

On a whim, Kelly attempted to make a trip to Black Mountain College, about 450 miles north of Jacksonville, by hitchhiking, a common means of transport for the poor artist during his early years. But after spending a whole day without getting a ride, he gave up on the idea. He ran into another returning soldier who had also been hitchhiking and who informed him that they were actually near an airport where they could fly for free on freight planes, a perk for fresh veterans. They were able to get on a flight to New York City that night. As Kelly recalled, "The next morning I said, 'Goodbye, Black Mountain.' I never got there."[21]

So Kelly went on his own fated path, choosing the School of the Museum of Fine Arts, Boston, then known as the Boston Museum School, of which he had learned on the troop ship back to the States from Europe. Unlike Black Mountain College, the Boston Museum School was a traditional institution, founded in 1876 and conceived as part of the museum, which opened that same year. When Kelly arrived in January 1946, the overriding artistic influence was that of Karl Zerbe, the German-born artist in charge of the painting department. Zerbe had joined the school in 1937, bringing his engagement and training in German Expressionism, and over the years would exert great impact on his students, teaching a painterly, gestural approach combined with the depiction of recognizable subject matter. During his tenure it had grown into a style called "Boston Expressionism" that would become marginalized as the dominance of abstraction, soon to be heralded as "Abstract Expressionism," held sway in New York City with the emergence of Jackson Pollock and his drips, splatters, and skeins. Unlike his abstract counterparts in New York and their championing critics such as Clement Greenberg, who decried representation and the use of figurative imagery, Zerbe firmly believed that depictions of the material world still had the power to communicate.

In the aftermath and trauma of World War II, such an approach to painting still resonated for Zerbe, and so he continued to teach this style to his students, which included a number of veterans like Kelly. In 1946, the year Kelly began his studies at the Boston Museum School, it was observed that sixty-nine veterans had enrolled that year. This large number was made possible because of the G.I. Bill of Rights, the vastly influential legislation officially called the Servicemen's Readjustment Act of 1944. Passed by Congress and signed into law by President Franklin Delano Roosevelt on June 22, 1944, the bill rewarded ex-G.I.s for their wartime service, allowing them to catch up on their education, while giving the U.S. some time to move away from a war-time economy. Between 1944 and 1956 nearly 50 percent of veterans attended college or a trade school. Such a policy would have an extraordinary impact on American society at large, and specifically on the development of American art in the years to come: besides Kelly, the bill supported the likes of Robert Rauschenberg, Roy Lichtenstein, and Kenneth Noland.

Kelly desperately needed the monies provided by the G.I. Bill. He now had to pay for his own education, having freed himself from the parental pressure of becoming a commercial designer. The G.I. Bill provided tuition and a monthly stipend, which was set at $65 per month in 1946. The industrious Kelly was able to procure free room and board, including a studio, at the Norfolk House Center, a settlement house in Roxbury, Boston. There he lived and earned his keep by teaching two evening classes a week to the elderly and children. The school was just two and a half miles away from the center, an easy commute. He took full-time classes in drawing, painting, sculpture, and design, a rather traditional curriculum. Like his fellow classmates, he learned how to paint in the school-sanctioned style, as seen in a 1947 self-portrait, *Self-Portrait with Bugle* (fig. 21).[22] Although Kelly was still painting figuratively—his works from this time are mostly studies done in class from the female nude—there exists one small abstraction from his Boston days, *Untitled (Abstraction)* (1946) (fig. 20), which he had painted for a design exercise, whereby each abstract shape was supposed to be given a different kind of texture.

The Museum School required students to take two hours of art history per week, a subject that Kelly relished, unlike many of his classmates. Years of looking through art books when he was a child and then during service fared well for him. A serious student, he received all As in art history. His notebooks for these classes no longer exist, but they were probably meticulously written and detailed, like his thorough lists and notes of museums, churches, and other sites made in preparation for his return to France in 1948 (fig. 29). Although he had visited museums such as the Metropolitan Museum of Art while in high school, and the National Gallery of Art while in camouflage training at Fort Meade, Boston offered Kelly close proximity to many museums, especially the Museum of Fine Arts, which was right at his fingertips, the Fogg Museum and the Germanic Museum (now the Busch-Reisinger) at Harvard University, as well as the Isabella Stewart Gardner Museum.

Just like the boy who went immediately to the woods after school to look at birds, Kelly the newly minted veteran spent whatever spare time he had in these museums, continually looking and sketching. An example of a modern painting that caught his eye at the Museum of Fine Arts was an early Henri Matisse, *Carmelina* (1903) (fig. 22), which he admired for the French master's treatment of light and shadow, especially the sharp contrasts on the model's body. He also appreciated Claude Monet's *Rouen Cathedral Façade and Tour d'Albane (Morning Effect)* (1894) (fig. 23) for its zoomed-in focus on the cathedral and the way in which Monet chose to paint its spires, as if they were pushing themselves into the air, up to the edges of the canvas. And at the Gardner Museum, he liked another early Matisse, *The Terrace, Saint-Tropez* (1904), because of a specific diagonal that the French master used to delineate the break between sun and shade.

Kelly was also taken by art from other periods and cultures. For his painting classes, he was given the classic assignment of copying Old Masters, so he spent many an hour in the Museum of Fine Arts, looking intently at works such as Ambrogio Lorenzetti's *Virgin and Child* (c.1337–43) (fig. 24) and Domenico Tintoretto's *Portrait of a Young Man* (c.1580–85). Lucas Cranach the Younger's *Portrait of a Woman* (1549) (fig. 25) captured his attention for the sharply contrasting areas of figure and ground, the dark contours of the woman's coat, and her white headdress painted crisply against the colored background. It is likely that

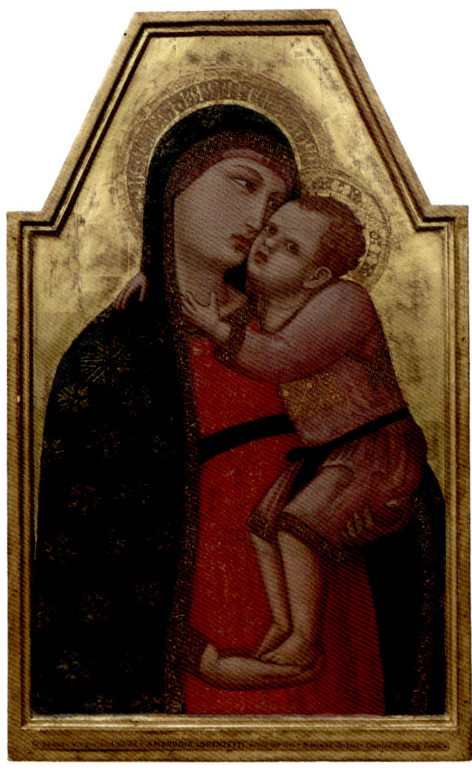

fig. 24: Ambrogio Lorenzetti, *Virgin and Child*, c.1337–43, tempera on panel, 29¾ × 17⅞ in, 75.5 × 45.4 cm

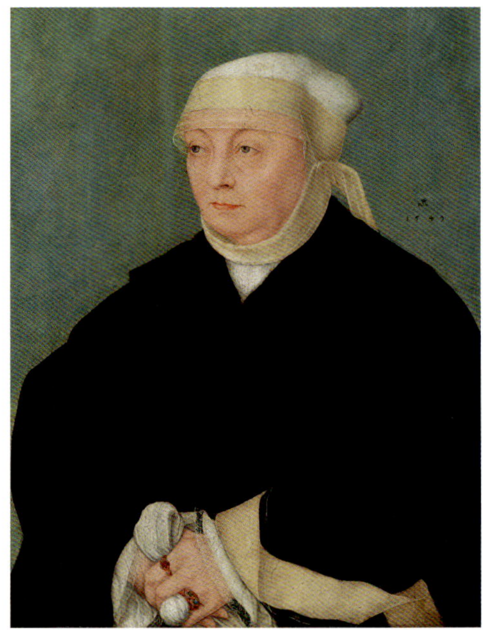

fig. 25: Lucas Cranach the Younger, *Portrait of a Woman*, 1549, oil on panel, 25⅛ × 18½ in, 63.8 × 47 cm

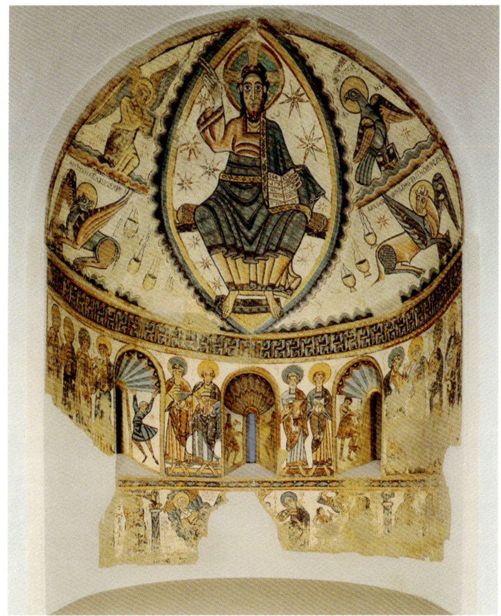

fig. 26: Unidentified artist, Spanish (Catalan), *Christ in Majesty with Symbols of the Four Evangelists,* from church of Santa Maria de Mur, 1150–1200, fresco secco transferred to plaster and wood, 253 15/16 × 150 3/8 × 111 in, 645 × 382 × 282 cm

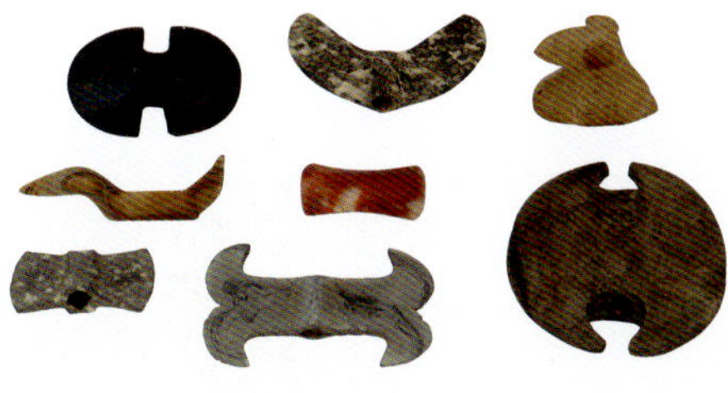

fig. 27: Ancient bannerstones and birdstones from the American Midwest, 500 B.C.– A.D. 1300

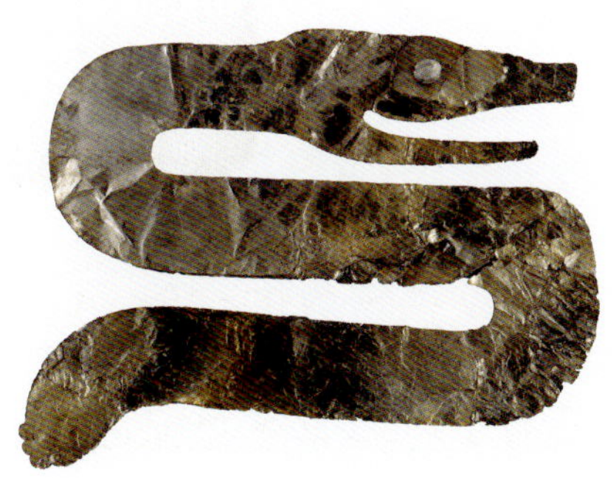

fig. 28: Serpent effigy, Turner Group Mound, Hamilton County, OH, 4200 B.C.– A.D. 200

he also appreciated the way her right arm just grazes the edges of the canvas, a tension between form and ground that he would develop in paintings made in New York, including *Black Curves* (1954) (p. 129), *Atlantic* (1956) (p. 139), and *Red Blue* (1964) (p. 164).

While Zerbe exerted great influence on his students, Kelly felt he learned more from his drawing teacher Ture Bengtz, whose lessons focused on contour drawing rather than illusionistic shading to render volume. Bengtz emphasized the perception of forms and their outlines in space, an approach that formed a great impression on Kelly the former camoufleur. He took these lessons and applied them to the study of works he saw on his museum outings, such as the Cranach painting at the Museum of Fine Arts, Boston. There he also encountered the twelfth-century frescoes from the Catalan church of Santa Maria de Mur (fig. 26) and was struck by the simplicity of their painted shapes, such as the mandorla, a form that he would explore in various incarnations (fig. 68) in the ensuing years. From this firsthand introduction, his appreciation of Romanesque art and architecture began and would continue to grow during his years in France.

What the Boston museums offered Kelly was continual opportunities to seek out a variety of forms. While finding these in painting, he also turned to objects. At the Peabody Museum of Archaeology and Ethnography at Harvard, he first came across ancient Native American artifacts, becoming intrigued by those made by Mississippian mound-building cultures from approximately A.D. 800 to 1600, such as carved stone lithics, known as bannerstones and birdstones. The Peabody had a plentiful collection of these small objects, displayed in hundreds of glass cases in which all were laid out for view.[23] Although Kelly had not yet realized he wanted to create an art of abstraction—that would come in late 1948, soon after arriving in Paris—the inklings of such an engagement can be identified here, in the way he was immediately drawn to these abstract curvilinear objects, carved from slate, granite, and porphyry.[24] In 1954, back in the States after his years in France, he would begin collecting such objects with great interest (fig. 27). Also on his visits to the Peabody, he was attracted by the flat, cutout silhouette of another ancient North American object, a mica serpent from the burial mounds of Madisonville, Ohio (fig. 28).

In the spring of 1948, the arrival of two guest speakers to the Boston Museum School would form a lasting impression on the student Kelly, who was nearing graduation. The first was German Expressionist Max Beckmann, who arrived that March for a three-day visit to the school. The previous year, Beckmann had come from Germany to teach at Washington University in St. Louis, and a major solo exhibition would open later that May at the Saint Louis Art Museum, then called the City Art Museum. Boston was also celebrating his art, with the school hosting a small Beckmann exhibition. On Zerbe's invitation, Beckmann flew to Boston for a visit that proved to be memorable for the twenty-four-year-old Kelly, who was already an admirer of the German's use of black contours and high contrasts. Instead of presenting a traditional lecture, Beckmann, an imposing figure and chain-smoker, chose to share with the students a letter he had written to an aspiring artist. Yet experiencing some difficulty speaking English, he asked his wife Quappi to read the words instead, which included the following passage:

> Don't forget nature, through which Cézanne, as he said, wanted to achieve the classical. Take long walks and take them often, and try your utmost to avoid the stultifying motor car, which robs you of your vision, just as the movies do, or the numerous motley newspapers. Learn the forms of nature by heart so that you can use them like the musical notes of a composition. That's what these forms are for ... The impression nature makes upon you must always become an expression of your own joy or grief, and consequently in your formation of it, it must contain that transformation which only then makes art a real abstraction.[25]

As a young man who had spent his childhood outdoors and who was now serious about becoming an artist, Kelly took in such words of advice and, in the years to come, would remember this lesson well.

Soon after Beckmann's arrival in April, the second guest speaker to visit the school was British art historian and critic Herbert Read, who lectured on modern art. What struck Kelly was Read's assessment that the tradition of "easel painting" was outdated, declaring it over for the time being; instead, a new collaboration between art and architecture was needed. Not surprisingly, the faculty was taken aback by such a statement, especially at a school so devoted to the tradition of figurative painting. Kelly, however, found Read's argument provocative, inspiring, and even validating, since he was already experiencing a great disaffection with the traditional lessons being taught there. Despite his appreciation of a number of the "easel paintings" he saw at the Museum of Fine Arts, Boston, such as those by Cranach and modern ones by Monet and Matisse, he found himself drawn to medieval mosaics and frescoes like those from the Santa Maria de Mur, presented within the setting of church architecture—in a similar collaboration to that proposed by Read. As he pondered Read's arguments, they continued to resonate, but with graduation upon him, he filed away such concepts for later. For now, he needed to think about his next steps.

1 Ellsworth Kelly, in conversation with the author, Spencertown, New York, August 2, 2001. Starting in the early 1970s, most notably in John Coplans, *Ellsworth Kelly* (New York: Harry N. Abrams, 1971), p. 20, Kelly began making related statements, published and unpublished, about "not inventing," or creating art not from "invented content."

2 This essay draws from biographical and art historical research provided in the following studies: E.C. Goossen, *Ellsworth Kelly* (New York: The Museum of Modern Art, 1973); Patterson Sims and Emily Rauh Pulitzer, *Ellsworth Kelly: Sculpture* (New York: Whitney Museum of American Art, 1982); Trevor J. Fairbrother, *Ellsworth Kelly: Seven Paintings (1952–55/1987)* (Boston: Museum of Fine Arts, 1987); Yve-Alain Bois, Jack Cowart, and Alfred Pacquement, *Ellsworth Kelly: The Years in France, 1948–1954* (Washington, DC: National Gallery of Art, 1992); Barbaralee Diamonstein, "Ellsworth Kelly" in *Inside the Art World: Conversations with Barbaralee Diamonstein* (New York: Rizzoli, 1994), pp. 121–24; Diane Waldman (ed.), *Ellsworth Kelly: A Retrospective* (New York: The Solomon R. Guggenheim Foundation, 1996); Philip Gerard, *Secret Soldiers: The Story of World War II's Heroic Army of Deception* (New York: Dutton, 2002); Stuart Steck, "Veiling the Subject: Ellsworth Kelly and the Discourses of Modernism," Ph.D. thesis, (Boston University, 2008). I also draw from published interviews quoted here, as well as this author's unpublished interviews and conversations with the artist from August 2001 through March 2015, some of which are cited in Tricia Y. Paik, "A Palpable Vision: Ellsworth Kelly's Years in New York, 1954–1969," Ph.D. thesis, (New York University, 2009).

3 Kelly, quoted in Diamonstein, 1994, p. 121.

4 Kelly cannot recall the exact publications he first saw at the library, but they may have included an edition of Audubon's classic publication, *The Birds of America*, which Audubon originally published in serial portfolios from 1827 to 1938.

5 Kelly would learn this fact after visiting the New-York Historical Society in 1954. Having discovered that the society owned Audubon's original drawings for his *Birds of America* engravings, Kelly went to study them.

6 Kelly, quoted in Ann Hindry, "Conversation with Ellsworth Kelly," in Hindry (ed.), *Artstudio: Spécial Ellsworth Kelly*, no. 24 (Spring 1992), p. 29.

7 Kelly, in conversation with the author, Spencertown, New York, August 2, 2001.

8 Kelly, quoted in Paul Taylor, "Ellsworth Kelly: Talking to America's Most Colorful Artist," *Interview* 21, no. 6 (June 1991), p. 102.

9 Kelly, quoted in "Ellsworth Kelly by Gwyneth Paltrow," *Interview* 41, no. 8 (October 2011), p. 130.

10 A.M. Homes, "Ellsworth Kelly," *Vogue Homme International* (spring/summer 2003), p. 144.

11 Kelly, quoted in Gerard 2002, p. 62.

12 Ibid., pp. 63–64.

13 Ibid., p. 64.

14 Ibid.

15 Ibid.

16 Kelly, quoted in "Ellsworth Kelly by Gywneth Paltrow," 2011, p. 129.

17 Kelly, quoted in Diamonstein 1994, p. 121.

18 Kelly, quoted in Gerard 2002, p. 63.

19 Kelly, in conversation with the author, Spencertown, New York, August 2, 2001.

20 Ibid.; italics added.

21 Kelly, in conversation with the author, Spencertown, New York, January 1, 2014.

22 Although about forty paintings exist from his two and a half years at the Boston Museum School, there is only one extant painting from 1946. Kelly had made many more canvases during this time. However, when he returned to the States after living in France from 1948 to 1954, he learned that his mother had destroyed or thrown away the rest of his Boston output.

23 Carol Diehl, "Birds, Beads & Bannerstones," *ARTnews* 95, no. 7 (summer 1996), p. 84.

24 For a statement by Kelly about his interest in ancient North American art, see "Ellsworth Kelly," *Cahiers d'Art,* no. 1 (October 2012), p. 52.

25 Max Beckmann, quoted in Goossen 1973, p. 104, n. 11.

In France, 1948–54

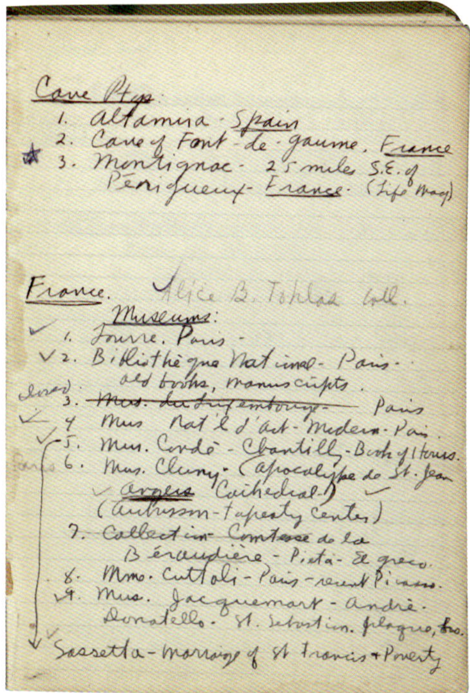

fig. 29: First page of Ellsworth Kelly's journal listing places to visit in Europe, 1948

Forming an Abstract Idiom

"Louvre." "Mus. Nat'l d'Art Modern [sic]." "Colmar, Alsace, Grünewald altar." "St. Savin frescoes": these are just a few of the many museums and sites in France that the twenty-five-year-old Kelly listed in a slim army-green journal in 1948 (fig. 29). The tried and true tradition of going to the French capital to study art was one he could not resist, so when deciding where to go after Boston, he chose Paris over New York. He had visited Paris only briefly during the war and had found the cultural atmosphere and architecture stimulating, despite the fact that the museums had been closed. The prospect of visiting the museums he had missed and returning to this city of great culture and history beckoned him. Hoping to visit these museums, churches, and other places of artistic pilgrimage in France and throughout Europe, he had diligently made, in advance of his trip, numerous lists by topic, country, and city, including Amsterdam, Barcelona, London, Mt. Athos, and Ravenna. He even listed Italian painters by the cities or regions for which they are known, for example, Tintoretto under "VENITIEN" and Cimabue under "SIENESE." This wide-ranging list spanning cave painting to the Alice B. Toklas collection reveals the curiosity the young artist already possessed, the knowledge gained from art-history classes and his own self-education, plus a wanderlust sparked by his travels during World War II.

Kelly arrived in Paris in October 1948, still a beneficiary of the U.S. government with an increased stipend of $75 a month, plus tuition covered by the G.I. Bill. Recovering from the war, Paris was not the most hospitable of places, with heating a luxury in the winter. Yet its rich artistic tradition combined with cheap rents made it enticing for aspiring American artists. This generation, however, was the last significant group of Americans to soak in the majesty of the City of Light, since its identity as a great arts capital was now starting to dim, with new attention on New York and the emergence of Abstract Expressionism. A month after his arrival, Kelly visited various schools and ateliers, finally selecting the École des Beaux-Arts. However, he rarely attended classes, as was the practice with other American veterans, who enrolled in schools only to qualify for the stipend. In his own estimation, he had already received sufficient academic training in Boston, so instead, equipped with his notebook of lists, Kelly turned Paris and beyond into his classroom. For excursions outside of the city, he would travel on his own or with friends from his Boston days such as Ralph Coburn or new Paris friends like Jack Youngerman, whom he met at the École des Beaux-Arts. After each trip made by bike, bus, train, or by thumbing a ride, he would record his mission accomplished, dutifully checking off the name of the place visited in his journal.

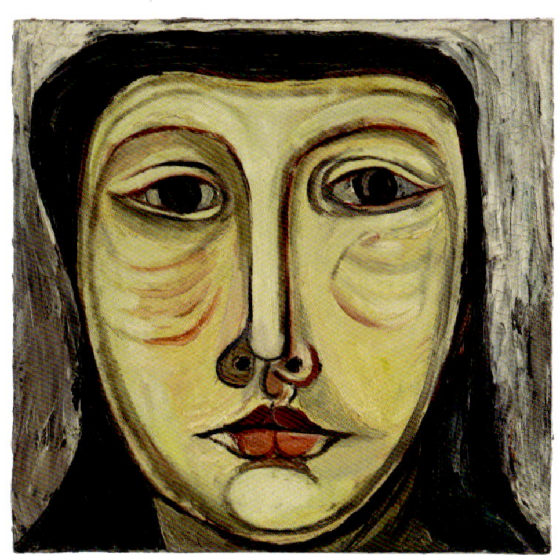

fig. 30: *Byzantine Head I*, 1948, oil on canvas, 15 × 15 in, 38.1 × 38.1 cm

Soon after his arrival in Paris, Kelly painted two works inspired by the Byzantine art he had already seen on display there: *Byzantine Head I* and *II* (1948). In both, but particularly *Byzantine Head I* (fig. 30), he focused on the details of the face. The painting reveals his interest in abstracting form through outline, instead of volumetric shading, as seen in the almond-shaped silhouette of the eyes. Indeed, it was around this time that he realized that figuration was not the path he wanted to take. As he would recollect in 1971 in his first major public statement,

I soon realized after arriving in Paris in 1948 that figurative painting no longer interested me. Looking for different ways to continue, I spent days at the Louvre and the Guimet Museum, where I studied the art of the Mediterranean and the East. The two things I admired most were an Egyptian stele in relief (fig. 31) ... and a Greek headless statue of Hera ... I also studied Chinese ceramics and bronzes, the decorative objects and sculpture of Luristan, Susa, and the Cyclades. At the Byzantine Institute, I studied mosaics and early manuscripts.[1]

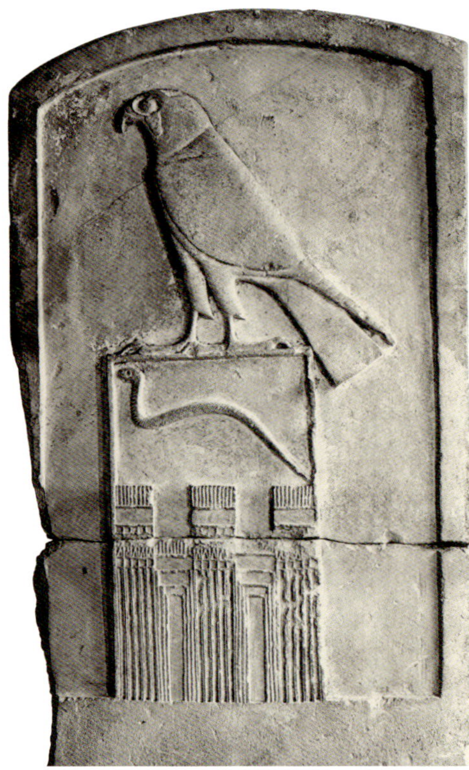

fig. 31: *Stele of the Serpent King,* from the tomb of the Serpent King, Abydos (Egypt), c.3000 B.C. (1st dynasty), limestone, $56\frac{1}{3} \times 25\frac{2}{3} \times 9\frac{7}{8}$ in, 143.1 × 65.2 × 25.1 cm

Other museums such as the Musée de Cluny, now the Musée national du Moyen Âge, engaged his interest in Romanesque and Byzantine art. He also visited the Musée Cernuschi and the Musée de l'Homme. All these museum visits whet his growing appetite for abstract forms.

Kelly was also able to make the acquaintance of many important artists and other cultural figures during his French sojourn. No wish lists seem to exist for such meetings, but, through eager industriousness as well as plain good luck, he met such crucial figures of European modernism as Jean Arp, Constantin Brancusi, Marcel Breuer, Alberto Giacometti, Joan Miró, Francis Picabia, Georges Vantongerloo, as well as Americans Alexander Calder, John Cage, and Merce Cunningham. According to Kelly, it was surprisingly easy to make the acquaintance of such luminaries: "everyone was available," even the great master Picasso, who once invited him into his car so that he could learn more about the young American. Even more reticent in Paris than in the U.S. because of his meager French, Kelly declined the offer.

Kelly was more confident in visiting Alice B. Toklas in the summer of 1949 and seeing the collection of her late partner, noteworthy writer and cultural figure Gertrude Stein. Having found her number in the phonebook, he simply called her up. Toklas answered, neither particularly friendly nor rude, but willing to hear why he had called. After being peppered with curt questions from Toklas, he was finally able to make his request clear: that he and a friend wanted to see the Stein collection. She agreed, so Kelly and his friend Coburn made their way to Toklas on rue Christine. Toklas and Stein had moved there in 1938 from their famed address of 27, rue du Fleurus, the setting of their legendary salon, where they entertained the likes of Picasso, Matisse, Georges Braque, and writers such as Ernest Hemingway, T.S. Eliot, F. Scott Fitzgerald, and Thornton Wilder.

The collection as it stood then was not as it was in its prime, having already been partially dispersed after Stein's death. But Kelly was enthralled by all the Picassos he saw on the wall, of which Toklas still owned twenty-seven. He has recalled, "I remember there was a small Picasso with a man's head and beret on it. The beret was pinned on to the head of the man—a paper cutout. I remember looking at it, and thinking that I've always loved that beret shape."[2] Already familiar with the Cubist collages that Picasso and Braque had first made in 1912 using newspaper print, wallpaper, and liquor labels, thus revolutionizing the practice of art through the addition of non-art materials, Kelly had begun experimenting with collage and readymade materials in 1949. His first paper cutout, ***Head with Beard*** **(1949)** (fig. 32), was a silhouette cut from an English-language

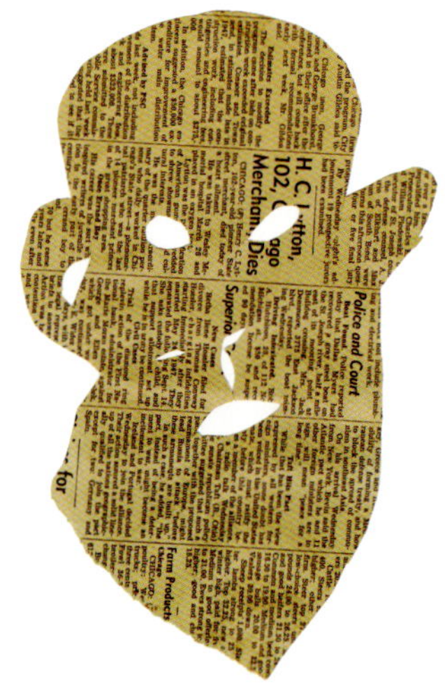

fig. 32: *Head with Beard,* 1949, newspaper cutout, $10\frac{1}{4} \times 6\frac{1}{4}$ in, 26 × 15.9 cm

newspaper. Wishing not to distract with the legibility of the written word, he turned the newspaper clockwise by 90 degrees, so that the lines of the print run vertically down the face, appearing like an abstract linear patterning. But not yet ready to truly relinquish figuration, he had cut out small shapes, indicating the eyes, nostrils, mouth, and ear.

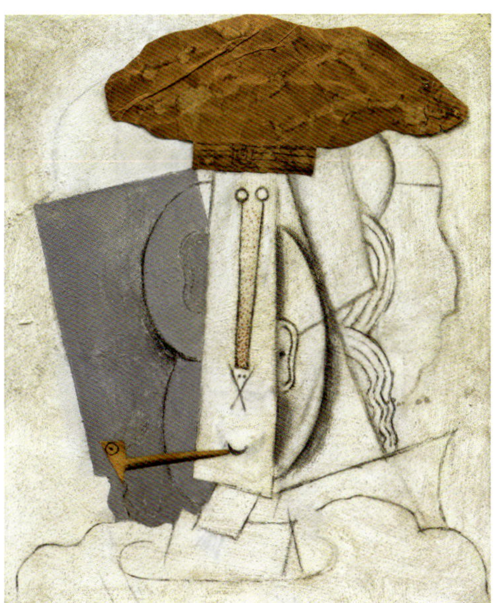

fig. 33: Pablo Picasso, *Student with a Pipe*, 1913–14, oil, gouache, cut-and-pasted paper, gesso, sand, and charcoal on canvas, 28¾ × 23⅛ in, 73 × 58.7 cm

Here in Toklas's house, he admired the Picasso collage before him, *Student with a Pipe* (1913–14) (fig. 33), the curvilinear silhouette of the beret and the use of brown paper for the cutout form. After looking at the collection, Toklas invited Kelly and Coburn to stay, since she was eager to learn more about them. During and after World War II, Stein had taken to inviting American G.I.s to see her collection, becoming so fond of the soldiers that she even referred to them as her godsons. It is thus no surprise that Toklas took an interest in these two young American men, one of them a former G.I. Unfortunately, when Toklas's dog became sick on the carpet, their visit was cut short.

During the summer of 1949, Kelly was on the cusp of abandoning figuration, still studying the world around him, a historical city filled with centuries-old architecture.[3] In his 1971 statement, Kelly reflected on these days:

> I became more interested in the physical structure of Paris, the stonework of the old buildings and bridges, and preferred to study and be influenced by it rather than by contemporary art. The forms found in the vaulting of a cathedral or a splatter of tar on a road seemed more valid and instructive and a more voluptuous experience than either geometric or action painting.[4]

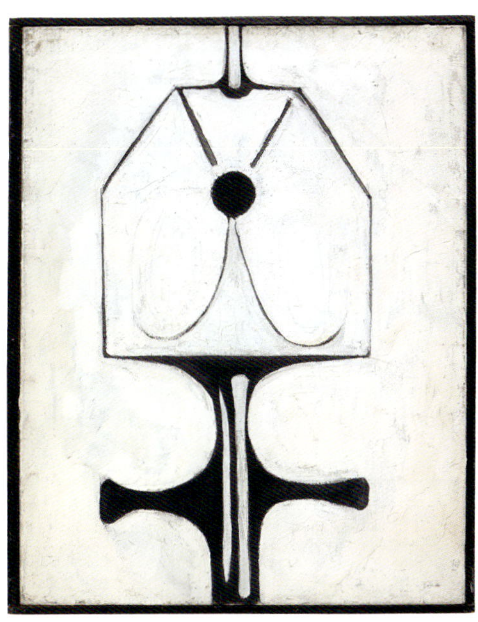

fig. 34: *Toilette*, 1949, oil on canvas with painted wood frame, 24¾ × 18¾ × ½ in, 62.9 × 47.6 × 1.3 cm

Kelly continued his search for forms in architecture, traveling in the spring of 1949 to the Romanesque sites of Poitiers, Saint-Savin-sur-Gartempe, and Tavant. The conceptual underpinnings of his art really began to emerge during this fruitful year. That May, he painted *Toilette* (fig. 34) in his studio at the Hôtel de Bourgogne on the Île Saint-Louis, where he would live for almost three years. This black-and-white painting seems to be a curious abstraction, its geometric and curvilinear forms not immediately identifiable. The title of the painting, however, gives the subject away: Kelly's source was indeed a Turkish-style toilet, unfamiliar to most Americans.

As identified by the artist, *Toilette* was the first painting he had made that was inspired by objects found in the real world. Kelly discussed its significance in 1971, for the first time going on record about how in France he intentionally chose to *find*, not *invent* his subject matter:

> Instead of making a picture that was an interpretation of a thing seen, or a picture of *invented content*, I found an object and presented it as itself alone. The first of the object-oriented works was *Toilette*, which was derived from a particularly French design of a floor toilet, which only Parisians and visitors to Paris will recognize. During the summer and fall of 1949, on an island off the coast of Brittany, I continued to explore the object quality of things seen. Picking up five white stones on a beach, I made a face in my

palm. Other works were done from the markings of a tennis court, a kilometer marker, a seaweed, a window frame.[5]

Such a distinction between "invented" and "found" is central to the development of Kelly's key artistic goals.[6] At the time of making *Toilette*, when he was about twenty-six, he was already an admirer of the great Picasso and felt a need to free himself from the pressure of having to create something entirely new. Leading Kelly scholar Yve-Alain Bois has explained, "No artist could be any more intimidating than Picasso, with his Protean inventive abilities. What is there left to do in the wake of someone who has invented *everything*?"[7]

Kelly realized that he needed instead to *resist* invention. Later that summer of 1949, he returned to the island of Belle-Île, where he had already been with Coburn. With a new confidence, having made *Toilette*, he created paintings from the sources listed above in his 1971 statement: *Window I* (1949) (p. 50), *Kilometer Marker* (1949) (p. 51), and *Tennis Court* (1949) (p. 54). As in *Toilette,* he singled out the specific forms or outlines observed in the found sources that intrigued him. By lifting the shapes from their original surroundings, he rendered them unrecognizable, distanced from their original contexts. He translated them into abstract shapes, akin to the memorable vision he had experienced when he fainted as a boy—when the world became abstract based on his inability to recognize what he saw. As Kelly explained in 1991, "Since birth we get accustomed to seeing and thinking at the same time. But I think that if you can turn off the mind and look at things only with your eyes, ultimately everything becomes abstract."[8]

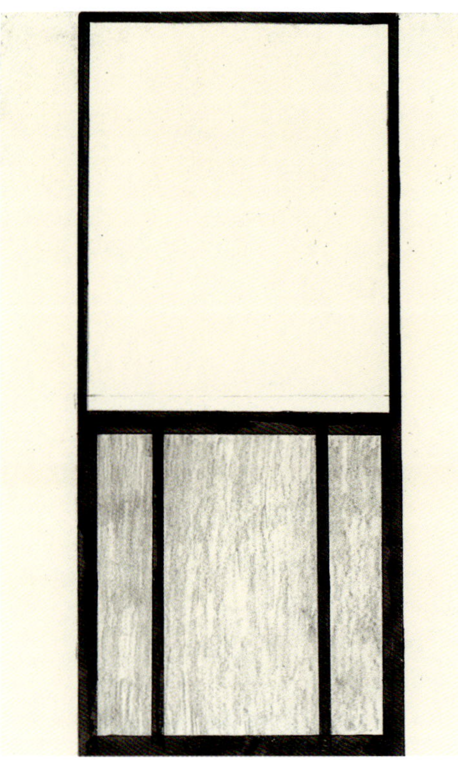

fig. 35: Study for *Window, Museum of Modern Art, Paris,* 1949, ink and graphite on paper, 13¾ × 8½ in, 34.9 × 21.6 cm

The "Already-Made" and *Window, Museum of Modern Art, Paris,* 1949

By the fall of 1949, Kelly had checked off many an item in his inventory of sites. He had been making regular visits to the Musée National d'Art Moderne, then housed at the Palais de Tokyo on the Right Bank in Paris. In October he returned to see an exhibition, but this time he found himself drawn to the elegant, elongated windows in between the small paintings rather than the art. What impressed him was the large scale and structure of these uniquely designed windows. Back in his studio, he made some drawings (fig. 35), playing with the proportions of the windows he had just observed, as well as the color scheme. From these studies, he constructed a scaled-down version of the actual window (p. 53).

Instead of painting a pictorial representation of the window, Kelly chose to make an actual object using two canvases, strips of wood, and paint. He painted the top canvas a monochrome white and the bottom one a monochrome gray, which is recessed, and thus not flush with the white canvas above. Each of the panels was flatly painted, without any sign of gesture, showing the beginnings of his wish to make "anonymous" works that did not register an artistic personality. To replicate the three-dimensional nature of the window with its frame and mullions, he used thin strips of wood painted black. The result was a sculptural object that diverged from the traditions of easel painting. In 1967, in a retrospective look at his French work, Kelly photographed one of the windows (fig. 36) that punctuate the slightly curved façade of the art-deco Palais de Tokyo building. In another retrospective

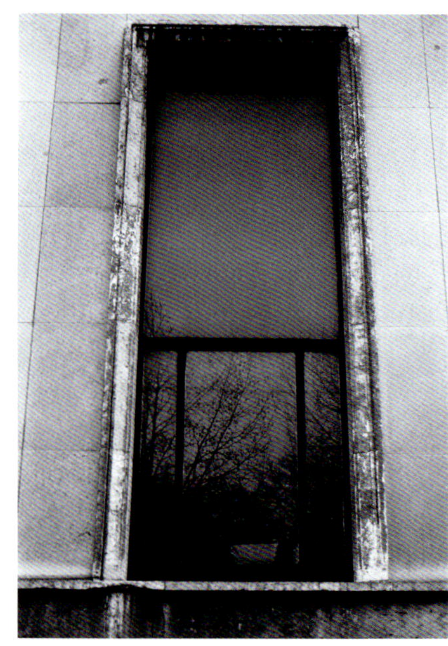

fig. 36: *Window, Musée National d'Art Moderne, Avenue du Président Wilson, Paris,* 1967, gelatin silver print

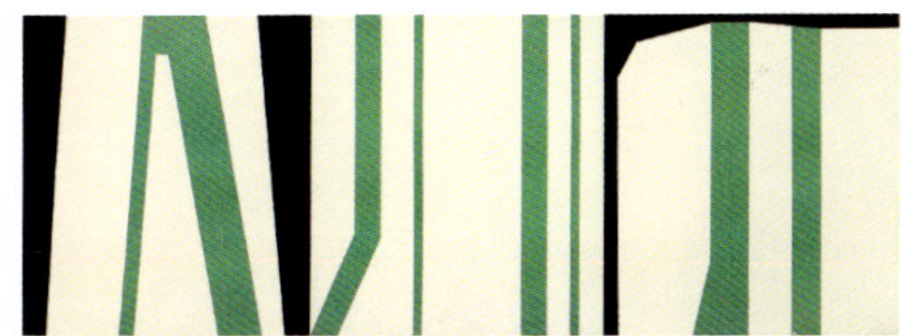

fig. 37: Study for *Ormesson,* 1950, collage on paper, 22 × 59 in, 55.9 × 149.9 cm

consideration, his 1971 statement, Kelly described how he arrived at the idea for this finished work, which he would later title *Window, Museum of Modern Art, Paris* (p. 53):

> In October of 1949 at the Museum of Modern Art in Paris, I noticed the large windows between the paintings interested me more than the art exhibited. I made a drawing of the window (fig. 35) and later in my studio I made what I considered my first object, *Window, Museum of Modern Art, Paris*. From then on, painting as I had known it was finished for me. The new works were to be painting/objects, unsigned, anonymous. Everywhere I looked, everything I saw became something to be made, and it had to be made exactly as it was, with nothing added. It was a new freedom: there was no longer the need to compose. The subject was there already made, and I could take from everything; it all belonged to me: a glass roof of a factory with its broken and patched panes, lines of a roadmap, the shape of a scarf on a woman's head, a fragment of Le Corbusier's Swiss Pavilion, a corner of a Braque painting, paper fragments in the street. It was all the same, *anything goes*.[9]

Still focusing on what he saw in the world, he discovered a way to translate his "already-made" sources into "painting/objects" that still drew from reality but in the end became abstractions. For example, *Ormesson* (1950) (fig. 37 and p. 64), made of three joined panels onto which he painted a vertical patterning of green and black, derived from the design of different chimneys that he had observed on Parisian building façades, and which he would document in 1967 (fig. 38). By extracting forms from their "already-made" contexts and intentionally not composing, Kelly recreated only their shapes and not their surroundings, ultimately eliminating identifying traits that linked his sources back to their referents.

In 1949, Kelly was not fully aware of what he had achieved with *Window, Museum of Modern Art, Paris.* By constructing a physical object rather than painting a depiction of what he had seen, Kelly was challenging the traditions of mimetic representation stemming back to the Renaissance, and the corresponding notion that painting should enact for the viewer the experience of looking through "a window opened onto the world." As Bois explained in 1992, "it took Kelly several years to digest the import of the blow he had dealt the pictorial tradition."[10] Prior to *Window, Museum of Modern Art*, Kelly had made three works inspired by the window, such as *Window I* (1949) (p. 50), and he continued with this series in 1950 with *Window V* (p. 57), one of his first examples of a shaped panel, inspired by light and shadows that he had witnessed on a December 1949 trip to Sanary, France.

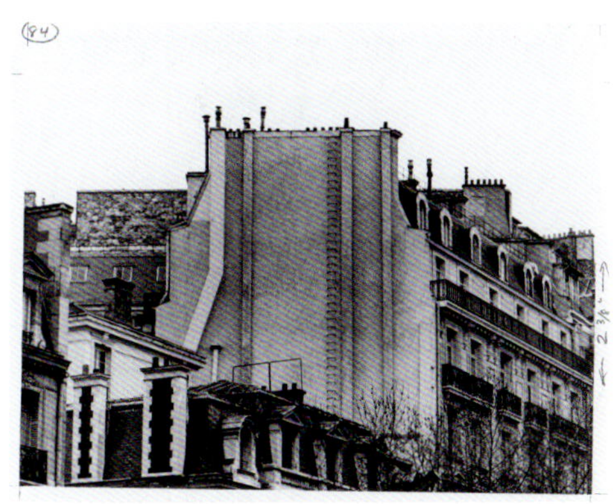

fig. 38: *Chimneys, Boulevard de Courcelles, Paris,* 1967, gelatin silver print

By moving away from the tradition of mimetic easel painting, of representational depiction, Kelly began to cast off the requirements of this tradition—composition, illusionism, and the use of the unitary canvas. Instead, he explored their opposite—non-composition, construction, and the deployment of multiple panels. There was, however, one key process connected to mimesis that he never attempted to cast off—looking at the real world, the experience of vision itself. But he would transform the reality of what he saw into something unidentifiable and abstract, distancing his "already-made" motifs from their original contexts.

Through this intriguing oppositional relationship between the real and the abstract, he began to take in the physical world by fragmenting the scope of the totalizing Renaissance window into selected units of vision through his "already-made" inspirations.

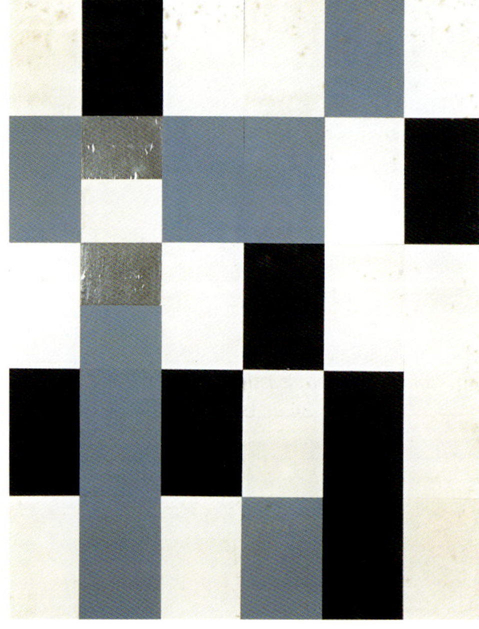

fig. 39: Sophie Taeuber-Arp and Jean Arp, *Untitled (Duo-Collage)*, 1918, colored paper collage, 32 5/16 × 24 7/16 in, 94 × 78.7 cm

Kelly's conception of the "already-made" must be clarified as quite distinct from Dadaist provocateur Marcel Duchamp's idea of the "readymade," such as his notorious *Fountain* from 1917, a readymade work because Duchamp signed an actual porcelain urinal with his alter ego's name, R. Mutt, turned it on its side, and declared the mass-produced object a work of art. In contrast, Kelly's *Window* is a *made* work of art, not a manufactured and *premade* found object like Duchamp's *Fountain*. Furthermore, Duchamp's precedent, even his own readymade featuring a window, *Fresh Widow* (1920), did not provide any conceptual inspiration for Kelly, who would not learn of Duchamp's readymades until a couple of years later.

Playing with Chance

Although Duchamp's concept of the readymade did not serve as a model for Kelly, other approaches developed by the Dada movement and by Surrealism did provide inspiration for the young artist. The goal of Dadaist practices was to abandon logic and reason and instead to access irrationality and chaos, and the Surrealists developed this notion of tapping the unconscious mind. These significant European modernist movements stemmed from an artistic critique of World War I, as avant-garde artists grew skeptical of reason in the face of tragedy. Dada first emerged in Switzerland in 1916, proposing an anti-war stance that in turn fostered an anti-tradition mentality and thus an anti-art aesthetic, setting the stage for Surrealism to develop in France. Kelly learned about these movements and their practices in the spring of 1949 on gallery visits with Coburn, newly arrived in Paris from Boston. They began to experiment with such concepts, collaborating on chance collages, automatic drawings made with their eyes closed, and drawings created by the Surrealist parlor game of "Exquisite Corpse."

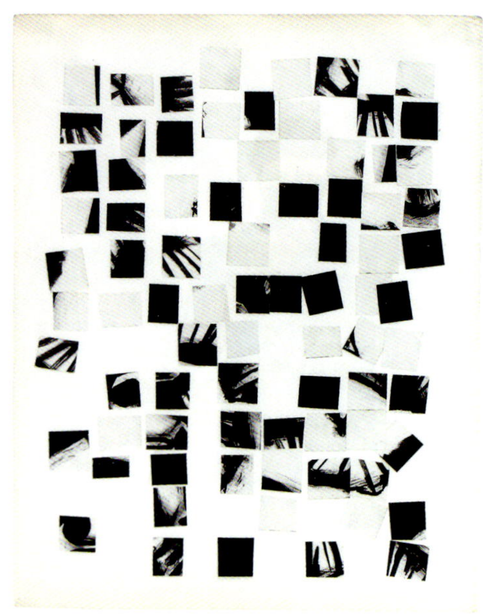

fig. 40: *Cut Up Drawing Rearranged by Chance*, 1950, ink and collage on paper, 25½ × 19½ in, 64.8 × 49.5 cm

What these modernist practices shared was the rejection of composition, of intentional decision-making to create a work of art. Instead, randomness and chance reigned supreme. Kelly found himself drawn to such methods, for they answered his growing wish not to compose and to create anonymous works that were "unsigned," revealing no trace of artistic authorship or personality. He realized that the "already-made" was random in its own nature, selected through chance observations of things he happened upon and to which he was drawn—from tangible objects like the Turkish toilet or the Palais de Tokyo window, to transient visual experiences such as the fragmented shadows for his "La Combe" series (pp. 60, 61). As he said in 1971, "It was all the same, *anything goes*," even the experience of theater. During a performance of *Hamlet* in the fall of 1949, Kelly observed the negative space between the stage curtains and admired how this void continued to be filled by different shades of colors depending on shifts in the set lighting. A year later, he would make this visual experience palpable in one of his first reliefs, *Relief with Blue* (p. 58).

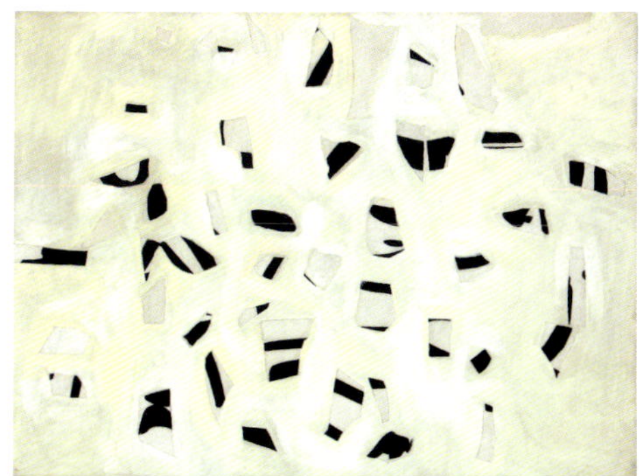

fig. 41: *November Painting*, 1950, oil on wood, 25½ × 34 in, 64.8 × 86.4 cm

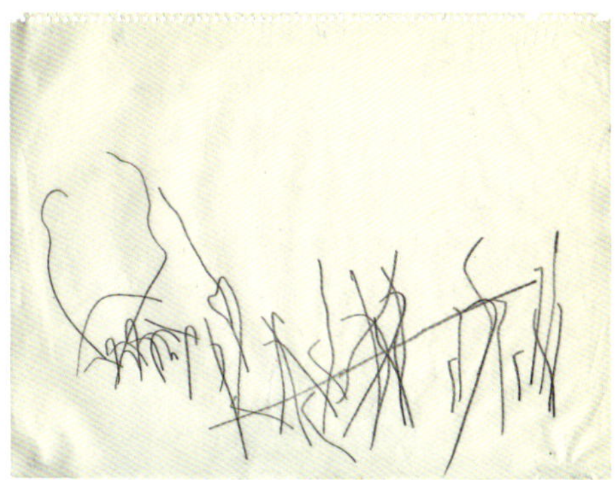

fig. 42: *Automatic Drawing: Shelled Bunker VI*, 1950, graphite on paper, 10½ × 13½ in, 26.7 × 34.3 cm

Appreciating this freeing notion of *finding* things by chance, Kelly soon became fully enthralled with *making* things by chance. Through French critic Michel Seuphor, in January 1950, he met Jean Arp, who subsequently invited Kelly, along with Coburn and Youngerman, to his studio in Meudon the following month. Although Kelly was already familiar with some of Arp's works, here he learned firsthand from the artist himself about his chance collages, as well as the lesser-known gridded collages that Arp had made with his first wife, Sophie Taeuber-Arp, which they called duo-collages. For these collaborative works, they used a paper cutter rather than scissors in order to eliminate the trace of the artist's hand, thus rendering their works more impersonal (fig. 39). Arp, a founder of the Dada movement in Zurich during World War I, had chosen chance as his guiding method in order to relinquish artistic creation and intention, whereby he would cut or tear pieces of paper and then let them fall to the ground or another recipient surface. He would then glue the resulting arrangement made "according to the laws of chance," similar to literary Dadaist Tristan Tzara's practice of forming poems from torn pieces of newspaper. Arp derived this concept of chance from his fascination with Zen Buddhism, specifically the ancient Chinese text the *I Ching* (*Book of Changes*), appreciating the impersonal, accidental approach and how the random configuration directed the final arrangement of his collages.

Meeting Arp at this time proved fruitful for Kelly. Arp's aesthetics and theories validated his developing ideas about creating an abstract art devoid of subjectivity and personality, but one still drawn from the empirical world. In particular, he found himself drawn to the gridded structure of the duo-collages he saw at Arp's studio. The visit also fueled Kelly's increasing reliance on the practice of collage to experiment with ideas quickly and effectively. He began to make his own chance collages that year, such as *Cut Up Drawing Rearranged by Chance* (1950) (fig. 40). He even made a painting inspired by this practice titled *November Painting* (1950) (fig. 41). Kelly also kept his hand and eye fully exercised, making his own kind of automatic drawings inspired by various subjects, from coat hangers to pine branches, and even the exposed rods of a shelled German bunker along the French coast (fig. 42).

By the summer's end in 1950, the funding Kelly received from the G.I. Bill was about to end, so he accepted a position at the American School in Paris. He took seriously this job of teaching art to young students, the children of American diplomats and businessmen. In the same pale green journal that contained his wish lists of places to visit, he jotted down ideas for art assignments and notes of things to say to his students. These reflect his willingness to allow the children to express their own abilities, with comments such as "what will be done depends greatly on the class." Perhaps taking a cue from his drawing teacher from his Boston days, Ture Bengtz, Kelly confidently wrote in his journal, "I can teach anyone to draw—first you must be able to see."[11] By this time, the artist had abandoned figuration in his "paintings/objects," but here one can observe how strongly he still believed in the act of drawing and the lessons he learned from Bengtz. Also keen on teaching his students the aleatory methods he had been currently exploring, he assigned exercises such as spattering watercolor or blowing ink onto absorbent paper.

He even gave them a drawing assignment inspired by his "La Combe" series and liked one of the student drawings so much that he made a new painting based on it. He titled it *La Combe IV—Collaboration with a 12-year-old Girl* (fig. 43), thus extending shared artistic credit to his student. He made this collaboration even more public when he showed it with a similar title at a group exhibition in the summer of 1951, the sixth Salon des Réalités Nouvelles in Paris.

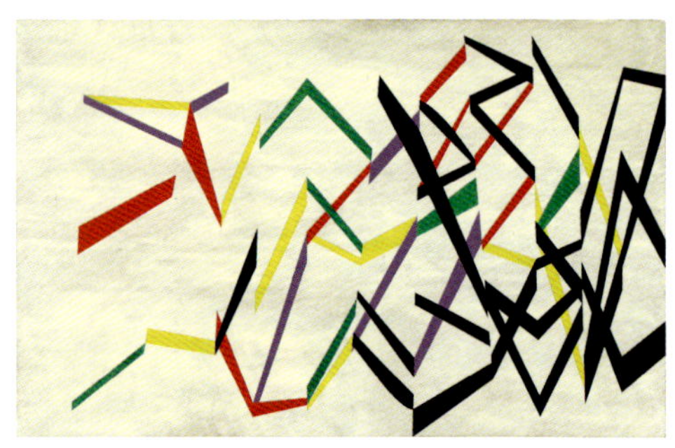

fig. 43: *La Combe IV—Collaboration with a 12-year-old Girl*, 1951, oil on wood, 39½ × 60⅜ in, 100.3 × 153.4 cm

Recently founded in 1946, the Salon des Réalités Nouvelles promoted geometric abstraction through annual exhibitions. It had grown out of Abstraction-Création, founded in 1931, which itself was a merging of two earlier artist groups, Cercle et Carré and Art Concret, both founded in 1929 to garner public interest in geometric abstraction while Surrealism was gaining new ground. The pioneering modes of European abstraction such as Dutch De Stijl, Russian Suprematism and Constructivism, movements that had actively disengaged from creating an art based on the observed world, continued to be upheld as the exemplary models to follow. By the time Kelly arrived in Paris, participation in the Salon des Réalités Nouvelles had grown, including representation by Americans, many there on the G.I. Bill like Kelly. For the fifth Salon in 1950, Kelly was first included with six works, among them *Window, Museum of Modern Art, Paris* (1949) (p. 53) and *Relief with Blue* (1950) (p. 58). Another work, *White Relief* (1950) (p. 59), was rejected because the artists of the Salon felt that it was "not art." These artists most likely scorned Kelly's use of a repetitive pattern, anathema to their commitment to formal composition and asymmetrical balance, as derived from the Neo-Plastic ideals of De Stijl. While Kelly appreciated the opportunity to exhibit his work, he felt restricted by the rigid tenets of this Salon.

After his first solo exhibition at the Galerie Arnaud in Paris in 1951, Kelly still felt boxed in. Critics immediately and wrongly assumed that his abstract-appearing work stemmed from the pioneering modes of European geometric abstraction. One reviewer stated, "The paintings and reliefs of Kelly at the Galerie Arnaud have the wherewithal to seduce the admirers of Mondrian and Vantongerloo."[12] Another critic compared his art to Malevich's Suprematism and the Bauhaus: "He returns to the old Russian suprematist strategy of white on white ... In him, the spirit of investigation that formerly reigned with such ruthlessness at the Bauhaus is reborn at Saint-Germain-des Près."[13] In a review of a group exhibition at Galerie Maeght in Paris the following year, Michel Seuphor, the leading art historian of Mondrian's work, said of Kelly that "Mondrian's patient instruction is bearing fruit."[14] In great contrast to Mondrian, however, Kelly's French output had nothing to do with creating an alternative world order or professing universalizing truths. Instead, the work he showed in Paris was fully engaged with *this* world, his own responses to the specificity and indeterminacy of lived experience.

Kelly was aware that his methods of creating works inspired by his "already-made" strategy as well as working things out in advance through studies and collages might not be accepted. Looking back at this time, he admitted in 1974, "I was scared people wouldn't see them as works of art. You had to be valid—you had to make 'A Painting.'"[15] And then when he was back in New York in the mid-1950s, he had to defend his own abstraction against a new backdrop of gestural American

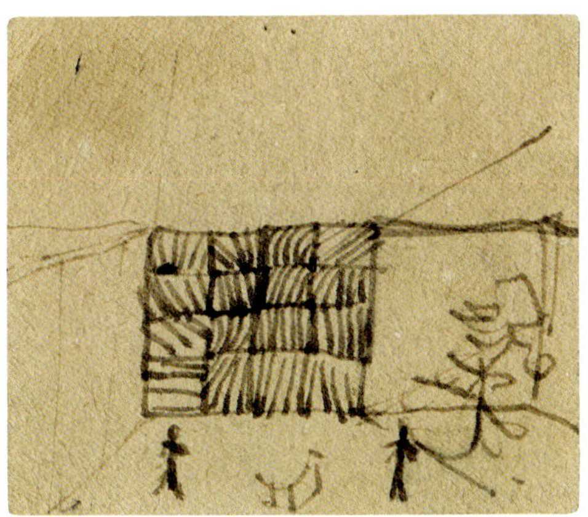

fig. 44: Original sketch for *Cité*, 1951, ink on paper, 1⅞ × 2⅛ in, 4.8 × 5.4 cm

abstraction: "Older, respected artists would tell me I wasn't really painting. I was just determining a shape and filling it with color. Because in those Abstract Expressionist days, it was not thought valid to plan a painting. You had to face the canvas as a battlefield."[16] The "older, respected artists" were, in fact, Adolph Gottlieb and Theodore Stamos, whom he had met one night in 1955. Riding on the subway, the older artists had expressed curiosity about his art. After listening to Kelly explain how he worked, Gottlieb coolly answered that this approach was "not painting." Regarding this negative response, Kelly recalled, "So I thought to myself, I can't talk to them."[17]

For many years, Kelly would remain intentionally quiet about his artistic strategies and subject matter, shunning opportunities to go on record about his art. Only in 1963 did he finally make a public statement about his art for a solo exhibition catalogue published by the Washington Gallery of Modern Art, and then in 1971 he began to open up more for the first two monographs written on his work by John Coplans and Diane Waldman respectively. His reluctance to participate in his own critical reception during the first few decades of his career would partially contribute to misunderstandings about his art in the years to come. And here, at the very beginning of his career in 1951 at Galerie Arnaud, where he showed *Window, Museum of Modern Art, Paris* (p. 53), he first hid the real inspirations for his abstract-appearing art, intentionally giving his 1949 work a vague, discreet title in French, *Construction—relief en blanc, gris et noir*, thereby not providing any descriptive hints as to the original source of the work.[18]

In 1951, concepts of chance continued to occupy Kelly, even chance derived from a dream—how very Surrealist! Perhaps unconsciously inspired by his great enjoyment of teaching his young students, one night he dreamt that he was working on a large mural with many children. With large brushes and on scaffolding, they were painting black bands onto square panels that comprised the mural. The next morning, not wanting to lose the idea, he dashed off a quick ink sketch on a café receipt (fig. 44). He then made a black-and-white brushstroke drawing, which he cut up into squares. Using the grid as his non-compositional format, he arranged the squares by chance. While staying at Meschers again that summer of 1951, he hired a cabinetmaker to cut twenty roughly square wood panels, each measuring 14½ × 14 inches. On each panel he painted similar black-and-white abstract patterns, though now on a much larger scale, ultimately creating *Cité* (p. 63).

Also made in 1951, *Seine* (p. 66) is another important black-and-white painting from this period. To get anywhere from his studio on the Île Saint-Louis, Kelly had to cross the Seine. On these walks over different bridges, he became attuned to plays of light and shadow skimming the surface of the water, a continually shifting "already-made" quite difficult to capture, in contrast to the more static "already-mades" that he had been creating. He studied such light effects through a variety of abstract loose sketches. In contrast, for one drawing he gridded out a total of 3,280 tiny rectangles on a sheet of paper measuring 4 × 15 inches. He developed an elaborate method of chance operations to direct whether each miniature rectangle would be colored black or white. He filled a box with pieces of paper numbered from one to forty-one, which matched the number of rectangles in each vertical row. Beginning with the first vertical row, he pulled out his first piece of paper at random, then filled in the corresponding rectangle in that row with pencil, afterward putting the piece of paper back into the box. For the second row, he drew two pieces of paper, then penciled in the two selected rectangles. He continued this method, increasing the pieces of paper he pulled until he approached the center vertical row, after which point he reversed his operation by decreasing the number of pieces of paper drawn from the box as he moved step by step to the outermost row on the right, which he left blank. When he transferred the black-and-white patterning of the completed drawing (fig. 118) to a much larger wood panel, the result, *Seine* (p. 66), did resemble the way light and shadow dapples on the water. Looking at it now, with twenty-first-century eyes, the work also registers the appearance of a malfunctioning pixelated computer or TV screen. Hence, we can say that in 1951 Kelly had already found a way to break down the visual experience into countless tiny units, thus prefiguring Roy Lichtenstein's Ben-Day dot paintings by a decade.

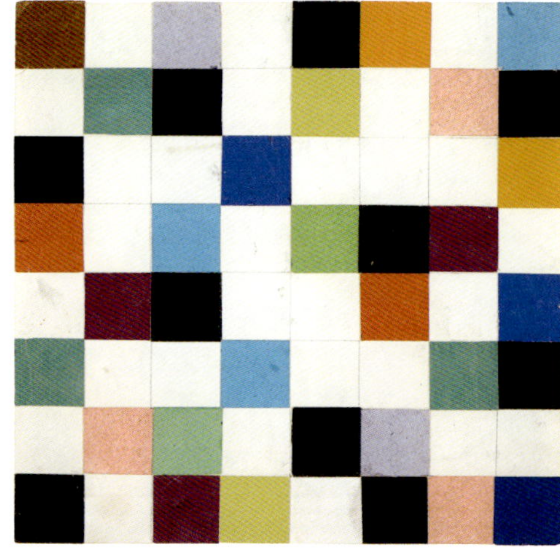

fig. 45: Study for *Colors for a Large Wall*, 1951, graphite and collage on paper, 7⅞ × 7¾ in, 20 × 19.7 cm

Seine led to the format of the first of his large-scale collage series, *Spectrum Colors Arranged by Chance I* (fig. 10), in which one-inch colored squares spread out horizontally from a denser center, also arranged according to chance. In the remaining six collages of this series, he returned to the square grid, as used in *Cité* (1951) (p. 63) and *Meschers* (1951) (p. 65), another gridded painting of broken patterns, which when shown at the Galerie Maeght in the fall of 1951 would be admired by Braque. Kelly's increasing involvement with grids at this time revealed his growing enthusiasm not to compose. Based on these collages, he would make a gridded painting of 1,444 tiny squares, *Spectrum Colors Arranged by Chance* (1951–53) (p. 67), fifteen years before Gerhard Richter started making his own gridded "Color Charts" in 1966. By using the predetermined layout of the grid and the indeterminate laws of chance, Kelly was able to resist composition in two ways. And through his colored collages, he also relinquished another aspect of composition—color choice. By this time, he had discovered colored gummed paper or *papier gommette*, used in French kindergarten classes, and he turned to this stash of paper for his collages. After cutting out countless one-inch squares, he was now faced with a bounty of readymade instant color, as he had been almost ten years before with the colored chips for his Munsell student charts at Pratt in 1942 (fig. 12).[19]

Later that fall 1951, in Sanary, a fishing village in the south of France, Kelly continued the ideas developed in his "Spectrum" collages, creating a much smaller stand-alone collage with the same colored gummed papers (fig. 45). Pleased with the result, he decided to make this into a painting, *Colors for a Large Wall* (p. 69), carrying over the chance color arrangement into the finished work, which at approximately 8 × 8 feet was his largest painting to date by late 1951. In contrast to *Seine*, in which he painted the individual rectangles of black and white onto a single canvas, here he chose to construct a physical, literal grid by joining sixty-four individually stretched canvases, each painted a single color flatly applied—a true "painting/object." When shown in his first solo exhibition at Betty Parsons in 1956, this gridded work would continue the false characterization of Kelly as a follower of Mondrian. In *The New York Herald Tribune*, Emily Genauer—the very same critic whom Kelly and his mother had visited to get advice on which art school to attend many years before—wrote,

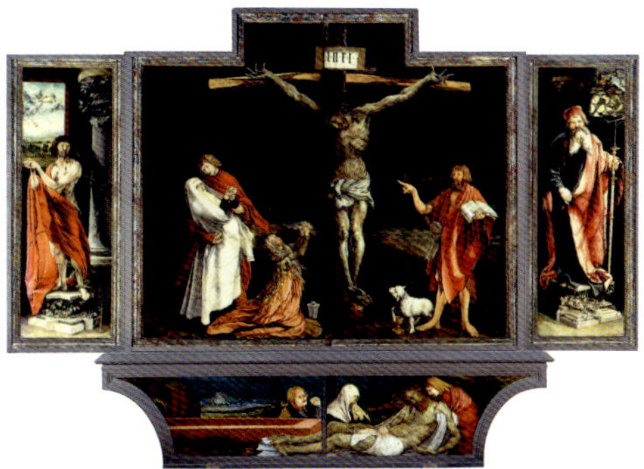

fig. 46: Matthias Grünewald, *Isenheim Altarpiece*, 1512–16, oil on panel, 115 × 211¼ in, 292.1 × 536.6 cm

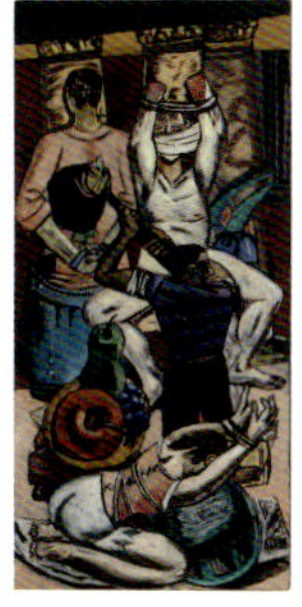
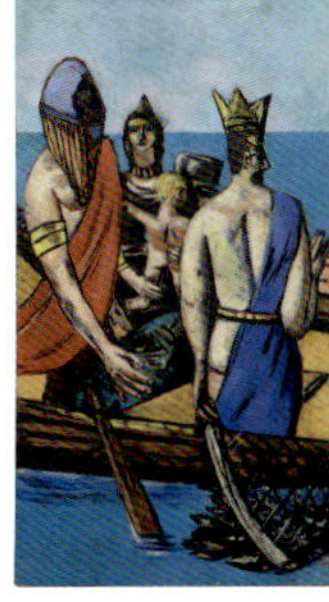
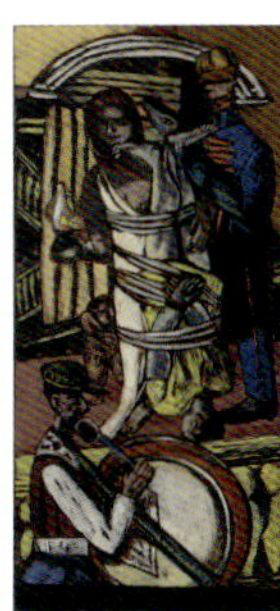

fig. 47: Max Beckmann, *Departure*, 1932–35, oil on canvas, 3 panels: side panels each 84¾ × 39¼ in, 215.3 × 99.7 cm; center panel 84¾ × 45⅜ in, 215.3 × 115.2 cm

"An austere taste for form and color reminiscent of Mondrian is his most conspicuous trait."[20]

Given Kelly's flat application of paint, crisp contours, and deployment of the gridded format, facile comparisons with Mondrian were inevitable, both by French observers and then by those in the U.S. Furthermore, his long sojourn in France led New York critics to assume incorrectly that he followed in the trajectory of European geometric abstraction. In 1950, he had even met De Stijl practitioner Vantongerloo, who lectured about formal aesthetics and how they could only be achieved by mathematical order rather than intuition. Looking back on this meeting, Kelly would later recall, "He made me understand that *his* kind of paintings had to have reasons. I was glad that mine didn't."[21] Instead, he developed his own artistic principles relying on chance, a method antithetical to De Stijl dogma. *Colors for a Large Wall* was an exploration of the fullness, specificity, and arbitrariness of color. Furthermore, each color exerts its own physical presence with a separate panel, contrasting with the singular canvas of a Mondrian and his interlocking armature of painted black lines to hold his colors in place. As Kelly stated in 1992,

> If I had painted the 64 panels on one canvas it would have been quite a different painting, reminiscent of a Klee or a Mondrian. But I wanted an edge for each color, I wanted it to begin and to end so that it had its own uniqueness ... [I]n the world, every object/form has its edges. If you copy it, you depict it, and that I knew: *I didn't want to depict.* In order not to depict I had to make the panels.[22]

Colmar and Multipanel Painting

By the time of *Colors for a Large Wall*, Kelly had already created a handful of joined panel works, such as *Window, Museum of Modern Art, Paris* (p. 53), *La Combe II* (1951) (p. 60), and *Cité* (p. 63). Yet with *Colors for a Large Wall,* he had finally arrived at a distinctive solution for his "painting/objects"—a work constructed from joined panels that asserted both their own presence as well as their own individual color. With *Colors for a Large Wall*, Kelly had thus frustrated the tradition of single-canvas painting stemming from the Renaissance. Of course, this had already been challenged by early twentieth-century predecessors such as Russian Constructivist Aleksandr Rodchenko with his radical monochrome canvases from 1921, *Pure Red Color, Pure Yellow Color and Pure Blue Color*. With these three monochomes, Rodchenko believed he was declaring the end of easel painting. These works, however, did not serve as a model for the twenty-eight-year-old Kelly.[23] Instead, Kelly had turned to a much older source for inspiration—the medieval tradition of the polyptych, that of the church altarpiece made of multiple panels.

Having learned during his Boston years about the celebrated Isenheim Altarpiece by Matthias Grünewald, soon after his arrival in Paris he had made a pilgrimage to Colmar in Alsace, France, to see this early sixteenth-century masterpiece (fig. 46). Upon seeing the work, he linked Grünewald's expressionist style to the two other artists he admired the most at that time, Picasso and Beckmann. Yet, despite his appreciation for these artists, it is clear that Kelly was not drawn to paint in their expressionist, painterly manner. Instead, what he focused on during this visit was the structure of the work, its hinged construction with paneled wings that could open and close. Kelly also connected this work to Beckmann's use of multiple panels, as in *Departure* (1932–35) (fig. 47), which Kelly had seen at MoMA while a student in Boston. From this trip to Colmar as well as others to many more churches while living in France, Kelly forged a deep appreciation for altarpieces and polyptychs and the way they functioned in the overall experience of church architecture. During his French years, he drew a number of studies exploring his own versions of the polyptych, such as one in a sketchbook from 1951–52, in which he jotted down ten different multipanel configurations, noting his intention of making them all white (fig. 48). In another study from the same sketchbook, he drew three other multipanel combinations, even writing down in blue pen the words "colors for a large wall" (fig. 49).

After making *Colors for a Large Wall*, Kelly continued to produce more multipanel works. *Red Yellow Blue White* (pp. 74–75), made in the spring of 1952, in another productive visit to Sanary, exemplifies the great experimentation and originality of his work at the time. He made five vertical columns of five squared panels in different combinations of red, yellow, blue and white. Instead of deploying a continuous gridded structure as in *Colors for a Large Wall*, he separated the vertical rows of *Red Yellow Blue White*, providing interstitial spaces along the wall. Kelly's act of separating these columns was a crucial development, yet one he did not recognize at the time. He would develop this concept in New York (pp. 134–35, 136–37, 180–81; fig. 111), but for the rest of the multipanel works he made in France, he returned to hinging his panels together. As was his diligent practice, Kelly planned in advance the production of *Red Yellow Blue White* in both his sketchbook (fig. 50) and through collage. In his sketchbook study, he identified at upper left the kind of material he would use for this work, "colored cotton." Such a choice was an unusual one for the artist. While in Sanary he had bought some fabric of dyed cotton. This material offered readymade color akin to his colored gummed paper. He stretched cut pieces of this fabric over twenty-five individual panels, about fifteen years before Blinky Palermo would do something similar in the mid-1960s with his "Stoffbilder" or cloth paintings, also made from commercially manufactured fabrics wrapped around his stretchers.

At the time, Kelly had a particular interest in textiles, since he had recently begun to design fabrics for a Swiss textile manufacturer, Gustav Zumsteg. An art collector, Zumsteg was a close friend of Aimé and Marguerite Maeght, who first showed Kelly's work in their October 1951 "Tendance" exhibition at Galerie Maeght. After viewing *Meschers* (p. 65) at this show—the same painting that Braque had also admired—Zumsteg invited Kelly to work for him. Kelly had recently lost his job teaching at the American School of Paris, after the school's director saw his 1951 exhibition at Galerie Arnaud and most likely considered his abstract work too radical. Needing money, the artist had taken on a night watchman's job under the aegis of the Marshall Plan, for which Kelly had to undergo an exacting FBI investigation, but which he was happy to give up for a job designing fabric (fig. 51). Thus in Sanary the following year, he found himself more attuned to textiles

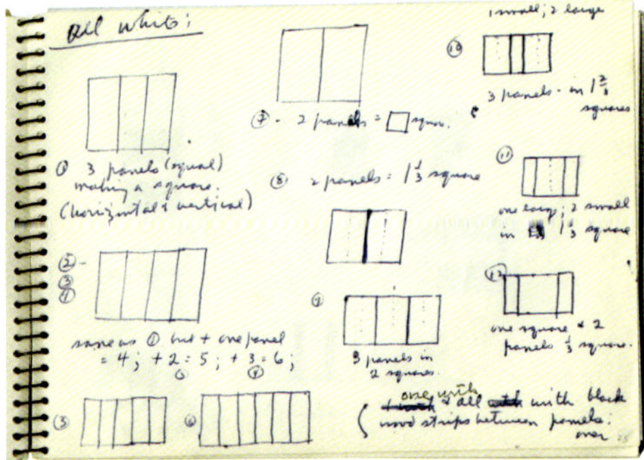

fig. 48: Sketches for white panels (from sketchbook 15), 1951–52, ink on paper, 5⅜ × 7½ in, 13.7 × 19.1 cm

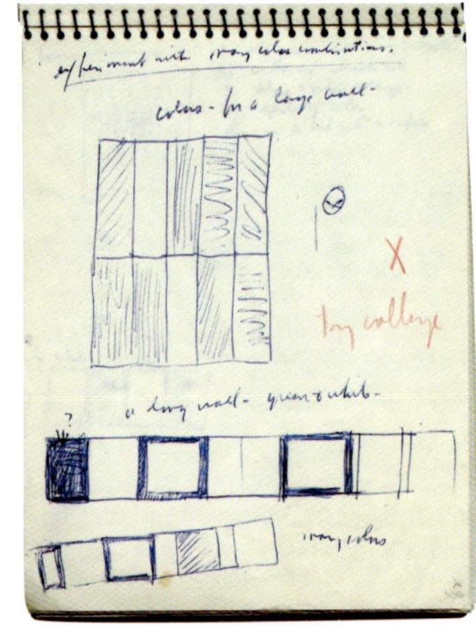

fig. 49: Sketches for paintings for a large wall (from sketchbook 15), 1951–52, ink on paper, 7 × 5¼ in, 17.8 × 13.3 cm

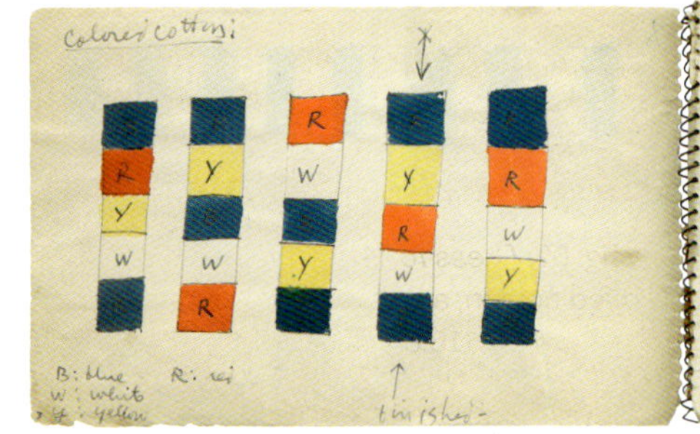

fig. 50: Study for *Red Yellow Blue White* (from sketchbook 18), 1952, 5¼ × 8¼ in, 13.3 × 21 cm

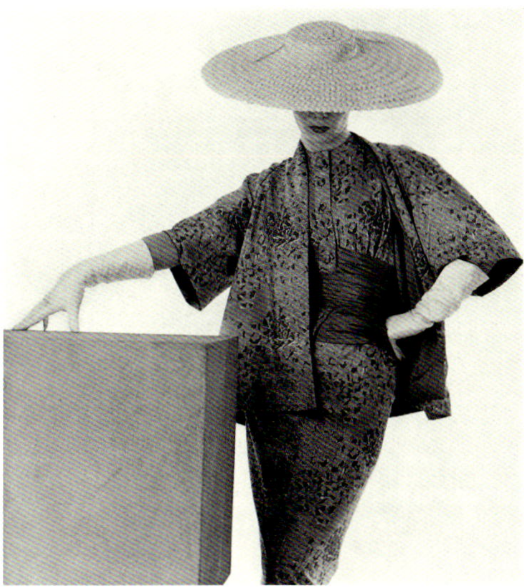

fig. 51: Dress by Pierre Balmain, with fabric designed by Ellsworth Kelly, photo published in *L'Art et la Mode*, 1952

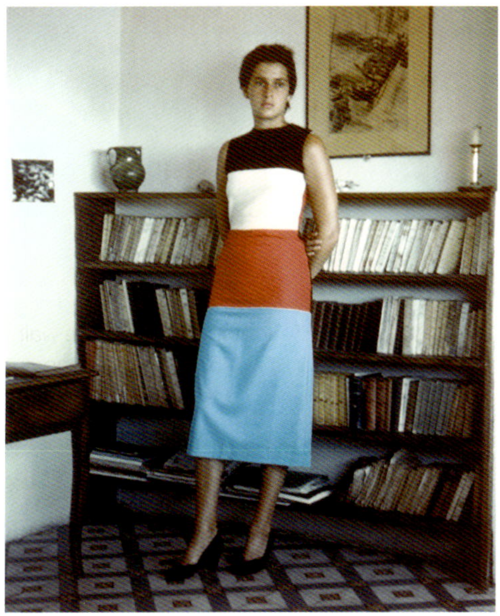

fig. 52: *Dress for Anne Weber*, 1952, dyed cotton, approximately 46 × 19 in, 116.8 × 48.3 cm

and thus inspired to buy the dyed cotton he had come across there. With this same fabric, he also designed a dress for his Boston Museum School friend Anne Weber. With his multipanel concept foremost in his mind, he carried over a similar idea to the design of the dress (fig. 52), which Weber sewed herself; however, she did not follow his instructions to make each panel of color the same height.

Kelly's examination of the multiple panel allowed for continued investigations of both color and structure. Still in Sanary in the spring of 1952, he made *Painting for a White Wall* (pp. 82–83), a work of five joined vertical panels with new colors of pink and orange, a color juxtaposition drawn from his Boston days of admiring the same color pairing in Ambrogio Lorenzetti's *Virgin and Child* (fig. 24). At the time, he was not feeling confident about how people would respond to this work. His 1950 *White Relief* (p. 59) had already been discredited by the Salon des Réalités Nouvelles as "not art," and his solo exhibition was the reason for his firing from the American School. So it was only natural to wonder then, as he recalled in 1996, "Can I make a painting with just five panels of color in a row? I loved it, but I didn't think the world would. They'd think, it's not enough."[24] In an earlier recollection from 1969, Kelly described how he decided to test the public, by installing the work outside of his studio:

> In 1952 I had a studio with a balcony overlooking a busy street. When I finished the first painting I had done in five horizontally grouped panels, I hung it on the balcony and went out to hear comments. A few people who noticed the painting were puzzled and said so. A child, pointing with his finger said, "black–rose–orange–white–blue—blue–white–orange–rose–black."[25]

Kelly appreciated the child's instinctive response to the work, how the boy simply stated what he saw rather than attempting to interpret what it was. This particular memory is one that Kelly has often recounted, as he did again in 1992: "People looked at it and said that it wasn't enough, that there were no marks on it, that it didn't say anything, and that there was no idea. They said it was just a presentation of colors. And I said, *'Well, that's what it is—the naming of colors.'*"[26] Although the boy "got" the work, Kelly still had concerns about whether an adult public would get it.[27]

This notion of "naming colors" is central to Kelly's experience of the empirical world and thus his overall approach to color. As discussed earlier, during World War II he had begun to chart out the color he saw in the world in his sketchbooks, as evidenced in his 1944 landscape sketch drawn in the south of Bastogne (fig. 17). One day in September 1953, near the end of his residence in France, he was traveling to Zurich for his fabric-design job. Sitting on the train from Paris, he looked out of the window and saw in the distance the fields of the French countryside, their colors passing quickly before his eyes. Through the window, which functioned as a framing device, he was still able to notice distinctions between the hues of the fields, appearing as separate planes. He took out his spiral sketchbook and started jotting down the colors that he had seen. Unlike the figurative sketch done in 1944 near Bastogne (which was incidentally just north of where he was on his 1953 train ride), he noted the colors in simple tripartite diagrams (fig. 53). In the first diagram he wrote down descriptions of color, “earth brown variance/lighter brown/earth brown,” while in the second he chose to note only the subject matter, “sky/earth/lettuce.” In the last one he referred to both, thus showing the quick translation of what he was seeing and the fluidity between color and subject, “lettuce/green (bluish/silver (light)/earth raw umber + white.”

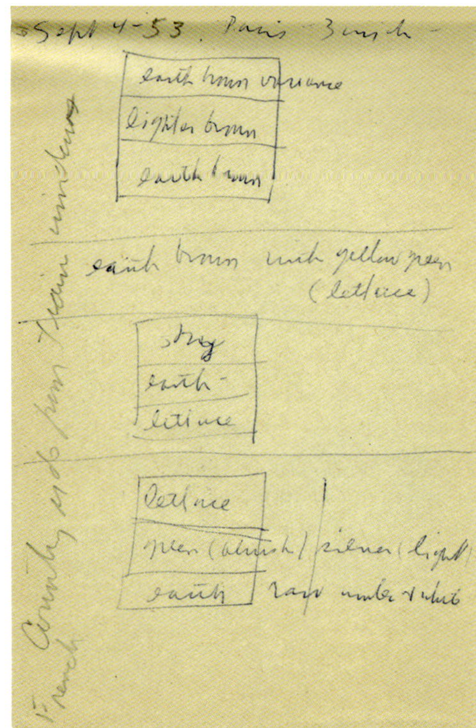

fig. 53: *Sketches from a train (Paris to Zurich)* (from sketchbook 21), 1953, ink on paper, 6½ × 4⅛ in, 16.5 × 10.5 cm

Back in his studio, he played with the color variations through collage, using his stash of *papier gommette*. Such explorations eventually led to a finished painting, ***Train Landscape*** (1953) (p. 77), a multipanel painting of three identically sized horizontal panels that basically follow his last diagram. At some point during or after this trip, Kelly wrote in pencil along the left edge of his sketchbook page, “French Countryside from train window.” *Train Landscape* can be understood as capturing not just the color he had observed, but also the passing of time on the train—a translation of a long duration into instant color. By not allowing gesture (and thus personality) to show in how he painted, Kelly had banished the visual evidence of how he made a painting (although if one sees his paintings close up, one can observe some of his brushstrokes). In contrast to canvases by Jackson Pollock or Willem de Kooning that reveal their processes through legible overlays of countless drips, splatters, or brushstrokes, Kelly’s paintings do not expose individual moments of creation, and thus the duration of their making. Instead, as in *Train Landscape*, the monochrome color of each of the three panels registers instantaneously, all at once, just like the readymade color of his gummed paper.

Art for Walls: Part I

Throughout his years in France, foremost on Kelly’s mind was how he could challenge and even bypass mimesis, depiction, subjectivity, gesture, and, as he has argued, even invention. To resist a number of these categories, he turned to methods of non-composition, such as chance operations, automatic drawing, the use of the grid, and his own unique strategy of the “already-made.” As we have seen, collage factored heavily in exercising these non-compositional strategies. Furthermore, his use of colored gummed paper allowed him to explore pre-made, hence anonymous, colors, which he then transferred to his finished work, painting them uniformly and flatly. Collage also helped him advance his approach to multipanel painting, since his initial studies allowed him to investigate such concepts on a small scale. All the while, however, he was also giving considerable thought to the overarching concepts of *what* he wanted his art to be, not just *how* he wanted to make it. While some of the titles he assigned to works of art do not convey any particular meaning, and others used at his exhibitions actually concealed his subject matter, a few of his titles from his French years do carry conceptual significance—namely ***Colors for a Large Wall*** (p. 69) and ***Painting for a White Wall*** (pp. 82–83). Here, he added an artistic purpose, a final destination for his works, even though it seems a rather obvious one. Aren’t paintings intended for walls? What exactly did Kelly mean by these titles?

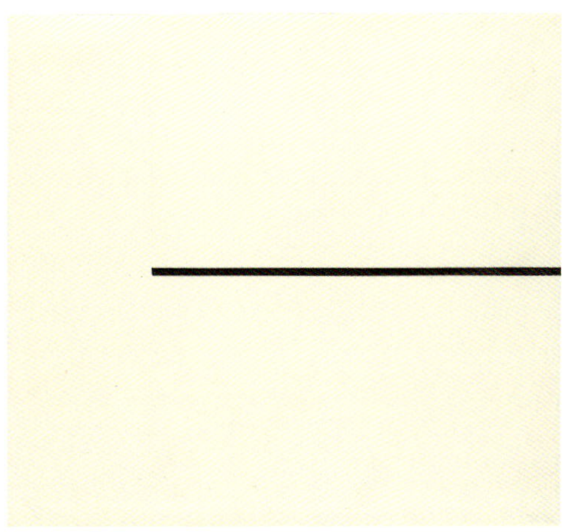

fig. 54: *Horizontal Line* (from *Line, Form and Color*), 1951, ink on paper, 7½ × 8 in, 19.1 × 20.3 cm

fig. 55: *Red* (from *Line, Form and Color*), 1951, collage on paper, 7½ × 8 in, 19.1 × 20.3 cm

Since the beginning of art's creation, or at least the earliest evidence deemed as such, the legendary cave paintings of Lascaux, France, from c.15,000 B.C., man painted onto a vertical surface, in this case the interior wall of the cave, the primitive architecture of prehistoric man. This tradition of painting onto a walled surface continued through time, from frescoes in Pompeii and mosaics in Byzantium to the Sistine Chapel by Michelangelo. When Kelly left Boston for Paris, he had already developed a true appreciation of such early models, specifically Byzantine and Romanesque art, which he had studied in two volumes he owned on the churches of Saint-Savin and Tavant, as well as the twelfth-century frescoes he had encountered at the Museum of Fine Arts, Boston (fig. 26). That installation had replicated in part the architecture of the original Catalan church from where the frescoes had been removed, most notably the partially domed apse. On visits to the museum, Kelly had admired how the frescoes were seamlessly integrated within the architecture itself. Such an interest was further sparked by the 1948 school lecture he had attended where Herbert Read called for a return to the collaboration between art and architecture.

Such ideas continued to gestate during Kelly's subsequent years in France as he visited various churches in and outside of Paris. He also paid close attention to the patterning and structure of walls he saw, to those who had actually constructed such walls, recollecting in 1971 how in France he had written, "Everything is beautiful but that which man tries intentionally to make beautiful. The work of an ordinary bricklayer is more valid than the artwork of all but a very few artists."[28] And in the fall of 1951, after he had made *Cité* (p. 63) and around the time he created *Colors for a Large Wall* (p. 69), he found the opportunity to formulate his thinking not only in studies and paintings, but in words as well. In need of funds, having been let go by the American School earlier that year, Kelly applied for a John Simon Guggenheim Memorial Foundation fellowship offered to those working in the fields of the natural sciences, social sciences, humanities, and the arts. He hoped the scholarship would furnish him with the money to publish a book project, *Line, Form and Color*, which he had begun that spring.[29] In the application he wrote, "I will create a book which shall be an alphabet of plastic pictorial elements, and which shall aim at establishing a new scale of painting, a closer contact between the artist and the wall, and a new spirit of painting to accompany modern architecture."[30]

Although Kelly was not granted the fellowship, preparing the application proved to be a beneficial and productive forum for him. Through his application statement, forty-six original maquettes (his proposed "alphabet of plastic pictorial elements"), and another text that he subsequently wrote, Kelly staked a claim to his burgeoning ideas and goals. First, in his collaged and drawn maquettes, he laid out the beginnings of his own vocabulary, primarily the focus on specific shape and the deployment of monochrome color (painted on individual panels) (figs 54–58). Through these maquettes and then in his written statements, he developed the concepts that became the foundation of his ongoing practice: to make an abstract, anonymous art based on the singular form, and one that would produce a new and vital relationship with the architectural wall. In a subsequent text he fleshed out his thoughts even further, declaring emphatically,

> Creative painting today means easel painting, "the original oil painting," sold through galleries to private collectors, and to museums, to be hung on walls. This painting has no relation to the architectural wall; it is an expression of the artist's separate personality. I believe that artists should work directly with the architect, building as the architect builds.[31]

Letters Kelly wrote around this time attest to the progression of his thinking, such as those sent to musician and composer John Cage, whom Kelly had met in June 1949 when Cage and choreographer and dancer Merce Cunningham were staying at the same hotel as Kelly, the Hôtel de Bourgogne on the Île Saint-Louis.[32] Cage had taken an interest in the younger artist's work, and for a period of time they would correspond until Kelly's return to the States in 1954.[33] In one such letter, dated September 4, 1950, Kelly shared his growing theories about art being in unison with the wall:

> My collages are only ideas for things much larger—things to cover walls ... I am not interested in painting as it has been accepted for so long—to hang on the walls of houses as pictures. To hell with pictures—they should *be* the wall—even better—on the outside wall —of large buildings. Or stood up outside as billboards or a kind of modern icon.[34]

About two years later, inspired now by modern architecture, Kelly went to Marseilles to see Le Corbusier's Unité d'Habitation, then nearing completion. It was the first time Kelly had seen the use of polychromy in modern architecture. Le Corbusier's designs incorporated bright pastel versions of red, yellow, and blue painted on the walls between the countless balconies. By this time Le Corbusier had become a leading champion of a total integration of the arts, similar to Herbert Read's call for collaboration between art and architecture, as well as those made by other avant-garde figures such as Fernand Léger. So Kelly was able to experience at firsthand a grand-scale realization of this utopian-inspired idea in Marseilles.

But to Kelly, the building and its use of color fell short of his expectations. As he retrospectively explained, "The wide slabs in primary colors on the balconies surprised me, but I thought that Le Corbusier was using color in a decorative way. I wanted to use color in this way, over an entire wall, but I didn't want it to be decorative."[35] The next year in 1953, Kelly's friend Alain Naudé, a South African pianist, was given the opportunity to show slides of Kelly's art to Le Corbusier, who responded well to *Méditerranée* (1952) (p. 71), and especially *Colors for a Large Wall* (p. 69). While looking at Kelly's examples, Le Corbusier remarked, "This kind of painting needs the new architecture to go with it."[36] In another letter written around this time to Baroness Hilla Rebay, the founding director of Solomon R. Guggenheim's Museum of Non-Objective Painting in New York (which would later become The Solomon R. Guggenheim Museum), and with whom he struck up a brief friendship, Kelly wrote, "I believe that the days of the 'easel' painting are fading, and that the future art will be something more than just 'personality painting' for walls of apartments and museums. The future art must go to the wall itself. And this is what I have been trying to do in my work."[37]

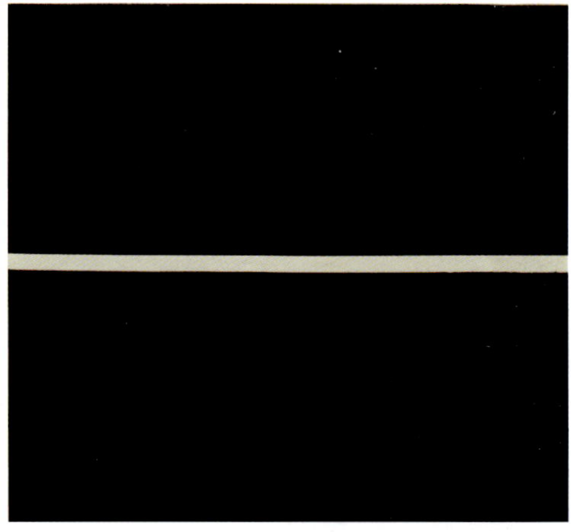

fig. 56: *Horizontal Band* (from *Line, Form and Color),* 1951, collage on paper, 7½ × 8 in, 19.1 × 20.3 cm

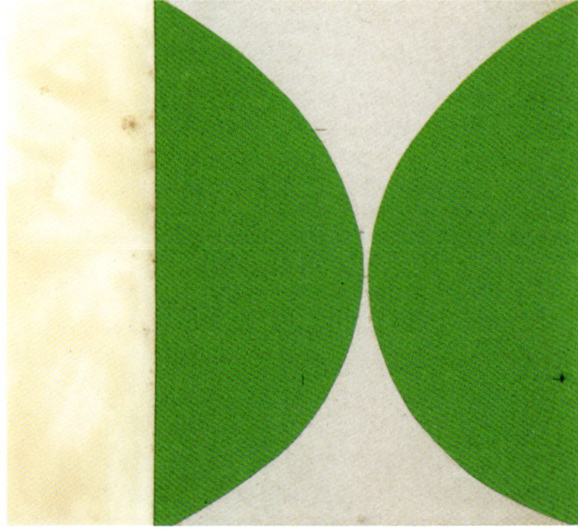

fig. 57: *Green Curves* (from *Line, Form and Color),* 1951, collage on paper, 7½ × 8 in, 19.1 × 20.3 cm

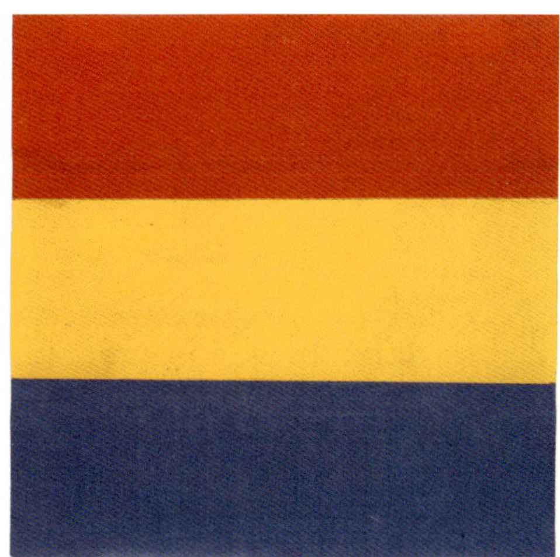

fig. 58: *Red Yellow Blue* (from *Line, Form and Color)*, 1951, collage, 7½ × 8 in, 19.1 × 20.3 cm

Later in 1952 Kelly visited Giverny, where Claude Monet had made his studio and home. Kelly had written to Monet's stepson, Jean-Pierre Hoschedé, who extended an invitation. There Kelly saw the late "Nymphéas," the now famed abstract paintings of water lilies that Monet had made at the end of his life. Seeing these large-scale works *in situ*, before they were acquired by American and European museums in the ensuing years, registered a great impact on the young artist. In 1991 Kelly recalled this visit he took with Naudé:

> In 1952, I began to wonder what ... happened to Monet in his last years. So I wrote to his stepson in Giverny and was invited to visit. He took us out to the big studio where all the paintings of water lilies were kept. There must have been at least a dozen huge paintings, each on two easels ... The paintings had been abandoned, really. And one of the things I remember most was one painting, a huge one, that was all white, very heavily painted. There was some orange and some pink maybe, and some pale green. And in the middle of it was a big, jagged cut. The stepson said that Monet had slashed it himself. And then we went into a second studio, and there must have been a hundred paintings there of medium size that were just jammed together. When we went back to Paris and talked to dealers about the paintings, everyone said that Monet was color-blind toward the end of his life and that these paintings were worthless. But we kept talking about them, and eventually the Museum of Modern Art purchased one of them.[38]

Inspired by Monet's late abstractions, Kelly painted *Tableau Vert* (1952) (p. 76) the day after his visit. Since he had already made paintings using different colored panels, he wondered if he could make a work of just one color. He incorporated texture and gesture, inflecting the surface with various brushstrokes and shifts in the green color, an approach quite unlike his usual flatly painted panels. Soon after he made this painting, he wrapped up the work, neither fully happy with it nor understanding its import. For a few decades he had forgotten about the work until he finally unwrapped it around 1985, after which point he realized *Tableau Vert* had been his first monochrome.

In the fall of 1953 Kelly was evicted from his studio at Cité des Fleurs, an event that would force him to come to terms with his immediate future. He had sold only one painting, *Antibes* (1950), and now had nowhere to make new work, let alone a place to live. The network of friends he had made in Paris came to his aid, offering temporary places to stay or even writing letters of encouragement, such as those sent to him by French critic Michel Seuphor.[39] Yet this support would not be enough. In the winter of 1954 Kelly became ill and was hospitalized for jaundice at the American Hospital in Paris. After convalescing outside of Rotterdam at the family home of a Dutch friend, Geert-Jan Visser, Kelly came back to Paris with the idea of returning to the U.S.

A trip to the local Brentano's bookstore helped confirm this decision. There he picked up a past issue of *ARTnews* from December 1953, which featured a review of Ad Reinhardt's exhibition at New York's Betty Parsons Gallery, a significant and early promoter of Abstract Expressionism. The reproductions of Reinhardt's abstract paintings resonated with Kelly, as well as the words written by critic

Thomas B. Hess, such as "The pigment is applied in flat, even, anonymous-looking coats. Rectangular shapes are spotted on monochrome backgrounds."[40]

Lacking funds and feeling utterly deflated by his current situation, Kelly found this article encouraging, since it made him think that New York City might be more receptive to his work. He began planning his return to the States, ignoring his mother's ill-advised suggestion of discarding the work he had made in France. Unable to afford the shipment of his art—by this time, over eighty-five paintings and reliefs, plus many drawings as well as sketchbooks—he selected the Cunard Line because it was the only steamship company willing to transport all his belongings on credit. In the summer of 1954, Kelly boarded the *Queen Mary* for the United States.

1 Kelly, quoted in Coplans 1971, p. 20.
2 Kelly, in conversation with the author, Spencertown, New York, January 2, 2014.
3 During his years in France, Kelly stopped bird-watching because the foreign birds were unfamiliar to his American eyes.
4 Kelly, quoted in Coplans 1971, p. 20.
5 Kelly, quoted in ibid., pp. 20–21; italics added.
6 Yve-Alain Bois, a leading scholar on Kelly, first observed this key aspect of his artistic practice in a seminal 1992 essay on the artist's years in France. In this essay, Bois was also the first to identify and analyze the conceptual foundations of Kelly's art as they were emerging during his French sojourn, most significantly, strategies of non-composition, such as chance operations, the use of the modular grid, and finding forms "already made" in the world, as Kelly first explained in 1971. The artist would then recreate such shapes in his paintings and reliefs by employing, in the words of Bois, the strategy of the indexical "transfer." See Bois, "Ellsworth Kelly in France: Anti-Composition in Its Many Guises," in Bois, Jack Cowart, and Alfred Pacquement, *Ellsworth Kelly: The Years in France, 1948–1954* (Washington, DC: National Gallery of Art, 1992), pp. 9–36.
7 Bois 1992, p. 16.
8 Kelly, quoted in Taylor 1991, p. 102.
9 Kelly, quoted in Coplans 1971, pp. 28, 30.
10 Bois 1992, p. 14.
11 Kelly, from notes in journal, sketchbook 6 (1948–51), Kelly studio archives, Spencertown, New York.
12 "Flâneur des Deux Rives," *Les Nouvelles Littéraires* (May 3, 1951, p. 5), quoted and trans. in Nathalie Brunet, "Chronology," in Yve-Alain Bois, Jack Cowart, and Alfred Pacquement, *Ellsworth Kelly: The Years in France, 1948–1954* (Washington, DC: National Gallery of Art, 1992), p. 189.
13 G.B., *Arts* (May 4, 1951) quoted and trans. in Brunet 1992, p. 189.
14 Michel Seuphor, *Derrière le miroir* ["Tendance" exhibition catalogue], no. 50 (October 1952), quoted (and trans.) in Bois 1992, p. 33, n. 16.
15 Kelly, quoted in Phyllis Tuchman, "Ellsworth Kelly's Photographs," *Art in America* 62 (January/February 1974), p. 60.
16 Kelly, quoted in Hindry 1992, p. 34.
17 Kelly, in conversation with the author, Spencertown, New York, August 2, 2001.
18 Kelly would not exhibit this work until seventeen years later, at the Museum of Modern Art's 1968 exhibition, "The Art of the Real: USA 1948–1968," now considered a seminal Minimalism exhibition, curated by E.C. Goossen, who would become a champion of Kelly's work. Following Goossen's premise for the exhibition that asserted the recent emergence of "the simple, irreducible, irrefutable object," Kelly revealed his original inspiration for the first time, exhibiting the work under a new title, by which it is now known, *Window, Museum of Modern Art, Paris*.
19 Kelly's deployment of collage, especially with bold color, undoubtedly brings to mind Matisse's cutouts made during the last decade of the French artist's life. While Kelly did see and was impressed by Matisse's large-scale cutout, *Zulma* (1950) at the Salon de Mai in Paris in May 1950, it must be noted that the collages made by Jean Arp and Sophie Taeuber-Arp, which he saw in January 1950 at Arp's studio (fig. 39), served as inspiration for the young artist's budding collage practice at this time rather than those by the French master.
20 E[mily] G[enauer], "Art Exhibition Notes: Kelly at Parsons," *The New York Herald Tribune*, June 2, 1956, section 1, p. 9.
21 Kelly, quoted in Goossen 1973, p. 29; italics his.
22 Kelly, quoted in Hindry 1992, p. 28; italics his.
23 Kelly was not aware of Rodchenko's three monochrome canvases from 1921 while living in France. According to the artist, he learned of the works in 1988 at the time of a Swiss and German exhibition exploring the primary colors, in which Kelly was also included, "*Rot Gelb Blau: Die Primärfarben in der Kunst des 20. Jahrhunderts*," which opened at the Kunstmuseum, St. Gallen.
24 Kelly, quoted in Holland Cotter, "A Giant of the New Surveys His Rich Past," *The New York Times*, October 13, 1996, section H, p. 43.
25 Kelly, quoted in "Ellsworth Kelly," *Art Now: New York*, 1, no. 9 (November 1969), n.p.
26 Kelly, quoted in Paul Taylor, "Ellsworth Kelly: Interview," in Hindry 1992, p. 155; italics his. Revised and expanded version of Taylor 1991.
27 Indeed, Kelly would not show *Painting for a White Wall* until sixteen years later in 1968 at MoMA's "The Art of the Real" exhibition where he also showed his 1949 *Window, Museum of Modern Art, Paris*, under its new title, thus divulging its connection to real things in the world.
28 Kelly, quoted in Coplans 1971, p. 30.
29 On May 28, 1951 Kelly wrote from Paris to his friend Ralph Coburn, "I am planning a book, perhaps a magazine, with no writing whatsoever, just (linoleum) prints." Kelly, quoted in Clare Bell, "At Play with Vision: Ellsworth Kelly's 'Line, Form and Color'," in Waldman (ed.) 1996, p. 66, n. 1.
30 Kelly, from his original application form in the Kelly studio archives, Spencertown, New York. Also quoted in Bell 1996, p. 66, n. 3. See also the publication, Ellsworth Kelly, *Line Form Color* (Cambridge, MA: Harvard University Art Museums, 1999), in which the artist finally published his 1951 maquette concepts as originally intended, in book form.
31 Kelly, quoted in "Project for a Book: *Line, Form and Color*," in Ellsworth Kelly, *Line Form Color* (Cambridge, MA: Harvard University Art Museums, 1999), n.p. In this 1999 publication, Kelly published a longer statement dated November 1951.
32 It must be noted that according to Kelly, his explorations with chance did not stem from his 1949 meeting with John Cage, who would not introduce chance operations in his own compositions until 1951.
33 For more information on Kelly and Cage, see Brunet 1992, pp. 182, 184, 187–88. For a more recent discussion, in particular of Kelly's correspondences with Cage, see Branden W. Joseph, *Random Order: Robert Rauschenberg and the Neo-Avant-Garde* (Cambridge, MA, and London: The MIT Press, 2003), pp. 73, 78, 96–97.
34 Kelly, quoted in Brunet 1992, pp. 187–88. It must also be noted that his inspiration to create large paintings came from studying masterpieces at the Louvre, "I liked the quality of the painting ... And the scale was also impressive. Of course, there are all the huge Davids and Géricaults in the Louvre, and when I saw them, I realized I wanted to do paintings their size, the size of walls. But if you don't have any money, and have only a small hotel room, you can't do things like that." Kelly, quoted in Taylor 1991, p. 102.
35 Kelly, quoted in Brunet 1992, p. 192.
36 As recounted by Kelly, quoted in Goossen 1973, p. 45.
37 Kelly, from a letter dated November 29, most likely from 1952, quoted in Michael Plante, "'Things to Cover Walls': Ellsworth Kelly's Paris Paintings and the Tradition of Mural Decoration," *American Art*, 9, no. 1 (spring 1995), p. 43, n. 14.
38 Kelly, quoted in Taylor 1991, p. 102.
39 Seuphor wrote to Kelly in 1953, "Of all the serious successors to Mondrian I think that you will be the best. It is a shame that we may not have access to your magnificent works for several months." Brunet 1992, p. 194.
40 Thomas B. Hess, "Reinhardt: The Position and Perils of Purity," *ARTnews* 52, no. 8 (December 1953), p. 26.

Plant II, 1949
oil on wood, 16½ × 13 in, 41.9 × 33 cm

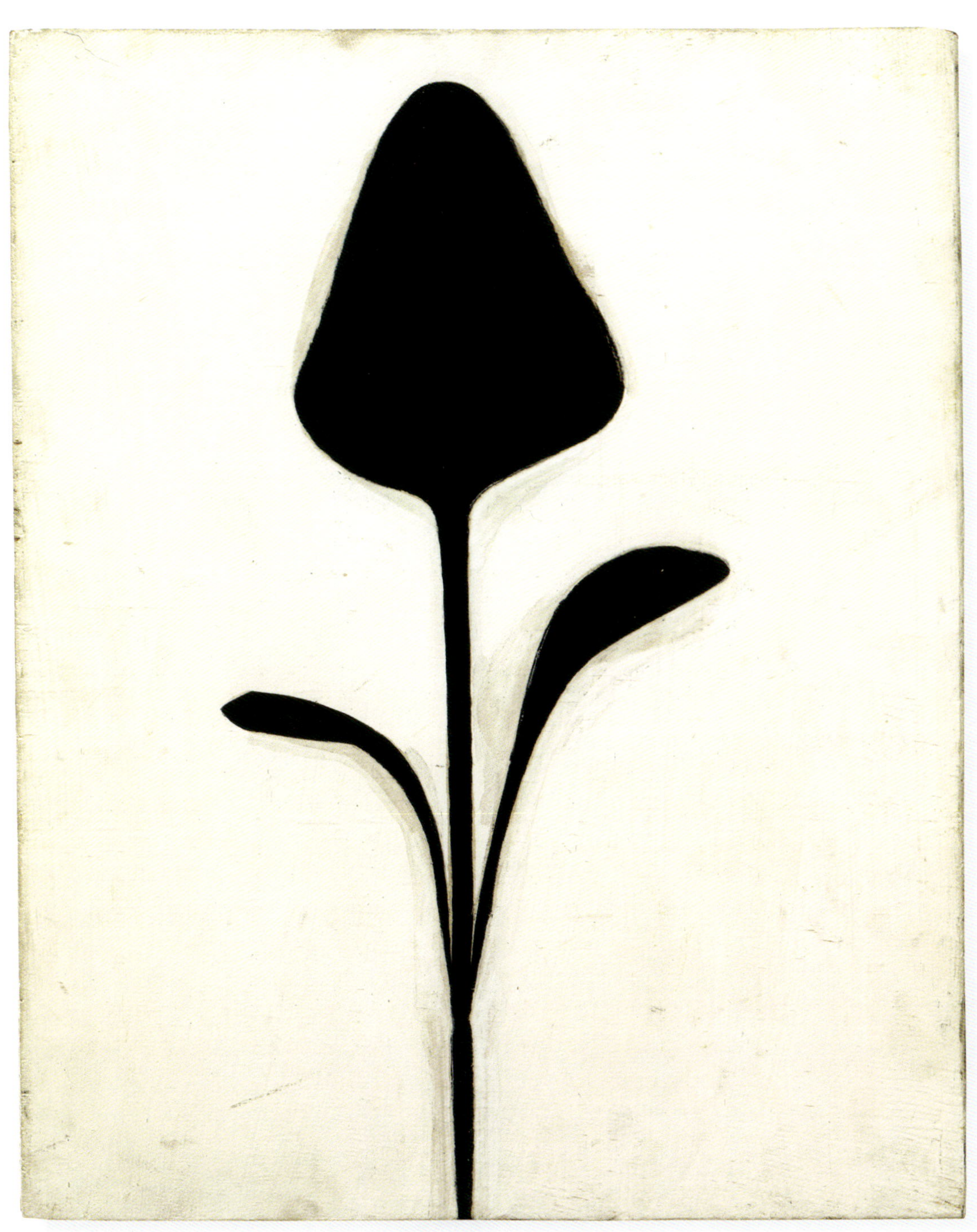

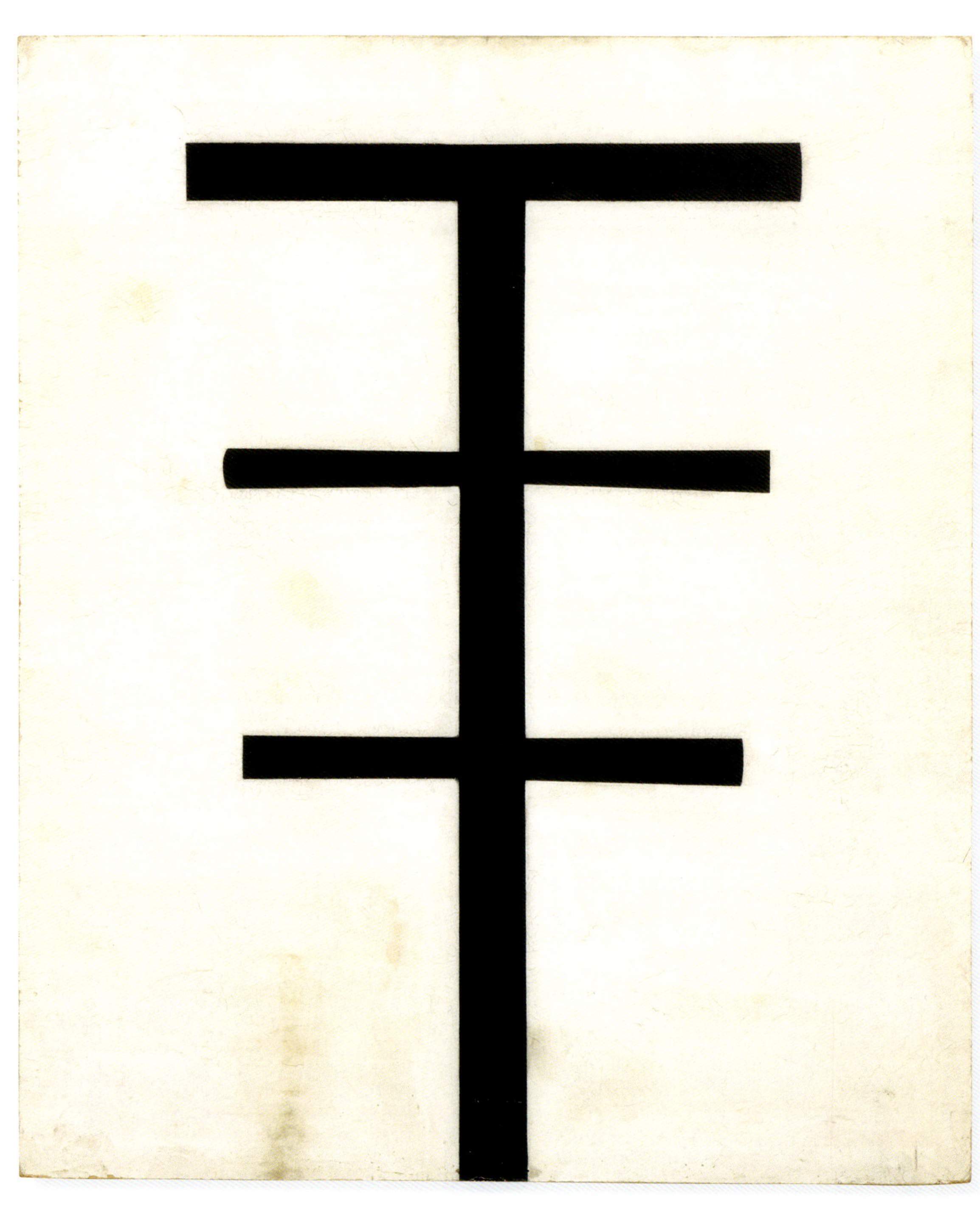

Window I, 1949
oil and gesso on wood, 25½ × 21 × 1½ in, 64.8 × 53.3 × 3.8 cm

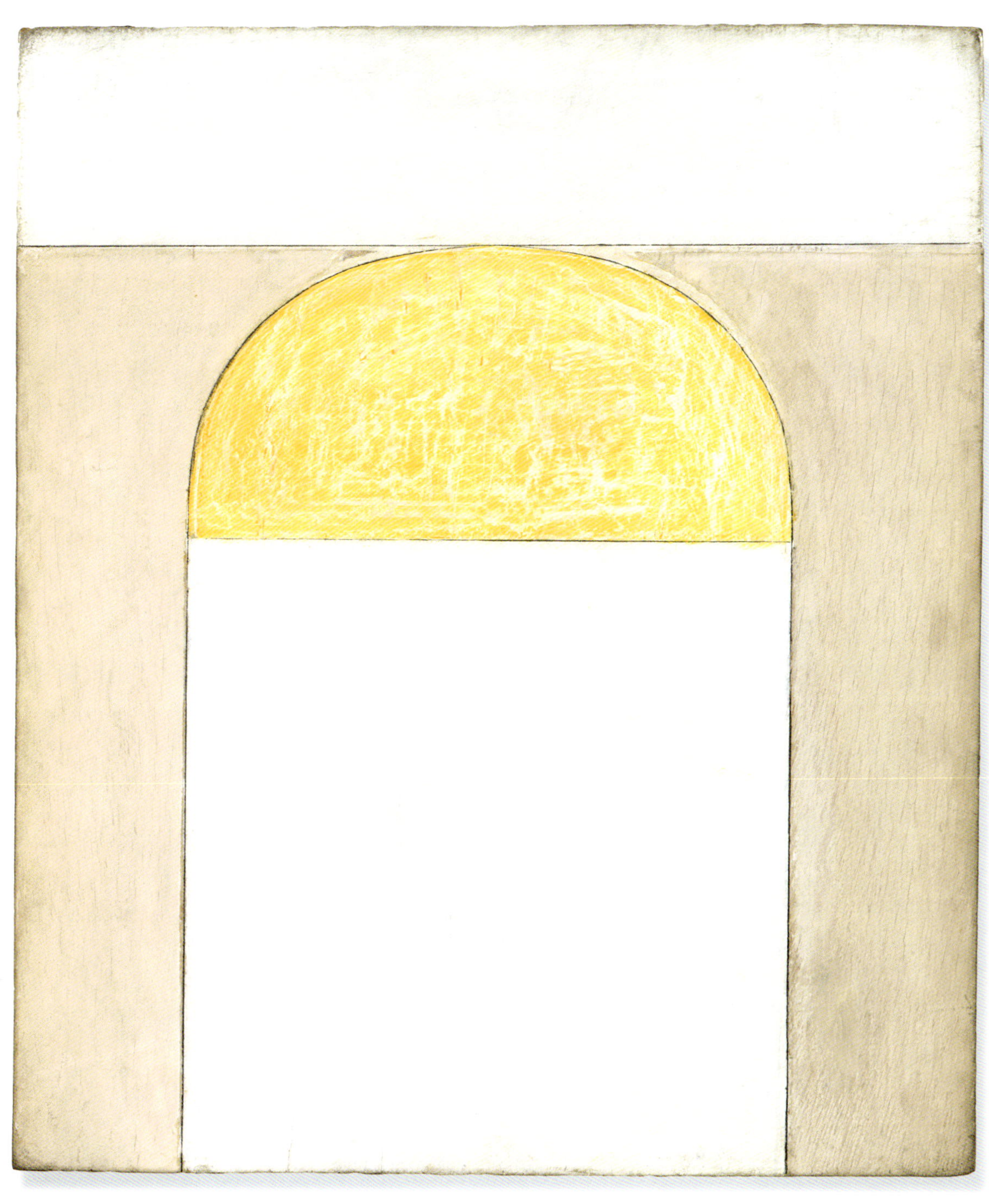

Kilometer Marker, 1949
oil, gesso, and graphite on plywood, 21½ × 18 × 1½ in, 54.6 × 45.7 × 3.8 cm

Window, Museum of Modern Art, Paris, 1949
oil on wood and canvas, 2 joined panels
50½ × 19½ in, 128.3 × 49.5 cm

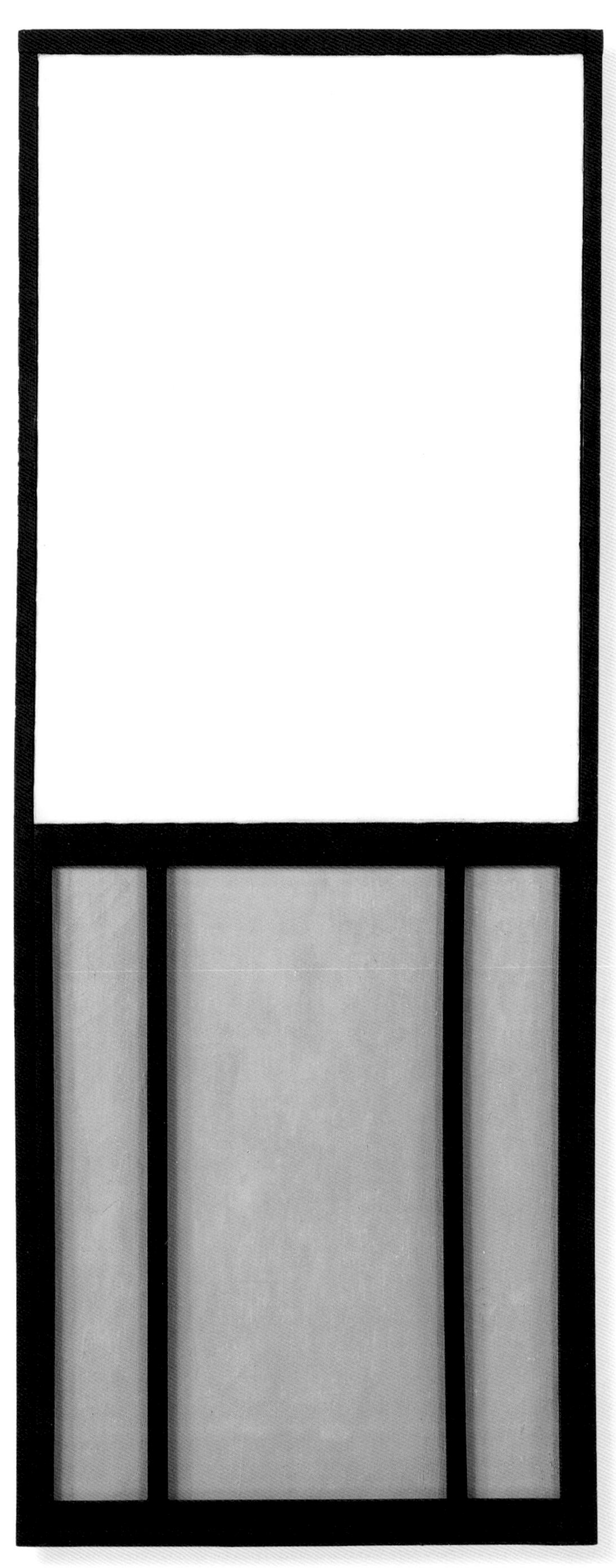

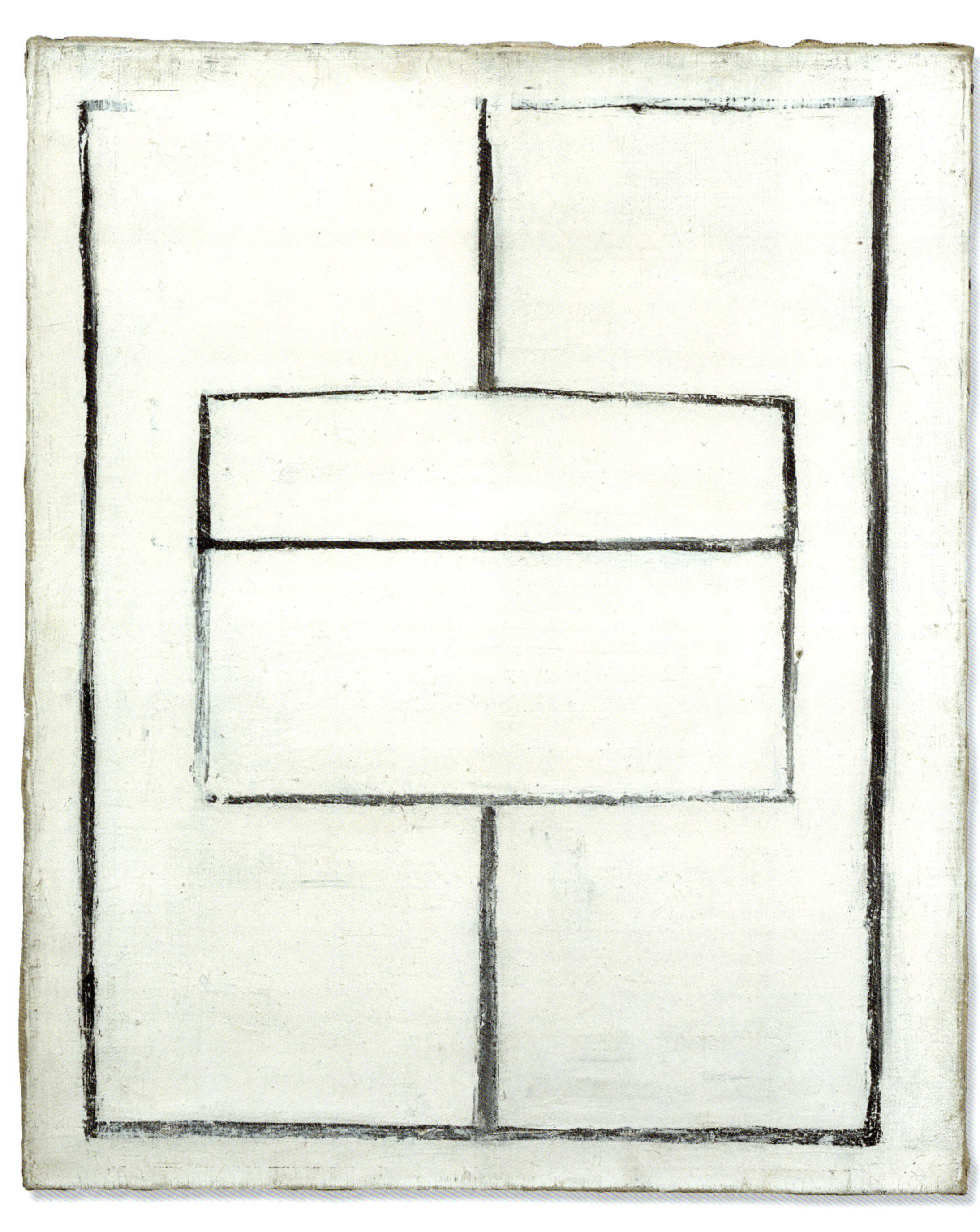

Tennis Court, 1949
oil on canvas, 24 × 19½ in, 61 × 49.5 cm

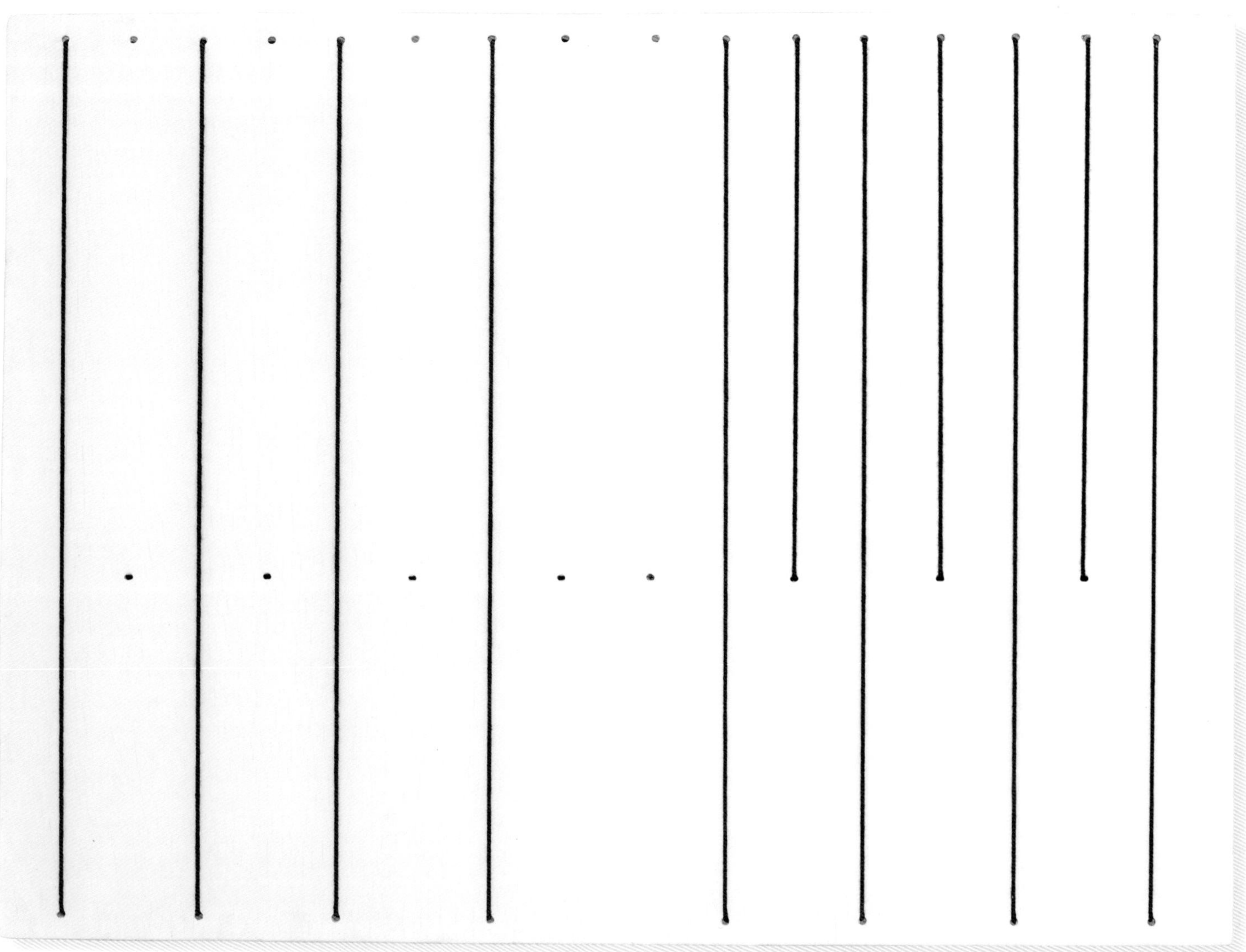

Gate-Board, 1950
oil on wood with string, 26¾ × 35¼ in, 67.9 × 89.5 cm

Window V, 1950
oil on wood, 27½ × 7¼ × ½ in, 69.9 × 18.4 × 1.3 cm

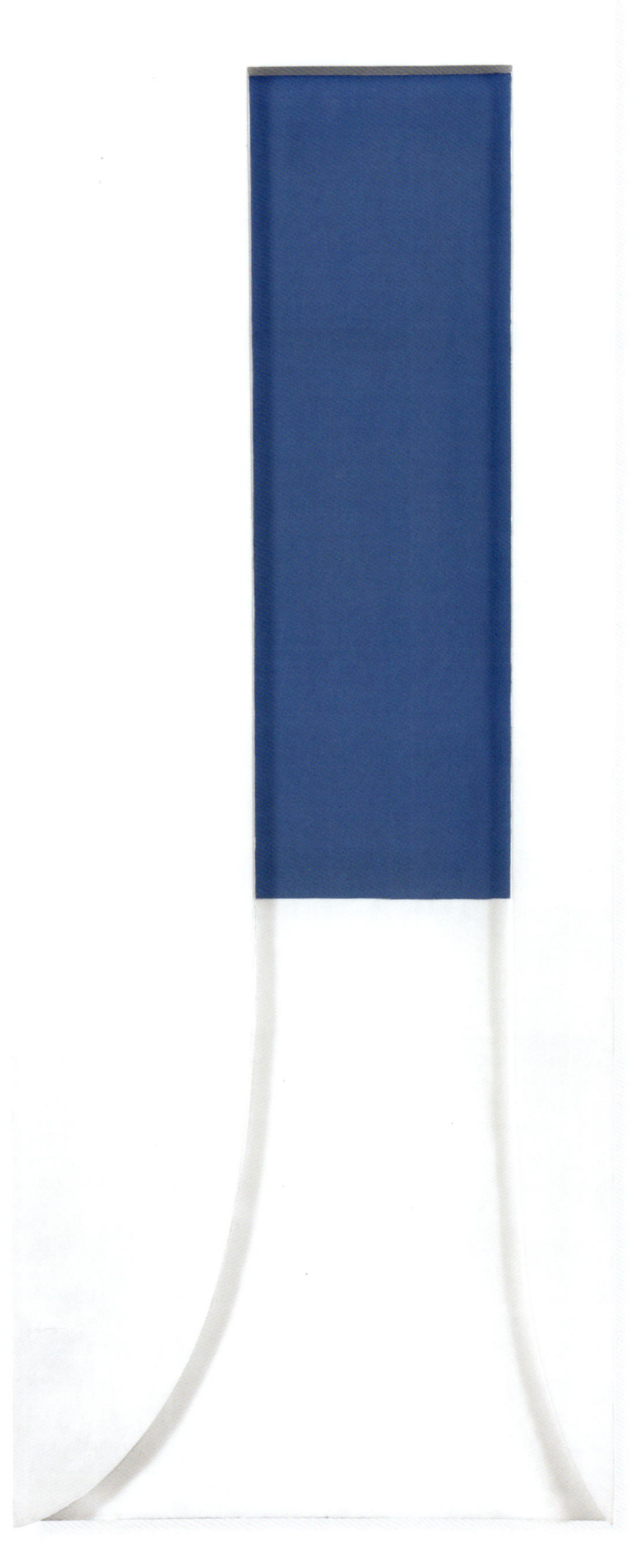

Relief with Blue, 1950
oil on wood, 44⅞ × 17½ × 1¼ in, 114 × 44.5 × 3.2 cm

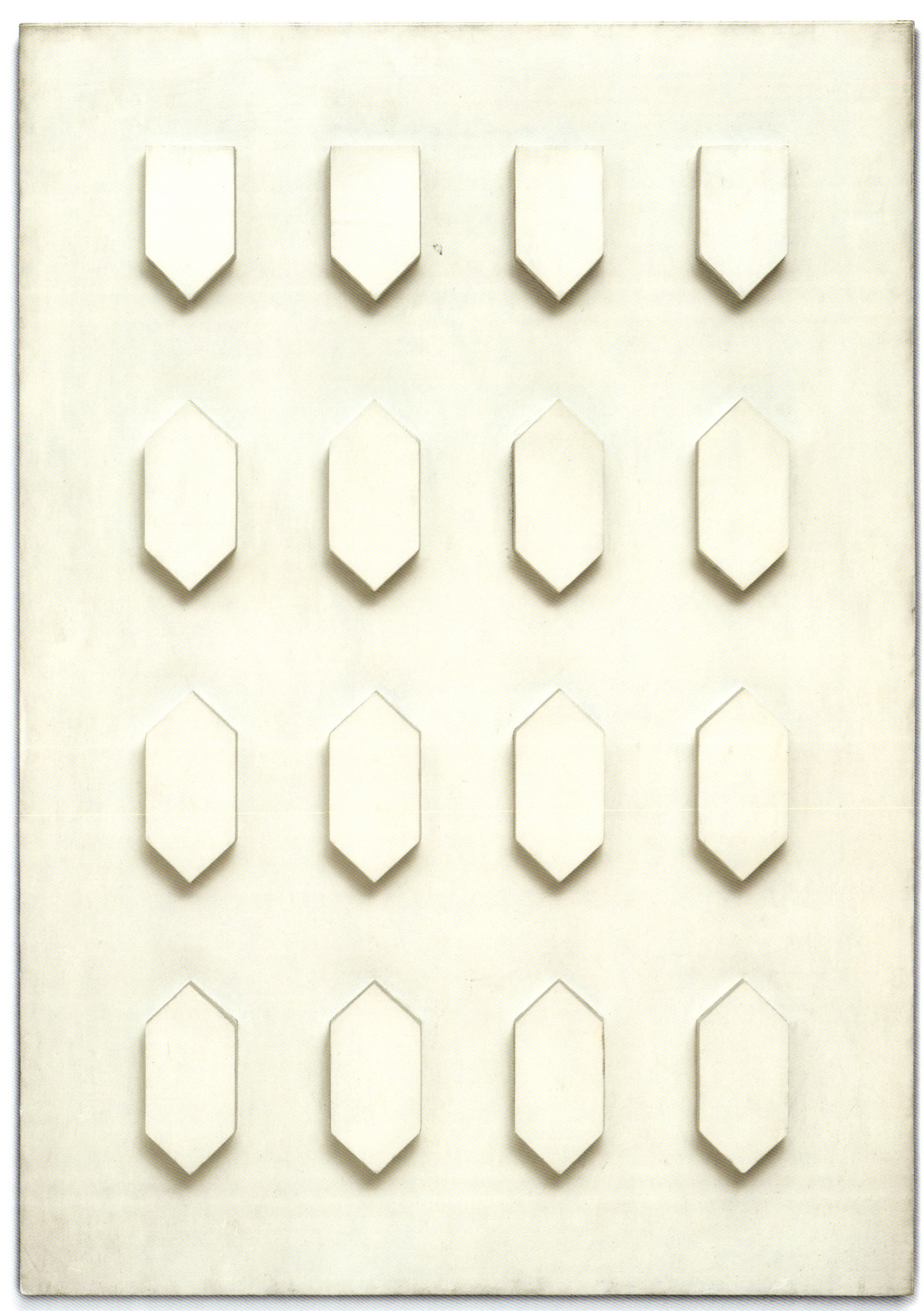

White Relief, 1950
oil on wood, 39⅜ × 27⅝ × 1⅞ in, 100 × 70.2 × 4.8 cm

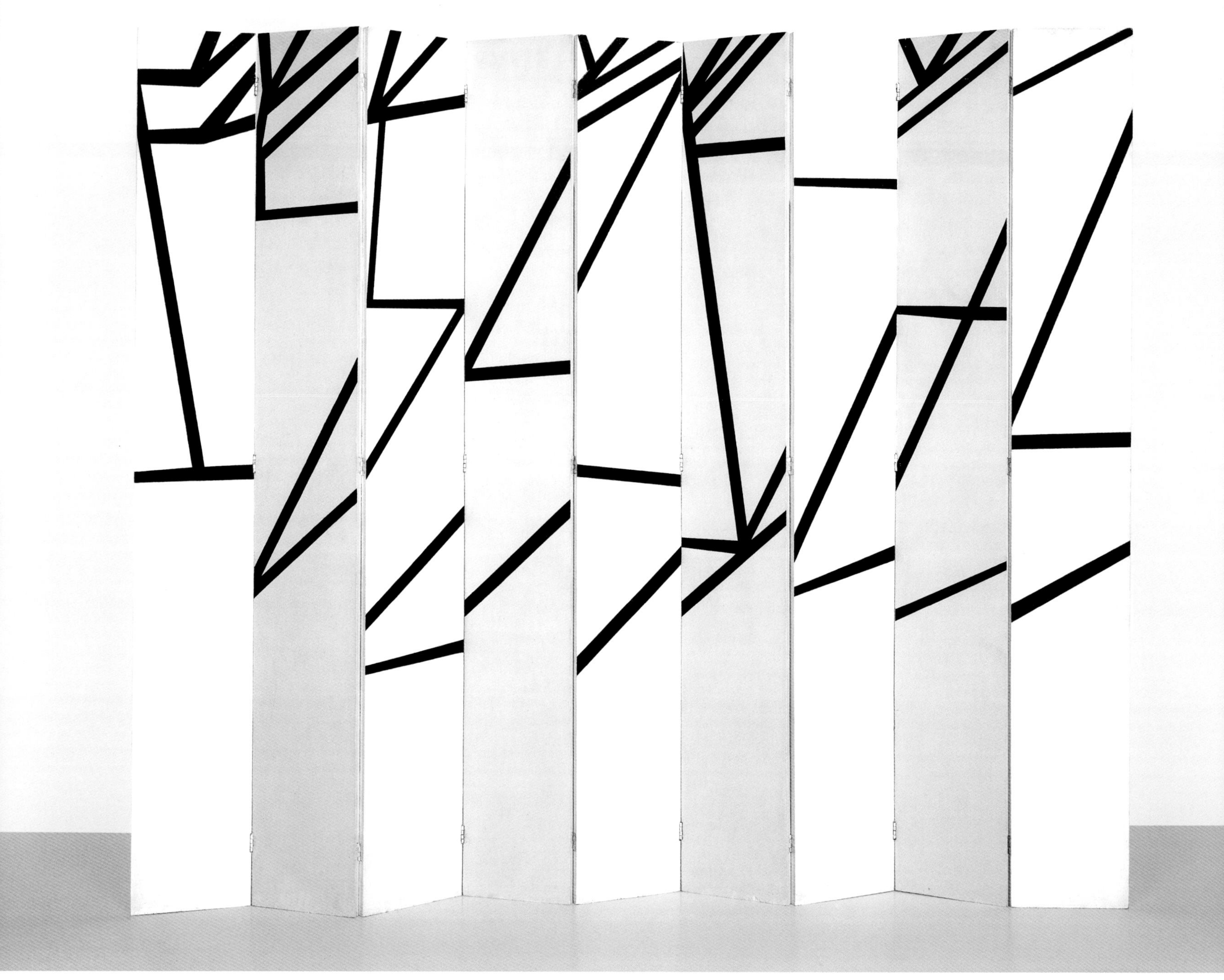

La Combe II, 1951
oil on wood, folding screen of 9 hinged panels
39¼ × 44½ × 2⅝ in, 99.7 × 113 × 6.7 cm

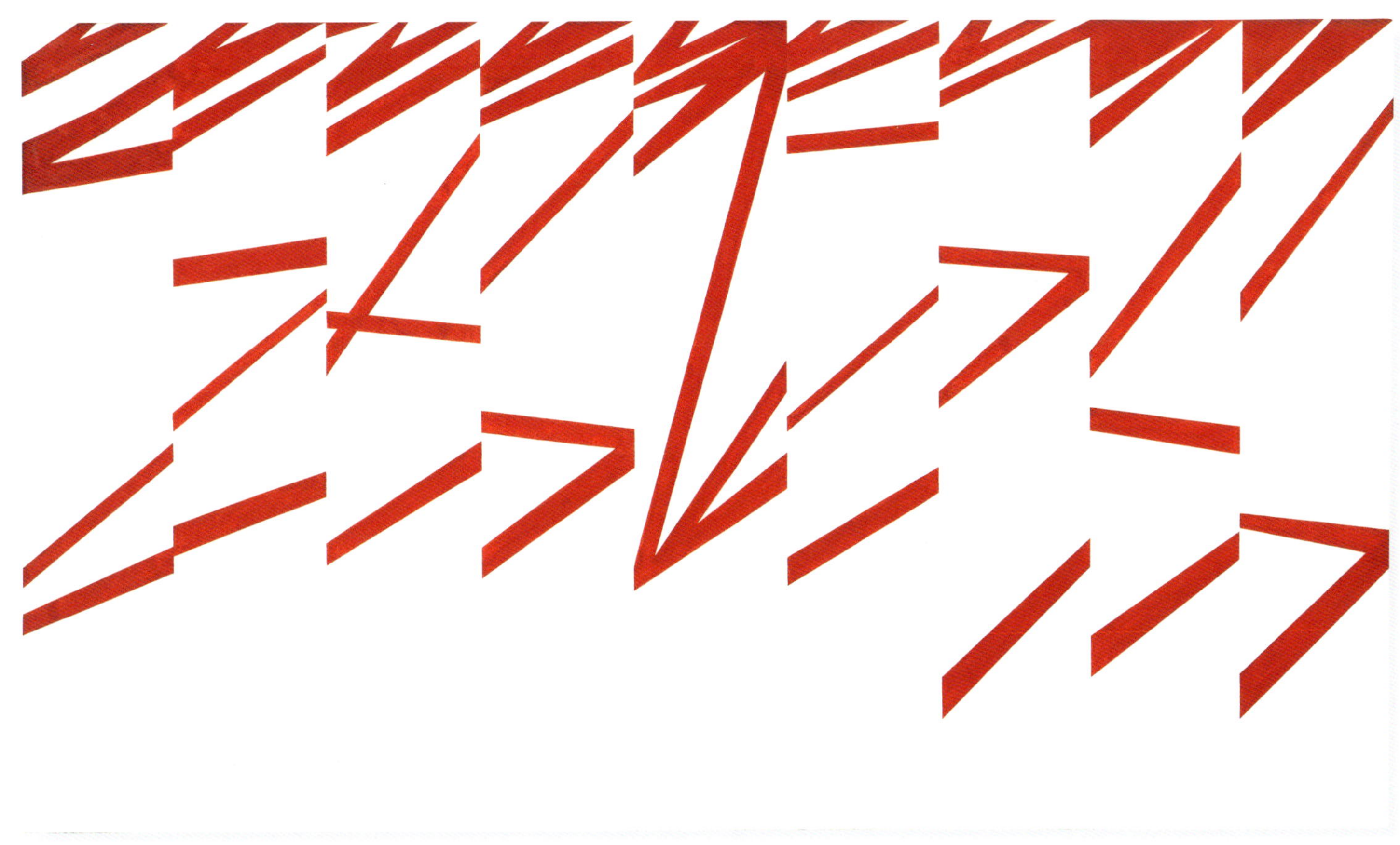

La Combe I, 1950
oil on canvas, 38 × 63½ in, 96.5 × 161.3 cm

Cité, 1951
oil on wood, 20 joined panels
56½ × 70¾ × 1¾ in, 143.5 × 179.7 × 4.4 cm

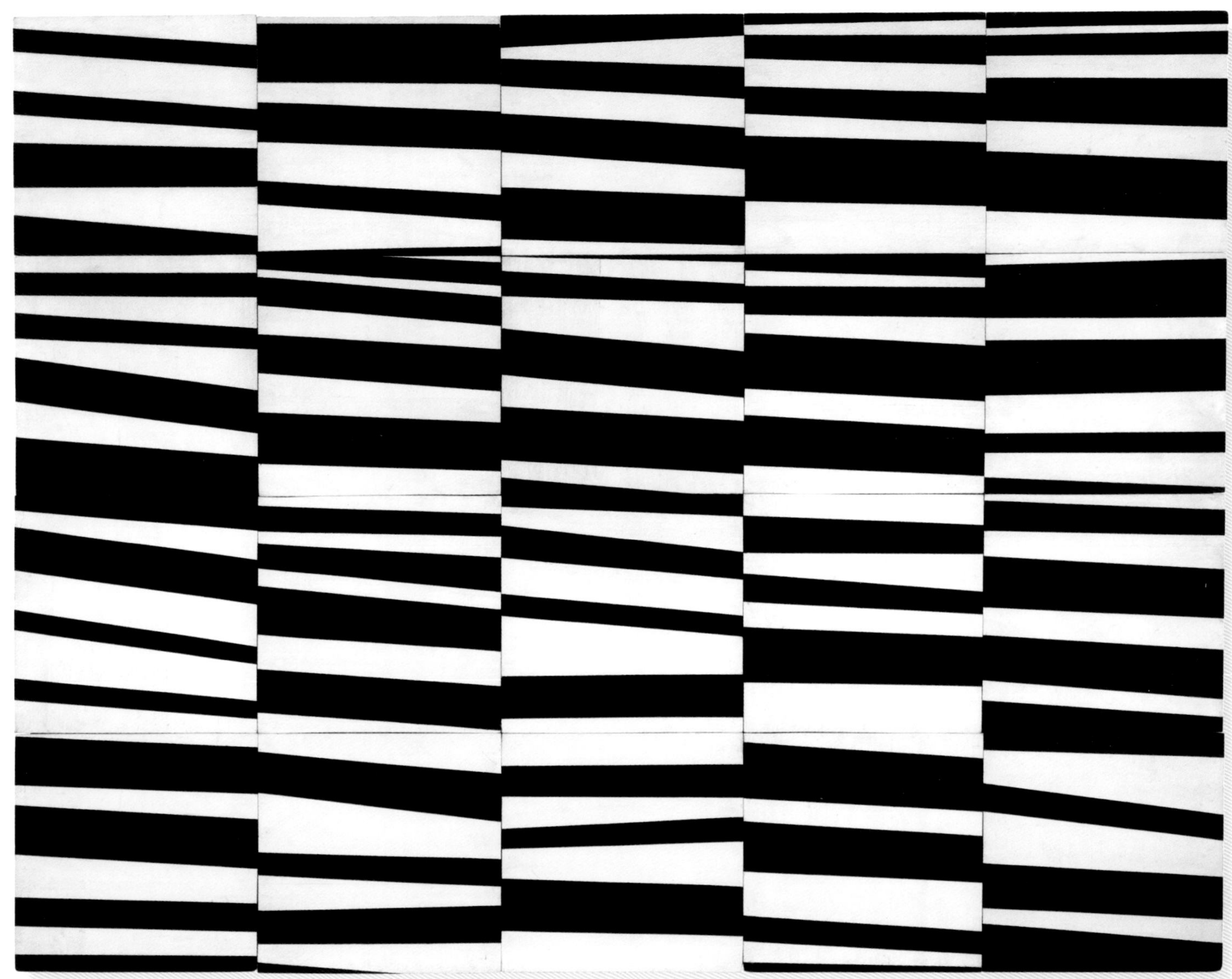

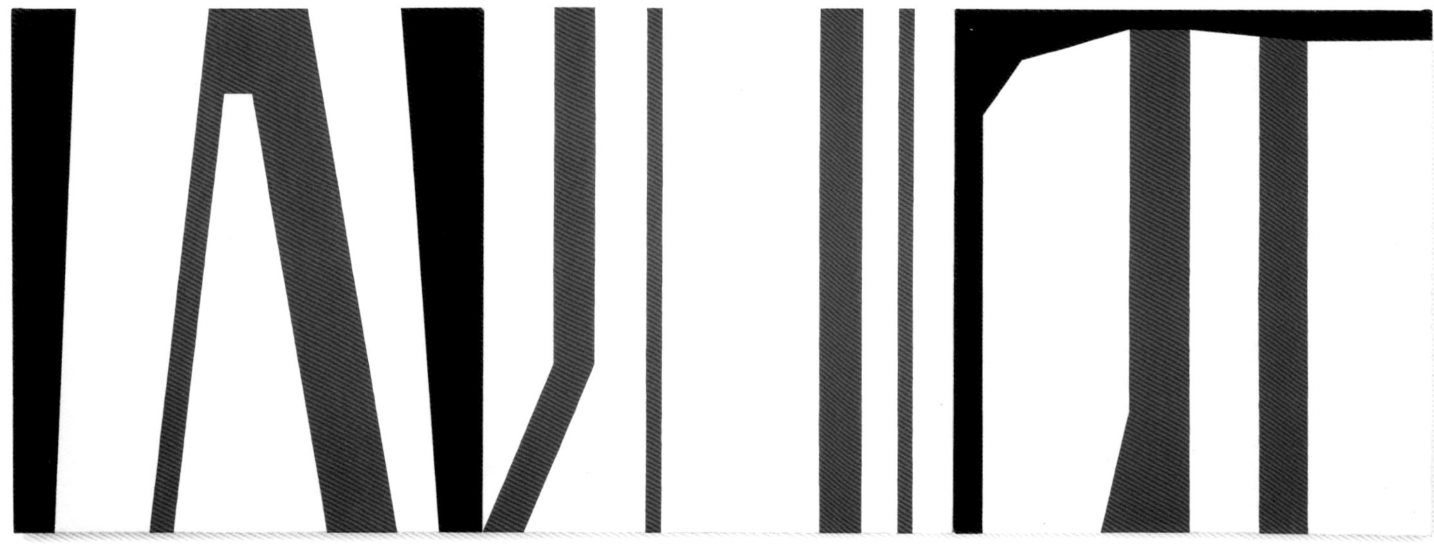

Ormesson, 1950
oil on canvas, 3 joined panels, 33 × 88¼ in, 83.8 × 224.2 cm

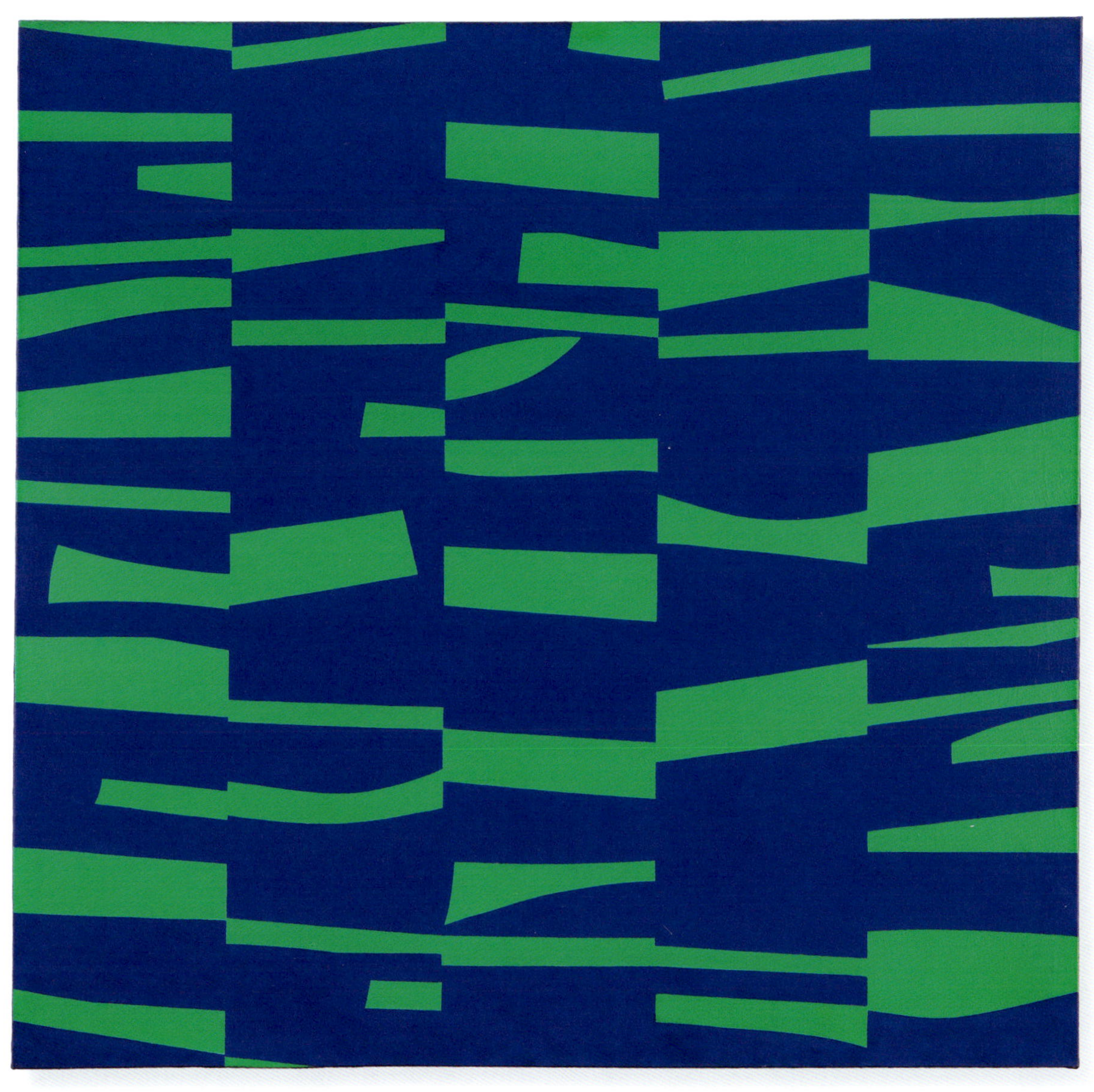

Meschers, 1951
oil on canvas, 59 × 59 in, 149.9 × 149.9 cm

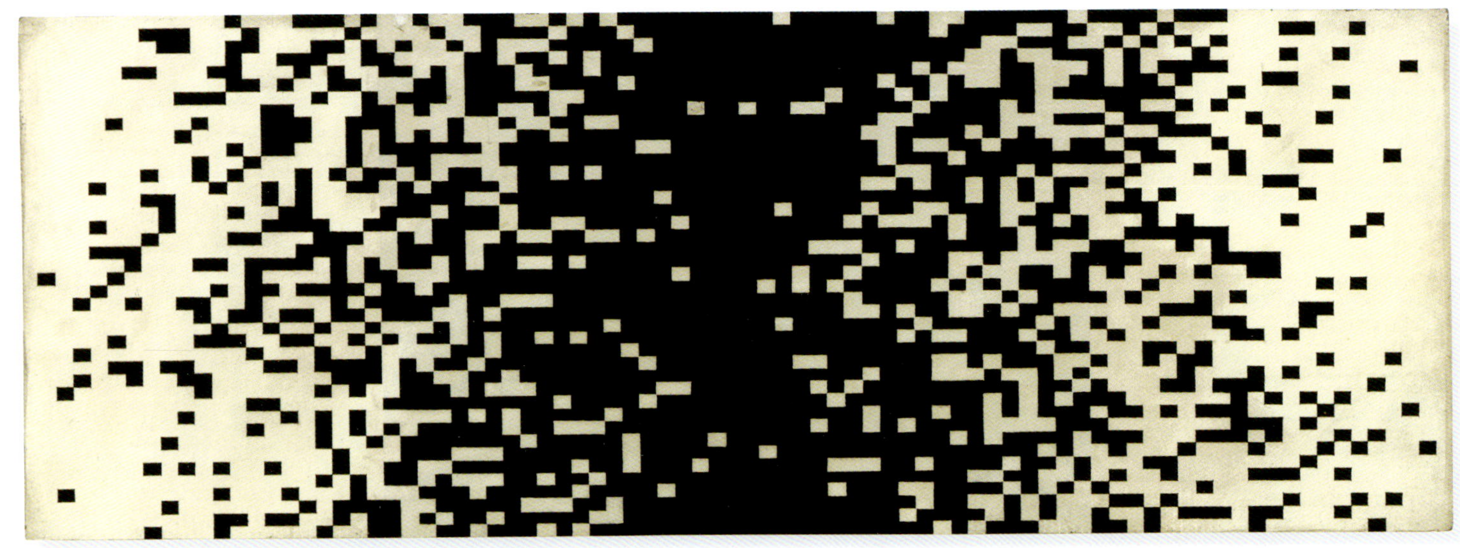

Seine, 1951
oil on wood, 16½ × 45¼ in, 41.9 × 114.9 cm

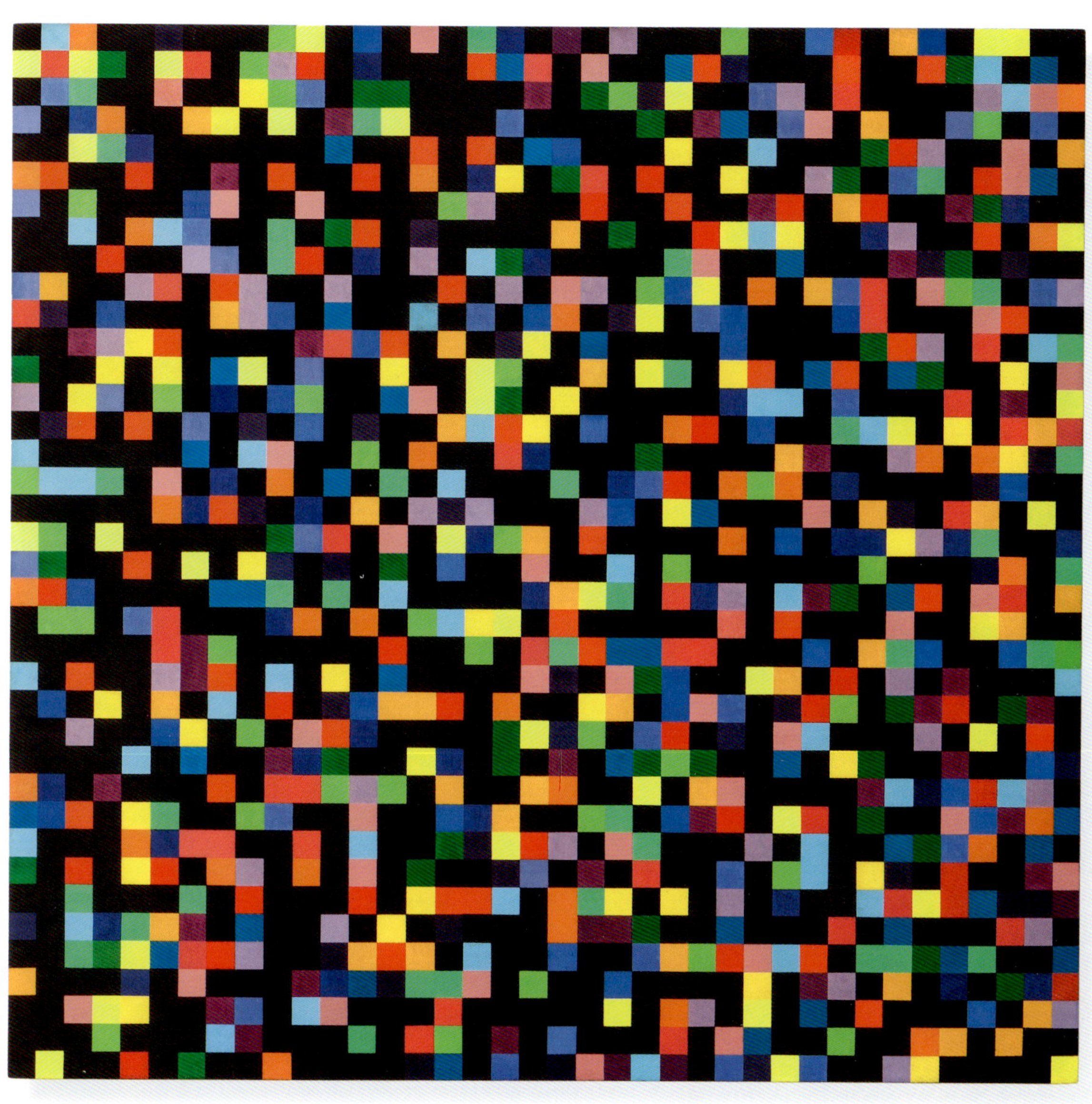

Spectrum Colors Arranged by Chance, 1951–53
oil on canvas, 60 × 60 in, 152.4 × 152.4 cm

Colors for a Large Wall, 1951
oil on canvas, 64 joined panels
94½ × 94½ in, 240 × 240 cm

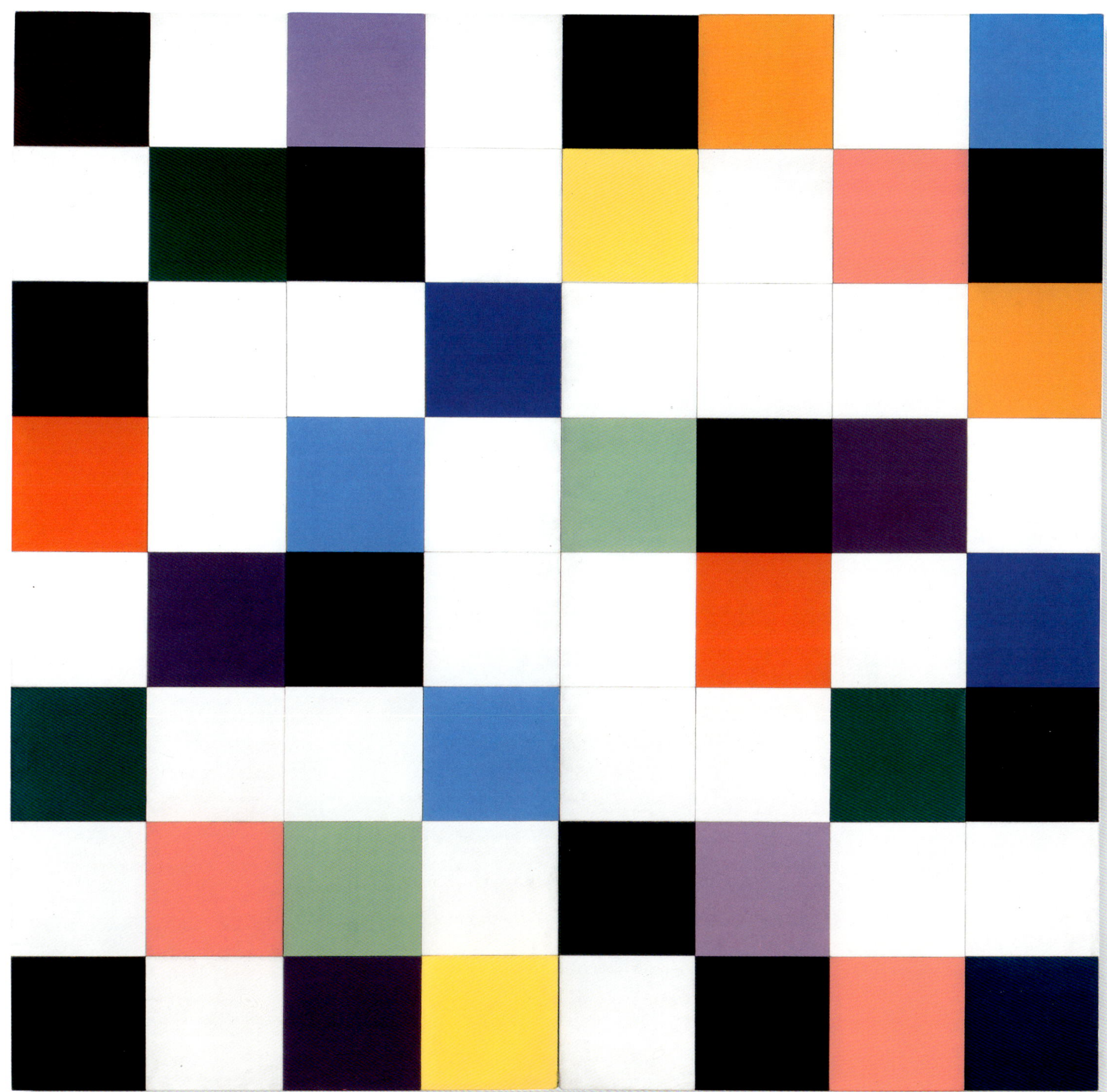

Méditerranée, 1952
oil on wood, 9 joined panels, 3 in relief
59¼ × 76¼ × 2¾ in, 150 × 195 × 7 cm

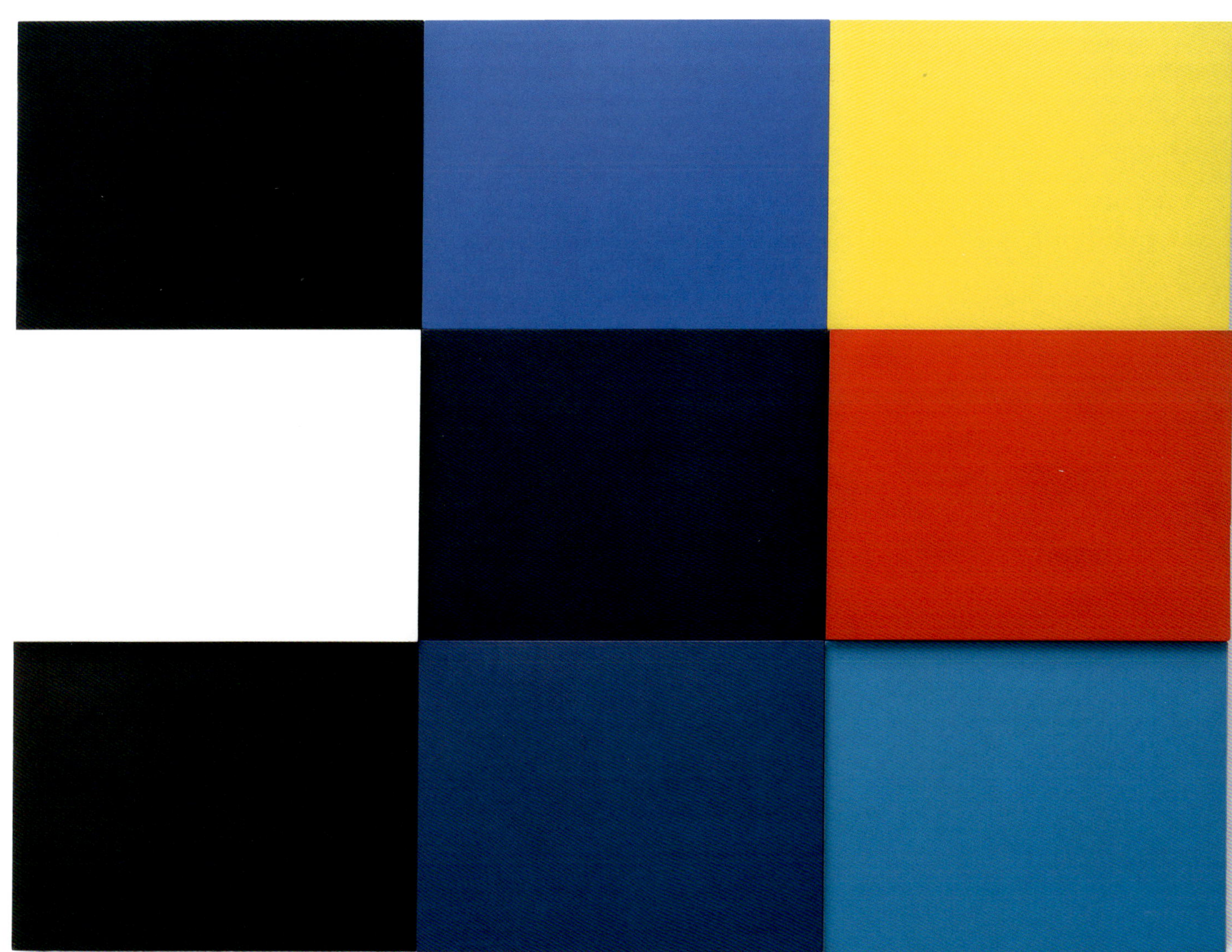

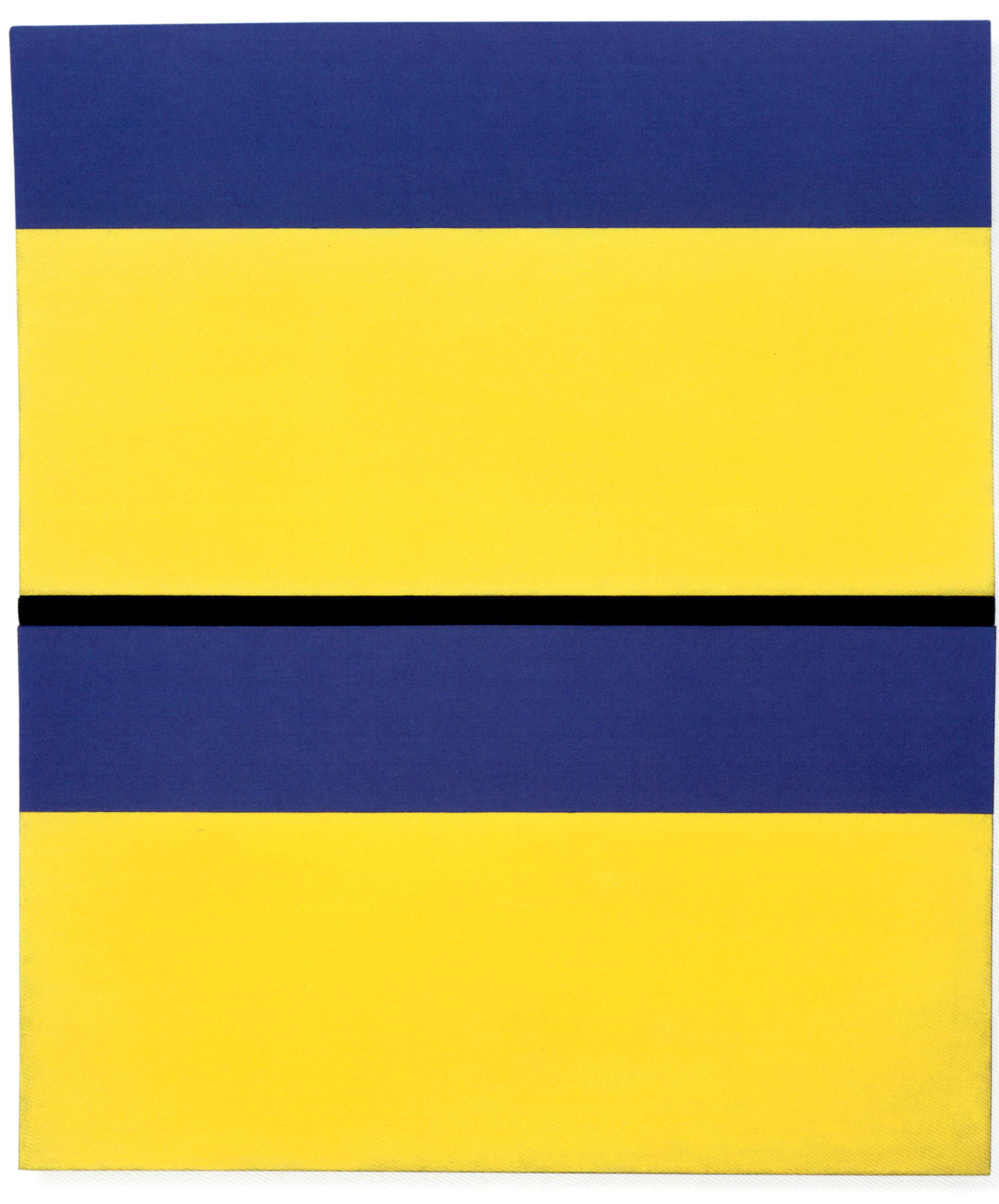

Fête à Torcy, 1952
oil on canvas and wood, 2 panels separated by a wood strip
45½ × 38¼ in, 115.6 × 97.2 cm

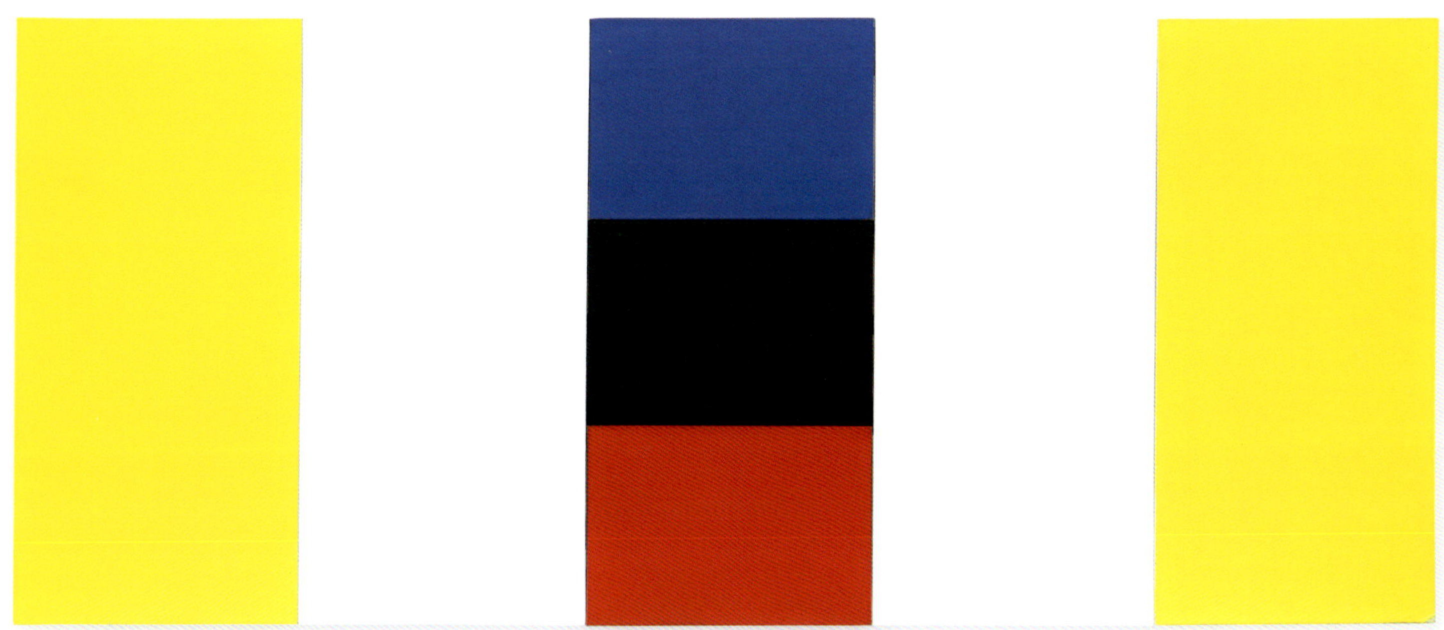

Kite I, 1952
oil on canvas, 7 joined panels
39⅜ × 91⅝ in, 100 × 232.7 cm

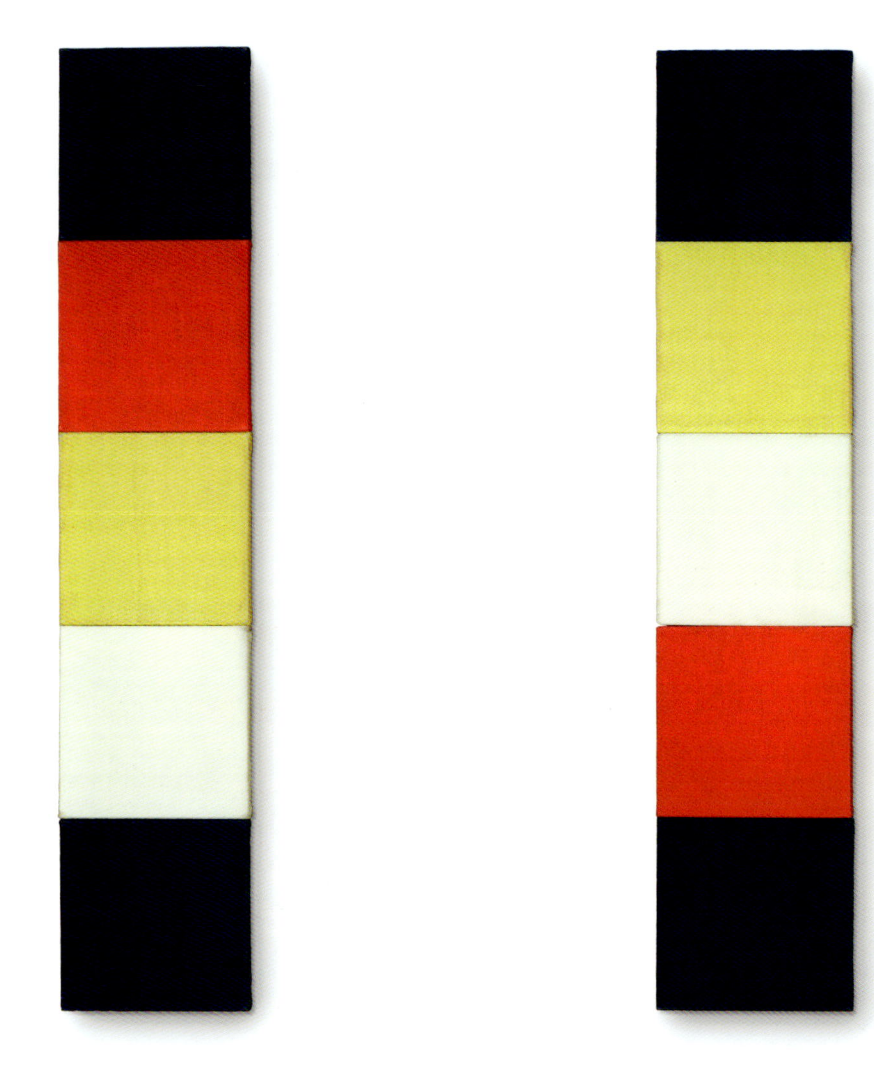

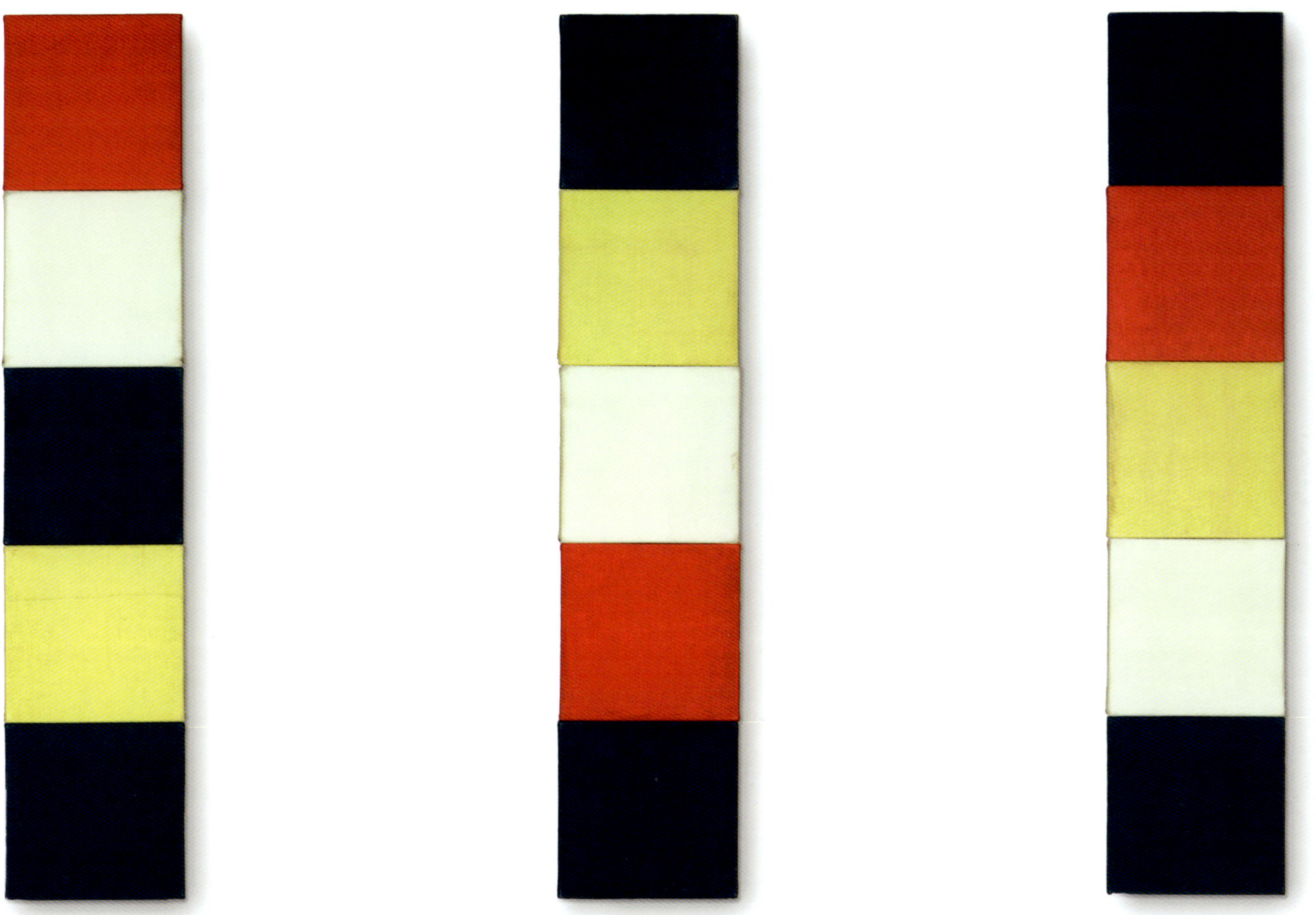

Red Yellow Blue White, 1952
dyed cotton, 25 panels in 5 parts
60 × 148 in, 152.4 × 375.9 cm

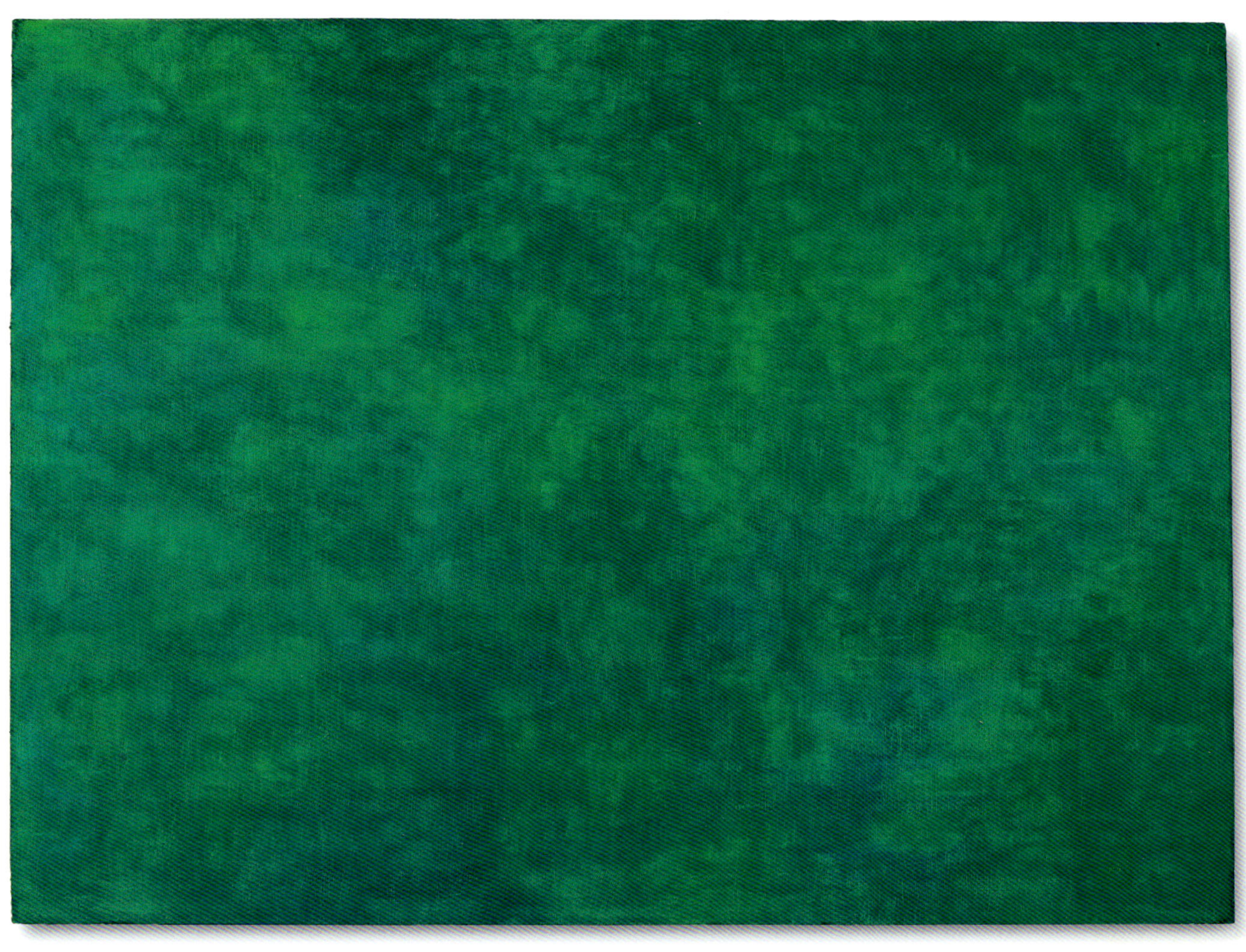

Tableau Vert, 1952
oil on wood, 29¼ × 39¼ in, 74.3 × 99.7 cm

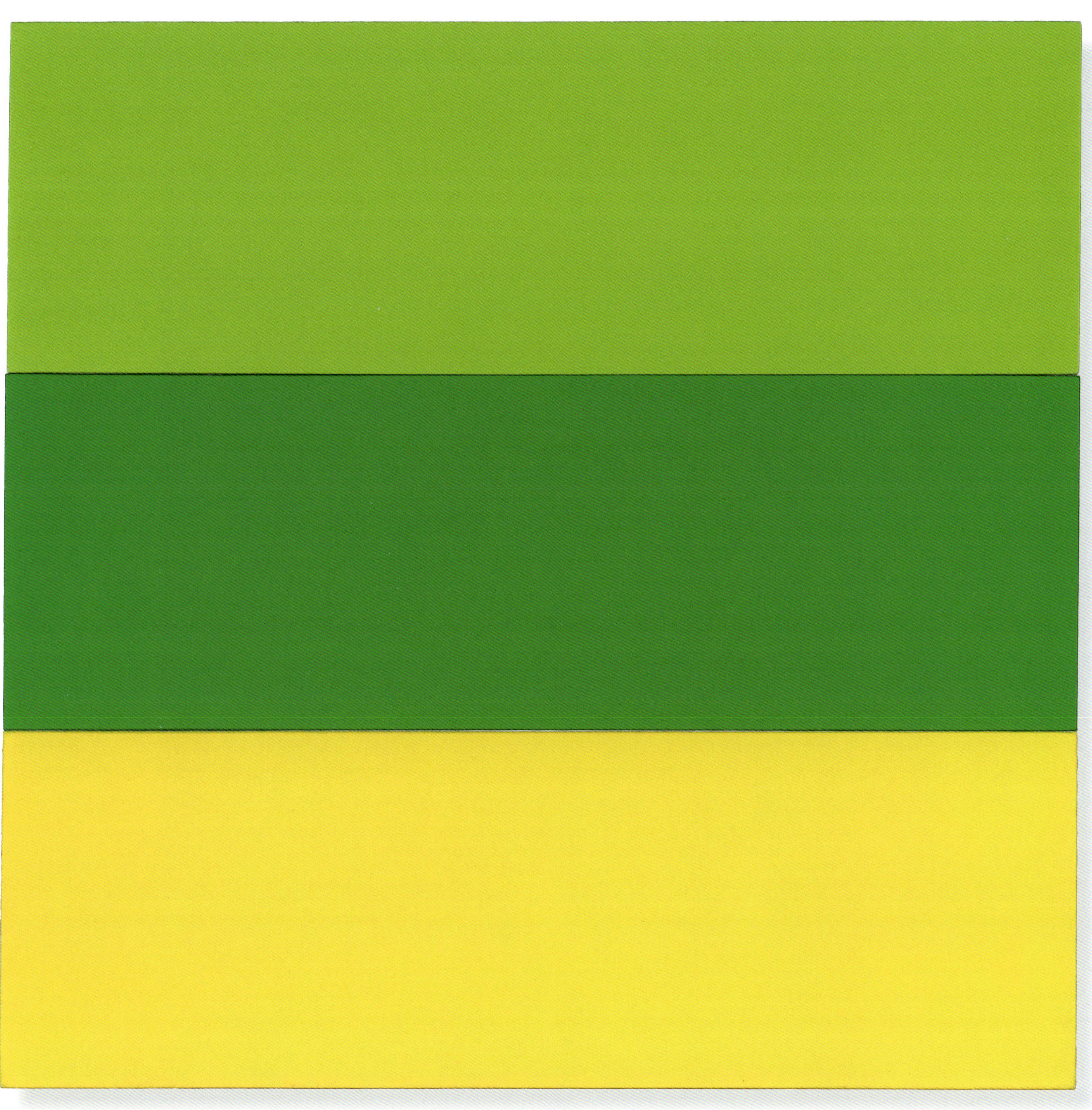

Train Landscape, 1953
oil on canvas, 3 joined panels, 44 × 44 in, 111.8 × 111.8 cm

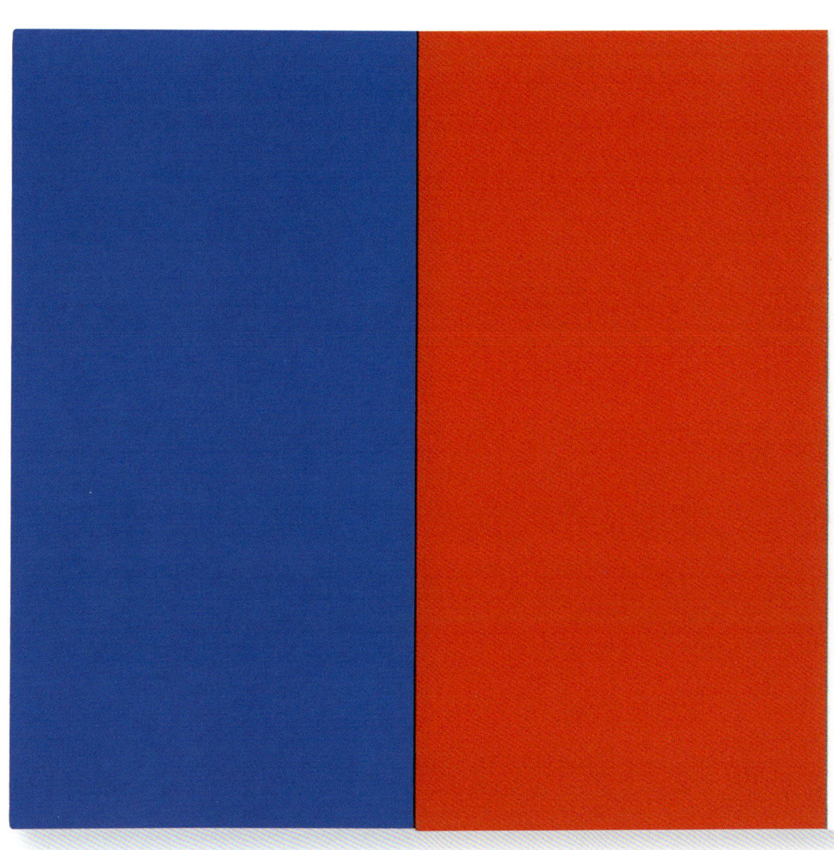

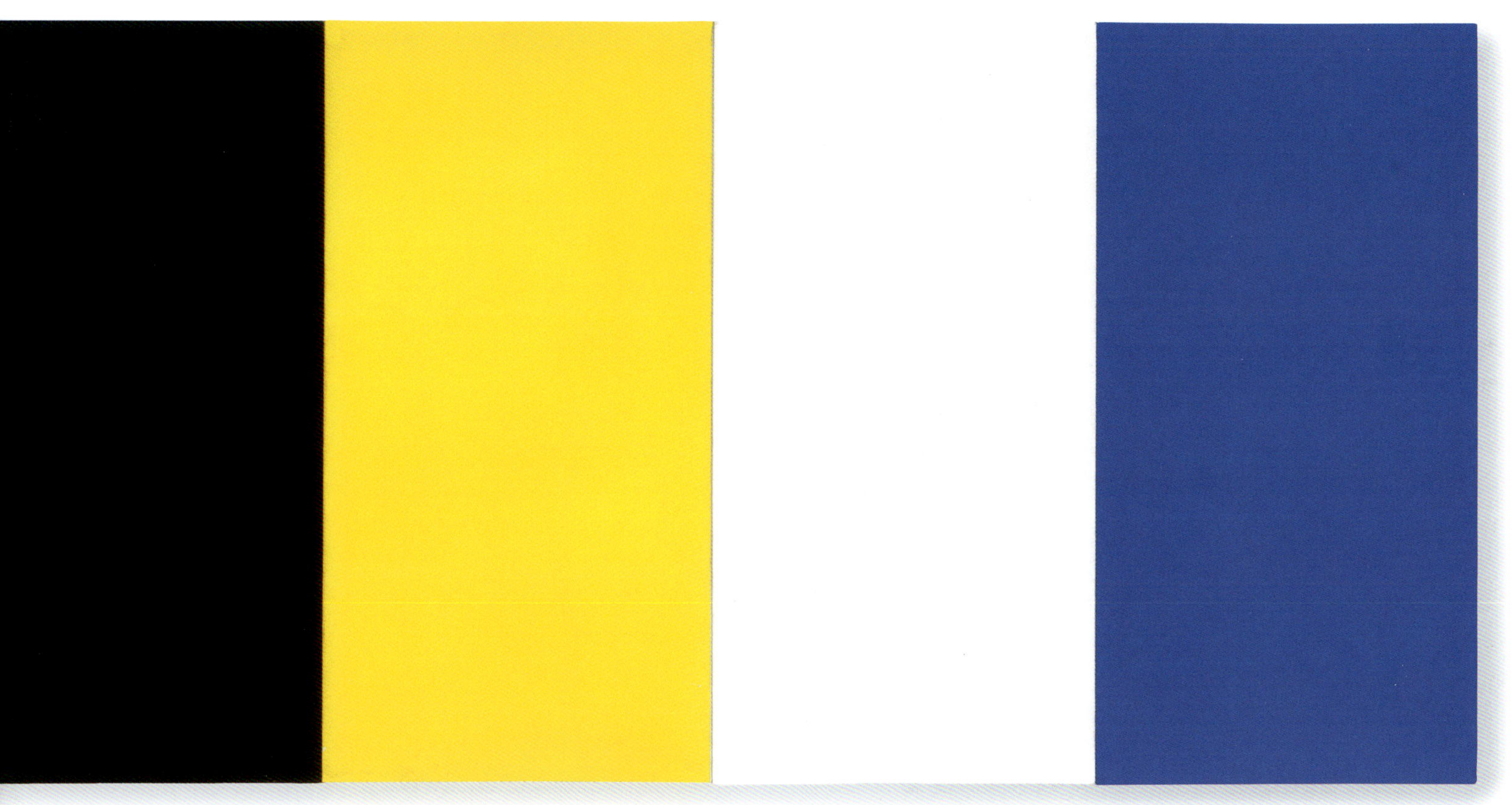

Red Yellow Blue White and Black II, 1953
oil on canvas, 7 joined panels, 39 × 138 in, 99 × 350.5 cm

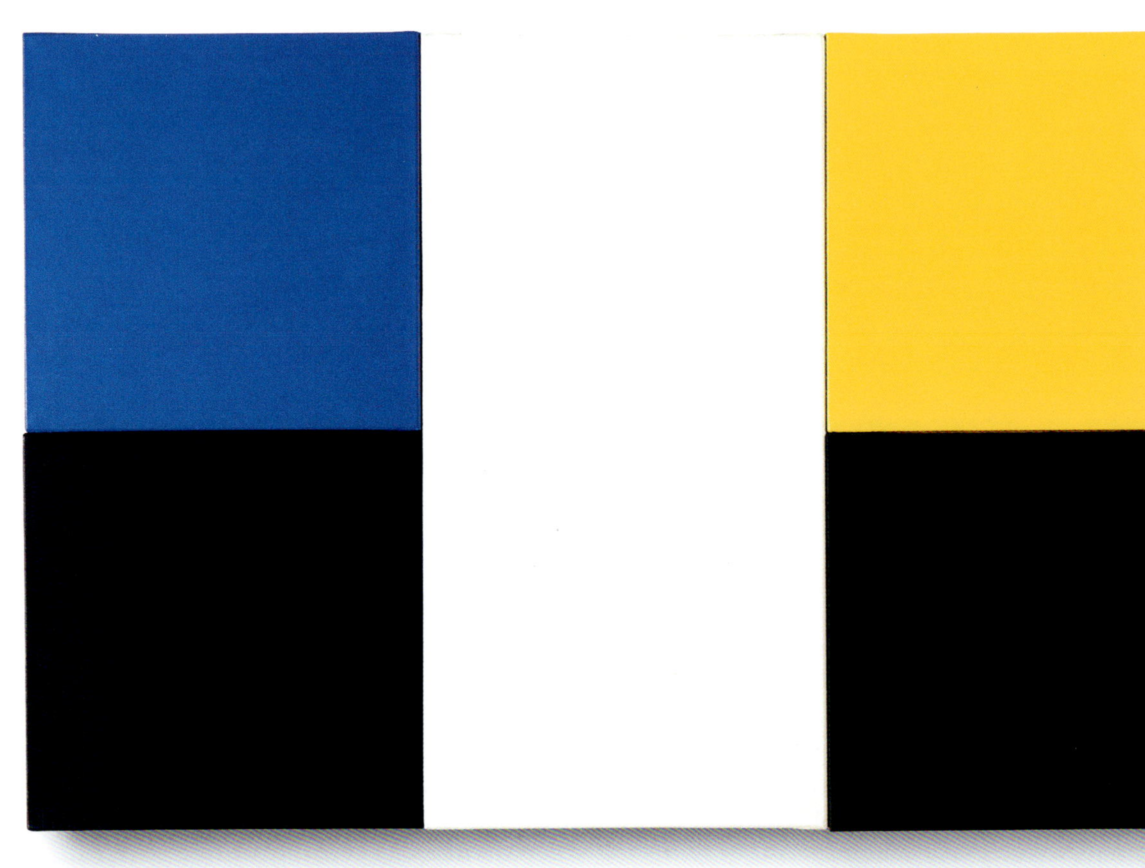

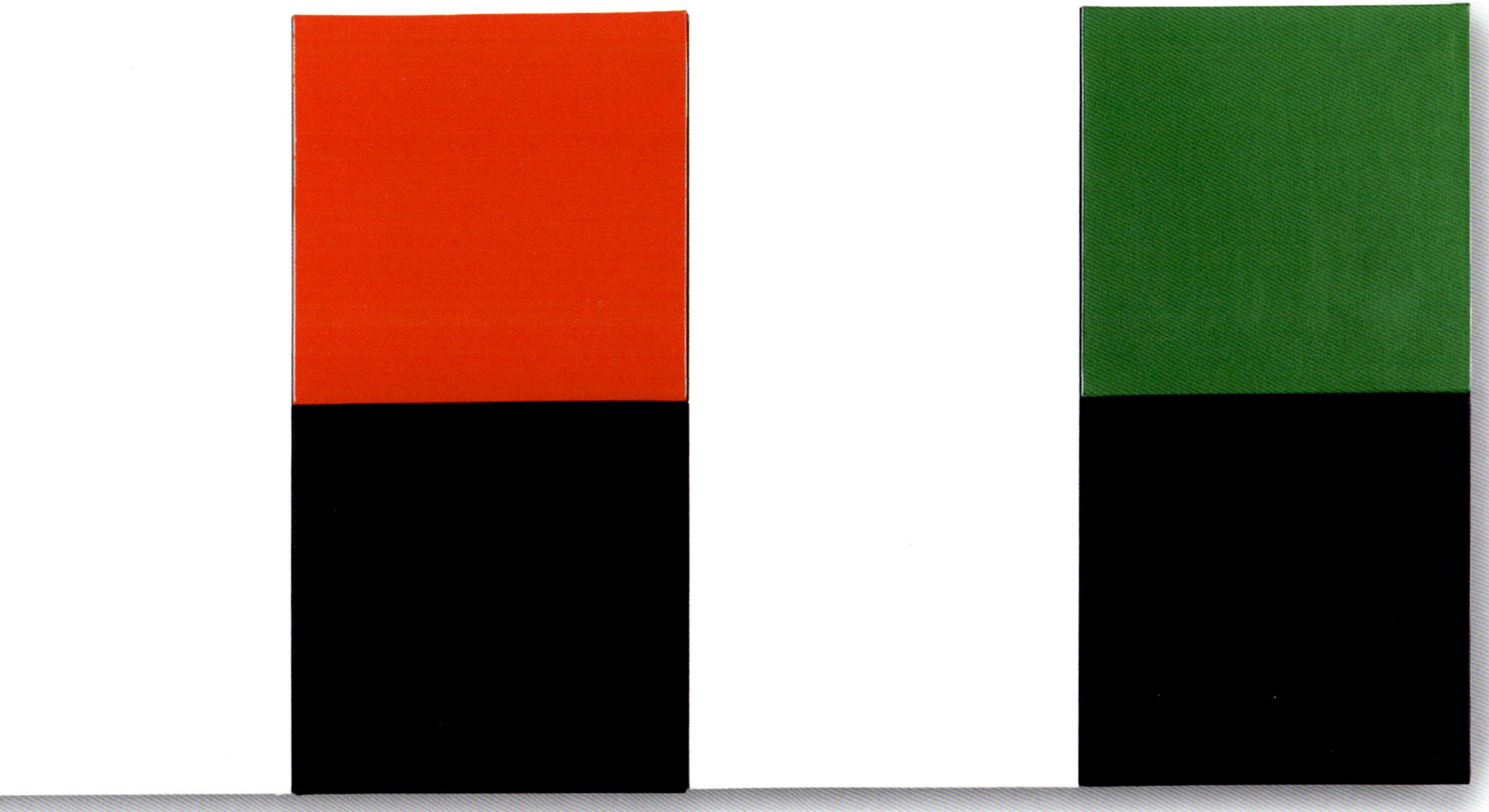

Kite II, 1952
oil on canvas, 11 joined panels, 31½ × 110¼ in, 80 × 280 cm

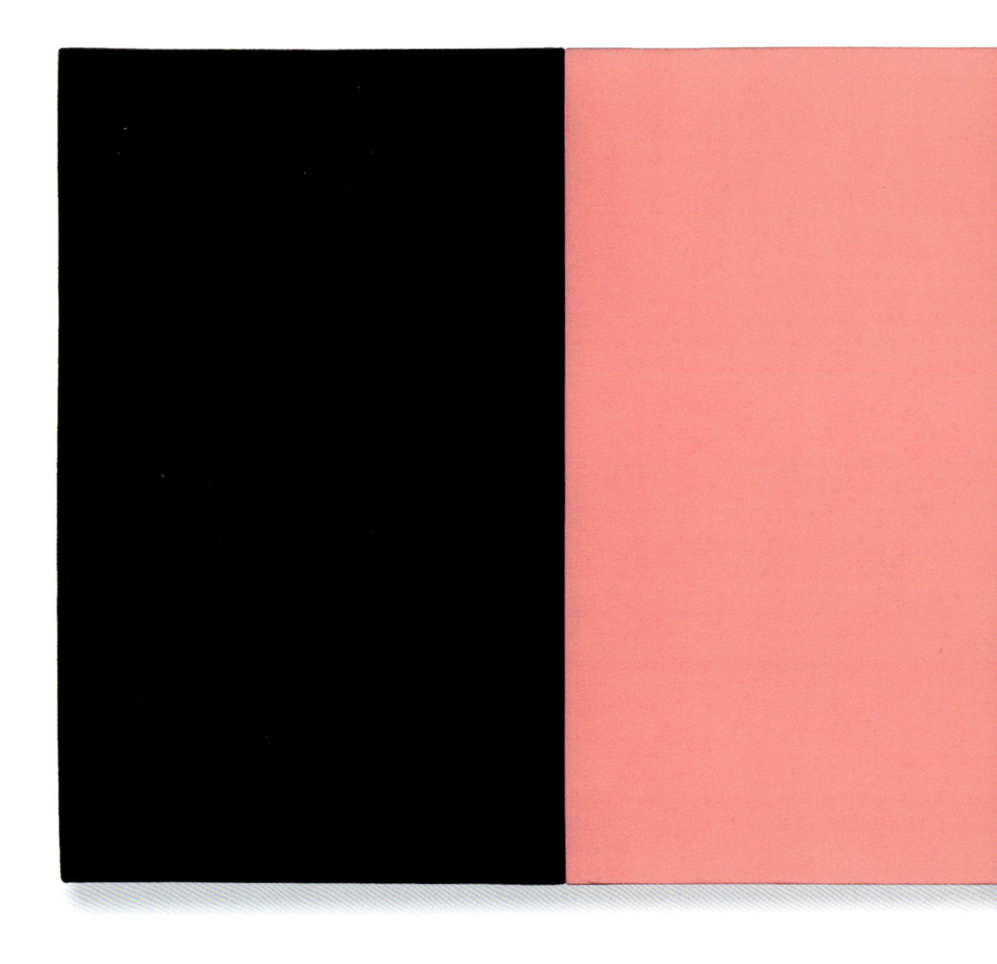

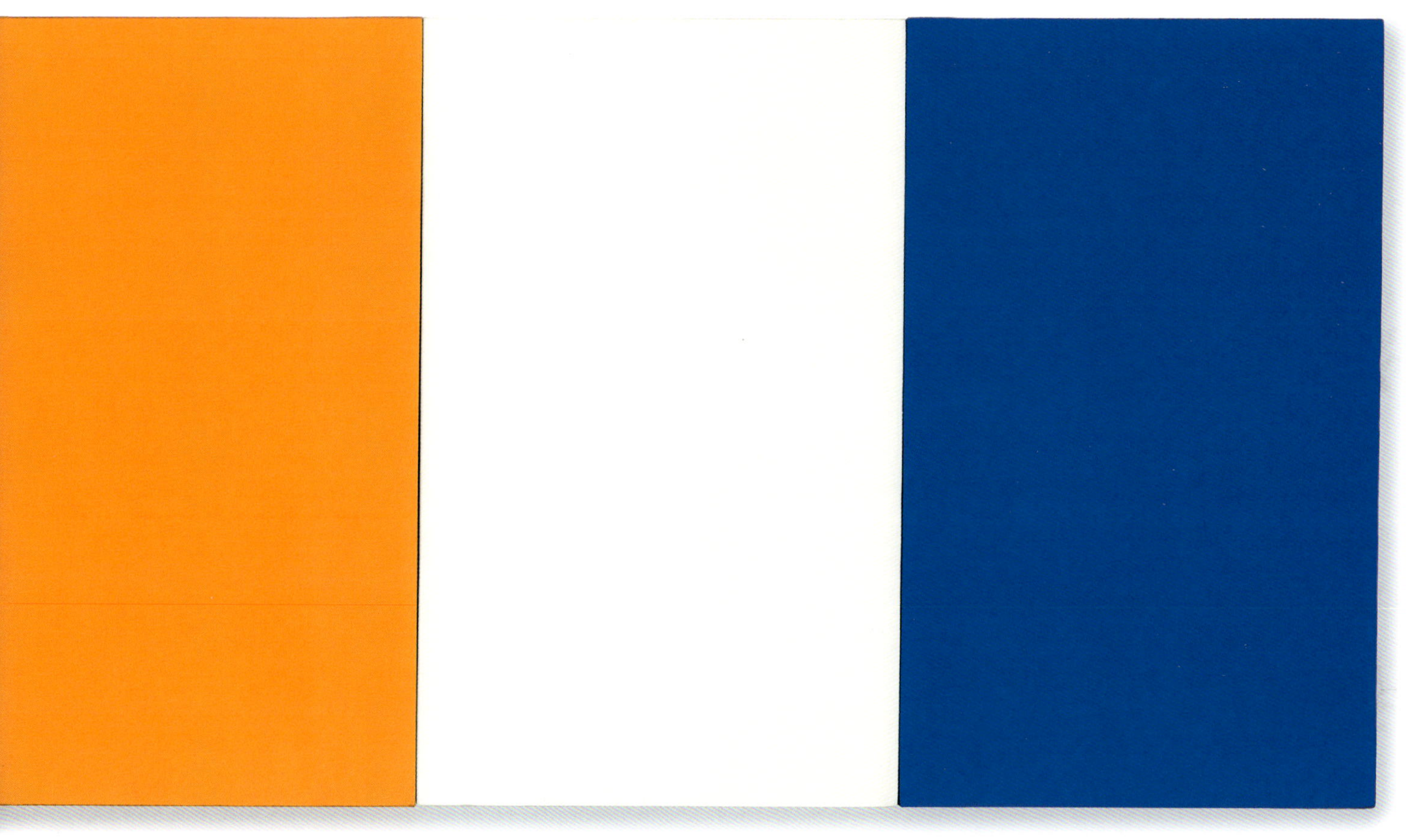

Painting for a White Wall, 1952
oil on canvas, 5 joined panels, 23½ × 71¼ in, 59.7 × 181 cm

Black Square, 1953
oil on wood, 43¼ × 43¼ in, 109.9 × 109.9 cm

White Square, 1953
oil on wood, 43¼ × 43¼ in, 109.9 × 109.9 cm

Spectrum I, 1953
oil on canvas, 60¼ × 60¼ in, 153 × 153 cm

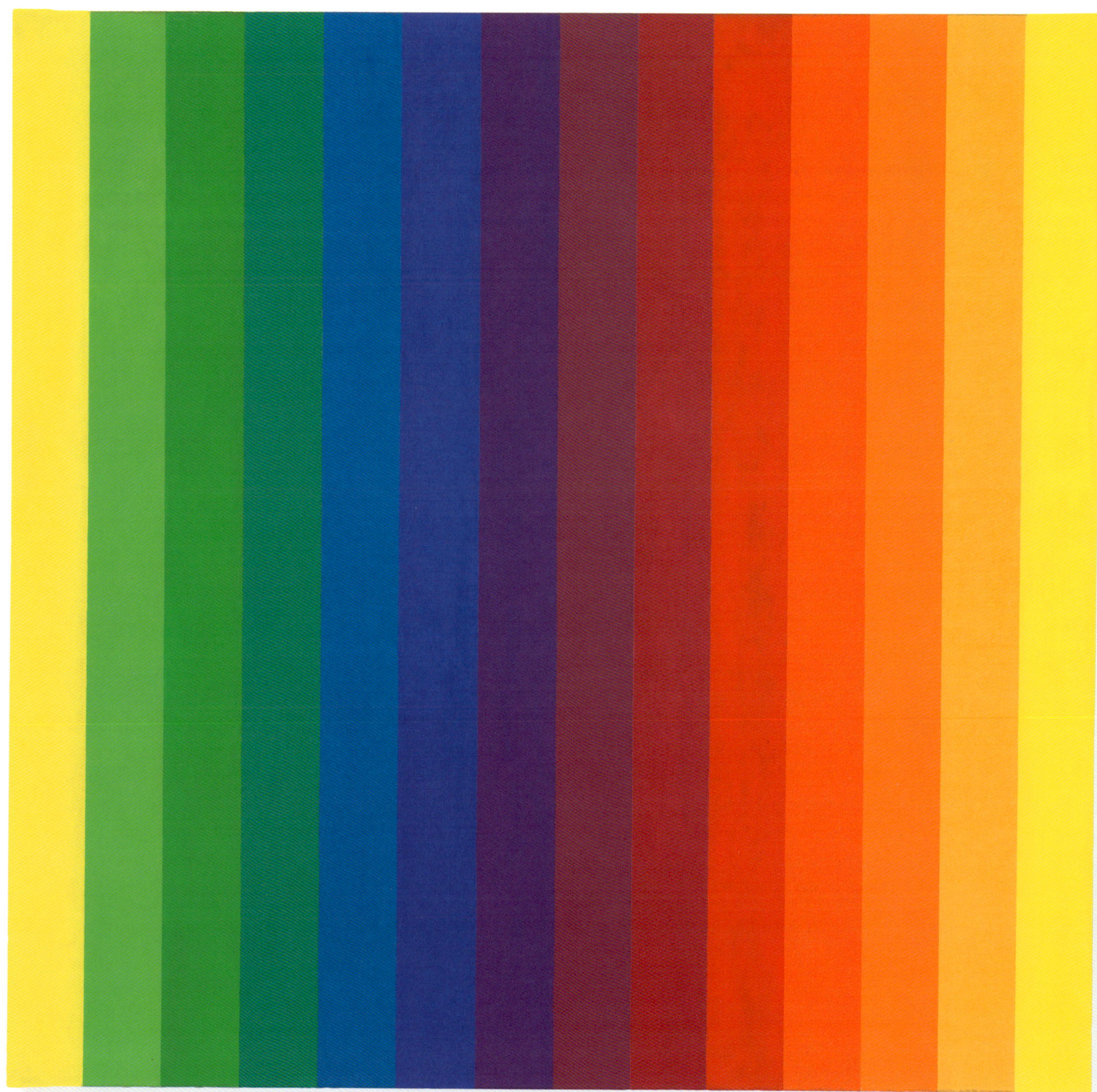

Starting Out—Starting Over

Robert Storr

"What is to be done?" It is the basic question that each generation of artists must ask itself. Often in the past those words have echoed broadly resonating cultural, social, and political urgencies. So it was when Russian radical Nikolay Chernyshevsky coined the phrase in his 1863 novel of that name, challenging Ivan Turgenev's more genteel examination of the conflict between young and old in *Fathers and Sons* (1862). In turn, Chernyshevsky's passionate plea for change so impressed the youthful Vladimir Ilyich Lenin that he used its title for his own revolutionary pamphlet of 1901, *What Is to Be Done?* Eventually, Mario Merz, a veteran of the Italian resistance to fascism in World War II, returned to the formula during the upheavals of 1968, fashioning the words "*che fare?*" in green neon and laying them atop a mound of beeswax packed into a galvanized steel tub in what became one of the icons of the Arte Povera movement.

Every young artist must also ask this question of him or herself, since the answer may not be collective, no matter how universal the imperatives of the moment appear to be. In the final reckoning the only issue that really matters to the individual artist—and ultimately to art—is what is there for *me* to do? Setting aside over-determining ideologies, there are as many ways of posing the problem and of solving it as there are artists. However, before an artist can provide or even imagine an initial response to such a sweeping call to action, there are bound to be detours and deviations from what might seem, with 20/20 hindsight, to be the obvious way forward, missteps that produce inexplicable anomalies within his or her career that most observers will choose to ignore once the overall direction becomes clear. Looking back with puzzlement over the trajectory of Jackson Pollock, New York School pioneer George McNeil mused:

> What was interesting about Pollock is that he came from very bad influences like [Thomas Hart] Benton and the Mexican muralists and other anti-painterly influences, and yet somehow, in a kind of alchemy, he took all the negatives and made them into a positive. It's a mystery. The rest of us were following the right path and therefore the magic didn't issue.[1]

But genius is never careless with its sources of invention; it wastes nothing. Not even time spent with possibilities that may appear unpromising to those who lack its adaptive, catalytic capacities—possibilities that look to such sidewalk supervisors more like *im*possibilities leading into historical dead ends. Such preemptive erasures of the inconvenient past are especially dubious when it comes to artists who assiduously preserve the record of their achievement and regularly double-back on their own course to re-examine the abiding potential of previously incomplete motions this way or that.

Well into his nineties and still busy in the studio creating vigorous new paintings, sculptures and architectural projects despite the ineluctable physical challenges of great old age, Ellsworth Kelly is just such an artist. Both the surprises and the palpable continuity of his most recent production with that which came before it issue from the almost daily practice of revisiting earlier phases of his career, either by looking at examples of his work that he has kept for himself for precisely this purpose, or by looking through old exhibition catalogues and magazines. For instance, Kelly's 2013 exhibition at the Matthew Marks Gallery in New York featured a relief like none other he had ever painted: *Gold with Orange Reliefs* (p. 311), now promised to the Museum of Modern Art in New York. For the first time ever, the ground color he employed was a metallic gold rather than black, white, gray or a spectral hue. And, for the first time as well, the panels superimposed on the bottom edge of the supporting rectangle were eccentrically contoured shapes, resembling blocky punctuation marks or horizontal rather than vertical parentheses, each of which had its own distinctive arc. In contrast to the shiny gold, these elements were a matte, deep daffodil or yellow-orange.

Spectators unfamiliar with Kelly's oeuvre, and even connoisseurs with intimate knowledge of its ups-and-downs and ins-and-outs, might surmise that he had been emboldened by his secure position within the canon of modern masters to strike out in a wholly unanticipated direction. (It is a position that has been his since the 1950s by virtue of his innovations of that decade, but one that has been a matter of critical consensus only since the 1980s due to a host of institutional factors and intellectual fads). They would be half right, but only half, because the study for this particular work is a small collage—*Orange Forms on Gold*—of 1962 (fig. 59), which Kelly had never reinterpreted as a painting and only recently rediscovered when going through his flat files. Why he hesitated to act on it when he

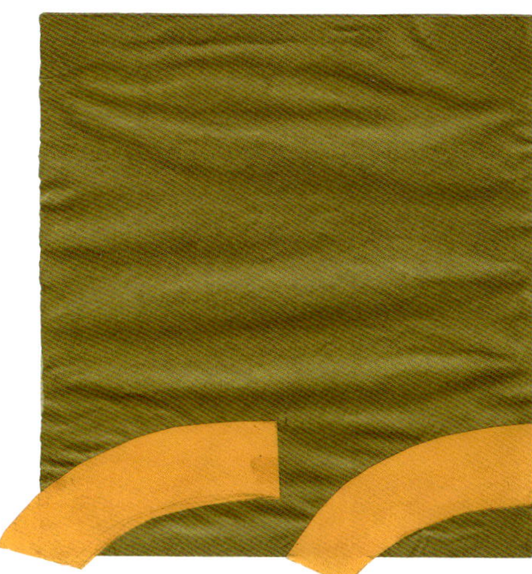

fig. 59: *Orange Forms on Gold*, 1962, collage, 8½ × 7⅞ in, 21.6 × 20 cm

originally made the study he has yet to say, though I have put the question to him. That he *has* acted on it at this late date is the more important consideration. Perhaps the simplest way to explain this delay is to point out the difference even for artists of recognized audacity between making something and being able to see in it—that is to say, fully grasp and accept—elements that are essentially new. Thus old images can resurface as new images that seem like the inevitable outgrowth of identifiable precedents although their actual genesis proves that such inevitability was, in the first instance, hardly obvious to their creator, and, were it not for a belated epiphany, that their full flowering was anything but guaranteed.

In truth, the staggered assimilation or ultimate avoidance of influences to which an artist has been exposed in his or her formative years is one of the least predictable aspects of the creative process. Why does this recognized artist miss the obvious ramifications of what he or she has previously achieved and a lesser talent seize upon them, thereby achieving full but previously elusive mastery? By the same token, such unanticipated leaps and lags are the hallmark of authentic artistic identity, the choices that render a given artist's work unique. The extraordinarily long and graceful arc of Kelly's oeuvre since he came into his own in the early 1950s would appear to be that of an artist with an uncomplicated sensibility assiduously pursuing a clearly laid out program. Which opens a trap for commentators with uncomplicated minds and dogmatic programs of their own to fall into. In that respect the puzzlement that McNeil expressed with respect to Pollock arises when we consider Kelly's apprenticeships and aesthetic associations before and just after World War II.

Kelly's military service counts among those apprenticeships in as much as he was assigned to the 603rd Engineers Camouflage Battalion while stationed in France shortly after the D-Day landings. Once the Germans retreated—which they did, circumventing a mass of inflatable rubber decoy tanks that Kelly and his cohort rigged to intimidate Nazi Panzers—this posting in the Île de France afforded him a chance to enter Paris following the liberation of the City of Light and to see it as it was when darkness settled over it during the Occupation. For a young painter fresh out of art school—before being drafted at twenty, Kelly had attended the Pratt Institute in Brooklyn, starting in 1941, the year the U.S. entered the war—it was a case of being in the right place at almost the right time. When Kelly resumed his studies after being demobilized in 1945, he skipped New York and headed to the School of the Museum of Fine Arts, Boston, where he completed his formal education.

Much has been made of Kelly's stint as a camoufleur, first and foremost by the curator of the artist's 1973 Museum of Modern Art, New York, retrospective, E.C. Goossen, who stressed the connection in his still-valuable catalogue. As everybody is aware, the techniques of visually dissolving men and machines into the background entail synthesizing designs consistent with that background, which are then used to cover the surfaces and objects one wants to make vanish into a fundamentally undifferentiated spatial gestalt. In turn, doing that involves "abstracting" some of the given characteristics of the environment and rendering them as consistent but irregular patterns. Thus, long before Andy Warhol started appropriating the prints on army tents and uniforms as the common denominator for self-portraits or as parodies of "all over" abstraction, Kelly mastered the art of adjusting areas of flat tones and tints into jigsaw puzzles, combinations that could, in principle, go on forever, enveloping anything and everything over which they were spread, and imparting to those things the ambiguous dimensionality of the basic graphic elements.[2]

Unquestionably, as Goossen was quick to point out, with a five-year delay between learning them "on the job" and applying them in his own work, these techniques inform Kelly's segmented grid paintings of 1950–51, works such as ***Cité*** (p. 63) and ***Meschers*** (p. 65), and even ***La Combe I*** (p. 61), the last of which was inspired by shadows falling on an exterior metal staircase of the house owned by the father of the

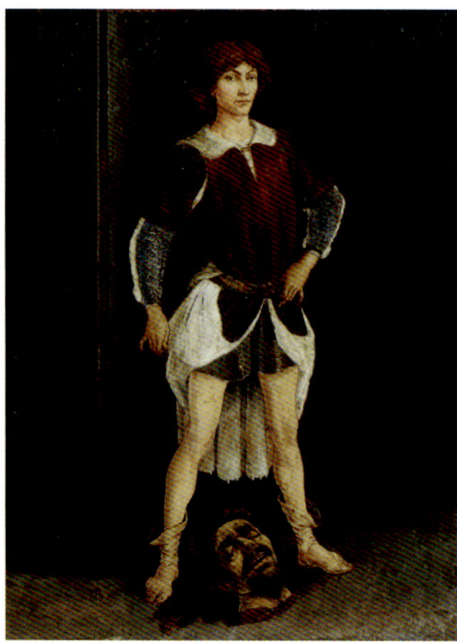

fig. 60: Antonio del Pollaiuolo, *David Victorious*, c.1472, tempera on poplar panel, 18⅛ × 13¾ in, 46.2 × 34 cm

actress Delphine Seyrig (wife of painter Jack Youngerman, one of Kelly's closest American companions during his crucial second sojourn in France), where the artist spent the summer that year. And, just as certainly, one of the turning points of Kelly's early development was his lucky encounter with John Cage in Paris in 1949. Fittingly, given the aesthetic they shared but pursued along parallel tracks, Cage and Kelly first met on the street accidentally; shortly thereafter Cage and his partner Merce Cunningham moved to the same hotel where Kelly was already renting a room. The Neo-Dada composer and theorist of chance operations reinforced Kelly's interest in aleatory composition, an approach he had previously explored with his friend, Ralph Coburn.

But a close reading of the chronology of those pivotal years, and careful scrutiny of the works produced during that interval, tell a more interesting story about what literary critic Harold Bloom called "the anxiety of influence." By which, Bloom understood the Oedipal need to escape the authority of one's artistic father figure or figures and reinvent the world as if they had never existed. Or, in the case of critics and historians, reinterpret such precedents in a manner that diminishes their dominion over the artist's own insights, while fostering a more complex feel for the multiplicity of influences that any given artist may have encountered and in some cases may have actually sought out. The names I am about to cite with regard to Kelly will come as no surprise to anyone who has studied the same material. Nevertheless, I hope to weigh the evidence somewhat differently than is customary in order to encourage a reading of Kelly's contribution that respects both its initially eclectic sources and its ultimate rigor. Such eclecticism is common for young artists trying to get their bearings, but such rigor is extremely rare inasmuch as few open-minded young talents are strong enough to resolve the competing claims and inherent contradictions among their promicuous artistic "first loves." In the process, I want to give greater credit to artists frequently passed over as incidental, if not dismissed as antithetical, to Kelly's self-realization—and in one important case off-handedly passed over as virtually irrelevant to it.

I'll start with the "irrelevant" mentor because, quite by chance, my own curatorial practice obliged me to re-evaluate his importance to Kelly. The project was a MoMA retrospective of which I was one of three curators, and its subject was the exiled German modernist painter Max Beckmann, who visited Boston during the last two years of his life at the invitation of his protégé Karl Zerbe, then a leading light of the heavily Germanophile local art scene. In his journal, Beckmann noted that the talk was attended by, "150 students, teachers, etc. Quappi [his wife] read very well, thunderous applause then a lot of sherry and very amusing feminine discussions." During an interview conducted by the author in 2001, Kelly, who was among those one hundred and fifty students, recalled:

> When Beckmann came to Boston to give a lecture in 1948 his wife delivered it because Beckmann's English was very limited. She read his "Letter to a Woman

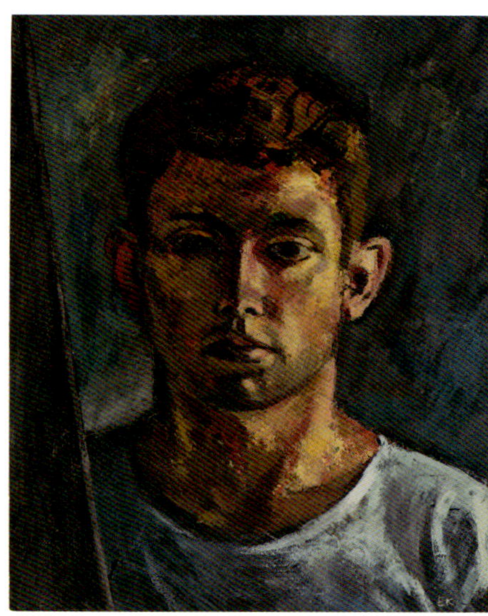

fig. 61: *Self-Portrait*, 1947, encaustic on Masonite, 20⅛ × 16 in, 51.1 × 40.6 cm

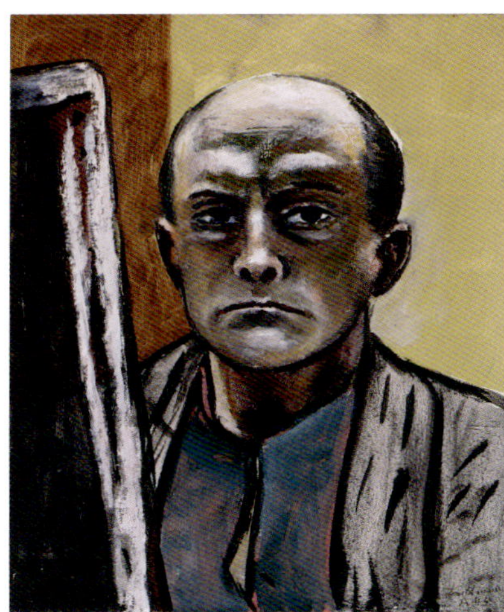

fig. 62: Max Beckmann, *Self Portrait in Olive and Brown*, 1945, oil on canvas, 23¾ × 19⅝ in, 60.3 × 49.8 cm

> Painter." He later visited the painting studio where we were all painting nudes from the model. I was disappointed at first since he only was interested in female students. But even this brief encounter made a deep impression on me. At that time he was the most important painter that I had come in contact with. It was a very significant event in my life.[3]

In a sense, Kelly had prepared for this unexpected meeting with works he had made the previous year, demonstrating the improbable hybrids that budding talents often concoct. Also in conversation with the author, Kelly remembered:

> There's a full-length portrait (fig. 21) I did that initially was inspired by Pollaiuolo's *David Victorious* (c.1472) (fig. 60). I used the stance of Pollaiuolo's *David* but the painting needed another element. I added a bugle I had in my studio referencing Beckmann's *Self-Portrait with a Horn* (1938). A smaller self-portrait from that year was done in encaustic (fig. 61) ... In this painting, the position of the head and the shoulders in relation to the easel—cropped at the left side forming a diagonal— is a device from Beckmann's *Self-Portrait in Olive and Brown* (1945) (fig. 62).
>
> I admired the intensity of his colors against their black outlines and his almost brutal and erotic subjects ... One of the things I did when I went to France ... was to go to Colmar to see Grünewald's *Isenheim Altarpiece* (fig. 46), which of course had an important impact on German Expressionism. Picasso and Beckmann were the most important artists to me during my student years ... Even though my work is not Expressionist, Beckmann's visual force has informed my painting and my admiration for his art only grows with time.[4]

It may come as a shock for some observers looking back on Kelly's oeuvre from the vantage point of his color cutouts and plant drawings to learn that Picasso rather than Matisse was first among his favorites in modern art. More surprising still may be the discovery that Beckmann came a close second and has remained a point of reference ever since his Boston days. Accordingly, it would be a serious lapse on the part of commentators if they failed to take honest account of Kelly's declared preferences and—*pace* Bloom—simply chalked his statement up to an Oedipal denial of the master to whose work his now bears the stronger resemblance. Just how enamored Kelly was of Picasso is anecdotally apparent when he recounts having almost been run over by the Spaniard's Hispano-Suiza as he walked down a street near the master's studio on Quai des Grands Augustins. After coming to an abrupt halt the apologetic Picasso opened his door and offered the younger man a lift, which the awestruck Kelly declined. Refusing a ride from one's idol is a telling indication of the extent to which he *is* an idol from whom one must keep a respectful distance.[5] Nevertheless, Kelly and a fellow American artist, Ralph Coburn, did visit Gertrude Stein's "widow" Alice B. Toklas—Stein had died of cancer in 1946—who received them in the apartment containing the legendary collection that she and her life-partner had occupied. According to Goossen, the work that most impressed Kelly was the Picasso collage *Student with a Pipe* (1913–14) (fig. 33). He seems to have mentioned none of the numerous Matisses that also occupied the walls, pictures that Stein and Toklas strategically hung in order to foment the rivalry between the two leaders of the School of Paris, such that at the dinner table each would be seated opposite a work by the other.

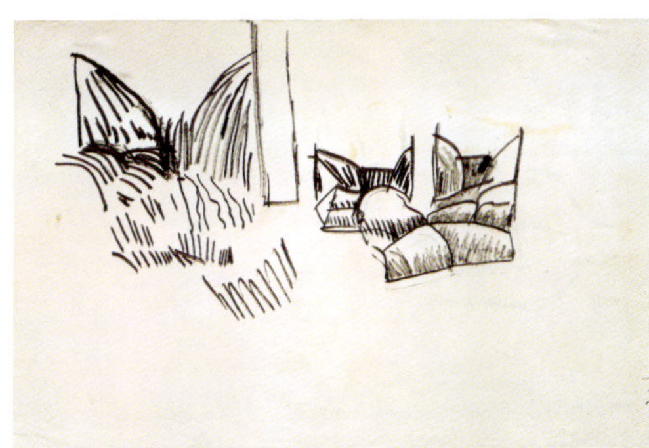

fig. 63: *Sluice Gates*, 1947, ink on paper, 12 × 18 in, 30.5 × 45.7 cm

As to why he regarded Picasso more highly than Matisse – who was by then a semi-invalid living on the Côte d'Azur rather than a vigorous presence in Paris – Kelly said, "I liked Picasso rather than Matisse because he made you want to paint. Because his paintings are sexy, exciting, orgasmic."[6] His feeling about Beckmann was much the same. Furthermore, then as later, Kelly's firm, decisive draftsmanship had a muscularity—dare one say, a masculinity—akin to both Beckmann's and Picasso's essentially sculptural, testosterone-charged approach but quite unlike Matisse's loose, discursive—I will refrain from resorting to a gendered binary by saying "feminine"—free-form improvisations.

Evidence for such a claim can be found in drawings and paintings made both during the war and immediately after, the self-portraits Kelly mentioned being exhibits A and B, as well as in the casual studies of fellow G.I.s and postwar friends relaxing, some of which bear a similarity to the sketches Beckmann made while serving as a medic in World War II—minus, it must be admitted, Beckmann's emotional vehemence. Still, Beckmann's frequently voiced contempt for modernist painting's flat, decorative qualities—qualities he disdainfully ascribed to Cubistic semi-abstraction as well as to the "pure" abstraction pioneered in Russia by Kandinsky and others—can hardly have escaped Kelly's notice. In fact, it must have hit a nerve. But in equal measure, Beckmann's lecture in Boston and the aesthetic and humanist articles of faith it contained must have resonated profoundly with the young American, habituated as he always had been to sharp observation of the world around him, as countless cityscapes of Paris attest, along with drawings of natural forms and portraits of intimate friends. Kelly arrived at abstraction without ever

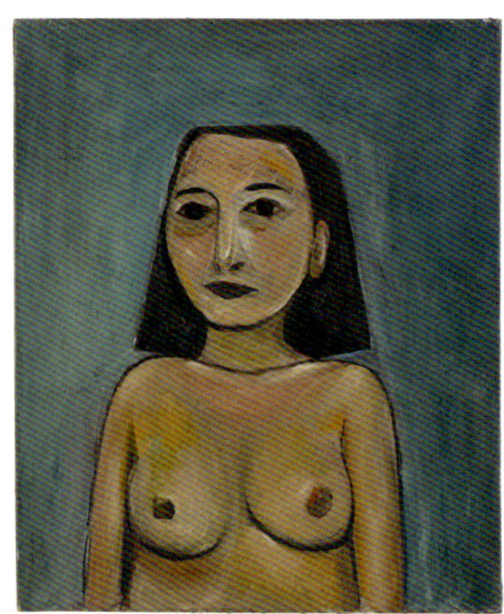

fig. 64: *Egyptian Woman*, 1949, oil on canvas, 24⅛ × 19¾ in, 61.3 × 50.2 cm

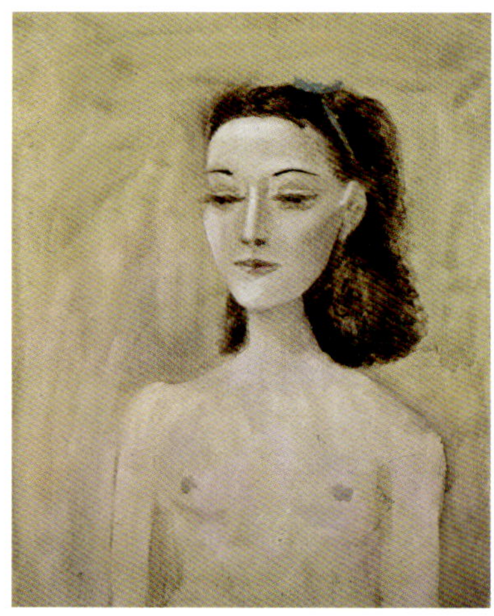

fig. 65: Pablo Picasso, *Portrait de Nusch Éluard,* 1941, oil on canvas, 28¾ × 23⅝ in, 73 × 60 cm

cutting its ties to looking. ***Sluice Gates*** **(1947)** (fig. 63) exemplifies his deft notational manner of structuring impressions of his surroundings while saving them up.

So when Quappi read the words of her husband's "Letters to a Woman Painter" in Boston, we can safely assume they fell on keenly attentive, if not instantly responsive, ears:

> The important thing is, first of all, to have a real love of the visible world that lies outside ourselves as well as to know the deep secret of what goes on within ourselves. For the visible world in combination with our inner selves provides the realm where we may seek infinitely for the individuality of our own souls. It has been, strictly speaking, a search for something abstract ... But we must not digress into metaphysics or philosophy ... One must have the deepest respect for what the eye sees ...[7]

Formalists would have it that the creative paradigms that truly matter to artists are essentially, if not exclusively, formal. So far as that goes, Kelly had avowedly studied the structure of Beckmann's paintings and drawings as closely as he had Picasso's, and freely borrowed from them. But of comparable if not greater importance to Kelly, it would seem, were Beckmann's motivations and his understanding of what art can do to marshal the forces of the artist's mind and spirit. Emotionally, Beckmann hit a nerve and unlocked pent-up energies that began to pour into Kelly's work. Without such permission or such a goad, a purely conceptual understanding of "what is to be done" is unlikely to reveal an artist to himself or herself. The conviction that seeing reality was the path of abstraction and that the visible could guide one to the invisible—or heavily sublimated—dimensions of one's true but hidden nature must have had a profound impact on multiple levels of Kelly's consciousness during his early manhood and artistic development. The many self-portraits he drew in this period, while unremarkable in their number given the natural self-absorption of youth (and the plentiful precedents in Beckmann), are nonetheless striking in their assurance, and—a full-length nude, especially—in their frankness. Beckmann's continuing effect on Kelly is such that as late as 2006 he could say, "Even though my work is not Expressionist, Beckmann's visual force has informed my painting and my admiration for his art only grows with time."

Still, Picasso's influence on Kelly's conception and realization of images is more obvious than Beckmann's, although as with Beckmann it derived both from the sensuality and verve of the elder's persona and from specific works that Kelly straightforwardly glossed, for example Picasso's highly stylized portraits of the lover he took at the very end of World War II, Françoise Gilot. Of particular interest in this regard is *La Femme Fleur* (1946) (fig. 66), whose bouquet of abstract petal or leaf-like shapes reappear in more subdued versions in Kelly's *Woman with Arm Raised* (1949) (fig. 67). A slightly earlier painting, *Egyptian Woman* (1949) (fig. 64) recalls Picasso's haunting wartime likenesses of Paul Éluard's wife, chief among them the one given by the poet to the Musée National d'Art Moderne *Portrait de Nusch Éluard* (1941) (fig. 65), as well as a bleaker bust of Gilot's predecessor made the year after, *Portrait of Dora Maar* (1942). Of more lasting consequence to Kelly, though, was

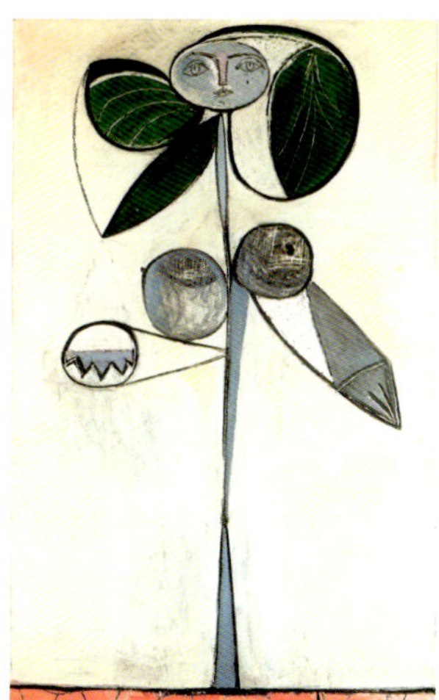

fig. 66: Pablo Picasso, *La Femme Fleur*, 1946, oil on canvas, 57½ × 35 in, 146 × 88.9 cm

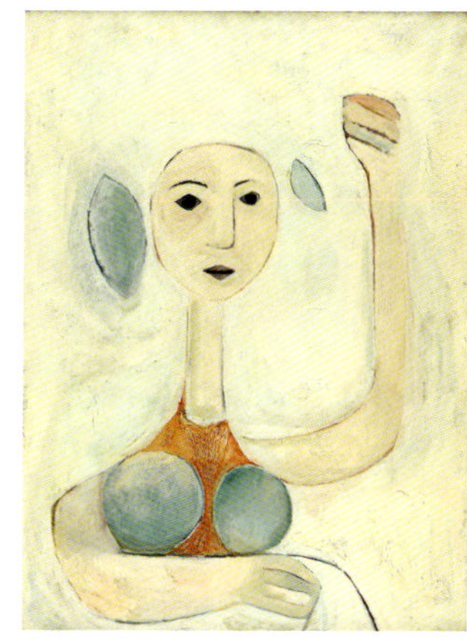

fig. 67: *Woman with Arm Raised,* 1949, oil on canvas, 33⅛ × 24 in, 84.1 × 61 cm

Picasso's engagement with the solid, powerfully articulated forms of Catalan Romanesque painting, sculpture and architecture—arguably as much of a primary source for the schematic faces and bodies of the *Les Demoiselles d'Avignon* (1907) and other "primitivizing" works as African tribal art—to which Kelly also was attracted. In time, his meditation on the almond-shaped formats of Byzantine altarpieces gave rise to Kelly's wholly secular burnished bronze wall relief *(Untitled) Mandorla* (1988) (fig. 68). According to Goossen, Kelly's interest in the Romanesque, far from being a widely shared passion among budding artists of that period, was "sparked by an apse seen at the Boston Museum." In the meantime, so Goossen tells us, Kelly's interest in Byzantine art—which converges with the Romanesque in its use of geometry—was stimulated by fellow Museum School student Bernard Chaet, later a force in the Yale School of Art following the tenure of Josef Albers.[8]

However, by the late 1940s, the force field surrounding Picasso in Paris had been significantly weakened by his increasingly long absences from the city and his correspondingly protracted sojourns in the South of France. It had also been diminished by the direct challenges posed to him by younger artists. Some were either closely or loosely associated with Existentialism—Alberto Giacometti and Jean Dubuffet front and center and more tangentially Jean Fautrier and Germaine Richier—because their rough handling of the human body evoked the suffering, destruction and spiritual isolation of the recent war and the threat of immanent nuclear annihilation. None held any special fascination for Kelly, who, incidentally, had seen more of the destruction of war than any of these artists except Fautrier. Neither, apparently, did the "informel" or "lyrical"

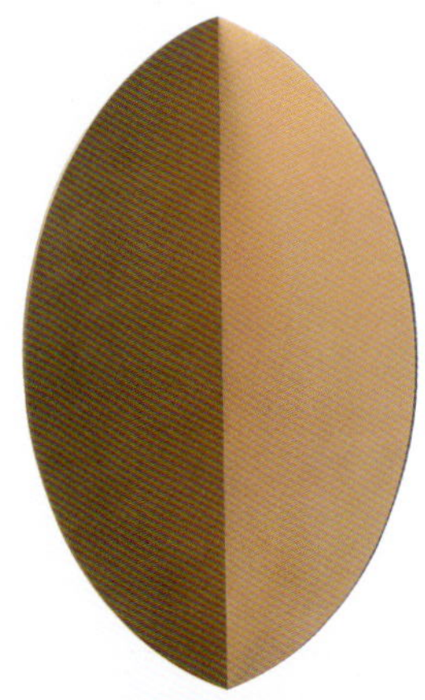

fig. 68: *Untitled (Mandorla)*, 1988, bronze, 101 × 54 × 21½ in, 256.5 × 137.2 × 54.6 cm

abstractionists such as Jean Bazaine, Camille Bryen, Alfred Manessier, Georges Mathieu, Pierre Soulages, or the maverick poet and painter Henri Michaux. Kelly's affinities lay elsewhere.

In crucial instances those affinities were historical—a 1952 visit to Claude Monet's studio in Giverny was a privileged peek at the recent past—and quasi-historical. In the latter regard, Kelly struck up an acquaintance with Alexander Calder, who had returned to France once the fighting had stopped. This friendship is commemorated by two gifts that Calder gave to Kelly and the encouragement his whimsical work set for pure but fundamentally intuitive abstraction. Indeed, Calder's gifts—a small sculpture (fig. 69) and a diminutive canvas (fig. 70)—epitomize those qualities and have been talismans in Kelly's studio ever since. In the same vein, Kelly's felicitous encounters with Dada abstractionist Jean Arp made a lasting impression on him, about which more later. As did Kelly's pilgrimage to the open door of Constantin Brancusi's studio in tandem with his artist friends Jack Youngerman and Alain Naudé. Constituting another direct connection to the surviving cohort of modernist pioneers the actual visit was something of a failure socially—Brancusi's obsession with a young woman who was also present limited conversation—even though the aged Romanian enjoyed his guests, was sorry to see them leave and invited them back, an opportunity that Kelly never took advantage of. Perhaps frustration with Brancusi's reluctance to discuss art was the reason, perhaps his age, perhaps—like Beckmann in Boston—his preoccupation with attractive women. In any case, Kelly had a good long look at one of the most extraordinary and aesthetically coherent studios in Paris and at the major examples of Brancusi's work that packed it. There can be no doubt that this brief but total immersion in Brancusi's austere, elegant environment had a profound influence on him.[9]

Kelly rubbed shoulders with other significant "moderns" during his second and most extended stay in France—1948 to 1954—and exposure to their work certainly helped him to better see and understand the emerging, on the whole contrasting, characteristics of his own. This was especially true when it came to artists associated with Non-Objective, Concrete, and Neo-Constructivist art of the late 1940s through the 1960s. A broad, cosmopolitan, trans-generational tendency, Neo-Constructivism—for economy's sake I will settle on that term—extended its hold on artists throughout both Eastern and Western Europe, from the North to the South of the Americas and across the Pacific. Although the culturally dominant modes of abstraction internationally during the same period were gestural, improvisatory or Expressionist—all of which Kelly flirted with in his formative years—Neo-Constructivism came a close second in terms of its aesthetic scope and geographic reach, though not in terms of its capacity to capitalize on the anxious Zeitgeist of the Cold War era.

A recent revival of interest in this work has yet to produce greater public demand for it, and that may remain the case for the foreseeable future. In part, it is because such art strikes much of the public as cold, cerebral and formulaic—which a considerable amount of it is, although that fact hardly disqualifies it as art and nor does it mean that it lacks a "humanistic" dimension as is so often said (what could be more exclusively a human invention than mathematics?) And in part the tendency lost traction as the result of the

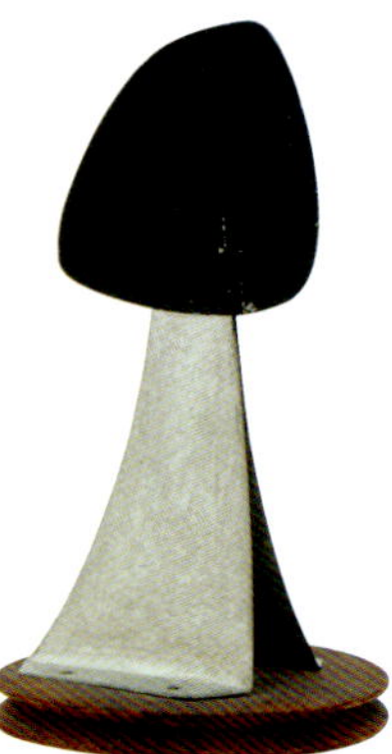

fig. 69: Alexander Calder, *Untitled* (alternate part from a maquette for Three Penn Center Plaza) [unrealized], 1955, sheet metal, wood, wire and paint, 12 × 7 × 7 in, 30.5 × 17.8 × 17.8 cm

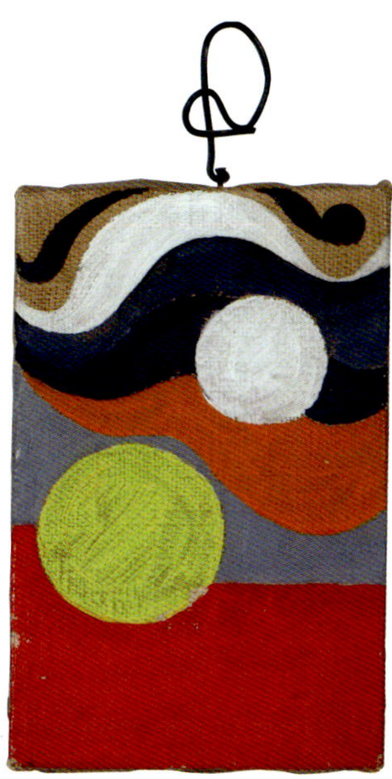

fig. 70: Alexander Calder, *Untitled*, c.1945, oil on canvas with metal hook, 5 × 3¼ in, 12.7 × 8.3 cm

fact that between the 1910s and 1920s, when geometric abstraction initially burst forth onto the scene in the context of social upheaval if not actual revolution, and the 1940s and 1950s, when it reappeared against the background of global devastation both actual and impending, Constructivist and Neo-Constructivist artists had abandoned much of their hope of totally redesigning and rationalizing the world and so jettisoned the movement's socially progressive rhetoric. Still, it retained a futuristic orientation. Kelly eschewed both politicized aesthetics and teleological ones. His commitment was to an art of intuitive complexity.

Nevertheless, he experimented with formal possibilities introduced to him by Constructivism and Neo-Constructivism. The "primitive" effigy or musical instrument-like string reliefs to which he devoted himself in 1949–50 may in this sense be simultaneously atavistic paraphrases of traditional forms—Goossen also suggests children's punched-card and yarn picture-making toys as a possible source—and idiosyncratic adaptations of the futuristic laced constructions of Naum Gabo.

Moreover, Kelly became familiar with the Belgian protégé of Piet Mondrian, Georges Vantongerloo. Alienated from many within the enclave of De Stijl artists still in Paris, not least from Theo Van Doesburg's widow, Vantongerloo took a liking to Kelly, as the latter recalled: "I think he liked me. People weren't friendly with him. I went to see him quite a bit and he was always pleased to have me around in the studio. And I became like a little pal."[10] Once again, the younger man cherished a present that the older, might-have-been mentor gave him—a small painting—and the nonagenarian Kelly cherishes it still. In spite of this bond, yet consistent with Kelly's claim not to have been tempted to become an epigone of Neo-Plasticism, Kelly steered clear of subscribing to the systems that Vantongerloo and his Neo-Plasticist cohorts devised and adhered to. It was a group that also included the artist, critic, curator, and Mondrian biographer Michel Seuphor, a denizen of the postwar Paris art world.

Their collective influence on Kelly can readily be traced to the project he conceived for the Guggenheim Fellowship in 1951 (figs 54–58). Eventually published by the Harvard Art Museums as *Line Form Color*, the maquette was Kelly's answer to the Constructivist and Neo-Constructivist concern with parsing the transformational grammar of visual language. Yet within those circles it was also his calling card:

> When I was introduced to [Jean] Arp by Michel Seuphor, he invited me to visit him, so I asked him to look at the project I proposed for the Guggenheim Fellowship [*Line, Form and Color* (1951)]. There are 40 pages. He went through every one. Toward the end, there was one that was pink and orange (fig. 123). And his only comment was "Where did you get this? Why did you want to do that?" I just said "These are two very close colors." But later I realized it was something that came out in several paintings.[11]

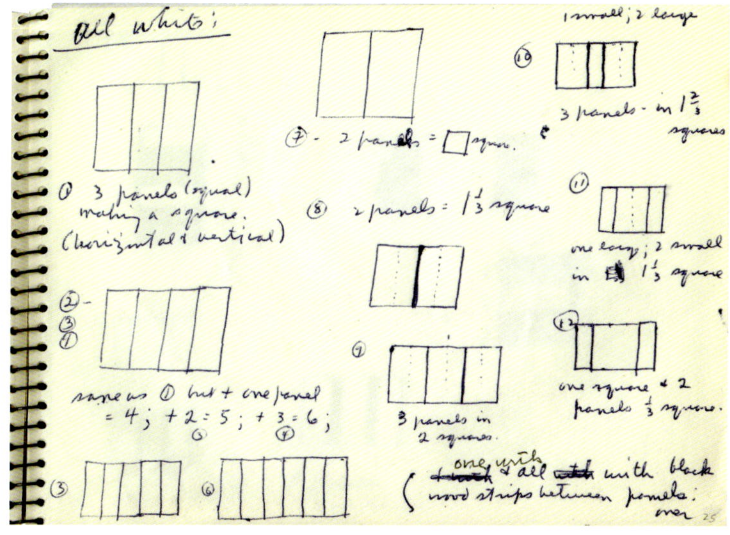

fig. 71: Sketches for white panels (from sketchbook 15), 1951–52, ink on paper, 5⅜ × 7½ in, 13.7 × 19.1 cm

In addition, Kelly's statement at the end of *Line, Form and Color* echoed Constructivist and Neo-Constructivist preoccupations with moving beyond traditional easel painting into public spaces, much as the muralist movement of the 1920s and 1930s had done for figurative painters of the Abstract Expressionist generations that preceded Kelly's own. In his explanatory notes to the forty, square, totally abstract pages that demonstrate the operating principles of line, form and color as presented in his eponymous portfolio, Kelly writes,

> I propose to create a book which will be an alphabet of plastic pictorial elements aiming to establish a new scale of painting, a closer contact between the artist and the wall, providing a way for painting to accompany modern architecture. There has been a growing awareness among young painters that painting return to the wall [sic] as in the days before the Renaissance ... It will speak to people anonymously as did the art of Egypt, the art of the great periods of China and India, of Byzantium, of Europe during the Middle Ages (the glass and sculpture of Chartres.)[12]

The reference to Chartres was prompted at least in part by Kelly's having seen it while stationed outside Paris in 1944, so the tenor of this atypically programmatic declaration stems, as does everything that really counts for him, from direct experience rather than from the "logic of History" as it was frequently invoked in other such universalist manifestos or from the nakedly grandiose ambition that was also common to them. Indeed, the near total sublimation of the artist's personality is a salient component of Kelly's concerns. Except, of course, insofar as his or her

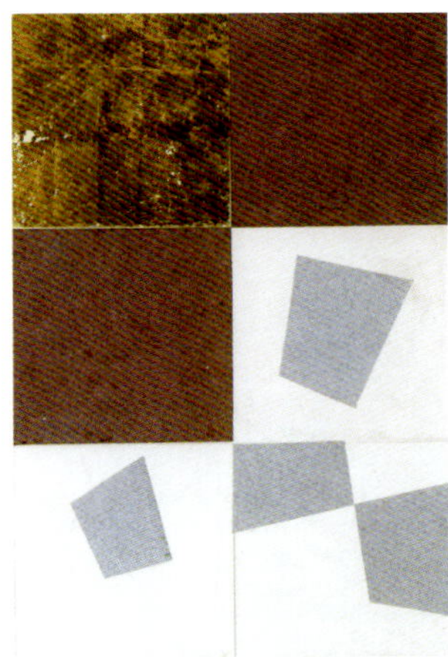

fig. 72: Jean Arp, *Collage Géométrique,* 1916, collage, 12 × 9¼ in, 31.8 × 23.5 cm

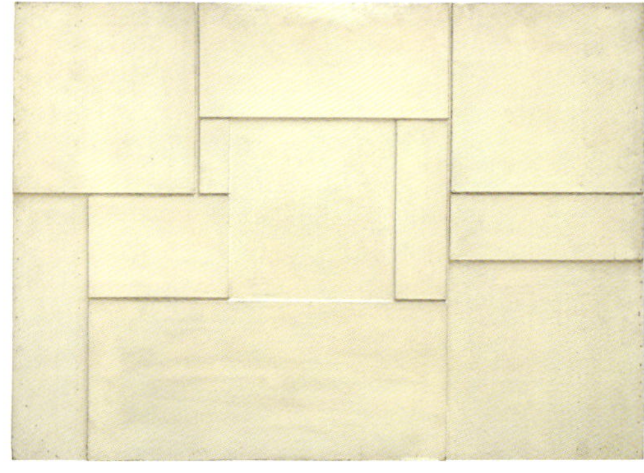

fig. 73: *Neuilly*, 1950, gesso on cardboard, plywood and wood, 23¼ × 31½, 59.1 × 80 cm

identity is readily discernible in distinctive choices about how to deploy the linguistic basics the books sets forth.

> Spirituality, the representation of nature, and the personality of the creator have been present in varying degrees, in all the art man has made ... Much of the art that has survived from ancient civilizations has been monumental, and compared with the art of today, appears anonymous. While the art of the twentieth century is personal on a very much smaller scale.[13]

Other than in self-portrait drawings, Kelly has rarely been tempted to make art *about* himself. Rather, his work is a forthright embodiment of his sensibility and spirit, in keeping with Beckmann's explanation of the dynamic fusion of objective reality and subjective nature. And so within five short years of writing the statement for *Line, Form and Color*, Kelly tested the proposition with a large architectural commission for the lobby of the new Transportation Building in Philadelphia: *Sculpture for a Large Wall* (1957) (pp. 140–41). Consisting of just over 100 tinted aluminum panels tipped at an angle to the existing wall on metal rails with carefully curved contours and precise intervals between each of the musical-note-like units, it was the first of many such public projects spanning his career over half a century from the mid-1950s into the middle of the second decade of the second millennium. In sum, Kelly lived up to the bold assertions made in *Line, Form and Color* and used it as the "manual of style" he had intended it to be.

Before making this leap, however, Kelly assimilated a crucial lesson taught to him by two very different artists. The first, already mentioned, was the Alsatian Jean Arp who, while in exile in Zurich during World War I, began to make collages by tearing up sheets of colored paper and dropping the

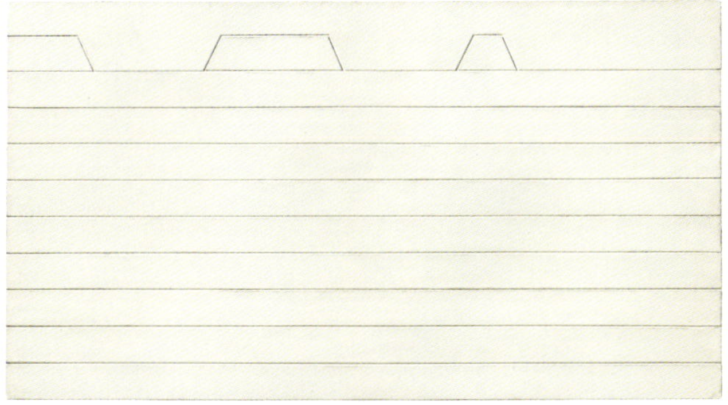

fig. 74: *Saint Louis II*, 1950, oil on cardboard and wood, 22 × 39¼ × 1 in, 55.9 × 99.7 × 2.5 cm

pieces on to another sheet of paper below to arrive at chance-determined anti-compositions. One of these early Arps, *Collage Géométrique* (1916) (fig. 72) was reproduced in black and white in *The Dada Painters and Poets*, published in 1951 by George Wittenborn and edited by Robert Motherwell. Previously published by Wittenborn and also edited by Motherwell was volume 6 of *The Documents of Modern Art* (1948), in which other aleatory Arps appeared. Meanwhile, in 1949, John Cage, fully cognizant of this Dada legacy, arrived in Paris on a Guggenheim Fellowship with the intention of meeting Olivier Messiaen and Pierre Boulez. He also crossed paths with Kelly—who came to know Boulez through Cage—and Cage's knowledge of Arp's randomizing procedures merged with his exploration of the *I Ching*. This reinforced Kelly's inclination to distance himself further from the regimented designs of the Neo-Constructivism and cast his lot with an alternative postwar avant-garde working beyond the precedents set by an early avant-garde. That is to say, Dada to Neo-Dada. Rejection by the Neo-Constructivists sealed Kelly decision.

> We would go to Denise [René]'s gallery and see what was going on. Jack sort of liked it better than I did. There were few artists I liked. There was one sculptor, Robert Jacobsen. He was feisty. Then there was one of Denise René's lovers, a stiff professor always dressed with a tie. I hated his work because they said "Oh, you're copying him." And I said "Oh, no, it's not like that." Anyway, once, when Jack and I went together to see something, Denise said "Why don't you bring some pictures and show them to my artists and see if we can do something? I won't choose you if they don't like you." This was quite early, probably in 1950. I had just made the white relief paintings—maybe a couple of them. They were a beginning, you know. Anyway, we were standing at the window and someone said "We're ready!" very quickly. They all did "Thumbs down." Later, I did sell her paintings.[14]

In all probability the "white reliefs" to which Kelly referred to were *Neuilly* (fig. 73), *Gate-Board* (p. 55), *Saint Louis I* (p. 14), *Saint Louis II* (fig. 74), and *White Relief* (p. 59) (all 1950). Perhaps the gallery artists balked at them as being insufficiently non-objective or not at all non-objective, in as much as at least two of them—*Saint Louis I* and *Saint Louis II*—are explicitly representational, depicting as they do masonry walls of buildings on the Île Saint-Louis in the middle of the Seine between the Left and the Right Bank. In effect, these objects, like others of this fertile, masterpiece-rich transitional period, are emblematic of the undisguised but fecund dualities of Kelly's aesthetic, which occupied a position halfway between the dominant aesthetic polarities of the day.

Even as he moved steadily in the direction of abstraction, and in particular of chance-determined abstraction, Kelly

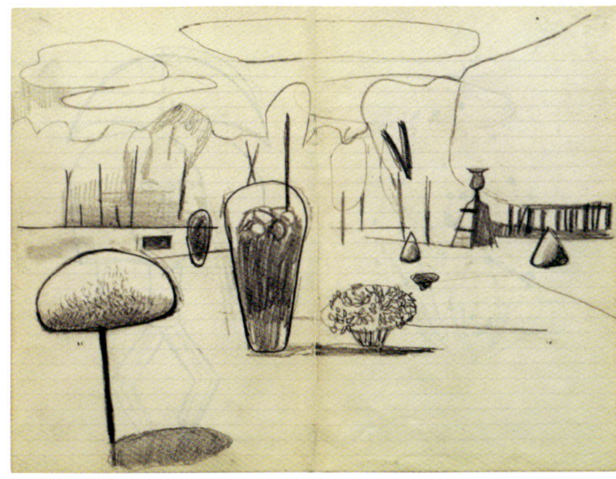

fig. 75: *Tuileries*, 1949, graphite on paper, 7¾ × 9⅞ in, 19.7 × 25.1 cm

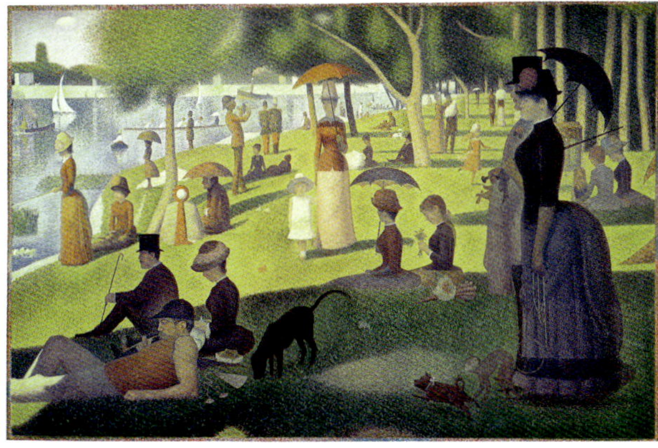

fig. 76: Georges Seurat, *A Sunday on La Grande Jatte–1884*, 1884/86, oil on canvas, 81¾ × 121¼ in, 207.5 × 308.1 cm

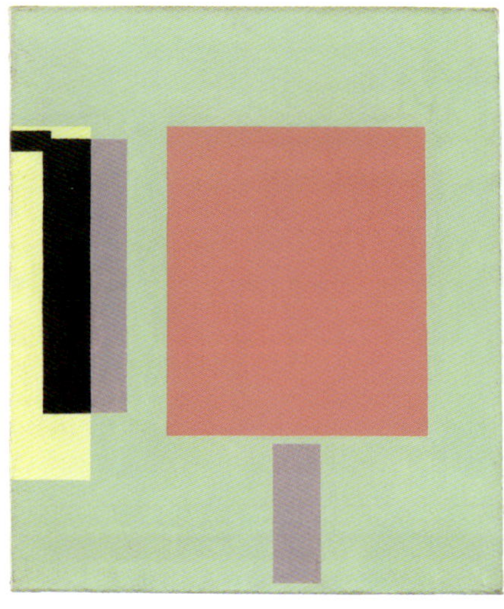

fig. 77: *Pink Rectangle*, 1950,
oil on canvas, 21¾ × 18⅛ in, 55.2 × 46 cm

continued to anchor his work in observed reality through constant sketching. Characteristic of these sheets is *Tuileries* (1949) (fig. 75), which might almost be read as a depopulated homage to the clear silhouettes and compact volumes in Georges Seurat's *A Sunday on La Grande Jatte—1884* (1884/86) (fig. 76). In others he extracted forms from lengths of seaweed, stacked café tables, the reflection of trees in the Seine, the previously mentioned shadows on the stairs in Meschers, side-walk grids, and the clustering of metro posters. Reminiscent of Mondrian's drawings of the found abstractions made visible when Parisian houses were torn down and the gridded interiors were exposed to view, the latter also coincide with the advent of Parisian "affichisme" and "decollage," as practiced by artists such as Jacques Villegle, François Dufrene, and Raymond Hains. And then there are Kelly's puckish homages to Turkish toilets, the then ubiquitous French amenity that he managed with tongue in cheek to transform into a cryptically hieratic emblem (fig. 34).

In collages, meanwhile, he seized upon and reconfigured a shadow falling on the Seine from an arc of the Pont Marie, the unevenly raised and lowered awnings of a shop on the posh Avenue Matignon, and the boundaries of fields in the French countryside. Furthermore, by 1949 the camera had become a key tool for capturing fleeting impressions—what Willem de Kooning called "slipping glimpses"[15]—of the artist's surroundings. Thus, the same Meschers stairs appear in a black and white photo of 1950, as do trapeze swings in a playground, rebar from a shattered seaside military bunker, the patched patterns of striped beach tents—roughly twenty years before Daniel Buren started to make "paintings" by mounting printed striped yard goods on stretchers—as well as other motifs that Kelly drew from life and/or translated in pencil or pen. In 1967 he went so far as to revisit and photograph some of the sites he had used for the "already-made" compositions of his early reliefs; specifically *Window, Musée National d'Art Moderne, Avenue Président Wilson, Paris* (fig. 36) and *Wall, rue Saint-Louis-en-l'Île* (fig. 9).[16] That said, and his connections to Arp and Cage duly taken account of, Kelly sought methodologies that would freshen his vision and devices for making art; anti-art, and more specifically the destructive subversion of painting, were the furthest things from his mind.

In sum, during a scant half decade between the end of World War II and the first years of the 1950s in which he made works as seminal and unmistakably his own as *Window V* (p. 57), *Saint Louis I* (fig. 8), *Saint Louis II* (fig. 74), *White Relief* (p. 59), *Relief with Blue* (p. 58), *La Combe I* (p. 61) (all 1950), and *La Combe II* (p. 60) and *La Combe III* (fig. 155) (both 1951), and Kelly managed to harness all the forces that he made available to himself during his various apprenticeships and via his many acquaintances without performing histrionic rituals of rebellion, without killing his aesthetic fathers or even his artistic uncles. To the contrary, even after his breakthrough, or while still in the course of its unfolding, he would test options that might retrospectively appear to belong to tendencies he had already put behind him.

For example, the pronounced asymmetries of *Fond Rouge* and *Pink Rectangle* (fig. 77) (both 1950) evoke the Neo-Constructivism on which he had just turned his back in favor of more unified pictorial gestalts, as do *Fond Jaune* and *Fond Noir* (also 1950). But, as decisive as he is in the studio, Kelly has never been an ideologue; in fact, the ideological aspect of Neo-Constructivism was one of the things that put him off it. However, a side-glance at what was going

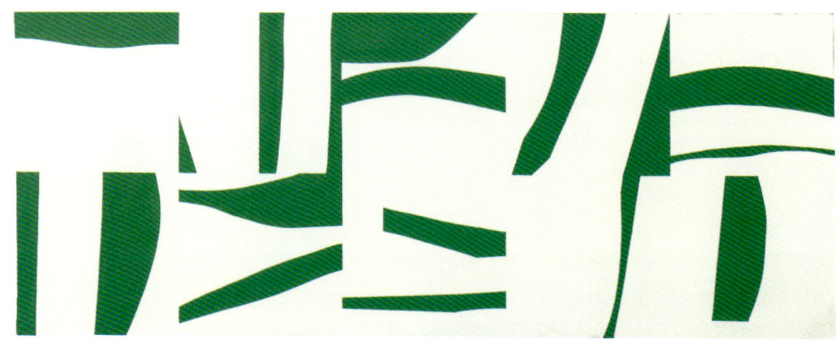

fig. 78: *Talmont*, 1951,
oil on canvas, 26 × 64¼ in, 66 × 163.2 cm

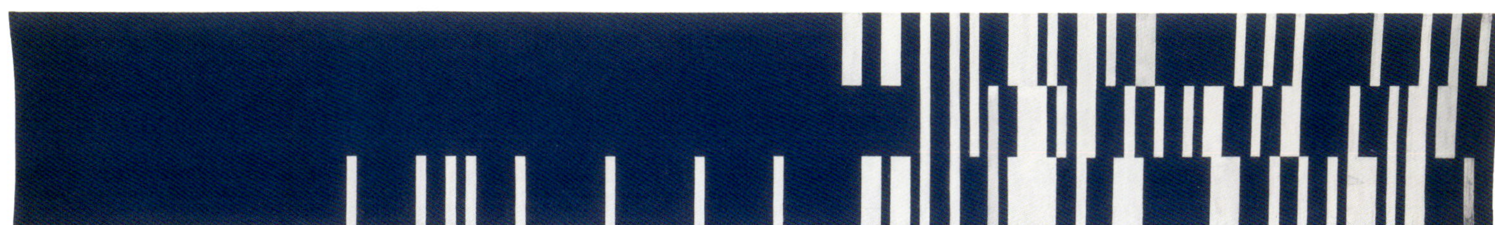

fig. 79: *Rouleau Bleu*, 1951, gesso on unstretched cotton, 17½ × 117 in, 44.5 × 297 cm

on around him, or even a look back over his shoulder at things he had surpassed, made sense to him when he thought he saw that there might still be something in it *for him*. Under those circumstances the only rational choice was to try that something out, and if the results did not demand the most of him—and they didn't—they are better, livelier by far than the Neo-Constructivist school norm at that time. Also of this ilk are the atypically scroll-like *Rouleau Bleu* (1951) (fig. 79) and scatter composition *Red Yellow and Blue* (1951), which seems quite literally to float between Arp-like randomness and Neo-Constructivist regularity if not regimentation. That the latter piece is owned by a collector in Venezuela, which like Brazil and other countries in South American embraced Neo-Constructivism during the 1940s, 50s and 60s, suggests that Kelly's affiliation with the movement is harder to shake off than words alone can accomplish—and not worth the effort since it in no way compromises or diminishes his huge achievement.

Thus when the authors of the tendentious, indeed egregiously overzealous 2004 textbook *Art Since 1900: Modernism, AntiModernism, Postmodernism* write of his formative years, "Kelly had no connection to what was happening in New York or to the spread of Piet Mondrian's legacy into an academic dogma at the hands of artists like Georges Vantongerloo and Max Bill," they protest too much. And in the process they falsify the historical record. Kelly *did* have such a connection, a warmly reciprocated personal one at that, which makes his resistance to entering the slip stream of orthodox Neo-Neo-Plasticism all the more remarkable as well as a testament to the acuity of his instincts and his strength of character in sticking to them.[17]

The years from 1951 to 1954, when Kelly finally left France, would yield both a consolidation and further elaboration of the formal principles at work in canvases and constructions such as *Meschers* (p. 65), *Cité* (p. 63), *Talmont* (fig. 78), *Seine* (p. 66), *Gironde* (fig. 80), *Colors for a Large Wall* (p. 69) (all 1951). These works incorporate ideas and procedure deriving from Arp and Cage that Kelly rehearsed in *November Painting* (1950) (fig. 41) and *Moby Dick* (1951) more or less without deviation, and then reconsidered and redeployed with breathtaking authority in previously cited paintings. By substituting fabrics that had been commercially dyed with the act of applying pigments to primed cotton duck with a brush in *Red Yellow Blue White* (1952) (pp. 74–75) opened up wholly new territory while anticipating Blinky Palermo's "Stoffbilder" by over a decade, even as *Spectrum Colors Arranged by Chance* (p. 67), foreshadows—or fore-scintiliates? —Gerhard Richter's chance-determined color grids of the 1970s onward. Elegantly proportioned and subtly luminous, *Dominican* (fig. 81), *Fête à Torcy* (p. 72), (both 1952) and *Train Landscape* (1953) (p. 77) are in a sense classic Kellys, with the latter providing a slipping glimpse of pure color bands that uncannily evokes the speed of train travel through fields. Although it is composed of subtly modulated hues and contains both a black and a white panel, *Painting for a White Wall* (1952) (pp. 82–83) effectively initiates Kelly's exploration of the spectrum, with *Spectrum I* being the first instance of such a composition consisting entirely of fully saturated colors. And with *White Plaque: Bridge Arch and Reflection* (1955) (p. 131) Kelly created the paradigm for the

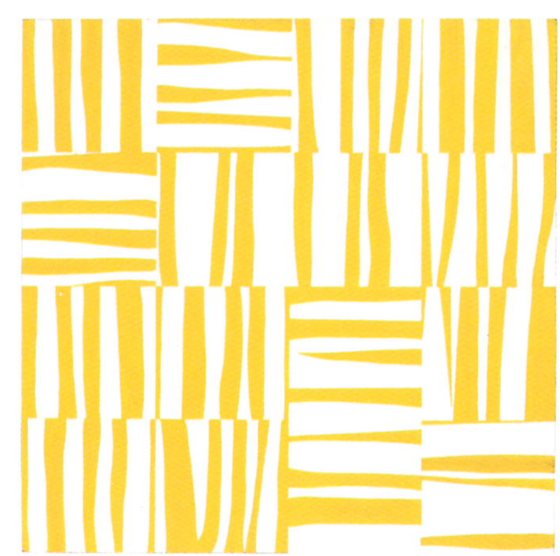

fig. 80: *Gironde*, 1951, oil and Ripolin on Masonite, 45⅝ × 45⅝ in, 116 × 116 cm

fig. 81: *Dominican*, 1952, oil on canvas and wood, 2 joined panels separated by a wood strip, 38½ × 25⅝ in, 97.8 × 65.1 cm

enormous number of monochrome and polychrome multi-panel paintings and reliefs that have preoccupied him from the mid-1950s until the present day, of which *Gold with Orange Reliefs* (p. 311) is just one, albeit the most surprising and eccentric example.

For much of the second half of the twentieth century, and despite abundant empirical evidence to the contrary, art criticism has been predicated on linear models of history that tend toward radical, not to say narrow and inherently erroneous, descriptions and analyses of how and why things happen and which of those many things is important because it buttresses a given model. Although undeniably a "mainstream" artist Kelly has through much of his career suffered from the misapplication of such paradigms to his work. In the U.S., the narrowness of which I am speaking sometimes resulted in bizarre twists, such that in the 1960s, when North American artists, succumbing to spasms of triumphalism, were at pains to prove they had freed themselves from European domination, and to that end invented formal categories and genealogies in support of what were in fact untenable ahistorical claims. Naturally enough, polemics of this kind can be invigorating, and occasionally the extra energy they release does engender genuinely new ways of thinking and doing. Arguably that was the case when, as a part of the rise of Minimalism, some artists essential to that tendency declared that the new American forms of geometric abstraction had once and for all parted company with the old Continental styles of abstraction by doing away with principles of composition based on balance and dynamic equilibrium. That, at any rate, was the contention of Donald Judd and Frank Stella when they answered questions posed to them by critic Bruce Glaser. After acknowledging a connection to Mondrian and the grand tradition of Neo-Plasticism and Constructivism, Judd and Stella, facing down their opponents like tag-team wrestlers, are quick to distinguish their motives from those of their predecessors—which is fair enough because they did differ fundamentally as I previously indicated. In the process, they turned to the relative lightweight Victor Vasarely to spell out just how much their own ideas about painting structure diverged from the European model. For them, Vasarely was a convenient and basically retrograde personification, although it must be admitted that he was having a significant impact on advanced art in South America even if few North American artists took notice at this time. The crucial difference, Judd and Stella maintained, was that whereas European art was based on a balance established among a variety of distinct pictorial elements, their art was predicated on the concept of the perceptual gestalt, which is to say on images that are instantly experienced as a whole rather than composed and read as parts organized in relation to one another.[18]

With distinctions drawn in this manner by ascendant Minimalists, Kelly's work fell into the gap between the two ostensibly conflicting approaches. While much of his work after 1950 was "composed," most of those compositions were based on chance operations such that despite the degree to which his abstractions like *Colors for a Large Wall* (p. 69), or in another vein *Fête à Torcy* (p. 72), may have superficially resembled what Judd, Stella and their followers considered "European" paradigms, the actual logic behind them was of an entirely different order.

fig. 82: *White, Two Blacks*, 1953, oil on canvas, 3 joined panels, 23⅝ × 70¾ in, 60 × 179.7 cm

(Kelly's two episodes abroad and his associations with School of Paris artists, which he refused to renounce for the sake of aesthetic chauvinism, only reinforced this misconception.) On the other hand, it is difficult to think of works that more fully embody the principles of the gestalt than *Black Square* (p. 84), *White Square* (p. 85), *Black, Two Whites*, *White, Two Blacks* (fig. 82) (all 1953) and *White Plaque: Bridge Arch and Reflection* (p. 131), although they are rarely if ever cited as precursors of Minimalism.

Why? There are a host of contingencies that might explain this strange disconnect and the ambiguous place Kelly was accorded in much of art history and criticism until quite recently. Among them are the "natural" shrugging off of immediate predecessors that attends the rise of a new generation—let's call them big brothers and stipulate that unlike fathers who must be killed (and can be when they weaken with age), it is usually safer to just ignore an imposing elder sibling. Typecasting Kelly as "too European" was a way of not talking about him. Yet, taking the long view now that those rivalries have exhausted themselves, we can see that he stands alone as a Janus-like figure looking both forward and back. His work represents a hub at which an exceptionally diverse assortment of sources converge—Beckmann and the Byzantine, Picasso and the Romanesque, Dada and Neo-Constructivism—and from which a truly astonishing array of inventions issue, forming vectors of influence that continue to widen and extend themselves: American Minimalism and Postminimalism of the 1960s and 1970s as exemplified by Robert Mangold, Brice Marden, Richard Serra, and Richard Tuttle, German abstraction of the 1970s as developed by Palermo and Richter, ironic American abstraction of the 1980s as conceived of by Peter Halley and Philip Taaffe, as well as millennial Hard-Edge abstraction worldwide. The question for young artists with which I began—"What is to be done?"—is always the same: to succeed, one must heed Ezra Pound's exhortation to "Make it new!" No artist of the twentieth century demonstrates more refreshingly how that is done, and, having done so, none poses a more daunting challenge, nor sets a more useful example to artists waiting in the wings to make their entry.

1 George McNeil quoted in Steven Naifeh and Gregory White Smith, *Jackson Pollock: An American Saga* (New York: Clarkson N. Potter, 1989), p. 338.

2 From the full transcript of "Conversation: Ellsworth Kelly & Robert Storr," in *Ellsworth Kelly* (Paris: Les Cahiers, Fondation Louis Vuitton, Manuela Editions, 2014), pp. 11–30. EK: I was in the Engineer Battalion, camouflage, in 1943. We worked in Normandy, right after the D-Day landings. To fool the Germans into thinking that we were something else we made an army of decoy tanks and planes that were hidden behind hedgerows, to provoke the Germans into attacking us. They took surveillance photographs and they couldn't tell the difference between a real tank and a fake tank. Then, toward the end, they did discover what was going on because they had these cameras that told that the equipment wasn't real. Still, when they *were* arranging to attack us, we were told: "Get out, get out now." But we couldn't get out in half an hour because we had all these rubber tanks and rubber planes. Everything was made of inflated rubber. When the Germans began to move against us, they attacked from behind and we had to get out fast. And I remember we were on a hill and the guys in our tanks had gone through our ranks so as to be hidden from the Germans and they hit the Germans' full line and realized they were outnumbered. So they turned and were screaming: "Why don't you join us; why don't you help us?" because they too thought the fake tanks were real. Yes. That was scary.

3 Ellsworth Kelly, quoted in "Boston, Beckmann and After," excerpts from an interview with Robert Storr, published in the catalogue of *Max Beckmann*, an exhibition jointly organized by Robert Storr at the Museum of Modern Art, New York; Didier Ottinger at Musée National d'Art Moderne at Centre Georges Pompidou, Paris, and Sean Rainbird at Tate Modern, London. The catalogue contains essays and interviews by all three curators, as well as contributions by other scholars. It was edited by Sean Rainbird. Kelly's words appear on p. 237 of the American edition.

4 Ibid. Note also that Grünewald's *Isenheim Altarpiece* was much later an inspiration for Jasper Johns' AIDS allegories of the 1980s and 1990s.

5 From an interview conducted for the archives of the Museum of Modern Art. "A friend of mine in the army, Bill Griswold [a student of architectural history] met Picasso on the street. Picasso invited him up. It was September of that year. Bill came back and I said 'And I am not going?'. He said 'Oh, I don't think you would function in that society.' You know, Gertrude Stein was there as well as other people involved with Picasso. And there were parties and stuff. Of course, that started my interest in Picasso. I remember seeing some paintings of his on posters as we left Paris and went to the country. The interest in Picasso was very strong for me. Later on when I went later to Boston to the Museum School, I put myself in Bill's spot and I said that I had been invited by Picasso. And that changed everything! [laughs] But then I felt badly about it. You know when you're young you want to do something to impress people." From the unedited transcript of the interview conducted for Les Cahiers, Fondation Louis Vuitton, 2014.

6 Ibid.

7 Max Beckmann, "Letters to a Woman Painter," in *Max Beckmann, On My Painting* (Madras & New York, Hanuman Books, 1988), pp. 63–66.

8 E.C. Goossen, *Ellsworth Kelly* (New York: Museum of Modern Art, 1973), p. 18.

9 From full transcript, *Ellsworth Kelly,* Les Cahiers, 2014.

10 Ibid.

11 Ibid. p. 28.

12 Ellsworth Kelly, *Line Form Color* (Cambridge, MA: Harvard Art Museums, 1999).

13 Ibid.

14 From full transcript of *Ellsworth Kelly,* Les Cahiers, 2014, p. 25.

15 Sarah Boxer, "In Short: A Slipping Glimpser" *The New York Times,* August 7, 1994, see also "Content is a Glimpse," excerpts from an interview with David Sylvester (BBC) reprinted from *Location*, Vol. 1, No. 1, Spring 1963 and *The Collected Writings of Willem de Kooning,* Hanuman Books, Madras & New York, 1988, p. 83.

16 All of the works mentioned in these two paragraphs and detailed discussion of the relation between photographs and drawings of particular sites appear in Yve-Alain Bois, Jack Cowart, and Alfred Pacquement, *Ellsworth Kelly: The Years in France, 1948–1954* (Washington, DC: National Gallery of Art, 1992) and in Diane Waldman, *Ellsworth Kelly: Drawings, Collages, Prints* (New York: Paul Bianchini Book, New York Graphic Society, 1971).

17 Hal Foster, Rosalind E. Krauss, Yve-Alain Bois, Benjamin H.D. Buchloh, *Art Since 1900: Modernism, Antimodernism, Postmodernism* (London: Thames & Hudson, 2004), p. 370. As to my claim about the book's tendentiousness, one example is the treatment accorded to Kelly's hero Max Beckmann. His considerable contributions to the history of modern painting are reduced to an ideological rant about one early canvas *The Night* (1918–19) which completely misrepresents Beckmann's politics and artistic intentions while missing the overt allusions he makes to the gruesome paintings of martyrdom and crucifixion that were common during the German Renaissance. "While Beckmann's work had clearly acknowledged the tragic experience of the failed German revolution of 1919 with its brutal murders of Marxist leaders Rosa Luxemburg and Karl Liebknecht among others, this depiction of a cryptic scene of the sadomasochistic mayhem positions the revolutionary worker (possibly a clandestine portrait of Lenin) on the same level of violent perpetration as a fascist petit bourgeois. Typically Beckmann's humanistic lament of universal bestiality fails to reflect on the painting's own heavily repressed but fully exposed indulgence in the sadistic scene it pretends to reveal." For what it is worth, although carelessly used, "humanism" is not a dirty word, the "revolutionary worker" looks nothing at all like Lenin though he might just as easily be a fascist thug caught in the act of murder, and almost everything said in this commentary could–with the same uninformed and indiscriminate malice–be said of Francisco de Goya's *Disasters of War*. For the record, in 1937 shortly after Hitler publicly attacked modern art as "degenerate" Beckmann and his wife Quappi left Germany for Holland. In 1947 he moved to the United States where he died in 1950.

18 "Questions to Stella and Judd," Interview by Bruce Glazer edited by Lucy Lippard, in Gregory Battcock (ed.), *Minimal Art: A Critical Anthology* (New York: E.P. Dutton & Co., 1968), pp. 149–50, 154, reprinted from *Art News,* September 1966. In the exchange between Stella and Judd, Vasarely basically serves as a whipping boy or straw man for the purposes of comparison with their work when in fact his work and theirs had very little in common, other than being hard-edged and abstract. As a consequence of occupying the demilitarized zone between

the two camps codified by Judd and Stella in this influential interview, Kelly is mentioned in passing a number of times and several of his works are reproduced, but there is scant attention paid to the formal dynamics or historical contribution of his work, except for a very curious observation by editor Gregory Battcock in the introduction to the anthology that is responsible for the interview's long-term impact: "For example, we know that the new Minimal style should not be considered a repudiation of the earlier Abstract-Expressionist aesthetic. Rather, modern artists, such as Ellsworth Kelly, emphasize the lingering vitality of certain Abstract Expressionist discoveries, and at the same time acknowledge the legitimacy of that movement." It was not until the publication of James Meyer's scholarly *Minimalism: Art and Polemics in the Sixties* in 2004 that a comprehensive and dispassionate account of the movement that gives proper credit to Kelly's influence on it became available.

In New York City, 1954–70

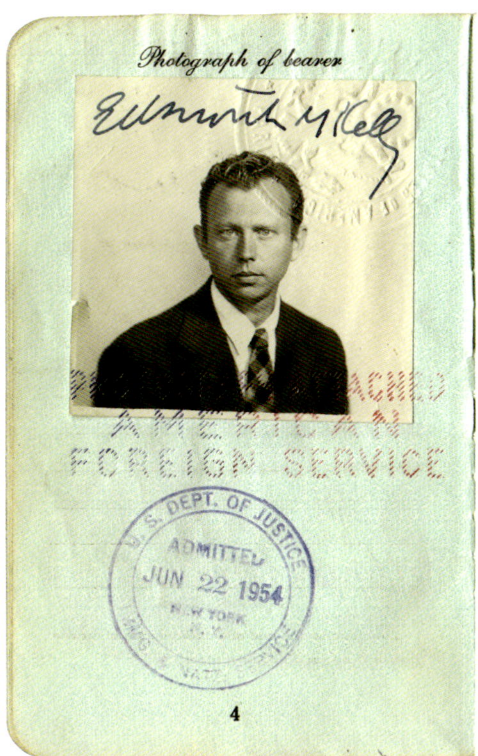

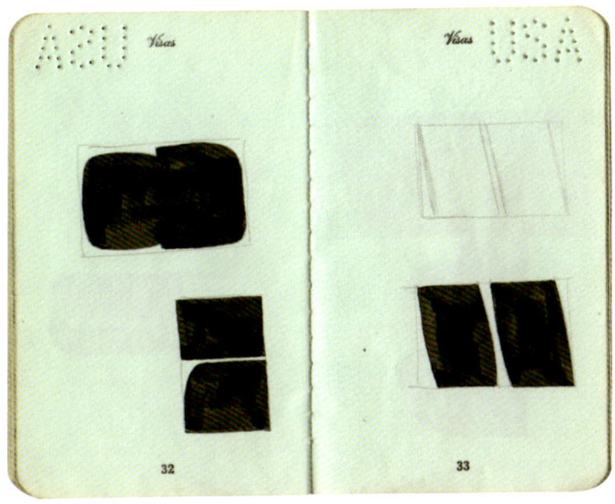

fig. 83: Ellsworth Kelly's U.S. passport (issued in 1952) with sketches for paintings

The Curve

After six formative and productive years in France, Kelly, now thirty-one, arrived in New York City on June 22, 1954. Always an artist who needed to jot things down as ideas came to him, he did so even in his passport (fig. 83). Having lived in Brooklyn while a Pratt student before World War II, this time he chose to settle in Manhattan. He rented a studio at 109 Broad Street at the southern tip of Manhattan Island, where he would live for about two years. Nearby was the Seamen's Church Institute, where he was able to pass as a sailor, allowing him to eat almost for free. Soon after his arrival, following the advice of John Cage, Kelly went to visit the studio of Robert Rauschenberg, the "interesting young painter"[1] whom Cage had described to Kelly, and there he saw Rauschenberg's "Red Paintings" from 1953–54 as well as the monochrome *White Painting* comprised of seven panels from 1951. While Kelly was surprised to see a multipanel work so akin to what he had already been exploring in France—he had mapped out a similar work around the same time in France, an all-white work of six panels, but had never made (fig. 48)—he also found it reassuring that others were examining similar concepts that intrigued him, since he had felt artistically isolated in France.

As in Paris, Kelly would meet a number of artists while living in New York City until 1970, many who in the coming years would contribute to the steady rise and varied breadth of postwar American art. With some he forged close friendships, such as Robert Indiana, Agnes Martin, and later Roy Lichtenstein. He also continued friendships with artists whom he had met in France, including Jack Youngerman and Alexander Calder. Kelly had met Calder in 1950, and their friendship would deepen through his contact with Youngerman's father-in-law, Henri Seyrig, an accomplished archaeologist who later served briefly as the director of the Musées de France in the early 1960s; Seyrig was the only one who had bought a work of Kelly's during his French years (*Antibes*, 1950). Taking a sincere, even fatherly interest in Kelly, Calder visited him at his Broad Street studio soon after the younger artist's return to the States. By the late fall of 1954, Kelly was struggling to pay his rent and Calder sent a letter to him on December 9, with a check to cover the younger artist's rent, explaining it was a "gift" meant to alleviate Kelly's *"soucis"* (French for "worries"). Calder also explained that he had written on his behalf to Alfred H. Barr, Jr., the founding director of MoMA, and James Johnson Sweeney, the director of the Guggenheim Museum. Calder closed his letter, "I hope something comes of it. Cordially, Sandy."[2]

Something did, rather quickly, showing Calder's sway with both directors. Sweeney wrote to Kelly on December 15 with a very kind letter, offering to visit and sharing the fact that Seyrig had also written on Kelly's behalf and that Calder's letter was a reminder for him to be in touch.[3] Sweeney would visit Kelly that month, but the Guggenheim would not acquire a work by Kelly until 1967 (pp. 170–71). Barr wrote to Kelly a week later on December 23, in a much less friendly letter, suggesting that Kelly deliver some of his paintings to the museum, because his busy schedule gave him no time to visit.[4] Disappointed and even offended by the director's half-hearted suggestion, Kelly chose not to deliver any works to MoMA for his review, saying he would prefer to wait for a studio visit.

Instead, curator Dorothy C. Miller, who by this time had curated the first three of her influential "Americans" shows at MoMA, came to visit Kelly before the end of 1954. Through these periodic exhibitions that spotlighted new American artists, the museum had become an integral force in championing contemporary American art. For example, "Fifteen Americans" in 1952 had brought together Jackson Pollock, Mark Rothko, Clyfford Still, and William Baziotes, among others, helping to solidify the dominance of Abstract Expressionism.

Miller's 1954 visit to Kelly's studio proved fruitful, although the fruits would not come until a few years later. In 1957, Miller would include Kelly's first painting made in New York, *Black Curves* (p. 129), in a group exhibition at the Time-Life Building in Manhattan, which traveled to eight other venues in the States, mainly universities, including Stanford University, and then ended its run at the Tate Gallery in London. (When *Black Curves* returned from its tour, Kelly jotted down in his journal that the painting had actually been shown incorrectly, on its side so that the curves protruded upward.) Miller would then invite Kelly to participate in her 1959 "Sixteen Americans," an exhibition now with minted historical status, one that heralded rising artists Jasper Johns, Robert Rauschenberg, and Frank Stella.[5] However, it must be noted that Kelly's first appearance at MoMA (as well as his first exhibition in New York) was actually three years earlier at a show titled "Recent Drawings USA" in 1956, upon the invitation of curator William Lieberman, where Kelly showed an ink study for *Black Ripe* (1955) (p. 130).

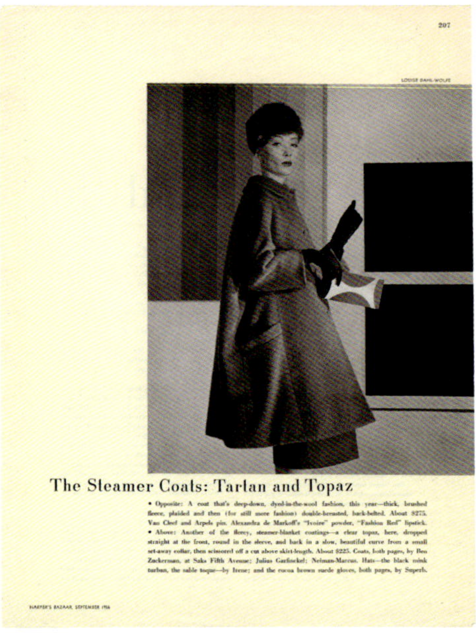

The Steamer Coats: Tartan and Topaz

• Opposite: A coat that's deep-down, dyed-in-the-wool fashion, this year—thick, brushed fleece, plaided and then (for still more fashion) double-breasted, back-belted. About $275. Van Cleef and Arpels pin. Alexandra de Markoff's "Ivoire" powder, "Fashion Red" lipstick. • Above: Another of the fleecy, steamer-blanket coatings—a clear topaz, here, dropped straight at the front, round in the sleeve, and back in a slow, beautiful curve from a small set-away collar, then scissored off a cut above skirt-length. About $225. Coats, both pages, by Ben Zuckerman, at Saks Fifth Avenue; Julius Garfinckel; Neiman-Marcus. Hats—the black mink turban, the sable toque—by Irene; and the cocoa brown suede gloves, both pages, by Superb.

HARPER'S BAZAAR, SEPTEMBER 1956

fig. 84: Model posing with works by Ellsworth Kelly, *Harper's Bazaar* ("Ripe for Fashion: Tomato Tweed"), September 1956

As Kelly had hoped, the New York art world did prove to be more receptive to his work, relatively soon after his return to the States. In 1955, dealer David Herbert, an associate at Sidney Janis Gallery (which had opened in 1948 on the same floor across the hall from Betty Parsons Gallery on East 57th Street) also took interest in Kelly's work, visiting his studio and recommending him to Betty Parsons herself. Soon afterwards, Parsons went to see Kelly, offering him a solo exhibition at her gallery the following year. What satisfaction Kelly must have felt after landing an exhibition at the same gallery where Ad Reinhardt had shown—the subject of the *ARTnews* review that had motivated his return to the States.

In May 1956, Kelly's first solo exhibition in the U.S. opened at Betty Parsons. The majority of the paintings shown here were new works made in New York, such as *Black Curves* (1954) (p. 129), *Yellow Black and White* (1955) (p. 128), *White Plaque: Bridge Arch and Reflection* (1955) (p. 131), *Bar* (1955) (p. 132), *South Ferry* (1956) (p. 138), and *Black Ripe* (1955) (p. 130). The artist also showed a handful of his French works, including *Cité* (1951) (p. 63), *Colors for a Large Wall* (1951) (p. 69), *Fête à Torcy* (1952) (p. 72), *Train Landscape* (1953) (p. 77), and *Spectrum Colors Arranged by Chance* (1951–53) (p. 67). Sale prices began at $150, with mid-range works around $600, the price for *White Plaque*, and the highest price at $1,500 for *Colors for a Large Wall*.[6] For his first solo outing in New York, the show garnered decent press, even landing Kelly's art in a fashion spread for *Harper's Bazaar* several months later. Photographer Louise Dahl-Wolfe, who worked closely with revered fashion editor Diana Vreeland, featured models dressed in stylish winter coats set against the backdrop of Kelly's work (fig. 84). Critics overall responded well to the artist's New York debut. In *Arts Magazine,* Barbara Butler described Kelly as "a new and forceful painter," whose work, "like those of Malevitch [sic] and Arp look deceptively simple." She continued, "Kelly's work reflects precision and control; its directness—unlike that of today's 'action' painting—is the result of this refinement, rather than of a method of addressing the canvas."[7] In *ARTnews* Parker Tyler referred to Kelly as an artist who was "ingenious in flexing the strict anatomy of large, mathematically divided areas" and stated that some of his works "suggest a heraldry of De Stijl and the Bauhaus." He explained how Kelly had "boldly colonized territory that Mondrian's ghost might claim but that this young artist is capable of holding on his own."[8]

As we have seen, being classified as reminiscent of Mondrian and of other early European geometric abstractionists was not a new occurrence for Kelly; he had grown used to this in France. And the American art world, for the most part, would continue to view the artist on basically the same terms over the next several years. For example, in a review of his 1959 exhibition at Parsons, his third solo show there, critic Dore Ashton wrote, "Kelly is one of the few painters who have been able to carry out Mondrian's program of neutrality in the special sense Mondrian meant it."[9] Future MoMA curator William Rubin, however, had a better grasp of Kelly's work. After the artist's appearance at Miller's "Sixteen Americans," Rubin, then a critic, attempted to clarify such misunderstandings in 1960: "Kelly has been wrongly related to Mondrian (on the basis of the flat, pristine surfaces and the hard edge) and Arp (flat curvilinear shapes). But being very much a colorist Kelly is opposed to both, particularly to Mondrian, against whose intellectual attitude he sets a thoroughgoing sensuous approach."[10]

Rubin had identified a key distinguishing trait of Kelly's work—its sensuousness. And while Kelly's first New York critics were, for the most part, positive in their assessment of his 1956 debut, they had failed to recognize this aspect of his work, both in color and form. This sensuousness could be found in the rich, delectable colors of his French works, but was harder to identify because of the gridded structure of such works as *Colors for a Large Wall* and *Spectrum Colors Arranged by Chance*. It was much clearer in his new works made in New York that incorporated curving, bulging forms, as in *Black Curves*, *White Plaque: Bridge Arch and Reflection*, and *Black Ripe*, an engagement antithetical to Mondrian's strict and rational aesthetics. In his 1971 statement looking back on his French years, Kelly even addressed this preference: "The forms found in the vaulting of a cathedral or a splatter of tar on a road seemed more valid and instructive and a more voluptuous experience than either geometric or action painting."[11]

Kelly has often described his time in France, as "voluptuous." Such an adjective, especially when applied to anything French, cannot help but bring to mind the famous line, *"luxe, calme et volupté"* from Charles Baudelaire's 1857 poem, *"L'Invitation au voyage,"* where all is luxury, tranquility, and pleasure (which, of course, inspired Matisse's 1904 painting created in the French Riviera, *Luxe, Calme et Volupté*). While taking in the visual world in France was indeed a "voluptuous experience" for Kelly, one of great pleasure and tranquil idylls as he walked about Paris and traveled around the French countryside and along its shores, his work made at this time did not necessarily register this appreciation, especially with his rectilinear multipanel paintings, despite their pleasing, alluring colors. Indeed, this interest in "voluptuousness" is ironically more readily identifiable in his paintings made after returning to the U.S., those featuring curvilinear shapes, for example.

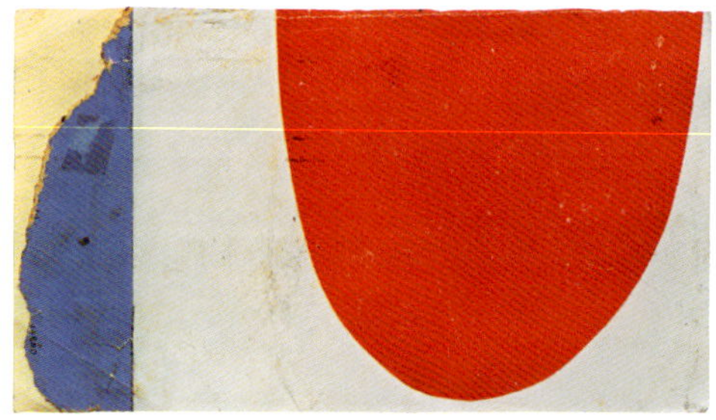

fig. 85: *Gauloise Blue with Red Curve,* 1954, postcard collage, 3¼ × 5½ in, 8.3 × 14 cm

Shortly after his return to the U.S., Kelly sent his friend Ralph Coburn from his Boston years his first collage made in New York. Made with a postcard, he would later title it *Gauloise Blue with Red Curve* (fig. 85). He introduced an upside-down bell-shaped curve in red against a white ground. Adding a blue paper scrap torn from a *Gauloise* cigarette pack, Kelly mimicked the color order of the French flag. About this 1954 collage, he later remarked, "To me the red curve ... was different from Paris";[12] "the blue was French; the red curve was the new world."[13] These first explorations of the curvilinear shape, including *Black Curves* (p. 129), heralded a departure from the rectilinear gridded and banded paintings that Kelly had made in France. He would focus on a variety of manifestations of the curve over the next decade: oblong versions as in *Black Curves*, more fragmented ones as in *Rebound* (1959) (p. 145) and *Red Blue Green* (1963) (pp. 156–57), and some even in sculpture, *Blue Red Rocker* (1963) (p. 160). Over the years, Kelly came to call this type of shape a "free curve," a term to contrast his paintings and reliefs that derive from a segment of a circle, works he calls "radiuses" or "radial curves," which can be seen in works including *White Plaque: Bridge Arch and Reflection* (1955) (p. 131), *Pony* (1959) (p. 148), *Red Curve II* (1972) (fig. 132), and *Yellow Curve* (1990) (pp. 256–57). While indeed a new direction for Kelly at this time in 1954, the "free curve" does in fact draw from a shape the artist had painted five years earlier in France, *Kilometer Marker* (1949) (p. 51). In this painting inspired by an "already-made" source, Kelly had rendered the silhouetted form of a kilometer marker seen along a roadside in France by drawing with graphite pencil, a linear treatment visible in the painting.

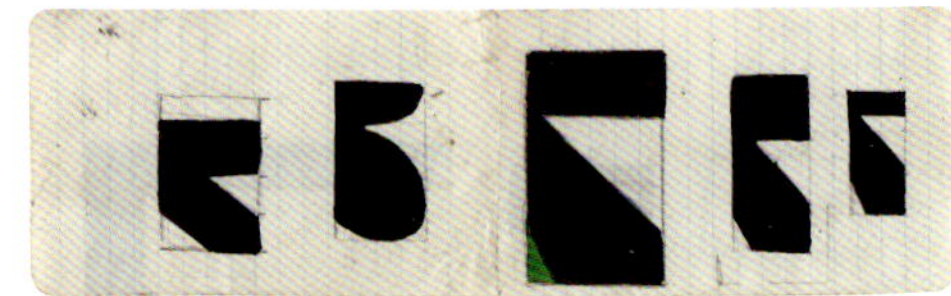

fig. 86: First study for *Painting in Five Panels*, 1955, graphite and ink on paper, 3 × 9½ in, 7.6 × 24.1cm

Soon after making this painting in France, Kelly relinquished the drawn line in his paintings, while maintaining this practice in his drawings of plant life and portraiture. For the artist, executing a form, even an abstract one, via the drawn line, continued the act of depiction, a mode he wanted to eliminate in painting during his years in France. He discovered, however, that he could never fully deny this mode, for he equated the act of painting edges of his abstract forms as a depictive, figural method. With *Black Curves*, Kelly thus returned to the act of *depicting* forms, albeit abstract ones, many of which investigate his new interest in the "free curve." Such an approach led to playing with color contrasts between figure and ground, like those he had admired in the paintings of Max Beckmann, as well as of the Old Masters while a student in Boston. Over time, he would begin calling these investigations his "form and ground" paintings. Beginning with *Black Curves* in 1954, this return to pictorial relationships would dominate his painted output over the next decade or so, as seen in *Bar* (1955) (p. 132), *Painting in Three Panels* (1956) (pp. 136–37), *Jersey* (1958) (p. 146), *Green Blue Black* (1963) (p. 161), and *Red Blue* (1964) (p. 164). To plan these paintings, he either made drawings where he would paint his shapes, as in an ink study (fig. 86) for *Painting in Five Panels*, or create collages where he worked out his shapes through colored cutouts, a method that firmly denies painted, depictive modes and instead relies on additive construction, as in a collage (fig. 87) for *Jersey*. Deploying these contradictory approaches simultaneously, Kelly would move steadily back and forth between painted depiction and literal construction, with form always tantamount.

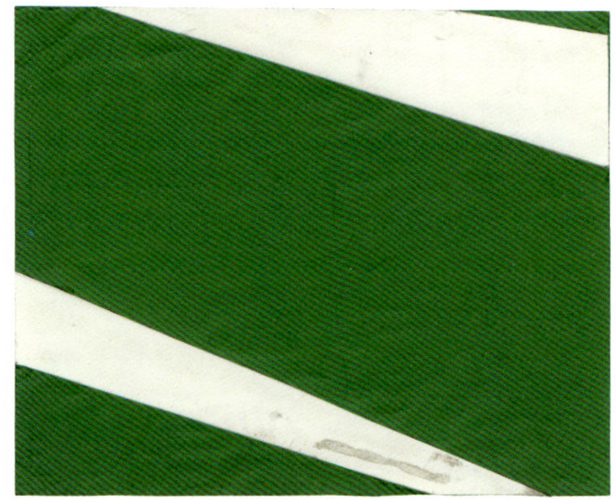

fig. 87: Study for *Jersey,* 1957, collage on paper, 7 × 8½ in, 17.8 × 21.6 cm

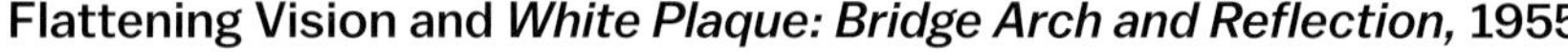

Flattening Vision and *White Plaque: Bridge Arch and Reflection,* 1955

During his first several years back in the U.S., Kelly created works inspired by “already-made” motifs observed in New York, thus continuing to draw from non-invented content for paintings such as *Atlantic* (1956) (p. 139) and *42nd* (1958) (fig 4). However, he also produced a handful of works that sprang from his time in France. Such an approach of retrieving earlier ideas would grow into a regular practice for the artist. Over the course of several decades, he would develop a rich and expansive vocabulary of shapes and concepts to which he could return as needed. *White Plaque: Bridge Arch and Reflection* (1955) (p. 131) exemplifies the beginnings of this method, revisiting an idea that had come about in the fall of 1951.

fig. 88: Study for *White Plaque: Bridge Arch and Reflection,* 1951, collage, 20¼ × 14¼ in, 51.4 × 36.2 cm

It stemmed from an experience that Kelly had one day in Paris, while walking in the garden behind the Cathedral of Notre Dame. He looked eastward across the Seine to the next bridge, the Pont de la Tournelle, which connects the Left Bank of Paris to the Île Saint-Louis, where he was living. A small arch at the base of the bridge captured his attention. He noticed how a dense black shadow filled the hollowed space of the arched opening, preventing him from seeing through it. He also observed how the light conditions that day had cast a reflection of the arch on the water. Instead of capturing this memorable vision through a sketched depictive drawing, Kelly constructed a shaped collage (fig. 88). Employing his strategy of the “already-made,” he cut out of matte black paper two shapes that recalled the black arched shadow and its mirrored reflection on the Seine, transferring only the shapes and colors from his observation to the collage. He then pasted a third element on top, a sliver of darker, glossy paper to stand in for the water line that he had also noticed that day. Afterwards, he left the collage alone, purposefully not adding any pigment to the paper. By producing a silhouetted collage free of any drawn or painted mark, Kelly moved beyond the notion of the two-dimensional support as a recipient surface for drawn description. In this study, the visual information that might link the collage to its natural referent was nearly eliminated, except for shape and color.

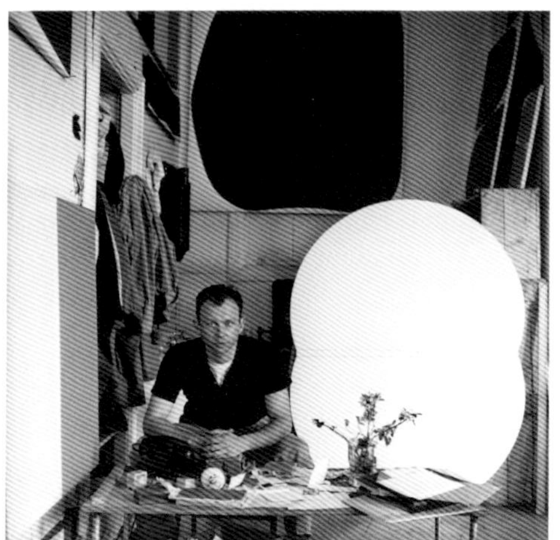

fig. 89: Ellsworth Kelly, Broad Street studio, New York, 1956

Now in New York in 1955, inspired by the cutout curved form again and perhaps reminded of the Seine by living near the East River, he revisited this study and decided to scale it up into a bigger work. With the help of a local carpenter, he used large pieces of wood with a thickness of half an inch to construct a form about three times the size of the original collage, as seen in a 1956 photograph of Kelly in his Broad Street studio (fig. 89). He copied the tripartite aspect of the collage, giving a physical identity to the shadow of the arch, its reflection, and the water line.[14] He did not, however, repeat the two-toned blackness in this final rendition. As he prepared the wooden surface with coats of gesso, Kelly realized that he preferred the new whiteness of this larger shape, and so he painted over the white gesso layer with more coats of white paint. The reliance on collage resulted in a work that asserted its own silhouetted structure in the study, and which was transferred to the final product. What Kelly had intriguingly done was given physicality to things he had seen that did not possess any mass—the negative space under the bridge, the reflection on the water, as well as the line of the water. Such a choice to give tangible form to usually ignored negative spaces predates Bruce Nauman's *A Cast of the Space under My Chair* (1965–68) (fig. 90), as well as Rachel Whiteread's sculptural practice of giving form to even much larger negative spaces starting in the early 1990s.

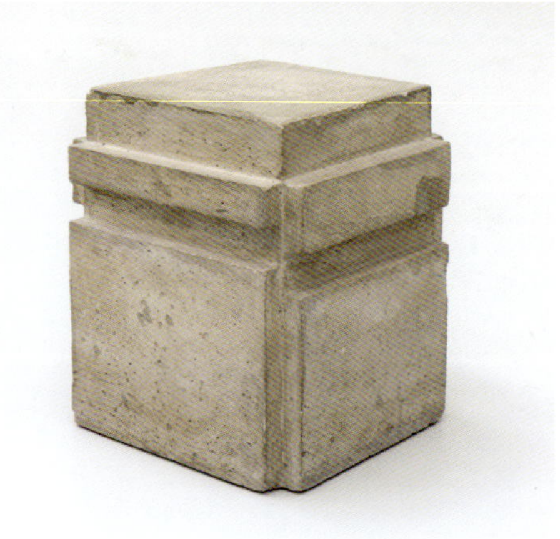

fig. 90: Bruce Nauman, *A Cast of the Space under My Chair*, 1965–68, concrete, 17½ × 15⅜ × 14⅝ in, 44.5 × 39 × 37.1 cm

Kelly's approach to materializing the non-material is, however, paradoxical. While cutting out his shapes for collage led the artist to create works that asserted a certain level of physicality, it also reinforced his drive to flatten his chosen forms. Kelly intentionally chose not to render the volumetric negative space under the bridge arch into something three-dimensional. In France, many of the "already-made" motifs that inspired his paintings and reliefs derived from things that were basically flat—a kilometer marker, a tennis court, wall patterns, shadows cast on flat surfaces. This "already-made" inspiration for *White Plaque*, however, is distinct for its three-dimensional nature, the perceived sense of volume in the original observation, yet which Kelly chose not to capture in both the collage and the final work. As he would explain years later about his impulse to create flat works, "What I have done is to take the space out."[15] To achieve this, he first condensed the volume of the negative space under the bridge. Then he made a distinction between the waterline and the reflection. After isolating all three elements, he brought them back together, unifying and flattening them out along a single plane, the vertical axis of the wall.

Constructed works including *White Plaque* and earlier examples from 1949–50, such as *Window, Museum of Modern Art, Paris* (p. 53), *Window V* (p. 57), and *Relief with Blue* (p. 58), thus function as intriguing dialectical opposites. They are works derived from the real that appear abstract, revealing the transformative capacity of his "already-made" strategy—how he distanced the motif from the original context by fragmenting and isolating the form, and then reinstated this perceptual moment back into the world, instead as a painted, abstract object. And while they are constructed physical objects, they are basically flat and hang on the vertical plane of the wall. Through its flattened silhouetted form, *White Plaque* thus corresponds with the wall and its surrounding space, no longer existing as a separate entity unto itself.

The unframed shaped structure of the work, in turn, produces a closer relationship with the wall in contrast to a rectangular canvas that maintains autonomy through its frame. While artists such as Jackson Pollock, Mark Rothko, and Barnett Newman had already abandoned their reliance on the frame (as Rodchenko had already done in 1921), the often large scale of their standard rectangular paintings eclipsed the walls on which they were hung, forcing the spectator to forge a relationship solely with the paintings. Unlike the kind of spectatorship that Newman had defined—one in which the viewer met his canvases face-to-face, a full immersion that denied the viewer an appreciation of his or her physical surroundings—Kelly facilitated an engagement that acknowledged the tangible nature of his artwork in relation to its environment. With *White Plaque*, an inventive work that prefigured the emergence of the shaped canvas in the 1960s by the likes of Frank Stella, Kenneth Noland, and Richard Tuttle, Kelly offered the spectator a new correspondence with an artwork—one that addressed both the visual and physical properties of the painted object in the context of its installation and surrounding architecture.

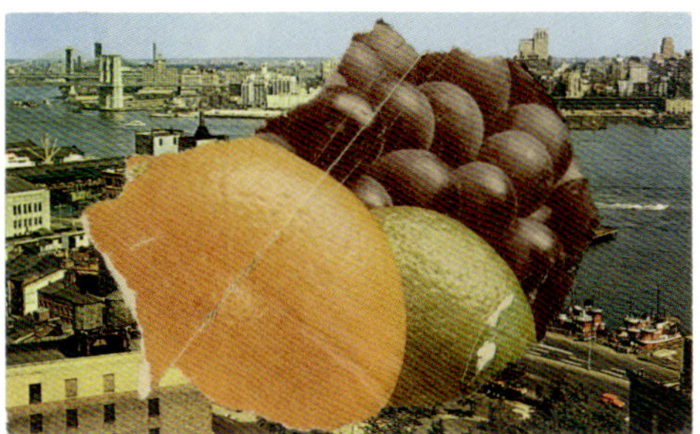

fig. 91: *Coenties Slip*, 1957, postcard collage, 3½ × 5½ in, 9 × 14 cm

It is thus important to note that when Kelly first displayed *White Plaque* at his 1956 debut show at Parsons, the novelty of its silhouetted shape went unnoticed, for the most part, by his reviewers. One critic did remark upon this unique aspect, yet only in a private conversation with the artist. As recounted by Kelly, while leaving his Parsons opening, he encountered a man in the elevator whom he had never met. The man declared, "Oh! You're the one who did the cutout!" Kelly acknowledged that he was indeed the artist. The man inquired, "Why did you do it?" Kelly replied brashly, "Well, if you don't understand why, then I can't help you." This curt response, not surprisingly, affronted the man, who then demanded gruffly, "Do you know who I am?" Kelly replied that he did not. The man said, "Clement Greenberg." In astonished embarrassment, Kelly shook hands with the renowned critic, a cordiality that ended the conversation. Kelly would later regret his quick dismissal of the critic's pointed question, realizing that a good discussion might have ensued regarding the cutout quality of *White Plaque* and how it had pushed him to move beyond painting into new artistic territory.[16]

Postcards from New York

In 1957, Kelly collaged a torn reproduction of fruit onto a postcard capturing an aerial view of Lower Manhattan (fig. 91), which included his new home of Coenties Slip, where he had moved in 1956. Partially obstructing the original vista, the close-up image of the fruit contrasts with the Lilliputian scale of the view still visible around the periphery. Located near the southeastern tip of Manhattan, Coenties Slip, a three-block long Y-shaped neighborhood, was once a shipping port, a deep-water inlet active during New York's maritime days of the eighteenth and nineteenth centuries. Named after an early Dutch settler in New York, Conraet Ten Eyck, Coenties Slip carried the romance of old New York, even memorialized by novelist Herman Melville in his classic *Moby-Dick* from 1851, "Circumambulate the city of a dreamy Sabbath afternoon. Go from Corlears Hook to Coenties Slip, and from thence, by Whitehall, northward. What do you see?—Posted like silent sentinels all around the town, stand thousands upon thousands of mortal men fixed in ocean reveries."[17]

A century later, the thousands and thousands of Melville's days had gone, along with the city's first publishing houses once located at Coenties Slip, which had brought in other writers such as Walt Whitman and Edgar Allan Poe. By 1870 the once bustling slip of Coenties had been filled in by land as the rise of steamships required new ports, and now at mid-twentieth century, the old lofts of sail-making factories remained abandoned. Poor artists soon made their way there, since these spaces were well-lit and could be rented for cheap, averaging $50 a month. Kelly's friend, Fred Mitchell, whom he had met in France, was the first to settle there in 1954, and in July 1956 Kelly relocated to the Slip from his Broad Street studio a block away. He chose the top floor of 3–5 Coenties Slip (two buildings joined by a staircase), greatly attracted by the skylights above, peace and quiet at night, and proximity to the East River and the Brooklyn Bridge.

There in the Slip, Kelly answered Melville's nineteenth-century invitation to circumambulate these downtown neighborhoods, which within the next few decades would start to transform into New York's Financial District.[18] On foot or by bike, he took in the sights along the way. A number of his paintings made during his early years in the city were named after places or streets in New York, such as *South Ferry* (1956) (p. 138), *42nd* (1958) (fig. 4), *Brooklyn Bridge II* (1958) (fig. 103), *Broadway* (1958) (p. 144); broader geographic expanses, including *Jersey* (1958) (p. 146), and *North River* (1959) (fig .99); or even something as expansive as the ocean, *Atlantic* (1956) (p. 139). And yet, it must be noted that most of these sites did not serve as one-to-one visual inspiration for their namesakes. Sometimes, only after the fact, Kelly would notice a visual likeness between a painting and a specific place, after which he would then name it after that site. Other times, Kelly assigned geographic titles for no particular reason, except perhaps to chronicle his new life in New York.

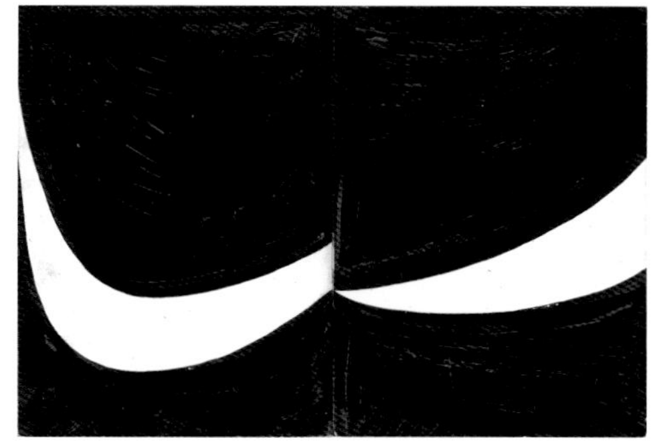

fig. 92: Study for *Atlantic,* 1954, ink on paper, 10½ × 15 in, 26.7 × 38.1 cm

For example, with the title of *Atlantic* (p. 139), one might conjecture that the two curves in this two-paneled work are abstracted shapes of waves caught in time, when in fact these silhouettes derive from an altogether different source. While riding a bus at night to visit a friend within the first several months of living in New York, Kelly set a book on his lap to read. As the bus drove through the city streets, he noticed how the paperback pages became a receptive surface for the changing light streaming through the bus window; he saw ever-changing patterns of black and white forming on the printed pages. Drawing from his practices of chance and automatic drawing from France, he began sketching the outline of the shapes as they morphed and shifted onto many spreads in his paperback, allowing the perimeter of the pages to dictate the cropping of his forms. Back in his studio, he transferred these quickly rendered ideas onto pages in a makeshift sketchbook—a dummy copy of Sigfried Gideon's book *Bauen in Frankreich, Bauen in Eisen, Bauen in Eisenbeton* (1928), which had been given to him by Hugo Weber, the husband of his Boston friend, Anne Weber (fig. 52). Kelly copied his pencil lines from his original paperback into this sketchbook, later filling them in with black ink (fig. 92).[19] With the forms that spread over two pages, the binding of the original book functioned as a structural divide, which he transferred into his Gideon sketchbook and then into a couple of duo-paneled paintings, one being *Atlantic*. A year later, Kelly exhibited this work in "Young America 1957" at the Whitney Museum of American Art, where he appeared as an outlier in contrast to the majority of artists painting in an expressionist, gestural style. His other work shown there, *Painting in Three Panels* (1956) (pp. 136–37) was considered radical in the way the three separate canvases spread across the wall. During the run of the exhibition, the Whitney purchased *Atlantic* for its collection, the first time a museum had acquired a work by Kelly.

From something as fleeting as two flickers of light passing along a paperback page, Kelly created a painting perhaps unmatched in his early New York period. Despite its utter simplicity, inspired by something ephemeral and weightless, he rendered this notion of lightness with startling opacity over two joined panels. It is often tantalizing to try to identify Kelly's "original sources" for his works, a practice of many scholars, including this author. Peeling back the curtain to reveal occasional glimpses of what Kelly once saw allows for deeper insight into the artist's transformative vision, how he perceived what he saw and what steps he took to turn these observations into finished works of art. But the fact that the artist was inspired by the visual world does not suggest the need to seek out and identify his iconographic sources one by one. For Kelly, retaining a level of mystery about how a work was made is crucial. As the artist explained in 1991,

> As we move, looking at hundreds of different things, we see many different kinds of shapes. Roofs, walls, ceilings are all rectangles, but we don't see them that way. In reality they're very elusive forms. The way the view through the rungs of a chair changes when you move even the slightest bit—I want to capture some of that *mystery* in my work. In my paintings I'm *not inventing*; my ideas come from constantly investigating how things look.[20]

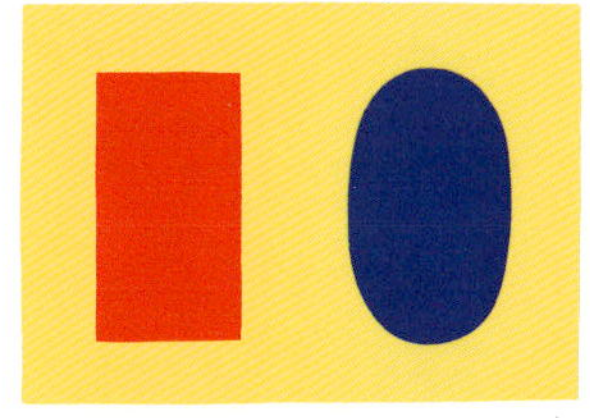

fig. 93: *Orange and Blue over Yellow (Orange et Bleu sur Jaune),* 1964–65, lithograph on Rives BFK paper, 23⅝ × 35⅝ in, 60 × 90.5 cm

After his return from France, Kelly continued to explore his ideas through drawing as with *Atlantic* and also through collage. The latter remained an effective method to experiment quickly, functioning as artistic shorthand, and soon he chose a new collage support, the postcard, as seen with *Coenties Slip* (1957) (fig. 91). In reverse of his strategy of finding motifs "already-made" in the world, he turned to ready-made views in picture postcards, predetermined templates of colors and shapes that he could manipulate with his own forms, cut or torn from colored paper as well as from newspapers, magazines, and other printed matter. The small uniform dimensions of the postcard allowed for easy experimentation, whether in the studio or not. Mass-produced and affordable, the postcard was an inexpensive option for a poor artist, and what began as playful experiments with a new support grew into a substantial artistic practice that lasted well over three decades.

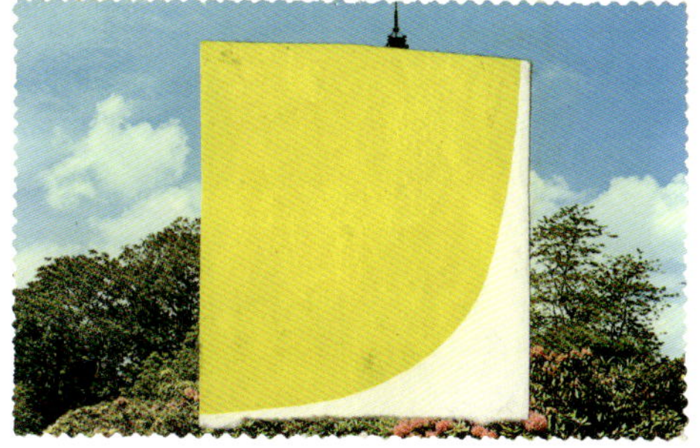

fig. 94: *Study for a Yellow and White Sculpture for the Eiffel Tower*, 1964, postcard collage, 3⅜ × 5⅜ in, 8.6 × 13.7 cm

As Kelly gained more recognition throughout the 1960s, his postcard collages became more international, marking trips to Europe as well as islands of leisure (fig. 95). In 1964, when he traveled to Paris for his second solo exhibition at Galerie Maeght, he made a postcard collage (fig. 94) blocking out the spire of the Eiffel Tower. While there, he began to make his first series of prints for Aimé and Marguerite Maeght, the owners of the Paris gallery who had included Kelly in group exhibitions during his French years. From this time onward, he would continue to practice printmaking, beginning a longstanding partnership with Gemini G.E.L., Los Angeles, in 1970. For his 1964 suite made in Paris, Kelly created twenty-seven brightly colored lithographic prints (fig. 93), some inspired by paintings that he had made by this time (pp. 154, 155). Turning to Parisian postcards during his 1964 extended stay, Kelly used his own working print proofs as a new source for collaged elements, pasting a yellow and white paper cutout onto the Eiffel Tower postcard.

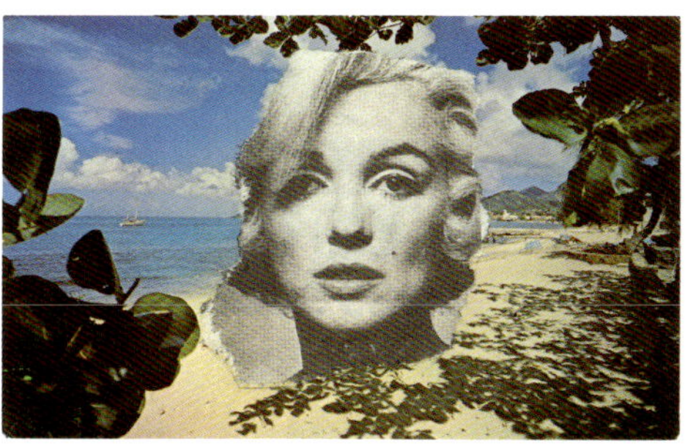

fig. 95: *Marilyn Monroe/Shadows*, 1974, postcard collage, 3½ × 5½ in, 8.9 × 14 cm

Kelly's postcard collages occupy a unique place within his oeuvre. They resist clear taxonomies, contrasting with both his figurative linear drawings of plant life or portraiture (figs 5, 109, 137, 192, 201) and his abstract collages, paper cutouts pasted onto a blank or colored support (figs 57, 87, 150). They are neither Duchampian readymades nor Kellyesque "already-mades," neither simply postcards nor finished works of art. His abstract paintings—uninterrupted surfaces of flatly painted color—staunchly abandon representational modes, while his postcard collages rely on the printed, realistic image of the postcard view. Kelly explained in 1973, "I've always felt competitive with reality."[21] By practicing collage with postcards, he had found the perfect support to enact this sensibility: his collaged abstract shapes literally collide with the representational views of the postcards. These postcard collages reveal much about the artist's perceptual relationship with the world, allowing entrance into his unique engagement with vision. Such altered objects dispel the mythology of the supposedly clean dichotomy between abstraction and representation. Instead, such opposing impulses meet head-on in these works, situating Kelly's cards squarely within one of the key debates of twentieth-century art. Just as the paper cutouts appear temporarily suspended within the postcards themselves, these collages linger in a perpetual state of flux, capturing specific moments between abstraction and representation.

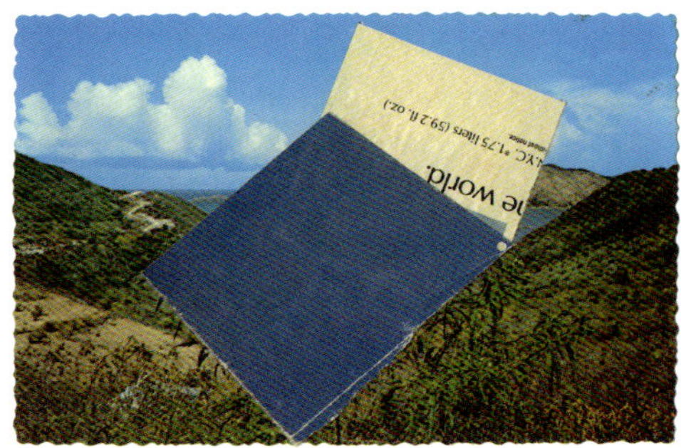

fig. 96: Study for *Blue White,* 1980, postcard collage, 4 × 6 in, 10.2 × 15.3 cm

Yet no matter to what extent Kelly altered their surfaces, he never obscured their identity as postcards. Keeping them whole, uncut, he maintained their original physical conditions and, thus, their inherent meanings and associations. Sometimes he utilized the original function of the postcards, mailing them in manipulated form to his friends. The U.S. Postal Service often refused to process the cards, which the mailmen deemed too altered; other mailmen, prescient enough to grasp their aesthetic and even potential value, stashed them. As Kelly has explained,

> I sent a lot of them out. It was a mail [art] thing, like Ray Johnson, whom I knew well. It was fun to do [it], but people didn't keep them. I sent one to Leo [Castelli], Betty [Parsons], Henry [Geldzahler] ... But then the postmen started to steal them. They warned me that they wouldn't send them so I would go to the post office and have them stamped ... and put them in an envelope.[22]

Kelly had become friends with Ray Johnson around 1955, before the Mail Art pioneer sparked the movement by the late 1950s. To earn money during his first years in New York, Kelly had actually sorted mail at Manhattan's main branch of the U.S. Post Office on Eighth Avenue. This experience undoubtedly played a role in both his use of postcards and the mail system. As someone clearly aware of postal regulations, he mischievously tested this system through his modified postcards. But when he realized that some of his own recipients, unlike the discerning mailmen, had failed to keep them, he stopped sending them out on a regular basis: "I said, 'To hell with them, I won't send them anymore'—in 1974–75. When I did send them to friends, [it was] to friends who would keep them, who wouldn't junk them. That's where I get my ideas from and I like to share them that way."[23] And he kept many for himself, especially those that functioned as souvenirs of specific ideas, mementos of what he once thought, saw, and experienced. Some postcard collages also served as ideas for finished works, for example, a 1980 collage (fig. 96), a study for ***Blue White*** (p. 242) made the same year.

Kelly created many of these postcard collages during his days of living in Coenties Slip, from 1956 to 1963. During this period, more artists had moved to the Slip, forming a community that at times included Charles Hinman, Robert Indiana, Agnes Martin, Fred Mitchell, Larry Poons, James Rosenquist,

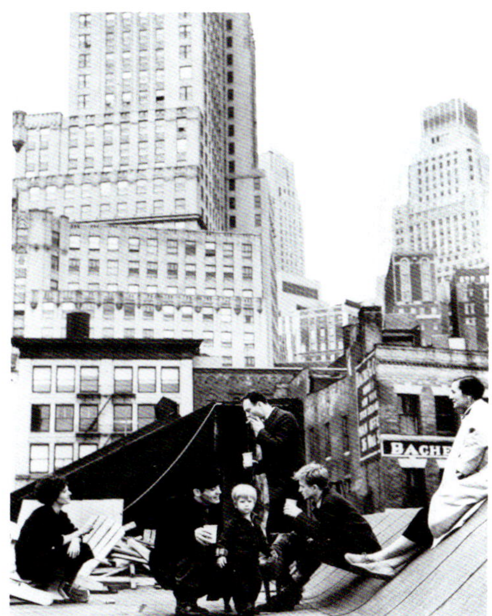

fig. 97: (left to right) Delphine Seyrig, Robert Indiana, Duncan Yougerman, Ellsworth Kelly, dog Orange, Jack Youngerman, Agnes Martin, Coenties Slip, New York, 1958

Lenore Tawney, Jack Youngerman, and Ann Wilson.[24] These artists living on the Slip separated themselves from the presence further uptown of the Abstract Expressionists, who held court in and around Tenth Street, drinking and smoking at their favorite hangout, Cedar Tavern, though Jackson Pollock had died in 1956. In the ensuing years, key artists from Coenties Slip would help shape the next generation of postwar American art during the 1960s, with Indiana and Rosenquist contributing to the emergence of Pop art, and Kelly and Martin asserting a new take on abstraction, a pared down and methodical approach versus the highly emotive and impromptu style of Abstract Expressionism.

In 1958, this moment in Coenties Slip was captured in a series of photographs taken by famed photographer Hans Namuth, best known for his documentation of Pollock painting in both stills and film. Namuth had been commissioned to take photographs of Kelly for a photographic essay featuring the artists showing in the American Pavilion at the Brussels World's Fair that year, where Kelly exhibited *Painting in Five Panels* (1955) (pp. 134–35). The majority of the American artists shown in Brussels exhibited paintings in a brushy, expressive style, with Pollock's impact still being felt despite his death. Kelly and the older Ad Reinhardt were among the few invited who painted clean-edged forms crisply and flatly. The best known of these photographs taken by Namuth on that day in 1958 featured Kelly and his friends on the roof of 3–5 Coenties Slip, where Kelly lived (fig. 97). Kelly is standing, taking a drag from a cigarette with a cup of coffee in his other hand. Youngerman is seated on the right, while his wife, the actress Delphine Seyrig—who would later star in Alain Resnais's influential 1962 film of the French New Wave, *Last Year at Marienbad*—is seated on the left. In the middle, Indiana is squatting, focusing on toddler Duncan Youngerman with partially seen dog Orange (the Youngerman family dog who would soon be given to Kelly), while Martin is seated farthest to the right.

By 1958, when Namuth photographed this group, Kelly and Indiana had become close friends, having met by chance in 1956 at an art-supply store on West 57th Street, a block away from the Art Students League of New York. Indiana had returned to the States in 1954 after living abroad and to make ends meet had been clerking at the art store. He was arranging the window dressings with art postcards and other reproductions when Kelly was walking by on West 57th Street and noticed a Matisse postcard in the display. Kelly went inside the store to purchase the card, and they struck up a conversation. Soon afterwards, both were living near each other in Coenties Slip. Five years older, Kelly was more established than Indiana, who was still searching for his own artistic language, but in time would, like Kelly, begin painting crisp abstracted forms against contrasting grounds such as *Gingko* (1957/59) (fig. 98). In his later years, Indiana would credit Kelly for this important shift in his art: "My painting life began with Ellsworth. Before Coenties Slip, I was aesthetically at sea. With Ellsworth, my whole life perspective changed. All of a sudden I was in the twentieth century."[25] Although Indiana would develop his own iconic style that figured prominently in the development of Pop art, his attention to silhouetted forms, and later on, letters rendered with sharp edges, was greatly informed by Kelly's example.

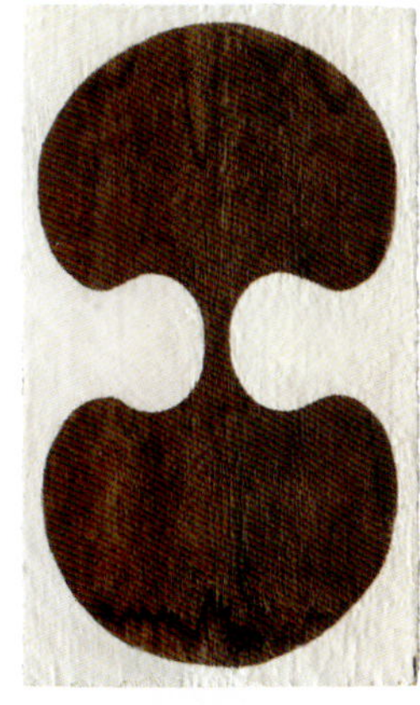

fig. 98: Robert Indiana, *Gingko*, 1957/59, gesso on wood panel, 15½ × 8⅞ × 2 in, 39.4 × 22.5 × 5.1 cm

Painting Figure and Ground

Beyond his circle of friends in Coenties Slip, where Kelly would live until 1963, critics, curators, and collectors continued to notice and admire his meticulous silhouettes, full color, and ripe forms. After "Sixteen Americans" in 1959, where Kelly showed *Rebound* (p. 145) and *North River* (fig. 99), both from 1959, plus seven other works, William Rubin declared,

> Kelly's work comes as a refreshing contrast to the fatiguing exploitation of impasto and brushwork typical of New York painting ... Kelly is a marvelous creator of shapes, bold shapes that seem very summary at first but that are really complex and elusive, full of subtle local decisions and unassimilable to formula and geometry. This last fact, plus the sensuousness of his colored surface, separates him completely from the geometricians of the Nouvelles Réalités and the still-born local followers of Mondrian.[26]

fig. 99: *North River*, 1959, oil on canvas, 78 × 70 in, 198.1 × 177.8 cm

By 1961, Kelly had exhibited for the second time at the Pittsburgh International (renamed the Carnegie International in 1982) at the Carnegie Institute, winning the Fourth Painting Prize of $750 for *Block Island II* (1960). (Mark Tobey won the first prize, Jules Olitski the second, and Adolph Gottlieb the third.) There, Kelly also presented his first foray into sculpture, *Gate* (1959) (p. 150). A local review of this exhibition heralded him as "one of the new looks in contemporary art,"[27] while *New York Times* critic Stuart Preston lauded his concurrently running solo exhibition at Betty Parsons, saying, "These dazzling and unambiguous pictures, excluding in their flawless surfaces any appearance of the artist's manual quirks, cannot fail to magnify Mr. Kelly's already considerable reputation ... These new paintings make a formidable impact."[28] Here at Parsons, his third solo outing, Kelly unveiled new paintings like *Black and White* (1960–61) (p. 152) and *Yellow White* (1961) (p. 153), works that displayed his ongoing exploration of figure-ground pictorial compositions.

Through his probing of the painted shape from the mid-1950s to the mid-1960s, Kelly produced internal relationships within the painting itself, something he had chosen to eliminate in France with his multipanel paintings, whereby he had fostered a relationship between the panels and the wall. As he would later explain, "I gave up panels and began seeing shapes in America."[29] In these paintings, he enacted a return to figure-ground dynamics, and for the most part, set aside the use of the monochrome panel. In creating paintings with pictorial relationships, he de-emphasized the relation of the work to the wall. Correspondingly, he created a primarily visual engagement with these works on the part of the viewer, a departure from the more palpable experience of his so-called "painting/objects."

Looking at the two examples of works shown at Betty Parsons in 1961, one can identify two distinct ways in which he rendered his forms. In *Black and White*, two slender white shapes are set against the black painted surface and extend to the top and bottom edges of the painting. Engaging with the limits of the canvas in order to truncate his forms, Kelly allowed the framing edge to halt the areas of white, thus fragmenting the linear shapes. In contrast, in *Yellow White*, he opted to present a shape in its entirety, resulting in the creation of a whole, unfragmented

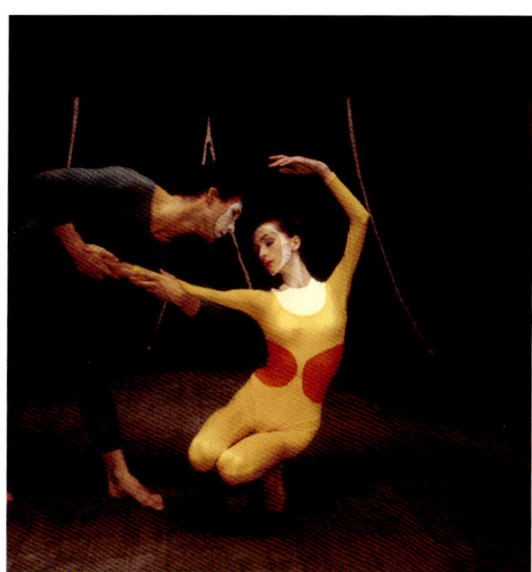

fig. 100: Costumes and curtain designed by Ellsworth Kelly for Paul Taylor's *Tablet* performed in Italy, 1960

bulging form. This symmetrical curvilinear form presses against the confines of the frame, with the most outer parts of the silhouette just grazing the inner edges of the canvas. In his figure-ground paintings, Kelly would choose either to fragment his forms or enclose a whole form in its entirety, yet both through dynamic tension along the edges of the canvas, a continued nod to Audubon. Kelly's attention to fragmented forms, of course, first appeared during his French years, but it now became a central focus, starting with his first painting made in New York, ***Black Curves*** **(1954)** (p. 129). Through the mid-1960s, Kelly continued exploring such cut-off forms, including ***Rebound*** **(1959)** (p. 145), ***Red Blue Green*** **(1963)** (pp. 156–57), which he debuted at Documenta III in 1964, and ***Red Blue*** **(1964)** (p. 164). Conversely, he painted singular whole forms starting with ***Black Ripe*** in 1955 (p. 130) and continuing with ***Blue Green*** **(1962)** (p. 155), and ***Blue Black Red*** **(1964)** (p. 166).

As he had done with *White Plaque: Bridge Arch and Reflection* (p. 131) in 1955, Kelly would also free his painted forms, whether fragmented or enclosed, letting them exist as cutout shapes. Turning to relief, he created constructions that allowed him to literalize his forms against another rectilinear support, sometimes in wood, as in ***Concorde Relief I*** **(1958)** (p. 143) or in painted aluminum, as in ***Blue over Blue*** **(1963)** (p. 167). With ***Gate*** **(1959)** (p. 150) and ***Pony*** **(1959)** (p. 148), his first sculptures, he also released his flattened cutout forms to the floor, into the three-dimensional space in which we live. He could thus move back and forth between producing figure-ground contrasts with the painted shape and examining the silhouetted form through the literal shape. His production of figure-ground paintings, freestanding sculptures as well as reliefs from the mid-1950s to the mid-1960s substantiates the adaptability and breadth of his methods and goals.

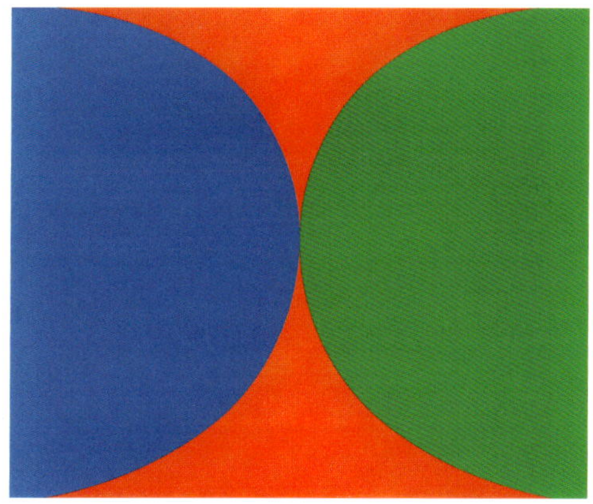

fig. 101: *Blue Green Red II*, 1965, oil on canvas, 88 × 102 in, 223.5 × 259.1 cm

During his New York years, Kelly even explored figure-ground relationships on the human figure itself, for avant-garde choreographer Paul Taylor who commissioned him twice to design costumes for his dance company. At the 1960 Festival of Two Worlds held in Spoleto, Italy, Taylor, who was on his first European tour, premiered his dance *Tablet*, featuring costumes and a curtain designed by Kelly as well as another performance with designs by Robert Rauschenberg. As seen in a 1960 photograph featuring dancer and future choreographer Pina Bausch (fig. 100), Kelly's linear curtain design relates to his interest in curved forms, while his costume design for Bausch makes an even stronger connection to his "free curves." Two small curves mirror each other at her waist, playfully creating the semblance of an extremely cinched hourglass figure, in contrast to the phallic singular form rising up the male dancer's body.

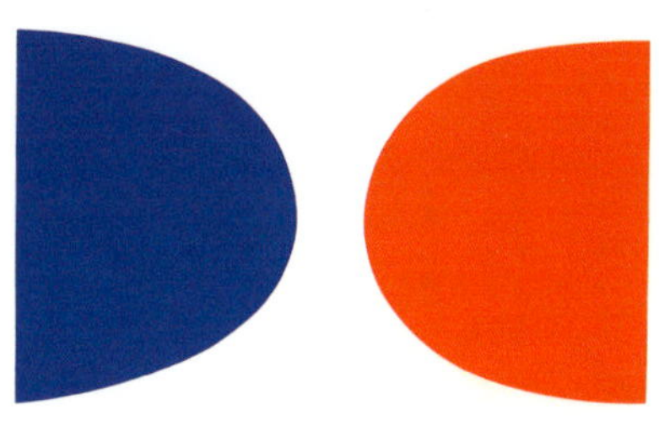

fig. 102: *Blue and Orange (Bleu et Orange)*, 1964–65, lithograph on Rives BFK paper, 23⅝ × 35⅝ in, 60 × 90.5 cm

This particular concept of paired curves stems back to Kelly's years in France, with mirroring curves found in *Toilette* from 1949 (fig. 34) and a maquette for *Line, Form and Color* in 1951 (fig. 57). A year after designing the costumes, Kelly would paint against a black background two white curvilinear forms that just touch at center, adjoining each other in *Rebound* (1959) (p. 145), and in the coming years, he would expand on this idea in other manifestations: in paintings (fig. 101), in collages and drawings, in prints (fig. 102), as well as in monumental sculpture (p. 165). And in 1958, the year he designed these costumes, Kelly explored a similar idea of mirroring curved forms on his *own* body (fig. 103). In a whimsical 1958 photograph taken in his Coenties Slip studio dotted with potted plants (for his ongoing plant-drawing practice), Kelly stands upright and almost nude, save for a small painting covering his torso and genitals. The white curved bands of this painting, *Brooklyn Bridge II* (1958) begin and end along the edges of the canvas, now matched perfectly to the silhouette of his torso and the outer sides of his thighs.

In 1968, Kelly was once again asked to design costumes for Taylor's company, for a new dance called *Lento.* In his studies for these designs, the outlines of both the male and female dancers are drawn in a similar way to the blocky silhouette that he had created for himself in the 1958 photograph. In preparatory studies he mapped out different colored forms onto sketches of full-body leotards in white (fig. 104). In order to produce these leotards, there was even a stage when Kelly had to draw the shapes directly onto them while worn by the dancers. Many of the dancers could not control their giggling as Kelly unintentionally tickled their bodies with his drawing instrument. As seen in a photograph with a kneeling Taylor (fig. 105), the ten dancers wearing Kelly's designs offer an intriguing parallel to the figure-ground paintings made from the mid-1950s through the mid-1960s. The way the elongated forms caress the bodies of the dancers is akin to the streaming, lengthened forms that make their way across the canvases in *Atlantic* (1956) (p. 139), *Jersey* (1958) (p. 146), and *Black and White* (1960–61) (p. 152). Designed in 1968, these costumes and their bright colors also resound with Kelly's renewed interest in his "Spectrum" paintings at the time. As the artist later reflected about the designs for these costumes, "It's a Spectrum... It's interesting to see the creative past. It's a summation of what I was doing in my paintings."[30]

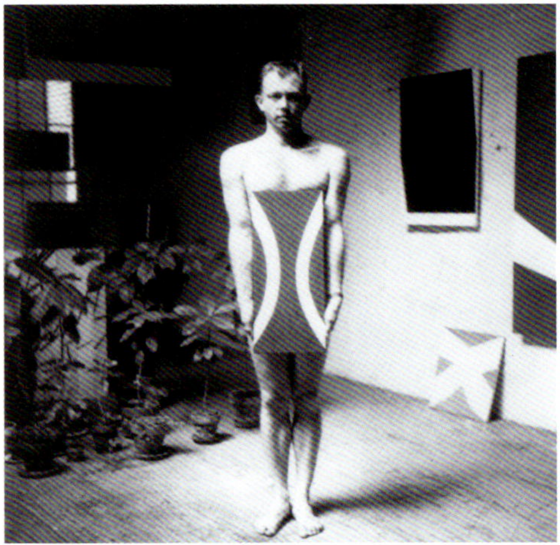

fig. 103: Ellsworth Kelly with *Brooklyn Bridge II* (1958), Coenties Slip studio, New York, 1958

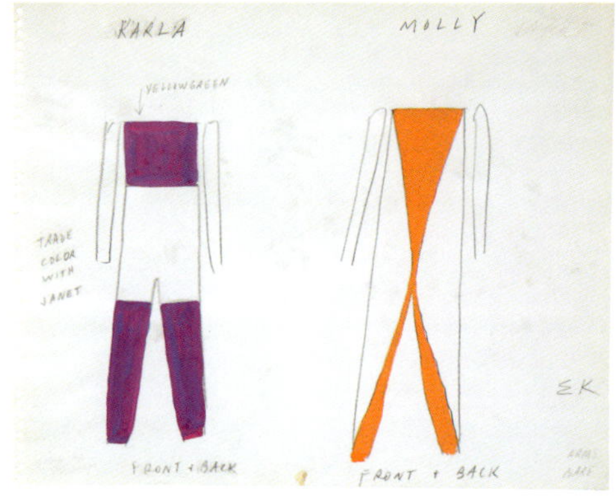

fig. 104: *Karla–Red Violet and Molly–Orange* (study for Paul Taylor's *Lento*), 1968, graphite and gouache on paper, 14 × 17 in, 35.6 × 43.2 cm

Sculpture for Walls and Floor

At the 1964 New York World's Fair held in Queens, New York, Kelly debuted one of the largest and most high-profile works he had made to date, *Two Curves: Blue Red* (p. 165), which was presented not just to the city itself, but to an international audience. Measuring a total of eighteen by eighteen feet with a depth of eight feet, *Two Curves: Blue Red* adorned the façade of the Theaterama, a circular theater that comprised a part of the New York State Pavilion. Designed by architect Philip Johnson, the pavilion featured a grand and festive open-air structure called the "Tent of Tomorrow," three observation towers of varying heights, plus the Theaterama, which inside projected a 360-degree film celebrating New York State.[31] For the exterior of this theater (fig. 106), Johnson had commissioned Kelly and nine other artists to create works of art: Peter Agostini, John Chamberlain, Robert Indiana, Alexander Liberman, Roy Lichtenstein, Robert Mallary, Robert Rauschenberg, James Rosenquist and Andy Warhol. (Warhol's controversial entry, *Thirteen Most Wanted Men,* was later eliminated.[32]) Looking back, the works installed on Johnson's Theaterama provide an instructive cross-section of the art made at the time, from Rosenquist's fragmented imagery and Indiana's letter-based, multipanel work to Chamberlain's abstraction of crushed metal and Kelly's planar, cutout shapes.

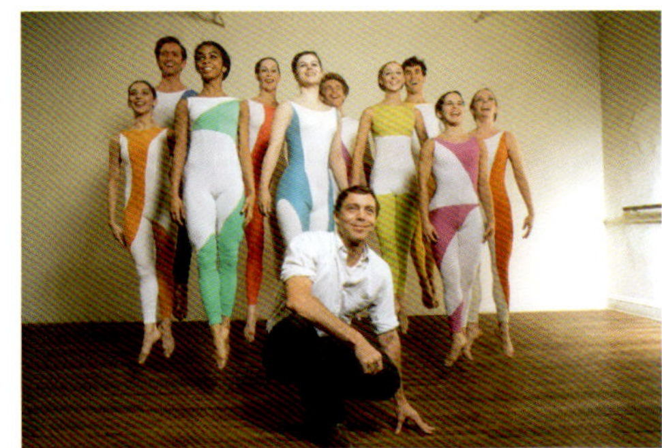

fig. 105: Costumes designed by Ellsworth Kelly for Paul Taylor's *Lento*, 1968

By this time, the public had accepted Pop art, welcoming back figuration after the dominance of Abstract Expressionism had given way. When referring to

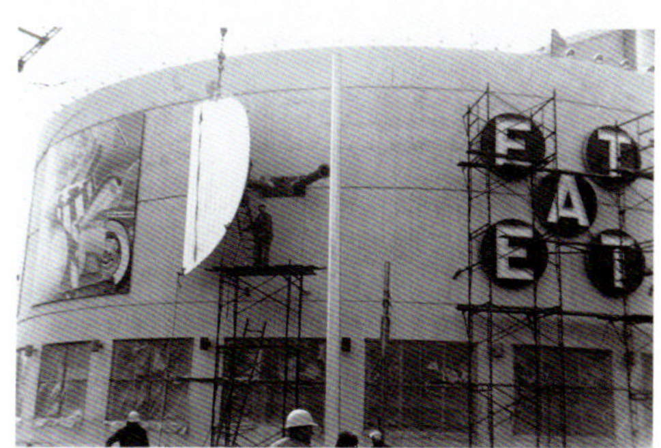

fig. 106: Installation of *Two Curves: Blue Red* at New York State Pavilion, New York World's Fair, 1964

the New York pavilion commissions, critics for the most part disregarded the abstract ones, focusing instead on the Pop works. In *The Nation*, critic Max Kozloff described how, "There is no more significant tip-off of the fair's character than Johnson's sophisticated choice of ten artists, mostly Pop, to decorate his set piece at Flushing Meadows,"[33] although the majority of the commissions were actually abstractions (those by Kelly, Agostini, Chamberlain, Liberman, and Mallary). Based on their lack of legible, figurative content, these abstractions were at a disadvantage when it came to attracting more attention than their Pop counterparts. For example, Kelly's *Two Curves: Blue Red* quietly contrasted with its neighbors, such as Indiana's white letters encased in black circular panels and lit up by clear neon lights that spelled out "EAT" in duplicate (fig. 106). Kelly's work, despite its own blown-up size, demanded a more subtle engagement through its abstract forms and monochrome treatment.

Installed on the circular edifice of the Theaterama, *Two Curves: Blue Red* embraced the architecture in a manner unlike most of the other commissions. Although Agostini and Mallary incorporated the façade by distributing separate units across their allotted wall space, the rest treated the surface of the structure as only a backdrop on which to display their work. Kelly's forms, on the contrary, responded to Johnson's building, echoing and reiterating the grand, curved wall of the theater. With *Two Curves,* Kelly accomplished one of the major goals he had set out for himself during his years in France: to make a new art for modern architecture—in this case, in conjunction with one of the most distinguished architects of the day. Kelly had conceived his commission only after considering Johnson's proposed structure for the building, thus establishing the wall as the integral ground upon which his work would be installed. In a small maquette study from 1963, he experimented with how these curved shapes, one colored blue, the other red, could adjoin each other and jut out from the wall (fig. 107). For the finished work, unlike in the collage study, he chose to make the curves symmetrical, mirroring each other. Cut from giant sheets of aluminum and then painted, they created a monumental two-part, two-toned structure in high relief.

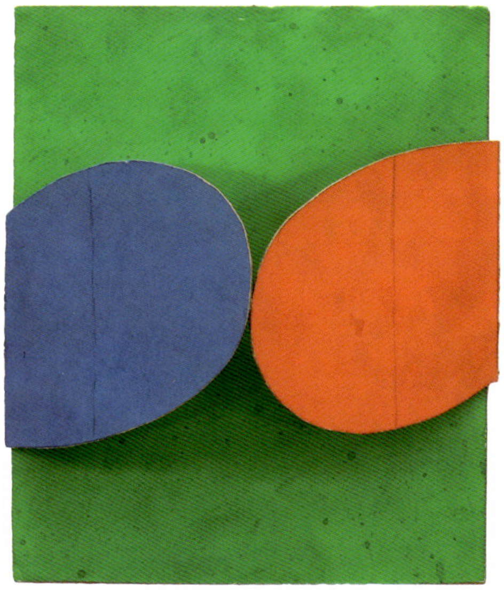

fig. 107: Preliminary study for 1964 World's Fair sculpture *Two Curves: Blue Red,* 1963, cardboard, 9 × 7¼ × 3¼ in, 22.9 × 18.4 × 8.3 cm

Kelly had made an even larger sculpture just three years after his return to the States, for a new development in Philadelphia, Penn Center, which opened in 1957. A part of this complex was the Transportation Building, and Kelly had been commissioned to make a large-scale sculpture installed high on the wall of this lobby.[34] Visible from outside, it spanned 65 feet across, almost 11½ feet high, and just over 1 foot deep (fig. 108). Kelly had planned this work with much thought and preparation, creating a number of studies as well as models. Made in deep relief, the work comprised 104 individual forms, curved shapes and trapezoids cut from aluminum panels installed at different angles between parallel poles. The silver panels were simply polished while the black, blue, red, and yellow shapes were colored using an anodizing process. For this work, Kelly introduced more subtle curves than the ones he had been creating at the time. As he once explained about the process of creating such shapes, "It was like a trance: my curves came at the right time. It was like writing."[35]

Architect Vincent Kling had commissioned Kelly for the lobby sculpture after the artist had completed a commission for the Post House restaurant (also located in the Transportation Building), a series of brass screens that were later destroyed. Around this time, Kelly had also secured a small commission in New York, for the lobby of a new apartment building in Manhattan, the Eastmore. His finished work, now called the *Eastmore Mural* (1957) (p. 142) and no longer located there, was made out of Micarta, a Formica-like material that came in a limited palette of colors, hence the muted hues of tan, taupe, orange, and gray, along with black and white.[36] These commissions came at an opportune time, since Kelly was in need of money; it also provided him with two separate forums to put into practice the goal he had envisioned in France, of creating art for modern architecture. The design process for both overlapped during the fall of 1956 into early 1957, and both incorporated variants of his developing curve. Kelly's commission for Penn Center became known as the *Transportation Building Lobby Sculpture*, and for many years, languished unnoticed in Philadelphia. In 1998, before renovations were undertaken in the building for a new tenant, the work was safely removed from its original site. Kelly retitled it *Sculpture for a Large Wall*, reiterating from forty-seven years earlier his first usage of his similarly titled *Colors for a Large Wall* (p. 69) in 1951.

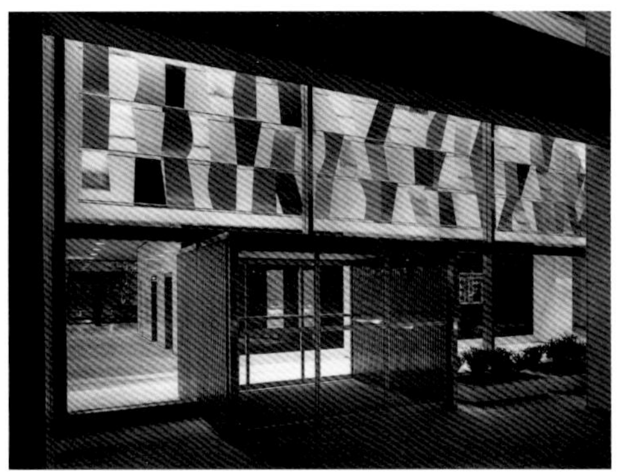

fig. 108: *Sculpture for a Large Wall* at Transportation Building, Penn Center, Philadelphia, 1957

Working on this project in 1956 and 1957 offered Kelly the opportunity to put his ideas into action, while it also allowed him to experiment with new materials, in conjunction with a sculpture fabricator, Edison Price. A couple of years later, when he was inspired to create his first freestanding sculptures, *Gate* (p. 150) and *Pony* (p. 148), he already knew to whom he could turn to fabricate his sculpture for the Transportation Building. Working on this Philadelphia commission, plus his growing interest in the cutout form set in relief, which he addressed in 1958 with works such as *Concorde Relief I* (p. 143), eventually led him to release his forms to the actual ground—the floor. As Kelly would recollect in 1992,

> At the beginning, I didn't feel this way of working was actually painting, so I called my works *reliefs.* I didn't think of sculpture then because sculpture to me was always in the round and I realized that I didn't necessarily want to see something from all directions. So that is why the relief work interested me and why later on my sculpture would remain planar.
>
> [...] After Paris, I thought I had exhausted what the painting in panels could express, so I started with painted curves. I had to experiment with painted forms on ground again—two forms first, then one, like *Black Ripe* (p. 130), which was beginning to squeeze the ground out—until I felt I could paint a big shape that could stand by itself. It was a turning point for me. A short while later, I cut it out in metal, let it exist for itself.[37]

With *Gate* and *Pony*, Kelly freed their shapes from the painted ground and thus the wall, asserting their own physical existences on the floor and in space. Into both works he carried over the two-dimensional planarity of his canvases, thus resisting the three-dimensional massed nature of traditional sculpture.

While using flat planes in sculpture was not a novel approach (Russian Constructivist Naum Gabo, for example, had already deployed a planarity in his sculptures during the first quarter of the century), Kelly's particular use of the flat plane took his work in an alternative direction. Unlike Gabo, Calder, or even Kelly's more recent predecessor David Smith, he allowed his flat planes to exist, silhouetted on their own and unhindered by layered or overlapping forms. Instead of a complex arrangement of various intersecting planes, he underscored a singular focus on the cutout shape. In many ways, the term "sculpture" is a misnomer for these works, as it was for other three-dimensional abstract works made by contemporaries such as Carl Andre, Donald Judd, and Richard Serra. The majority of these "objects"—the term that began to be applied with greater frequency in the 1960s to abstract works that blurred the boundaries between painting and sculpture—did not represent or refer to anything. They were three-dimensional, physical things, no longer possessing any correlation to quotidian, modern living (for example, as with Pop objects).

At the Venice Biennale in 1966, Kelly showed *Blue Red* (1966) (p. 173), a work that exemplifies more fully this blurring of the lines between painting and sculpture. Two rectangular monochrome canvases of equal size, each measuring 81 × 60 inches, join at a perpendicular angle. The blue canvas is parallel to the wall, while the red one rests on the floor (although a horizontal support makes the red canvas appear to float). Henry Geldzahler, the U.S. Commissioner to the Venice Biennale and a dynamic promoter of contemporary American art, had chosen four artists—Helen Frankenthaler, Roy Lichtenstein, Jules Olitski, and Kelly—to represent the U.S. at this significant international gathering. In an accompanying catalogue, he described Kelly's work in a brief entry: "The wall-floor painting (*Blue Red*) is an incursion into our own space; it is painted on canvas, hangs on the wall and lies on the floor."[38] Geldzahler's two-word adjective "wall-floor" derived from Kelly's own terminology and pinpointed the complex in-between nature of the work, addressing both the vertical plane of painting and the horizontal plane of sculpture. Although this work embraced real space, it still depended on the frontal experience of painting, leading Geldzahler to describe it as, "a paradox (painting or sculpture?)."[39] *Blue Red* reveals how Kelly could expand his multipanel practice in novel ways.

At the Met

In October 1969, the Metropolitan Museum of Art opened "New York Painting and Sculpture: 1940–1970," a sweeping exhibition organized to celebrate its centennial. Curated by Geldzahler, who had become the Met's first curator of contemporary art in 1967, it was a survey of mammoth scale, colonizing the thirty-five galleries usually devoted to eighteenth- and nineteenth-century European painting, a great exception for the museum. Kelly was among the forty-three American artists chosen, including Willem de Kooning, Dan Flavin, Helen Frankenthaler, Jasper Johns, Roy Lichtenstein, Robert Morris, Claes Oldenburg, Jules Olitski, Robert Rauschenberg, and Frank Stella. Now considered a landmark show, it initially stirred controversy and notoriety. John Canaday of *The New York Times*, for example, described the exhibition as "a booboo on a grand scale."[40] Others fervently lambasted Geldzahler's criteria for his selection of the artists. Detractors found that the absence of artists such as Louise Nevelson, Larry Rivers, Tom Wesselmann, and Jim Dine highly problematic.

A staggering total of over 400 works of art were shown. Forty-two of these were works by Kelly, the most of any artist, of which thirty were his plant drawings.

Geldzahler dedicated a whole gallery to the display of these drawings. Although the artist had been making his plant drawings since his years in France, this exhibition was the first time Kelly had shown them publicly, finally revealing the importance of this longtime practice. As mentioned earlier, Kelly had eliminated the drawn line from his paintings, but kept the tradition of contour drawing for his studies of plant life and portraiture (figs 5, 109, 137, 192, 201). Drawing from plants affirmed his attachment and reliance on nature as well as his commitment to the visual experience. While living in New York, he maintained this ritual by drawing from potted plants he had kept in his different studios (fig. 103) or from plants he grew outside on his Coenties Slip studio roof (fig. 180). He would also find time to draw from nature on domestic and foreign travels as his success grew during the 1960s.

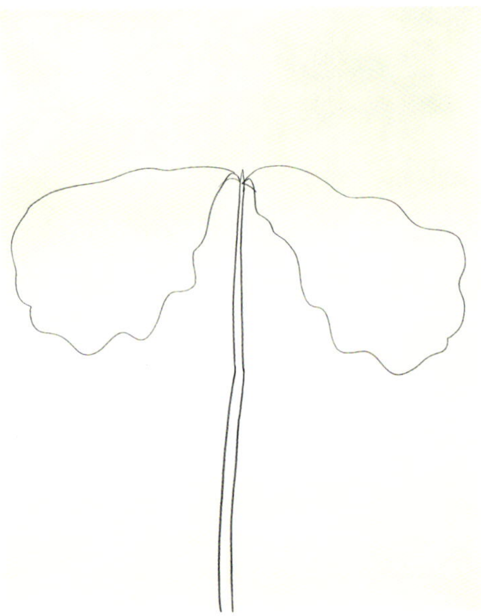
fig. 109: *Oak*, 1964, graphite on paper, 28½ × 22½ in, 72.4 × 57.2 cm

In his plant drawings, one can identify Kelly's unwavering focus on form. For example, *Oak*, 1964 (fig. 109), shown at the Metropolitan exhibition, demonstrates the artist's attraction to the curving outline of oak leaves and their vertical stem. Drawn with only a few strokes of pencil and without any shading, the depiction of these forms appears somewhere in between representation and abstraction. Kelly has abandoned any attempts to make the forms look three-dimensional and realistic. Instead, he has chosen to flatten out their shapes. As the artist explained about his plant life drawings in his retrospective treatise, "Notes from 1969" (which he did not publish until 1979), "I began to draw from plant life and found the flat leaf forms were easier to do than thighs and breasts. I wanted to flatten. The plant drawings from that time until now have always been linear."[41] Despite his decision to "flatten" and not depict his chosen forms volumetrically, it can be said that Kelly's plant drawings still retain the vital experience of vision, his connection to shape as existing in the world. Kelly would continue this commitment to drawing plant life throughout his career, especially after he moved to upstate New York the following year in 1970.

At Geldzahler's exhibition at the Met, Kelly also displayed his newest work created that year, *Spectrum V* (1969) (pp. 180–81), an exuberant celebration of color. Its thirteen separate panels, each painted a single color and spaced a foot apart, spread across an approximate total of fifty feet of wall space. Measuring 7 feet tall by about 3 feet wide, each panel offers its own field of monochrome color that relates to its neighboring panels and to the overall chromatic scheme. This work continues the color progression begun with Kelly's 1953 painting, *Spectrum I* (p. 87), produced in France—one that starts with yellow, moves through the spectrum to shades of green, blue, purple, violet, magenta, red, orange, and ends with another yellow. For *Spectrum I*, Kelly had painted within a single canvas fourteen vertical stripes of color, the borders of each delineated only with a painted edge—what Kelly has referred to as a "depicted edge"—rather than the literalized edge of his multipanel works. As he would later recollect, "It's very difficult to do a spectrum because each color has to be the right red, the right purple, and they have to blend together."[42] As his statement suggests, Kelly wanted to achieve as fluid a passage as possible between each color. In this first attempt (except his

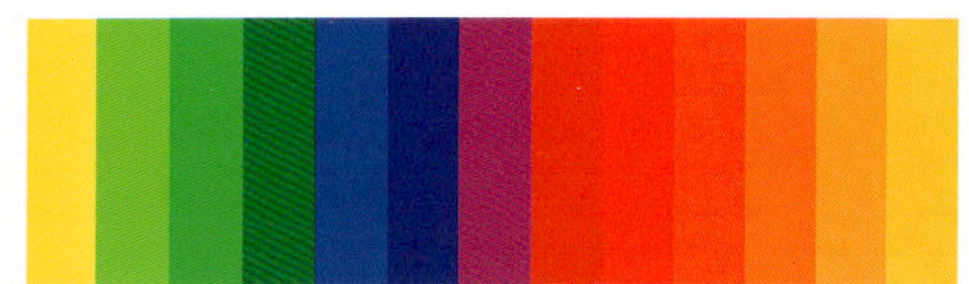

fig. 110: *Spectrum II*, 1966–67, oil on canvas, 13 joined panels, 80 × 273 in, 203.2 × 693.4 cm

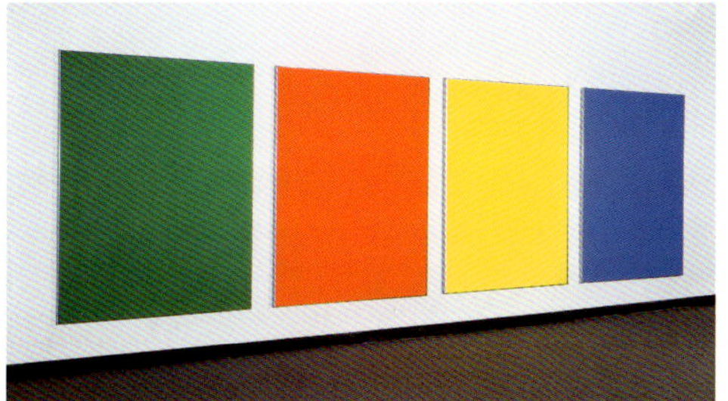

fig. 111: *Green Red Yellow Blue*, 1965, acrylic on canvas, 4 panels, 76 × 255 in, 193 × 647.7 cm

mini spectrum collaged onto one of his 1942 Munsell student charts [fig. 12]), he felt that he was far from accomplishing a seamless progression, and so he set this concept aside. In the years to come, Kelly would discover that for him arriving at the "right" color is an intuitive process, an act of trusting his eye.

In 1966, Kelly returned to his "Spectrum" concept, with *Spectrum II* (1966–67) (fig. 110). By the mid-1960s, he had felt he had given significant attention to his "form and ground" investigations, having produced over 200 paintings of this type. Thus, he returned to working with rectilinear multiple panels, as originally begun in France. He would later remark about these works in 1984, "The canvas panels were painted solid colors with no incident, lines, marks, brushstrokes or depicted shapes; the joined panels became a form, and thereby transferred the ground from the surface of the canvas to the wall."[43] This renewed multipanel investigation returned to a focused reexamination of the monochrome canvas, which he had basically set aside during his production of figure-ground paintings, except for only a handful of works that used monochrome panels including *White Plaque: Bridge Arch and Reflection* (1955) (p. 131), *Gaza* (1956) (p. 133), and *Orange Red Relief* (1959) (p. 149).

Among the first of these reengagements with the multiple panel was a quartet of four separated canvases, *Green Red Yellow Blue* (1965) (fig. 111), which he debuted at the 1966 Venice Biennale. He then made *Blue Green Yellow Orange Red* (1966) (pp. 170–71), which eventually led him back to his "Spectrum" idea. After Sir Isaac Newton first discovered the color spectrum in 1666, proving that sunlight was comprised of many colors, as refracted through a prism or observed naturally as a rainbow in the sky, he then divided this spectrum into seven colors: red, orange, yellow, green, blue, indigo, violet. Three centuries later, Kelly translated this ordering of color into his own sequence, assigning thirteen colors, beginning and ending in yellow, to *Spectrum II* (fig. 110). Featuring thirteen panels hinged together, *Spectrum II* forms a large vertical polyptych, the first of its kind in scale as well as in number of panels. Of course, Kelly had made *Colors for a Large Wall* comprising sixty-four square panels, but this was the first time he had ever attempted a multipanel painting of thirteen large vertical panels set side by side. Kelly made two more *Spectrums*, *III* and *IV*, both in 1967, also of thirteen joined panels.

With *Spectrum V*, he chose to separate his panels along the wall, an idea first explored in 1952 in *Red Yellow Blue White* (pp. 74–75) but one to which he returned in 1965, first with *Red Yellow Blue II* (pp. 168–69)—made a year before Barnett Newman's 1966 *Who's Afraid of Red, Yellow and Blue I*—and then with *Green Red Yellow Blue,* which he showed at the 1966 Venice Biennale. Geldzahler's invitation to Kelly to be included in the huge Met survey resulted in the large-scale format of *Spectrum V.* The artist had devoted the entire summer to making the work at his studio in Bridgehampton. When displayed for the first time at the Met, *Spectrum V* placed new demands on the spectator, a temporal unfolding of changing color interrupted by interstices along the wall. Each monochrome panel registers its own physicality, its own presence. As Kelly said two years before making *Spectrum V*, "I am less interested in the marks on the panels than the presence of the panels themselves."[44] The overall wall also unifies the panels while the spaces in between function as pauses between each color, here in new pastel hues.

By this time, Kelly had been invited to participate in several major exhibitions that attempted to define the increasing impact of Minimalism and its emphasis on the physical object and seriality, such as "Primary Structures" in 1966 at the Jewish Museum and "The Art of the Real" in 1968 at MoMA. Through inclusion in such thematic shows, Kelly had been folded into the dominant theoretical debate that emerged during the mid-1960s. The Minimalist camp, predominantly sculptors such as Carl Andre, Donald Judd, and Dan Flavin, promoted a new kind of three-dimensional art that would allow the viewer to experience artworks as real objects in their own embodied space, freeing art of traditional attitudes, such as the attachment to the pedestal. The other camp, with the likes of Color Field painters Morris Louis, Kenneth Noland, and Jules Olitski, created a type of abstract painting that their defenders such as Clement Greenberg asserted would inspire in the viewer a purely optical, disembodied experience and thereby affirm the preeminent status of the two-dimensional picture plane. At "Primary Structures," Kelly displayed *Blue Disk* (1963) (fig. 112), a uniquely shaped and planar work, intentionally not showing his multipanel paintings at this exhibition in order to distinguish his work from the others—to reiterate his commitment to specific shape and color, and *not* seriality. Kelly, however, would not turn away from the opportunity to exhibit, and misunderstandings, however, continued. For example, his five-panel work, *Blue Green Yellow Orange Red* (1966) (pp. 170–71), shown at the Guggenheim's "Systemic Painting" in 1966 contributed to the wrong notion that Kelly's use of the multiple panel was simply a recent development, and thus a response to the emergence of Minimalism.

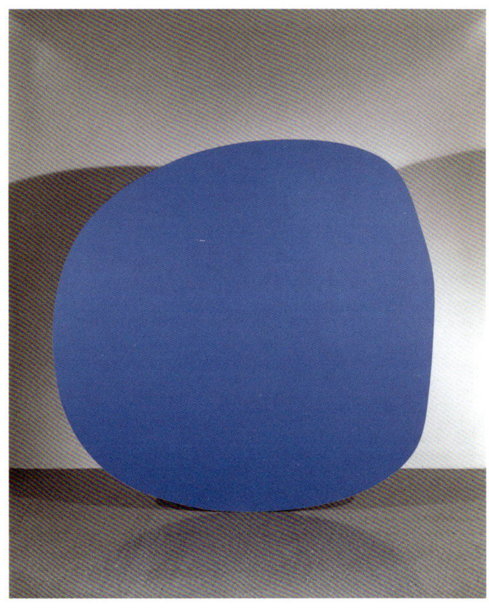

fig. 112: *Blue Disk*, 1963, painted aluminum, 70 × 72 × ⅛ in, 177.8 × 182.9 × 0.3 cm

Kelly's deployment of the multiple canvas, of course, had begun fifteen years earlier in France, first driven by non-compositional strategies of chance and experimentations with shape and color. His dependence on the multiple panel was far removed from the so-called Minimalist prescription of repeating into continuity, to add "one thing after another," as asserted by Judd.[45] Kelly's multipanel paintings utilized color in a non-serial, non-systematic way. In *Spectrum V*, he was clearly motivated by a specific color progression that offered a beginning, middle, and end, a goal that was anathema to Minimalist theory. Through his deployment of the monochrome and separating the panels along the wall, Kelly affirmed the rectangle as an individual shape worthy of investigation. These canvases existed as fields of monochrome hues, separate panels that "named" specific colors and produced a new, distanced structure as they spread across the wall.

Two years after the exhibition, "New York Painting and Sculpture," critic Calvin Tomkins wrote a profile on the inimitable Geldzahler in *The New Yorker*, lauding his Met show as "a valedictory to the decade."[46] Despite the criticism hurled at the show just two years earlier, this exhibition had indeed solidified the relevance and standing of American art. It celebrated a significant period of growth in the New York art world, a period of rich innovation when artists were, according to Tomkins, "optimistic, open, experimental, and feverishly intense; artists felt free to question every previous assumption of the purpose and function of art."[47] "Henry's show," as it became known, helped bring the 1960s New York scene to a close. In turn, about a month after the show ended in February 1970, Kelly's own New York chapter would also come to a close.

1 Goossen 1973, p. 49.
2 Letter to Kelly from Alexander Calder, dated December 9, 1954, Kelly studio archives, Spencertown, New York. Kelly would give Calder a painting, *Charmettes I* (1956), in January 1957.
3 Letter to Kelly from James Johnson Sweeney, dated December 15, 1954, Kelly studio archives, Spencertown, New York.
4 Letter to Kelly from Alfred H. Barr, Jr., dated December 23, 1954, Kelly studio archives, Spencertown, New York.
5 The other artists included were Jay DeFeo, Wally Hedrick, James Jarvaise, Alfred Leslie, Landès Lewitin, Richard Lytle, Robert Mallary, Louise Nevelson, Julius Schmidt, Richard Stankiewicz, Albert Urban, and Jack Youngerman, Kelly's close friend from France.
6 Price list from Betty Parsons Gallery papers (1941–1968), Reel No. 68–65, Archives of American Art, Smithsonian Institution.
7 B[arbara] B[utler], "Ellsworth Kelly," *Arts Magazine* 30, no. 4 (June 1956), p. 52.
8 P[arker] T[yler], "Ellsworth Kelly," *ARTnews* 55, no. 4 (summer 1956), p. 51.
9 Dore Ashton, "Arts," *Arts & Architecture* 76, no.12 (December 1959), p. 7.
10 William Rubin, "Younger American Painters, *Art International* 4, no.1 (January 1960), pp. 28–29.
11 Kelly, quoted in Coplans 1971, p. 20.
12 Kelly, in telephone conversation with the author, November 13, 2002.
13 Kelly, in conversation with the author, Spencertown, New York, August 25, 2003.
14 Kelly utilized a similar thin strip of painted wood in his multipanel painting, *Fête à Torcy* (1952) (p. 72), a year after making the black collage in Paris.
15 Kelly, quoted in Elizabeth C. Baker, *Ellsworth Kelly: Recent Paintings and Sculptures* (New York: The Metropolitan Museum of Art, 1979), p. 9.
16 As recounted by Kelly, in conversation with the author, Spencertown, New York, October 9, 2008.
17 Herman Melville, *Moby-Dick or, The Whale* (1851; repr., New York: Penguin Books, 1992), pp. 3–4.
18 While in France after reading Melville's novel, Kelly made a red-and-white painting titled *Moby Dick* (1951).
19 Using movement to dictate how forms are created on the receptive surface of the sketchbook page looks forward to William Anastasi's more conceptual, chance-based drawings from the 1960s where he allowed the movement of the subway train to dictate how his hand would move on the surface of his paper sheet.
20 Kelly, quoted in Charles Hagen, "The Shape of Seeing: Ellsworth Kelly's Photographs," *Aperture,* no. 125 (fall 1991), p. 45; italics added.
21 Kelly, quoted in Piri Halasz, "He Brightens Up the Spectrum of Contemporary Art," *Smithsonian* 4, no. 8 (November 1973), p. 42.
22 Kelly, in telephone conversation with the author, November 13, 2002. For a fuller discussion of Kelly's postcard collages, see Tricia Y. Paik, "A Green Mound for Ground Zero: Ellsworth Kelly's 9/11 Proposal" [ch.7], in Elizabeth Pergam (ed.), *Drawing in the 21st Century: The Politics and Poetics of Contemporary Practice* (Burlington, VT: Ashgate, 2015), pp. 101–22. See also "Chapter Two: Postcards from New York," in Paik 2009, pp. 71–121.
23 Ibid.
24 For a discussion of this community, see Stephanie Barron, "Giving Art History the Slip," *Art in America* 62, no. 2 (March/April 1974), pp. 80–84; Mildred Glimcher, *Indiana, Kelly, Martin, Rosenquist, Youngerman at Coenties Slip* (New York: The Pace Gallery, 1993); Holland Cotter, "Where City History Was Made: A 50's Group Made Art History," *The New York Times*, January 5, 1993, pp. C11, C16; and Robert A.M. Stern, Thomas Mellins, David Fishman, *New York 1960: Architecture and Urbanism between the Second World War and the Bicentennial* (New York: The Monacelli Press, 1995), pp. 206–07.
25 Robert Indiana, quoted in Barbara Haskell, *Robert Indiana: Beyond Love* (New York: Whitney Museum of American Art, 2013), p. 18, n.42.
26 William Rubin, "Younger American Painters, *Art International* 4, no.1 (January 1960), p. 29.
27 Ralph Brem, "Much on Display High in Quality; Some Just Nonsense," *The Pittsburgh Press*, October 26, 1961, p. 21, section 2.
28 Stuart Preston, "Art: At Opposite Poles," *The New York Times*, October 21, 1961, p. L11.
29 Kelly, in conversation with the author, Spencertown, New York, August 2, 2001.
30 Kelly, in conversation with the author, Spencertown, New York, January 3, 2014.
31 For a summary of the art and architecture at the Fair, see Robert A. M. Stern, Thomas Mellins, and David Fishman, *New York 1960: Architecture and Urbanism between the Second World War and the Bicentennial* (New York: The Monacelli Press, 1995), pp. 1026–57.
32 Warhol's choice of subject matter, twenty-five photographic images of the New York City Police Department's most-wanted list, was deemed too controversial for the World's Fair, and the work was covered with a coat of silver paint. See ibid., p. 1036.
33 Max Kozloff, "Pop on the Meadow," *The Nation* (July 13, 1964), p. 17. In Kozloff's lengthy review of the Fair, he describes only the work of Lichtenstein, Indiana, Rauschenberg, and Rosenquist, without even mentioning the presence of the abstract commissions. It must be noted that in this review and in others, Rauschenberg's piece was usually rolled into the Pop category.
34 The work was featured as the cover image of the May 1957 *Architectural Record*, "Penn Center Transportation Building and Concourse," *Architectural Record* 121, no. 5 (May 1957), pp. 190–96.
35 Kelly, quoted in James Meyer, "Art for the City: Sculpture for a Large Wall, 1957," in *Ellsworth Kelly: Sculpture for a Large Wall, 1957* (New York: Matthew Marks Gallery, 1998), p. 38 n. 48.
36 The material Micarta was suggested to Kelly by the friend who had recommended him for the commission.
37 Kelly, quoted in Hindry 1992, pp. 22, 32; italics his. In his first published interview in 1963 with Henry Geldzahler, Kelly had addressed the subtle distinctions between these three different approaches: "The paintings are flat and are meant to be flat. The sculpture has its own space. The reliefs are frontal and flat but they're something I couldn't do with painting." Kelly, quoted in Henry Geldzahler, "Interview with Ellsworth Kelly," in *Paintings, Sculpture and Drawings by Ellsworth Kelly* (Washington, DC: Washington Gallery of Modern Art, 1963), n.p. Reprinted in *Art International* 8, no. 1 (February 1964), pp. 47–48.
38 Henry Geldzahler, "Ellsworth Kelly," in Geldzahler, *XXXIII International Biennial Exhibition of Art Venice 1966 United States of America* (Washington, DC: National Collection of Fine Arts, Smithsonian Institution, 1966), p. 29.
39 Ibid.
40 John Canaday, quoted in Calvin Tomkins, "Profiles: Moving with the Flow," *The New Yorker* (November 6, 1971), p. 58.
41 Kelly, "Notes from 1969," in *Ellsworth Kelly: Paintings and Sculptures 1963–1979* (Amsterdam: Stedelijk Museum, 1979), p. 32.
42 Kelly, in conversation with the author, Spencertown, New York, October 9, 2008.
43 Kelly, in 1983 statement quoted in *Ellsworth Kelly: Painted Aluminum Wall Sculpture/ Weathering Steel Wall Sculpture* (Los Angeles: Margo Leavin Gallery; New York: Leo Castelli Gallery: 1984), n.p.
44 Kelly, quoted in Lucy R. Lippard, "Homage to the Square," *Art in America* 55, no.4 (July/August 1967), p. 57.
45 Donald Judd, "Specific Objects," *Arts Yearbook* 8 (1965), p. 82.
46 Tomkins 1971, p. 59.
47 Ibid.

Yellow Black and White, 1955
oil on canvas, 72 × 59¼ in, 182.9 × 150.5 cm

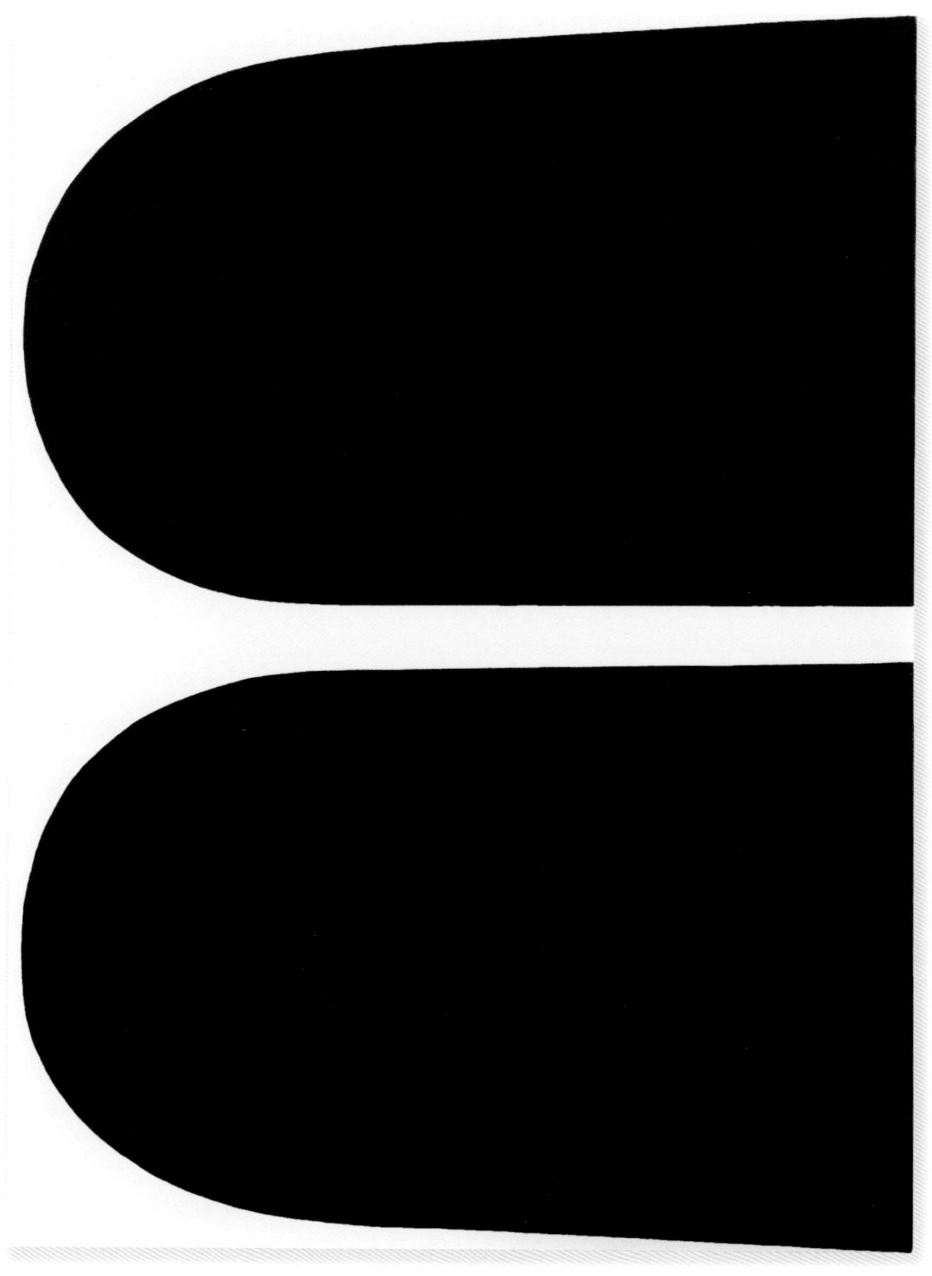

Black Curves, 1954
oil on canvas, 36 × 26 in, 91.4 × 66 cm

Black Ripe, 1955
oil on canvas, 63¼ × 59⅜ in, 160.7 × 150.8 cm

White Plaque: Bridge Arch and Reflection, 1955
oil on wood, 2 panels separated by a wood strip
64 × 48 × ½ in, 162.6 × 121.9 × 1.3 cm

Bar, 1955
oil on canvas, 32⅝ × 96 in, 82.9 × 243.8 cm

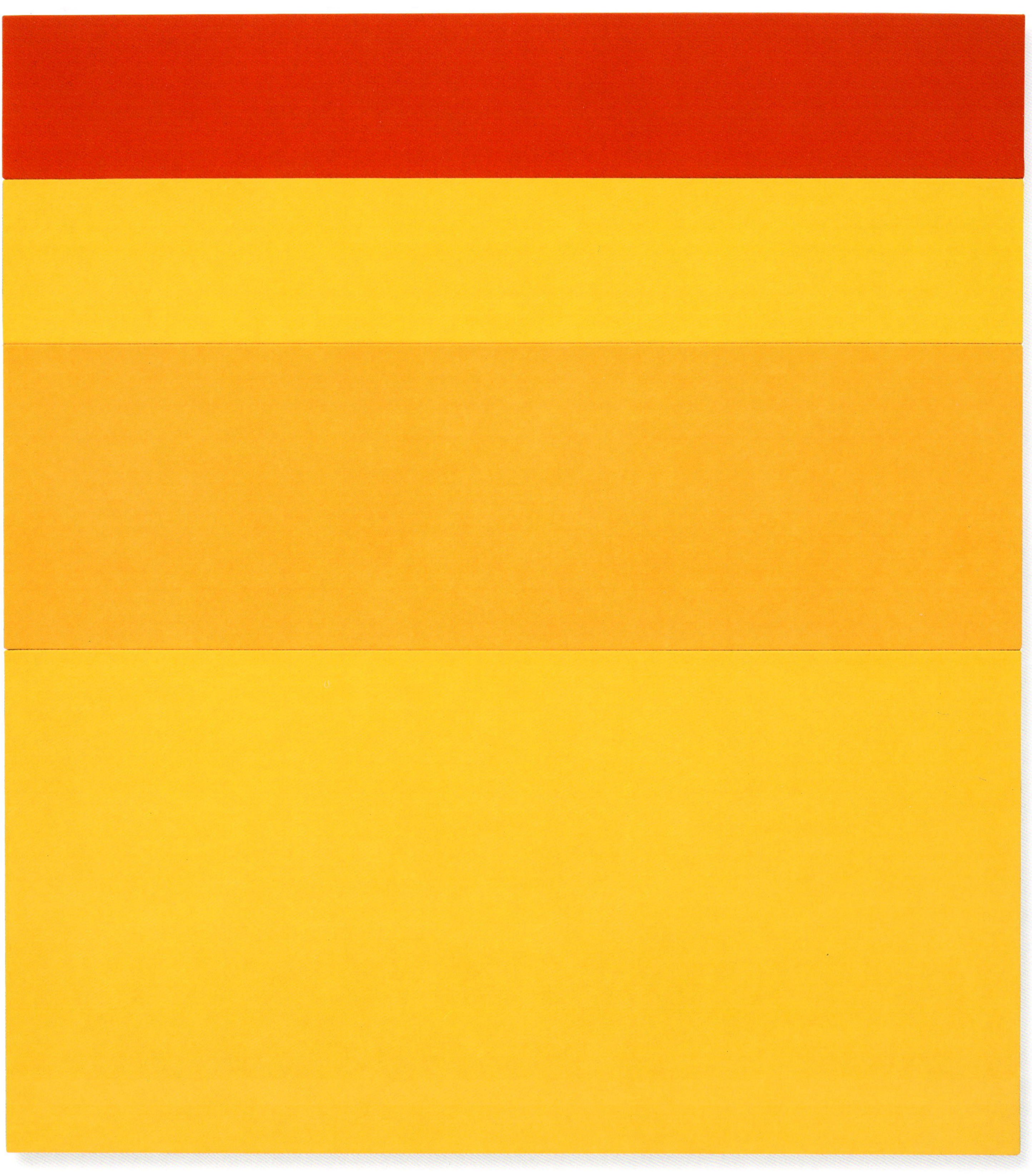

Gaza, 1956
oil on canvas, 4 joined panels, 89¾ × 79 in, 228 × 200.7 cm

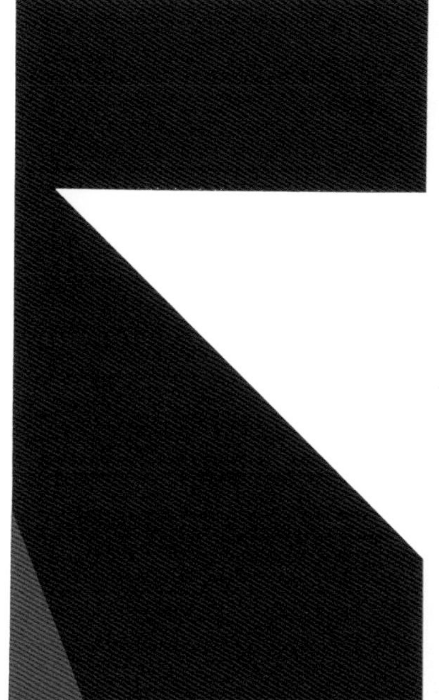

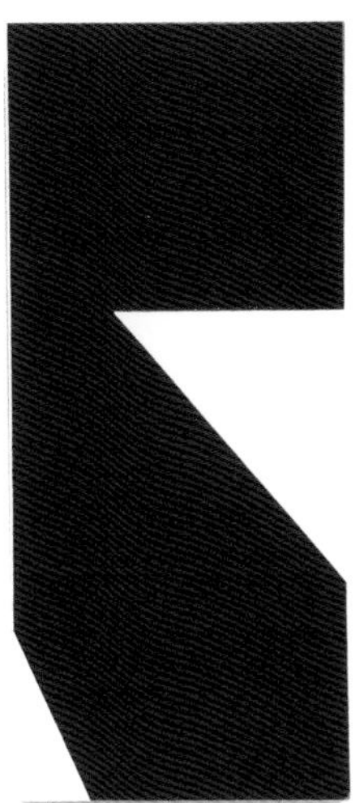

Painting in Five Panels, 1955
oil on canvas, 5 panels, 36 × 144 in, 91.4 × 365.8 cm

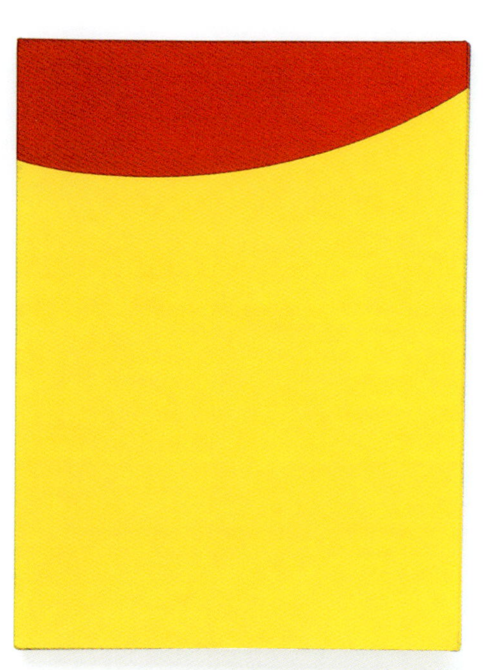

Painting in Three Panels, 1956
oil on canvas, 3 panels, 80 × 139 in, 203.2 × 353.1 cm

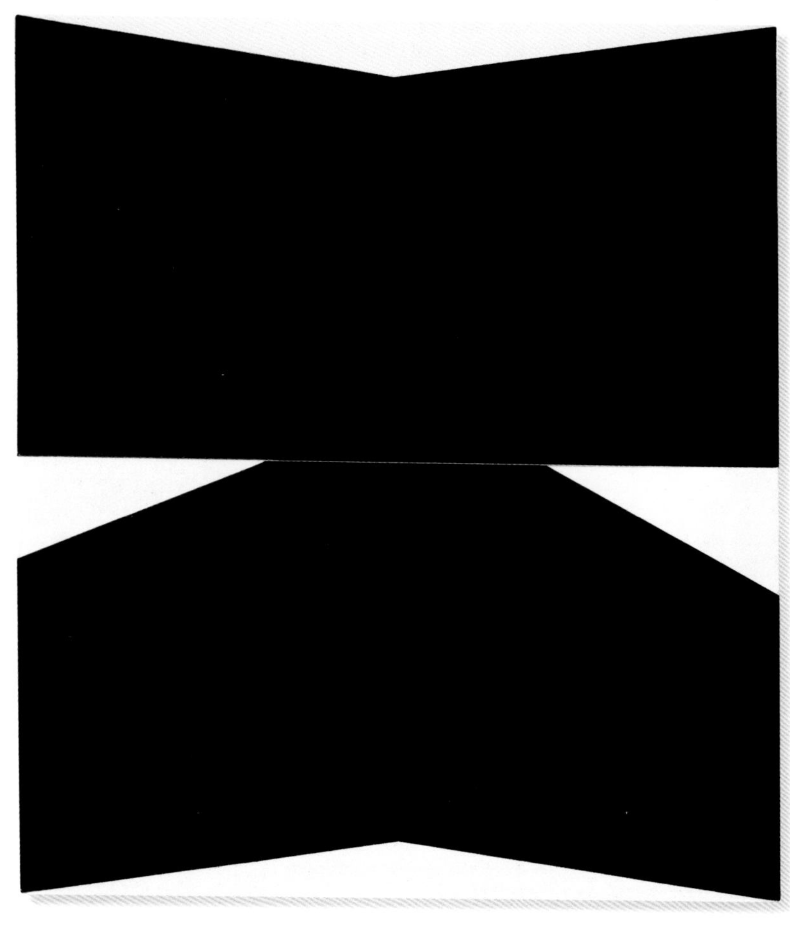

South Ferry, 1956
oil on canvas, 2 joined panels, 44 × 38 in, 111.8 × 96.5 cm

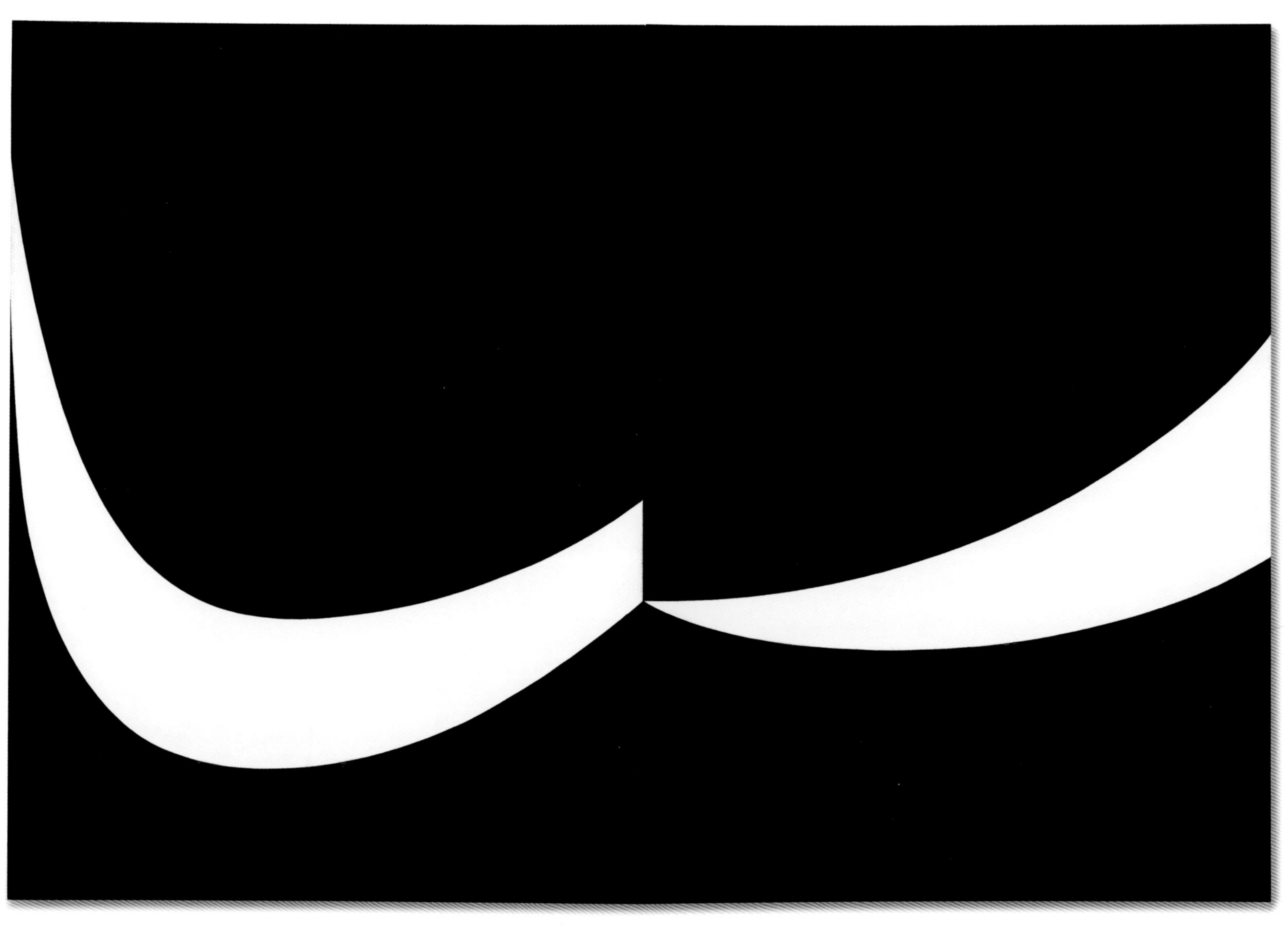

Atlantic, 1956
oil on canvas, 2 joined panels, 80 × 114 in, 203.2 × 289.6 cm

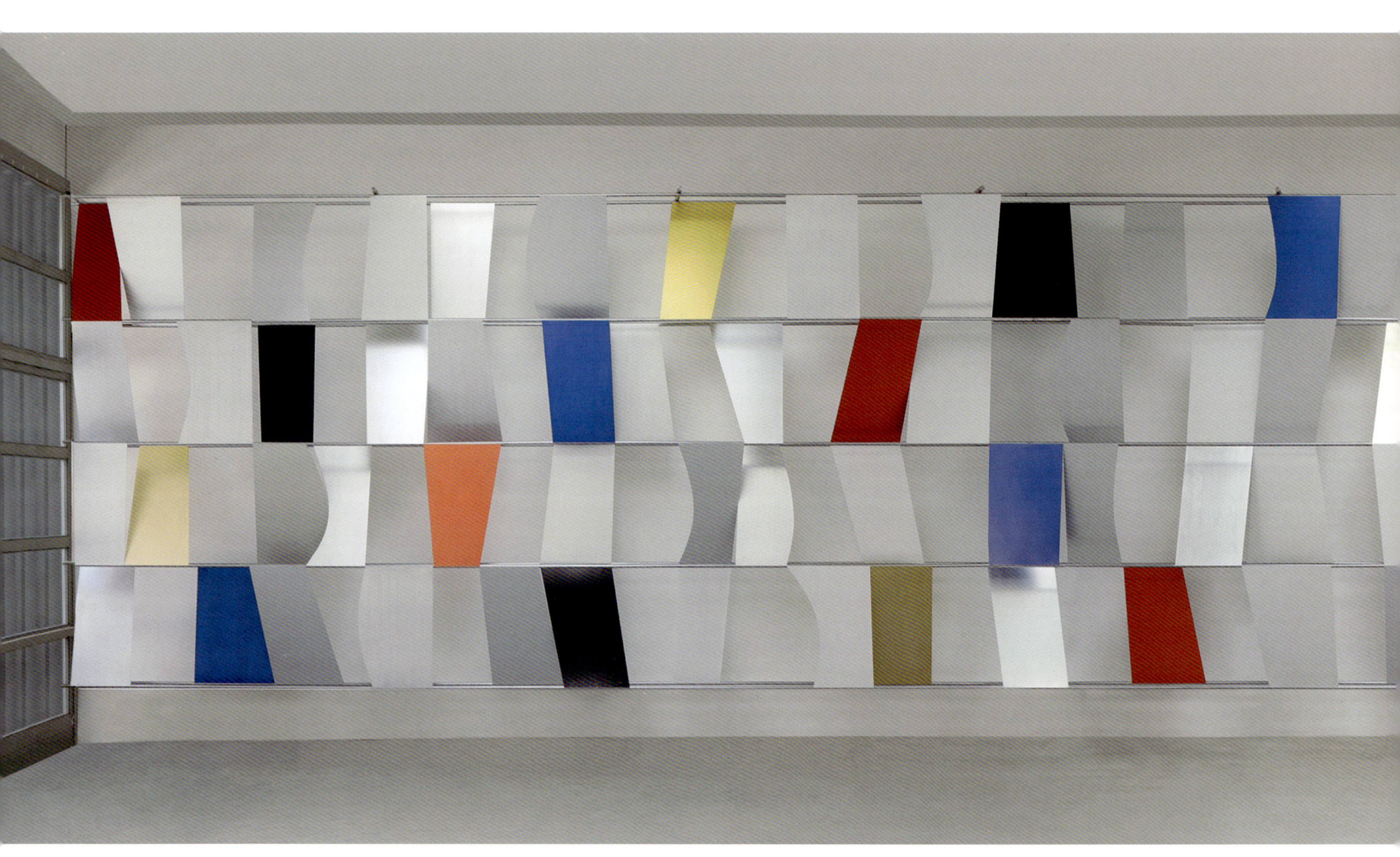

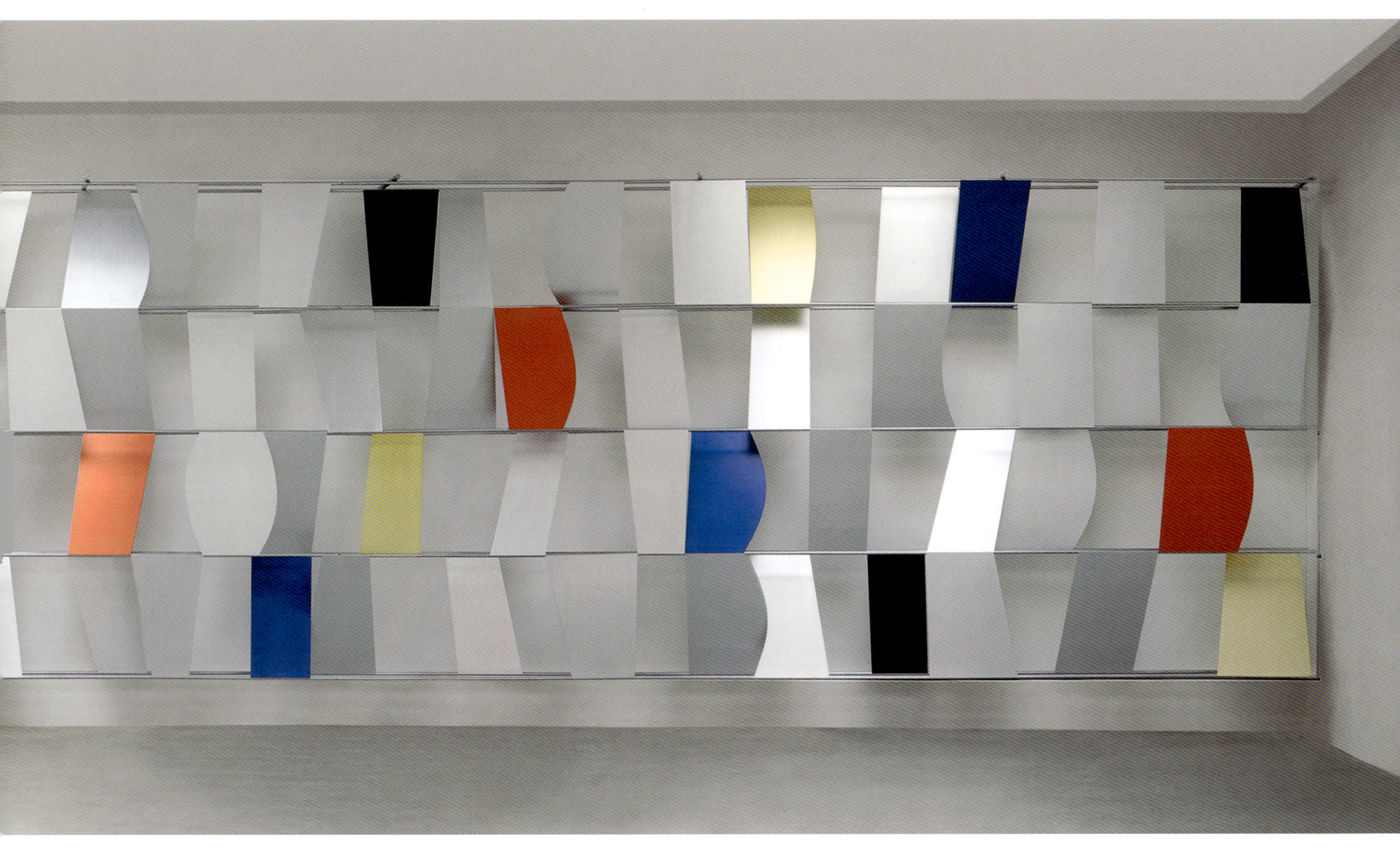

Sculpture for a Large Wall, 1957
anodized aluminum, 104 panels, 138 × 785 × 13 in, 3.5 × 19.9 × 0.3 m

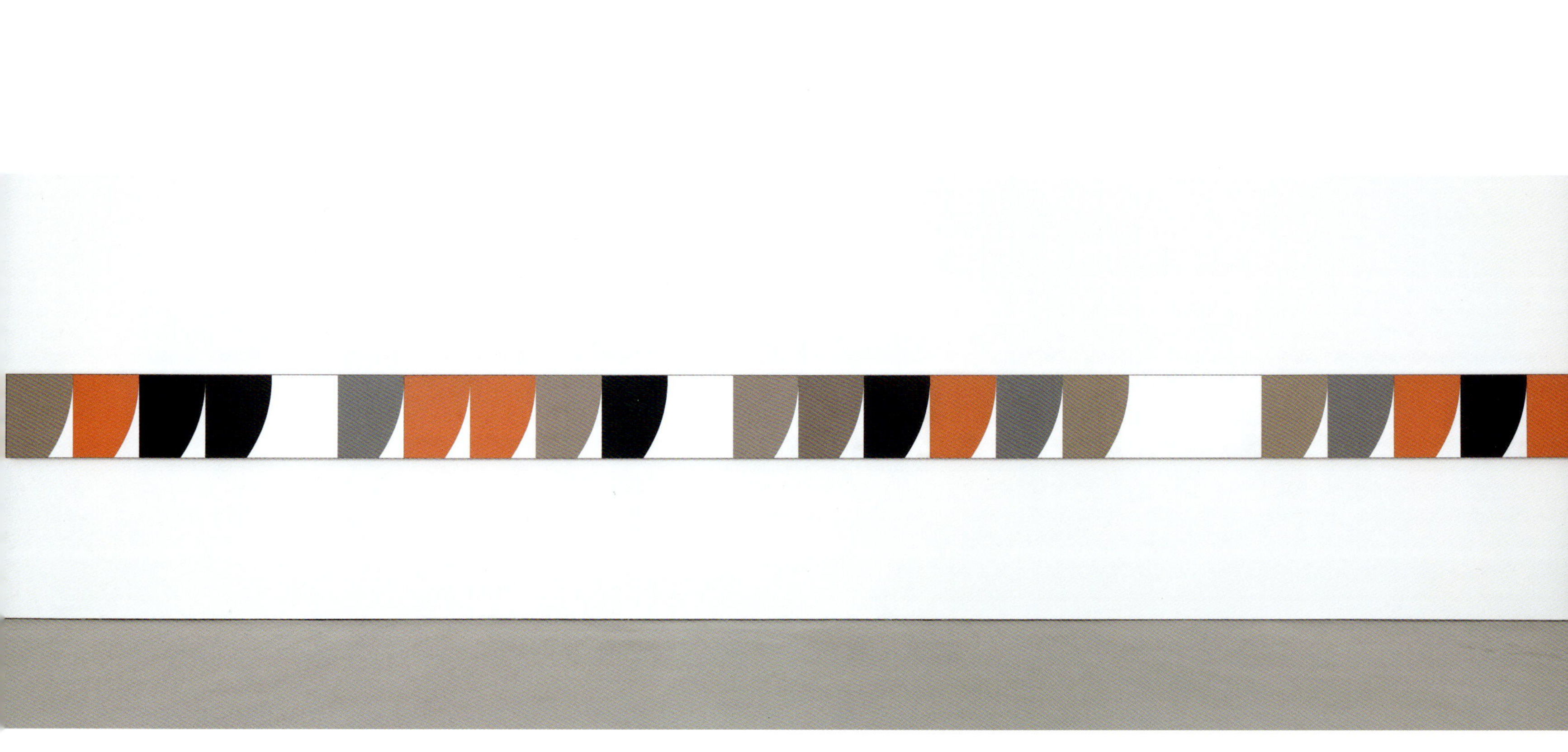

Eastmore Mural, 1957
Micarta, 24 × 408 in, 61 × 1036.3 cm

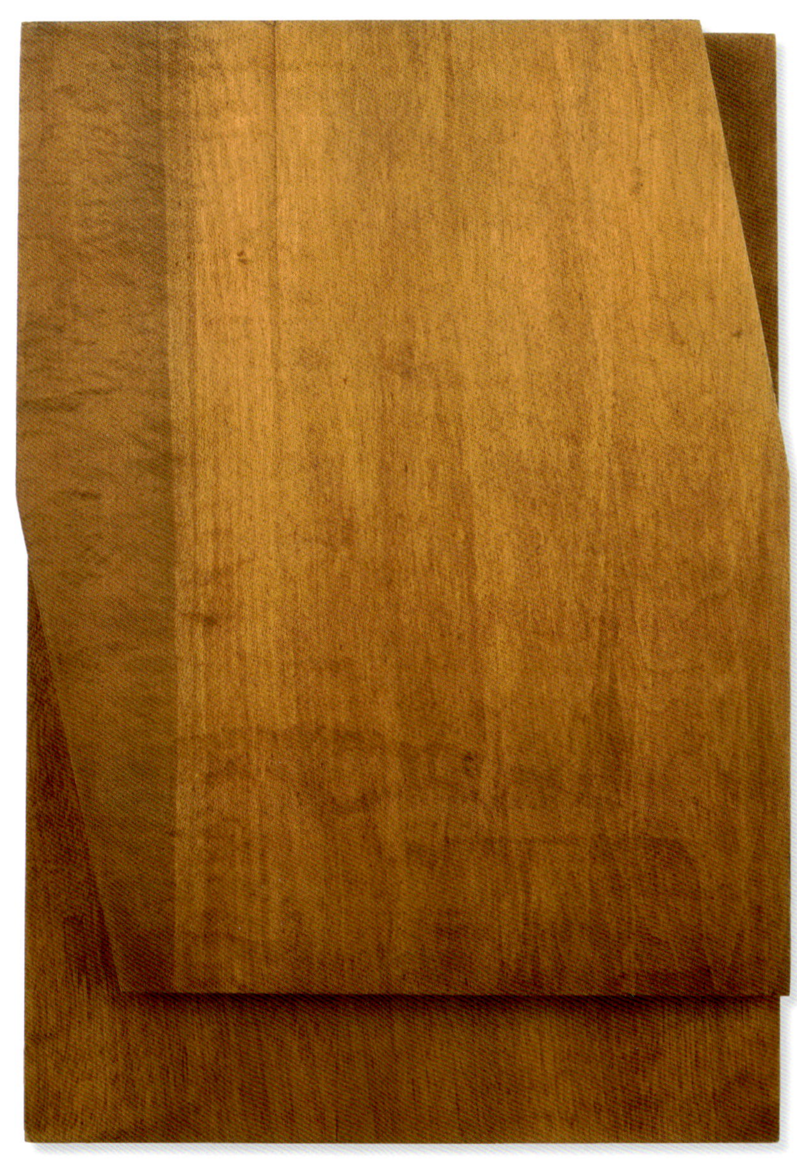

Concorde Relief I, 1958
elm, 11½ × 7¾ × 1¾ in, 29.2 × 19.7 × 4.4 cm

Broadway, 1958
oil on canvas, 78 × 69½ in, 198.1 × 176.5 cm

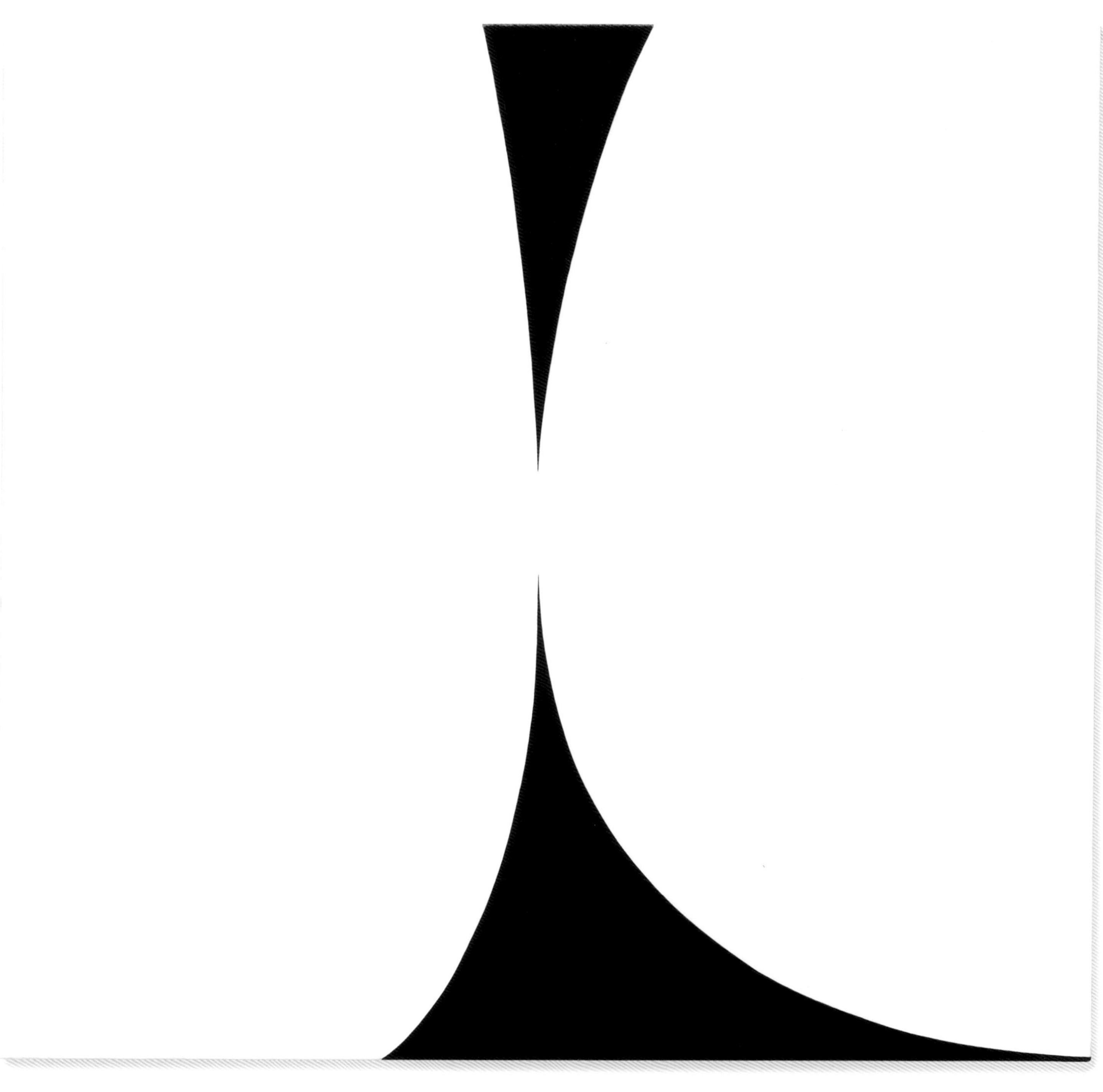

Rebound, 1959
oil on canvas, 68¼ × 71½ in, 173.4 × 181.6 cm

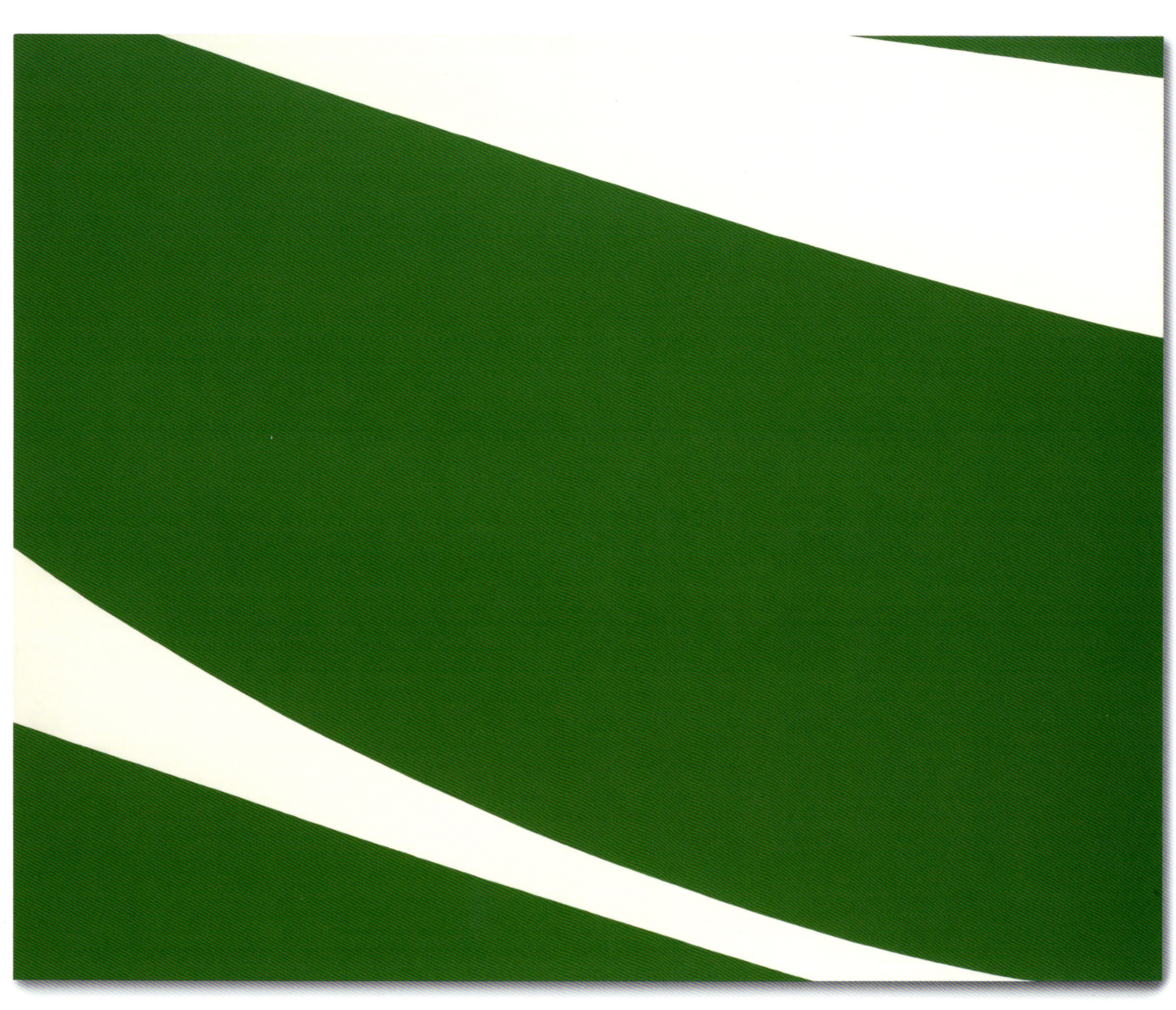

Jersey, 1958
oil on canvas, 60 × 72½ in, 152.4 × 184.2 cm

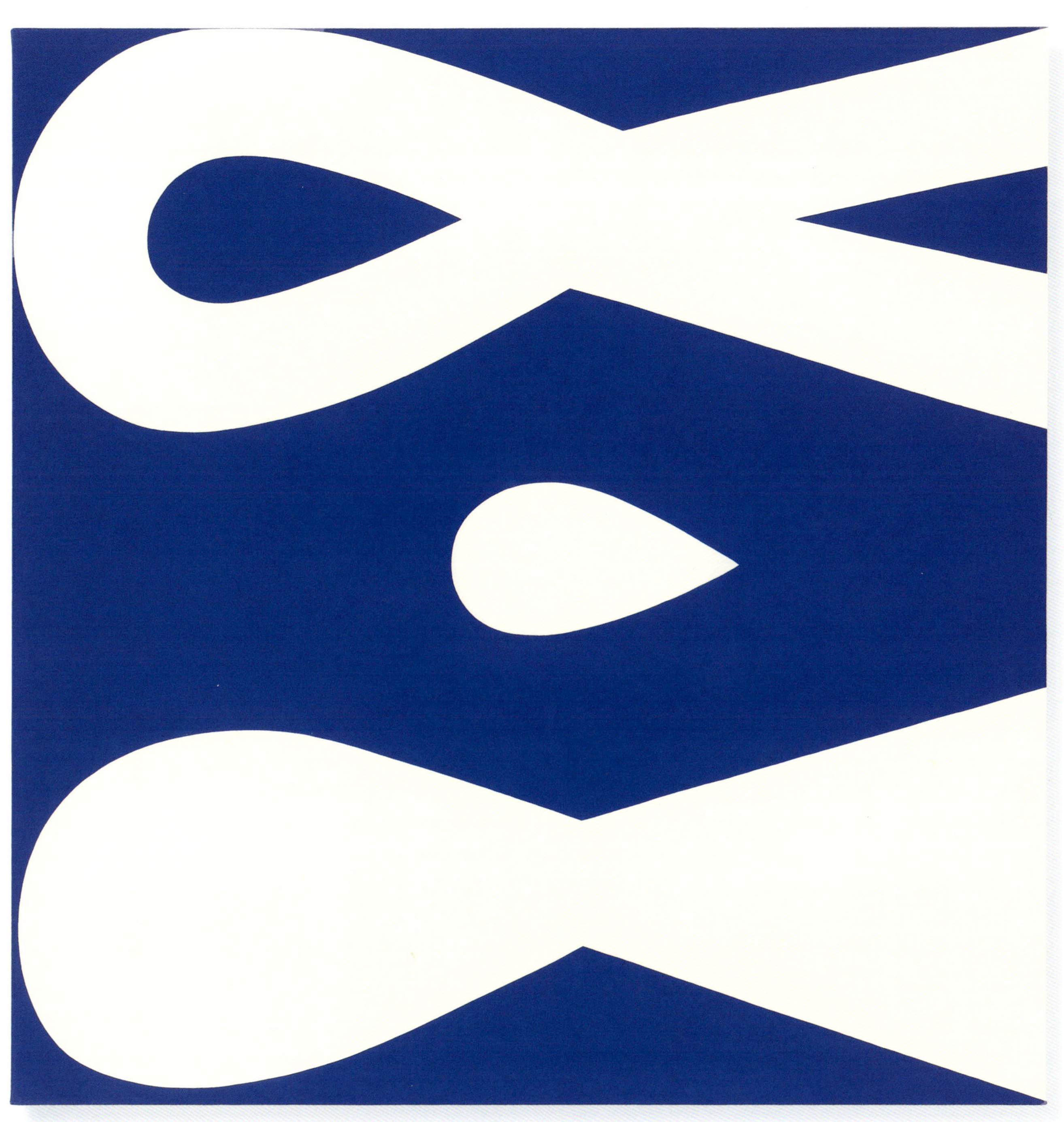

Loop, 1959
oil on canvas, 68¼ × 70½ in, 173.4 × 179.1 cm

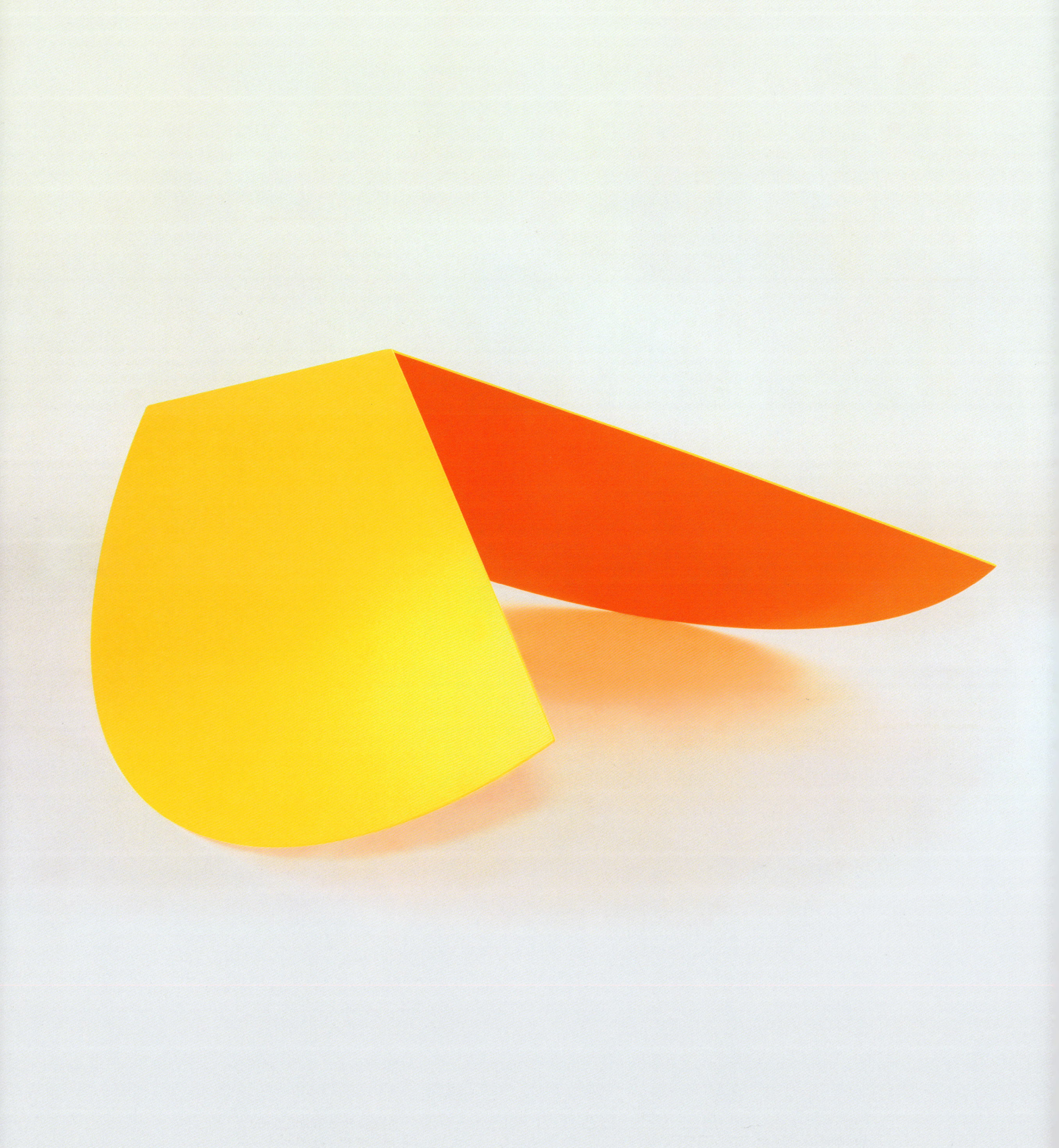

Pony, 1959
painted aluminum, 31 × 78 × 64 in
78.7 × 198.1 × 162.6 cm

Orange Red Relief, 1959
oil on canvas, 2 joined panels
60 × 60 × 3 in, 152.4 × 152.4 × 7.6 cm

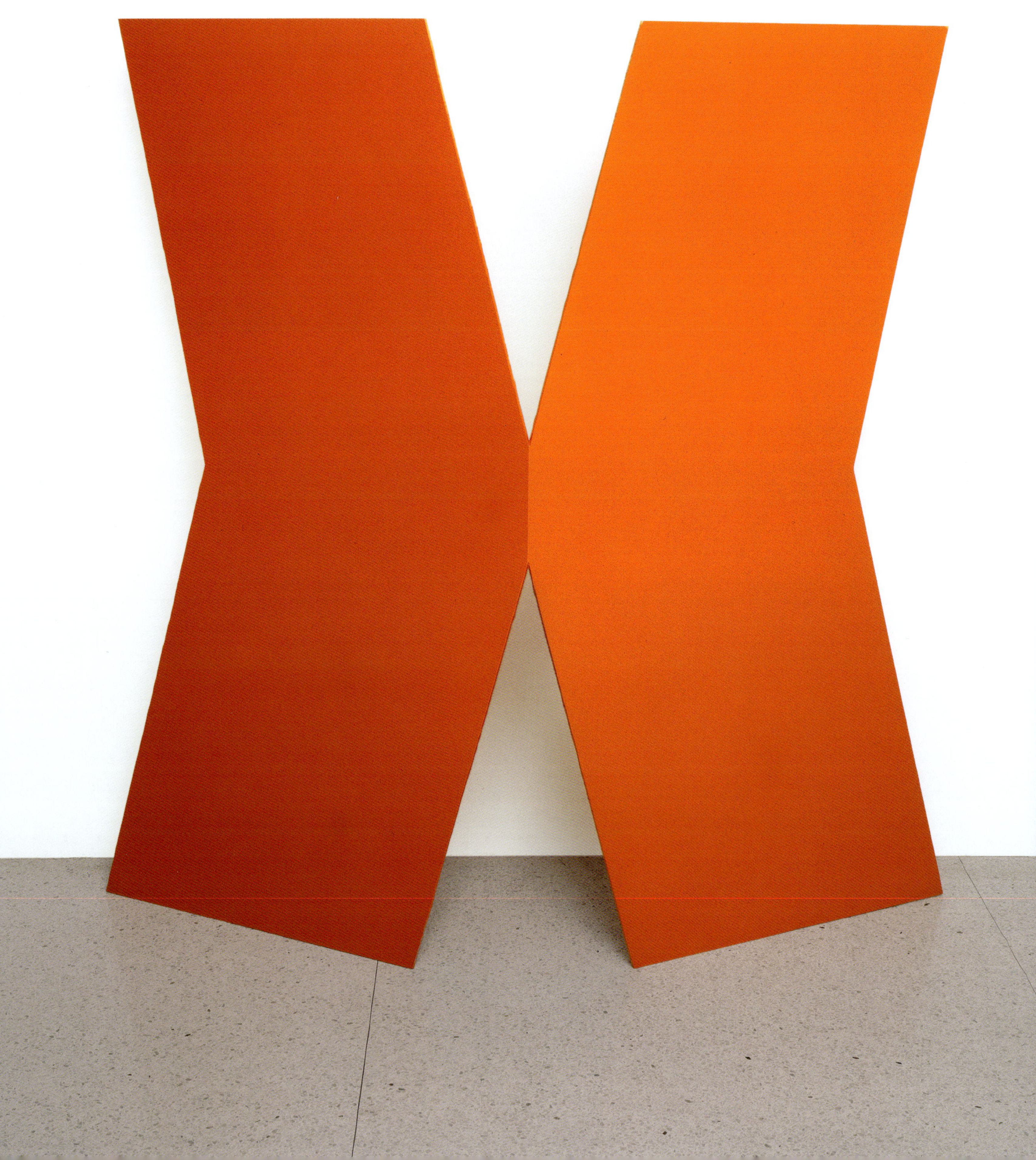

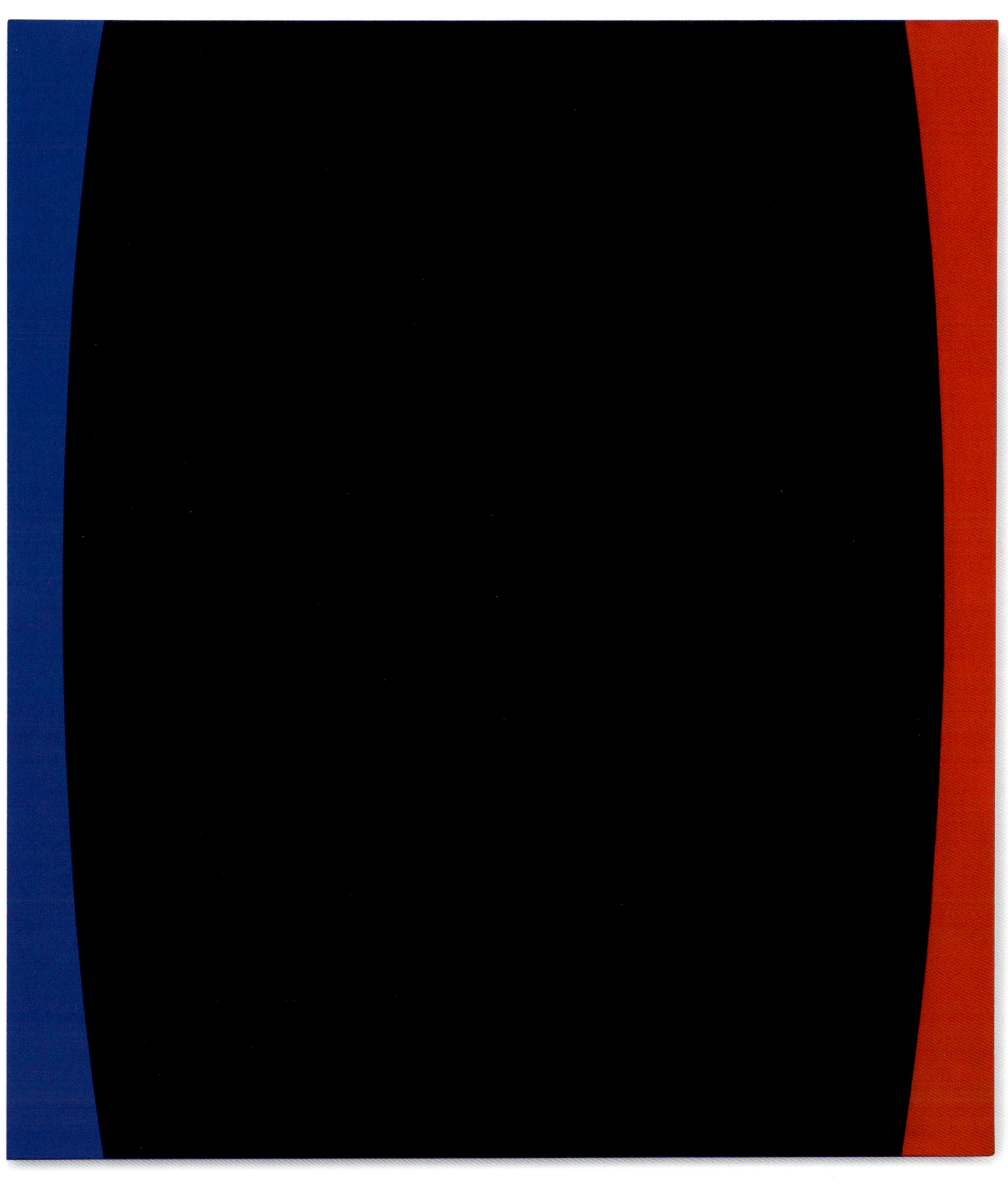

Gate, 1959
painted aluminum
67 × 63 × 17 in, 170.2 × 160 × 43.2 cm

Black Blue Red, 1960
oil on canvas
76½ × 66 in, 194.3 × 167.6 cm

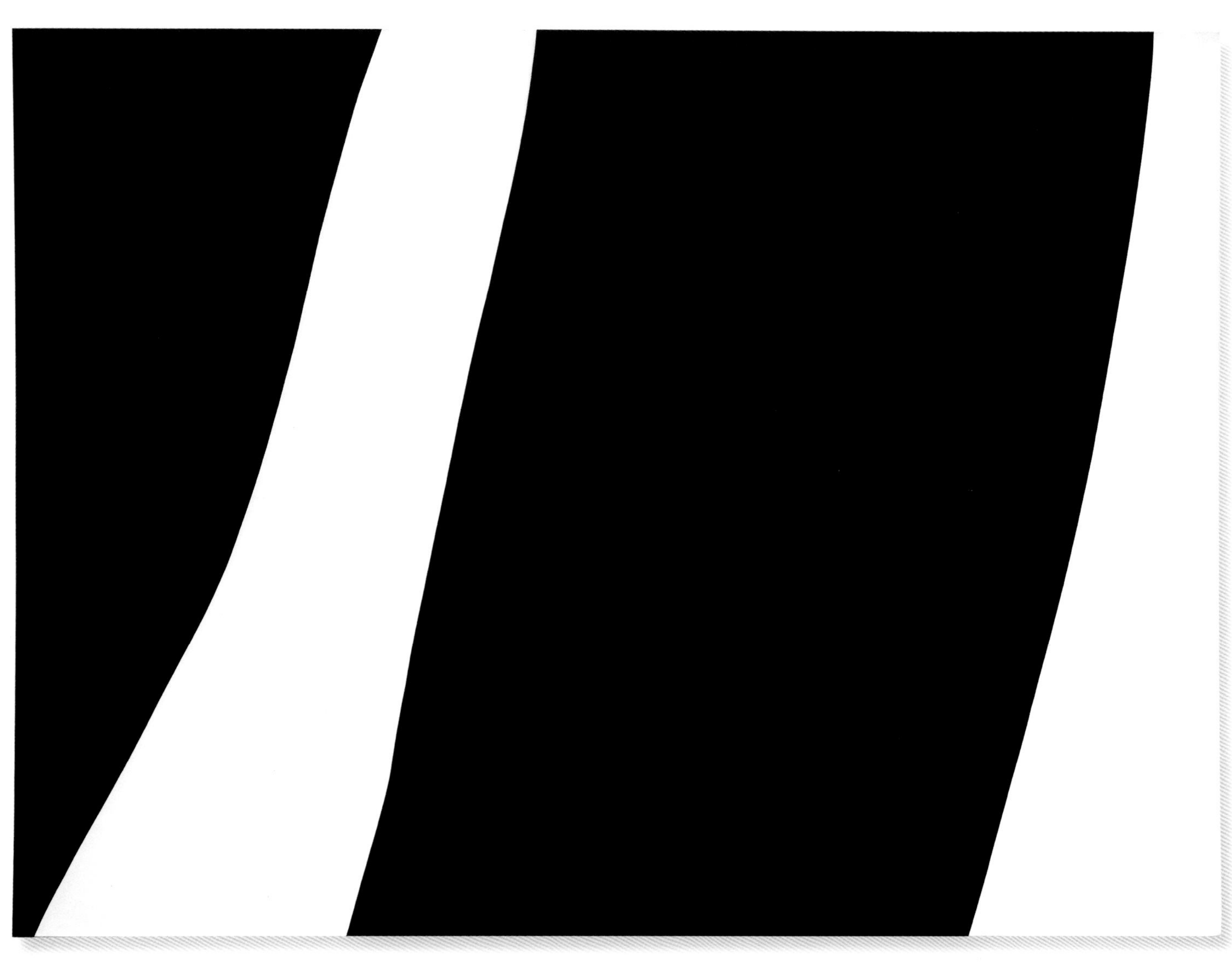

Black and White, 1960–61
oil on canvas, 90 × 120 in, 228.6 × 304.8 cm

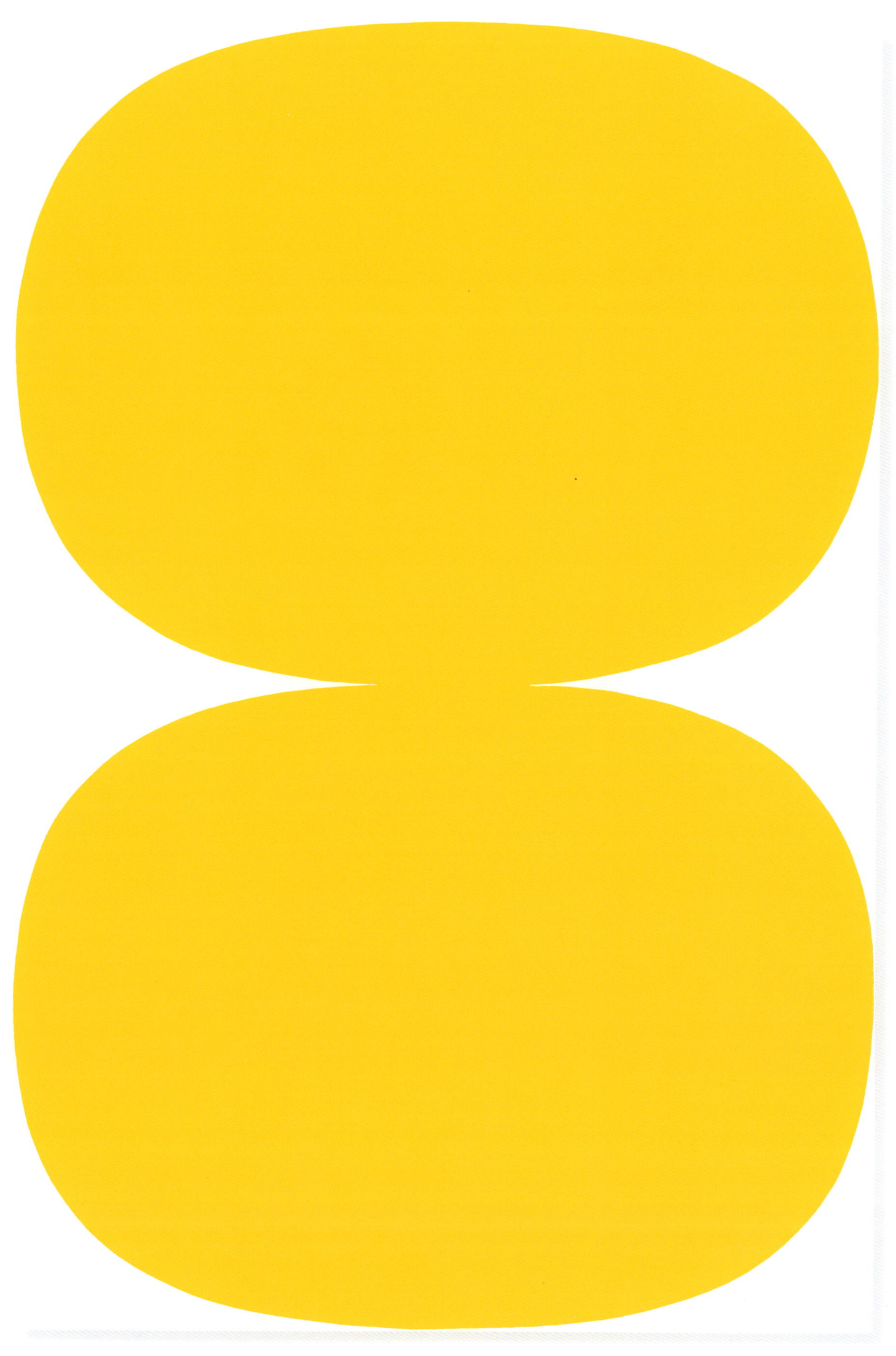

Yellow White, 1961
oil on canvas, 84¼ × 55¾ in, 214 × 141.6 cm

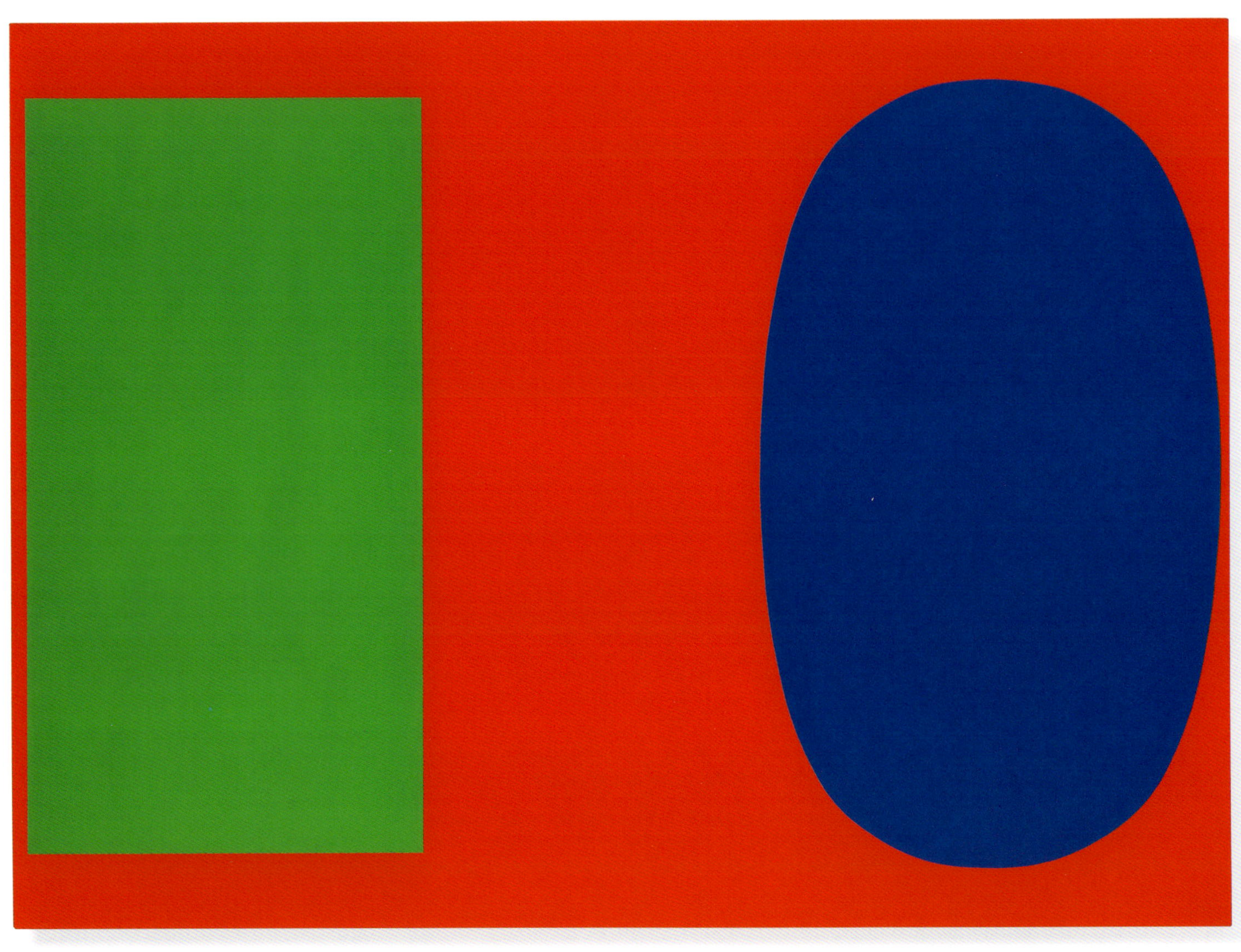

Green Blue Red, 1963
oil on canvas, 67½ × 90 in, 171.5 × 228.6 cm

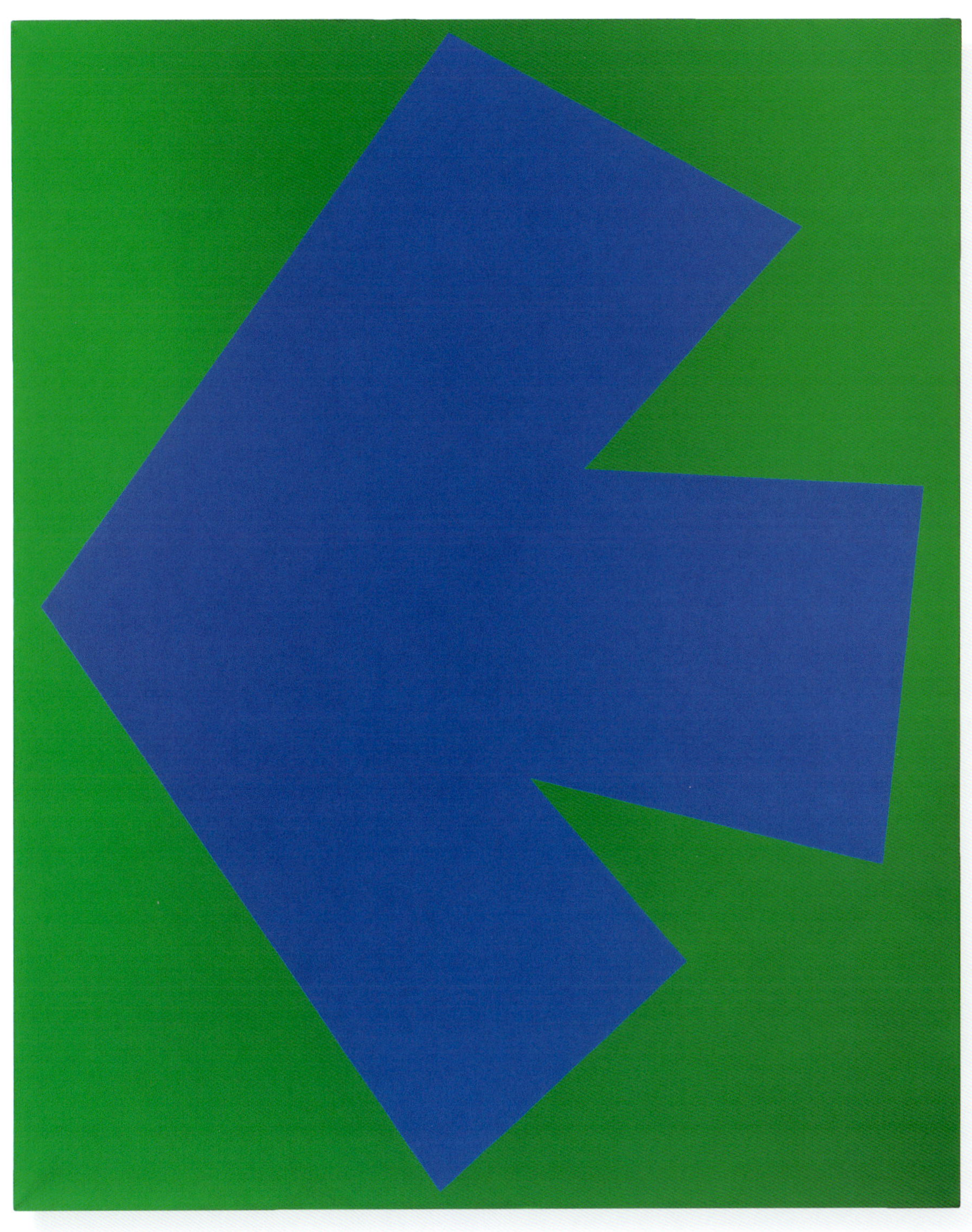

Blue Green, 1962
oil on canvas, 86½ × 68 in, 219.7 × 172.7 cm

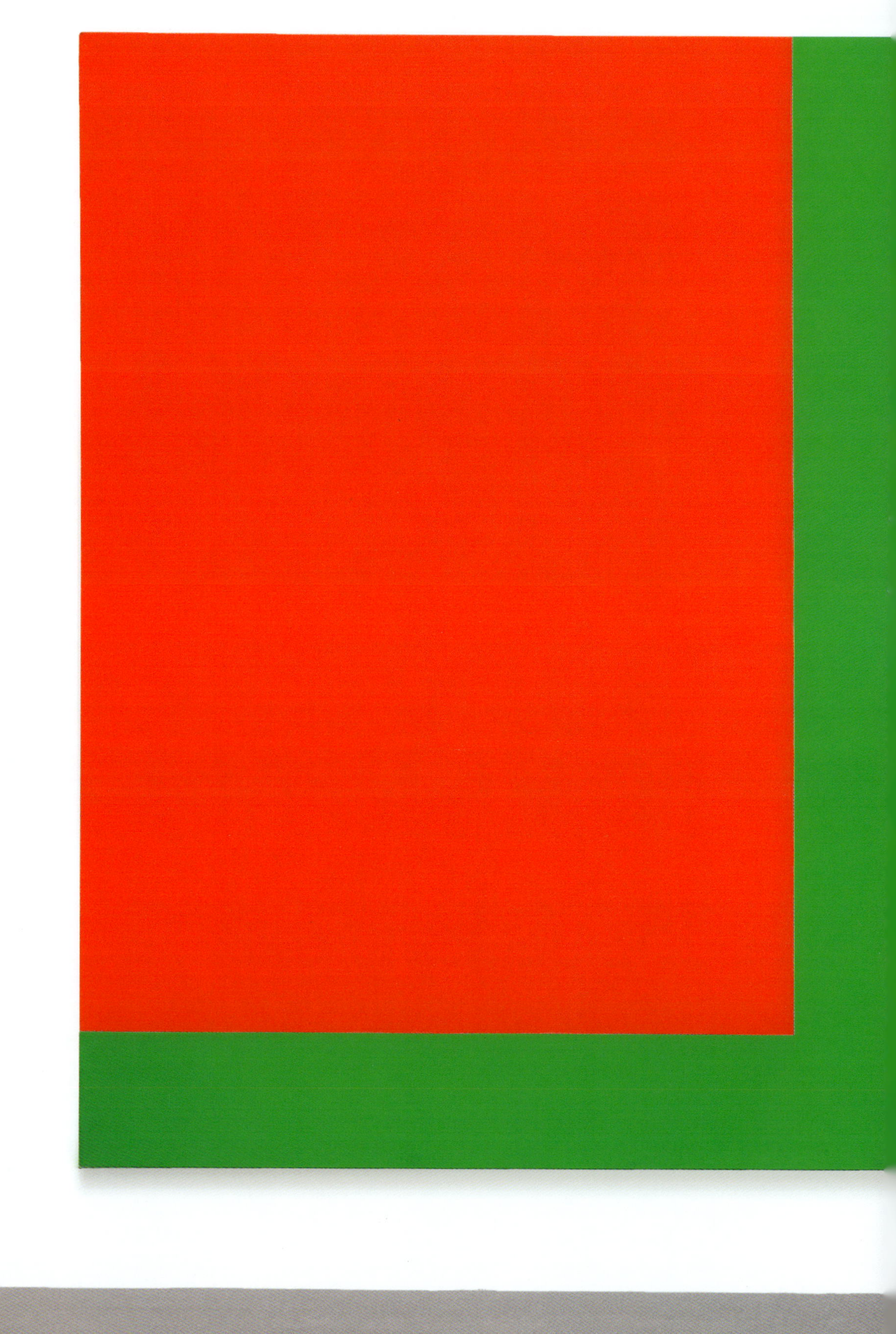

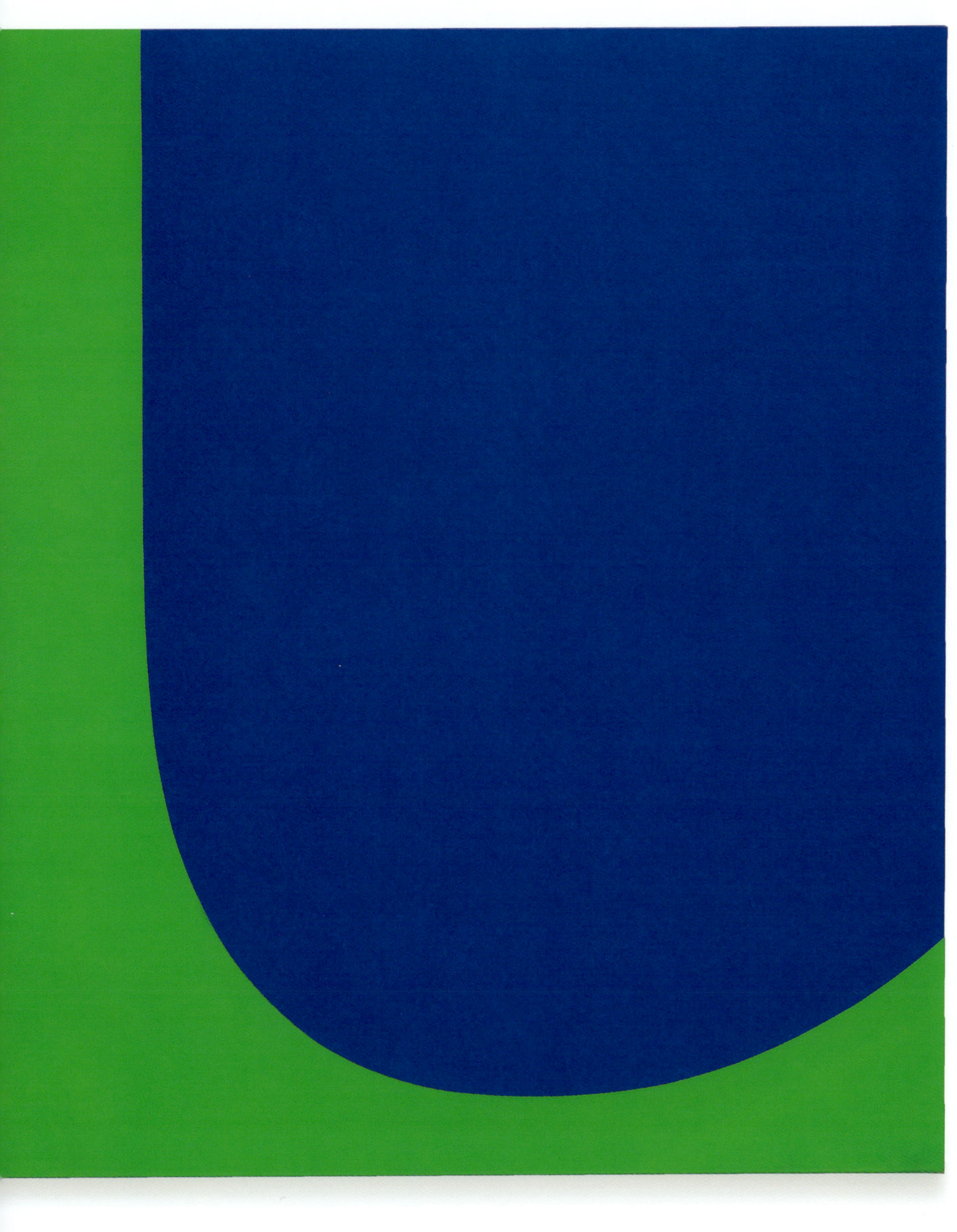

Red Blue Green, 1963
oil on canvas, 83⅝ × 135⅞ in, 212.4 × 345.1 cm

White Ring, 1963
painted aluminum, 70 × 72 × ¼ in, 177.8 × 182.9 × 0.6 cm

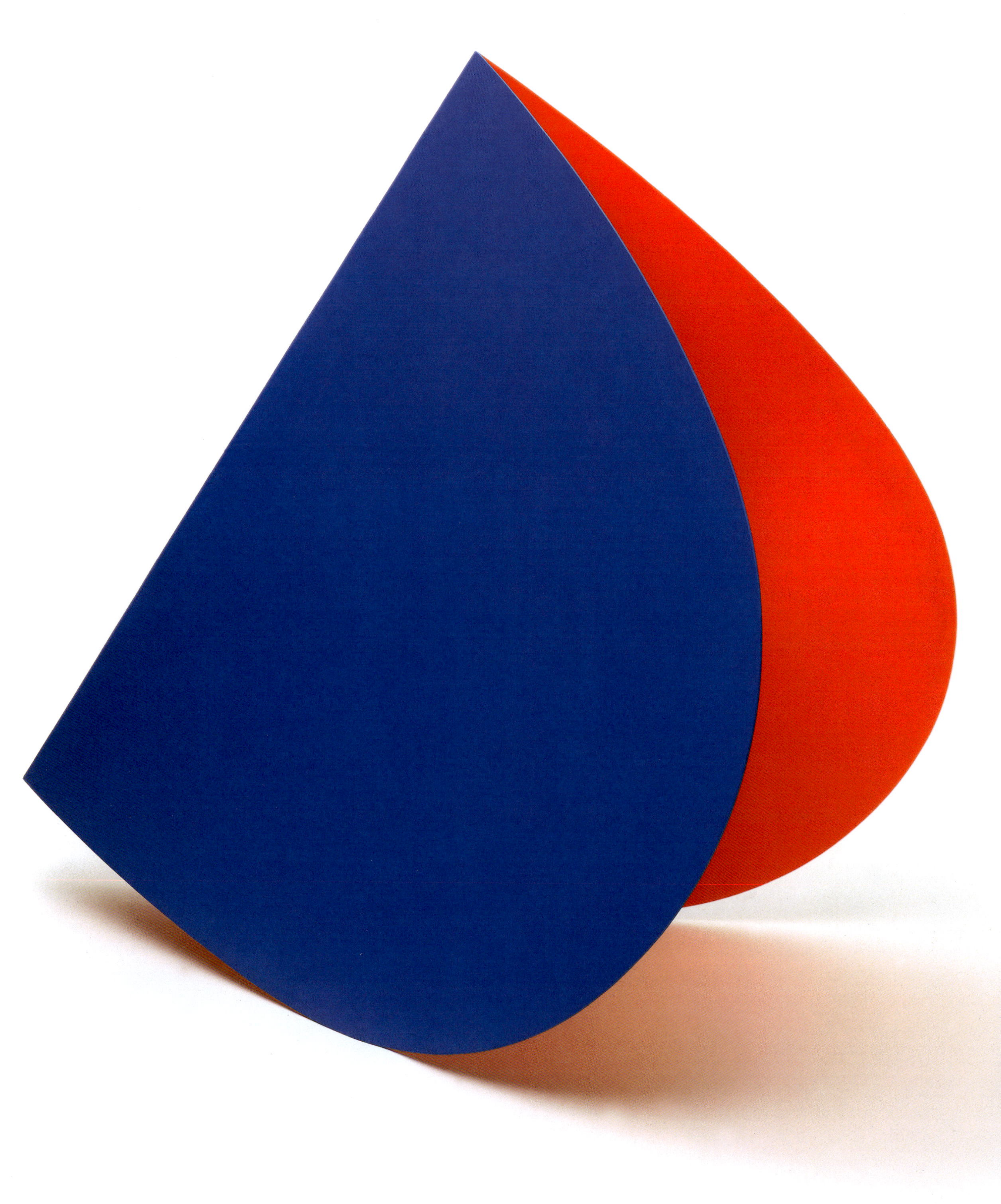

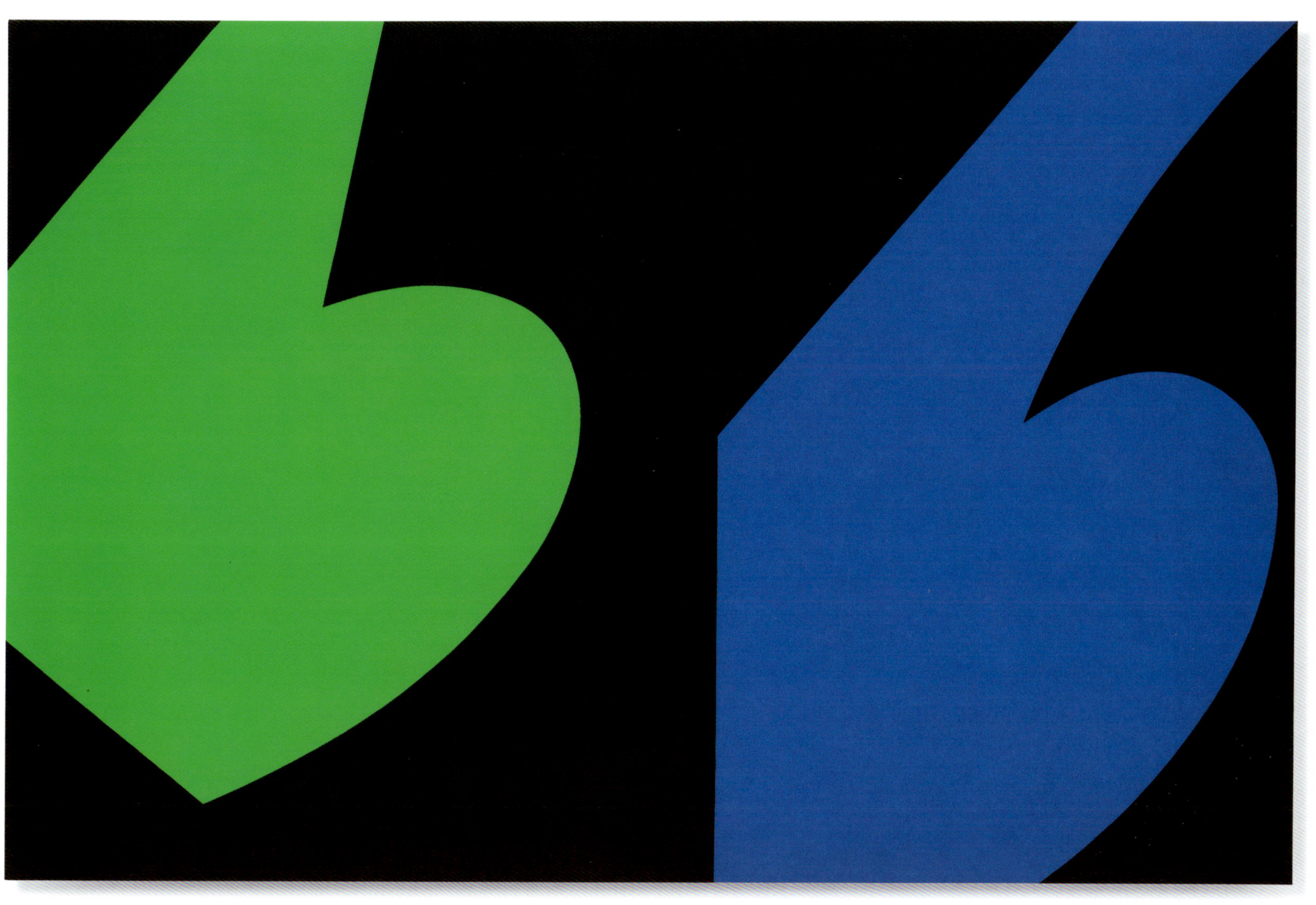

Blue Red Rocker, 1963
painted aluminum
72 × 66½ × 37½ in, 182.9 × 168.9 × 95.3 cm

Green Blue Black, 1963
acrylic on canvas
97 × 144 in, 246.4 × 365.8 cm

Red Yellow Blue I, 1963
acrylic on canvas, 3 joined panels
90 × 90 in, 228.6 × 228.6 cm

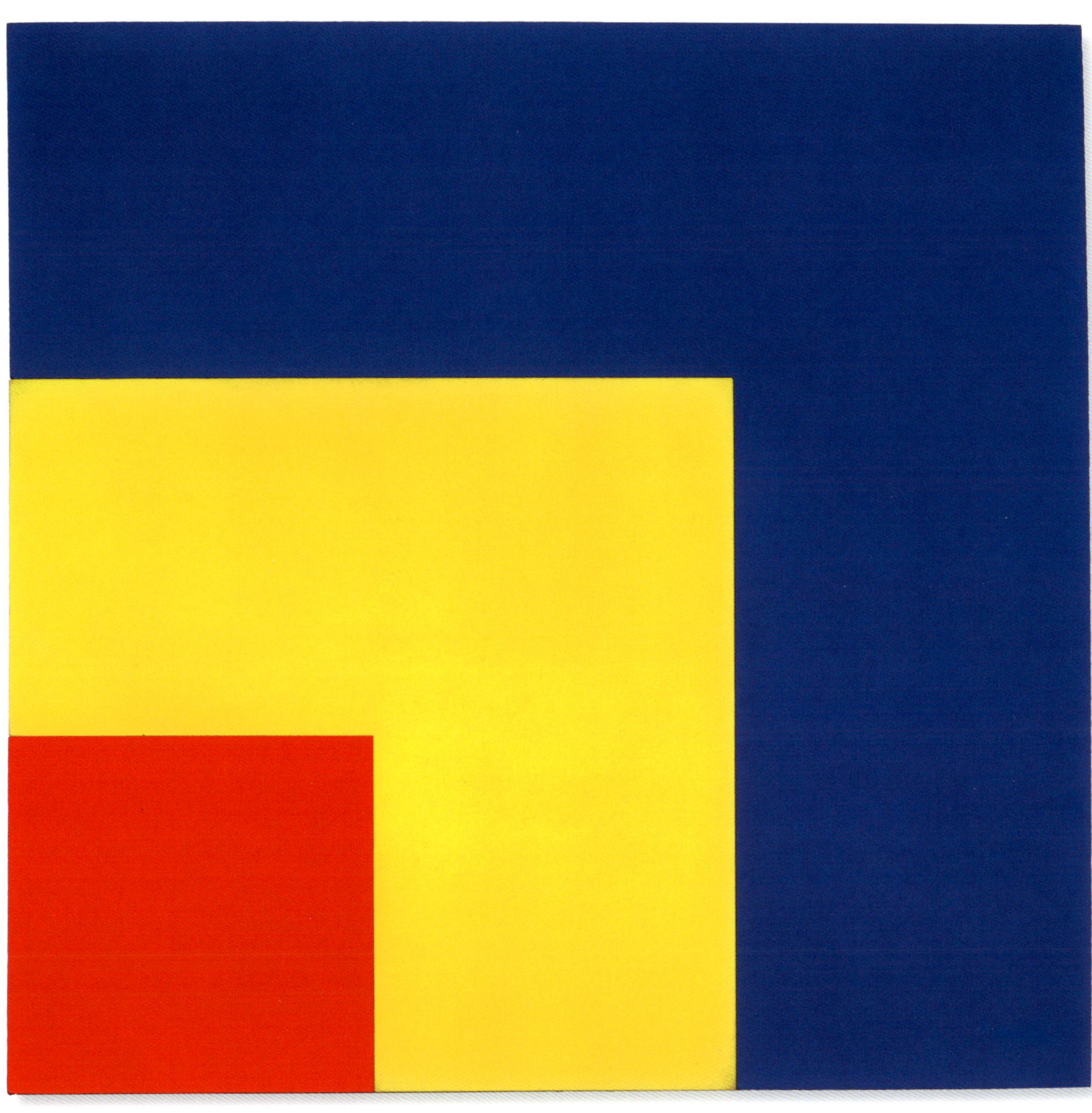

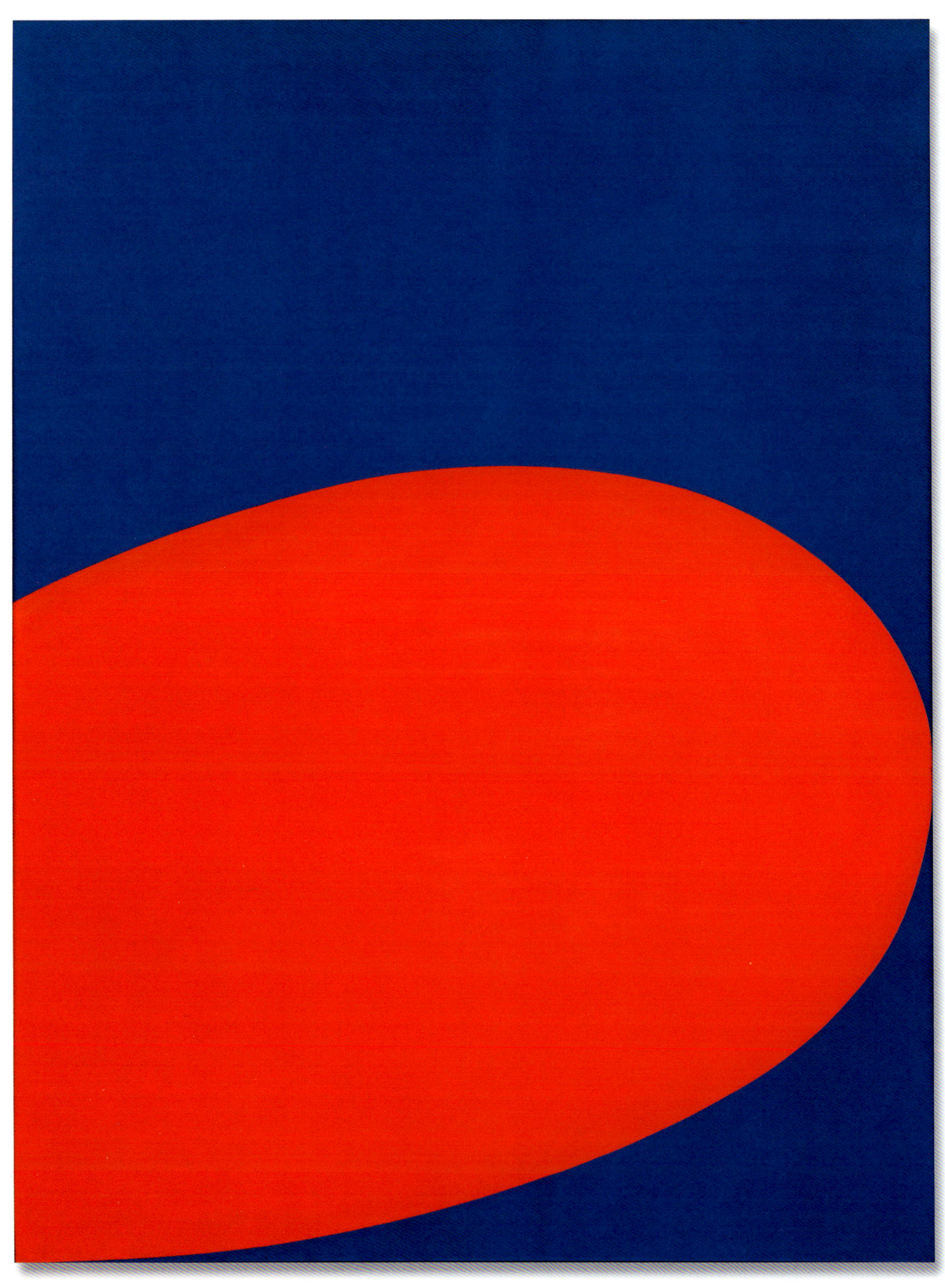

Red Blue, 1964
oil on canvas, 90 × 66 in, 228.6 × 167.6 cm

Two Curves: Blue Red, 1964
painted aluminum,
× 216 × 96 in
548.6 × 548.6 × 243.8 cm

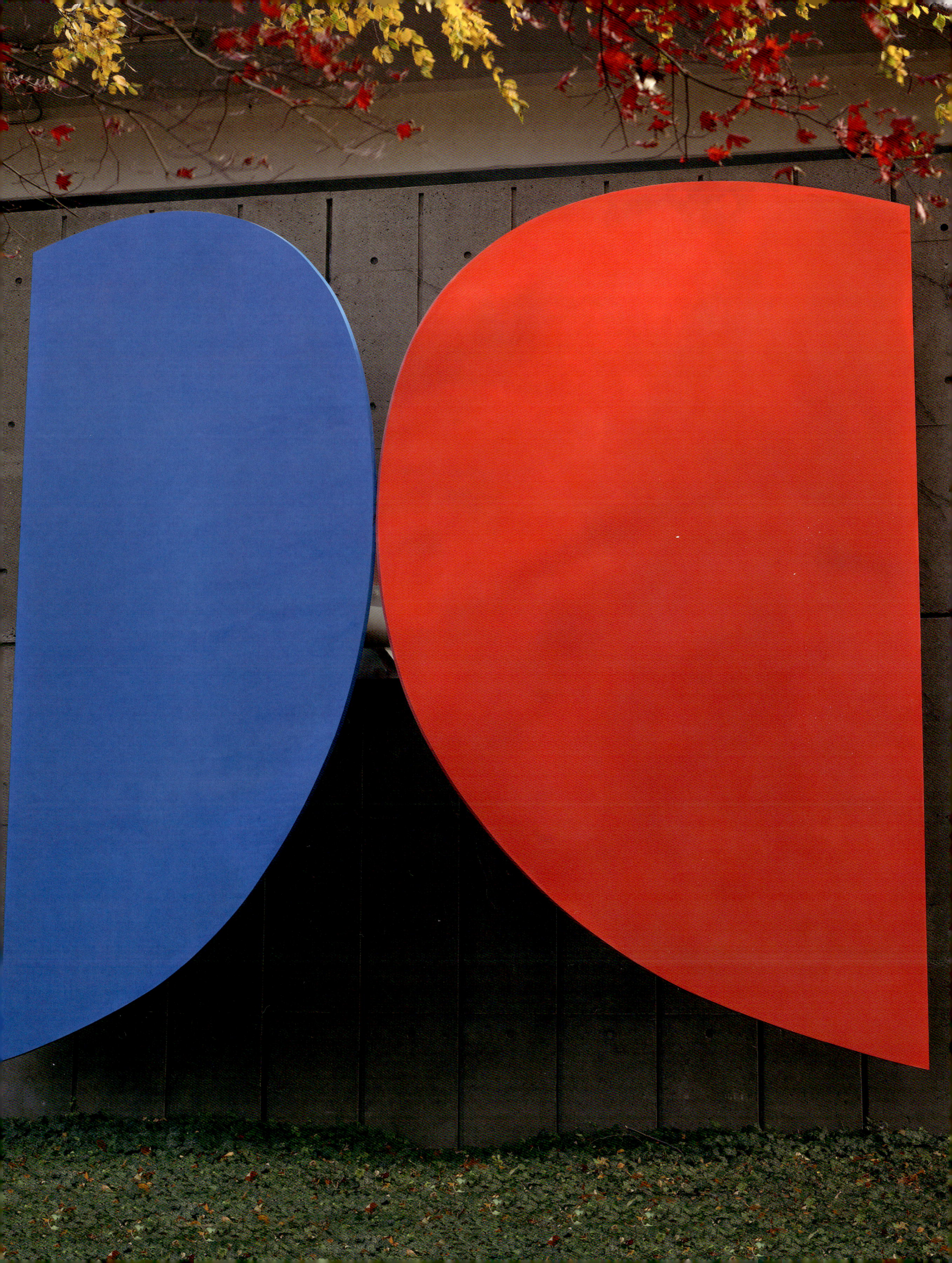

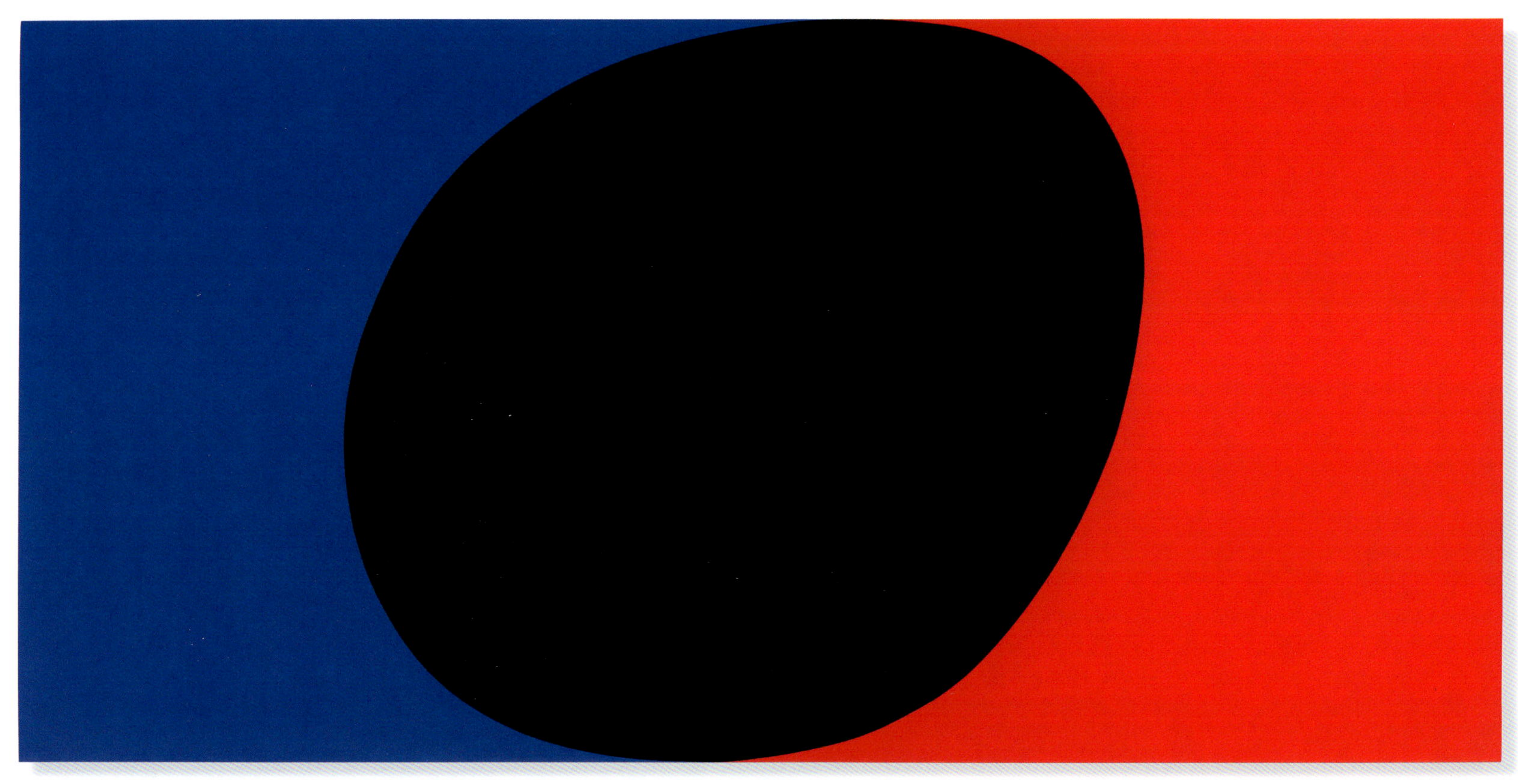

Blue Black Red, 1964
oil on canvas, 91 × 180 cm
231.1 × 457.2 cm

Blue over Blue, 1963
painted aluminum, 88 × 60 × 7½ in
223.5 × 152.4 × 19.1 cm

Red Yellow Blue II, 1965
acrylic on canvas, 3 panels
82 × 189 in, 208.3 × 480.1 cm

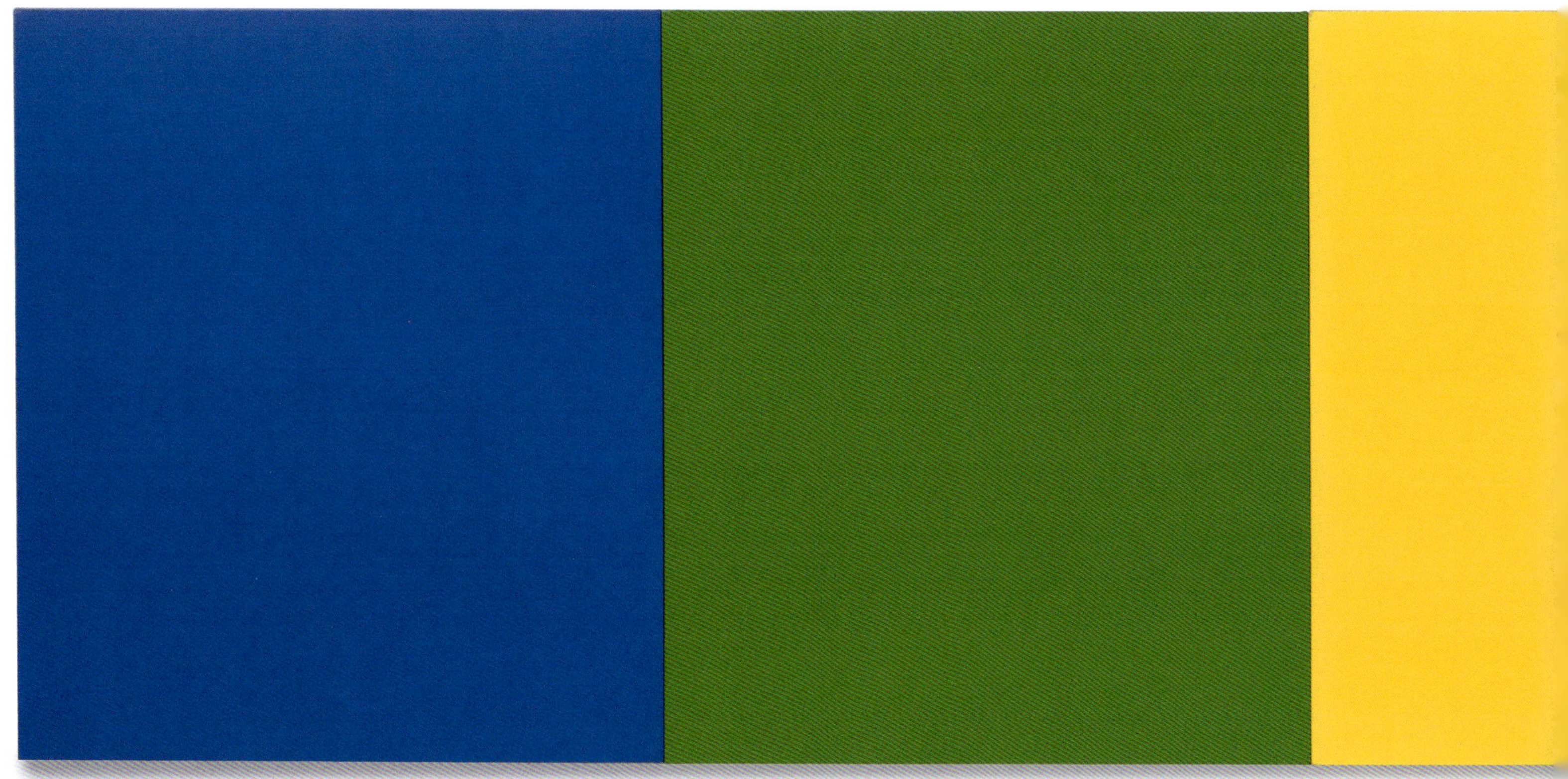

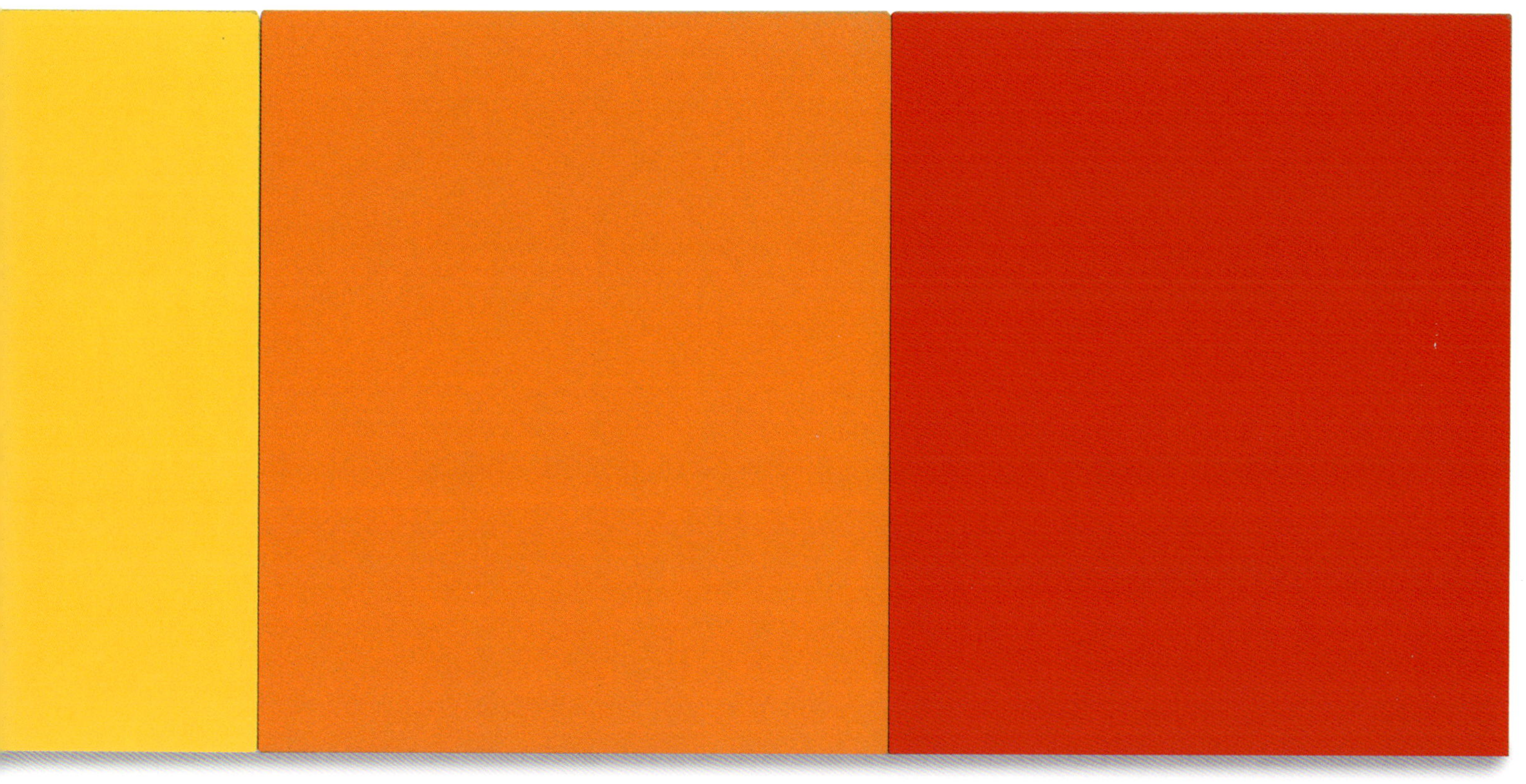

Blue Green Yellow Orange Red, 1966
oil on canvas, 5 joined panels
60 × 240 in, 152.4 × 609.6 cm

Blue Red, 1966
acrylic on canvas, 2 joined panels
81 × 60 × 81 in, 205.7 × 152.4 × 205.7 cm

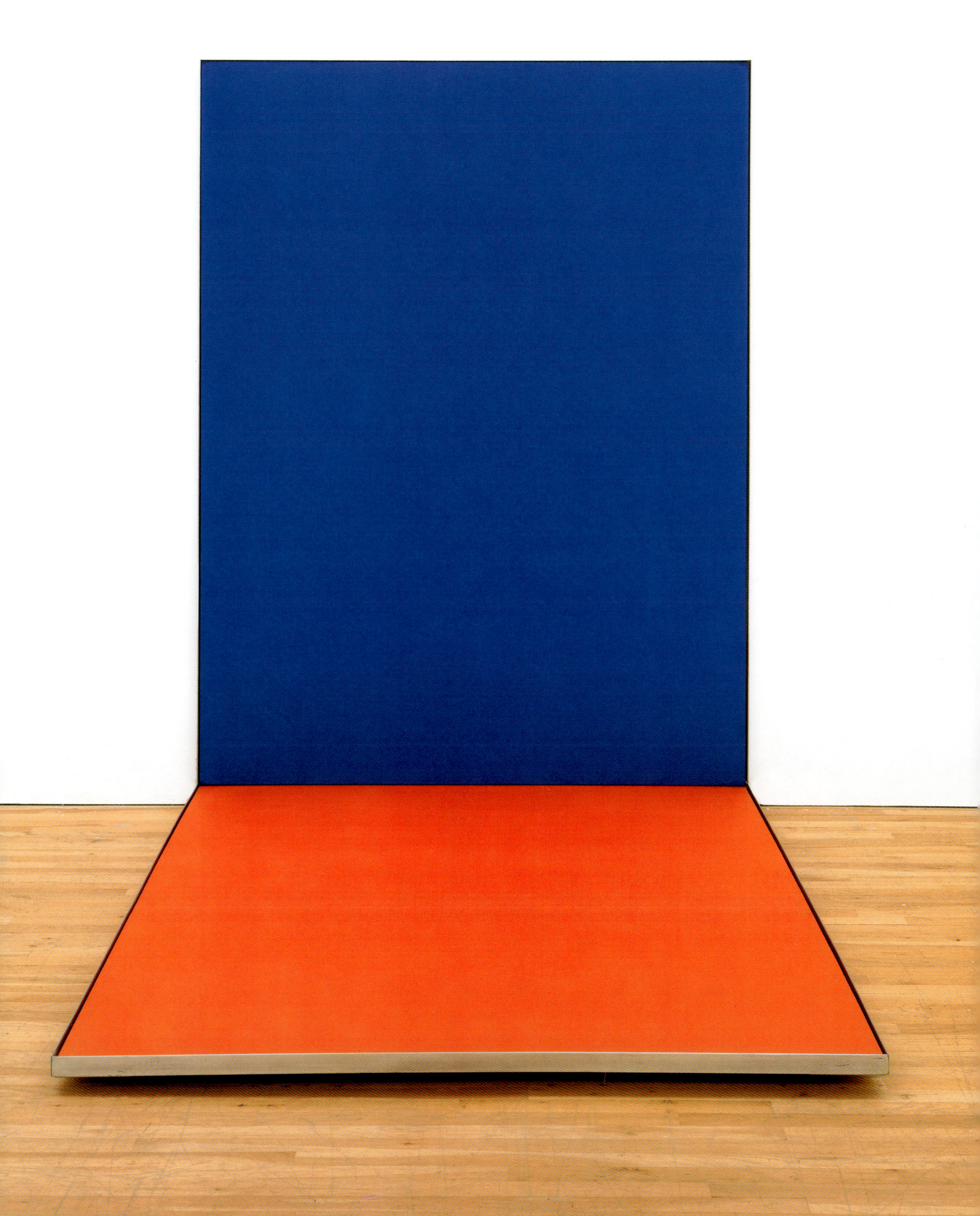

Yellow Piece, 1966
acrylic on canvas, 75 × 75 in, 190.5 × 190.5 cm

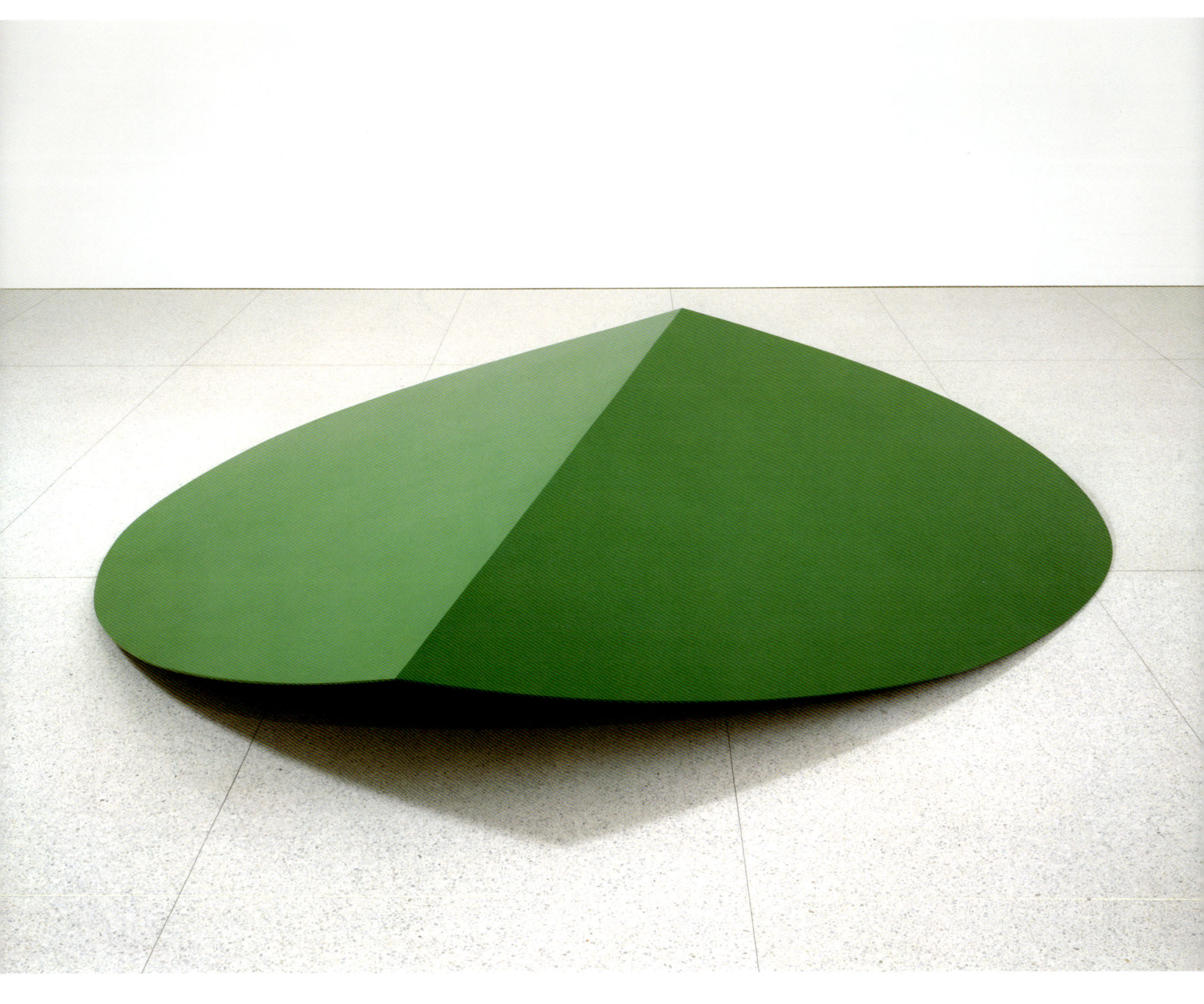

Black over White, 1966
oil on canvas, 2 joined panels
86 × 80 in, 218.4 × 203.2 cm

Green Rocker, 1968
painted aluminum, 21 × 105 × 112 in
53.3 × 266.7 × 284.5 cm

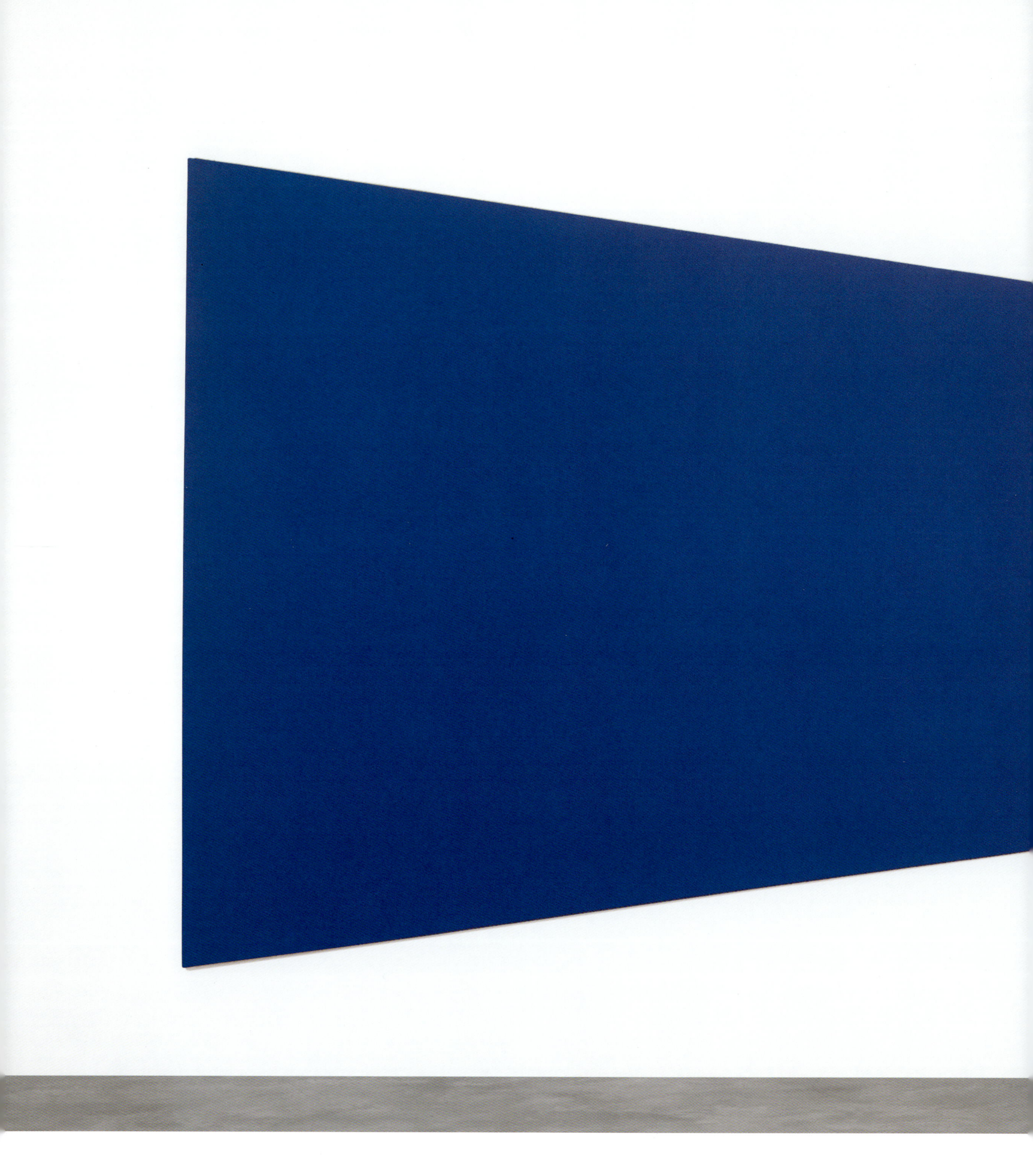

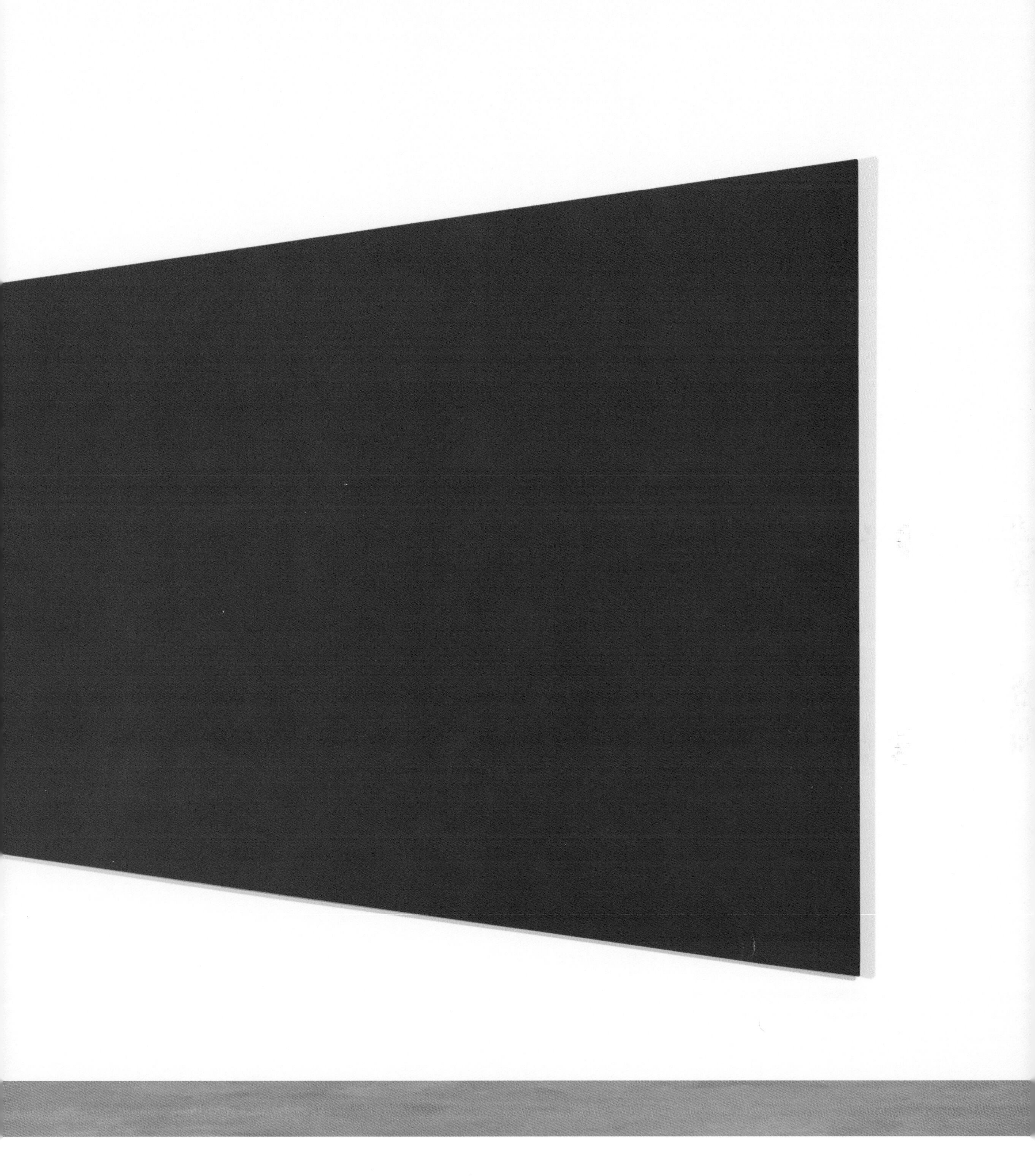

Blue Red, 1968
oil on canvas, 2 joined panels, 73 × 160 in, 185.4 × 406.4 cm

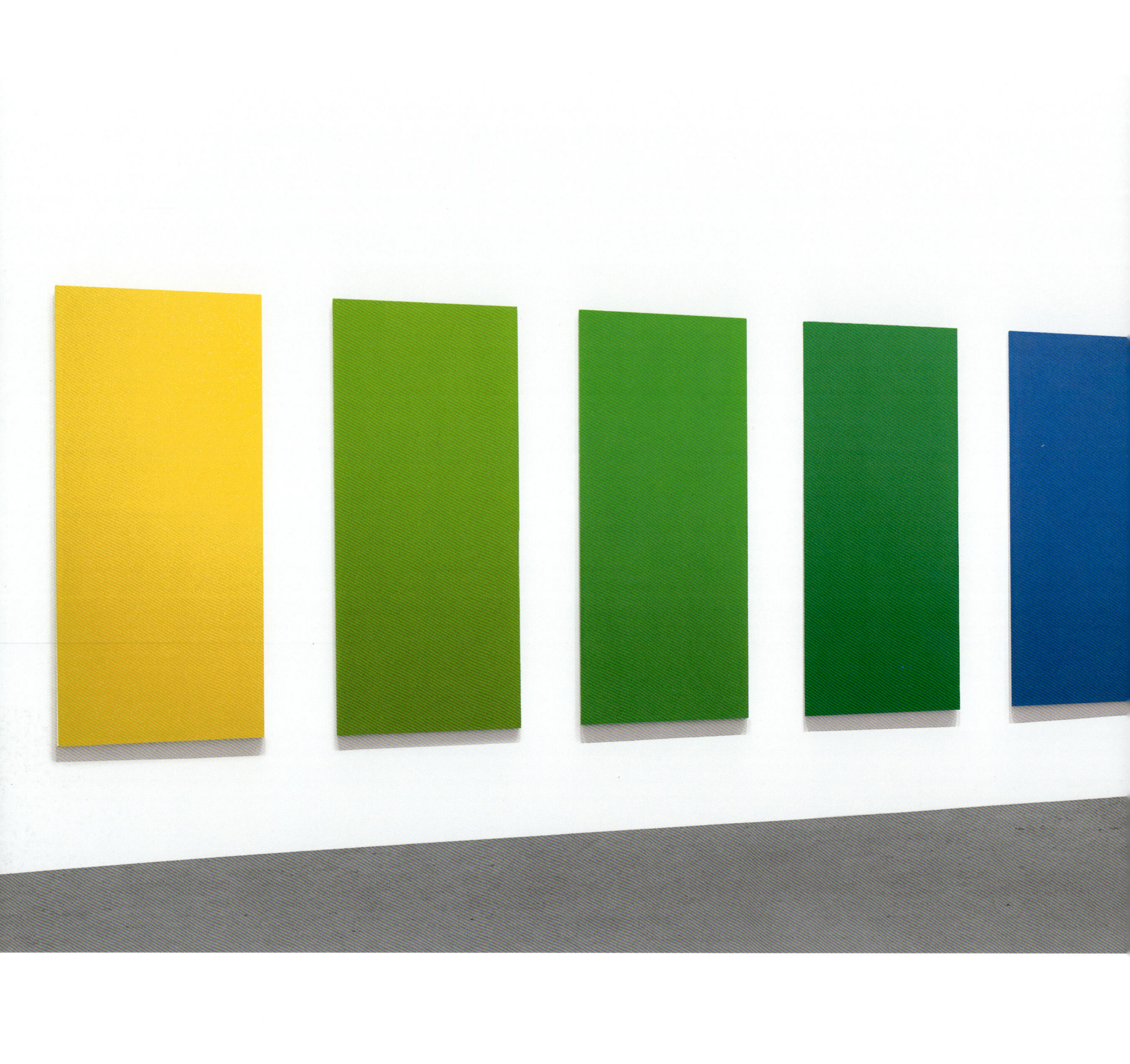

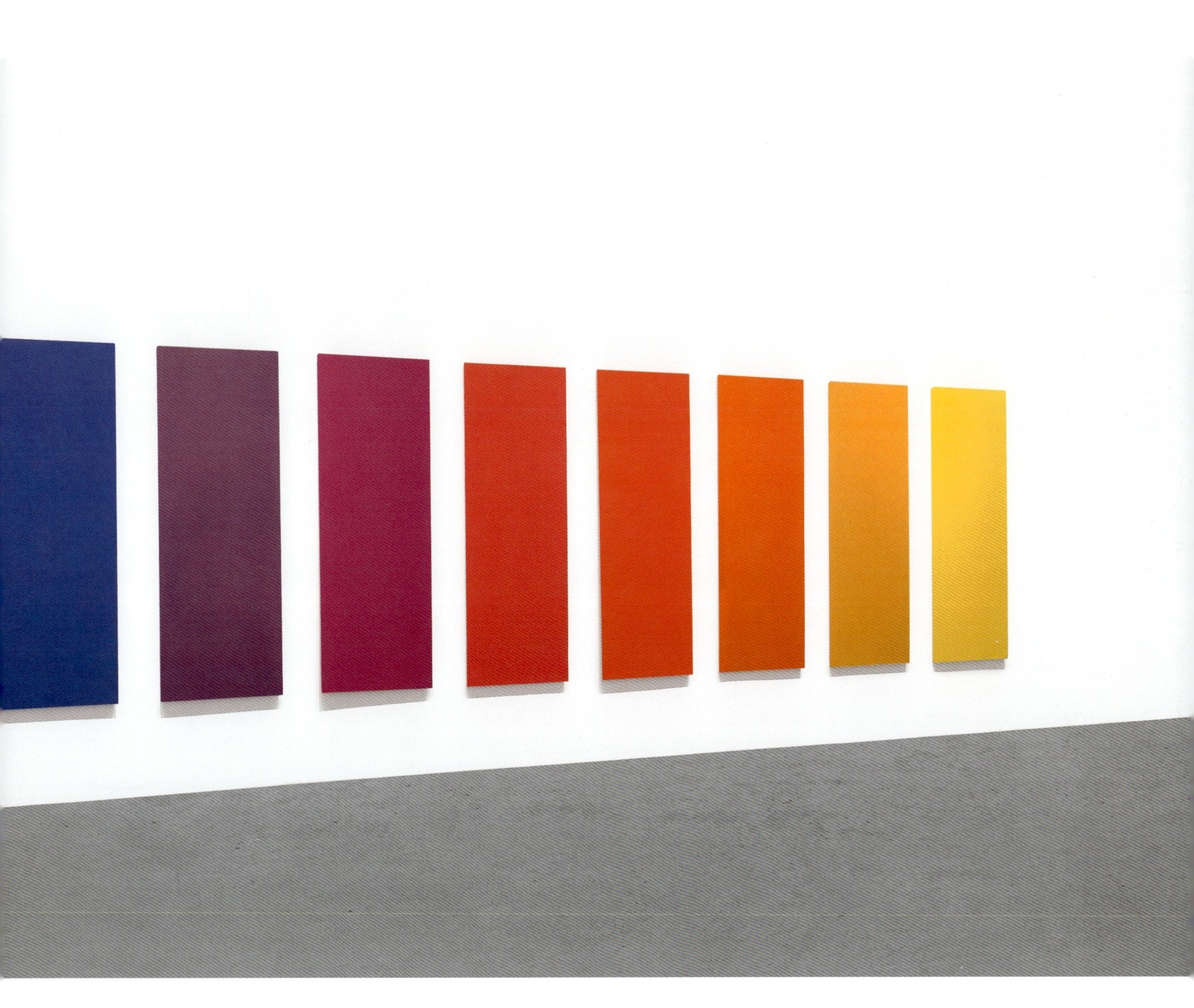

Spectrum V, 1969
oil on canvas, 13 panels, 84 × 588 in, 213.4 × 1493.5 cm

Memory Recorded and Transferred

Gavin Delahunty

Man's memory shapes its own Eden within
—Jorge Luis Borges, *Dreamtigers*

"Are there other, less narrow, descriptions of post-expressionistic art possible than that proposed by Greenberg?" enquires Lawrence Alloway in the catalogue accompanying his 1966 exhibition "Systemic Painting" held at the Guggenheim Museum.[1] Alloway's exhibition responded to one curated by Clement Greenberg two years earlier at the Los Angeles County Museum of Art, which like his own show, included the work of Ellsworth Kelly. He argued that Greenberg, in a hurried attempt to make art-historical sense of the post-Abstract Expressionist era, had inaccurately pooled a rich spectrum of styles of different emotional tone beneath the umbrella term "Post-Painterly Abstraction." The imprecision of Greenberg's term stemmed from his effort to sustain an uninterrupted line in the development of painting, specifically one that proudly asserts its two-dimensionality as a way to maintain its medium-specificity and relevance. The problem with this, according to Alloway, is that it leads us into a critical cul-de-sac of formal relations that ignore the possibility that painting's destiny may not be so linear. Moreover, Alloway proposes, "the pressing problem of art criticism now is to re-establish abstract art's connections with other experience without, of course, abandoning the now general sense of art's autonomy."[2] Some fifty years on, the flaws in Greenberg's teleological narrative of art history and his formalist method of analysis have been much discussed. But although Alloway stresses the importance of re-establishing abstract art's connections with "other experience," he is less explicit about what forms that "other experience" might take. In this essay, I will suggest that mnemonic experience is key to understanding Kelly's artistic process, the trajectory of his career, and the challenge his work poses to the kind of developmental narrative favored by Greenberg. Rather than operating according to a model of causation whereby the past results in the present, Kelly's practice has more in common with a retroactive model whereby the present acts upon and re-activates the past.

Since his earliest exhibitions, the exercise of formal analysis, at the expense of other properties of art, has been conveniently applied to Kelly's paintings. But his abstraction "developed from nature"[3] has routinely dodged this limiting parameter, allowing him to steer clear of a formalist cul-de-sac and into a unique position in contemporary critical perception. As early as 1963, the uncertainty of Kelly's status was being flagged by Henry Geldzahler: "What read at first as clear and simple forms rapidly become ambiguous and remain ambiguous." He continues, "we never see enough ... for a complete and final explanation ... the information given is insufficient to lock the painting in."[4] Take, for example, *Black Curves* of 1954 (p. 129). Two identical black forms are placed on a white ground, one suspended over the other—each has been made by joining a curvilinear form with a rectangle. When confronted with the work, one finds that one cannot approach it from left to right, owing to the curves on the left, which offer weight and structure; nor from the right to the left because of the irrefutable vertical black lines on the right of the canvas. From up to down or from down to up is irrelevant, since the forms are equivalents. Alert to Kelly's propensity for shrewdly reorganizing the negative space around and between objects, one sees the white ground in this instance as a bridge-like structure, composed of two arches, that has been placed at a right angle. Aside from this representational observation it does invite re-examination as to the nature of the forms. The uncertainty created is somewhat unsettling. It is a puzzling painting, where Kelly allows us to be carried away by the rhythmic amplitude of the two black forms that are somehow both an instrument to draw our attention to the white ground and autonomous entities possessing a definitive power over the painting.

Geldzahler strategically avoided direct association. Openly linking Kelly to Hard-Edge painting, for example, would

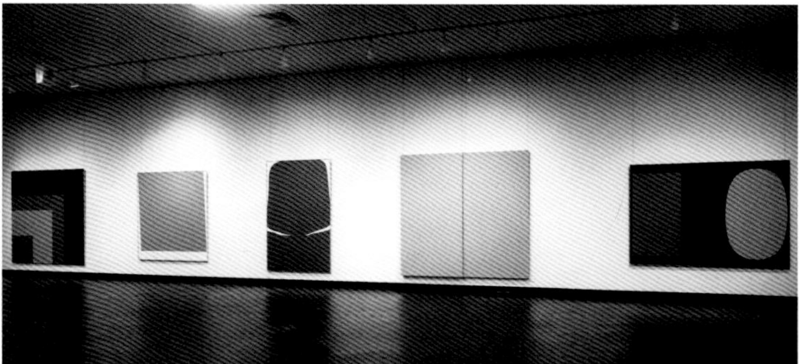

fig. 113: Installation view of Ellsworth Kelly paintings in "Toward a New Abstraction," The Jewish Museum, New York, 1963

fig. 114: *Red Blue*, 1962, oil on canvas, 90 × 69½ in, 228.6 × 176.5 cm

be oppressively simplistic and perhaps more of a hindrance than a help to our understanding of his work.[5] He recognized in Kelly a radical alternative to mainstream models of American abstraction. Kelly had picked up the baton of European geometric abstraction during six formative years in Paris and set out to address, by his own means, the burden of Cubism and the precursors of abstract art including Wassily Kandinsky, Kazimir Malevich, Piet Mondrian, František Kupka, and Johannes Itten. He had returned to New York in 1954 a relative outsider with a liberated palette. His brilliantly hedonistic use of color, exemplified by *North River*[6] of 1959 (fig. 99) (exhibited in Geldzahler's Jewish Museum exhibition [fig. 113]) found no correlation in New York. Kelly was promptly invited to participate in several other exhibitions that would turn out to be some of the most significant group shows of the early 1960s. He included *Red Blue* (1962) (fig. 114) in Greenberg's "Post-Painterly Abstraction" and *Blue Green Yellow Orange Red* (1966) (pp. 170–71) in Alloway's exhibition. These exhibitions revealed a growing critical and public interest in what Greenberg called a "move towards a physical openness of design, or towards linear clarity, or towards both"[7] and were where the reductive style later named Minimalism emerged. They inadvertently became the dominant framework for discussions of Kelly's art.

Red Blue in particular seems to evade the "hardness" that Greenberg claimed was the rationale for his selection of artists. The painting unashamedly refers to the earlier blue-black painting *Bay* (1959) (fig. 115). Its curvilinear blue line or wave naturally brings to mind a coastal inlet, and together with *Sumac* (fig. 116) (referring to a flowering plant) and *Blue Ripe* (fig. 117), both painted in 1959, indicates the artist's interest in abstracted, mnemonic impressions of visible reality. Despite the fact that by the early 1960s Kelly had moved away from referential titles that promised to uncover the works' "meaning," the curvilinear line of *Red Blue* refutes something that was fundamental to Greenberg's concept of "Post-Painterly Abstraction": that is, color uninterrupted by pressures of the hand. While economy of form, neatness of surface, and fullness of color certainly pervade *Red Blue*, there is no doubt that the energy of Kelly's hand is present—a trait that was stylistically and theoretically at odds with the poured and stained canvases of exhibiting artists Helen Frankenthaler, Morris Louis, and Jules Olitski. Alloway's inclusion of Kelly in "Systemic Painting" was not an attempt to reasonably explain the "new art" as attempted by Greenberg in "Post-Painterly Abstraction," or to define it, as was the case with Kynaston McShine's "Primary Structures" (which took place at the Jewish Museum in 1966 and included Kelly's 1963 *Blue Disk*) (fig. 112). On the contrary, Alloway—hyper-aware of both shows—was skeptical of what he saw as emergent and sweeping generalizations.[8] From these shows the word "minimal" increasingly began to reference any stylistic austerity and it is no wonder that Kelly started to be associated with art lacking emotional or narrative content. Speaking directly to this point less than a year later in 1967 in his review of Kelly's exhibition at Sidney Janis Gallery,

fig. 115: *Bay*, 1959, oil on canvas, 70 × 50 in, 177.8 × 127 cm

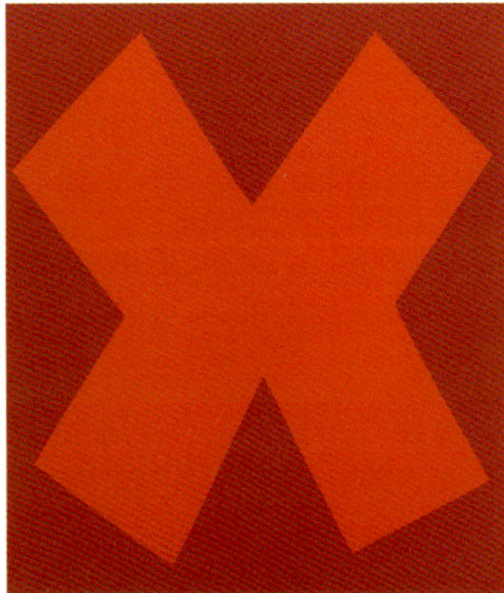

fig. 116: *Sumac*, 1959, oil on canvas, 74 × 63 in, 188 × 160 cm

John Perreault points out that "though superficially related to minimalist styles, Kelly's compositional and even coloristic austerity makes a warmth and sensuousness that separates him from younger, more ice-bound painters."[9] Having contributed an essay to an early and important solo exhibition of Kelly's work in London in June 1962, Alloway was familiar with his more biomorphic work. One might reasonably ask, then, why he chose to include *Blue Green Yellow Orange Red* in "Systemic Painting," as opposed to another work that might have made his point more explicitly.

For example, the abstract format yet figurative suggestion of *Rebound* (1959) (p. 145) addresses head on the question of drama as a structural component of Kelly's work. Defined as "to bound or spring back from force of impact; to recover, as from ill health or discouragement; to move from one relationship to the next right away to avoid the pain of a breakup,"[10] the polysemous title consents to a number of interpretations: an emotional narrative, an intense kinetic force or a mnemonic and reflective process. Compositionally the two swelling white forms relate to one another in such a lucid fashion that the viewer is immediately absorbed and wholly unaware of anything other than their balloon-like mass. The black fragments, however, play a decisive role. They contribute to the qualities of the white forms, which without them could be interpreted as being mere silhouettes that are translucent and weightless. The most straightforward instinctual interpretation of the painting is to understand the white as the principal form and the black as its ground. In this basic reading the two round parts take on an organic quality that suggests the gentle pressing of two supple forms against one another. Inverting this analysis by handing over the compositional authority to the black forms creates a visual tension between that hanging from the upper part and the one rising from the lower part of the canvas. The two masses appear to be under some gravitational, electrical or magnetic force. Whatever the impulses at play, push or pull, their relative proximity to one another creates a single powerful effect. Writing for *Arts Magazine* in 1976, Kenneth Baker similarly chose to highlight "the white gap at the center of the canvas." He points out Kelly's reliance on the conventions of linear perspective as a tool to guide the viewer's interpretation by referencing a "recognizable" system of viewing. Arguing convincingly for the "painting's deep and deliberate affinity with figurative art," he states that it "offers the paradoxical sensation of seeing something in an utterly characteristic aspect without being able to say what you see ... yet the sensation of seeing something essential stands."[11] A flirtation with deductive reasoning is at the heart of *Rebound*, where Kelly compounds the impression of the vaguely familiar with something totally nameless. The suspension impulsively binds the viewer to the painting in a cycle of interrogative thinking that repeats, or rebounds, over and over again.

In his introduction to the catalogue accompanying "Systemic Painting," Alloway reminds us that in Kelly's early work—for instance *South Ferry* (1956) (p. 138), *Broadway* (1958) (p. 144), and *Jersey* (1958) (p. 146)—the city of New York was used as a point of reference, drawing comparison between Kelly and the likes of Malevich and Mondrian, both of whom considered their forms to be from and of the man-made environment of the city. As already mentioned, Kelly had found it mostly unnecessary to title his paintings after 1960 and Alloway held that "they retain a sign-quality that relates them to the world as a place we live in and know. They do not call upon the other worldly resources

fig. 117: *Blue Ripe*, 1959, oil on canvas, 60 × 60 in, 152.4 × 152.4 cm

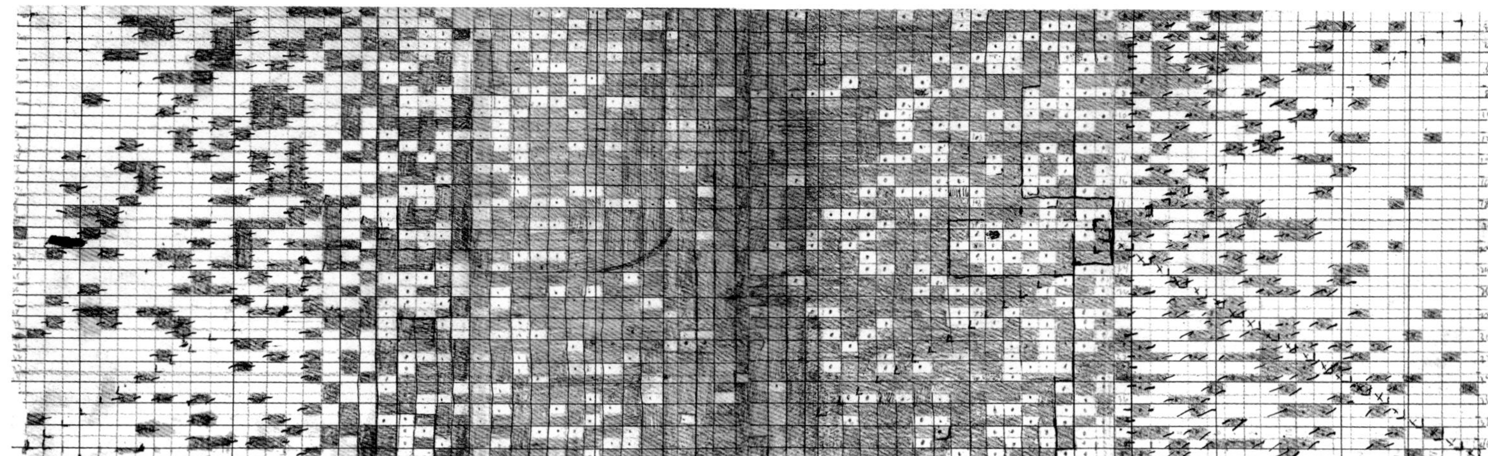

fig. 118: Study for *Seine,* 1951, graphite and ink on paper, 4¾ × 15⅞ in, 12.1 × 40.3 cm

of modern painting."[12] Perhaps with this knowledge, Alloway selected *Blue Green Yellow Orange Red* as an extreme example of Kelly's defamiliarization, confident that its visual warmth would single it out as separate from the "minimal" abstract art with which he was being connected.

The true roots of Kelly's modular framework as a carrier of form can be traced from *Seine* (1951) (p. 66) through *Train Landscape* (1953) (p. 77) to the likes of *Blue Green Yellow Orange Red*. In *Seine*, Kelly described how he was investigating the question of randomness and atomization. He gridded the wood on which he was working proportionally into forty-one vertical units by eighty horizontal, adding up to 3,280 units in eighty columns. The outermost right column, was left unfilled. Gradually working toward the center, Kelly populated the gridded field by hand-painting each black square: the second column, "column 1," with one black square, the third, "column 2," with two, the forth, "column 3," with three, and so on. Increasing one unit per column predetermined that the fortieth column would be an unbroken black band (fig. 118). Irrespective of reading the work from left to right or right to left, the power of *Seine* is created by its ordering system and sustained by its central black stripe. *Seine* relates factually and visually to the Parisian river. Encountering this arresting pictorial effect one evening, Kelly opted, when planning the composition, to reverse the specular reflection—black where the moonlight struck the river and white for the cold matte black of the river's surface. This playful reordering of information adds a further dimension to the work; it activates the visual material that would typically be discarded by the novice eye. Kelly, however, reminds us of the interdependency of black and white when experiencing the phenomenon of shimmering moonlight. The awareness and sensitivity required to complete *Seine* led him to investigate in greater depth the potency and specificity of spatial relations. As a result, he decided to enlarge each visual element; consequently, the visual potency of each color and its individual strength and identity is enhanced.

Train Landscape is composed of three horizontal panels. The colors of the painting were inspired by neighboring fields of lettuce, spinach, and mustard seen through the window of a train by Kelly *en route* to Zurich from Paris, in the same way that grass or trees when viewed *en masse* are normally seen not as discrete entities but as blocks of color. Kelly intensifies the color of each plant, raises the flat landscape into an upright position, and levels the crops into three equal yet contrasting bands. The division between each species intended by the farmer to avoid cross-pollination is removed by Kelly, who closes the borders so that the distance between the fields is more or less eliminated. His hybrid is dynamic and persuasive. In their new arrangement, the lettuce, spinach, and mustard colors mutually benefit from one another. Kelly succeeds in generating a vivid mode of pictorial representation that distills the chromatic essence of his experience. *Train Landscape* is based on fact and is therefore convincing. In his text for the catalogue accompanying the exhibition "The Art of the Real: USA 1948–1968," E.C. Goossen asserts, "although it is not necessary to know Kelly's sources to experience his art as art, knowing them helps one understand why his work has such structural integrity."[13] Goossen is correct that it is not essential to have the narrative account behind each artwork (although there often is one); this is because certain emotions are triggered by Kelly's use of color that supersede the necessity for the narrative component. Observing a changing landscape by train or the flickering reflections of light on water are powerful somatic and mnemonic experiences. That emotional information is accessed, reactivated, and reconstructed by Kelly in his abstract paintings.

It is fair to say that abstraction has a remarkable range and that Kelly's paintings have been from time to time obscured by persistent concepts from other fields: Minimalism's severe geometry and conceptual frameworks, for instance, or, not much better, a comparison to Hard-Edge painting or Post-Painterly Abstraction. From his earliest days in New York, Kelly was ambivalent to such forms of labeling. He respected the Abstract Expressionist painters who frequented the Cedar Tavern, but his practice stood apart from theirs and he was never fully accepted into—nor at home within—their social circle. Speaking in a recent interview, he described how Franz Kline had attended his first Betty Parsons show in 1956 and had looked visibly puzzled by his painting *Bar* (1955) (p. 132). In 1958, when Kelly took part in the Pittsburgh International Exhibition of Contemporary Painting and Sculpture at the Carnegie Institute, he was introduced to Kline by Jack Youngerman at the after-party. Kline turned to Kelly and said "You're the one who makes these beautiful color paintings." Shocked, Kelly thought he was being made fun of, but Youngerman quickly assured him, "He means it, he means it!," making Kelly weep.[14]

Kelly's is an abstraction derived from fragmented perceptions of nature with a bias towards the discovery of beauty. In this sense, his paintings are representational, though in the sense of "re-presentation" rather than of copying; "they bear the traces of perceptual experiences."[15] He re-presents the world with a singular perspective delineated through blocks of color. The natural and man-made world is a material for Kelly and his capacity to abstract and manipulate elements from it flows from a deep appreciation of it. As Christoph Grunenberg has noted, the paintings' "oblique references to nature go beyond the direct abstraction of visual forms and present a wider sensual repertoire of memories, impressions, and sensations."[16] They invoke the artist at work, his energy and temperament. The personal becomes somehow tangible in his paintings, his elementary shapes turning into live expressive forms. For the sensitive eye, Kelly's paintings have an active, articulate quality.

The difficulty with Kelly's art, like that of all great art, is that it is not easy to define. It doesn't play by the rules; it must be discovered in a sustained experience of looking. The demand for it to fall in line—to be neatly categorized, organized, quantified—is a demand for a certain kind of order, familiar and reassuring. In his groundbreaking 1969 appeal for Kelly's art to be understood in another way, John Coplans claimed that "the morphology of Ellsworth Kelly's art remains virtually unknown," indicating that the work made prior to his return to New York was critical to the discussion and understanding of the artist's practice. Several pieces of the Kelly puzzle were missing, said Coplans, and in order even to begin to grasp the nature of his abstraction,its impetus and momentum, we must loop back to fully appreciate the degree to which his "early art overtly reveals his typical predisposition for a non-linear development."[17] This would seem to suggest that it was misleading to include Kelly in either "Post-Painterly Abstraction" or "Systemic Painting" without emphasizing his painterly and coloristic complexity.

This argument was later picked up and notably advanced by Yve-Alain Bois in 1999 and 2004. Bois points out the pleasure that Kelly takes in revisiting sketches or collages he has made decades ago, and how he is persistently drawn to them—so much so that he faithfully brings them to fruition in painting and sculpture.[18] Kelly's paintings have overturned the clear-cut path of abstraction. Recalling sketches or collages for re-production allows him to re-access memories from the past. It can take several years, even decades, for him to replay a memory of that precise moment when he captured a shape from some undetected area of the visual world. Of course, these recollections are not identical to the original experience, but are an echo of that instant—one that has been stimulated by some current situation. The upshot of this is that Kelly's memories are not ossified in time. They are accessible by some *aide-mémoire* from the present or an associative object from the past. Somewhere within this arc, new information is also incorporated. Thwarting conception in terms of a linear progression, this retroactive movement is indicative not only of Kelly's artistic process, but of the way in which his work troubles established art-historical categories and developmental narratives.

1 Lawrence Alloway, "Introduction," in *Systemic Painting* (New York: The Solomon R. Guggenheim Foundation, 1966), p. 16.
2 Ibid., p. 20.
3 John I.H. Baur and Rosalind Irvine (eds), *Young America 1957: Thirty American Painters and Sculptors under Thirty Five* (New York: Whitney Museum of American Art/Clark & Way, Inc.), p. 41.
4 Henry Geldzahler, "Ellsworth Kelly," in *Toward a New Abstraction* (New York: The Jewish Museum, 1963), p. 16.
5 "Hard-Edge painting" was a term coined by curator and *Los Angeles Times* art critic Jules Langsner in 1959.
6 *North River* was initially titled *Blue White.* See p. 17 of *Toward a New Abstraction* (New York: The Jewish Museum, 1963)
7 Clement Greenberg, "Post-Painterly Abstraction," Los Angeles County Museum, April 23–June 7, 1964.
8 "Systemic Painting" had been scheduled to open in 1964. However, the show was postponed to gain critical distance from "Post-Painterly Abstraction."
9 John Perreault, "Color as Light," *The Village Voice* (March 9, 1967), pp. 12–13 (review of "Ellsworth Kelly," Sidney Janis Gallery, New York, 1967).
10 http://dictionary.reference.com/browse/rebound
11 Kenneth Barker, "Ellsworth Kelly's 'Rebound'," in *Arts Magazine* (September, 1976), p. 111.
12 Lawrence Alloway, "Introduction," in *Ellsworth Kelly* (London: Arthur Tooth & Sons, Ltd., 29 May–23 June, 1962), n.p.
13 E.C. Goossen, in *The Art of the Real: USA 1948–1968* (New York: The Museum of Modern Art, New York, 1968) p. 8
14 Interview with the author, Spencertown, August, 2014.
15 Briony Fer, "Utopia," in *The Infinite Line: Re-making Art After Modernism* (New Haven: Yale University Press, 2004), p. 190.
16 Christoph Grunenberg, "Modern Icons: the Contradictions of Ellsworth Kelly," in *Ellsworth Kelly in St. Ives* (London: Tate Publishing, 2006), p. 34.
17 John Coplans, "The Earlier work of Ellsworth Kelly," in *Artforum* (summer, 1969), p. 48.
18 For two excellent descriptions of this see Yve-Alain Bois, *Ellsworth Kelly: The Early Drawings, 1948–1955* (Cambridge, MA: Harvard University Art Museums, 1999) and *Ellsworth Kelly: Tablet 1948–1973* (New York: The Drawing Center, 2004).

That Will Be That

Richard Shiff

Imagine walking briskly through an urban environment. A paper cup—flattened, abraded, its surface printed bright blue on white with graphic figures and lettering—draws your eye to the pavement (fig. 119). You experience involuntary, heightened awareness. If you believe that litter of this sort would never divert your attention, accept the fact that any object can distract eyes attuned to looking. The blue pigment of the cup is arresting. The conical profile also has allure: two straight edges fan out from their acute angle, joined by the curve of a graceful arc, the segment of a much larger circle—an inherently curious form. The span of the curved edge (not the linear curve itself) equals the length of each of the two straight edges. This in turn implies that the three-sided object is either equilateral or not, depending on how you figure it—angle to angle (yes), line against line (no). But only if you do figure it. The object itself demands looking, not figuring. Its symmetry is virtual symmetry, sufficient to generate virtual interest—an unconscious attraction that erupts into consciousness. It can break a walker's stride. You pause to look at the cup.

Abstract Us

The surface figuration of the flattened cup affords an alternative focus. "Look at me," the top-hatted snowman seems to say. Its inscription ("double flavor") alludes to snow cones, otherwise known as Italian ices, an American street food. To attend to this figure is to read the culture of the image, perceiving a theme (sweet, cooling refreshment)

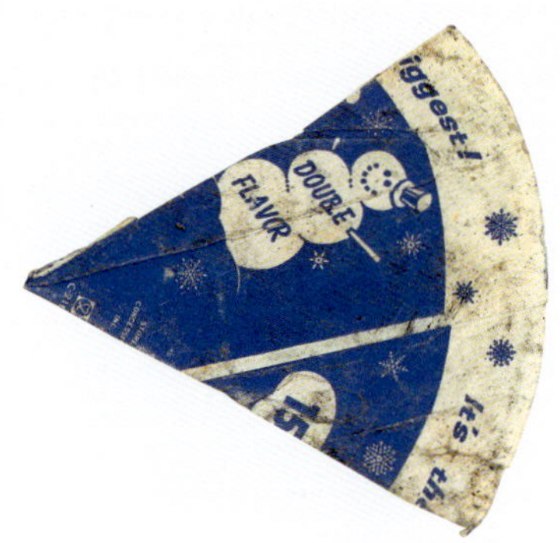

fig. 119: *Tablet 34* (detail), found crushed paper cone cup

abstracted from various semiotic parts: cartoons, lettering, a "snow" pattern. And within this emergent interpretive context, blue will signify "cold" just as the conical shape becomes the container of shaved Italian ice. But to fix instead on the color or the shape—to be distracted by these qualities alone, isolated from thoughts of summertime treats—would prove satisfying enough. If qualities are to be abstracted from the incident of the cup, the first among them must be those of the immediate sensation. An ironic reversal is likely to occur. The visual effect has the potential to *abstract us*, that is, to draw us as viewers away from our typical, culturally conditioned patterns of observation. From the primary experience, we might never pass to secondary concepts. We see variation on a conical shape in lieu of fantasizing over flavored ice. Sensations first distract and then they abstract. They deflect the drive to meaning.

What, precisely, is distraction? And what is abstraction? Prefixes matter: abs-traction and dis-traction must differ. In what respect? In common usage, the verb *abstract* and the noun *abstraction* suggest an economy of forms or a process of conceptualization (as in the abstractions of higher mathematics). Both verb and noun retain the directional force of their prefix. Abstraction refers to the action of drawing away: *ab(s)-*, from, away; *trahere* (*tractus*), to draw, to drag. If abstraction draws away, then *dis*-traction draws apart. Both are actions of separation and differentiation. Everyday logic dictates that whatever element is drawn, dragged, pulled or otherwise transferred from one state or location to another amounts to less than the initial undifferentiated mass. Abstraction and distraction are reductions, actions that remove something from something greater.

In the case of abstraction, the loss is motivated by expectation of a gain. Abstraction accomplishes reduction to an essence, and essences are worth more than their unrefined sources. This, at least, is the general assumption: whether materially or conceptually, abstraction distills, clarifies, epitomizes. It eliminates only what had little value to begin with. Not so with distraction. We assume that lesser things, trivialities, distract from things of greater value, including the essence of a matter of interest. Distractions lead attention astray or adrift. But consider people who experience one distraction after another. Are they mentally removed, distanced, or (as we say) "distracted"? Do their faces bear an "abstract look"? Probably not. Their senses are acute. Their experience is negative only according to the philosophical notion that a distracting sensation counteracts whatever state of mind preceded the current sensory intervention: "It is the compulsion, the absolute constraint upon us to think otherwise than we have been thinking that constitutes experience."[1] Most likely, people who are easily distracted find ordinary features of the environment stimulating to an extraordinary degree. They sense new sensations, think new thoughts. An artist capitalizes on experience that arrives by distraction, abstracting it.

The Impersonal Personal

It was Ellsworth Kelly who noticed the flattened paper cup. He had no need to speculate on whether its aesthetic quality might be arresting: it had already arrested him before he could think. As it happened, the shape of the object held his interest more than any other feature; the asymmetrical symmetry of the conical form compelled his moment of sensory distraction. This cup, this form, eventually found its appropriate place among the studies collected within his *Tablet*, a visual archive of his sketches of found ideas (*Tablet 34 (Five Sketches)*, 1950s, 1960s [fig. 120]). "I wait for ideas to come to me," he states, reflecting on a principle of much longer standing.[2] His art, he says, is a matter of "painting what has always been there."[3] The cup existed to be observed; and whether its flattening occurred months or only hours before he chanced upon it would be irrelevant to his immediate experience. He recognized the formal value of the object and abstracted that value in his vision, removing it from its context of a castaway, preserving it in the studio. Every moment of Kelly's distraction has the potential to generate an abstraction of this sort, lifting a shape or a color from the totality of a scene or the function of an object, as well as from any general meaning associated with the initial situation of its finding. Kelly's attention intensifies through distractive and abstractive acts that isolate visual elements.

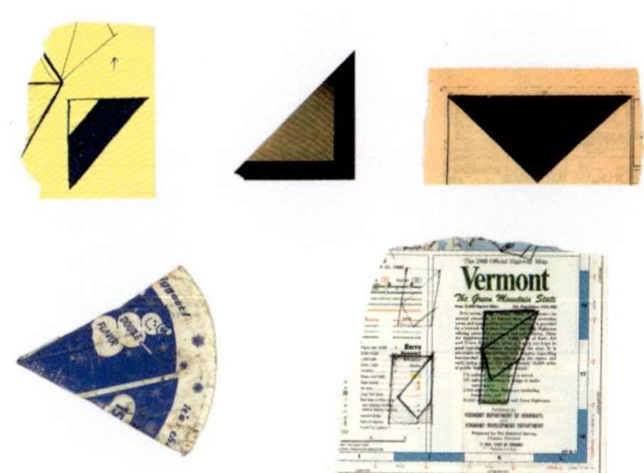

fig. 120: *Tablet 34 (Five Sketches)*, 1950s, 1960s, ink, printed paper, 15½ × 21 in, 39.4 × 53.3 cm

A painting of 1994, *Blue Curve* (p. 264) is one of a number of distant reflections of Kelly's interest in the paper cup. It adds an element of idiosyncrasy that complicates any suggestion of symmetry: the two straight sides are of unequal length, though the span of the curved side approximates the length of the vertical edge. Yet to summarize the play of the dimensions in this manner is misleading. Approximation means little, since each element of the object has its own sensory value—*its own*, not a likeness to some other value. The effect of *Blue Curve* is particular to itself and should not be generalized by assigning values to proportions, angles, or other features. Kelly is known for insisting on the slightest adjustments to the dimensions of a monochrome panel or the spacing of a multiunit work, which may involve eccentricities such as variation in the height of the horizontal axis of each constituent element.

For example, in *Green Blue Black Red* (2007) (pp. 290–91), the second of four panels (blue) has the greatest verticality and determines the upper and lower levels of the work as a whole. Its central horizontal axis establishes the line of sight at 58 inches above the floor plane. But none of the three other panels has a central horizontal axis corresponding to that of the blue panel. And the spacing between the panels varies, though an unexpected factor of symmetry appears: between green and blue, 28 inches; between blue and black, 30 inches; between black and red, again 28 inches. The symmetry probably goes unnoticed because all other relationships are peculiar: the hanging heights of the panels vary; the black panel is nearly square but not quite (37 × 36 inches); the dimensions of the horizontal green panel and the vertical blue panel are nearly corresponding but not (23 × 46 inches and 45 × 20 inches). Kelly stymies any search for ultimate rationality. Each work is its own person. Take its shapes and colors as they are.

A moment of distraction is the personal possession of whoever experiences it; but it need not feel personal in any slanted, subjective way. All feelings feel objective when felt. "Don't tell me how I feel," we sometimes say, in response to suggestions that we fail to evaluate our subjective sensations and emotions with sufficient objectivity. What we *feel* is that we have been objective from the start. Individual experience derives from reality: "A painter," the phenomenologist declares, "cannot accept our opening to the world being illusory or indirect, that what we see is not

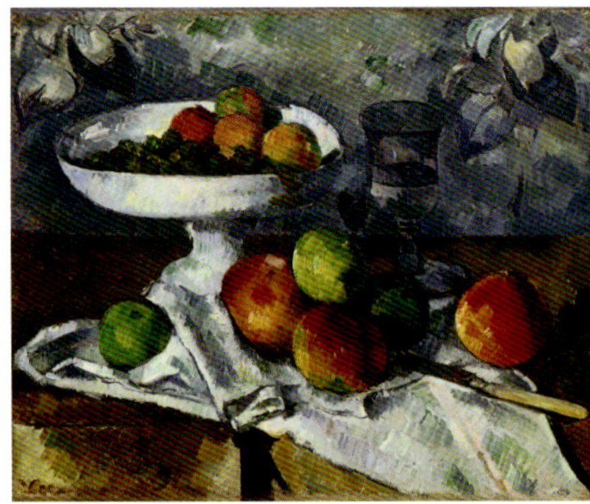

fig. 121: Paul Cézanne, *Still Life with Fruit Dish*, c.1880, oil on canvas, 18¼ × 21½ in, 46.4 × 54.6 cm

the world itself."[4] Kelly recalls two primary instances when distraction opened the world to him. "When I was about ten or twelve years old I was ill and fainted. And when I came to, my head was upside down." He had been seated, so his fainting spell left him bent over: "I looked at the room upside down, and for a brief moment I couldn't understand anything ... But for the moment that I didn't know where I was, it was fascinating."[5] Just then, as if waking from a dream, Kelly lacked all orientation. He was lost in sensation, which came—as he would say of the imagery of his future art—"from outside myself."[6] Reality rushed *at* him. A world bent-over was Kelly's subjective—no, objective—feeling. But it failed to correspond with the identity of the studied, acculturated person he already was. It existed outside his behavioral orientation, internalized predilections and cultivated desires. This new world became Kelly's by the inescapable realization of its reality. The experience of the senses is never a dream.

Bodily inversion generated a distraction from which the artist could abstract an aesthetic desire to be fulfilled in the future. Another moment of reorientation did the same:

> Looking through an aperture (a door or a window) is a way that I have been able to isolate or fragment a single form. My first memory of focusing through an aperture occurred when I was around twelve years old. One evening, passing the lighted window of a house, I was fascinated by red, blue and black shapes inside a room. But when I went up and looked in [eliminating the aperture effect], I saw a red couch, a blue drape and a black table. The shapes had disappeared. I had to retreat to see them again.

From this experience, Kelly learned "to see objectively, to erase all 'meaning' of the thing seen. Then only, could the real meaning of it be understood and felt."[7] Cultural practices—the conventions of domestic furnishing—established the meaning that the aperture eliminated. The "real meaning" was the affinity Kelly felt with visual form, the "red, blue and black shapes." From his two early experiences, he recognized his desire for distractive sensation.

What often appears to a critic as evidence of an artist's willful, subjective choice may have appeared to the artist as an application of objective observation. Traditional theories of naturalistic, representational practice have it both ways: the style of rendering and even of seeing is the artist's own; yet, aiming for scrupulous objectivity, the artist depicts what would be seen by anyone. The mark we recognize as characteristic of the artist's hand—in Paul Cézanne's apples a blunt diagonal bar (*Still Life with Fruit Dish*, c.1880) (fig. 121), in Claude Monet's aquatic vegetation a linear sinuosity (*The Rowing Boat*, c.1889–90) (fig. 122)—is the mark that records the struggle to keep pace with empirical experience.[8] Kelly has admired these two modern painters of the view outside themselves.[9] Their observations followed their emotions even as these same observations generated those emotions. For the painter, objectivity becomes subjective. The impersonal signifies a personal effort, if only because the painter seeks an impersonal physicality in the material process, designed to match this quality in nature. Kelly asks, "What is the world?" And answers like the phenomenologist: "It's what your eyes see. But as you move, everything changes. If you move a little, the whole world adjusts."[10] Cézanne had made an

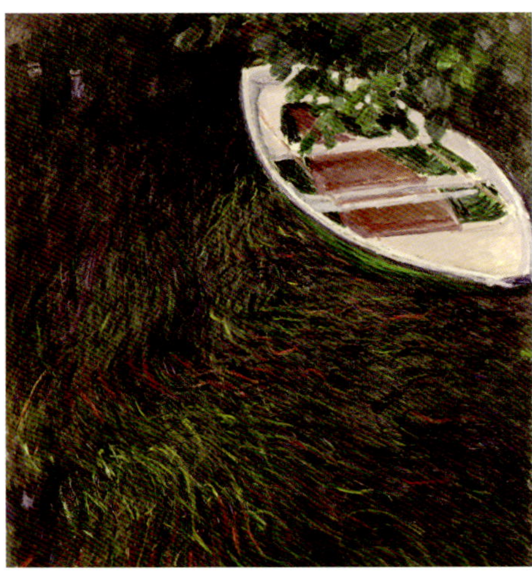

fig. 122: Claude Monet, *The Rowing Boat*, c.1889–90, oil on canvas, 57½ × 52⅜ in, 146.1 × 133 cm

analogously objective observation of his subjective perspective: "The motifs multiply, the same subject seen at a different angle takes on the greatest interest, and there is such variation that I believe I could work away for months without changing position but just by leaning a little to the right and then a little to the left."[11] Whatever Cézanne saw and painted was the only reality, the felt one, the objective one. A more generalized reality that would adhere to cultural or scientific regulation might signify objectivity by societal agreement but would hardly correspond to objective experience.

Kelly recognizes the divide between, on the one hand, types of subjectivity and objectivity that can be distinguished in theory and, on the other hand, the holistic life-experience that theories fail to articulate. He recalls his impression upon seeing Monet's late, unfinished water lily compositions at Giverny in 1952: "I felt that these works were beautiful, impersonal statements. ... I wanted to make visually engaging, impersonal works. Seeing the "Nymphéas" affirmed what I was doing."[12] Kelly perceived the impersonal aspect of Monet's art because the unfinished paintings in his estate seemed to have been dedicated to appearances, as if directly extracting the color values, including rendering effects that Monet suspected were "impossible to do" (such as capturing the underwater grasses seen in *The Boat*, unfinished like many of the "Nymphéas").[13] As the abstraction of appearances, Monet's painting was either subjective or objective or both (take your pick). More to the point, Kelly realized that it was impersonal as well. He could, so to speak, pick up where Monet left off.

Reflecting on his early development (corresponding to his years in France, when he visited Giverny), Kelly told an interviewer in 1991, "I didn't want [a] personal look ... I wanted something outside of myself, to get away from my personality ... away from the business of choice. Instead I wanted to *recognize* things."[14] To a different interviewer at nearly the same moment, he justified his kind of abstraction: "Panel paintings were the result of my wanting to completely abandon making lines or marks on the canvas, to eliminate a personal signature through brushwork ... When you make a line or mark on a panel, you are involved in depiction, and what I wanted expressed was the form of the painting itself."[15] Form (shape) became the bearer of sensations abstracted from the material world—feelings sufficiently impersonal to allow others, along with Kelly himself, to recognize their own perspective, seeing that "as you move ... the whole world adjusts." Kelly's paintings had bold shape and color analogous to the paper cup, but without its snowman, snowflakes or lettering. His art would communicate sensory experience rather than cultural messaging.

Impersonal Intensity

Each of Kelly's paintings and sculptures—beyond any possible representational reference and any subtle geometric or chromatic order—reflects a condition of sensory intensification. As an example, *Horizontal Curve I* (1996) (p. 269) is a bronze bar extending across a supporting wall to a length of 20 feet, long enough to induce a viewer to scan the bar horizontally, end to end. Its top edge is straight and parallel to the ground plane. Its bottom edge is an arc, a curve with a radius great enough to maintain a sense of this same curve as horizontal—yet only approximately so, because we continue to acknowledge the actual curvature. Strictly speaking, curving edges are neither horizontal nor vertical, though the greater the radius of the curve and the shorter the segment, the straighter the edge and the more likely that it falls into orthogonal order. The top edge of *Horizontal Curve I* leads the bottom edge into a horizontal state, as if the first were setting a goal or limit for the second.

Was Kelly thinking of the contradiction inherent in any distant view of the natural landscape, the perceptual experience that at its horizon (to be drawn as an edge) the land appears both straight and curved? A viewer with open, unprejudiced eyes will have no idea whether Kelly was abstracting a distant view or abstracting a geometrical configuration of interest to him, the creation of a studio process. If the latter, his bar of straight edge and curved edge would seem to capitalize on a fundamental perceptual distinction that he had articulated in 1951, as he sketched the design of a book "having no written word."[16] His manuscript consisted solely of abstract drawings and collages, which nevertheless bore a verbal title: *Line, Form and Color*. There the drawing of a single compass arc follows several different configurations of straight-edge lines—among them a single horizontal, a single vertical, and a single diagonal. Kelly was not drawing essences but establishing elements. Elements are impersonal.

Paradoxically, Kelly's set of elements of visual design is quirky, as if some were products of moments of chance distraction rather than logical deduction. Yes, as he states, his presentation amounts to an "alphabet of lines, forms, values and colors." But the book was very much Kelly's personal creation—for instance, among its limited number of color demonstrations, it included an odd, close-valued combination of pink and orange, which particularly interested him (fig. 123). He had been struck by the viability of this combination when he studied a painting by Ambrogio Lorenzetti at the Museum of Fine Arts, Boston (*Virgin and Child*, c.1340 [fig. 24]).[17] Having been seen elsewhere, pink-and-orange was to Kelly impersonal and could be used for *his* projects, without calling attention to his personality—he had learned that he liked this combination, a desire coming from the outside, like a distraction. In addition to using it for *Line, Form and Color*, he incorporated pink-and-orange into *Painting for a White Wall*, which consists of five joined panels: black, pink, orange, white, blue (1952) (pp. 82–83). Given this set of geometrically regular forms of equal dimensions, the color combination seems peculiar. The juxtaposition of pink and orange connotes subjective choice if only because the far more primary effect of black, white, and blue connotes systematic objectivity. Kelly found pink-and-orange; he did not invent it. Perhaps he re-invented it. Regardless of such a factor of eccentricity, he intended his book to lead art back to anonymous principles of design suited to large-scale public decoration. It was a book of findings. He announced clearly his dismay at the excess of "personality" in modern art. His creative process, like his book on design, was distinctively personal for the very fact that it conveyed its impersonal forms of expression in uniquely (re-)inventive ways.

Horizontal Curve I intensifies sensitivity to straight and curved edges, while it heightens the emotional force of these elemental features of the visual environment.

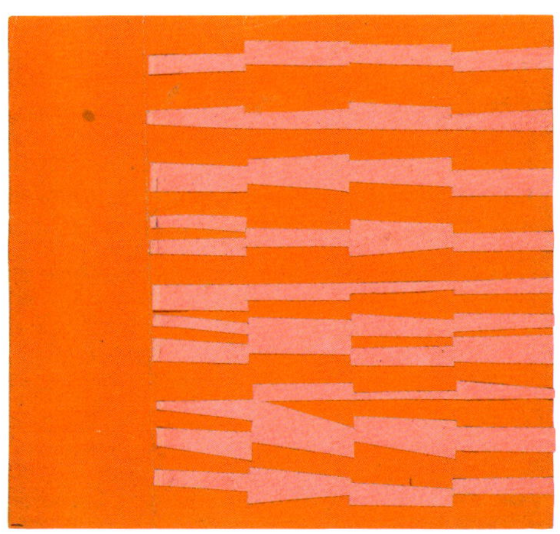

fig. 123: *Pink and Orange* (from *Line, Form and Color*) 1951, collage on paper, 7½ × 8 in, 19.1 × 20.3 cm

Perhaps what is most "personal" to Kelly is his ability to take a familiar form to extremes while preserving its inherent grace, avoiding any suggestion of grandiosity and bombast. At any dimension, he masters scale. A number of his works resemble *Horizontal Curve I* in developing an effect of tension-in-extension. *Red Curve* (1986) (pp. 248–49) is an elongated fan-like shape in which opposing edges constitute a gradual curve and a flattened obtuse angle. Each aspect of the form, top and bottom, stretches in its particular way, across the viewer's line of sight and toward the position of its counterpart, until both meet at the extreme left and right in an angle that is part curved, part straight. To face this eccentric form—over 17 feet wide, but only 3½ feet at its highest—is to respond viscerally, perhaps with an empathetic gesture of the hand, tracing the curve, marking the angle. *Red Curve* is an extreme variation on the shape of *Blue Curve*, not to mention its remote link to Kelly's flattened conical cup. Intensification is the result of his acts of abstraction—no reduction to an essence but enhancement of both sensation and emotion. In these instances, to abstract is to draw straightness and curvedness out of geometrical banality and into art.

The Feel of Color

From among various candidates for the inaugural moment of abstraction in painting, historians have often chosen an exchange between Paul Gauguin and Paul Sérusier in 1888. It resulted in works such as Sérusier's *The Talisman* (fig. 124), which viewers of the twentieth-century sometimes mistook for a composition solely of colors, devoid of the representational elements of a wooded park by a stream, references to the Bois d'Amour where the two painters worked *en plein air.* Gauguin offered instruction to his young companion: "How does that tree look to you? Is it decidedly green? Then use green, the most beautiful green of your palette. And that shadow—is it bluish? Don't fear painting it as blue as possible."[18]

No wonder that the look of *The Talisman* is ambivalent, for so was Gauguin's method. He sought to shift Sérusier's mimetic effort from capturing the nature of the tree to expressing the sensory look and feel of its colors—green overall, becoming blue in shadow. The identity of the green (the actual wave-length that would stimulate the eye) and the feel or emotional valence of this color would not present the same appearance, nor be expressed by the same hue. When the feeling of a color or a form in living perception dominates its commonplace identity, then (as Gauguin was arguing) a painter should extend representation in the direction of feeling. Subjective feeling distracts from the reality known as representational reference, yet feeling is the reality of life: *objective*. By leaving all reality aside other than its own, art sometimes—certainly not always—assumes the side of life in the conflict between immediate feeling and culturally inculcated expectations (our doxa). In Gauguin's era, the isolation of feeling, both sensory and emotional—the extraction of feeling from a general practice of representation—would come to be called "expression."[19] With increasing frequency, the process and its result were labeled "abstraction."[20]

A half-century after Gauguin instructed Sérusier, Kelly was instructing himself. As a student at the Pratt Institute in 1942, it was his responsibility to master the Munsell system of color (fig. 12) . Early in the century, art professor Albert Munsell devised a way of organizing colors in terms of their relative hue, value (degree of lightness) and chroma (degree of chromatic saturation, purity, intensity). Kelly took an initiative with the Munsell chart, locating the most saturated colors for each of the common hues, the colors with the greatest chroma (among them, the greenest green—what Gauguin sought from Sérusier). With each of his select colors brought to full saturation, Kelly created a spectrum—reds to oranges to yellows to greens to blues to violets—demonstrating how an artist's palette might look if each element were at maximum intensity.[21]

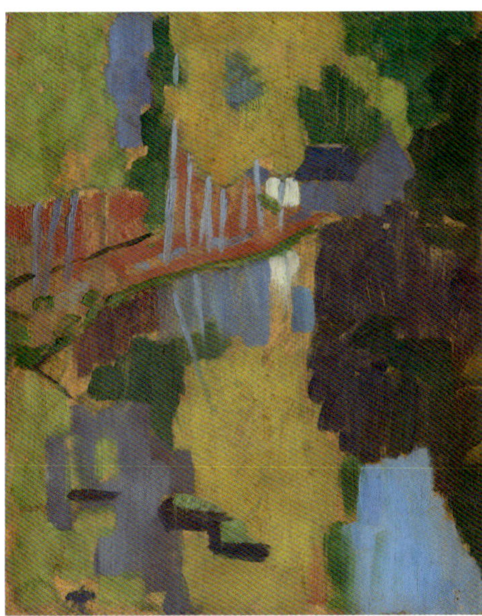

fig. 124: Paul Sérusier, *The Talisman, the Aven River at the Bois d'Amour*, 1888, oil on wood, 10⅝ × 8¼ in , 27 × 21 cm

Even as a student, Kelly avoided personal invention, preferring to "find things and develop them" (just as he had "found" abstraction through inversion and an aperture). He would develop his discoveries just as they appeared, not with measured precision but true to the affect—the objectively experienced, subjective feel of the objective look—or, as could just as well be said, the subjectively experienced, objective feel of the subjective look. Among his findings was the phenomenon of saturation: "I liked the [colors] with the most chroma."[22] Art is a matter of what you like, what attracts and distracts you. For *his* art, Kelly used the saturated colors that his study introduced to him. An impulse to intensify, when applied to Munsell's existing theory, generated a palette in accord with the young artist's recognition of what proved aesthetically satisfying. We do not question our likes, having discovered them; the trick is to find what we like, which may be different from what tradition and prevailing fashion suggest we ought to have desired. "In my paintings," Kelly has said, "I'm not inventing; my ideas come from constantly investigating how things look."[23] Such empirical study is also self-study.

In 1969, years after his involvement with Munsell's theory, Kelly painted a set of thirteen large vertical panels—each a spectral color in sequence, beginning with a yellow, passing through green, blue, violet, red, orange, and returning finally to yellow (*Spectrum V* [pp. 180–81]). He aimed for a set of colors that coordinated value and chroma. He strove to make the colors as uniform as possible in both aspects, even though the two qualities, value and chroma, normally remain at odds. The challenge was to make a luminous yellow look as weighty as a deep violet, while rendering a violet as brilliant as a yellow. All would hinge on the relations among the specific hues (variations on primary and secondary spectral colors), and these relations could be discovered only by painting and looking. Kelly's implicit question was this: At what uniform value do all colors reach uniform saturation—not the greatest saturation, but one successfully coordinated with the value? A solution could be approached, but not without pragmatic compromise. Kelly allowed the value of his blues and violets to darken in relation to the other hues, lest their saturation weaken.[24] The adjustments were sensory, a set of ad hoc judgments of the eye. He did not impose a theory, nor did he impose his will: "I didn't want to invent."[25] He discovered what was there to be found, responded to conditions, and did what intuition suggested. That was it. That was that. Or—as the expression goes when we venture a conclusion for which no precedent exists—*that will be that*. The colloquialism projects into an indefinite future the end of work already completed.

Sensations surprise even artists. Sensations distract. Some of our feelings derive from sensing the immediate environment. Other feelings reflect transitory states of emotion. Those who seek emotional and sensory security—most of us? most of the time?—treat the unpredictable aspects of our human situation as if all occurrences had underlying causes that could be analyzed. Not only as scientists, but also all the more as mythologizers and ideologues, we invent the rational, predictive systems that chance sequences of lived sensation lack. Following our rational fantasies, our inventions, we remove much of the uncertainty from living.

An alternative attitude is possible, less naive, less passive than it may seem: let occurrences occur; let things come into play as they do; keep explanation to the minimum required for continuing to process experience. A view befalls the viewer, complete with shape, color, light, and other sensory qualities. Let the distraction re-focus the senses as it de-focuses all thought of likeness and classification. Derived from distractive experience, a work of art becomes an abstraction of bits of the world rendered objectively real. Art will catch the attention and hold it, but will not force experience into a cultural mold. Each viewer will remain free to project a personal fantasy of meaning, or apply a collective one, or recognize that sensation alone can be enough. This is my guess at a characterization of art, given Ellsworth Kelly's achievement in creating it. If his art did not exist, I might see and think otherwise. And that will be that.

1 Charles Sanders Peirce, "Phaneroscopy: or, the Natural History of Concepts" (c.1905), in Charles Hartshorne and Paul Weiss (eds vols 1–6), and Arthur W. Burks (ed. vols 7–8), *Collected Papers of Charles Sanders Peirce,* 8 vols (Cambridge, MA: Harvard University Press, 1958–60), vol. 1, p. 170. I thank Ellsworth Kelly, Jack Shear, and the Ellsworth Kelly Studio for generously conveying information and documentation on numerous occasions. I am grateful to Jessamine Batario and Jason A. Goldstein for aid in research.

2 Kelly, conversation with the author, May 22, 2009.

3 Kelly, conversation with the author, July 7, 2012.

4 Maurice Merleau-Ponty, "L'oeil et l'esprit," *Art de France* 1 (1961), p. 204 (author's translation).

5 Kelly, in Paul Taylor, "Ellsworth Kelly: Interview," *Artstudio* 24 (Spring 1992), p. 154. This version of Kelly's statement is more extensive than the corresponding one published by Taylor in *Interview* 21 (June 1991), p. 102.

6 Kelly, in Martin Gayford and Ellsworth Kelly, "Where the Eye Leads," *Modern Painters*, Summer 1997, p. 63.

7 Kelly, "Notes of 1969," in Kristine Stiles and Peter Selz (ed.), *Theories and Documents of Contemporary Art* (Berkeley: University of California Press, 1996), p. 93.

8 See Richard Shiff, "To Move the Eyes: Impressionism, Symbolism, and Well-Being, c.1891," in Richard Hobbs (ed.), *Impressions of French Modernity: Art and Literature in France 1850–1900* (Manchester University Press, 1998), pp. 190–210.

9 On Kelly and Cézanne, see Katherine Sachs, "Cézanne and Kelly: Painting Form through Color," in Joseph J. Rishel and Katherine Sachs (eds), *Cézanne and Beyond* (Philadelphia Museum of Art, 2009), pp. 433–45. On Kelly and Monet, see Sarah Lees and Yve-Alain Bois, *Monet/Kelly* (Williamstown: Clark Art Institute, 2014).

10 Kelly, in Gayford and Kelly 1997, p. 62.

11 Cézanne, letter to his son Paul, 8 September 1906, in John Rewald (ed.), *Paul Cézanne, correspondance* (Paris: Grasset, 1978), p. 324 (author's translation).

12 Ellsworth Kelly, statement (August 12, 2001), in Karin Sagner-Düchting (ed.), *Monet and Modernism* (Munich: Prestel, 2001), p. 214.

13 Claude Monet, letter to Gustave Geffroy, June 22, 1890, in Geffroy, *Claude Monet, sa vie, son oeuvre*, 2 vols (Paris: Crès, 1924), vol. 2, p. 47. Kelly might have seen *The Boat* in 1952 because it remained in the possession of the Monet family at Giverny. His*Tableau Vert* (1952) [p. 76], inspired by the "abstraction" in Monet's art, represented in part a response to the effect of underwater grasses, the profound greenness he observed in Monet's pond. He painted *Tableau Vert* impulsively, without intending to make its surface as mottled as it appears (statement to the author, August 4, 2014).

14 Kelly, in Taylor 1992, p. 154 (original emphasis).

15 Kelly, interview by Nathalie Brunet (May 1991), quoted in Nathalie Brunet, "Chronology, 1943–1954," trans. Thomas Repensek, in *Ellsworth Kelly: The Years in France, 1948–1954*, p. 184.

16 The quoted fragment and those in the paragraph to follow are from Kelly's proposal of 1951 to the Guggenheim Foundation (which was denied). His statement appears as an addendum to a subsequent reconfiguration of his project: Ellsworth Kelly, *Line Form Color 1951* (Cambridge, MA: Harvard University Art Museums, 1999), n.p.

17 Kelly, conversation with the author, August 4, 2014.

18 Paul Gauguin's words, as reported by Paul Sérusier to Maurice Denis; see Maurice Denis, "L'influence de Paul Gauguin" (1903), *Théories, 1890–1910: Du symbolisme et de Gauguin vers un nouvel ordre classique* (Paris: Rouart et Watelin, 1920), p. 167 (author's translation).

19 Denis credited Sérusier for insisting on "expression by means of the [sensory qualities of the] work itself and not the represented subject"; Maurice Denis, "Le peintre Paul Sérusier," *L'Occident* 14 (December 1908), p. 279 (author's translation).

20 See Richard Shiff, "Dream of Abstraction," in Terence Maloon (ed.), *Paths to Abstraction 1867–1917* (Munich: Prestel, 2010), pp. 52–69; "From Primitivist Phylogeny to Formalist Ontogeny: Roger Fry and Children's Drawings," in Jonathan Fineberg (ed.), *Discovering Child Art: Essays on Childhood, Primitivism, and Modernism* (Princeton: Princeton University Press, 1998), pp. 157–200; "Expression: Natural, Personal, Pictorial," in Paul Smith and Carolyn Wilde (eds), *A Companion to Art Theory* (Oxford: Blackwell, 2002), pp. 159–72.

21 Kelly still possesses his original Munsell materials, used at Pratt; Kelly, conversation with the author, August 4, 2014.

22 Kelly, conversation with the author, August 4, 2014.

23 Ellsworth Kelly, "The Shape of Seeing: Ellsworth Kelly's Photographs" (excerpts from a conversation between Kelly and Charles Hagen, August 1991), *Aperture* 125 (Fall 1991), p. 45.

24 Kelly, conversation with the author, 4 August 2014.

25 Kelly, interview by Mark Rosenthal (June 1990, January 1991), in Mark Rosenthal, *Artists at Gemini G.E.L.: Celebrating the 25th Year* (New York: Harry N. Abrams, 1993), p. 70.

In Spencertown, 1970 to today

fig. 125: *Curve seen from a highway, Austerlitz, NY*, 1970, gelatin silver print

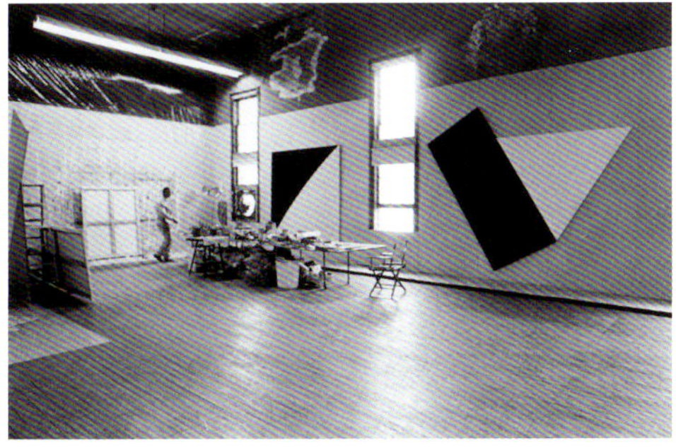

fig. 126: Ellsworth Kelly, Cady's Hall studio, Chatham, NY, 1973

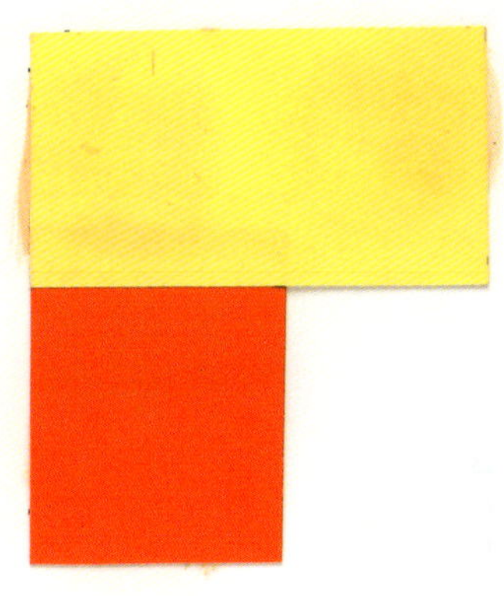

fig. 127: Study for *Chatham XIII,* 1971, collage, 7⅝ × 6⅞ in, 19.4 × 17.5 cm

Taking Stock

By the end of 1969, a significant year for American art in New York City as well as for Kelly himself, the artist came to the conclusion that a change was needed. Spurred on by the fact that the historic Hotel des Artistes at 1 West 67th Street where he had lived for about seven years (and which was originally built for artists in 1917), wanted to turn his studio rental into a residential apartment, Kelly had to come up with a new plan, since he was not interested in purchasing his studio; his works had also grown to such a scale that they could no longer fit inside the elevator in the Hotel des Artistes, forcing him to transport them by resting them on top of the elevator itself. Although he enjoyed forming close friendships with fellow artists, such as Lichtenstein (in the late 1960s he spent summers in Bridgehampton, Long Island, with Lichtenstein and his wife Dorothy), as well as with cultural figures such as Geldzahler, he still liked spending time on his own, just like the young boy who escaped to the woods after school. Feeling the social pressures of living and working in New York, he decided it was time to move out of the city. He chose to move upstate to Spencertown in Columbia County, a town about 130 miles north of the city, and coincidentally about 80 miles north from where he was born in Newburgh. The great change in scenery he experienced upon moving to the country can be noted in the photographs he took around this time. No longer did he see buildings that rose to the sky from the dense Manhattan grid, but now vast horizons in the distance, long roads and sloping hills that stretched out across the land (fig. 125). He had finally found the space and freedom that he had been wanting.

In Spencertown, he moved into a small Victorian house and learned about a century-old theater, Cady's Hall, on the main street of the next town, Chatham (fig. 126). After some industrious inquiring and gentle persuasion—he always researched thoroughly when trying to find a new studio, asking friends as well as local people on the ground—the artist was able to rent the upper floor of this moderately sized, low-rise brick building, which had served as an opera house in the early twentieth century. It needed a lot of work, but it offered much more space than his most recent studio, including four tall windows and easy convenience for moving his work.

Among the first works he made there were *Green Orange* (1970) (p. 222), and *Black with Red Bar* (1970) (p. 220). Two-paneled works, they form new geometric shapes, both in terms of the panels and the way he joined them. Kelly had begun doing something similar in the late 1960s, creating triangles and parallelograms, as well as other unique shapes, such as *Blue Red* (1968) (pp. 178–79). This kind of pairing of two panels diverged from the rectangular outline achieved by earlier multipanel paintings. His creation of his thirteen-paneled *Spectrum V* (1969) (pp. 180–81) for "Henry's Show" at the Metropolitan seemed to close the book at the time on making paintings out of *many* panels, and in the coming years in Spencertown, he created primarily duo-paneled works when he chose to use his multipanel approach. Some of the new shapes he created out of two panels were inspired by the vistas and architecture upstate. For example, *Black with Red Bar* derived from cantilevered structures that he had seen locally.

Such a pairing of two rectilinear panels of different proportions would lead to the beginnings of his "Chatham" series begun in 1971, where he addressed the cantilever more fully, and if one can say, more correctly, as in *Chatham X: Black Red* (p. 225), where the black bar is held in place at its left end and projects out to the right, a true cantilever. Kelly spent a considerable amount of time on this series, making a total of fourteen paintings, all of which follow the basic structure of an upside-down backwards L. Every version, however, offers changes in length and width to each of its two panels, as well as adjustments to its color pairing. In both collages and sketches (fig. 127), Kelly played with his proportions until he felt that the scale seemed right. Although he had to calculate varying measurements—so he could correctly order his different canvases—his decisions on size had nothing to do with mathematics, but rather with intuition. Kelly has often stated that when making a painting or sculpture, his forms and colors must look "right," "honest," or even "necessary." For these integral aesthetic decisions, he ultimately relies on vision, even explaining, "I don't know what I want, my eye does."[1]

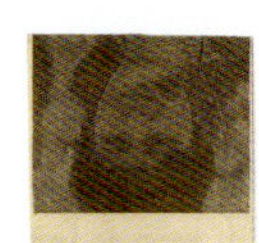
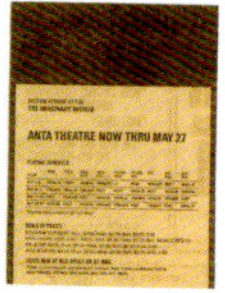
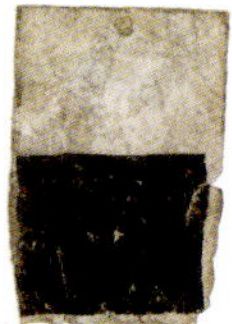

fig. 128: *Tablet 191 (Three Sketches)*, 1960s, ink, graphite, printed paper, 15½ × 21 in, 39.4 × 53.3 cm

According to Kelly, he was not as productive within his first year or so upon moving upstate. He was now forty-seven years old and had just closed a very active decade of showings at major exhibitions, such as Documenta in 1964 and 1968, the Venice Biennale in 1966, and "New York Painting and Sculpture: 1940–1970" in 1969. Recognized by influential tastemakers in the States and abroad, including Geldzahler, the British curator and critic Lawrence Alloway, and the German curator Arnold Bode (the founder of Documenta in Germany in 1955), Kelly had also been shown in solo gallery exhibitions annually throughout the 1960s, whether in New York, Los Angeles, London, or Paris. By 1965 he had moved over to Sidney Janis Gallery down the hall from Betty Parsons and had started to show with Irving Blum, first at Ferus Gallery and then Blum's own gallery in Los Angeles. In 1970, at mid-career, Kelly was indeed an artistic success, nationally and internationally.

Thus, now accommodated in larger quarters, Kelly had the space, both physically and mentally, to look back and take stock of his career. Within his first couple of years of living in Spencertown, he found himself faced with crates of artwork, boxes of drawings, sketches, and doodles, as well as many sketchbooks, plus journals and notebooks that carefully documented his paintings, reliefs, and sculptures. While in Paris, he had begun to inventory his output, assigning "EK" numbers to finished works, numbers that are still used today by him and his studio. He continued this practice in New York City, and acting as his own art historian, had even started keeping track of his exhibition histories as he began to show more and more during the 1950s and 1960s. At times, he kept track of new work he was making by drawing miniature sketches in his journal and noting how many coats of paint he had applied to a particular painting as well as the color mixture used. Over these years, he had kept practically everything related to his career—letters, photographs, exhibition announcements, diaries, calendars. So he began to sift through some of this material that he had collected, focusing a little bit less on creating new works as he started reflecting on the past.

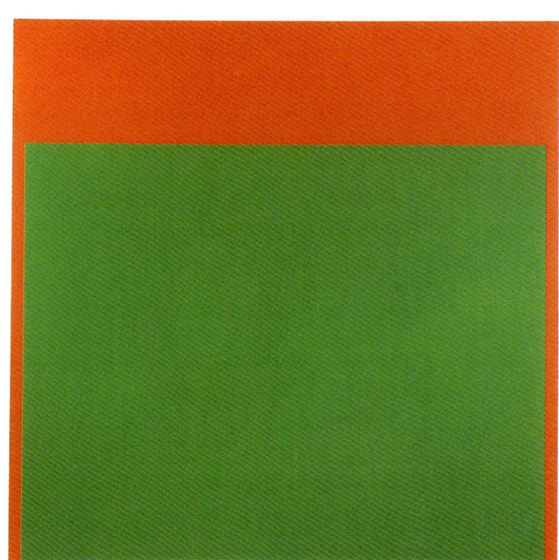

fig. 129: *Green Red*, 1965, oil on canvas, 90 × 90 in, 228.6 × 228.6 cm

Commentators in the art world were interested in doing the same. At the time of Kelly's move upstate, both John Coplans and Diane Waldman were researching

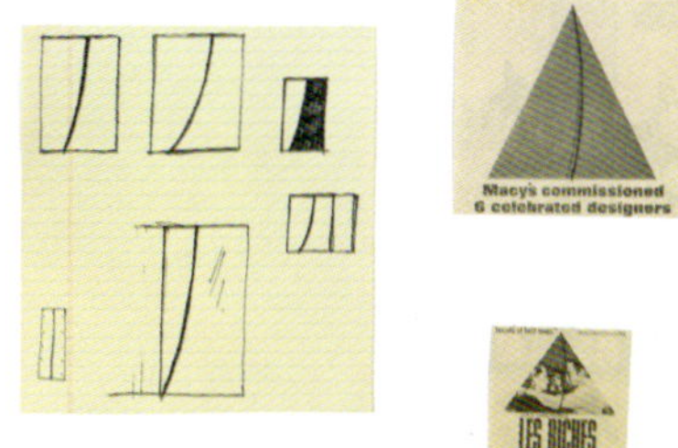

fig. 130: *Tablet 94 (Three Sketches)*, 1960s, ink, graphite, printed paper, 15½ × 21 in, 39.4 × 53.3 cm

and writing their respective studies on the artist, the first monographs on Kelly, which were both published in 1971.[2] Coplans, critic and the editor of *Artforum* by 1971, had included him in a 1968 show he had curated for the Pasadena Art Museum (renamed the Norton Simon Museum in 1975) titled "Serial Imagery" that presented artists from Claude Monet and Josef Albers to Andy Warhol and Yves Klein; and in 1969 he had penned the first scholarly article on Kelly's works made in France.[3] Guggenheim curator Waldman, who many years later, in 1996, would curate a major retrospective on Kelly, had also been following Kelly's work, having written a review of a solo exhibition at Sidney Janis Gallery in 1968. Then there was a third person also calling upon Kelly. Critic and curator E.C. Goossen, who had first written on Kelly's art in 1958 for *Derrière le Miroir* (a prestigious arts magazine published by dealer Aimé Maeght), was in discussions with Kelly about a mid-career retrospective at MoMA, which would open in September 1973.

Thus, with all these art-world people knocking on Kelly's door and requesting interviews, the artist was further compelled to ponder his past and career trajectory. He did this in many ways, but one specific approach resulted in a substantial and tangible outcome: a thorough ordering of over 800 small-scale sketches, doodles, and collages that he had amassed over the years and stored in shoeboxes. By this time, Kelly had made and collected many more than these 800 small sketches and jottings, but the ones he had deemed more successful or satisfactory had already made their way into his sketchbooks, pasted in diligently as studies for new works or preparatory studies for works completed. The trove that remained was the accumulation of behind-the-scene glimpses, of raw ideas quickly drawn, sketched, painted, or collaged, all still worthy of being kept.

The majority of these items, a number of them made on scraps of newspaper, letters, brochures, envelopes, and other ephemera of daily living, spanned the mid-1950s through the 1960s, along with a smaller selection of items that he had brought back from France. After thoroughly studying these visual snippets by theme or shape, he pasted, with an assistant's help, groupings of approximately three to six of each onto 217 uniform-sized sheets of mat board measuring 15½ × 21 inches. The end result was a visual record of plentiful ideas, the origins of concepts that eventually came to fruition as well as many others that did not. These sheets capture what caught Kelly's eye, how he looked at the world.

This process of reviewing the remnants of his artistic past proved revelatory for the artist at this point in career. He discovered correspondences and recurrences in shape, such as his ongoing interest in the curve, as well as his engagement with flat planes of rectilinear color as seen with a trio of related vertical rectangles (fig. 128). Each are duo-toned, each featuring a larger rectangle with a smaller rectangle inset that he either drew or found already printed, as in the center form that he cut from an advertisement for a theater production in Greenwich Village. In 1965, Kelly had made a painting inspired by this exact configuration, *Green Red* (fig. 129) and in 1970, before he moved upstate, he had made a related painting, *Black Yellow-Orange* (p. 221). What can be gleaned from comparing these sketches and collages with his finished works is the way in which Kelly would find a specific form and then hone and shape it into something that was his own.

Another proven lesson from this visual archive of 217 groupings, now known as *Tablet*[4] (the same name as the 1960 Paul Taylor dance for which he designed the costumes and curtain), is how Kelly continued to look back to past ideas in order to propel him forward with new ones. Indeed, he collected ideas wherever he went, storing them for later. Even while walking on the street, he would pick up the odd object that fascinated him, such as a flattened cigarette wrapper, with its top-left corner folded over, a gritty, soiled white triangle set against red. The fold was deeply creased, the wrapper most likely having been stepped upon many times before Kelly chanced upon it. Many years later, in 2002, he returned to this idea when he made a large-scale version of this concept, attaching a small white triangular panel that mimicked the folded over white area of the cigarette wrapper onto a red shaped panel (fig. 131).

fig. 131: *Red with White Relief*, 2002, oil on canvas, 2 joined panels, 81 × 63 × 2⅝ in, 205.7 × 160 × 6.7 cm

Another Kind of Curve

Following this practice of returning to earlier ideas, Kelly, within his first years of living in Spencertown, circled back to his appreciation for the curved form, which he had abandoned for a while as his focus on rectilinear multiple panels grew during the mid-to-late 1960s. In 1972, he made *Red Curve II* (fig. 132) and *Blue Curve III* (pp. 230–31), which each feature an elongated curve painted within a canvas shaped as a parallelogram. Kelly continued with this painted curve in *Yellow Blue Curve I* (1972) (p. 223), but here, he distributed color more evenly between the blue and the yellow, in contrast to the way the red and the blue areas dominate against the sliver of white in *Red Curve II* and *Blue Curve III*. He also chose another shape from geometry, this time not a parallelogram, but a triangle. On one of his *Tablet* sheets (fig. 130), one can find the beginnings of this concept from the 1960s. Grouped together are two cutouts featuring triangles that he had found from two advertisements—one for Macy's and one for a 1968 Claude Chabrol movie. Onto each triangle, Kelly had drawn in pen a slight curve from the apex of the triangle down to the center of its base. *Yellow Blue Curve I* is almost an exact translation of this curve performed in those two cutouts.

All three of these paintings marked a new approach for the artist: the merging of the painted curve with the shaped canvas. Kelly had already created a handful of shaped works during his years in New York, including *White Plaque: Bridge Arch and Reflection* (1955) (p. 131), and *Yellow Piece* (1966) (p. 175), works that had veered from the tradition of the neutral rectangular canvas, but these were painted a single color. *Red Curve II*, *Blue Curve III*, and *Yellow Blue Curve I* are among the first instances where he introduced painted shape and figure-ground contrasts within a shaped canvas. He showed a sampling of these curved works in his first exhibition at Leo Castelli Gallery in April 1973. What all these works had in common was the appearance of his so-called "radial curves." Contrasting his paintings of "free curves"—the voluptuous and organic forms he painted from the mid-1950s through the mid-1960s, and to which he would return many years later in 2004—Kelly's "radial curves" derive from fragmenting large circles. While *White Plaque* can be identified as radial as well, made from truncated circles, the radial curves of *White Plaque* are greatly distinct in their rounded nature in contrast to the attenuated radial curves that appear in these new paintings.

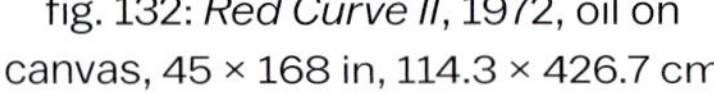

fig. 132: *Red Curve II*, 1972, oil on canvas, 45 × 168 in, 114.3 × 426.7 cm

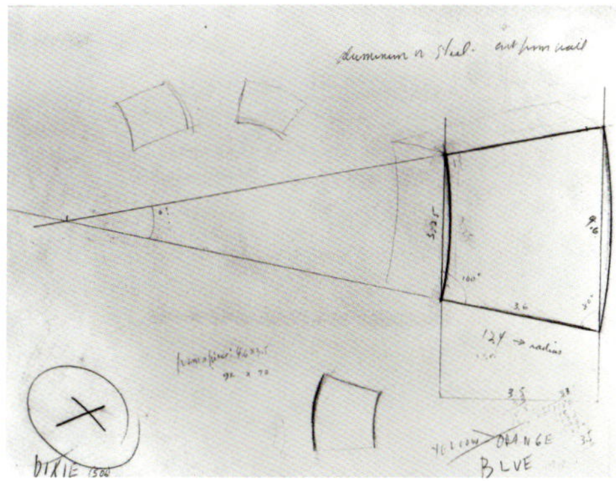

fig. 133: Study for *Curve I*, 1968, graphite on paper, 10¾ × 14⅛ in, 27.3 × 35.9 cm

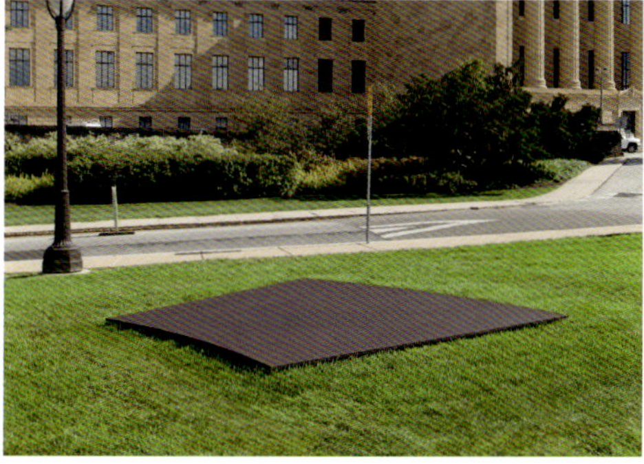

fig. 134: *Curve I,* 1973, weathering steel, 1 × 144 × 118¼ in, 2.5 × 365.8 × 300.4 cm

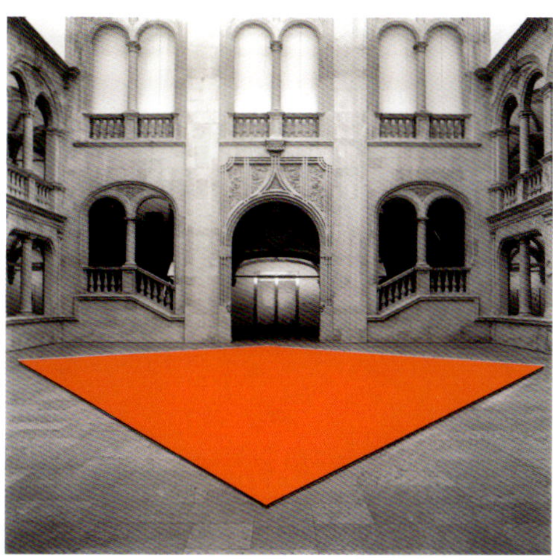

fig. 135: *Red Floor Panel*, 1992, acrylic on canvas on wood, 1 × 316½ × 478¾ in, 2.5 × 803.9 × 1216 cm

By creating this geometric curve from very large circles, Kelly began producing newly lengthened shapes that allowed him to spawn other distinct forms in the ensuing years, such as the asymmetrical pie-shaped *Blue-Violet Curve I* (1982) (p. 244), the greatly elongated *Diagonal with Curve XIV*, measuring sixteen feet wide (1982) (p. 250), and the symmetrical fan-shaped *Red Curve* (1986) (pp. 248–49). Produced from weathering steel, *Diagonal with Curve XIV* offers a subtle but distinct departure, its bottom-left point just gracing the floor. Other renditions of the radial curve moved his work to the ground itself, most notably with *Curve I* (1973) (figs 133, 134), based on a flattened paper cup that Kelly had found on a street in 1968. One of his first outdoor works made in upstate New York, *Curve I* rests flatly on the ground on which we walk, like a Carl Andre grid. Related to this embrace of the ground, Kelly would make seventeen years later an indoor monumental curve measuring approximately 25 × 24 feet for the gallery floor, *Yellow Curve* (1990) (pp. 256–57), at Portikus, in Frankfurt am Main, Germany, a contemporary art space founded by curator Kasper König. The artist would develop this further in three other similarly scaled versions in 1991 and 1992, including one for the Westfälisches Landesmuseum in Münster (fig. 135) and another in honor of his longtime dealer Leo Castelli (fig. 159), with whom he showed from 1973 until 1992.

At MoMA

In the fall of 1973, Kelly presented *Curve I* along with more than fifty other works of art, at his solo exhibition at MoMA (fig. 136). Opening on September 10, 1973, this midcareer retrospective was indeed a great achievement for the artist, now fifty years old, and the show would travel across the country, to the Pasadena Art Museum, the Walker Art Center in Minneapolis, and conclude at the Detroit Institute of Arts the following year. Curated by E.C. Goossen, this presentation spanned Kelly's French years to the present, starting with *Window I* (1949) (p. 50) and ending with *Curve II* (1973), an upright counterpart to *Curve I.* During that fall of 1973, the Solomon R. Guggenheim Museum and the Whitney Museum of American Art had opened retrospectives featuring the work of two other key contemporary artists, respectively, Richard Hamilton and Jules Olitski—the latter of whom also represented the U.S. at the 1966 Venice Biennale with Kelly, Frankenthaler, and Lichtenstein.

This moment in the New York art world offers a time capsule of how art historians, critics, and curators were evaluating Kelly's position in postwar art, as well as those of his contemporaries. For example, *The New Yorker* critic Harold Rosenberg (the critic who came up with the term "action painting" associated with Abstract Expressionism) noted in his review of Kelly's exhibition how these three shows represented the styles that dominated the 1960s—abstraction and Pop art—and how Kelly, Hamilton, and Olitski were indeed leaders of these modes. After quickly disparaging Pop art, going so far as to say that it had "earned an honorable burial," Rosenberg gave a positive assessment of the current state of abstraction, albeit with circumspection. He expressed displeasure with "the ritualistic drumming in art magazines" that allowed for only one acceptable kind of abstract painting to be admired, namely that of Olitski. He also criticized the assertion made by Kenworth Moffett, curator of the Olitski retrospective, that

"[Olitski] is like a block, *the* influence that has to be gone through or overcome if any fundamental innovation or breakthrough is to be achieved." Rosenberg claimed that Moffett's elevated view of Olitski did not advance the path of art, but functioned, ironically, as a literal "block." He concluded his review by defending and praising Kelly's originality:

> It is Kelly, rather than Olitski, who represents something new in the art of the seventies ... He has the feeling of rightness of the first-class designer, a fine sense of proportion, a sensitivity of shape and scale, and satisfying juxtapositions of colors and tones. Add the finesse of his paint surfaces, and it is undeniable that he repeatedly deserves an A.[5]

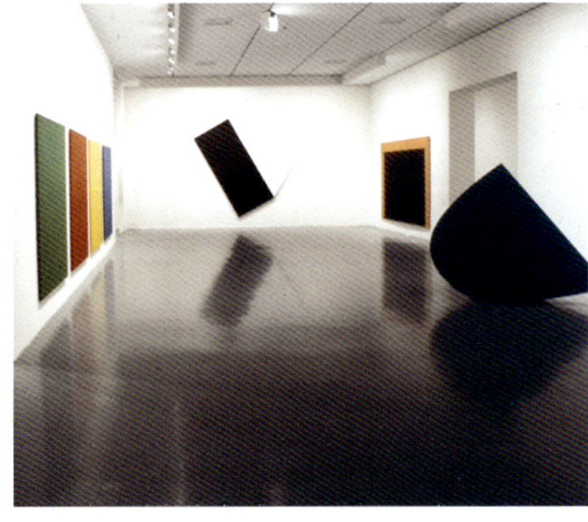

fig. 136: Installation view of "Ellsworth Kelly," The Museum of Modern Art, New York, 1973

So in the fall of 1973 at MoMA, fourteen years after his "Sixteen Americans" appearance in 1959, Kelly had finally arrived and had been given his public critical due. Just two years earlier, Coplans and Waldman, in each of their 1971 monographs on the artist, had remarked on a noticeable delay in the critical recognition of Kelly's art. As Waldman had pointed out,

> Kelly's work has suffered not only from insufficient exposure but also from the need of most critics to classify art as part of common thought processes. By side-stepping identification with a particular group or school, more a matter of instinct than intent, Kelly has often been misinterpreted and his work confused with issues with which it has only a tangential relationship.[6]

Both Waldman and Coplans argued that Kelly's work did not fit neatly with the abstract movements that had emerged in the 1960s, such as Minimalism, Color Field painting, Op art, and Hard-Edge painting. Based on the variety of approaches that he had undertaken in painting, sculpture, and relief during the 1960s, Kelly was included in many of the major thematic shows of the decade, such as those dedicated to abstract painting: "Toward a New Abstraction" at the Jewish Museum in 1963, "Post Painterly Abstraction" curated by critic Clement Greenberg at the Los Angeles County Museum of Art in 1964, and even "The Responsive Eye" in 1965, MoMA's exploration of optical art. Invitation to these painting shows was based on his "form and ground" works, in which he examined painted shape and where the visual experience was given primacy. In great contrast, he also appeared, as mentioned earlier, in significant shows that first addressed Minimalism, including the Jewish Museum's "Primary Structures" and the Guggenheim's "Systemic Painting," both in 1966, the Los Angeles County Museum of Art's "American Sculpture of the Sixties" in 1967, and MoMA's "The Art of the Real" in 1968. At these outings Kelly's works were either his multipanel paintings or the freestanding sculpture he had begun to make in the late 1950s, those that revealed his interest in the physical "presence" or object quality of a work.

While inclusion in these varied exhibitions reveals the critical misinterpretations of Kelly's art at the time, it also underscores the complexity of his production and his ability to progress fluidly between painting and sculpture, through shapes contained by the rectangular limit of the canvas, to those that function within the unlimited space on the wall or on the floor. While many of his contemporaries felt compelled to choose between painting and sculpture, Kelly developed a complex model of artistic production that still relied on the vertical plane of art but that had also expanded into real space. Indeed, Kelly was the only artist of his generation to exhibit in these varying shows of painting and sculpture, including his foreign presentations at Documenta, first in 1964 and then in 1968, and at the Venice Biennale in 1966. One of the few trends with which he was not associated was Pop art. Yet, if curators and critics had been privy to the extent of his post-card practice and his plays with such popular ephemera, it is quite possible that they would have found a way to fit him in the Pop box as well.

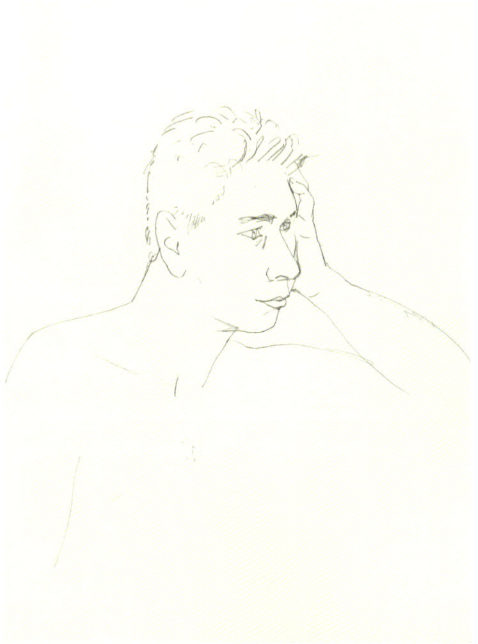

fig. 137: *Jack Shear,* 1984, graphite on paper, 30 × 22 in, 76.2 × 55.9 cm

In each of their books, Coplans and Waldman had attempted to clarify how, for example, Kelly's multipanel paintings, works that aligned him with Minimalism through a superficial connection to seriality, prefigured this movement by an entire decade, during the early 1950s when he lived in France. In a review of his 1973 retrospective, critic and later curator Thomas B. Hess (who wrote the 1953 *ARTnews* Reinhardt article that inspired Kelly's return to the U.S.) testified to these writers' assessment of Kelly's work by referring to "the prophetic nature" of his earlier work: "He was doing stripes and monochromes long before they became vanguard currency."[7] Yet, despite Kelly's successful outing at MoMA in 1973, and invitations for solo exhibitions, group shows, and more public commissions over the next few decades, one can still observe that his level of renown did not match the broad critical and curatorial attention afforded to contemporaries like Johns, Rauschenberg, or Lichtenstein.

And if the art world resisted a full understanding of the breadth of Kelly's art, Kelly also resisted the art world to a certain degree. His early reluctance to talk about his art had not made it any easier for critics. He remained particularly quiet about the subject and methods of his work during his New York years, with his first public statement made only in 1963.[8] His retreat from the New York art scene, by moving to Spencertown in 1970, also factored into his resistance. However, following his discussions with Coplans, some of which the author published in his 1971 monograph, Kelly became more comfortable about going on record. In 1979, at the time of his solo exhibition at the Stedelijk Museum in Amsterdam (his first major show in Europe), he revised and expanded his 1971 statements in Coplans's monograph into an important artistic treatise, "Notes from 1969," which was published in the Stedelijk catalogue. Kelly became more vocal during the 1980s, as writers and curators asked for more interviews. This growing willingness can also be attributed to the support and encouragement he received from his relationship with photographer Jack Shear (fig. 137), whom the artist met in Los Angeles in 1982 and with whom he still shares his home today.

Yet, misunderstandings and recognition of the scope of Kelly's work continued to a certain degree until an important exhibition took place in 1992, first in Paris at the Galerie nationale du Jeu de Paume and then at the National Gallery of Art in Washington, DC. Curated by Jack Cowart and Alfred Pacquement, "Ellsworth Kelly: The Years in France, 1948–1954" extensively explored the artist's French production, which, at the time, was not well known and barely represented in museum collections.[9] After showing some of his French works at MoMA in 1973,

Kelly would present a small selection of his French output at only two major solo exhibitions during the 1980s—"Ellsworth Kelly: Sculpture," curated by Patterson Sims and Emily Rauh Pulitzer in 1982 and "Ellsworth Kelly: Works on Paper," curated by Diane Upright in 1987. Although both of these shows traveled, the 1992 exhibition featuring his French work was a revelation. Furthermore, scholar Yve-Alain Bois wrote a seminal essay in the accompanying catalogue that identified and addressed the major strategies of Kelly's French practice without attempting to force his work into a specific box or category.[10] Also in 1992, Kelly started showing with Matthew Marks Gallery in New York, a successful partnership that continues to this day. And in 1996 the Solomon R. Guggenheim Museum, New York, mounted "Ellsworth Kelly: A Retrospective." Curated by Waldman, it traveled to the Museum of Contemporary Art, Los Angeles, Tate Gallery, London, and Haus der Kunst, Munich, and the floodgates finally opened, resulting in a consistent flow of significant museum exhibitions devoted to his art and thus a corresponding increase in critical attention, scholarship, and museum acquisitions.

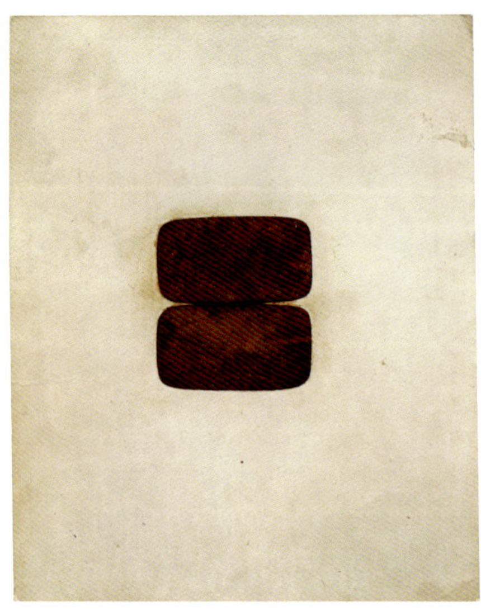

fig. 138: *Study for a sculpture*, 1959, metal on paper, 11 × 8½ in, 27.9 × 21.6 cm

Single Shape and Sculpture

In the years that followed his 1973 retrospective at MoMA, Kelly continued to settle into his life in Spencertown. Over the next two decades, he would be featured in several important solo exhibitions, as mentioned previously, such as his 1979 show at the Stedelijk Museum, Amsterdam, which traveled to the Hayward Gallery, London, the Centre Georges Pompidou, Paris, and then finally the Staatliche Kunsthalle, Baden-Baden, in 1979, broadening his renown in Europe. All the while, Kelly kept his consistent focus while working in Spencertown. Growing acclaim also led to more museums and collectors acquiring his work, so that in 1978 he was able to begin construction of a new studio adjacent to his Spencertown home. Gone were the days of having to seek out already existing spaces for his next studio. Now, he was able to design one to his own liking in concert with an architect. He also began to acquire parcels of land near his house.

Just as the surrounding domestic architecture had informed some of the shapes he explored in paintings from the early 1970s, such as his "Chatham" series (1971) (p. 225) and *Yellow with Red Triangle* (1973) (p. 229), the expansive landscape he found before him while walking on his property or driving to and from town influenced his choices in sculpture, such as *Curve I* (fig. 134) and *Curve II*, both from 1973. Shown at MoMA, they were his first to be made of weathering steel, in conjunction with fabricator Lippincott, Inc.; they were, however, not his first outdoor sculptures. His first outdoor work was, in fact, *Two Curves: Blue Red* (1964) (p. 165), his commission for the 1964 New York World's Fair. The next two outdoor works were made in 1968, *Green Blue* and *Black White*, his first collaborations with Lippincott, Inc. after working with his prior fabricator Edison Price. All three of these works were made of painted aluminum, the same material that he had been using for the indoor sculptures he began making in 1959, *Gate* (p. 150) and *Pony* (p. 148).

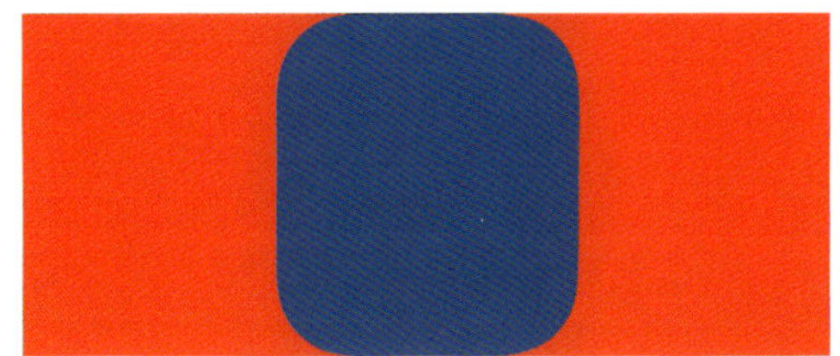

fig. 139: *Blue Red*, 1965, oil on canvas, 65 × 150 in, 165.1 × 381 cm

When Kelly returned to making outdoor sculptures in 1973, he decided to explore new materials, such as weathering steel. A kind of steel alloy first developed

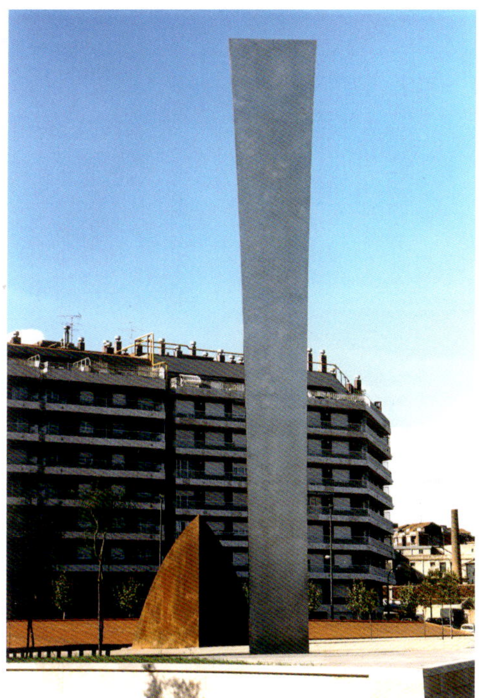

fig. 140: *Barcelona Sculpture at General Moragues Plaza,* 1987, stainless steel and weathering steel, totem: 588 × 86 × 7 in, 14.9 × 2.2 × 0.2 m; 260 × 260 × 227 in, 6.6 × 6.6 × 5.8 m

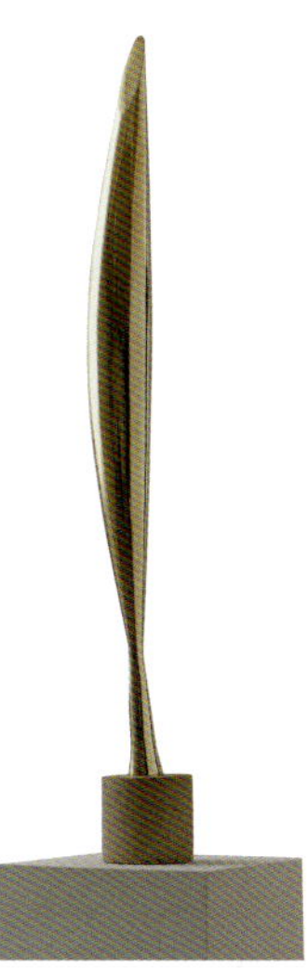

fig. 141: Constantin Brancusi, *Bird in Space*, 1928, bronze, 54 × 8½ × 6½ in, 137.2 × 21.6 × 16.5 cm

in the 1930s for railway coal wagons, weathering steel gained popularity in the 1960s when artists such as Carl Andre, Richard Serra, and Barnett Newman turned to this metal to make their sculptures, favoring the fabricated, industrial appearance of the material in order to remove the trace of the artist's hand. For Kelly, too, the choice of weathering steel offered a new color and texture. As seen with *Stele I* (1973) (p. 233) and *Stele II* (1973) (p. 235), a patina of corrosion develops as the steel literally weathers over time. In the development of these large-scale outdoor sculptures, Kelly relinquished painted color for found color that then altered over time. Attention to a new shape is also apparent in the outline of both these works. Although their titles help to identify this particular form in Kelly's work—that of a stele, for example, the Egyptian stele he had admired at the Louvre during his French years (fig. 31)—these sculptures resist the original purpose of such a form, which in ancient times was an upright stone slab inscribed with imagery or text. Instead, Kelly presents his steles as blank, emptied of any information except for the weathering passages of time.

Unlike his fragmented curves, these steles exist in their entirety, as a closed form unto itself. Earlier investigations into a related shape can be seen in a collage that Kelly made in 1959 using two metal cutouts (fig. 138), prefiguring in many ways the look of his future stele sculptures. The treatment of a similarly rounded rectilinear form appears in his painting, such as *Blue Red* (1965) (fig. 139). What Kelly did was literally free one of his collaged stele shapes from their white-paper background in the 1959 collage and allow it to exist in weathering steel form, now much enlarged and more square-like in *Stele II* (p. 235). With this attention to a much larger cutout shape, Kelly began to create entirely new forms in sculpture, namely his totems, starting in 1974 with *Curve X* (p. 236), for example. He created these totems in weathering steel, aluminum, and even wood, such as *Untitled* (1996) (p. 268). He also varied their shape, scale, and proportion, while making his lengthened curved outline either convex or concave. In 1987, he installed a totem measuring 49 feet tall in the city of Barcelona (fig. 140), one that remains his tallest to date, even compared to more recent ones, such as a 2008 totem commissioned for the U.S. Embassy in Berlin and a 2011 rectilinear totem designed for the new Barnes Foundation in Philadelphia (p. 304).

As an artist knowledgeable and curious about various fields of art history, Kelly could not have chosen his stele and totem forms lightly. The totem pole once featured prominently in certain Native American traditions, and in some, continues to do so today. Usually a symbol for a family or clan, the totem pole, carved and painted with animal figures, materializes connections with one's lineage or ancestry. As with his stele sculptures, Kelly abstracted his own totems down to a silhouetted shape, allowing his chosen material to speak its own specific color and texture. When installed on public grounds for museums or parks, his totems become meaningful markers of place, set firmly on the ground, but also rising up to the sky. Kelly once said that seeing the purified simplicity of Constantin Brancusi's sculptures, such as his *Bird in Space* (1928) (fig. 141), at the sculptor's Paris studio in 1951 affirmed his own growing approach to making art: "For me, his art was an affirmation; it strengthened my intention to make an art that is spiritual in content."[11] Kelly's totems, in particular, answer this intention. It is thus notable that when Lichtenstein passed away in 1997, Kelly chose the totem form to honor their special friendship, indeed their artistic clanship (fig. 200). He gave this totem a prominent place at his 1998 sculpture exhibition at the Metropolitan Museum of Art, "Ellsworth Kelly on the Roof," curated by Nan Rosenthal, an installation that inaugurated the tradition of showing the work of living artists on the Met rooftop, high above the skyline of Manhattan (fig. 142).

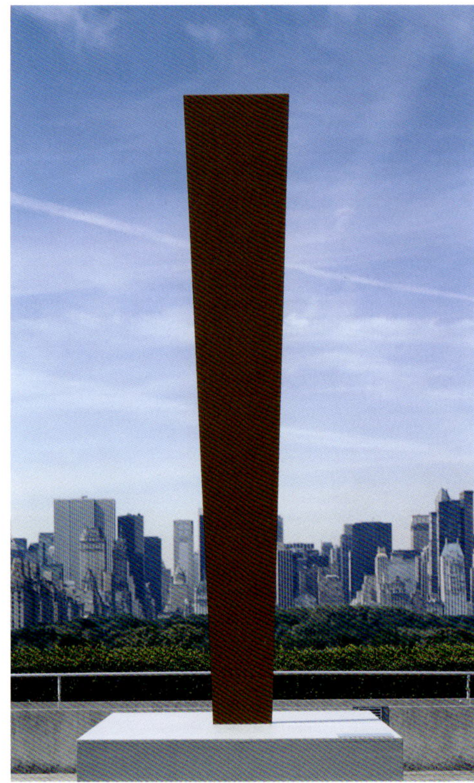

fig. 142: *Totem (for Roy Lichtenstein)*, 1998, bronze, 168 × 28 × 1¼ in, 426.7 × 71.1 × 3.2 cm

By the late 1990s, Kelly had risen in stature as an artist admired for both large-scale sculpture as well as monumental panels and reliefs. And with more success came more commissions. In the early 1960s he had begun to make white sculptures using painted aluminum, as with *White Ring* (1963) (p. 159). Such examples were human scale and intended for indoor viewing. He also made monochrome white reliefs with the same material during the 1970s and 1980s. With new sculptural commissions, he returned to his earlier all-white concept, in concert with his longtime sculpture fabricator since the late 1970s, Peter Carlson. For the first of these white monumental sculptures, commissioned by the Fondation Beyeler, Riehen, near Basel, Switzerland, Kelly produced a freestanding work (p. 271), a 2001 sculpture that soars 19 feet into the air, like his totems.

However, in contrast, *White Curves* (2001) (p. 271) at the Beyeler functions in the round like his rockers, *Pony* (p. 148) and *Untitled (Rocker)* (1997) (p. 270). It embraces the space around it in a new way, its folded structure producing dynamism and movement. Made out of painted aluminum and stainless steel, *White Curves* also introduced a polished surface that, unlike the predominantly matte textures that Kelly had created before for public sculpture, subtly reflects its environs or visitors standing or walking in front of it. Soon, on the request of collectors, Kelly continued creating other white monochromatic sculptures for their property, all on a monumental scale. In three of these examples, *Two Curves* (2001) (pp. 276–77), *Untitled* (2004) (p. 287), and *Untitled* (2013) (p. 313), Kelly incorporated a newly lengthened form: a continuous band of white that bends near the ground or in mid-air to create an altogether different shape. Like the Beyeler sculpture, all three are installed in verdant settings, their crisp man-made white offering a pristine and peaceful contrast to the organic colors of nature.

Art for Walls: Part II

As with the increasing demand for his large-scale outdoor sculpture, invitations for wall commissions by Kelly have grown since the late 1980s. For cultural and educational institutions including the Morton H. Meyerson Symphony Center in Dallas (fig. 143), the Pulitzer Foundation for the Arts in St. Louis (p. 275), the Art Institute of Chicago, Dartmouth College in Hanover, New Hampshire (p. 298), and the new Fondation Louis Vuitton in Paris (pp. 320–21; fig. 11), Kelly found distinctive solutions for the particular requirements of each building as well as his clients. For example, for the Dallas commission in 1989, he produced a quartet of monumental panels, each measuring 34 feet high in a different color, to reiterate the grand space and high ceilings of the symphony hall lobby, as designed by I.M. Pei. Similarly, at the Pulitzer Foundation, designed by Tadao Ando, which opened in 2001, Kelly paralleled the majestic rise of a floor-to-ceiling wall measuring approximately 37 feet tall (p. 275). To prepare for all his commissions, Kelly spends

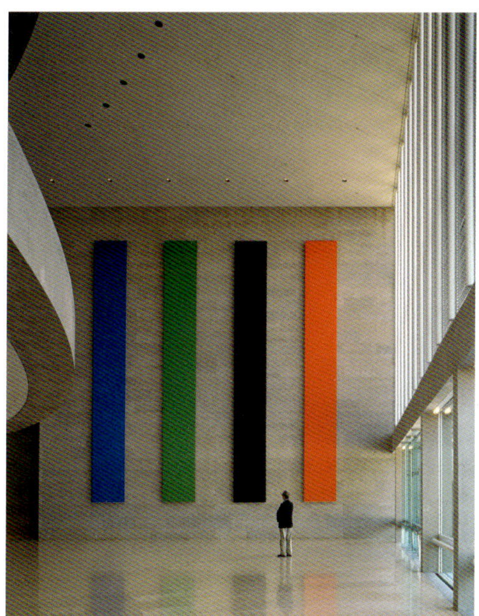

fig. 143: *Dallas Panels*, 1989, fiberglass, 4 panels, 408 × 375½ × 2½ in, 103.6 × 95.4 × 0.6 cm

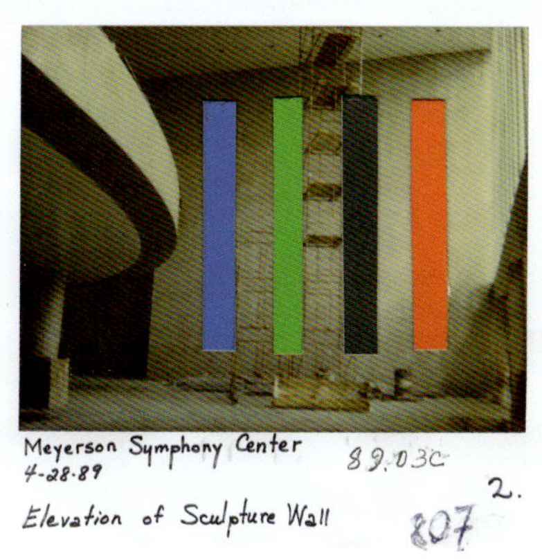

fig. 144: Study for *Dallas Panels*, 1989, Polaroid collage, 4 × 4 in, 10.2 × 10.2 cm

considerable time and effort conceiving his ideas, rendering many studies, through both drawing and collage. One small study for the Dallas project is revelatory of Kelly's working process for such large-scale commissions. In order to envision the scale of his panels, he pasted four small, rectangular paper cutouts onto a Polaroid image of the building under construction (fig. 144) so that he could test out the proportions until they felt "right" to him. Such a process stems from his longstanding practice of postcard collage, where in some he envisioned monumental sculpture on the same scale as the monuments depicted in the cards (fig. 94).

Just as he had dreamed in 1951 in Paris, when he wrote the words, "I believe that artists should work directly with the architect, building as the architect builds" (see p. 43), Kelly has indeed been able to build as each architect builds. In the case of the commissions mentioned above (except the one for Dartmouth, which was for a preexisting building designed by Wallace Harrison), he has done so with leading architects Pei, Tadao Ando, Renzo Piano, and Frank Gehry, respectively. Kelly had already been offered earlier opportunities during his years in New York—most notably, his commission for the Transportation Building in Philadelphia (pp. 140–41) and *Two Curves: Blue Red* with Philip Johnson for the 1964 World's Fair in New York (p. 165)—but these prestigious and ambitious commissions gave Kelly the second condition he had originally envisioned in Paris on a more monumental scale than his early New York commissions: to create works for walls of *large* buildings, as described in his 1950 letter to Cage (see p. 44). It is doubtful that the young artist who wrote this letter could have imagined the scale and variety of walls he would be offered later in his career.

Within the past two decades, governmental bodies have also invited Kelly to create work for their new buildings. In 1998, his seventy-fifth birthday year, Boston's United States Courthouse unveiled the artist's largest wall commission to date, a total of twenty-one panels installed throughout the building (fig. 162), which included a grouping of nine adorning the central rotunda (fig. 161) of the courthouse, designed by architect Henry N. Cobb, of Pei Cobb Freed & Partners. Such a commission was indeed a meaningful nostalgic return for Kelly, who had experienced his artistic beginnings in this city. Two years later, he was invited to conceive a work for another building project, this time for the German parliament in Berlin, the Bundestag at the Paul-Löbe-Haus, designed by Stephan Braunfels. In this enormous building, meant to communicate grandeur as well as power, Kelly was given two monumental lobby walls measuring seven stories high and which are visible from far beyond its exterior through an ambitious set of glass curtain walls. *Berlin Panels* (2000) is a quartet of asymmetrical shapes that harmonize with the dynamic diagonal geometry of the staircases installed along the two expansive walls. Diverging from his use of rectilinear panels, these uniquely shaped panels draw from related forms that he began making in the late 1970s, and which he continued to make into the 2000s—for example, *Blue Black Red Green* (2000) (pp. 272–73).

In 2003 came another esteemed commission, for the new U.S. Embassy in Beijing, under the auspices of the Foundation for Art and Preservation in Embassies (FAPE)—a non-profit organization committed to presenting the work of American artists in U.S. embassies around the world. In this new embassy complex designed by Skidmore, Owings & Merrill (SOM) and dedicated in 2008, Kelly was given both sides of a monumental wall. Inspired by the format of a 2002 work, *White Relief over Black* (p. 278), he installed on one side of the wall a large-scale relief of overlapping panels featuring the colors of the American flag (fig. 145) and on the other, a matching relief with the colors of the Chinese flag (fig. 146), a fitting and eloquent color decision that reflected the diplomacy between the two nations. As in other aspects of life, whereby symbolic color associated with one's country, school, or even favorite sports team can possess the iconic power to foster loyalty, these abstractions communicate national identity as well as pride. Indeed, through these works, Kelly accomplished another goal that he had first declared in his 1950 letter to Cage: that his works for large walls function as "a kind of modern icon."

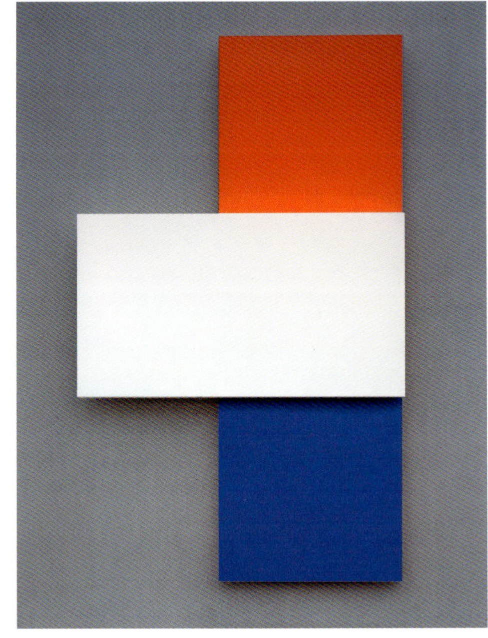

fig. 145: *Beijing Panels,* 2003, painted aluminum, two joined panels, 1 of 2 reliefs, 225 × 132 × 8 in, 571.5 × 335.3 × 20.3 cm

As seen through the variety of these significant commissions, Kelly was easily able to adapt to what was needed for each project, revealing the range and flexibility of his artistic methods. Depending on each commission, he employed a different model of his multipanel practice, choosing rectilinear or shaped panels, joined or separate, a couple or many, all combined with his sensitivity to color, proportion, and scale. Such large-scale commissions are also the culmination of many years of thinking and theorizing about what his art could be: his longstanding belief that it could exist as something beyond the limits of his chosen support, and instead correspond with its environs, with the walls of modern architecture. At the start of his career, the walls that Kelly first addressed were those of the private studio and the commercial gallery in Paris, those of domestic scale. During his years in New York, his choices extended to museum walls at various significant exhibitions as well as a couple of notable public wall commissions. And with the high-profile invitations from the past two decades, he developed thoughtful solutions to address the new kinds of walls he was offered: the judicial walls of the Boston courthouse, the parliamentary walls in Berlin, and the embassy walls in Beijing. Through these projects, he moved beyond the type of walls that exist within the sphere of art, and into the broader arenas of life, spaces endowed with perhaps more potent meaning, where people gather for the governance of a city, state, or nation.

Through these examples, it can be asserted that Kelly's abstract lexicon speaks more successfully on these civic and national walls than representational depictions of a leader, a mode of nationalist art that has lasted for countless centuries and continues today. Of course, Kelly's choice of abstraction was far from new at mid-century: the early twentieth-century avant-garde, such as Malevich, Rodchenko and Mondrian, were among the first to shun realism in order to reject materialism, selecting instead a modern language of abstraction that they believed possessed the power to shape a new society and world. And it was Rodchenko's radical act to declare the end of easel painting with his three monochrome canvases, *Pure Red Color, Pure Yellow Color, Pure Blue Color,* in 1921. While Kelly had not been familiar with this work while forming his multipanel practice in Paris, he had become aware of the philosophy behind the Russian's theorizing about the end of easel painting. The messages of Rodchenko's significant art movement, Constructivism, founded two years after the Russian

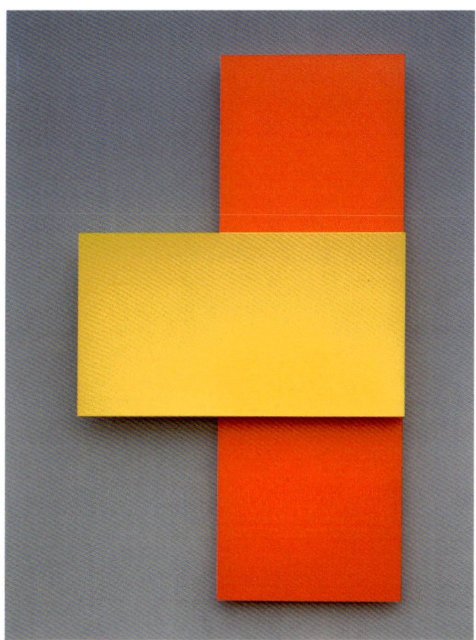

fig. 146: *Beijing Panels,* 2003, painted aluminum, two joined panels, 1 of 2 reliefs, 225 × 132 × 8 in, 571.5 × 335.3 × 20.3 cm

Revolution in 1917, continued to be echoed in different manifestations by architects, artists, critics, and theorists during Kelly's French years and into his New York period. In 1957, Kelly drafted another statement about his thoughts on art and architecture that refers directly to Constructivism and the limits of the easel painting tradition, a concept to which he had been first introduced as a student at Herbert Read's 1948 lecture in Boston:

> Today there is very little collaboration of the plastic arts with architecture producing anything of real value. Perhaps the reason for this is that most contemporary painting is too personal for large wall spaces and the easel painting artist is more involved in his painting as an end itself ... However, there is an awakening among some artists to the demands made upon them by the new architecture. This movement in painting is called Constructivism; an art using pure colors expressed in simple monumental forms adapts itself easily to modern building. The glass and steel reinforced concrete structures have created a new form and a new space to work upon. The monochrome buildings demand color, and the spaces demand an image on a large scale—powerful statements which are very much alive.[12]

Despite this easy adaptability of abstract art to modern architecture that Kelly described in 1957, it is arguably not the case that all abstract artists can achieve such goals, commanding attention on the gallery and museum wall, as well as the civic and national wall, at varying scales and with such fluency and breadth as Kelly has done. It is perhaps why Kelly has been able to stay so relevant and current, nationally and internationally.

Though not a political artist, Kelly is deeply sensitive to the world around him, and there have been times when current events have influenced or reinforced his ideas and thinking. For example, during the mid-to-late 1960s, the topic of space travel was ever present, leading to the success of the first moon landing in 1969 and dreams of more ambitious travel in the decades to come. He found himself drawn to fragmented views of the moon that he saw in news photos as well as in movies like *2001: A Space Odyssey* from 1968 as these images reminded him of his increasing interest in "radial curves." Even as early as 1960, he painted a small canvas called *Yuri Gagarin*, after the Russian pilot chosen to be a part of the Soviet space program that year, and who in 1961 would become the first human to travel into space and orbit the earth. And during the mid-1970s, while the U.S. was confronting the ongoing challenges of the Vietnam War, Kelly felt that his bold colors appeared too celebratory, neither matching nor respecting the mood of the country at the time. Thus, for his second solo exhibition at Leo Castelli in 1975, he presented muted works only in hues of gray, such as *Three Grays* (1975) (p. 237).

More recently, in 2003, Kelly entered the fervent dialogue about how to memorialize the 9/11 attacks and those who died that day in 2001. By fall 2003, a competition had already been called for the 9/11 memorial in downtown Manhattan, and approximately 5,200 proposals had been received. Kelly had not submitted a concept for the official competition, but he still felt compelled to contribute a proposal unofficially. He sent his concept in the form of a collage (fig. 149), plus a letter to *The New York Times* architectural critic Herbert Muschamp, who had become an active voice in the controversy over the rebuilding of the World Trade Center. Muschamp in turn published Kelly's collage, *Ground Zero* (2003), in a *Times* article that appeared on the second anniversary of 9/11. Kelly had taken the front page of a recent *Arts & Leisure* section of *The Times*, featuring an aerial photograph of the destruction at ground zero and the neighboring buildings, and collaged a large green trapezoidal cutout onto the image at center, the silhouette of the form echoing the foreshortened outlines of ground zero as captured in the photograph. In his letter to Muschamp, Kelly explained how "what is needed is a 'visual experience,' not additional buildings, a museum, a list of names or proposals for a freedom monument." According to the artist, these were "distractions from a spiritual vision for the site: a vision for the future."[13]

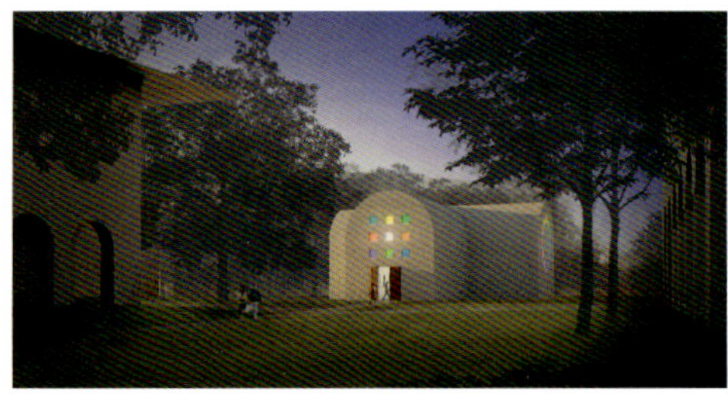

fig. 147: *Austin*, 1986/2015, (digital rendering) artist-designed building with colored glass windows and interior installation, 28 × 63 × 76 ft, 8.6 × 19.3 × 23.3 m

What Kelly had proposed was the presence of "a large green mound of grass" at the site of ground zero. Muschamp praised this concept, stating that Kelly's trapezoid "turned the disjointed cityscape into a symbol of the complex emotional and ideological forces that have been raging around ground zero."[14] Muschamp also connected Kelly's mound to that of the burial-mound tradition, since the site of ground zero had become, in effect, a hallowed burial ground for those who perished that day. This interpretation was apt: Kelly had indeed been inspired by the ancient mound tradition, both burial and ceremonial, stemming from his ongoing appreciation of Mississippian mound-building cultures, an interest awakened during his Boston years. In fact, the year prior to making the collage, he and Jack Shear had visited Cahokia, the site of the largest and best-preserved ancient mounds in the U.S., located just outside St. Louis.

Drawing from his longstanding fascination with ancient Native American artifacts and traditions as well as the visit to Cahokia, Kelly had imagined for his 9/11 proposal a monumental mound standing about 30 feet tall. He had also proposed different plantings depending on the season, offering a living and forever changing memorial at ground zero. However, he had collapsed his three-dimensional, monumental mound into a flat green trapezoidal cutout as performed in his postcard collages. Liking this shape so much, he would also transform it into a painted aluminum shaped panel in 2011 (p. 296). To this day, his unofficial 9/11 memorial proposal remains much admired, as disseminated first in *The New York Times* and then digitally dispersed on the internet.

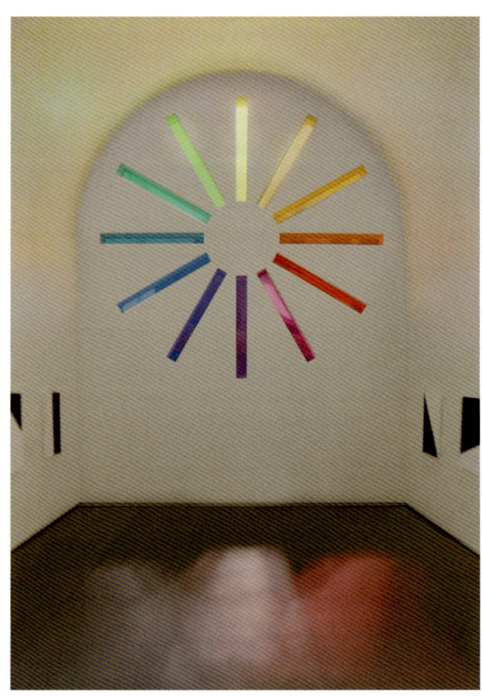

fig. 148: *Austin*, 1986/2015, (scale model) artist-designed building with colored glass windows and interior installation, 28 × 63 × 76 ft, 8.6 × 19.3 × 23.3 m

While Kelly's 30-foot tall mound remains a visionary proposal, there is always the hope that one day it could become a reality, for that is what will happen with an ambitious project Kelly conceived almost thirty years ago. In 1986, Kelly was commissioned to design a chapel for a private ranch in southern California. Despite the detailed plans the artist envisioned for a freestanding chapel, it was not constructed. In the near future, Kelly's original concept will be erected on the grounds of the Blanton Museum of Art at the University of Texas at Austin. Titled after its new site, *Austin* will be a 2,715-square-foot stone building (fig. 147), featuring interior components all designed by the artist: three bays of colored glass windows, a redwood totem, and a series of fourteen black-and-white panels made of marble (fig. 148). Although the cruciform layout and glass windows were inspired by the artist's longtime appreciation for Romanesque architecture and

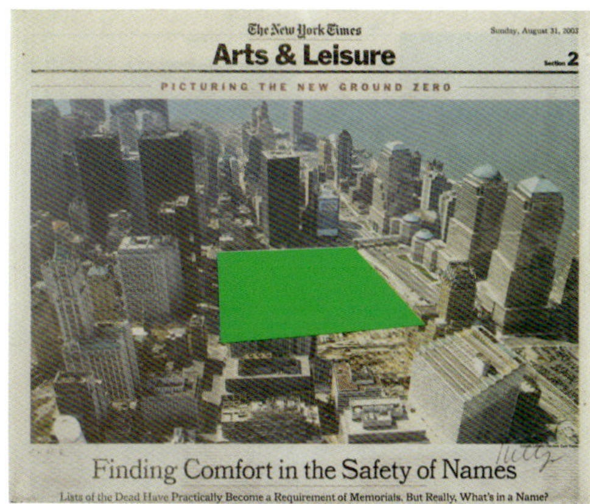

fig. 149: *Ground Zero*, 2003, newsprint collage, 8 × 12¾ in, 20.3 × 32.4 cm

art, Kelly's conception for this building does not include a religious program. Instead, he has abstracted the traditions of church architecture, also eliminating its original Christian functions to produce a non-denominational space for spiritual contemplation as well as the appreciation of art. As Kelly reflected in 1990 about his visit to Brancusi's Paris studio in 1951, "it strengthened my intention to make an art that is spiritual in content" (see p. 207). With the planning for *Austin*, Kelly has moved beyond his standard practice of making art for walls, of "building as the architect builds"; in this particular and remarkable case, he has become his own architect, building art for the walls of his own building.

Kelly in the Present Tense

Kelly once said, "My later paintings have all the early paintings inside them. An artist starts from an idea and builds on it."[15] Such a statement is applicable to all his art, in whatever medium, whether painting, relief, sculpture, print, drawing, or collage. His career of almost seven decades has allowed observers, as well as the artist himself, to note the correspondences and continuities in his art. For example, if one takes the trapezoidal form in his collage, *Ground Zero* (fig. 149), and imagines flipping it horizontally, one is surprised to see a stunning resemblance to a shape that he had painted while a student in Boston in 1947, when asked by his teacher to experiment with painting different textures. In this small 1946 study on wood (fig. 20), Kelly explored varied shapes as well as textures, and at center is a small green trapezoid, arrestingly similar to the one that the mature and seasoned Kelly would create in 2003. One also cannot help but notice the pairing of a red shape with a white one seen to the left of the green trapezoid and make a connection to his later duo-paneled works, such as *White and Dark Gray Panels I*, made in 1977 (p. 245) and more so with *Blue White*, made in 1980 (p. 242).

As quoted near the start of this essay, Kelly stated in 1992, "My painting is about the memory of things."[16] Many or even most of his works exemplify this statement, existing as new recollections of what came before, as seen throughout this study. Within the past several years, he has continued this practice, perhaps with even more fervor, tapping into a reserve of ideas that he has been collecting for almost seven decades. In 2009, he made *Blue Curves* (p. 294), a single shaped work that relates to another silhouetted example from 2004, *Two Curves* (p. 281). These two paintings mark a return to his "free curves," the voluptuous and sensuous forms that Kelly had begun to paint in the mid-1950s in New York, and which he had left behind for the most part, as he focused on developing his "radial curves" starting in the late 1960s. For *Blue Curves* in 2009, he mined his past again, inspired by a collage he had made in 1956 (fig. 150), which features a similar cutout shape in black, with one straight edge on the left, and the appearance of two curves protruding to the right.

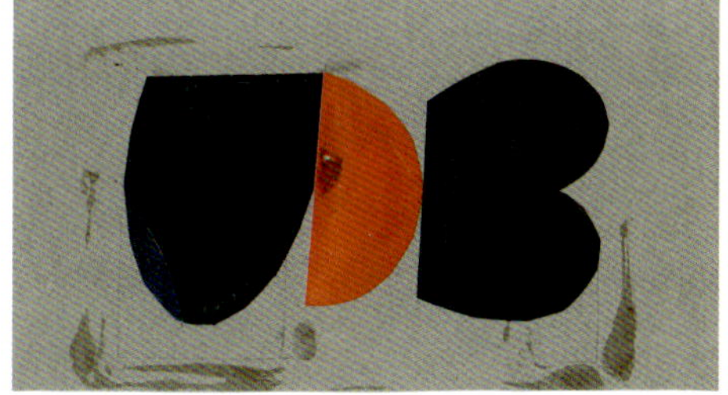

fig. 150: *Black Forms with Red*, 1956, collage on paper, 6¾ × 12¼ in, 17 × 31.1 cm

In this same calendar year, 2009, Kelly was also honored with a public and prestigious nod to his past in France. He was promoted to rank of *Officier* of the French Legion of Honor, an even higher award than the French knighthood already bestowed on him in 1992, *Chevalier de l'Ordre National de la Légion de Honneur et Patrie* by the French Republic. This 1992 award correlated to the important traveling exhibition devoted to Kelly's French years, a seminal period in his artistic development that French governmental officials had recognized, for it was there in France that the artist first laid out his artistic goals. At the time, starting out in 1948, he was unsure of how to proceed; he grasped that his growing resistance to a realistic representation of the world around him was not a new idea, but his sustained reliance on and compelling attraction to the visual experience proved to be a great obstacle for him. As he would later recall about these first years in France, "My problem was vision. What I got from vision didn't line up with new ways of making paintings."[17] Instead, he developed his own means of connecting with vision—one that still depended on what he saw, thus freeing him of the pressure to invent new content. There in France, Kelly discovered a number of ways to reconcile both his reliance and resistance to reality—"I've always felt competitive with reality" (see pp. 115–16)—by creating an art that did not achieve a likeness but nonetheless retained the perceived experience through form and hue. In doing so, he fostered a new kind of visuality, one that addressed not how we recognize things, but how they appear as shape and color. Thus we have seen that Kelly did invent a new brand of abstraction at mid-twentieth century by intentionally, even radically, choosing not to invent.

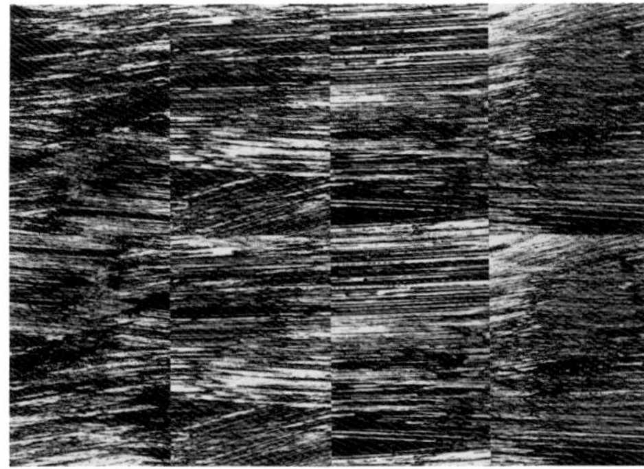

fig. 151: *River II*, 2004, 2 four-color lithographs, on Rives BFK paper mounted on aluminum, 80 × 109 in, 203.2 × 276.9 cm

Of course, it must also be stated that Kelly did indeed arrive at great moments of artistic invention. He was among the first to develop multipanel painting among his peers (though for him it was a *reinvention* of the medieval polyptych tradition that he greatly admired). He endowed new meaning to the wall, to the vertical surface on which art had hung for centuries, by integrating his art with architecture and thereby complicating the notion that a painting alone was the work of art. While the Abstract Expressionists before him had painted abstract worlds within each of their canvases, Kelly produced new paintings that incorporated the world in which we live. He created silhouetted, shaped works many years before it became currency during the 1960s. And it can be observed that over the years he did invent his own vocabulary of unique and plentiful shapes, ones that now read as characteristically Kelly, as can also be said of his bold brilliant colors.

While some might say that his art is one of distillation or purification, his approach is far from that. His work does partake in some levels of reduction, such as his use of singular forms, a palette of only a few colors, plus a paint application absent of a personal brushstroke and tonal inflections. Kelly, however, has remained thoroughly engaged by specificity and singularity, by the particulars and plenitude of vision, the exact opposite of a purified, distilled essence. Vision continues to factor significantly in his art-making while he still enjoys retrieving ideas from the past. In 2005, he completed an ambitious series of lithographs, unparalleled in his print oeuvre, called *The Rivers*, which include different renditions of the same theme, such as *River II* (2004) (fig. 151), the biggest in this series. *River II* features enlarged painterly gestures in black and white, a great surprise for an artist who abandoned gesture in his paintings many years ago. In the four separate vertical panels, a grid of eight separate images starts to appear on closer inspection.

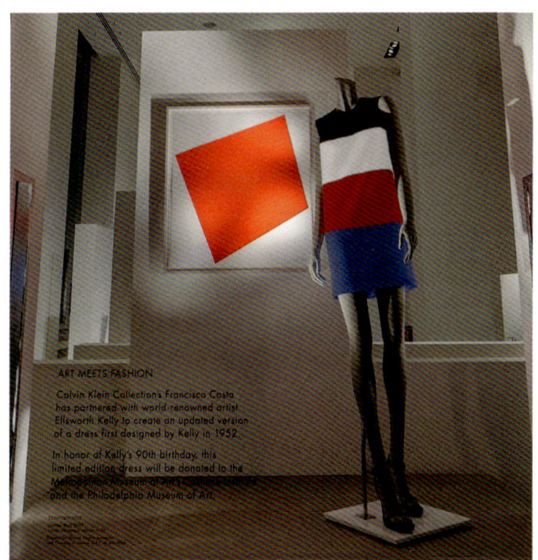

fig. 152: Ellsworth Kelly's *Dress* (2012) at Calvin Klein's Madison Avenue flagship store, 2013

The creation of *River II* was the consequence of both visual inspiration and retrieval of past concepts. Starting in 2002 when studying some printed cards of impressions that he had originally rejected for an earlier print series using black, Kelly discovered how he liked the gesture in these sample cards sent to him by Gemini G.E.L. These cut-up versions reminded him of the gridded work he had made in France, such as *Cité* (p. 63) and *Seine* (p. 66). Soon afterwards, he visited Basel, Switzerland, and while standing on his hotel balcony, he observed the flickering of lights on the Rhine, reminding him of his Paris days when he studied similar light effects on the Seine; he realized how his printed cards back at his studio related to such contrasts of light and dark. Inspired by this experience of looking at the Rhine, he requested Gemini to increase some of the small cards to a much larger size. Following more experiments as well as some happy accidents that Kelly liked, *River II* came into being, a work that fuses his memories of the past with the present.

Perhaps when one has lived as long as Kelly has, the past becomes more alive. At his 2013 Matthew Marks exhibition celebrating his ninetieth birthday, a number of works shown there stemmed from ideas and shapes that he had first developed in New York, including *Curves on White (Four Panels)* (2011) (pp. 300–01), although the distinction between then and now was his decision to make them in cutout relief form at this show. However, a few of the works in this exhibition were almost exact translations of sketches or collages he had made in 1962, such as *Gold with Orange Reliefs* (2013) (fig. 59 and p. 311) and a work similar to *Black Form I* (2011) (p. 299), ideas that either did not speak to him then many years ago, or for which he had simply run out of time. Also during his birthday year, a very unique Kelly creation was unveiled at Calvin Klein's flagship store in Manhattan (fig. 152), an updated version of the dress he had first designed in 1952 (fig. 52). After making *Red Yellow Blue White* (pp. 74–75) out of fabric that year, he had material leftover, which he then gave to his Boston friend Anne Weber with directions for making a four-paneled dress, with bands of equal height. Weber, however, did not listen to her friend's instructions, and instead made the fourth panel the longest, following current fashion, "the new Dior length."[18] Kelly was not pleased at the time with Weber's decision, and about sixty years later he was given the opportunity to correct his friend's disregard of his directions, this time with Francisco Costa, the women's creative director at Calvin Klein. With this dress, Kelly was able to renew his ideas from many years ago.

It does seem that Kelly, more than other artists, has always been willing to engage with his past readily, easily, and compellingly. He is also an artist inspired by the art-historical past, often saying that one must not forget the art of the Old Masters. As someone who has never veered from his overarching artistic drive—an honesty of vision—Kelly has stayed true and committed to the ideas first formed as a young man in Paris and then in New York. The memories of his life—experiences serving in the camouflage battalion, recollections of paintings seen in Boston, stories about artists met in France, books borrowed from the American Library in Paris, among many other pivotal and not-so pivotal memories—have accumulated over time, informing and literally shaping who he has become and what he still makes today. At his ninetieth birthday exhibition at Marks (fig. 154), his art looked just as fresh, crisp, and bold as his first solo show in New York at Parsons must have appeared in 1956 (fig. 153). In 1994 Kelly reflected on one of his early goals about his art that he thought at the time he had not achieved:

> I wanted to make art that wouldn't date, that would live in the present tense. Now, of course, you know that you can't avoid that, no matter how anonymous something can be. You're always part of your own time ... I thought that my large panels of primary colors separated on a wall was a modern statement. And I felt that in a hundred years it could still be a modern statement. It wouldn't change. But now when I look at those paintings, I see that they, like all art, are part of their time.[19]

While it cannot be denied that all art belongs to a particular time (and, of course, ages with the passing of years), it can be convincingly asserted that Kelly has indeed accomplished his goal of making an art that continues to look modern. The currency and elasticity of his art is profound, whether for museums or private collections, civic or national walls, for something as tragic and historical as 9/11, or something as beautiful and functional as a dress. Through the breadth of his exceptional vision and his diverse methods, he has been able to create an art that is still relevant almost seventy years from when he first started. And if that is not a hundred years, it is close. Ellsworth Kelly is our Old Master making art in the present tense.

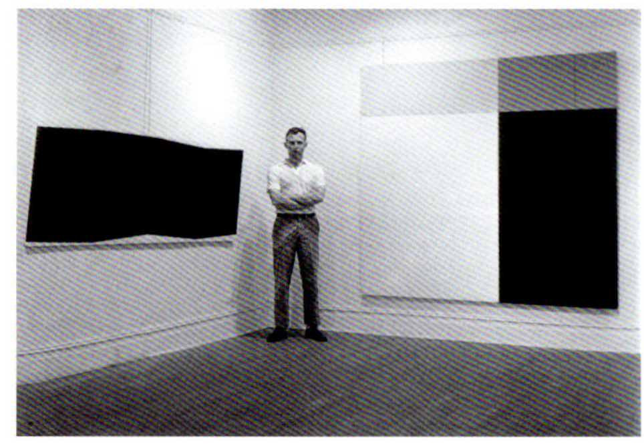

fig. 153: Ellsworth Kelly with *Bar* (1955) and *Tiger* (1953), Betty Parsons Gallery, New York, 1956

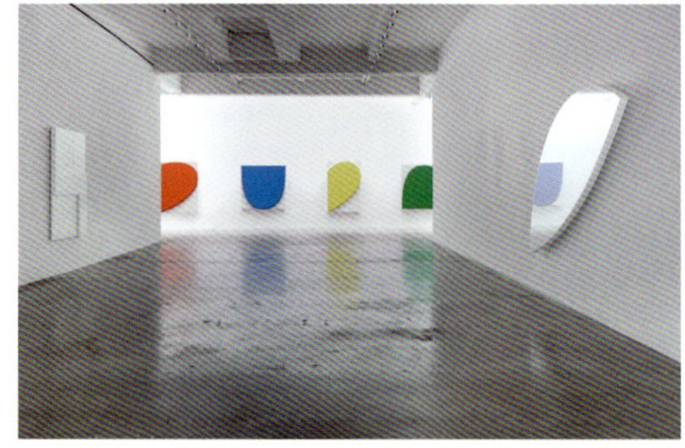

fig. 154: Installation view of "Ellsworth Kelly at Ninety," Matthew Marks Gallery, New York, 2013

1 Kelly, in conversation with the author, Spencertown, New York, August 2, 2001.
2 John Coplans, *Ellsworth Kelly* (New York: Harry N. Abrams, Inc., 1971); Diane Waldman, *Ellsworth Kelly: Drawings, Collages, Prints* (Greenwich, CT: New York Graphic Society Ltd., 1971).
3 John Coplans, "The Earlier Work of Ellsworth Kelly," *Artforum* 7, no. 10 (Summer 1969), pp. 48–55.
4 These large-scale sheets were displayed for public view in 2002 at the Drawing Center, New York, in an exhibition curated by Yve-Alain Bois. At the time of the exhibition, the first to show a large grouping together, the artist assigned the title *Tablet* to this body of work. See Yve-Alain Bois, *Ellsworth Kelly: Tablet, 1948–1973* (New York: The Drawing Center; Lausanne: Musée Cantonal des Beaux-Arts, 2002).
5 Harold Rosenberg, "The Art World: Dogma and Talent," *The New Yorker* (October 15, 1973), pp. 113–18.
6 Diane Waldman, *Ellsworth Kelly: Drawings, Collages, Prints* (Greenwich, CT.: New York Graphic Society Ltd., 1971), p. 11.
7 Thomas B. Hess, "Sincerely Yours, Ellsworth Kelly," *New York Magazine* (October 15, 1973), p. 98.
8 Henry Geldzahler, "Interview with Ellsworth Kelly," in *Paintings, Sculpture and Drawings by Ellsworth Kelly* (Washington, DC: Washington Gallery of Modern Art, 1963), n.p. Reprinted in Geldzahler, *Making it New: Essays, Interviews, and Talk*s (New York: Turtle Point Press, 1994), pp. 68–73.
9 By 1992, only two French works belonged to museums: *Colors for a Large Wall* (p. 69), which the artist gifted to MoMA in 1969; and *Kite II* (pp. 80–81), which the Centre Pompidou acquired in 1987, the first time a museum purchased a work from his French years.
10 See Bois 1992. Coinciding with this exhibition, the French publication *Artstudio* devoted its spring 1992 issue to the artist, with essays by Bois, Tiffany Bell, Roberta Bernstein, Christophe Domino, Carter Ratcliff, Nan Rosenthal, Claire Stoulig, and artist interviews each by Paul Taylor and Ann Hindry. See Hindry (ed.), *Artstudio: Spécial Ellsworth Kelly*, no.24 (Spring 1992).
11 Kelly, *Artist's Choice: Ellsworth Kelly: Fragmentation and the Single Form* (New York: The Museum of Modern Art, 1990), n.p.
12 Kelly, from a 1957 statement quoted in Meyer 1998, p. 5.
13 Kelly, quoted in Herbert Muschamp, "Critic's Notebook: One Vision; A Hill of Green at Ground Zero," *The New York Times*, September 11, 2003, p. E1.
14 Ibid. For an analysis of *Ground Zero* (fig. 149), see Tricia Y. Paik, "A Green Mound for Ground Zero: Ellsworth Kelly's 9/11 Proposal" [ch.7], in Elizabeth Pergam (ed.), *Drawing in the 21st Century: The Politics and Poetics of Contemporary Practice* (Burlington, VT: Ashgate, 2015), pp. 101–22.
15 Kelly, quoted in Taylor 1991, p. 102.
16 Kelly, quoted in Hindry 1992, p. 29.
17 Kelly, in conversation with the author, Spencertown, New York, August 2, 2001.
18 Kelly, quoted in Carol Vogel, "Inside Art: Galleries Celebrate Ellsworth Kelly at 90," *The New York Times*, April 26, 2013, p. C26.
19 Kelly, quoted in Diamonstein 1994, pp.122–23.

White Black, 1970
oil on canvas, 2 joined panels
111 × 64 in, 281.9 × 162.6 cm

Black Green, 1970
oil on canvas, 2 joined panels
110 × 84 in, 279.4 × 213.4 cm

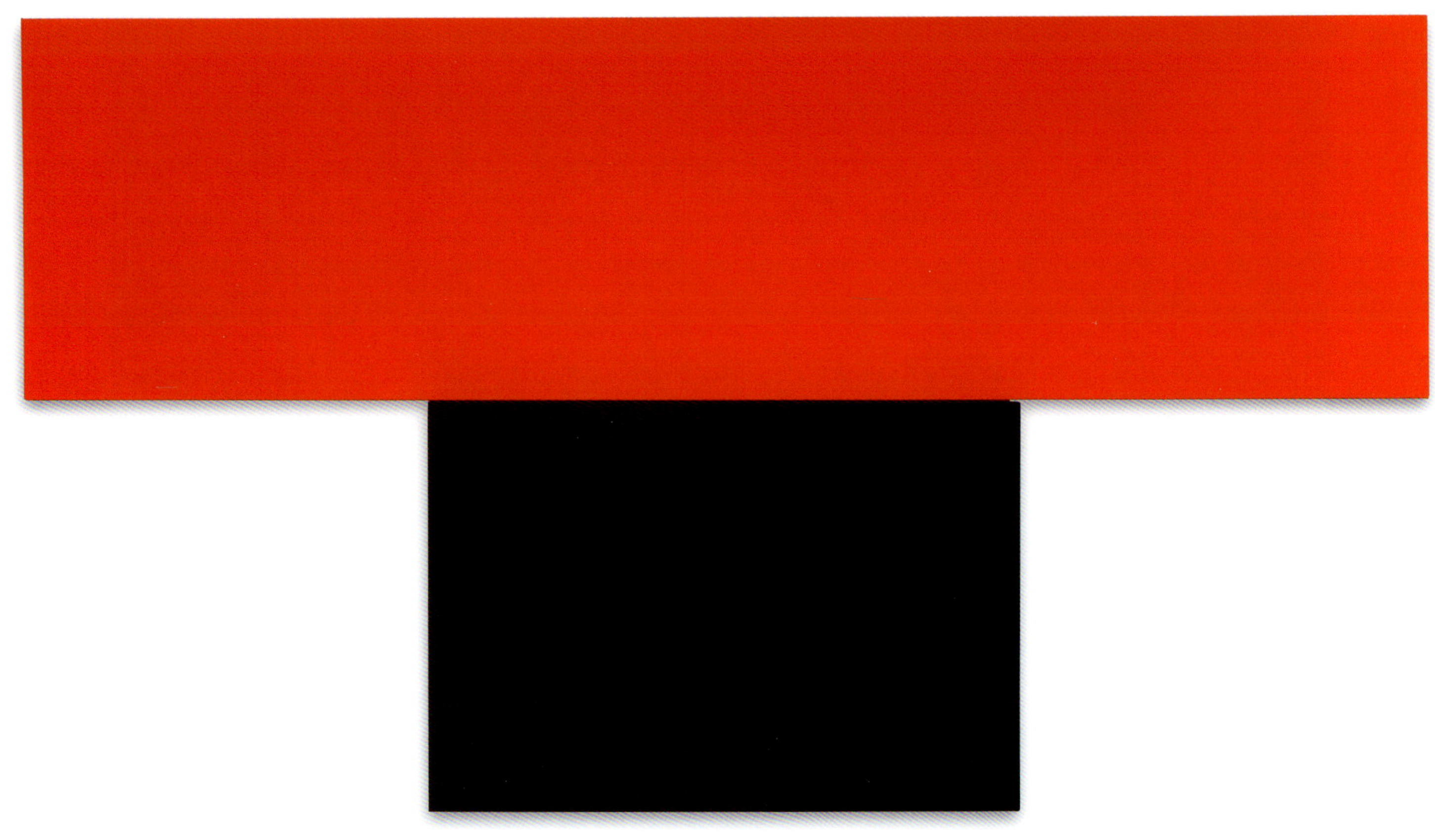

Black with Red Bar, 1970
oil on canvas, 2 joined panels, 68 × 120 in, 172.7 × 304.8 cm

Black Yellow-Orange, 1970
oil on canvas, 85 × 117 in, 215.9 × 297.2 cm

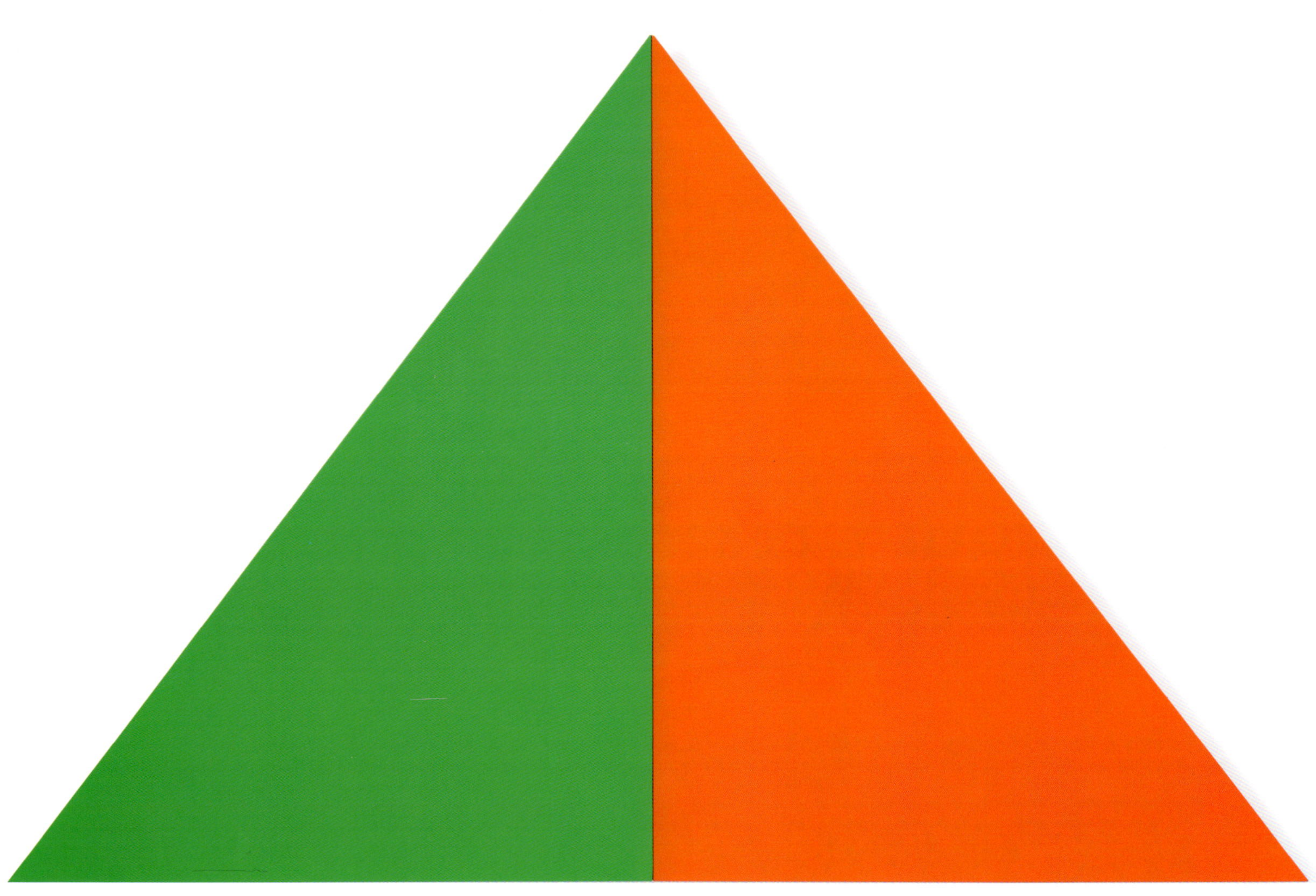

Green Orange, 1970
oil on canvas, 2 joined panels, 70 × 107 in, 177.8 × 271.8 cm

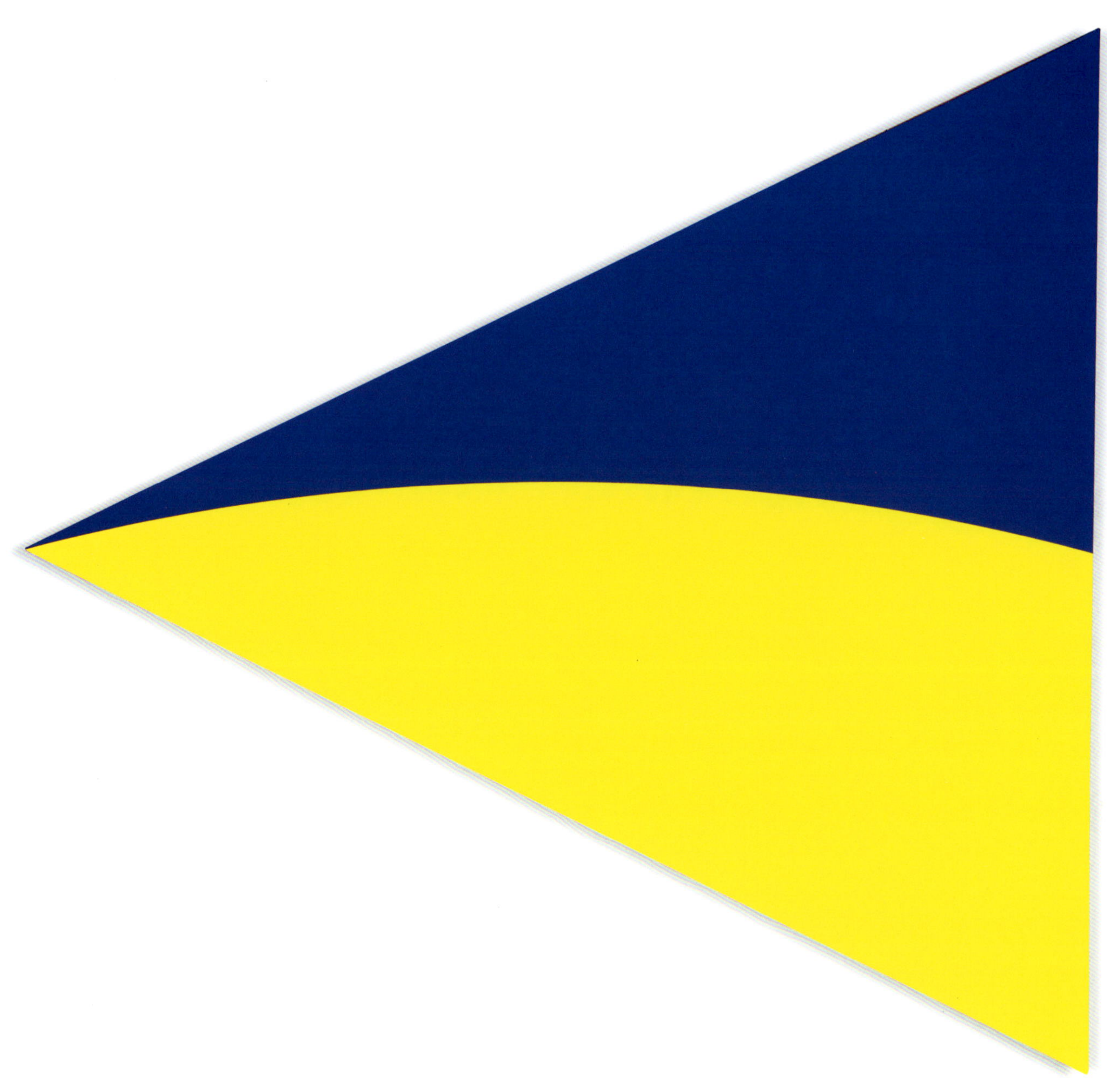

Yellow Blue Curve I, 1972
oil on canvas, 100 × 100 in, 254 × 254 cm

Chatham X: Black Red, 1971
oil on canvas, 2 joined panels
108 × 95¾ in, 274.3 × 243.2 cm

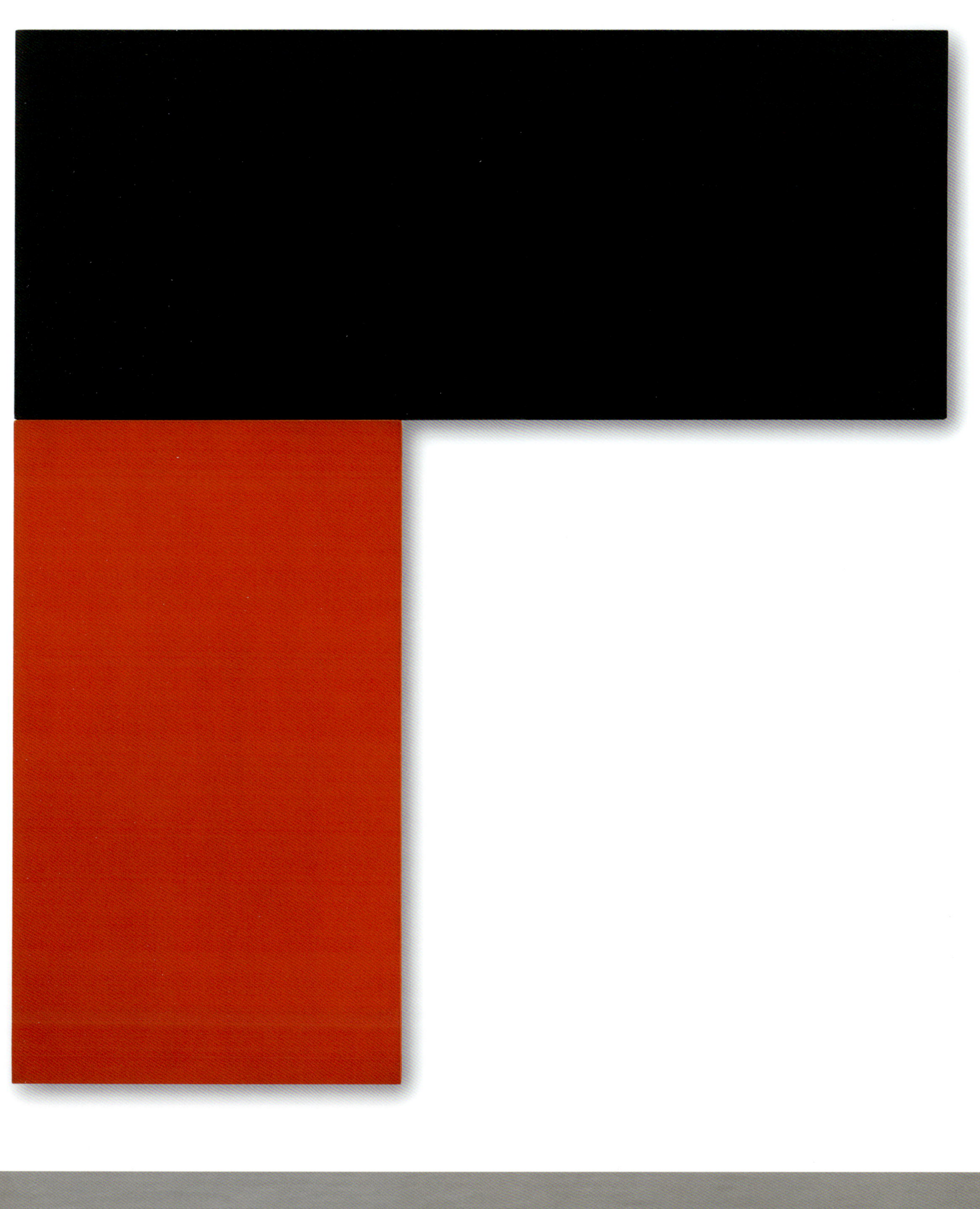

Blue Yellow Red III, 1971
oil on canvas, 3 joined panels
72 × 74 in, 182.9 × 188 cm

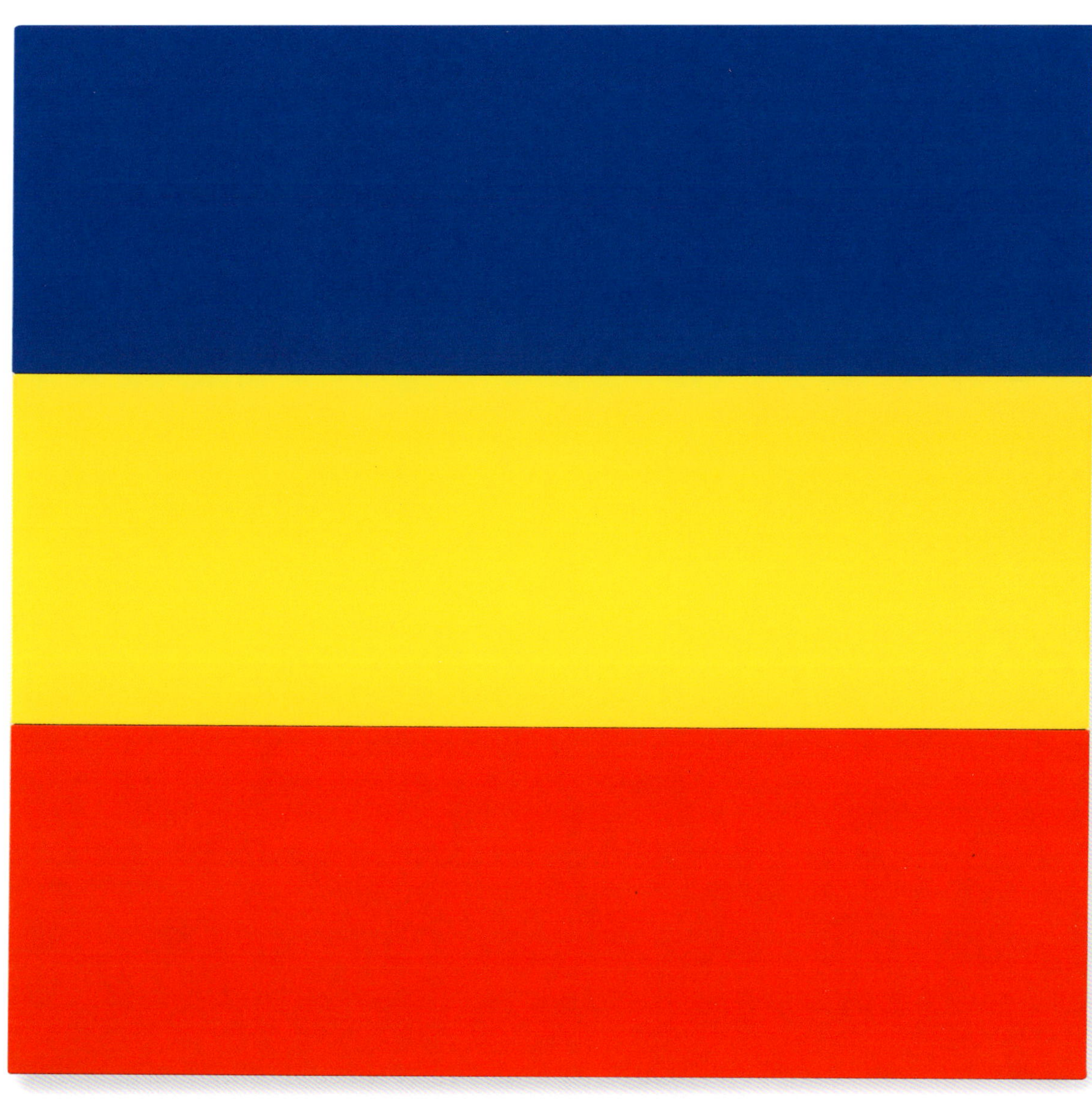

Black White, 1967
oil on canvas, 2 joined panels, 82 × 144 in, 208.3 × 365.8 cm

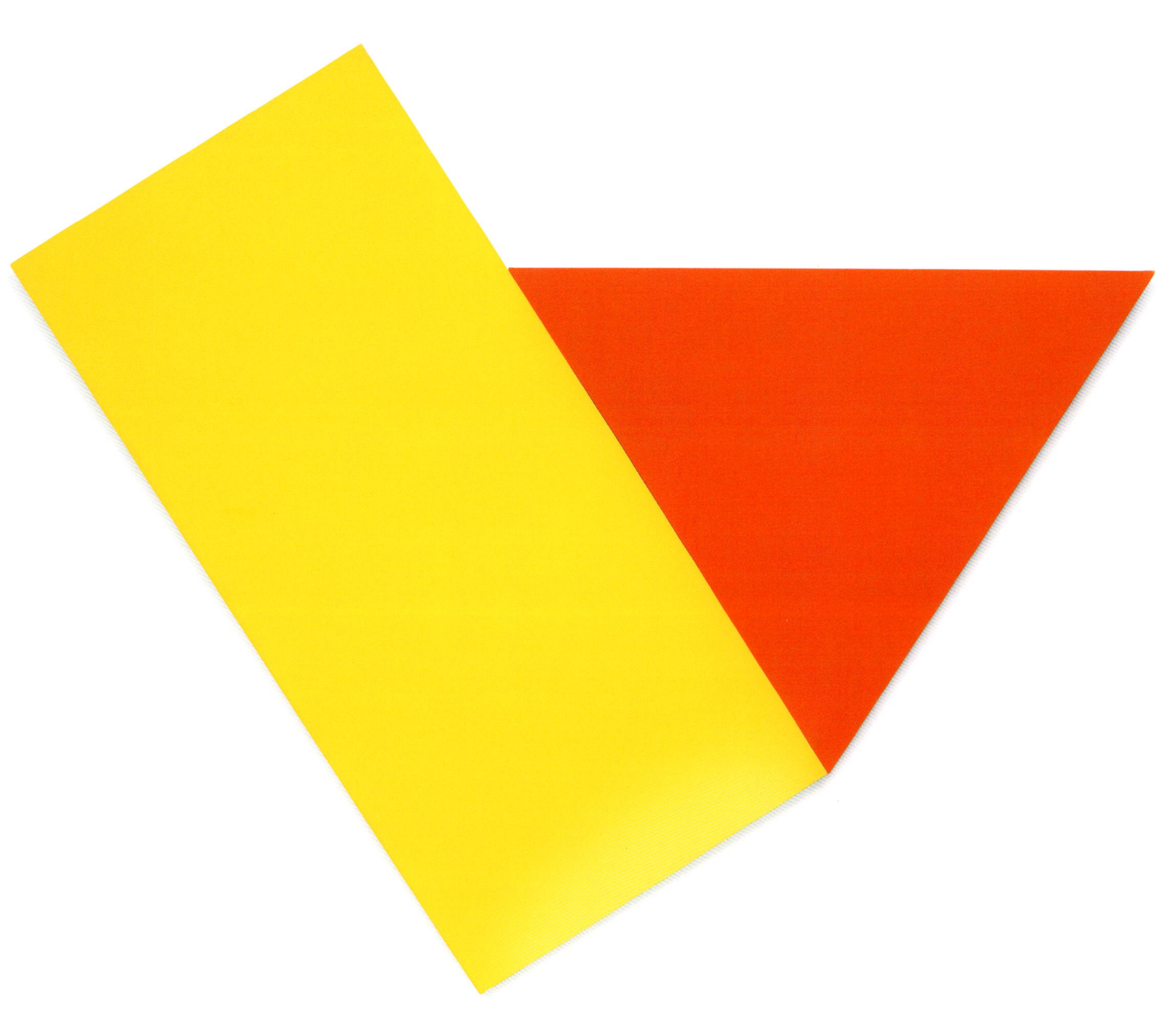

Yellow with Red Triangle, 1973
oil on canvas, 2 joined panels, 119 × 145½ in, 302.3 × 369.6 cm

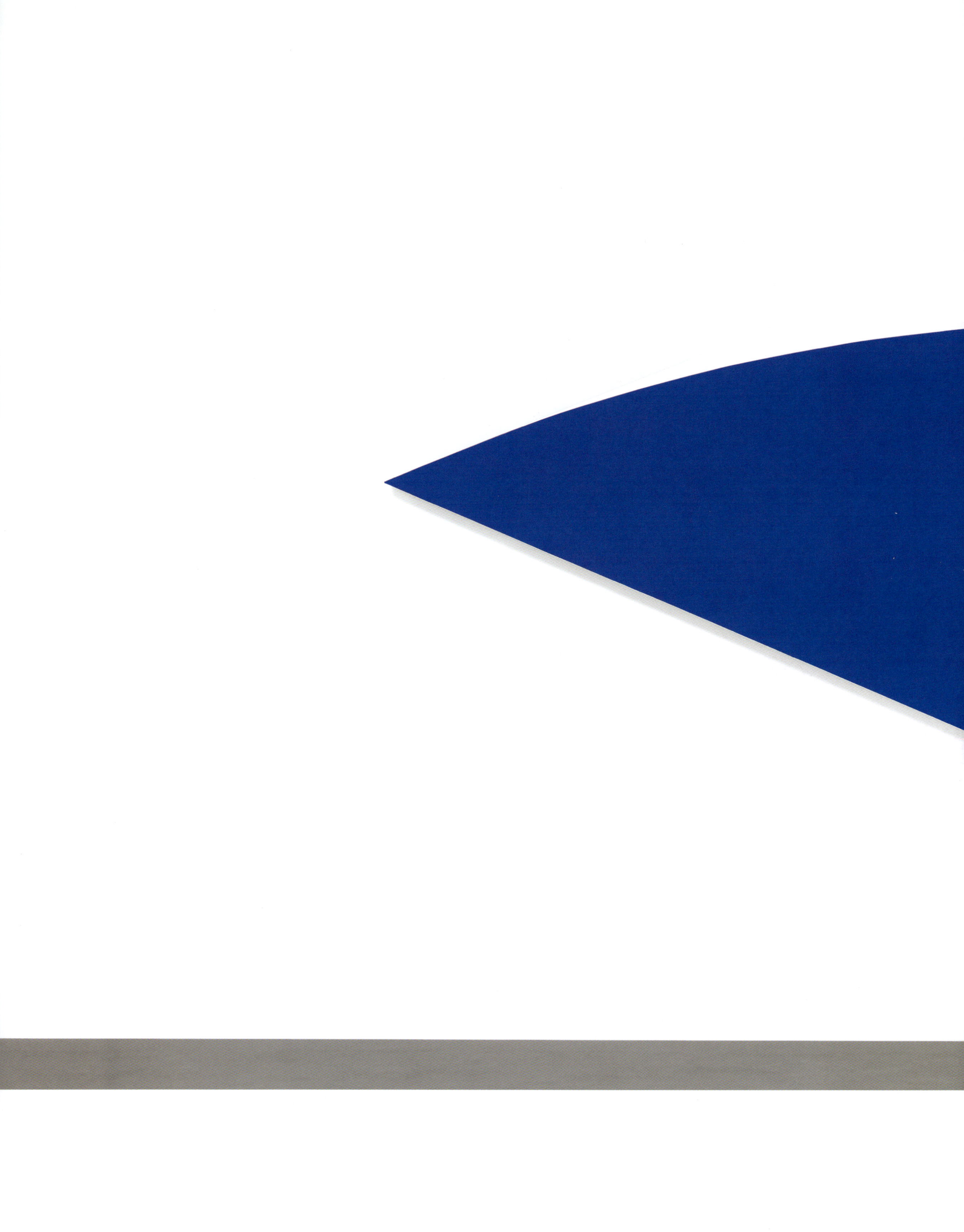

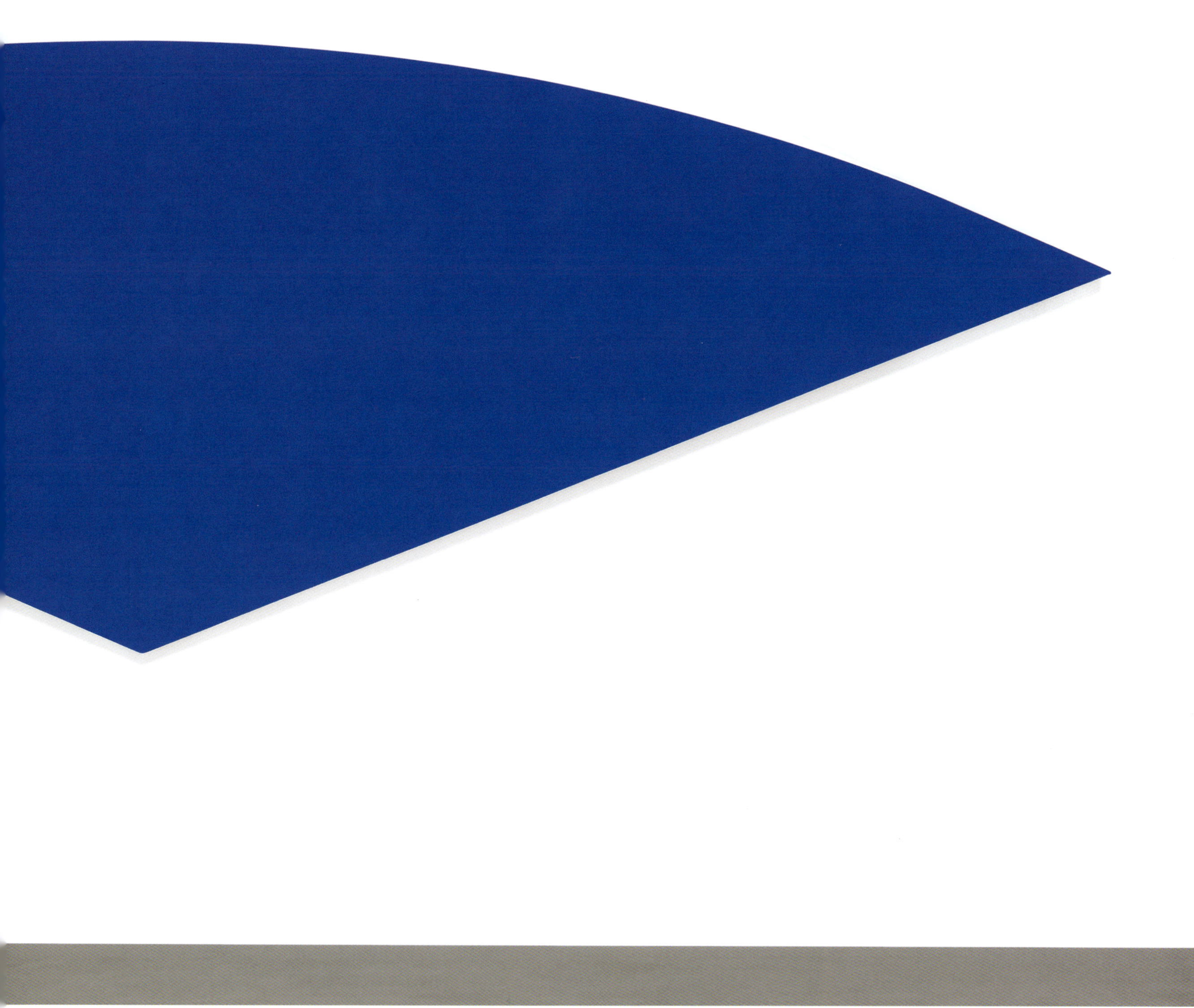

Blue Curve III, 1972
oil on canvas, 67¾ × 166½ in, 172.1 × 422.9 cm

Stele I, 1973
weathering steel, 216 × 120 × 1 in
548.6 × 304.8 × 2.5 cm

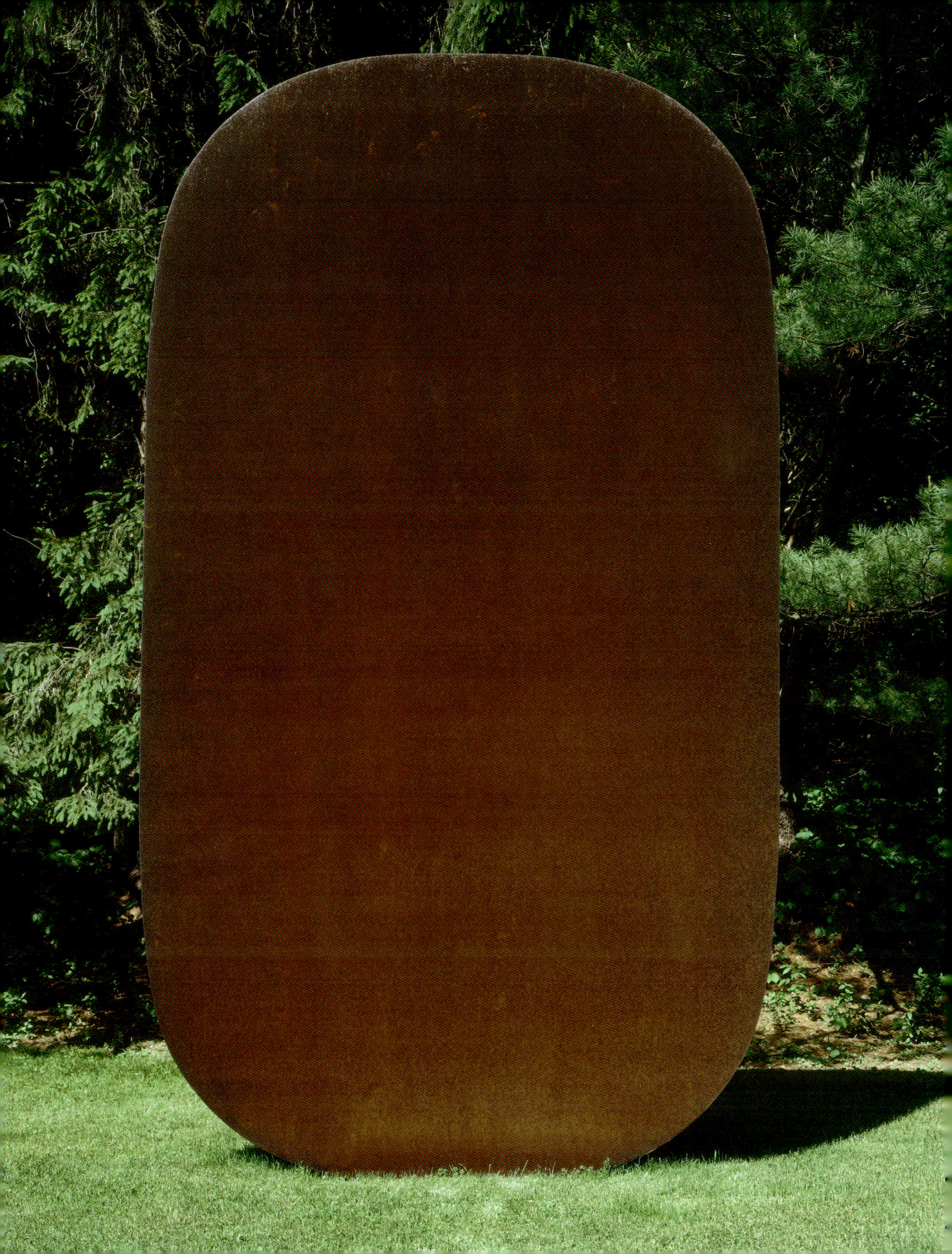

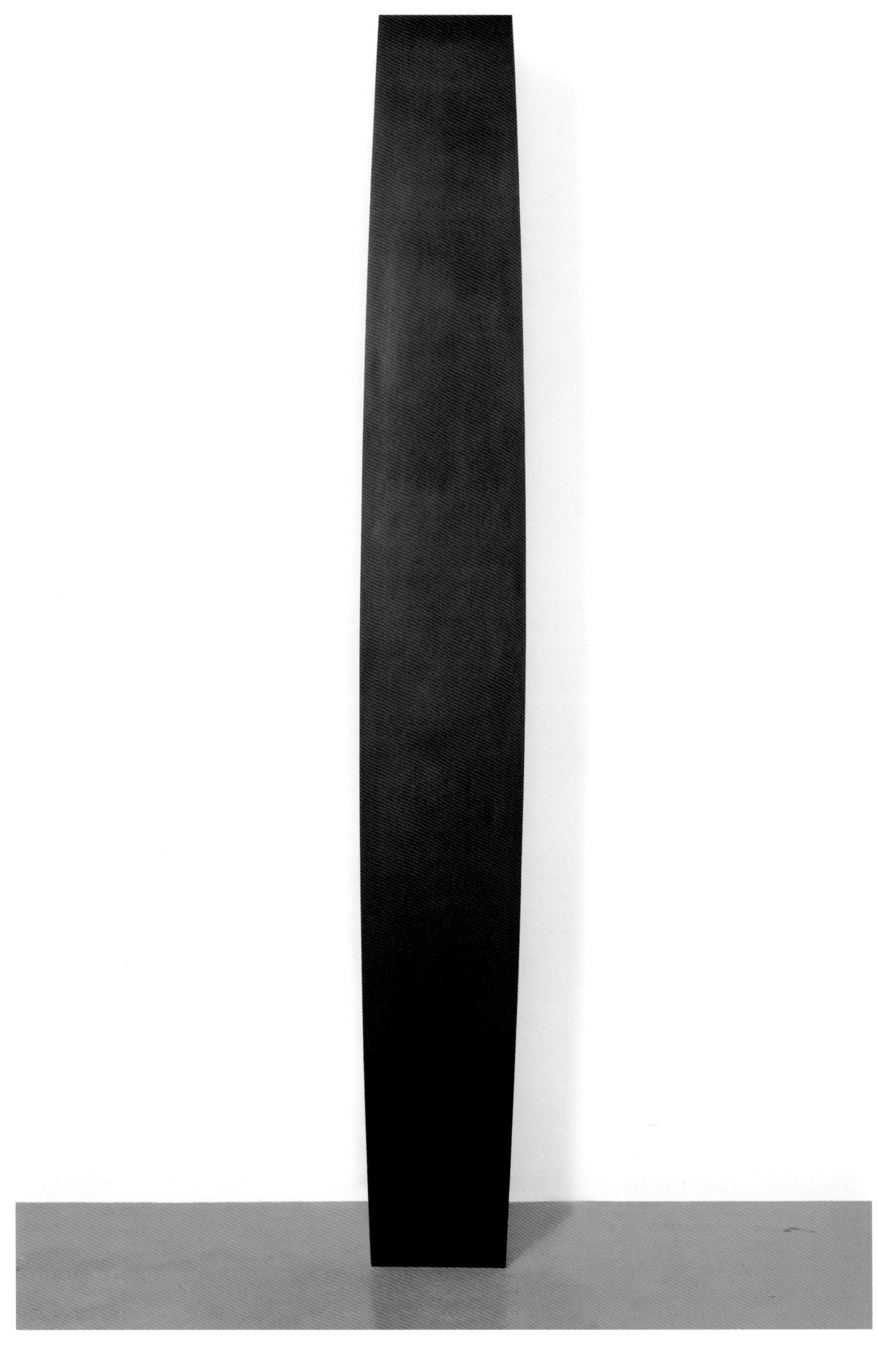

Curve XI, 1974
weathering steel
120 × 16 × ¾ in, 304.8 × 40.6 × 1.9 cm

Stele II, 1973
weathering steel
126 × 118⅛ × 1 in, 320 × 300 × 2.5 cm

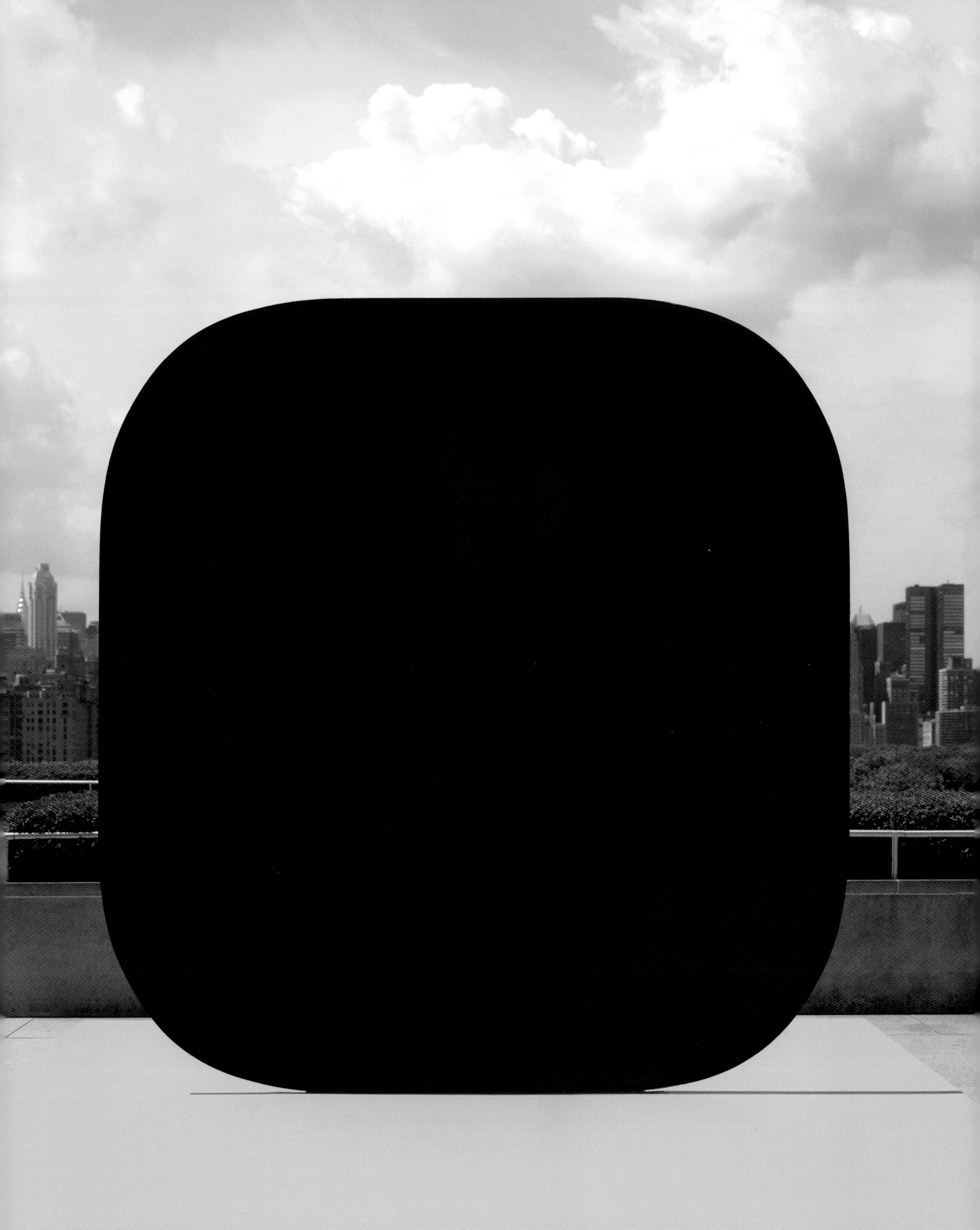

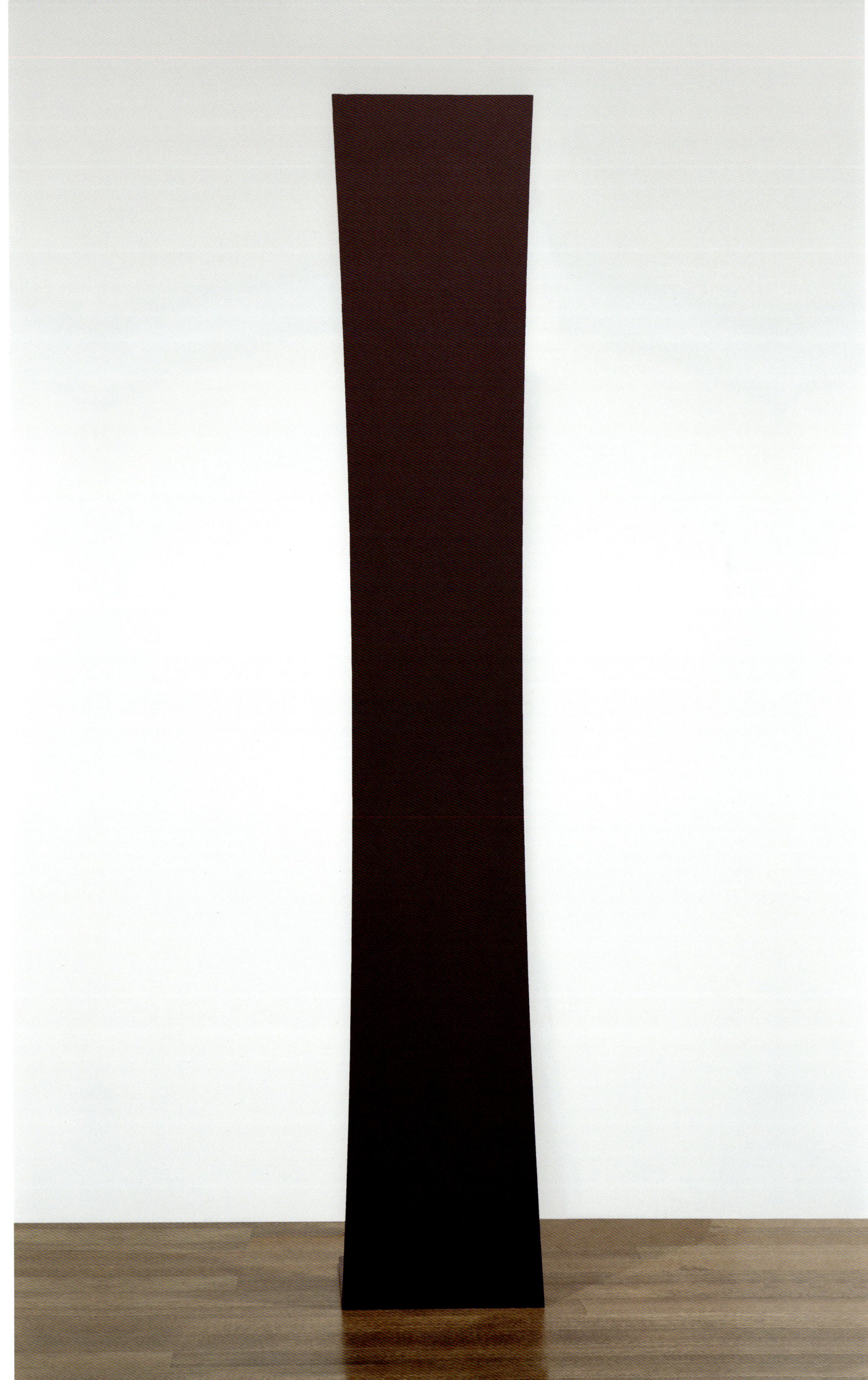

Curve X, 1974
weathering steel
120 × 20 × ¾ in, 304.8 × 50.8 × 1.9 cm

Three Grays, 1975
oil on canvas, 3 joined panels
108 × 108 in, 274.3 × 274.3 cm

Concorde IV, 1976
oil on canvas, 2 joined panels, 96 × 80 in, 243.8 × 203.2 cm

Black Curve I, 1970
oil on canvas, 41⅞ × 39¼ in, 106.4 × 99.7 cm

Gray Panels, 1976
oil on canvas, 4 joined panels, 69 × 180 in, 175.3 × 457.2 cm

Blue White, 1980
oil on linen canvas, 2 joined panels
112¼ × 115 in, 285.1 × 292.1 cm

Diagonal with Curve XIII, 1980
stainless steel
107½ × 47 × ½ in, 273.1 × 119.4 × 1.3 cm

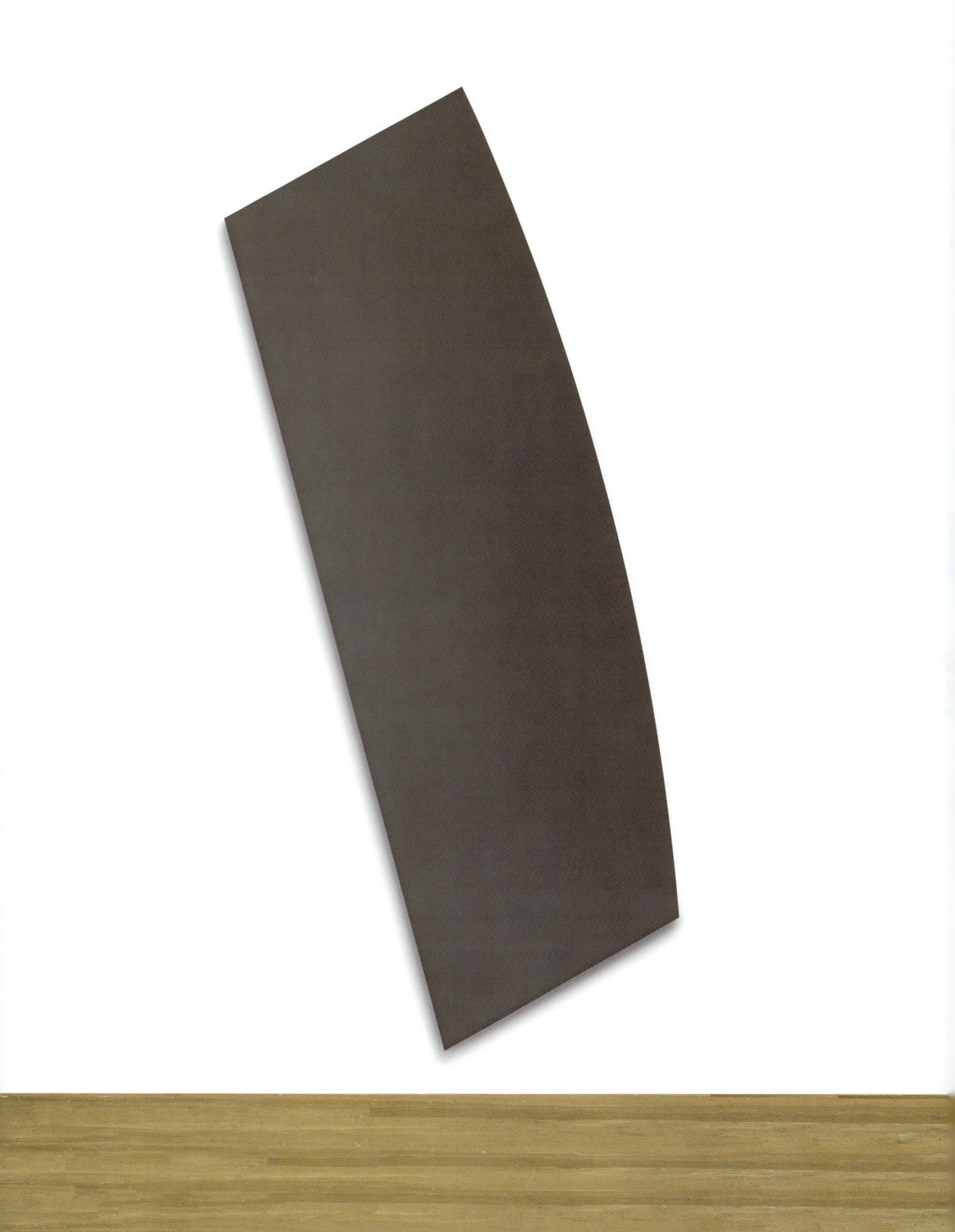

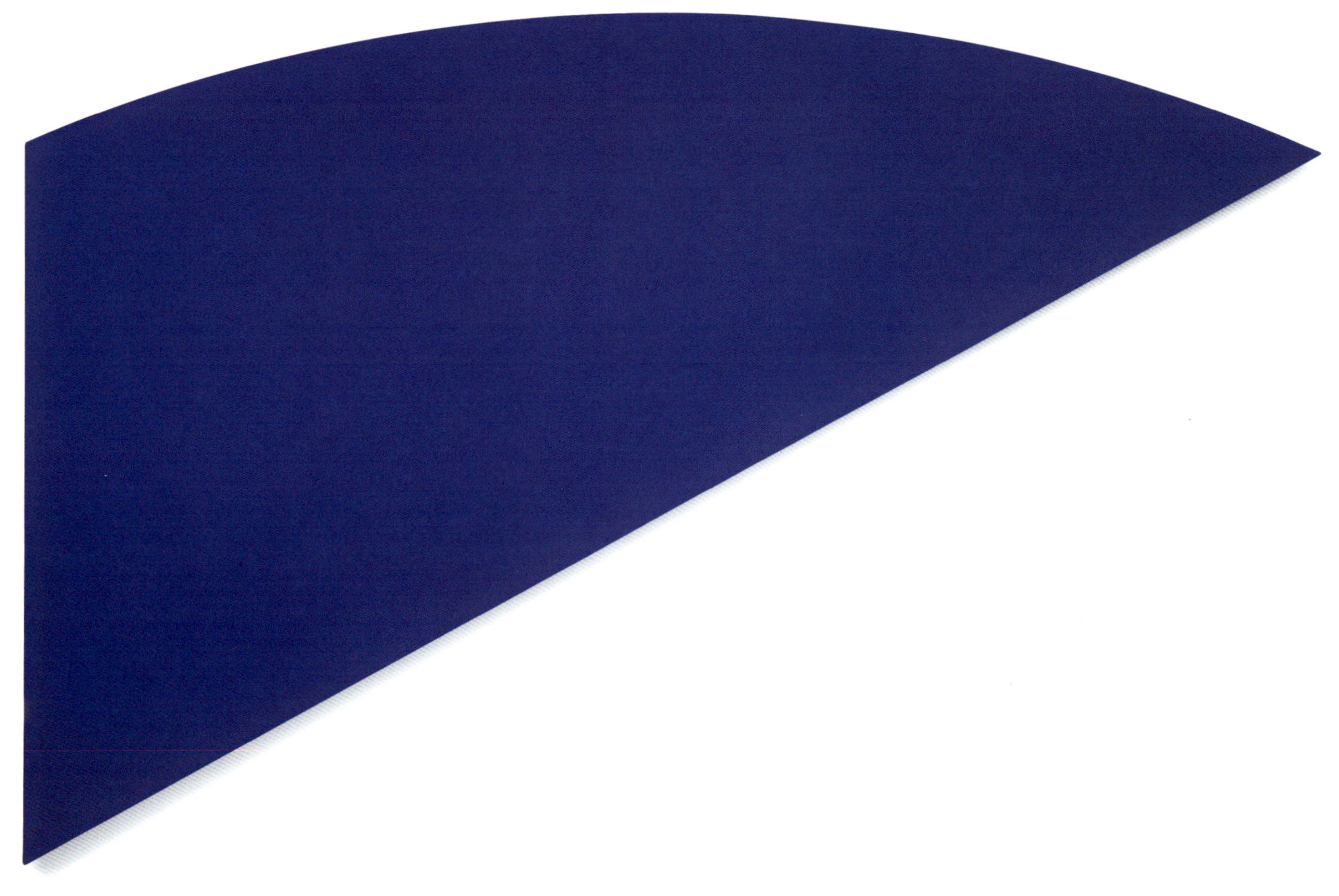

Blue-Violet Curve I, 1982
oil on canvas, 79¾ × 120¼ in, 202.6 × 305.4 cm

White and Dark Gray Panels I, 1977
oil on canvas, 2 joined panels, 106 × 144 in, 269.2 × 365.8 cm

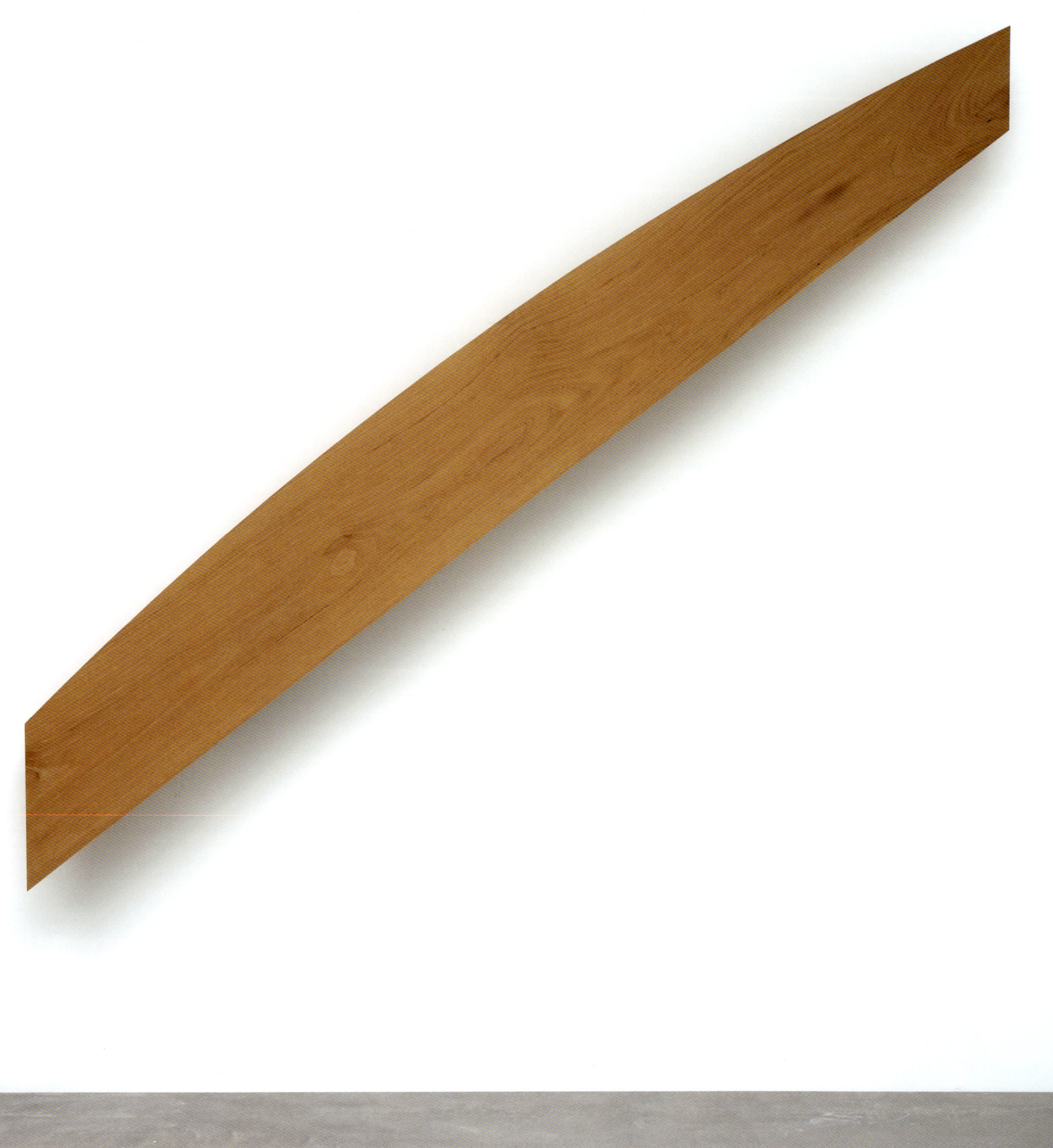

Diagonal with Curve XV, 1984
red oak, 75⅜ × 86½ × 1¾ in
191.5 × 219.7 × 4.4 cm

Curve XXXIII, 1982
weathering steel, 128 × 125½ × 1 in
325.1 × 318.8 × 2.5cm

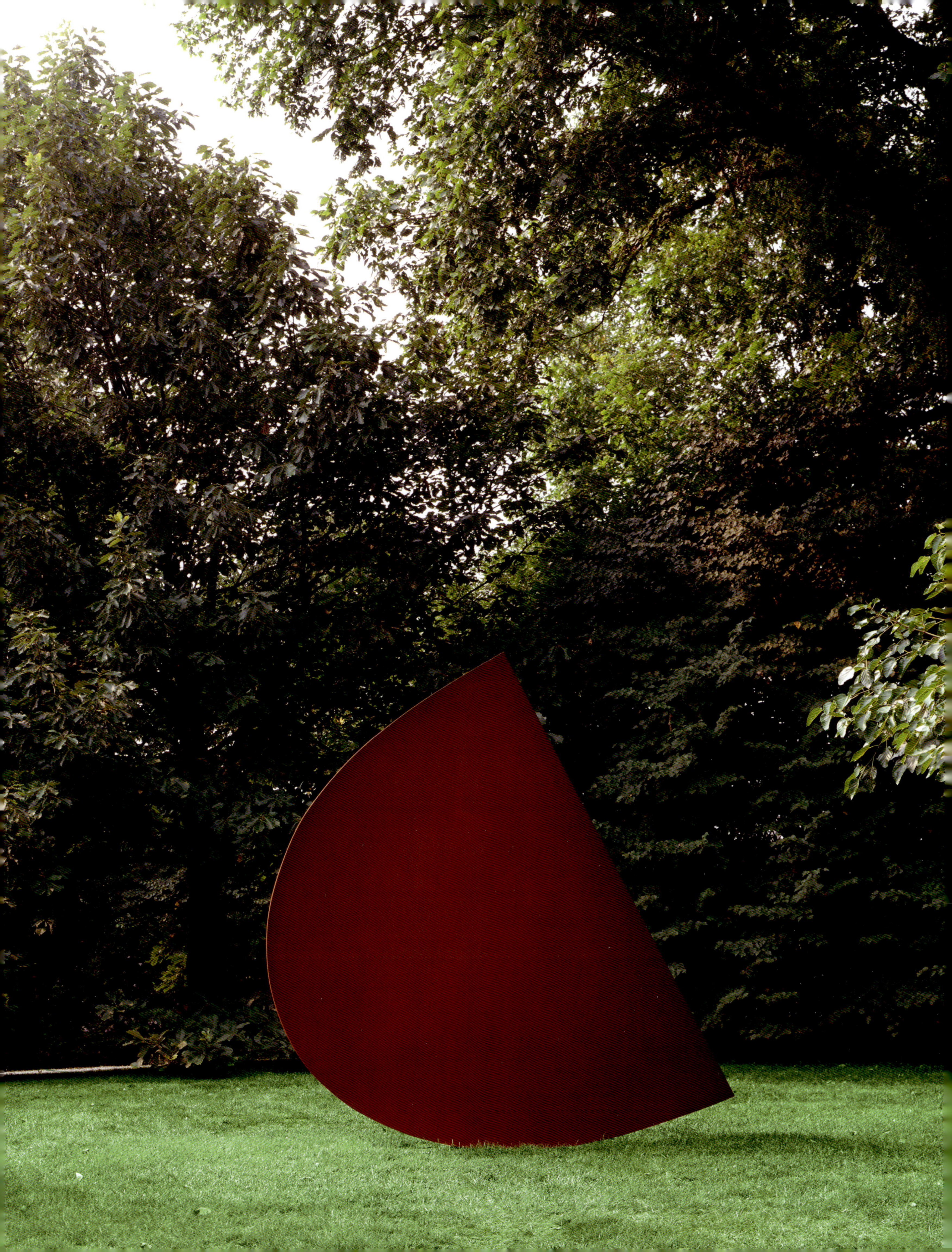

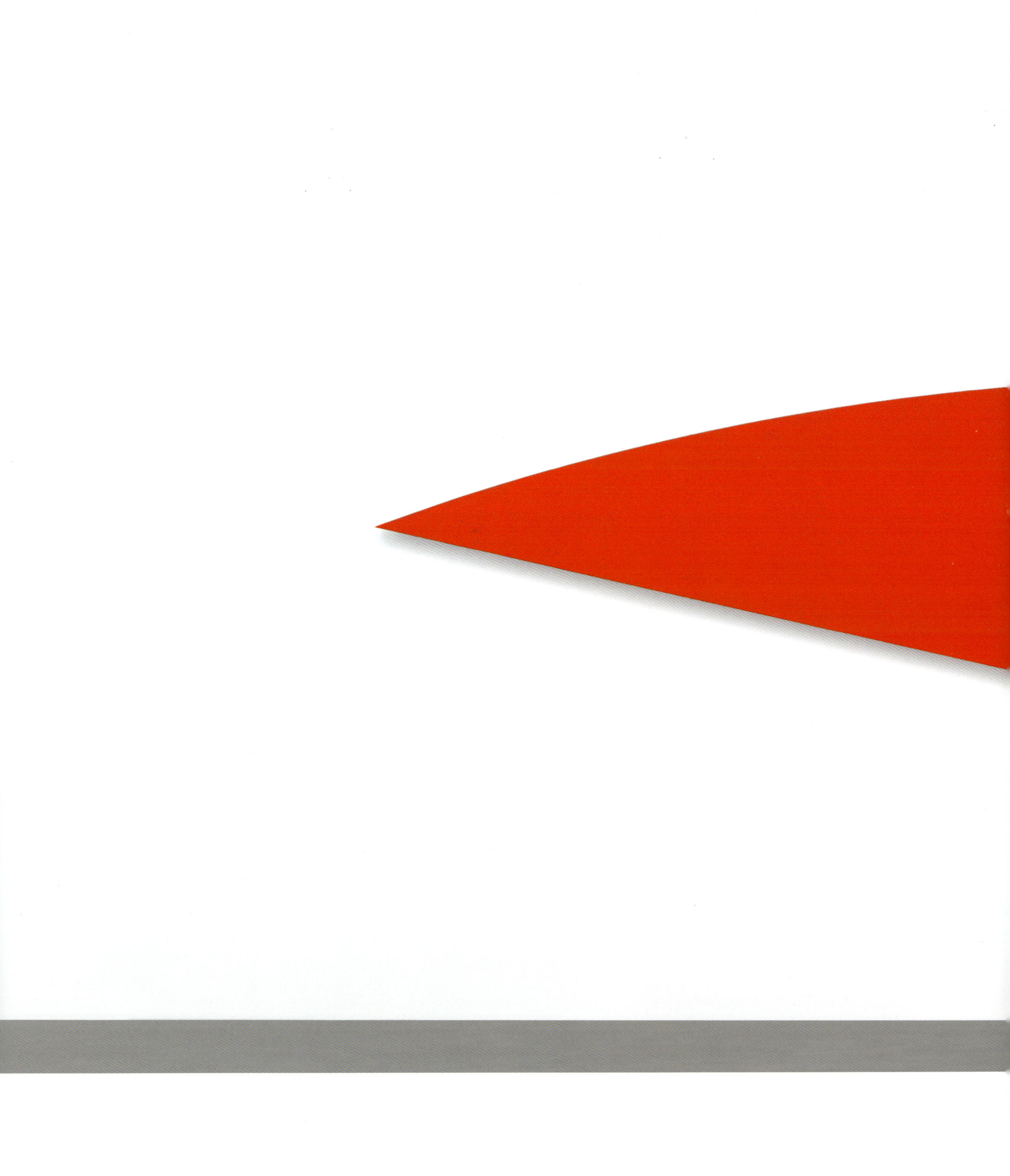

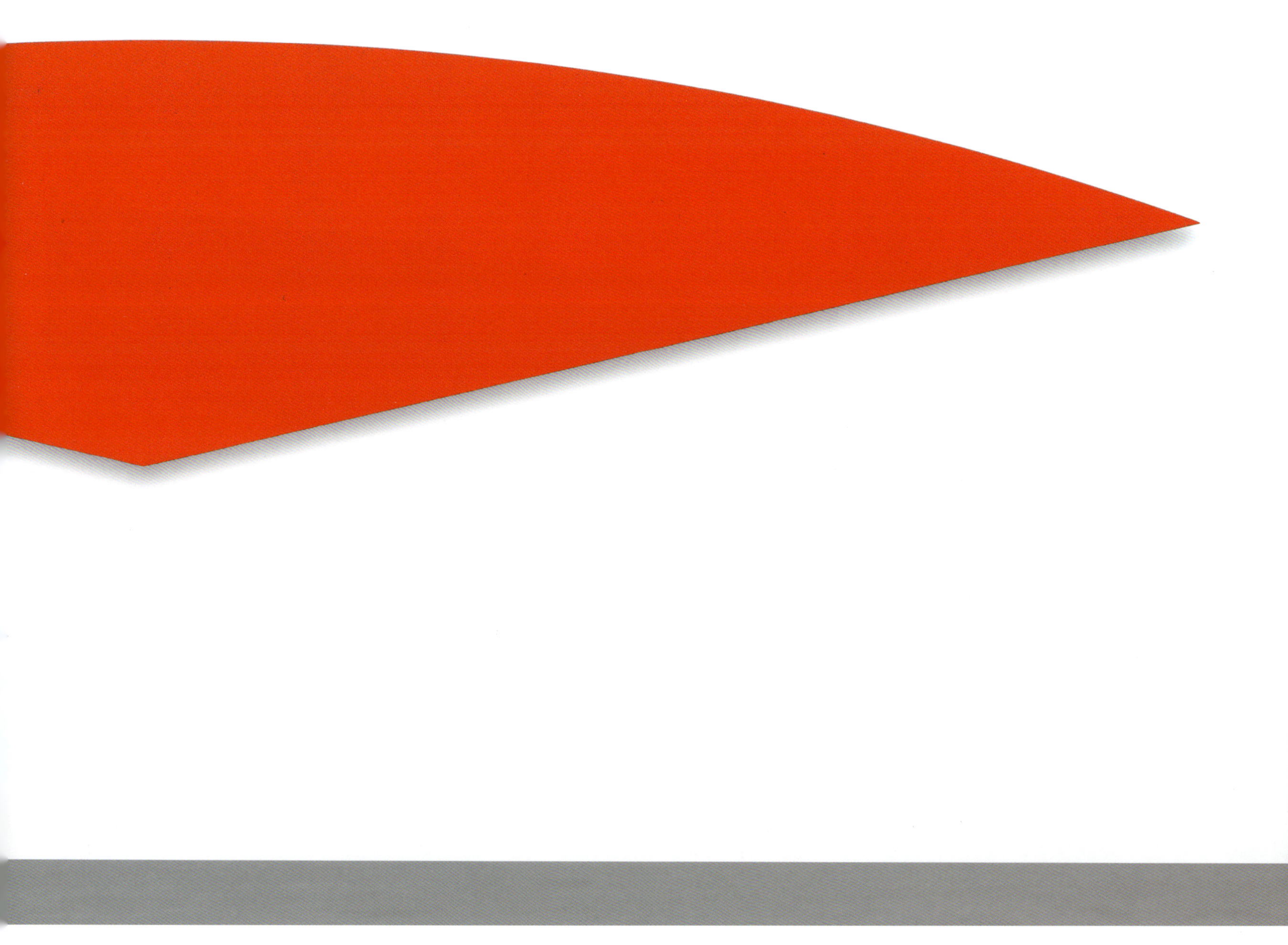

Red Curve, 1986
oil on canvas, 42⅛ × 205¾ in, 107 × 522.6 cm

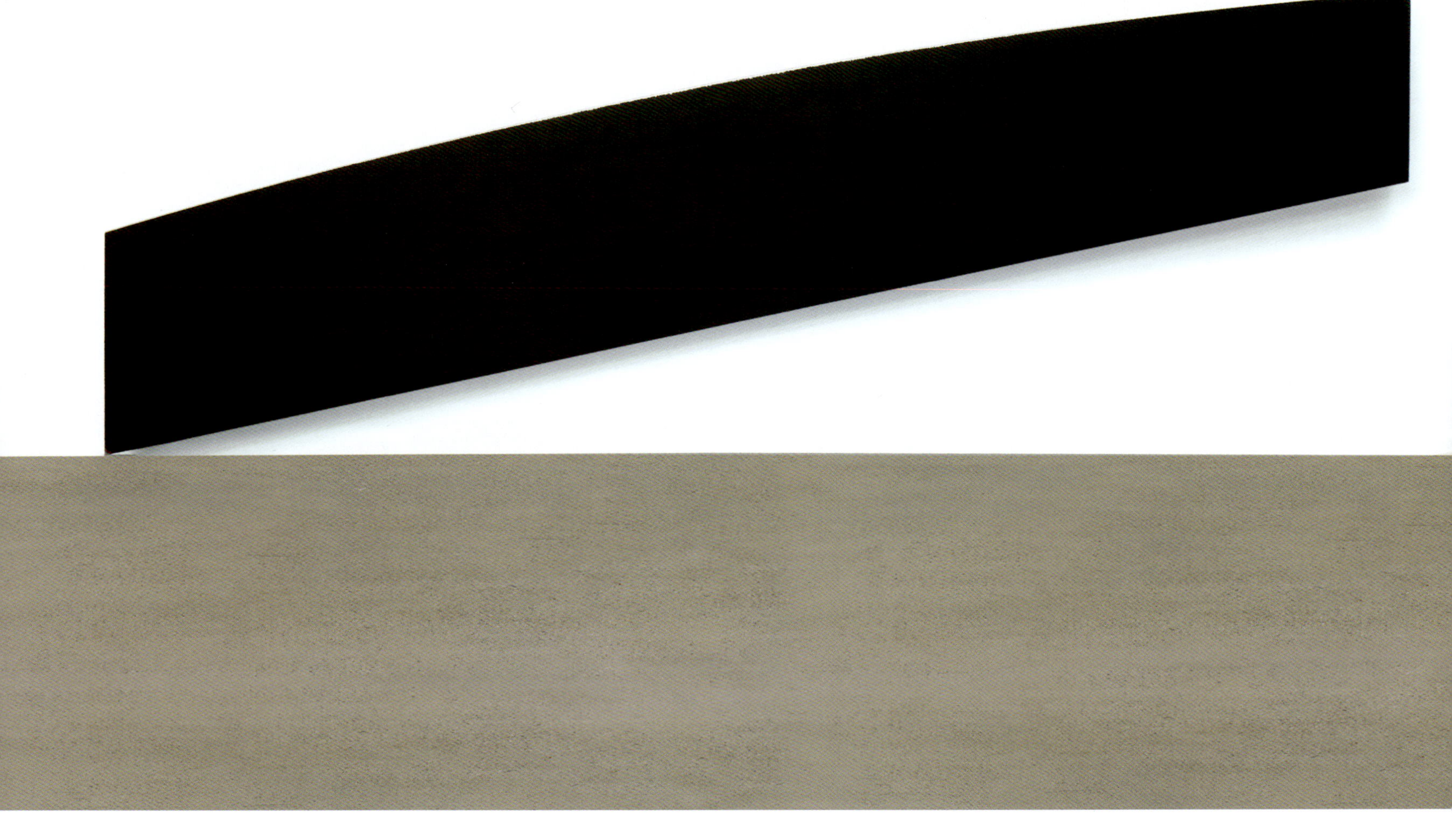

Diagonal with Curve XIV, 1982
weathering steel, 67 × 192 × ½ in
170 × 488 × 1.3 cm

Dark Blue Panel, 1985
oil on canvas, 97 × 111 in, 246.4 × 281.9 cm

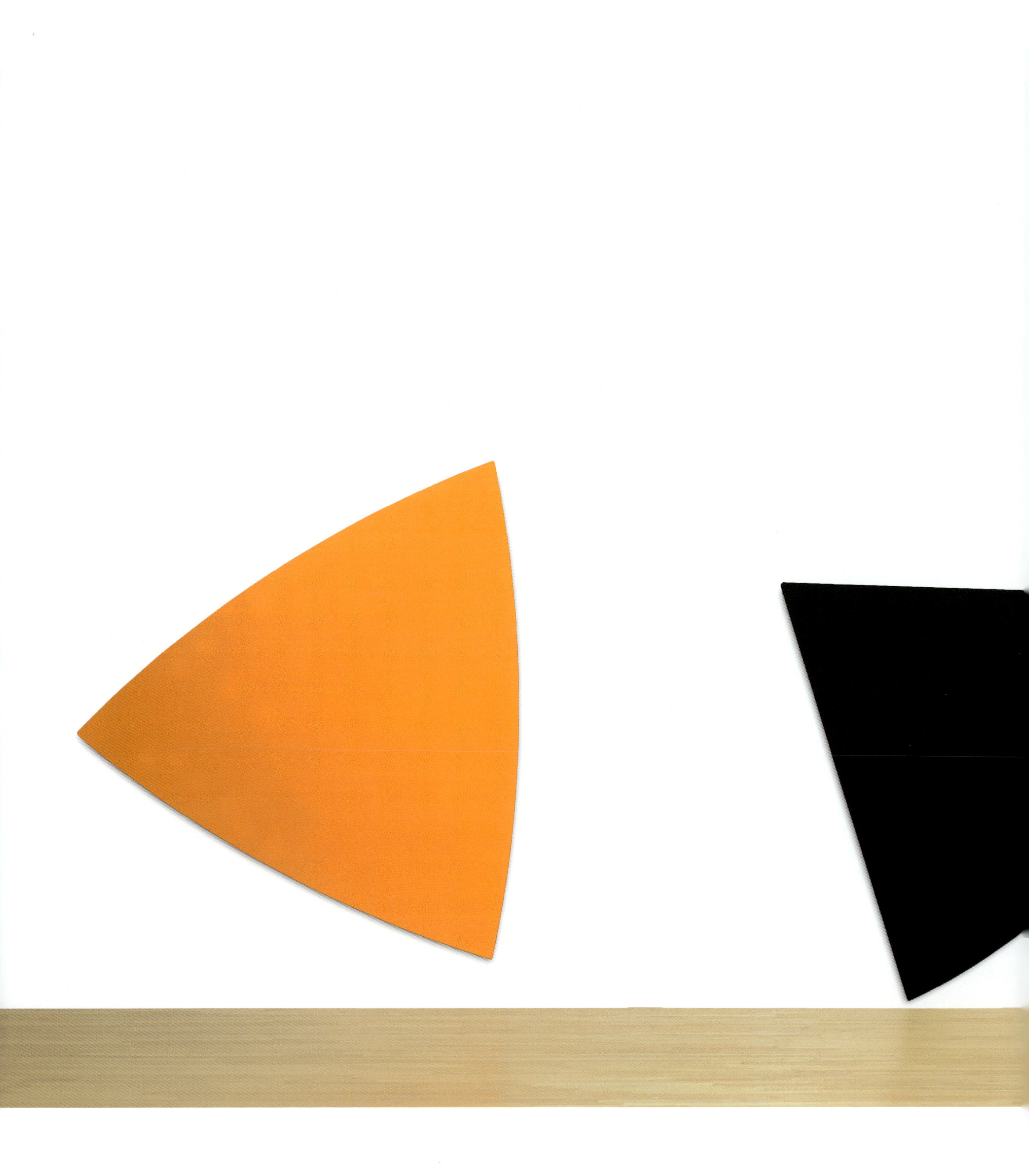

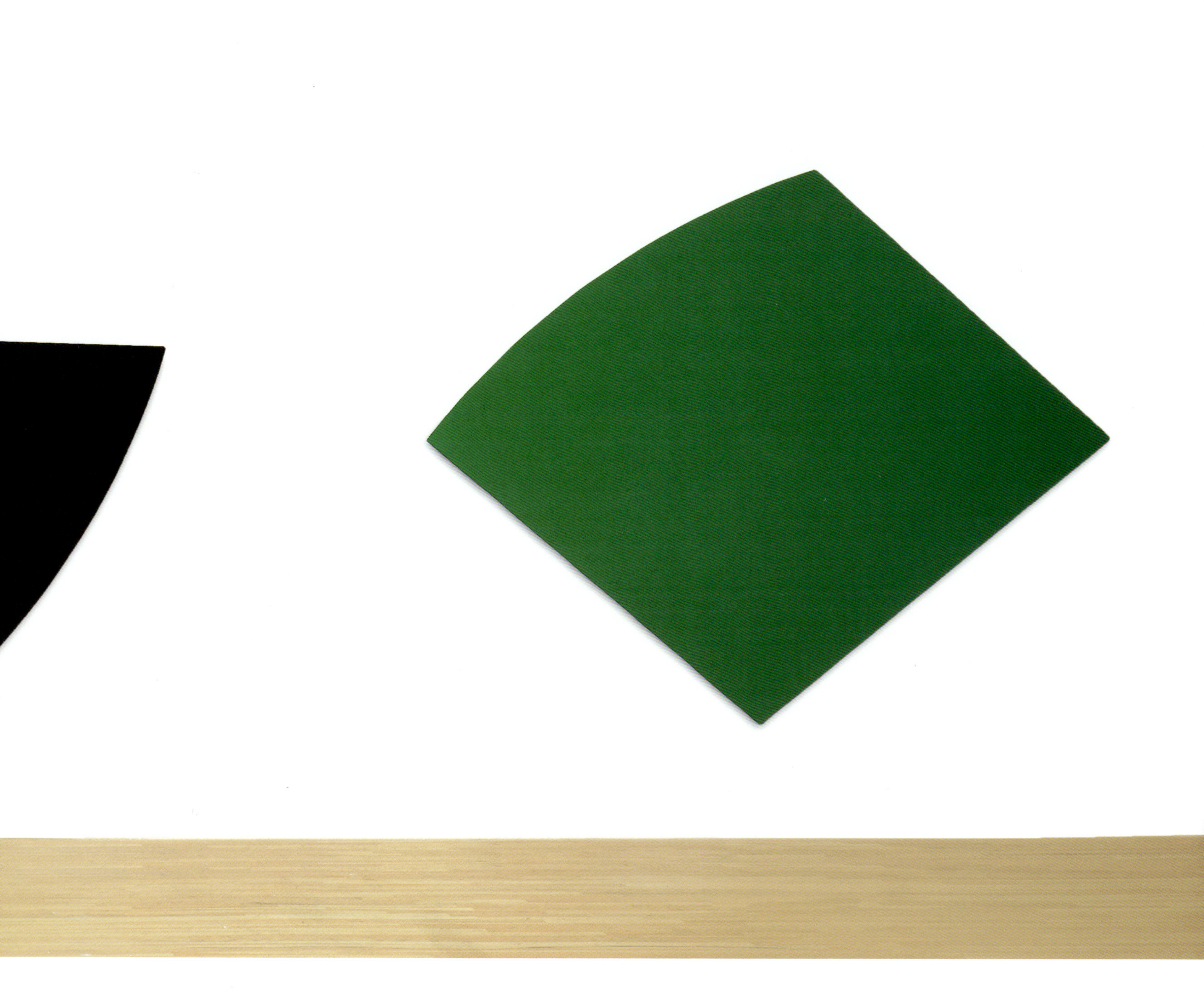

Three Panels: Orange, Dark Gray, Green, 1986
oil on canvas, 3 panels, 116 × 412½ in, 294.6 × 1047.8 cm

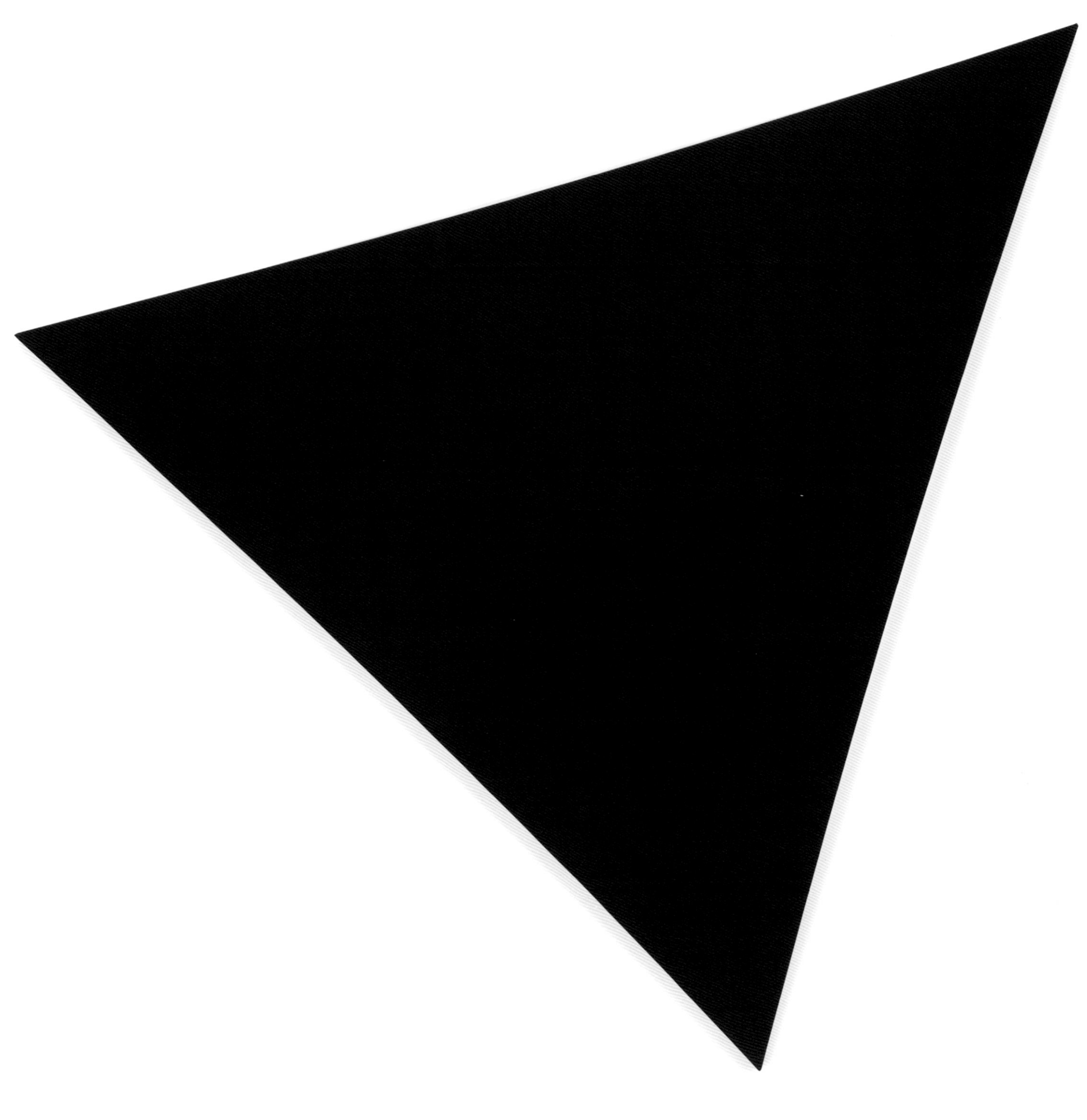

Untitled, 1987
bronze, 104 × 79 × ¾ in
264.2 × 200.7 × 1.9 cm

Purple Panel, 1988
oil on canvas, 111½ × 111½ in
283.2 × 283.2 cm

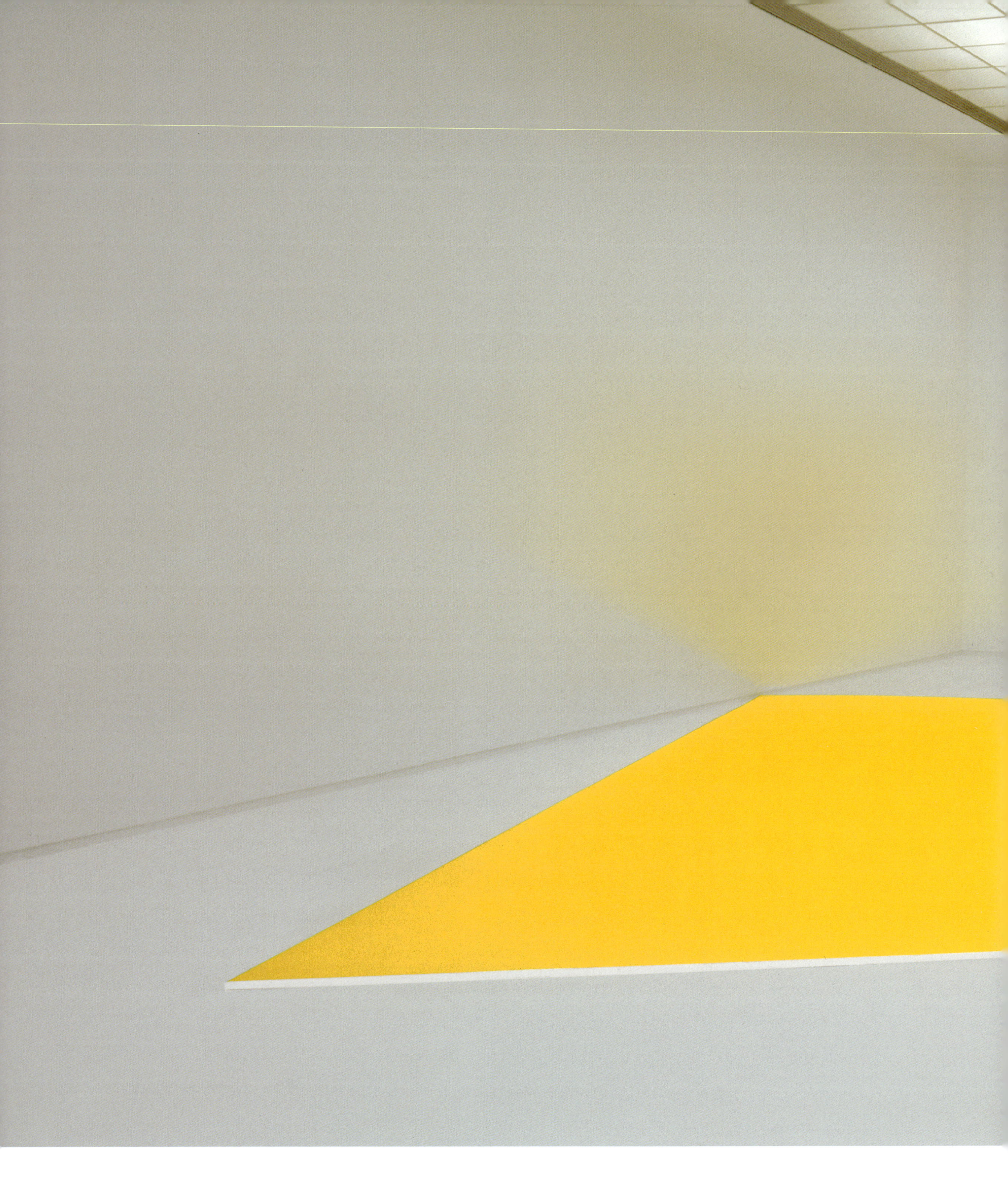

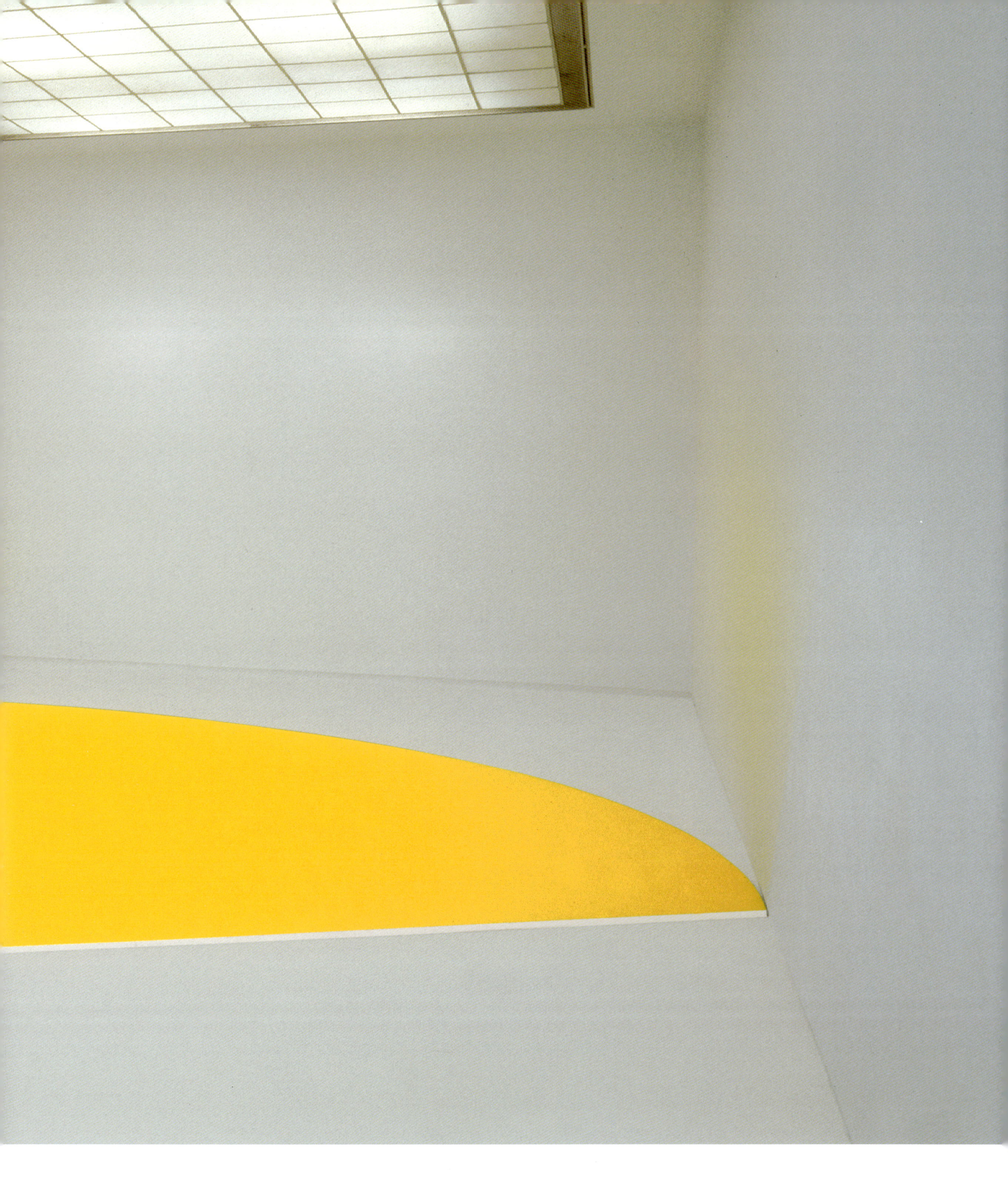

Yellow Curve, 1990
acrylic on canvas on wood, 1 × 306 × 292 in, 2.5 × 777.2 × 741.7 cm

Orange Red Relief (for Delphine Seyrig), 1990
oil on canvas, 2 joined panels
120¼ × 98½ × 2⅝ in, 305.4 × 250.2 × 6.7 cm

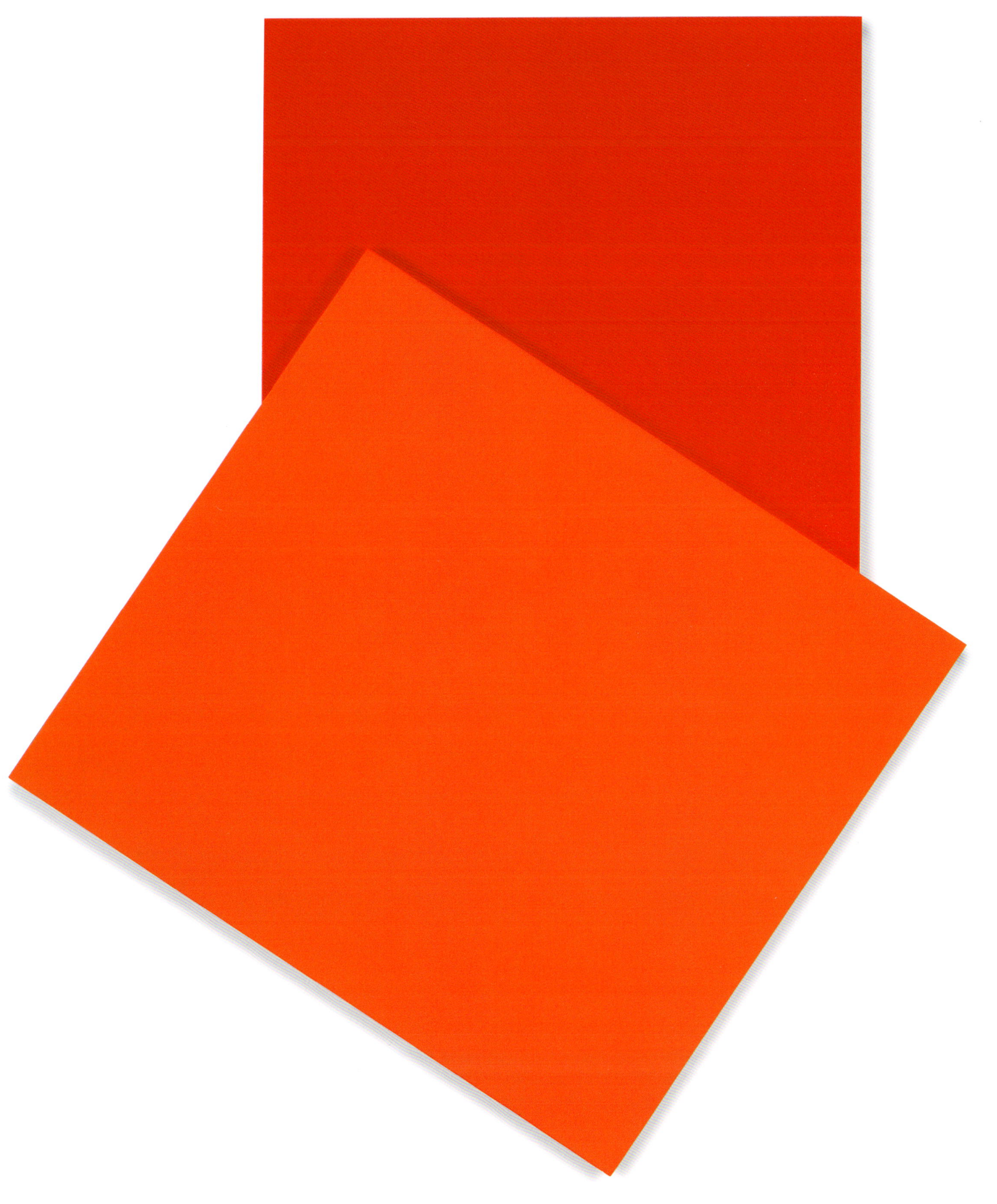

Yellow Relief with Blue, 1991
oil on canvas, 2 joined panels,
120 × 52 × 2⅝ in, 304.8 × 132.1 × 6.7 cm

Blue Relief with Black, 1993
oil on canvas, 2 joined panels,
98¼ × 89 × 2⅝ in, 249.6 × 226.1 × 6.7 cm

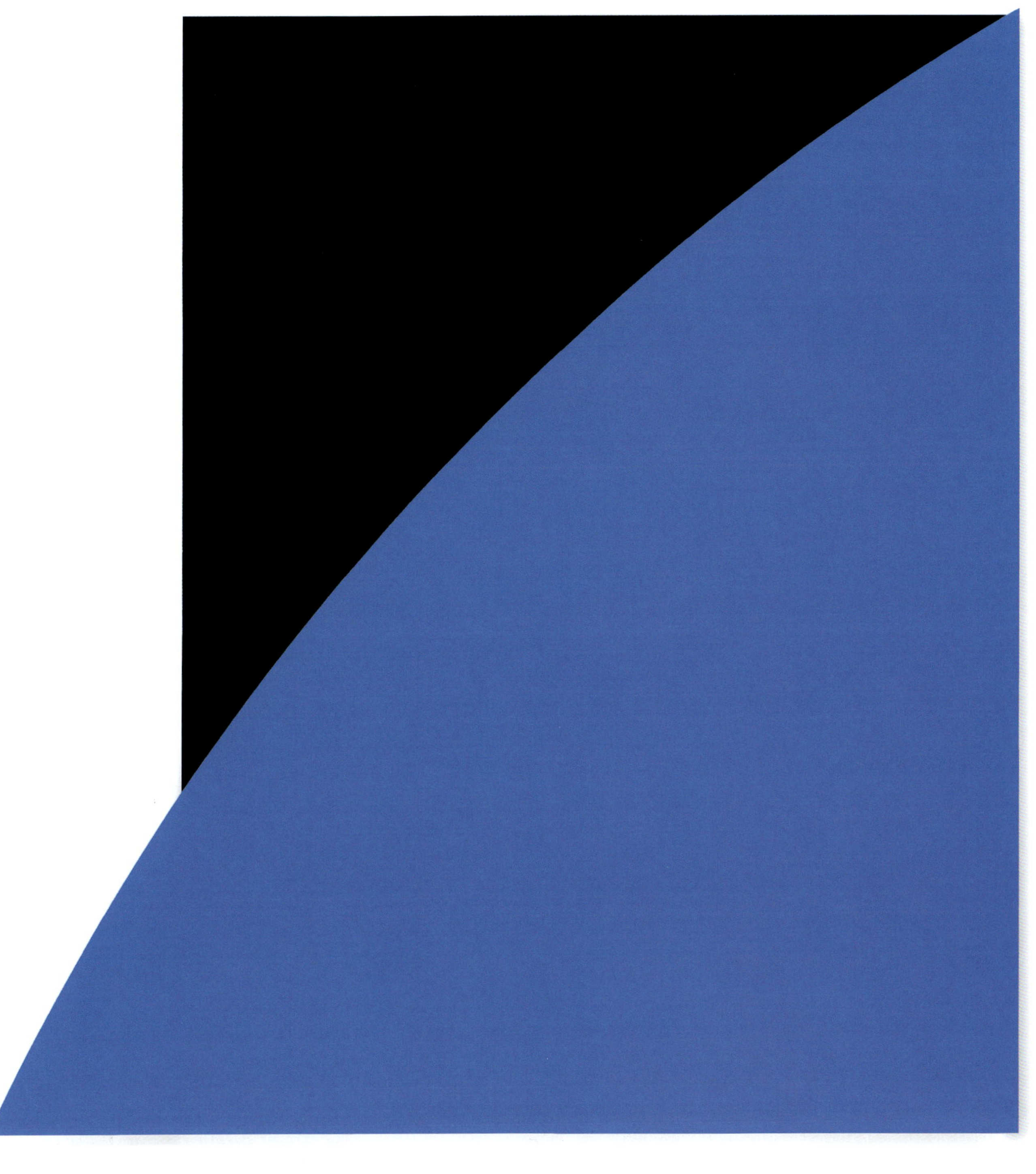

Orange Relief with Green, 1991
oil on canvas, 2 joined panels
93½ × 84¾ × 2⅝ in, 237.5 × 215.3 × 6.7 cm

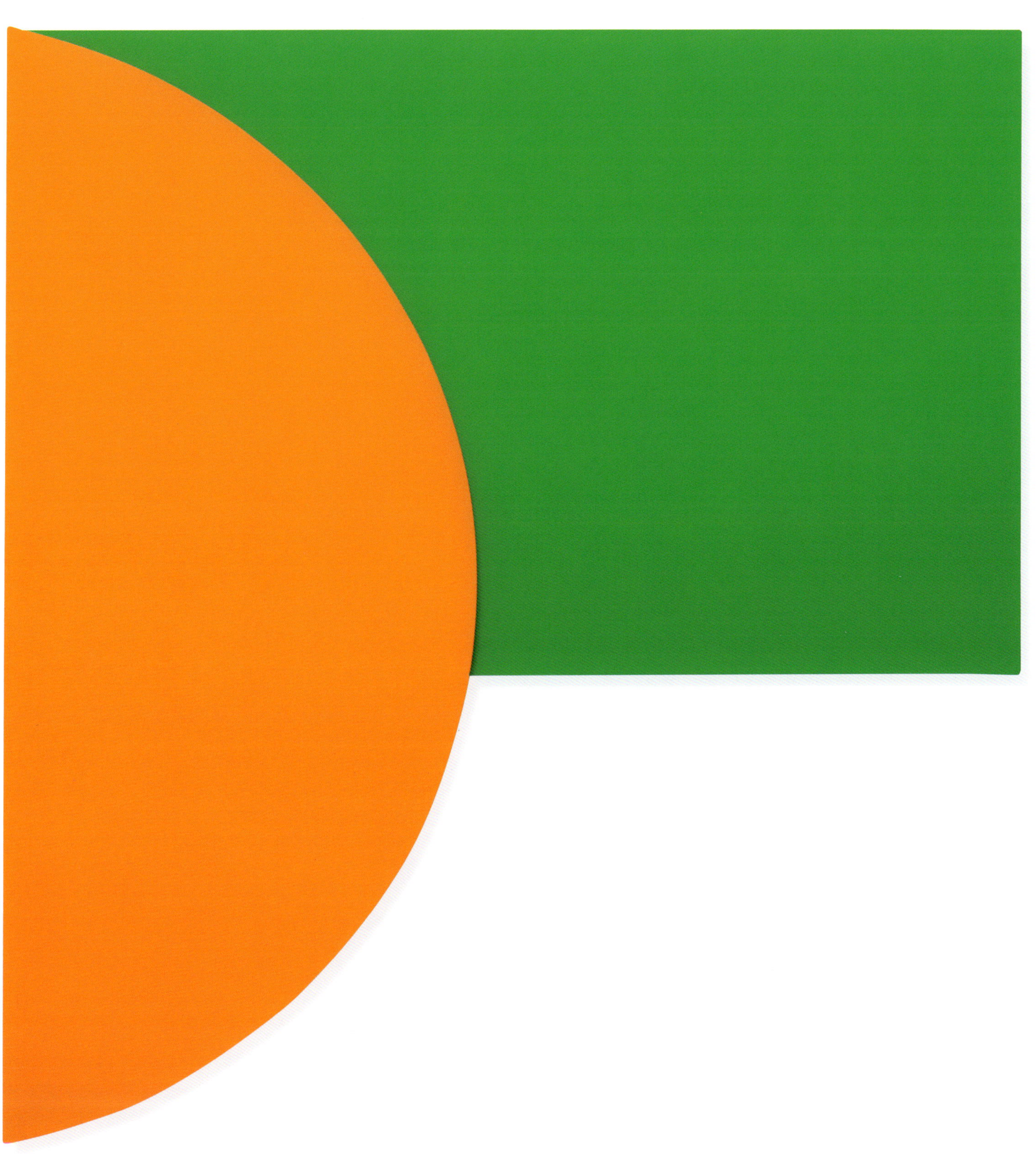

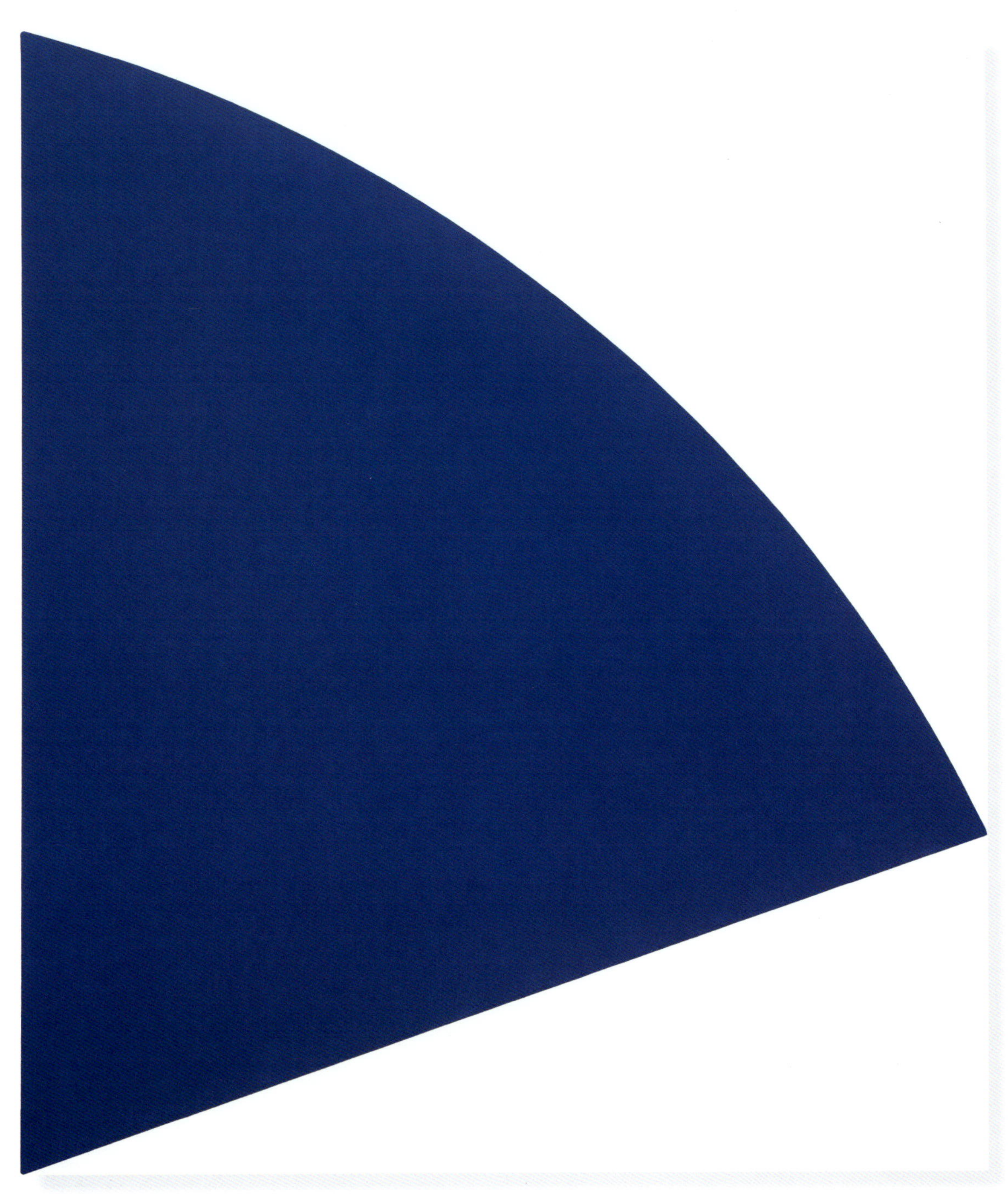

Blue Curve, 1994
oil on canvas, 86 × 72 in, 218.4 × 182.9 cm

White Relief with Black III, 1993
oil on canvas, 2 joined panels
120 × 98 × 2¾ in, 304.8 × 248.9 × 7 cm

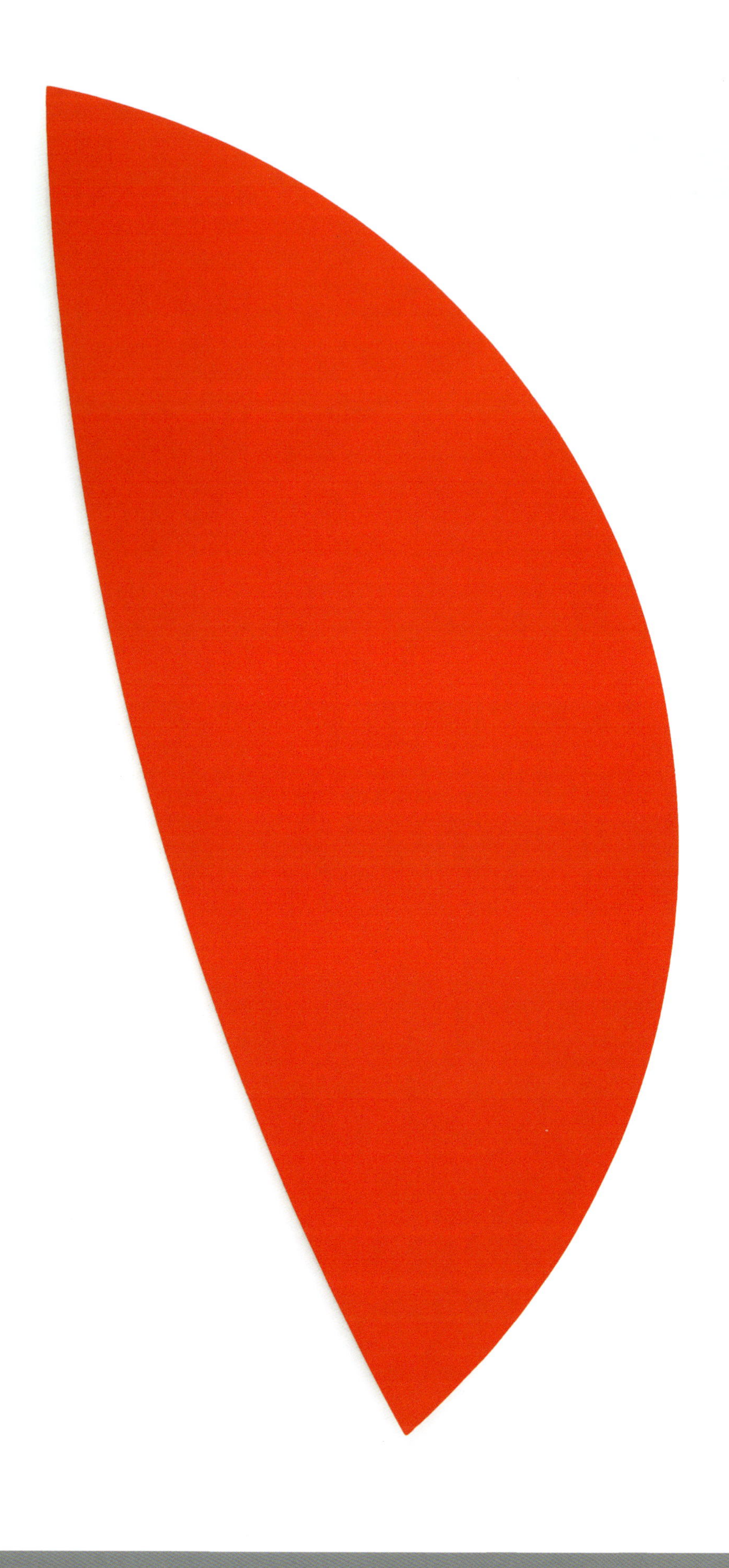

Red Curves, 1996
oil on canvas, 142 × 65½ in, 360.7 × 166.4 cm

Black Curves, 1996
oil on canvas, 144 × 42½ in, 365.8 × 108 cm

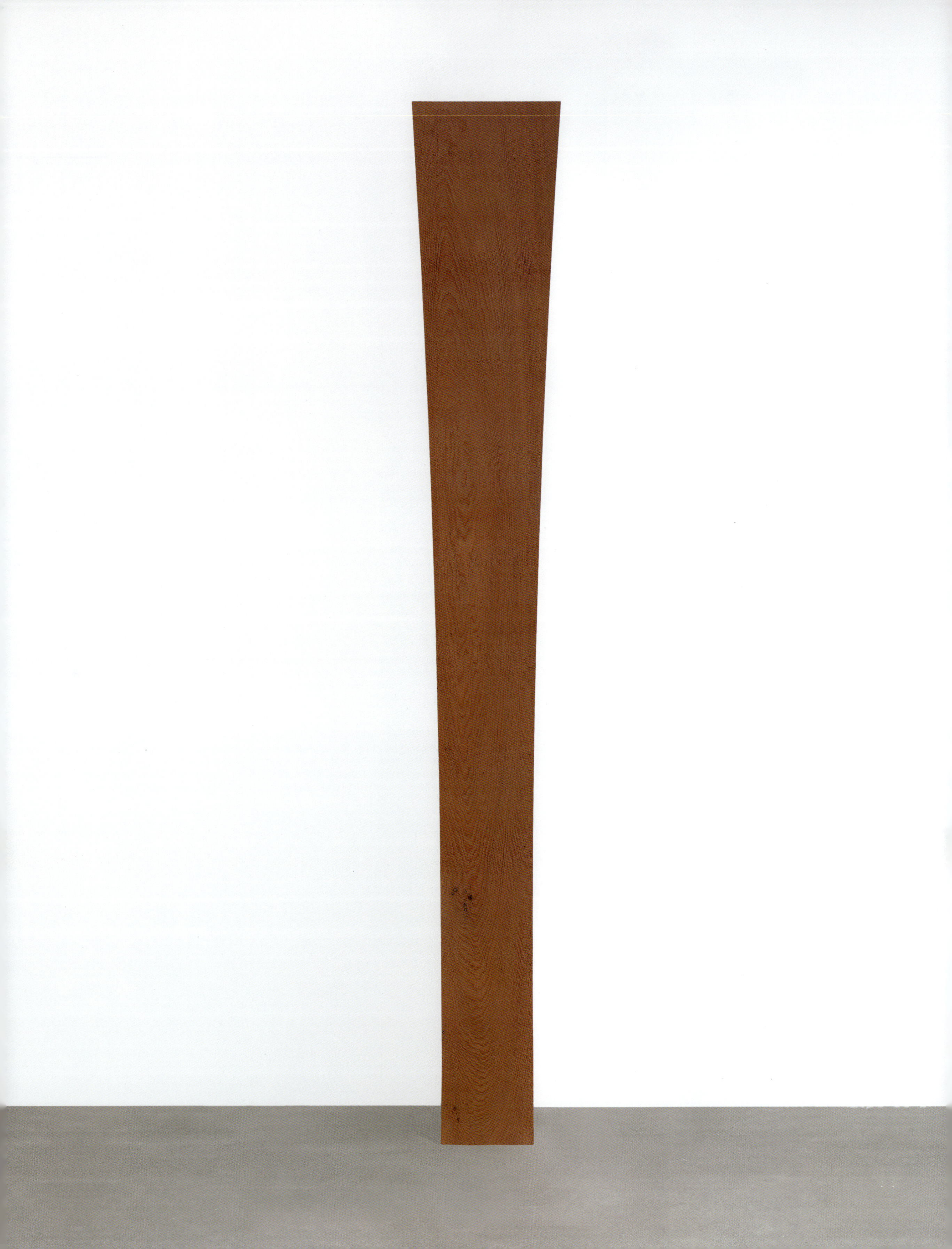

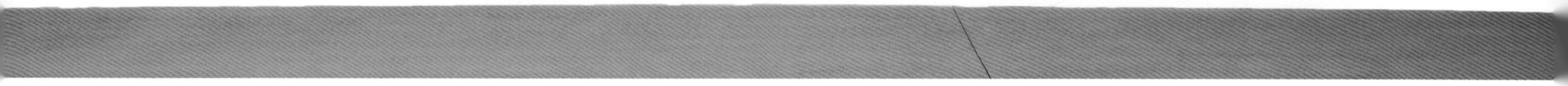

Untitled, 1996
redwood, 176 × 25¼ × 4½ in
447 × 64.1 × 11.4 cm

Horizontal Curve I, 1996
bronze, 13¾ × 240 × 1¼ in
34.9 × 609.6 × 3.2 cm

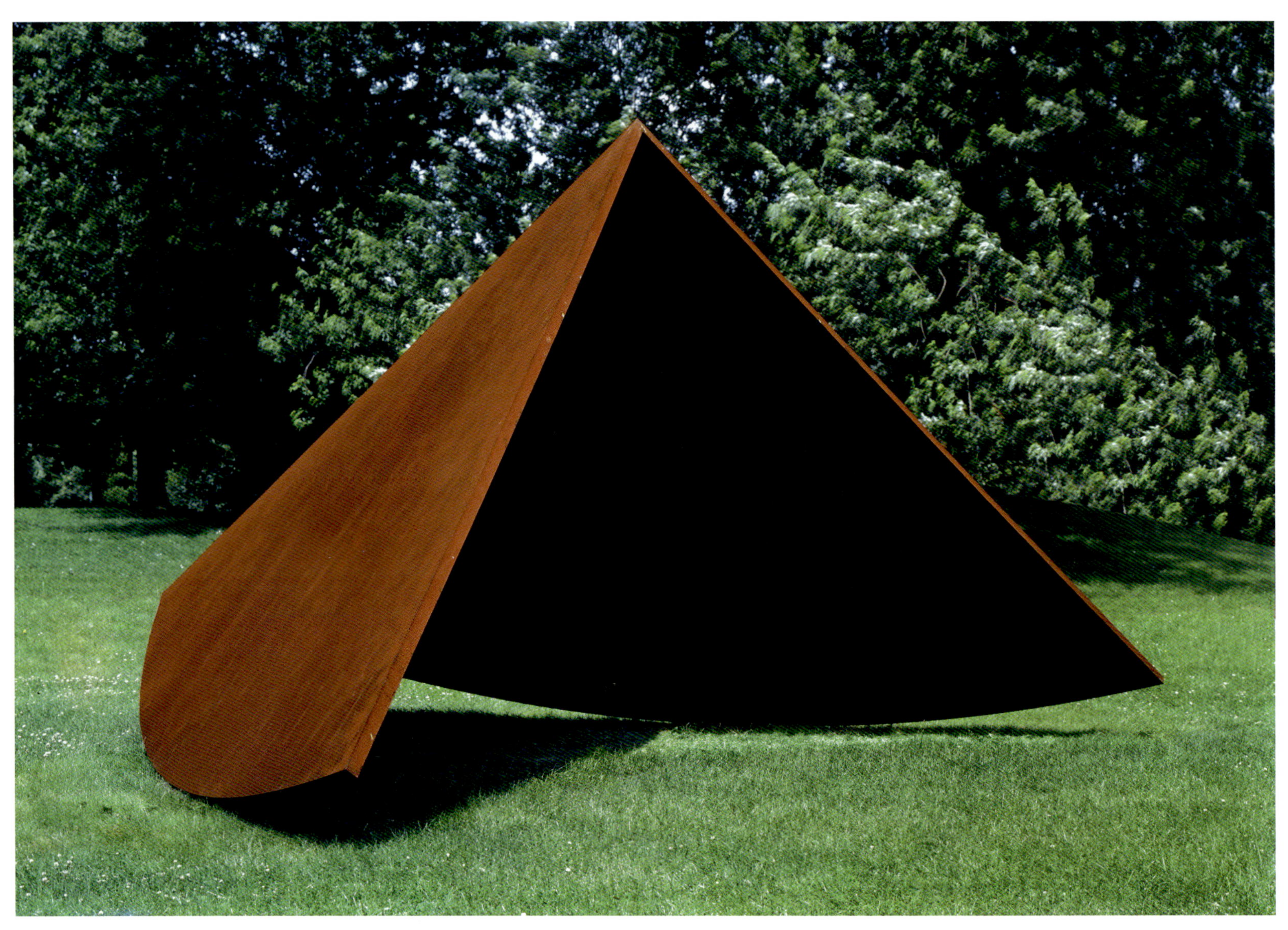

Untitled (Rocker), 1997
weathering steel, 114 × 221 × 208 in
289.6 × 561.3 × 528.3 cm

White Curves, 2001
painted aluminum and stainless steel
234 × 131⅞ × 49½ in, 594.4 × 335 × 125.7 cm

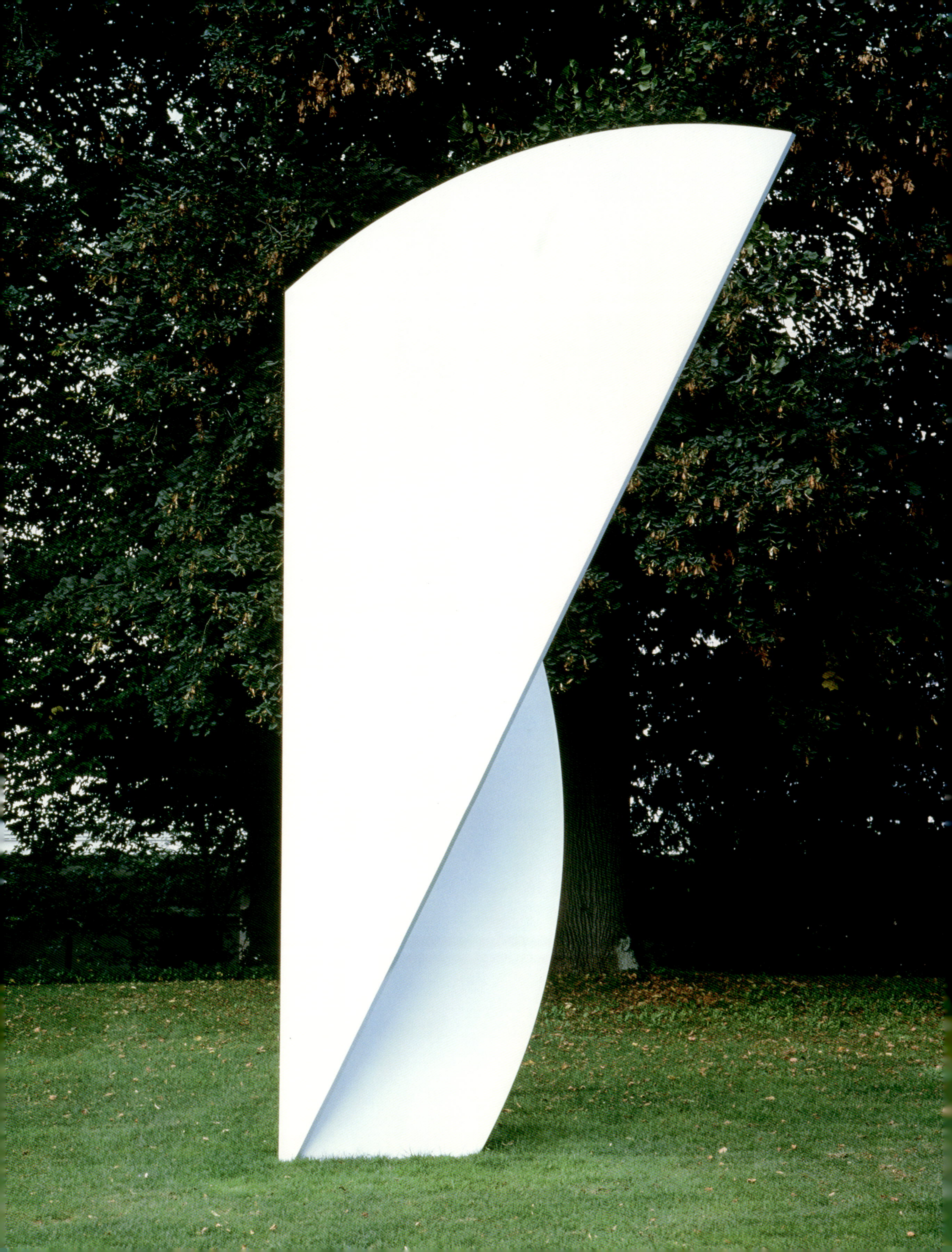

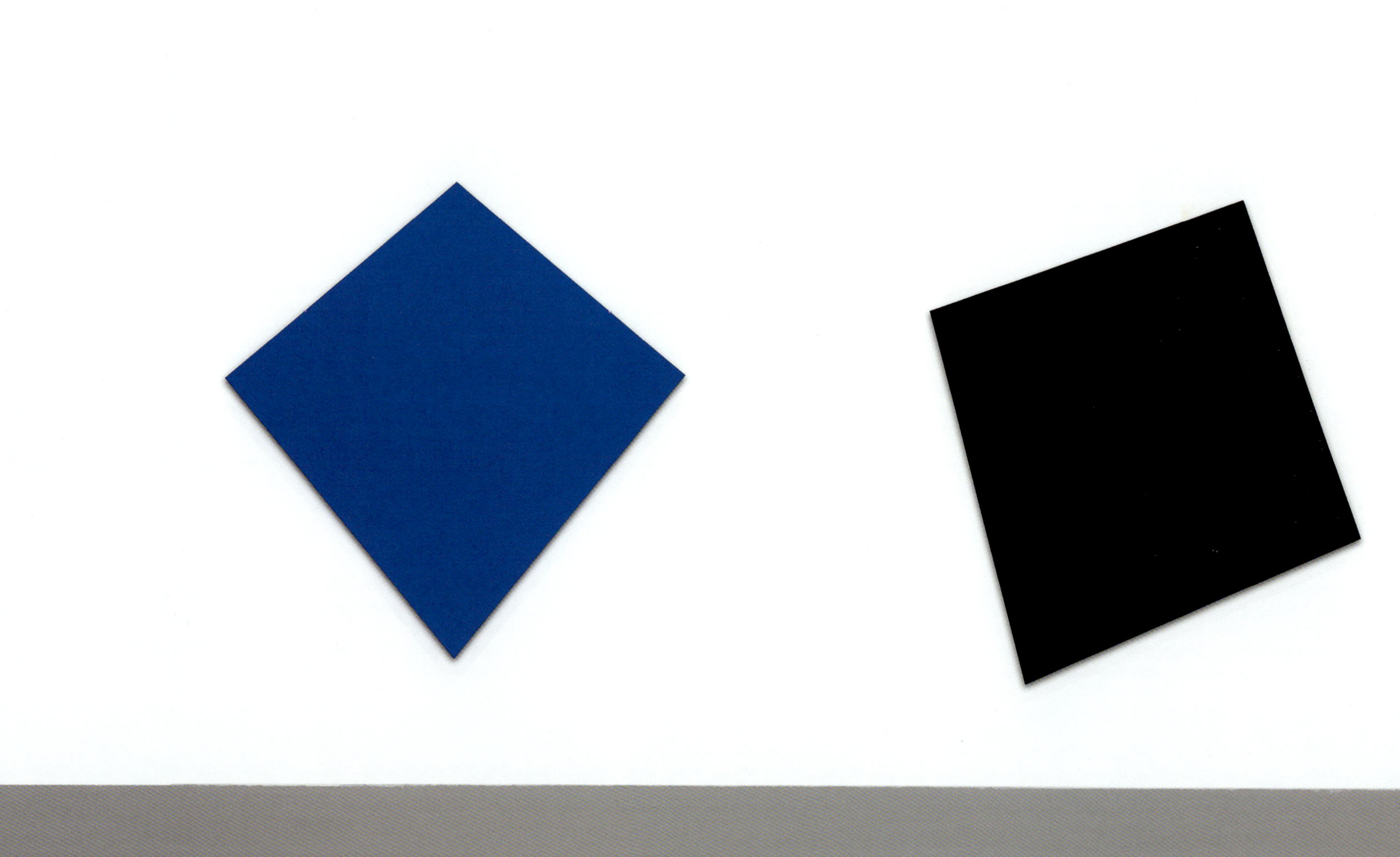

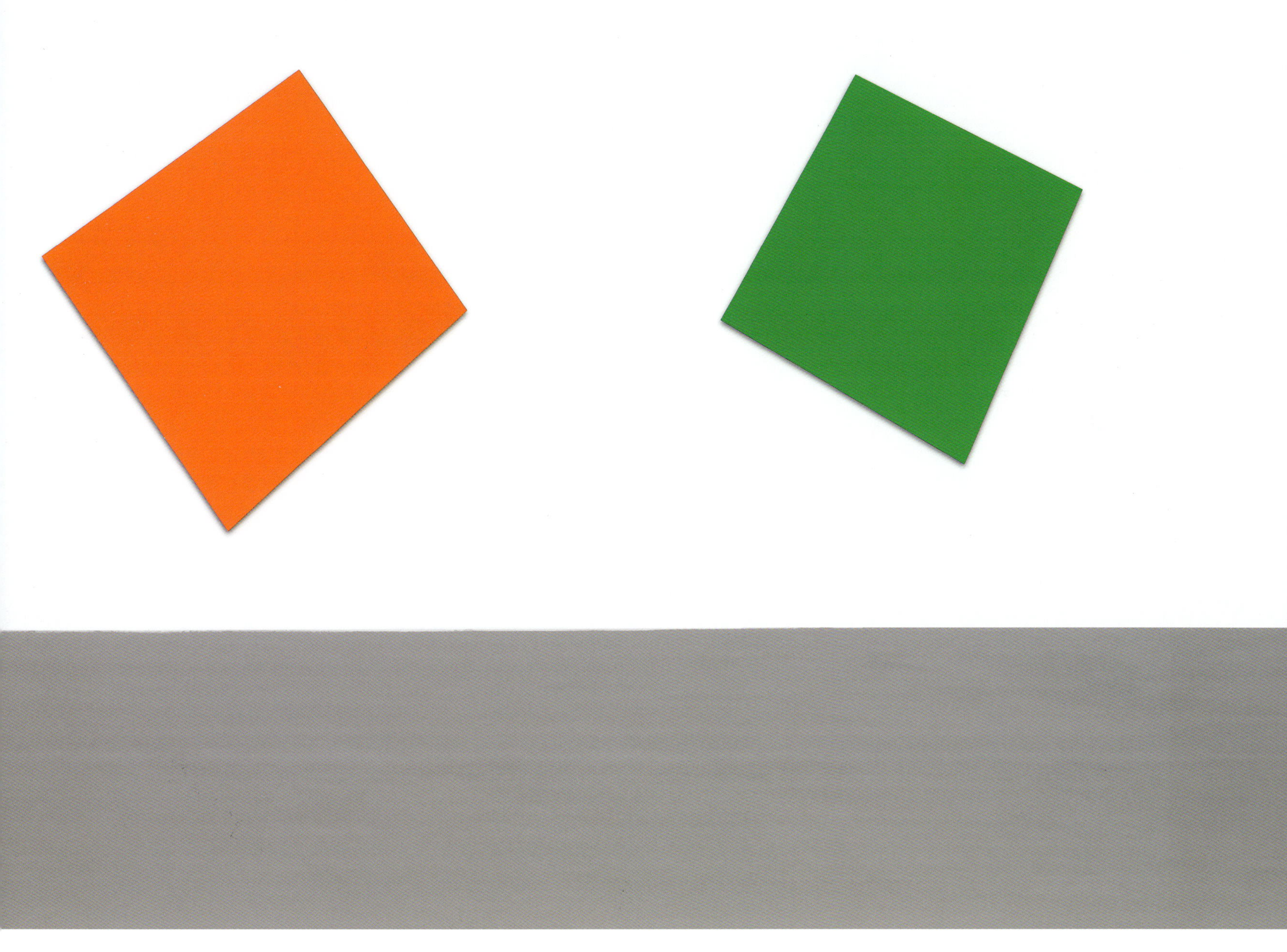

Blue Black Red Green, 2000
oil on canvas, 4 panels, 100 × 484 in, 254 × 1229.4 cm

Red Green Blue, 2002
oil on canvas, 3 joined panels
40 × 181 in, 101.6 × 459.7 cm

Blue Black, 2001
painted aluminum
336 × 70 × 2½ in, 853.4 × 177.8 × 6.4 cm

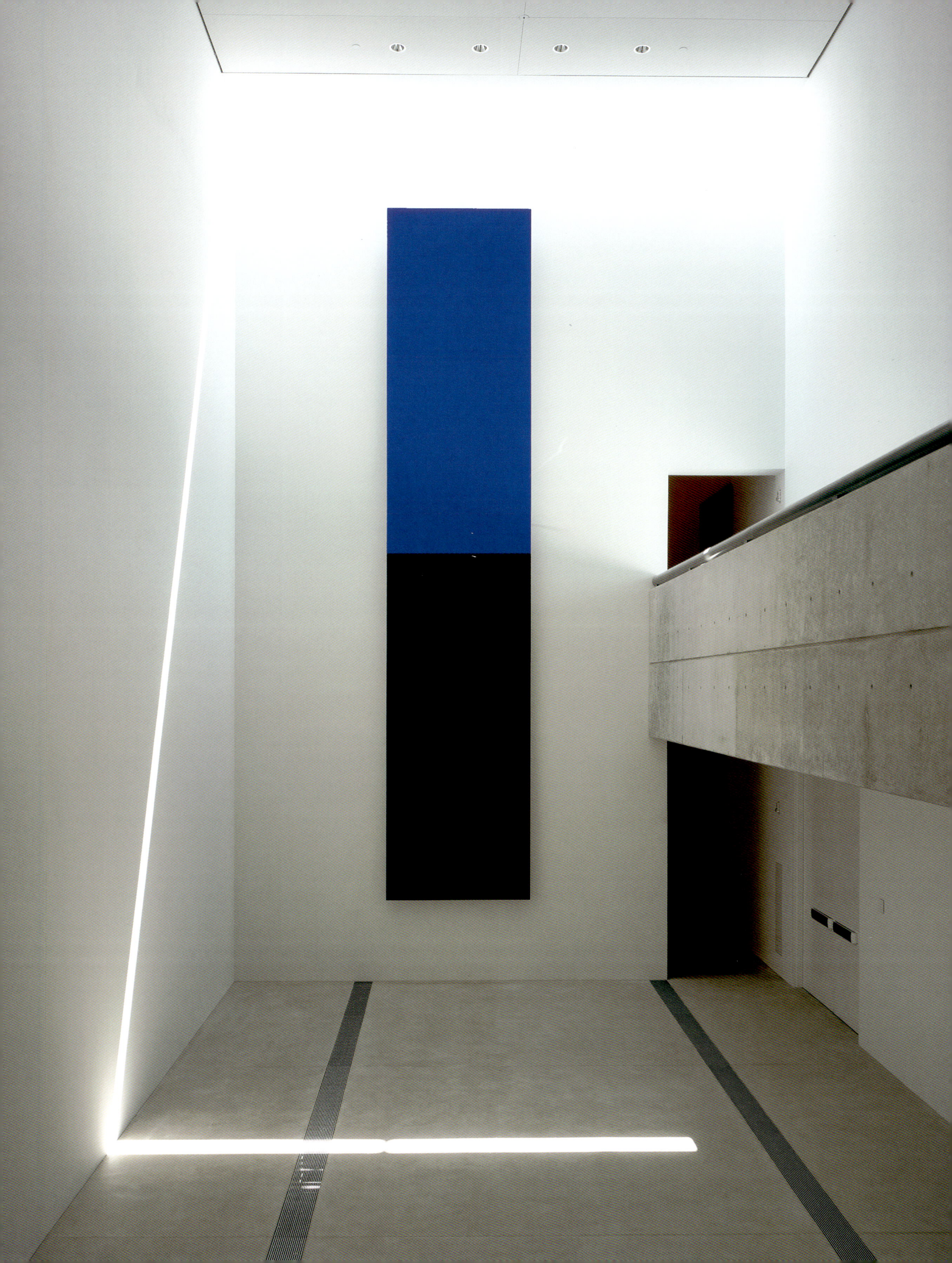

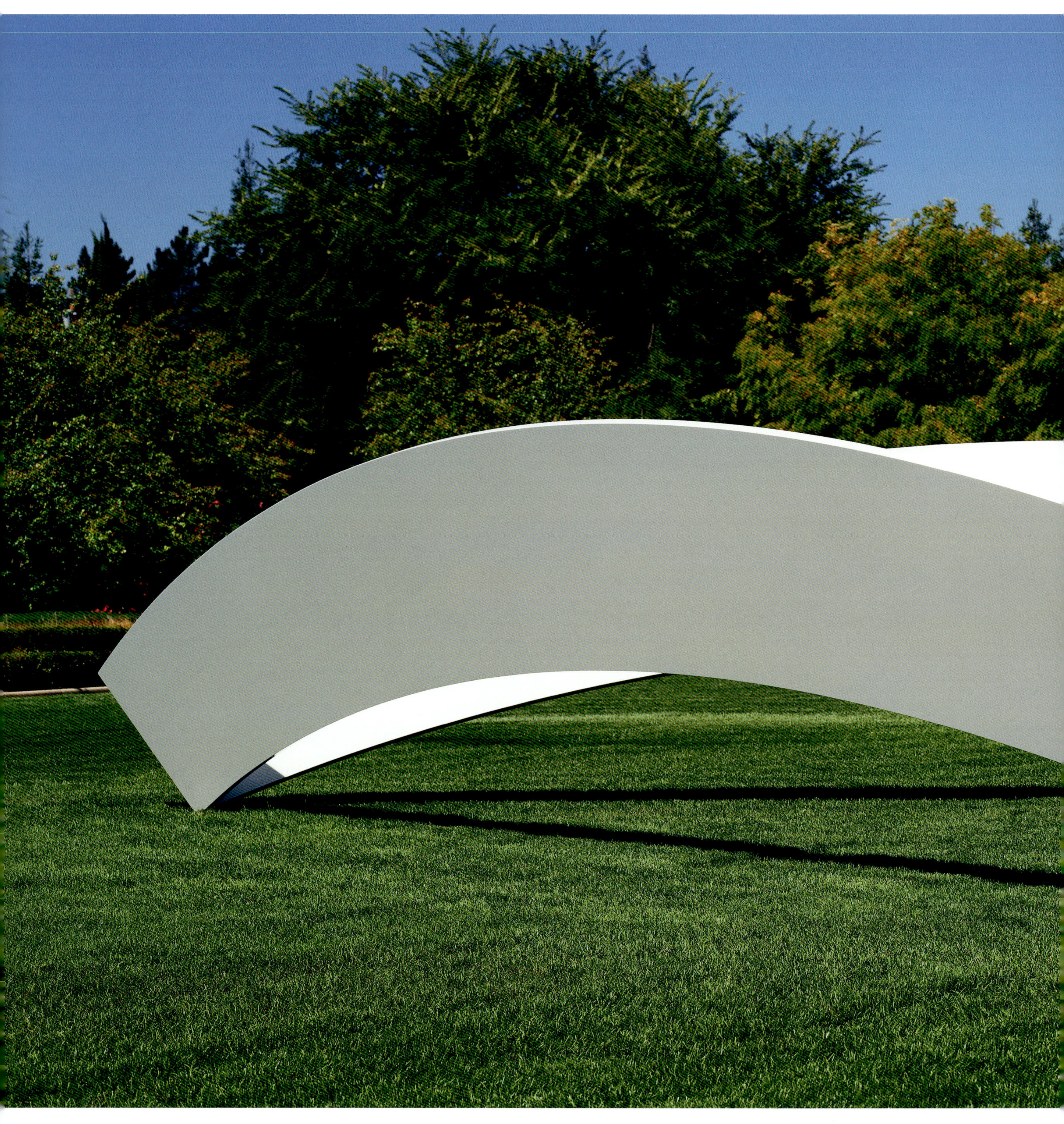

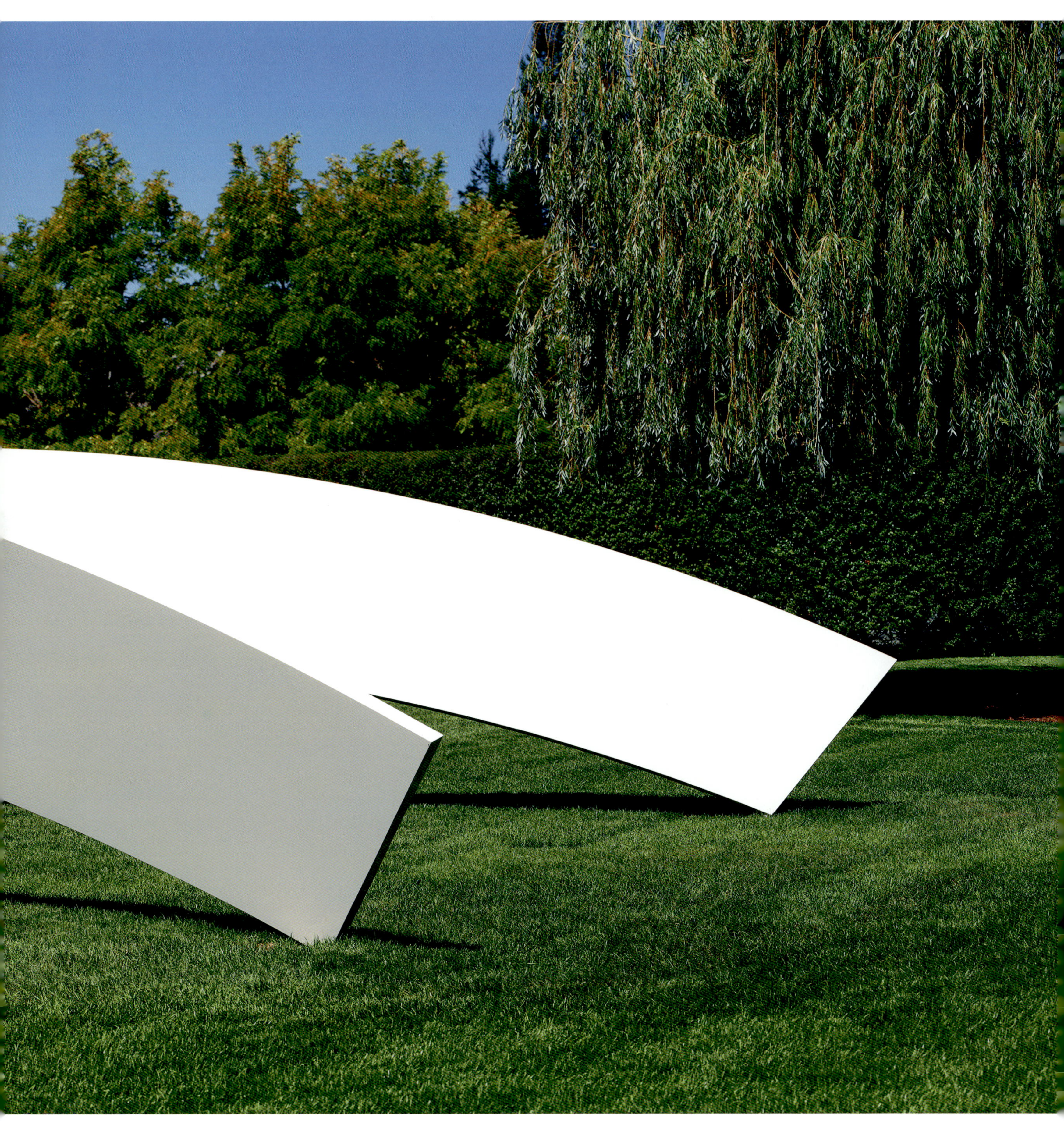

Two Curves, 2001
painted aluminum, 91 × 452 × 328 in, 231.1 × 1148.1 × 833.1 cm

White Relief over Black, 2002
oil on canvas, 2 joined panels
80 × 77½ × 2⅝ in, 203.2 × 196.9 × 6.7 cm

White Black Red, 2004
oil on canvas, 3 joined panels
81⅜ × 40½ in, 206.7 × 102.9 cm

Green Relief over Blue, 2004
oil on canvas, 2 joined panels
80 × 74 × 2¾ in, 203.2 × 188 × 7 cm

Two Curves, 2004
oil on canvas, 82 × 77 in
208.3 × 195.6 cm

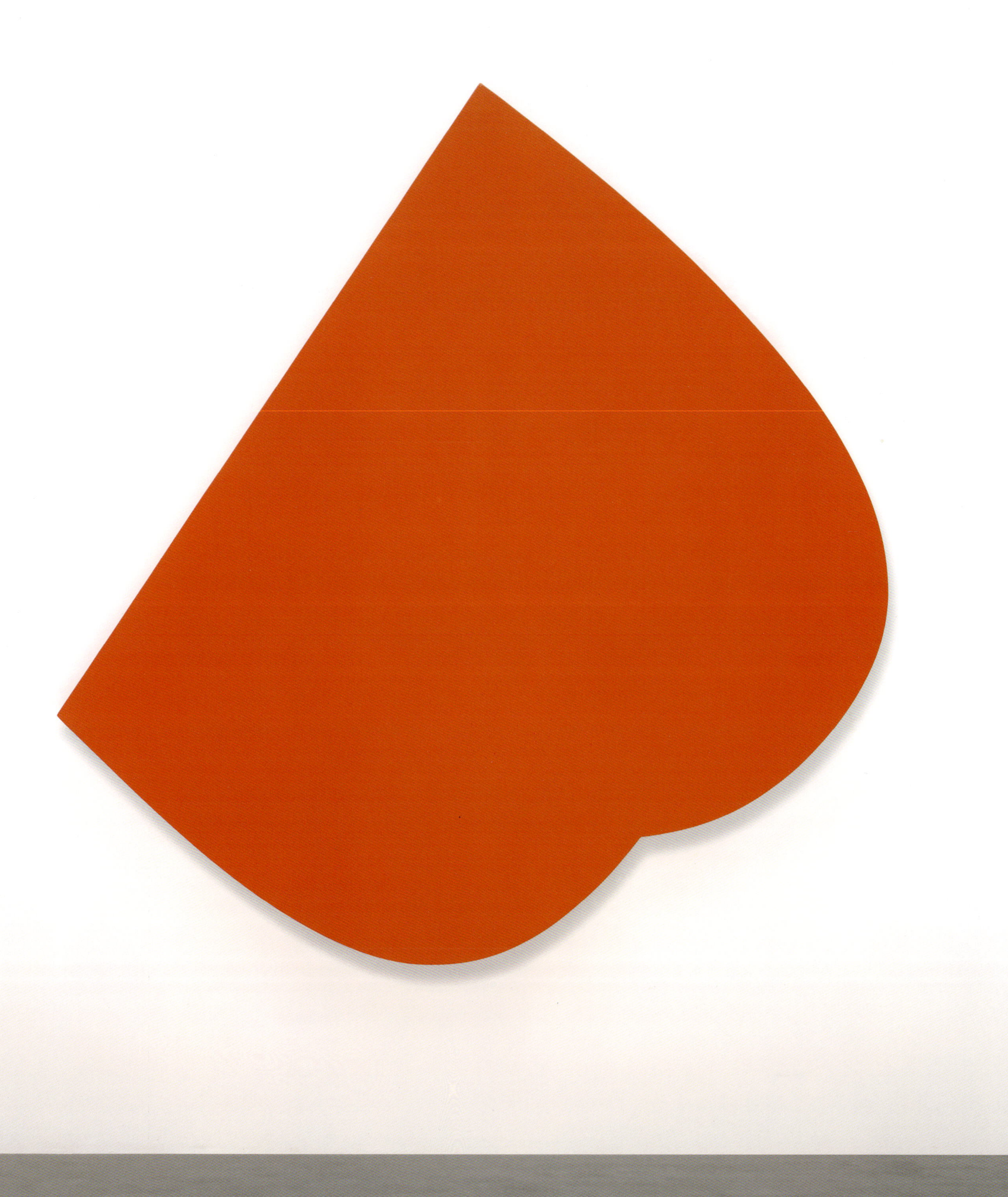

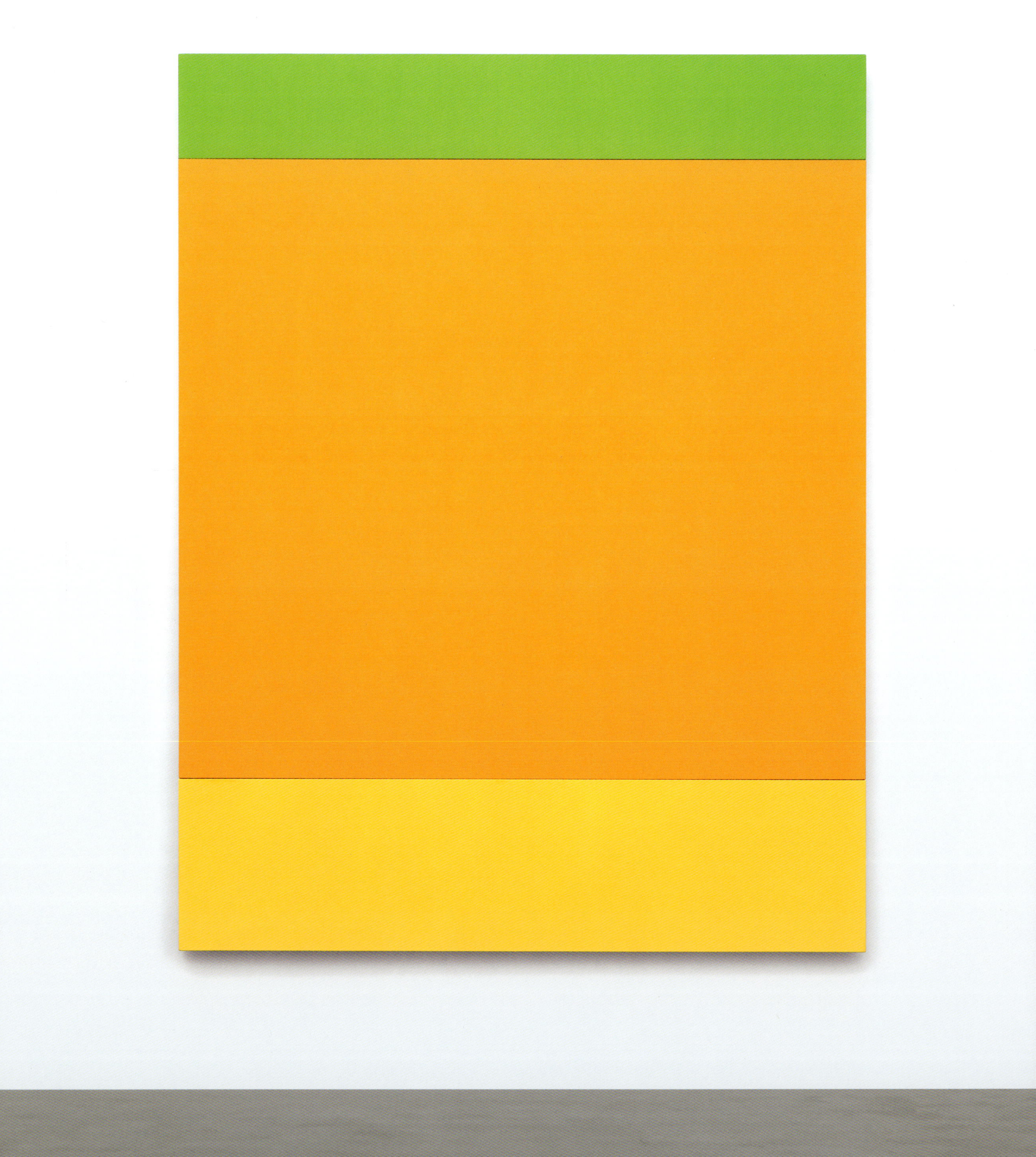

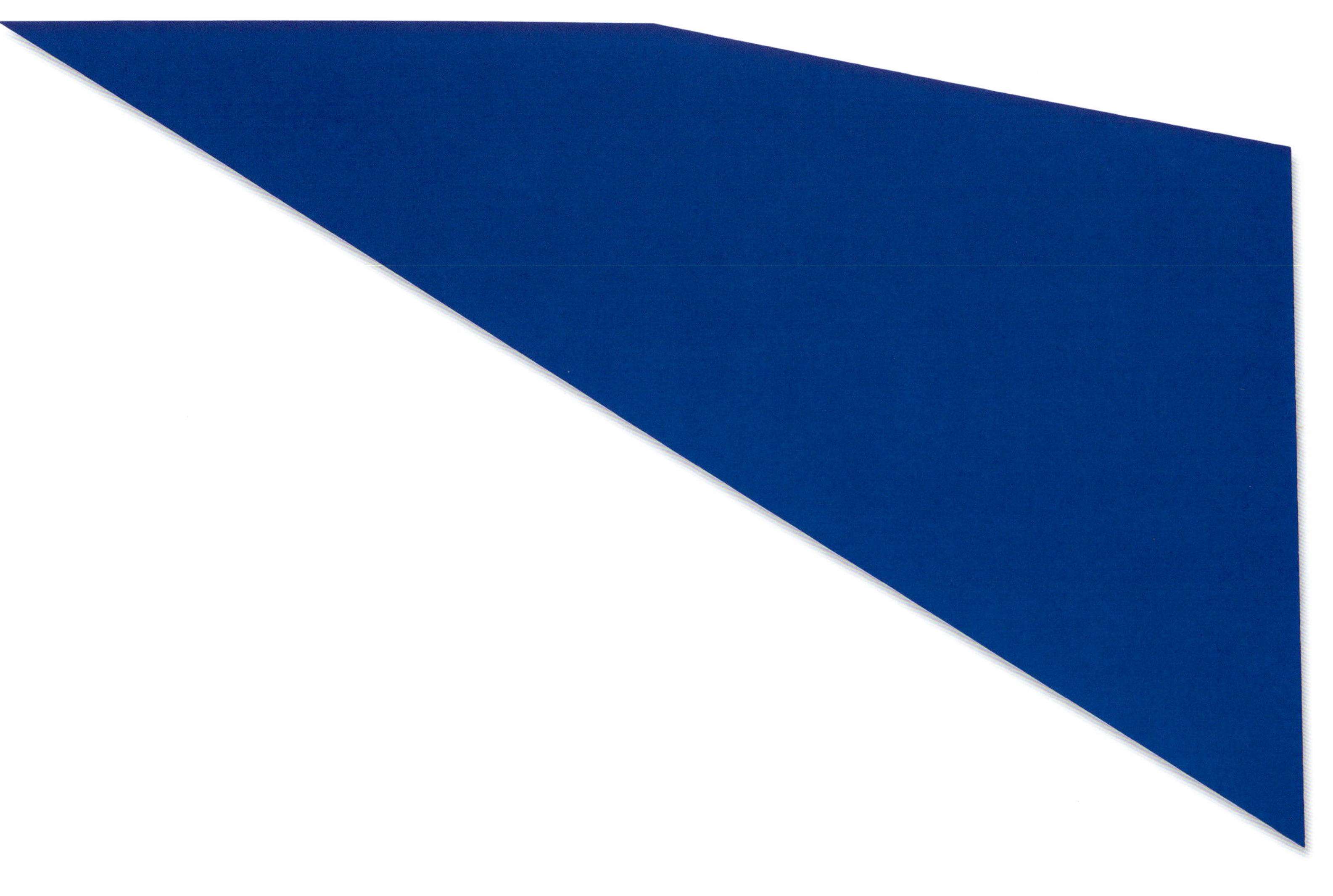

Green Orange Yellow, 2004
oil on canvas, 3 joined panels
86¼ × 65¾ in, 219.1 × 167 cm

Lake II, 2002
oil on canvas, 95 × 149⅜ in
241.3 × 379.4 cm

Purple Relief over Black, 2002
oil on canvas, 2 joined panels
80 × 77½ × 2⅝ in, 203.2 × 196.9 × 6.7 cm

Untitled, 2004
painted stainless steel and aluminum
314 × 195½ × 78½ in, 797.9 × 496.6 × 199.4 cm

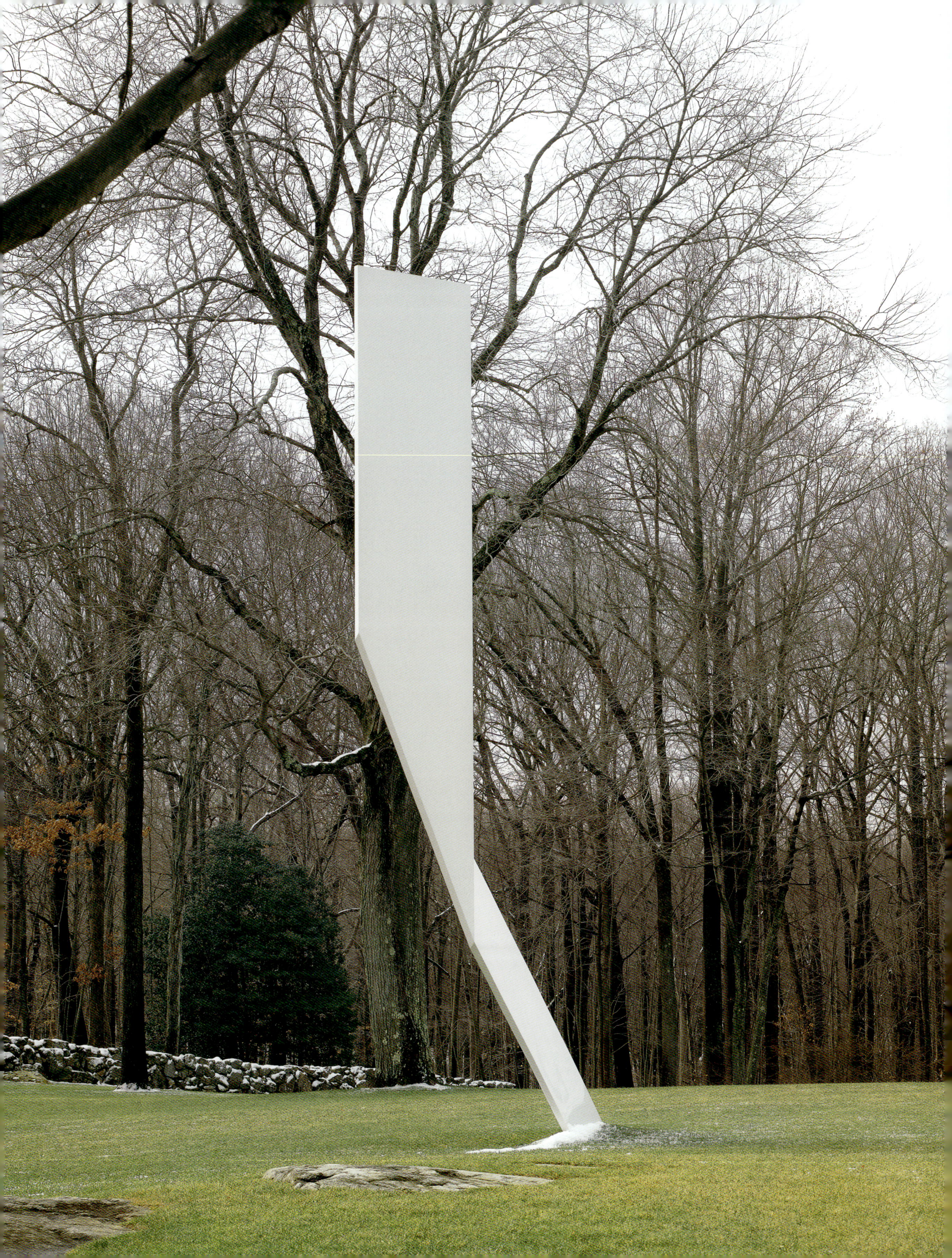

Green Black White, 2007
oil on canvas, 3 joined panels
80⅛ × 66 in, 203.5 × 167.6 cm

Black Relief with White, 2007
oil on canvas, 2 joined panels
65½ × 108 × 2¾ in, 166.4 × 274.3 × 7 cm

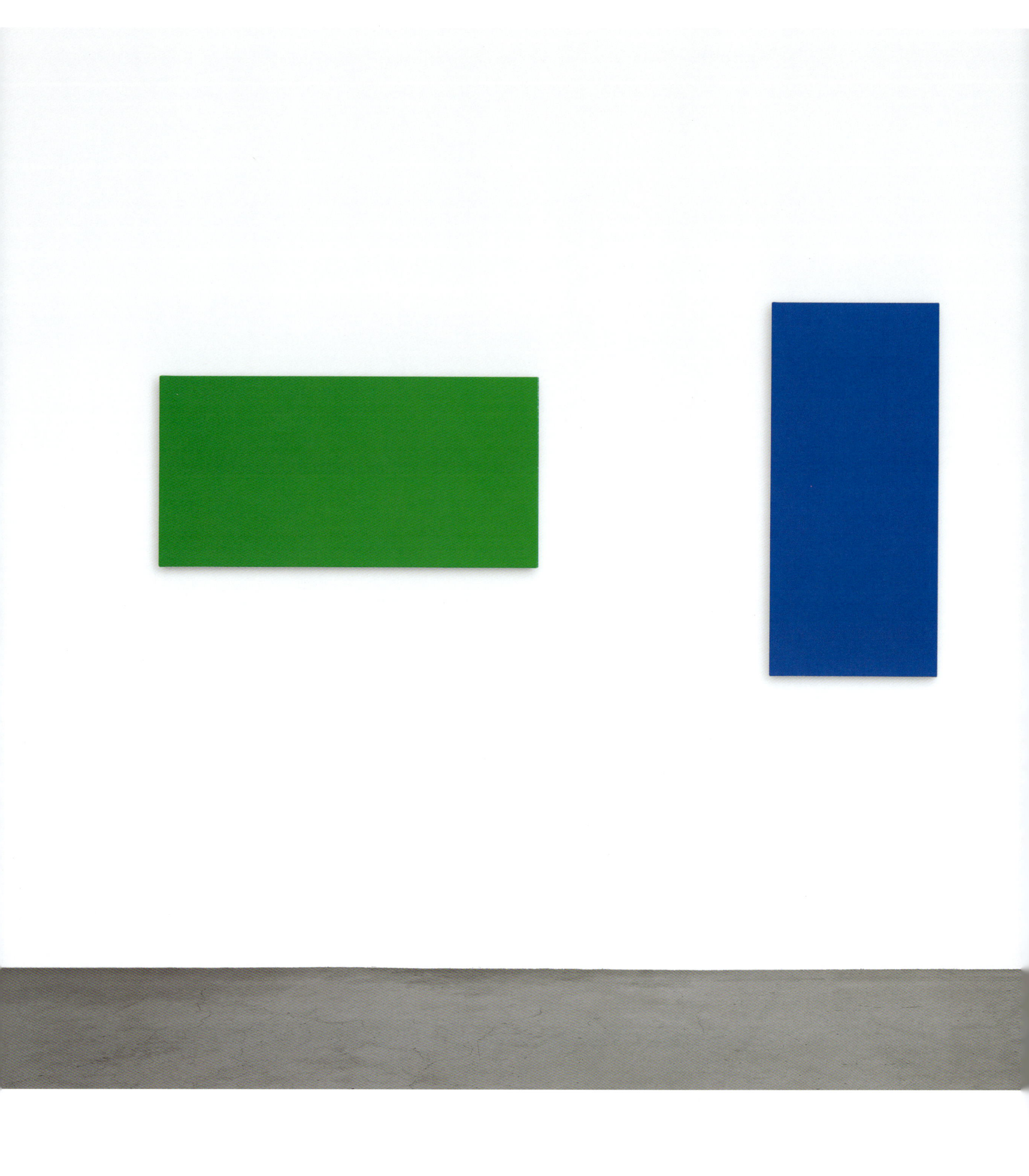

Green Blue Black Red, 2007
oil on canvas, 4 panels, 45 × 217 in, 114.3 × 551.2 cm

Black Curve Diagonal, 2010
oil on canvas, 2 joined panels
40¾ × 120 × 2⅝ in, 103.5 × 304.8 × 6.7 cm

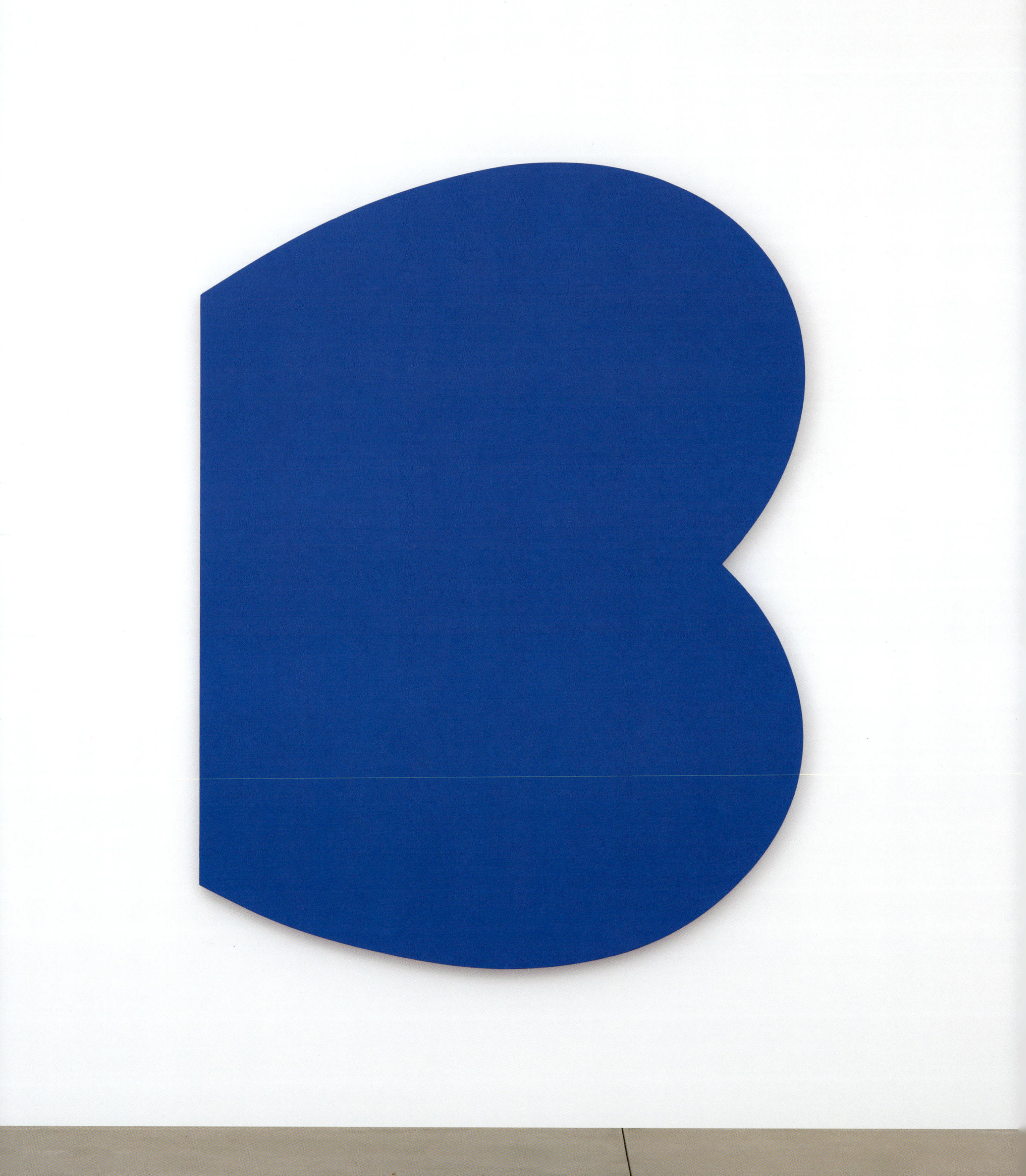

Blue Curves, 2009
oil on canvas
80 × 59¾ in, 203.2 × 151.8 cm

Black Relief II, 2010
oil on canvas, 2 joined panels
74 × 70 × 2⅝ in, 188 × 177.8 × 6.7 cm

Green Panel (Ground Zero), 2011
painted aluminum, 23⅝ × 50 × ½ in
60 × 127 × 1.3 cm

Black Bar for a Wall, 2011
painted aluminum, 96 × 473 × 6 in
243.8 × 1201.4 × 15.2 cm

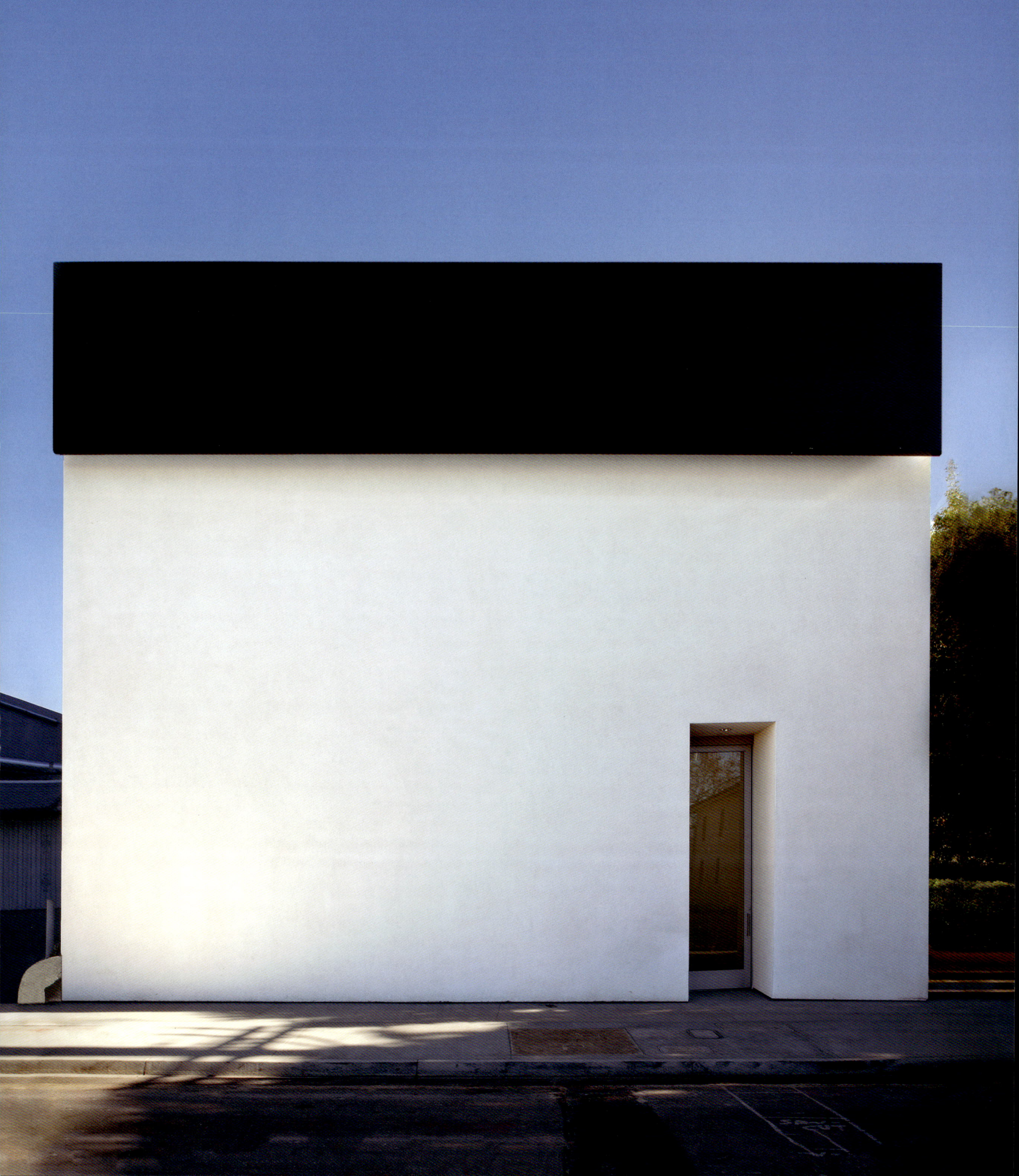

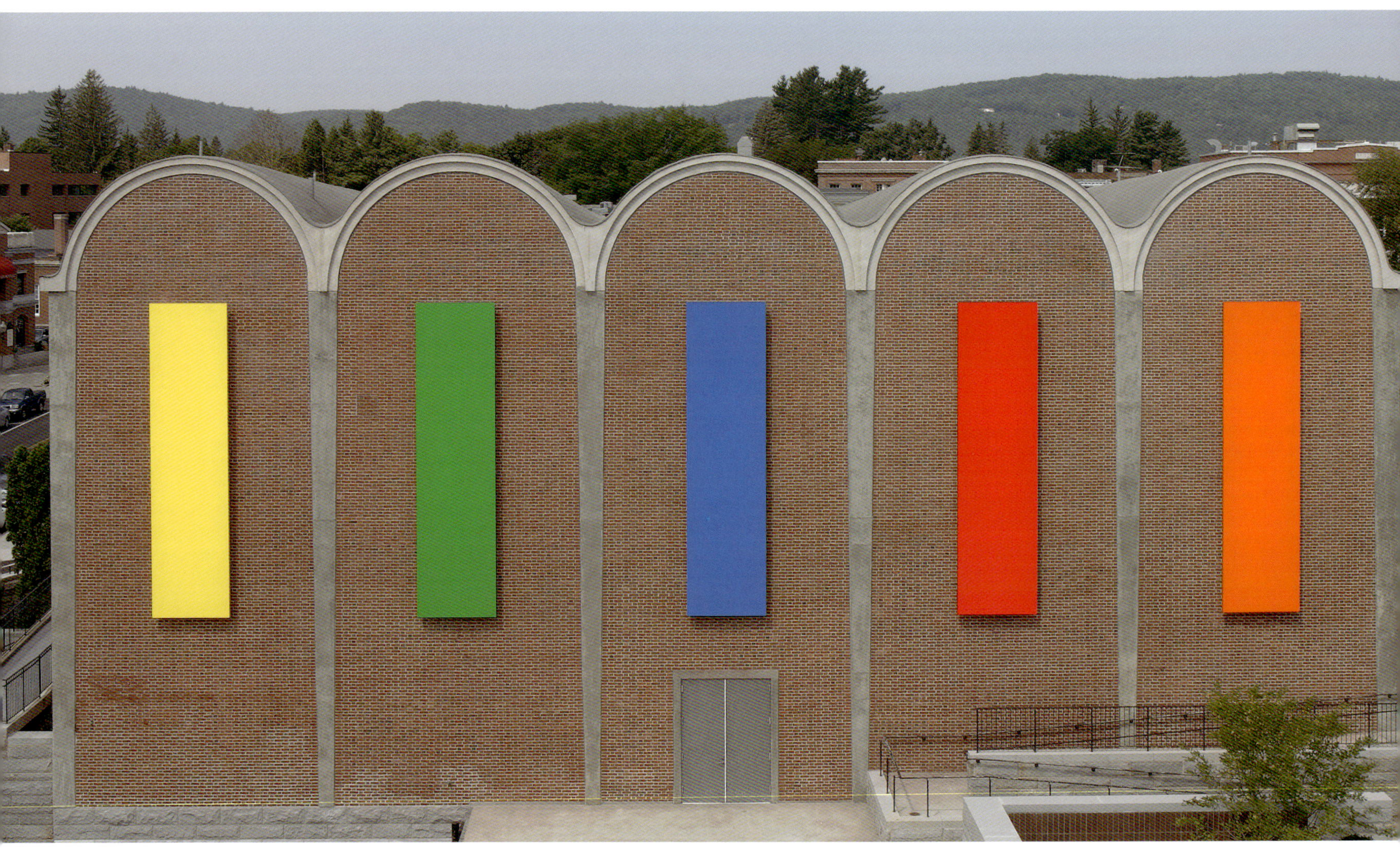

Dartmouth Panels, 2011
painted aluminum, 5 panels
266 × 1080 × 3¾ in, 6.7 × 27.4 × 0.1 m

Black Form I, 2011
painted aluminum
80 × 71¾ × 4¼ in, 203.2 × 182.2 × 10.8 cm

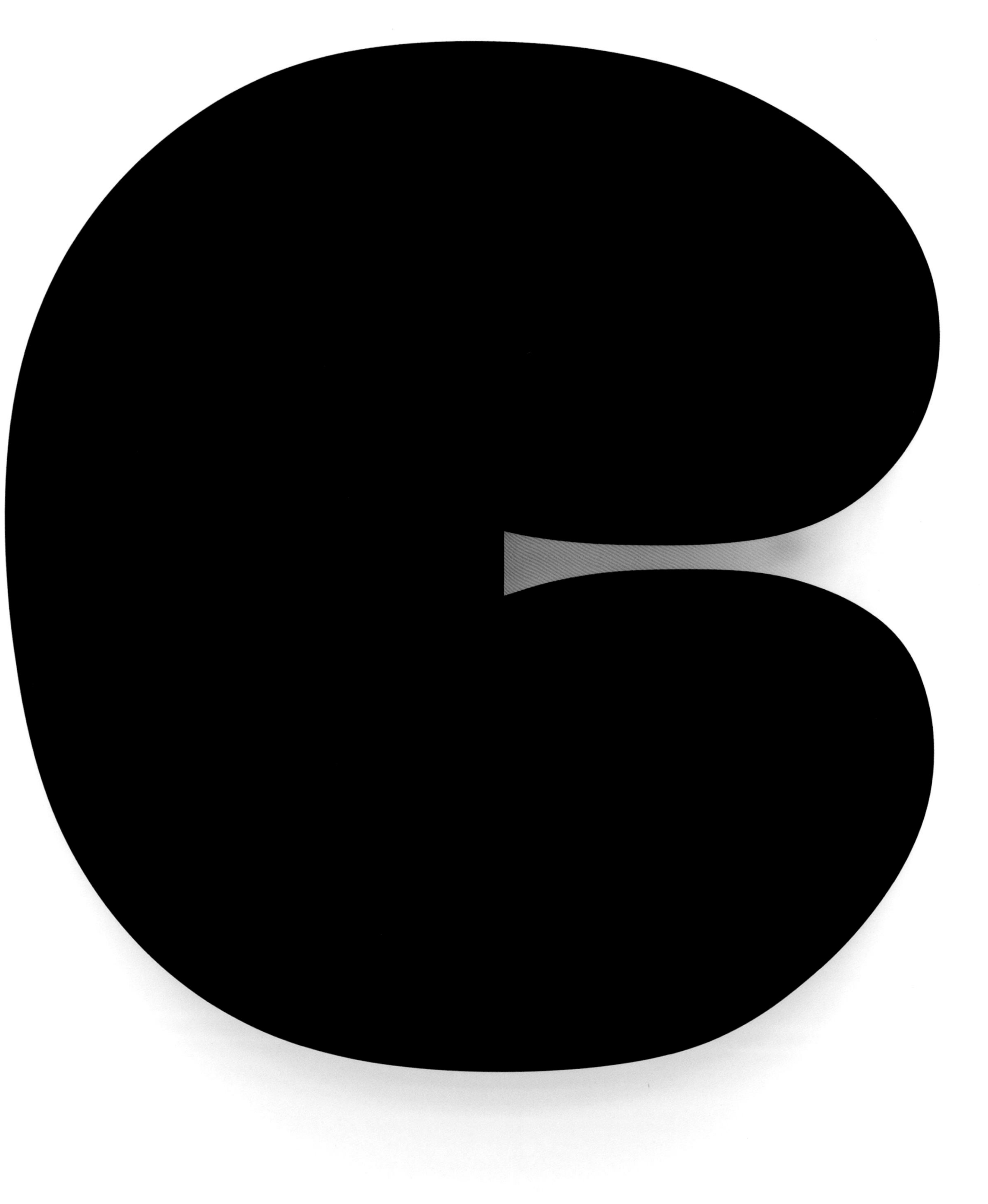

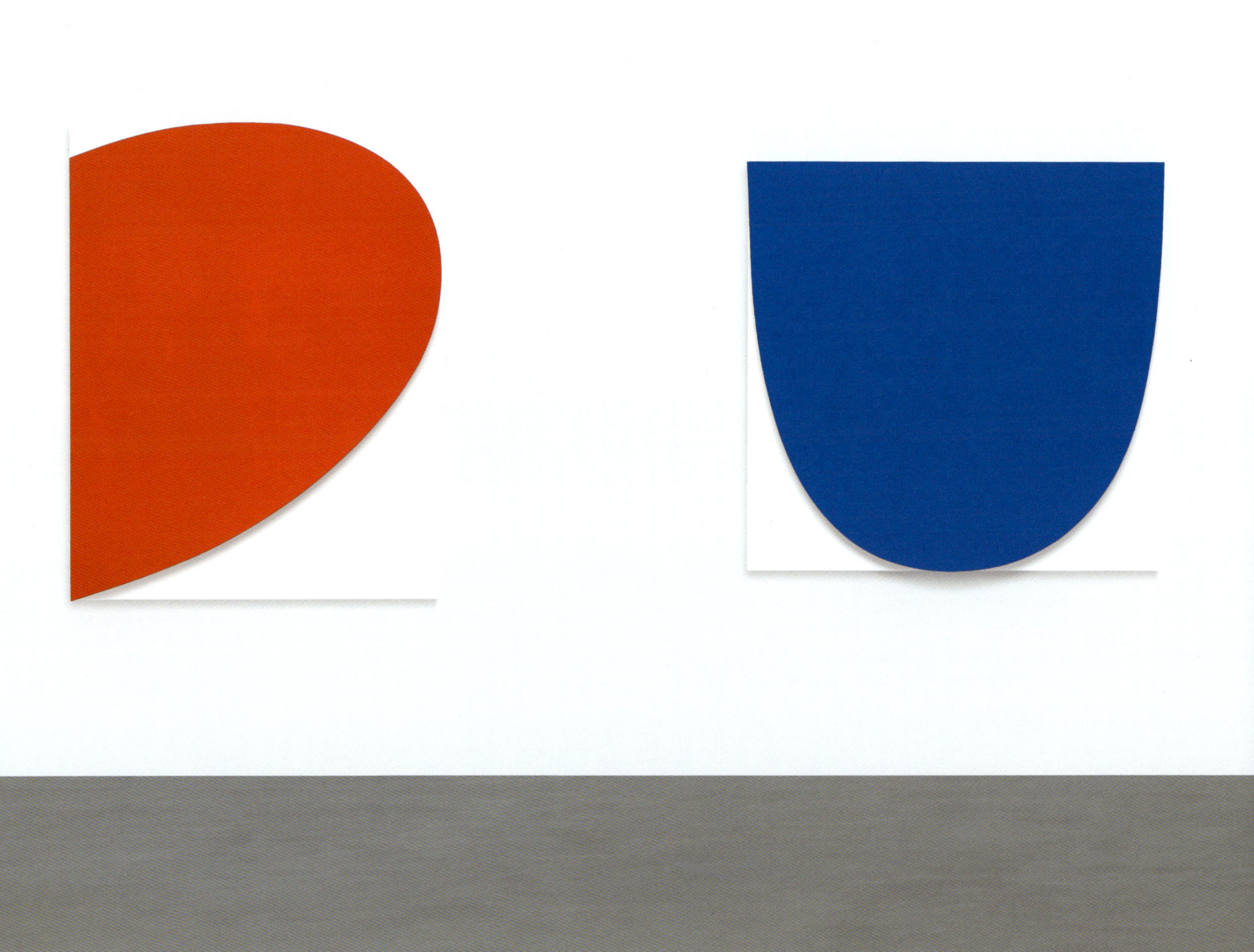

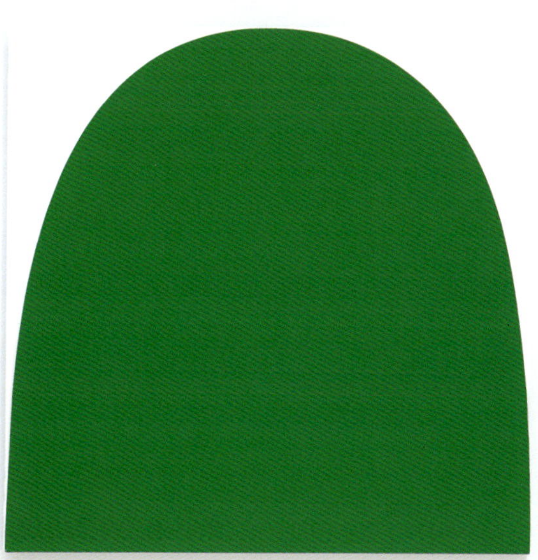

Curves on White (Four Panels), 2011
oil on canvas, 4 panels each comprised of 2 joined panels
70 × 328 × 2⅝ in, 177.8 × 833.1 × 6.7 cm

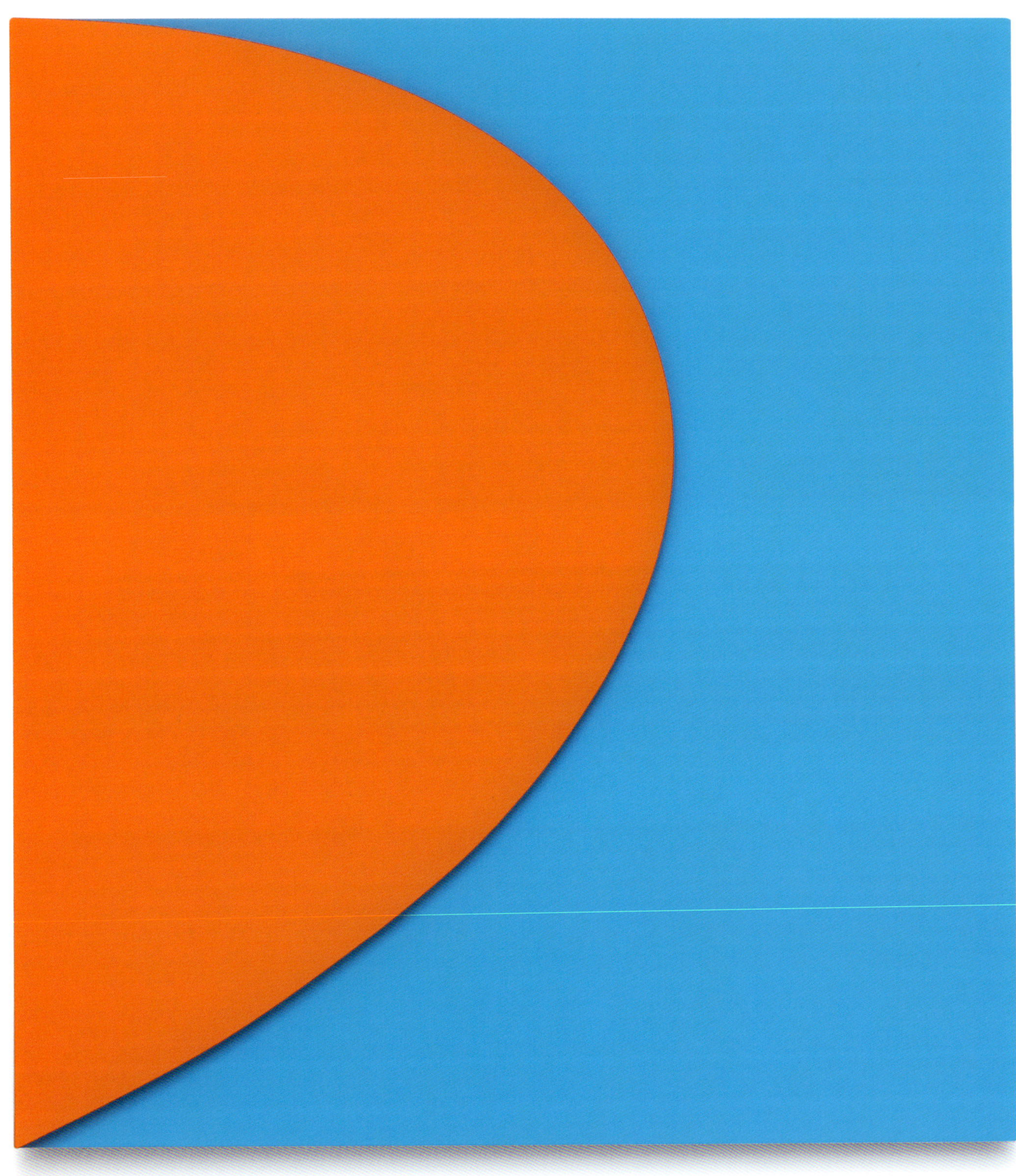

Orange Relief with Blue, 2011
oil on canvas, 2 joined panels
70 × 62¼ × 2⅝ in, 177.8 × 158.1 × 6.7 cm

White Relief with Black, 2011
oil on canvas, 2 joined panels
54¼ × 90 × 2⅝ in, 137.8 × 228.6 × 6.7 cm

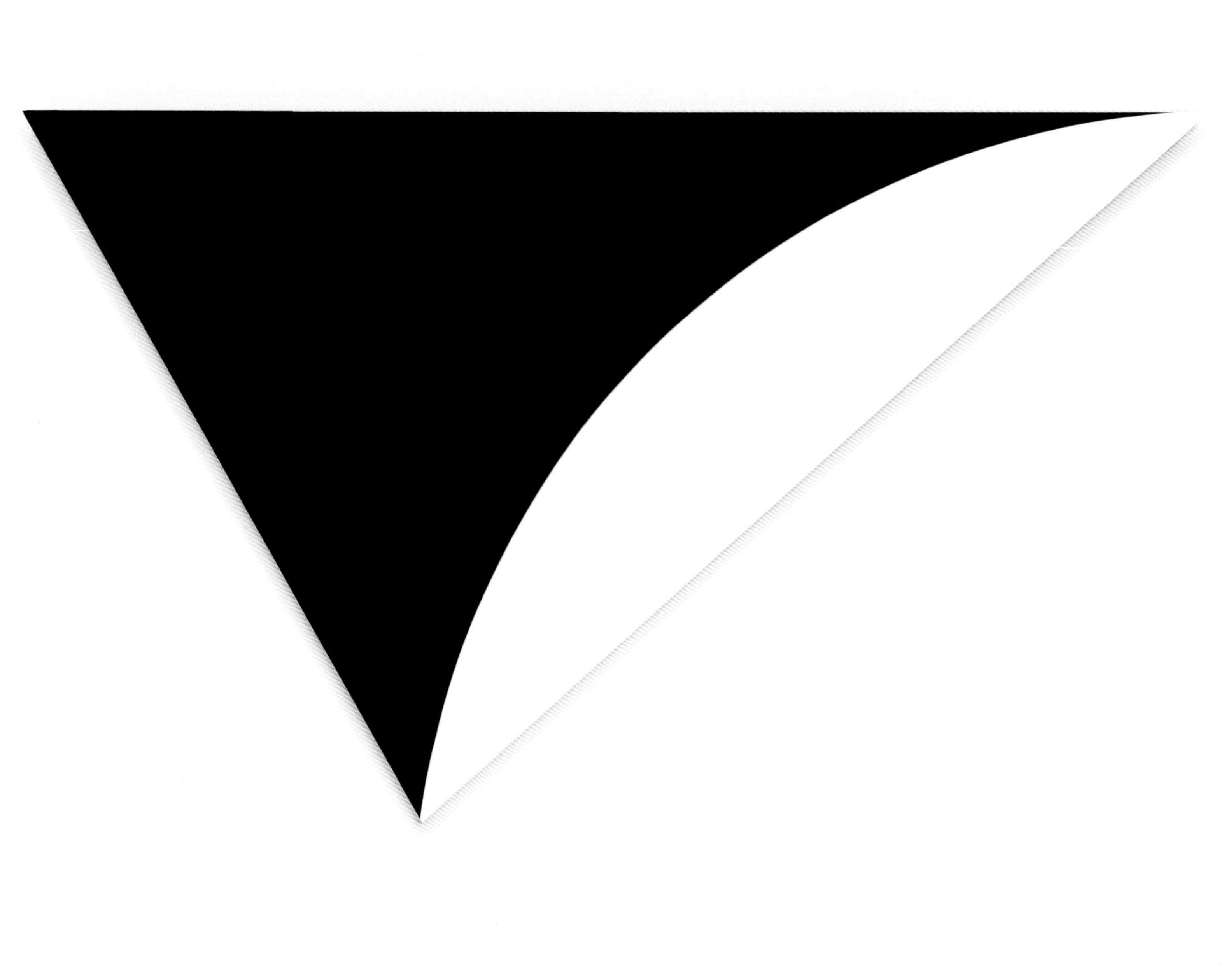

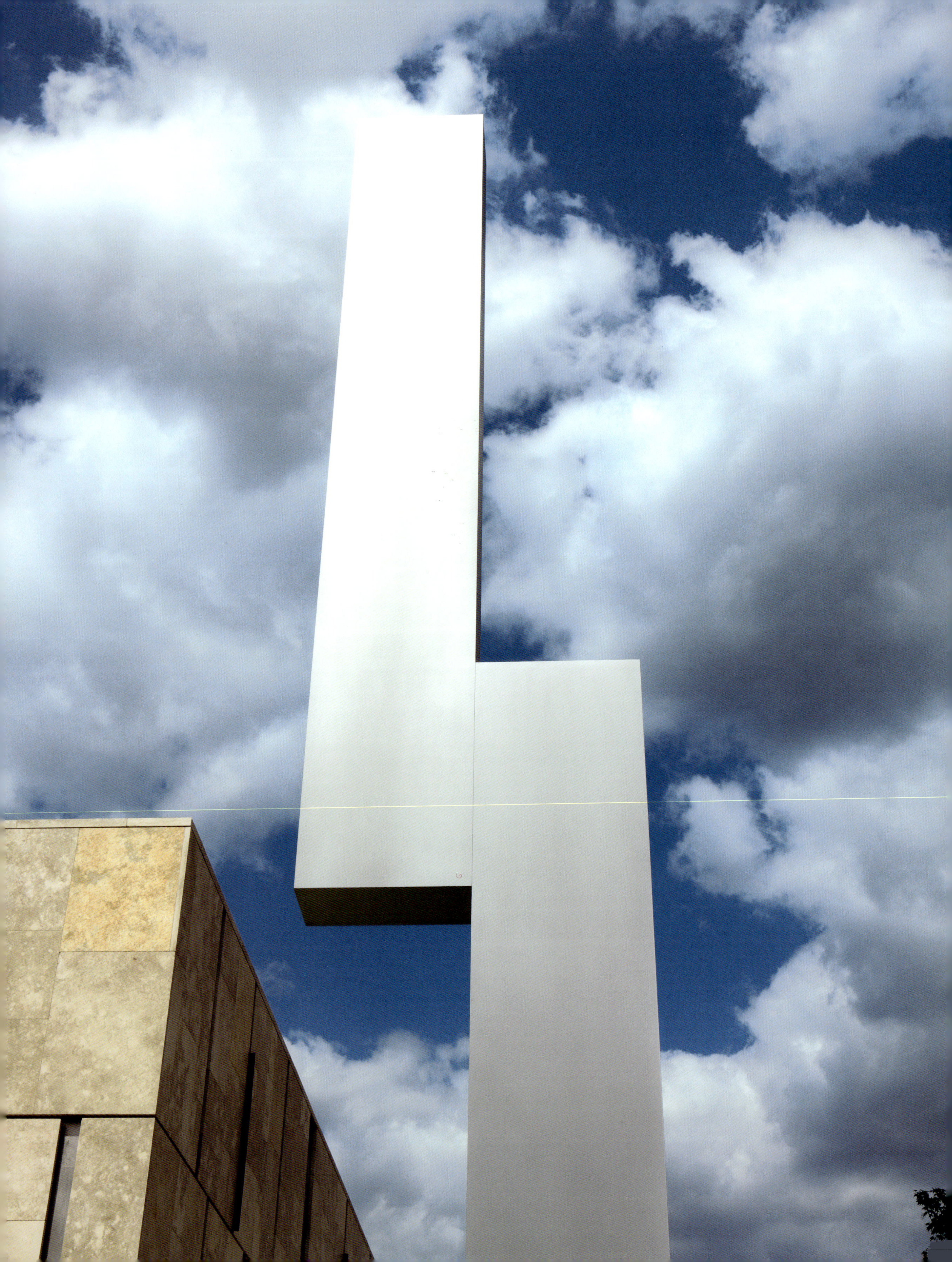

Barnes Totem, 2011
stainless steel, 480 × 80 × 20 in
1219.2 × 203.2 × 50.8 cm

Red Relief over White, 2012
oil on canvas, 2 joined panels
70 × 51¼ × 2⅝ in, 177.8 × 130.2 × 6.7 cm

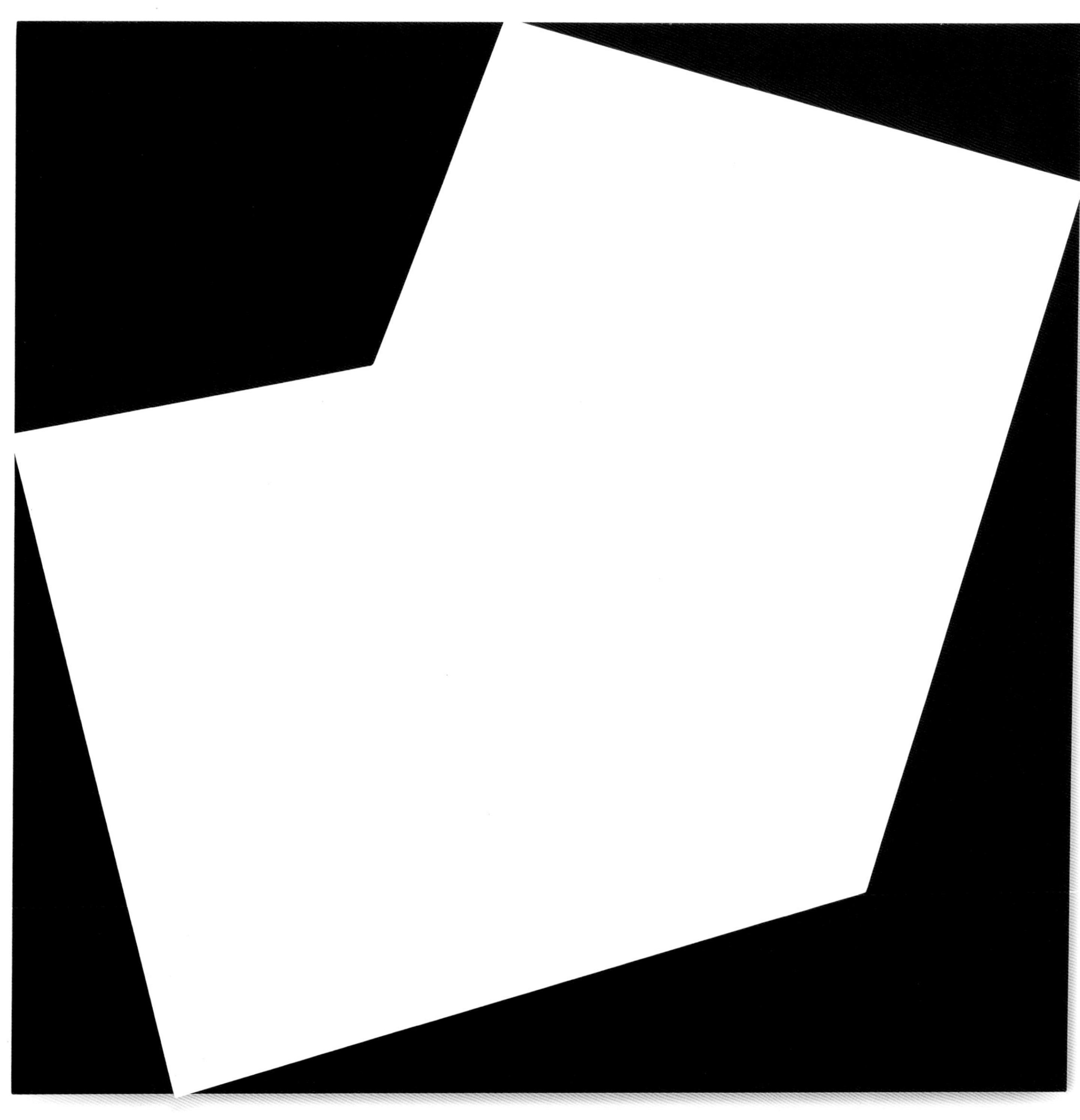

White Relief over Black, 2012
oil on canvas, 2 joined panels
70 × 70 × 2⅝ in, 177.8 × 177.8 × 6.7 cm

Untitled, 2011
painted stainless steel
240 × 34¼ × 3½ in, 609.6 × 89.5 × 8.9 cm

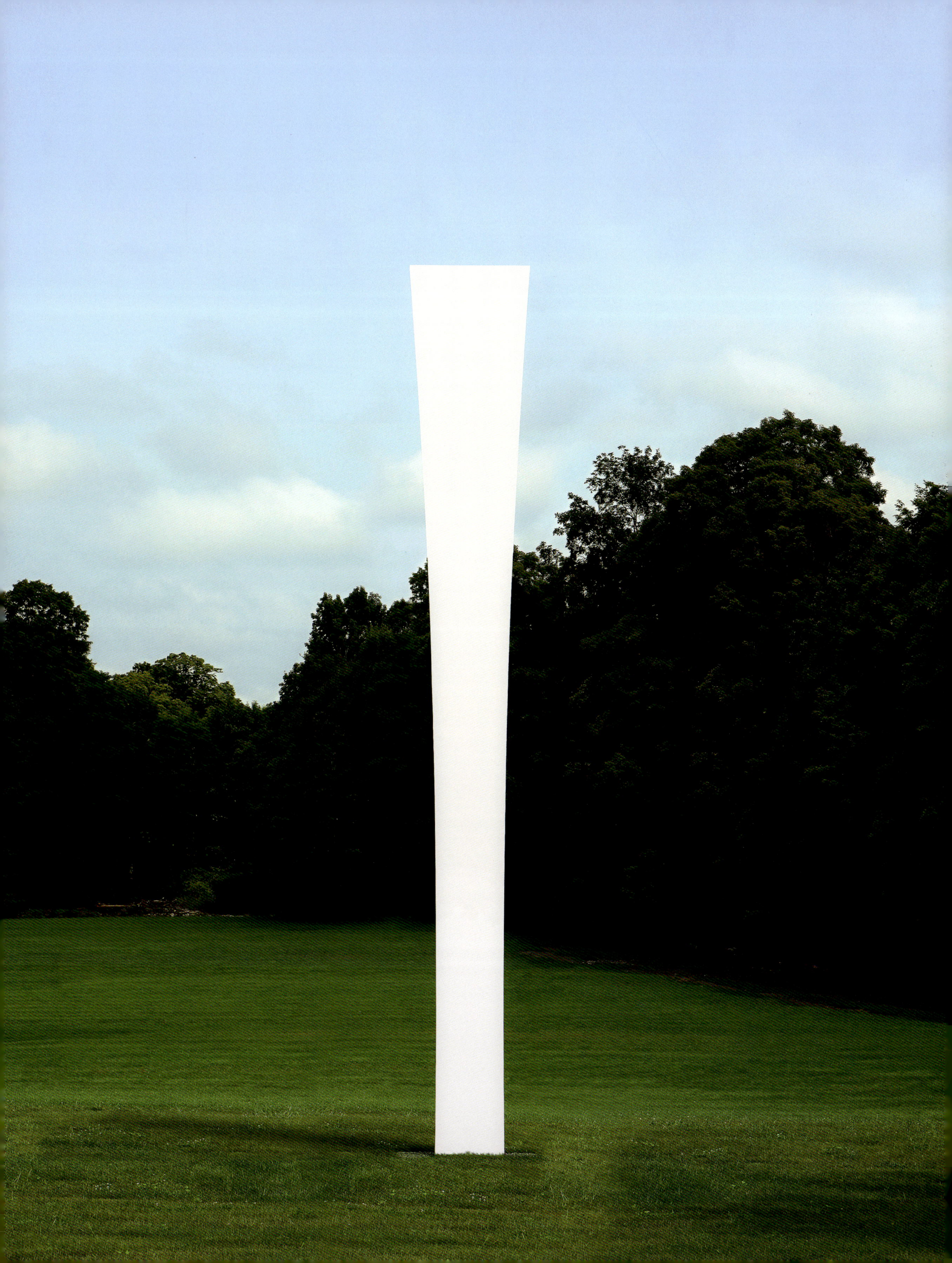

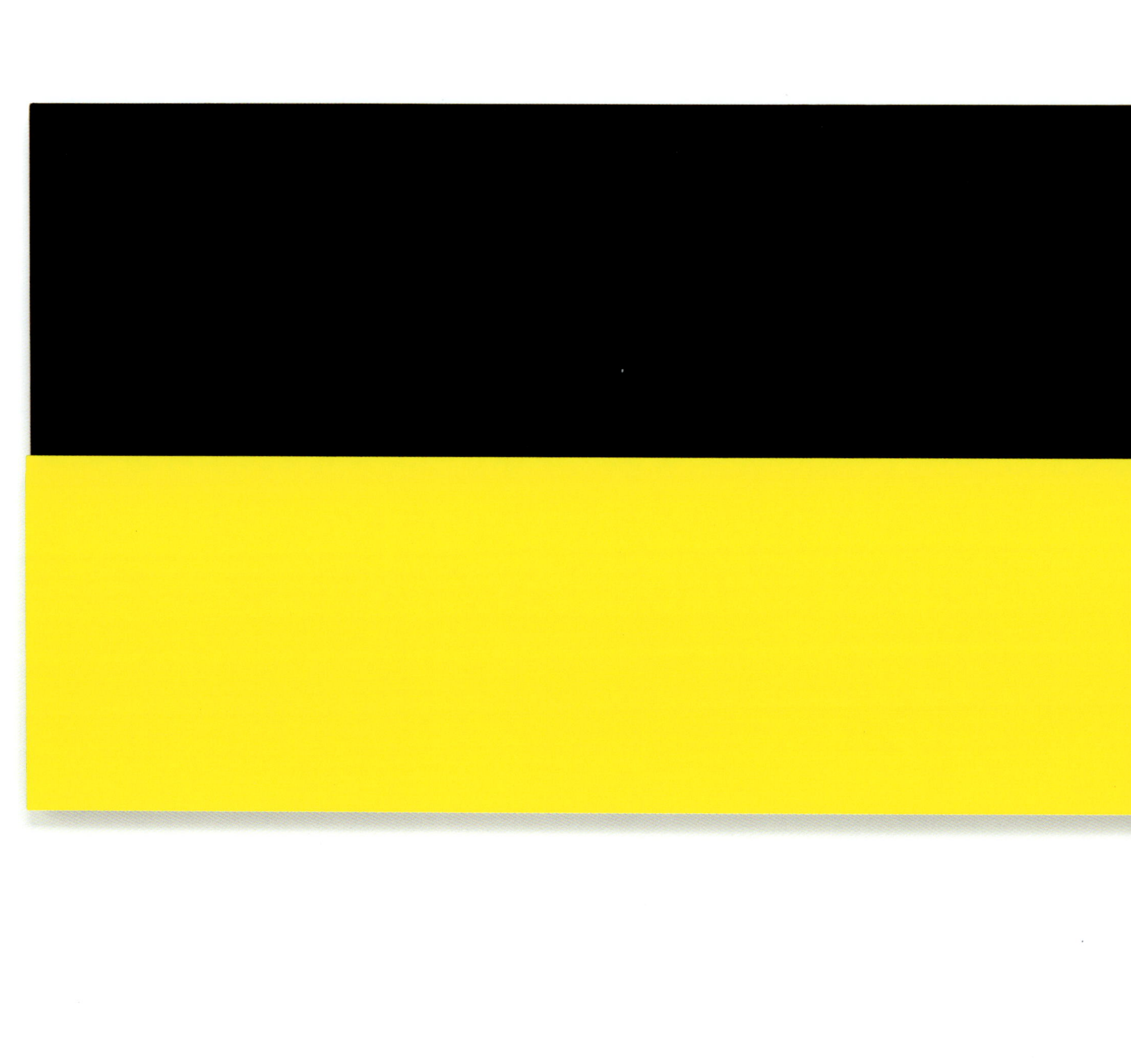

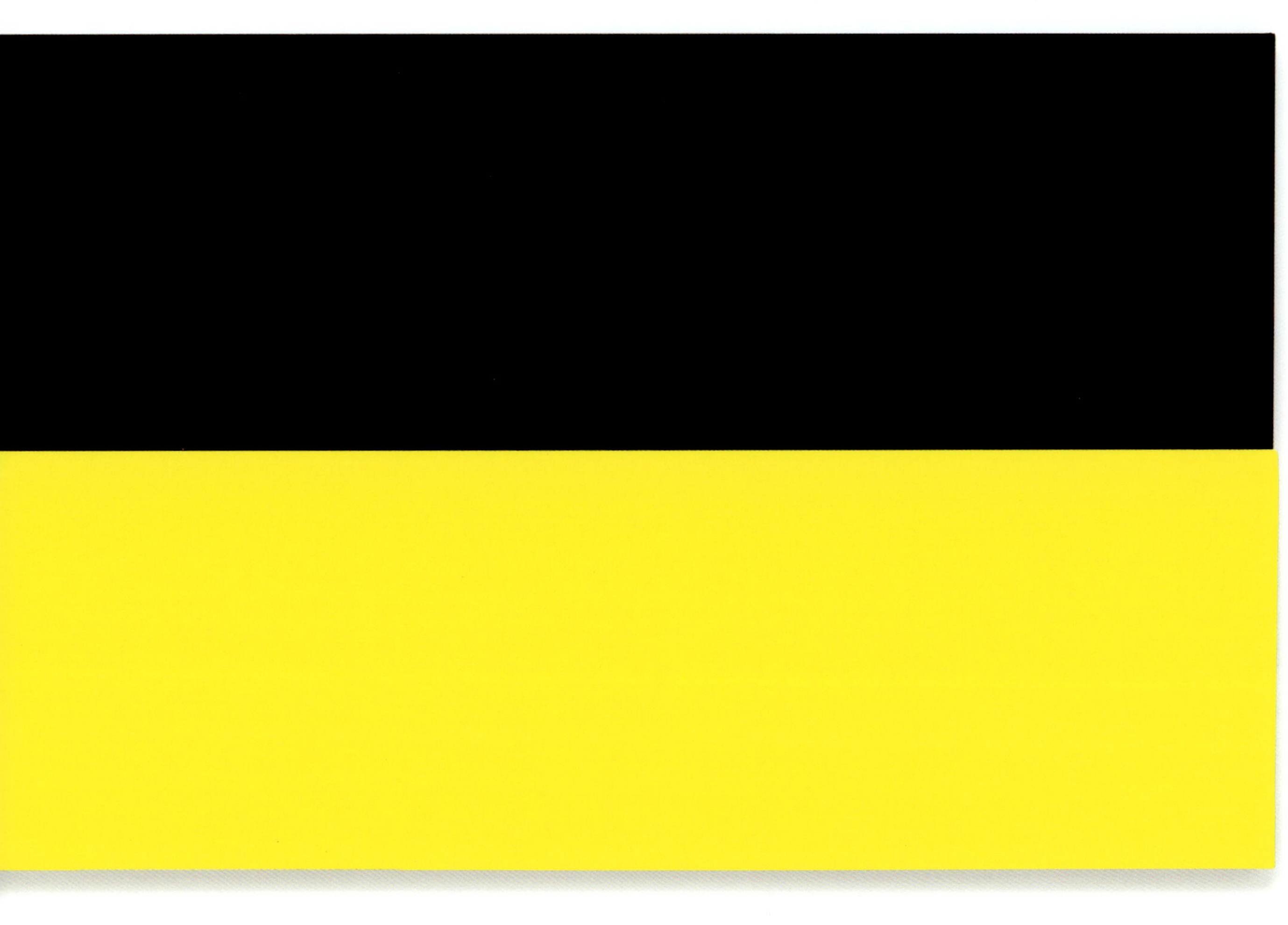

Yellow Relief over Black, 2013
oil on canvas, 2 joined panels, 40⅛ × 130 × 2⅝ in, 101.9 × 330.2 × 6.7p cm

Gold with Orange Reliefs, 2013
oil on canvas and wood, 3 joined panels
79¼ × 72¾ x 2⅝ in, 201.3 × 184.8 x 6.7 cm

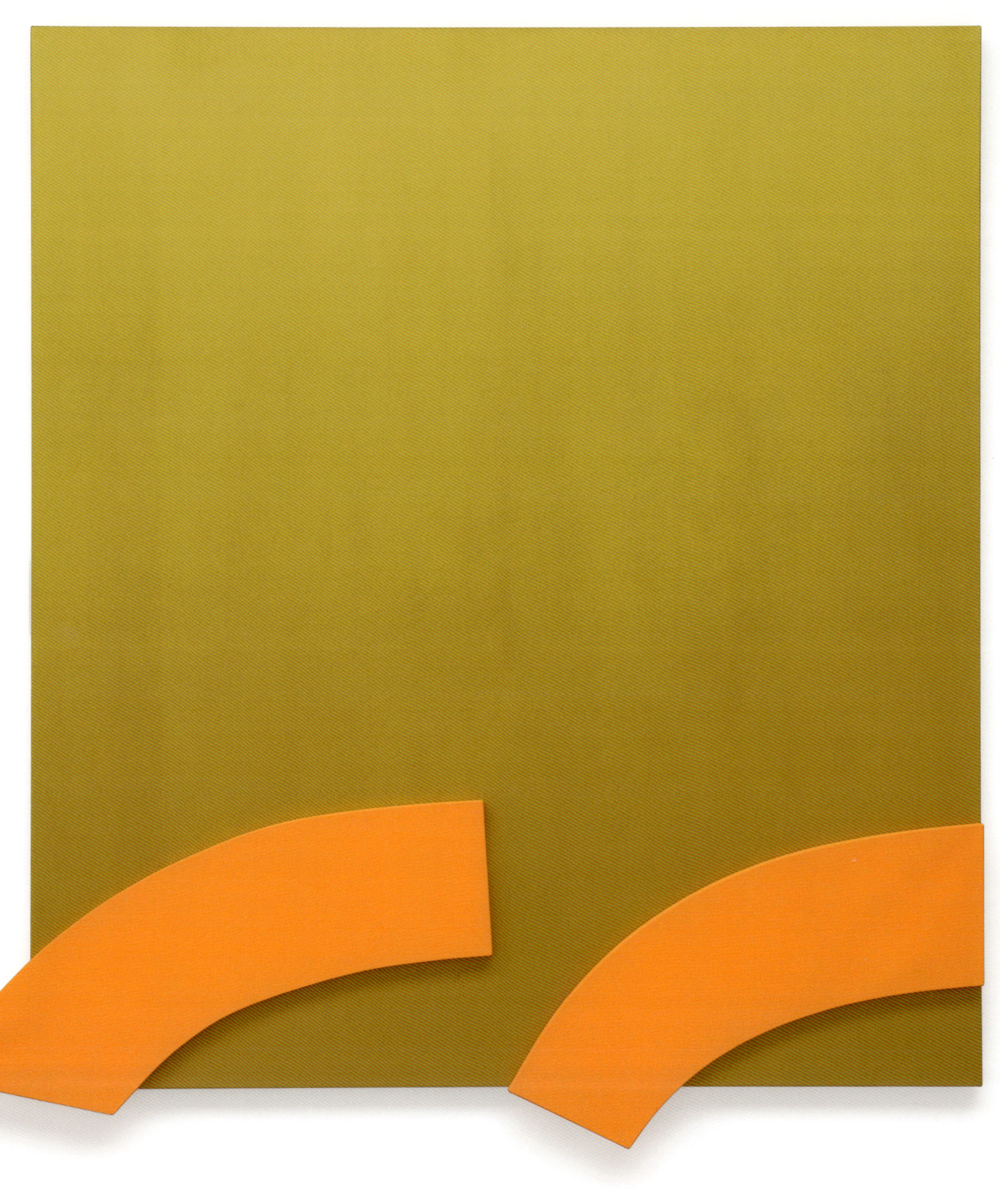

Untitled, 2013
painted stainless steel and aluminum
270 × 240 × 129 in, 685.8 × 609.6 × 327.7 cm

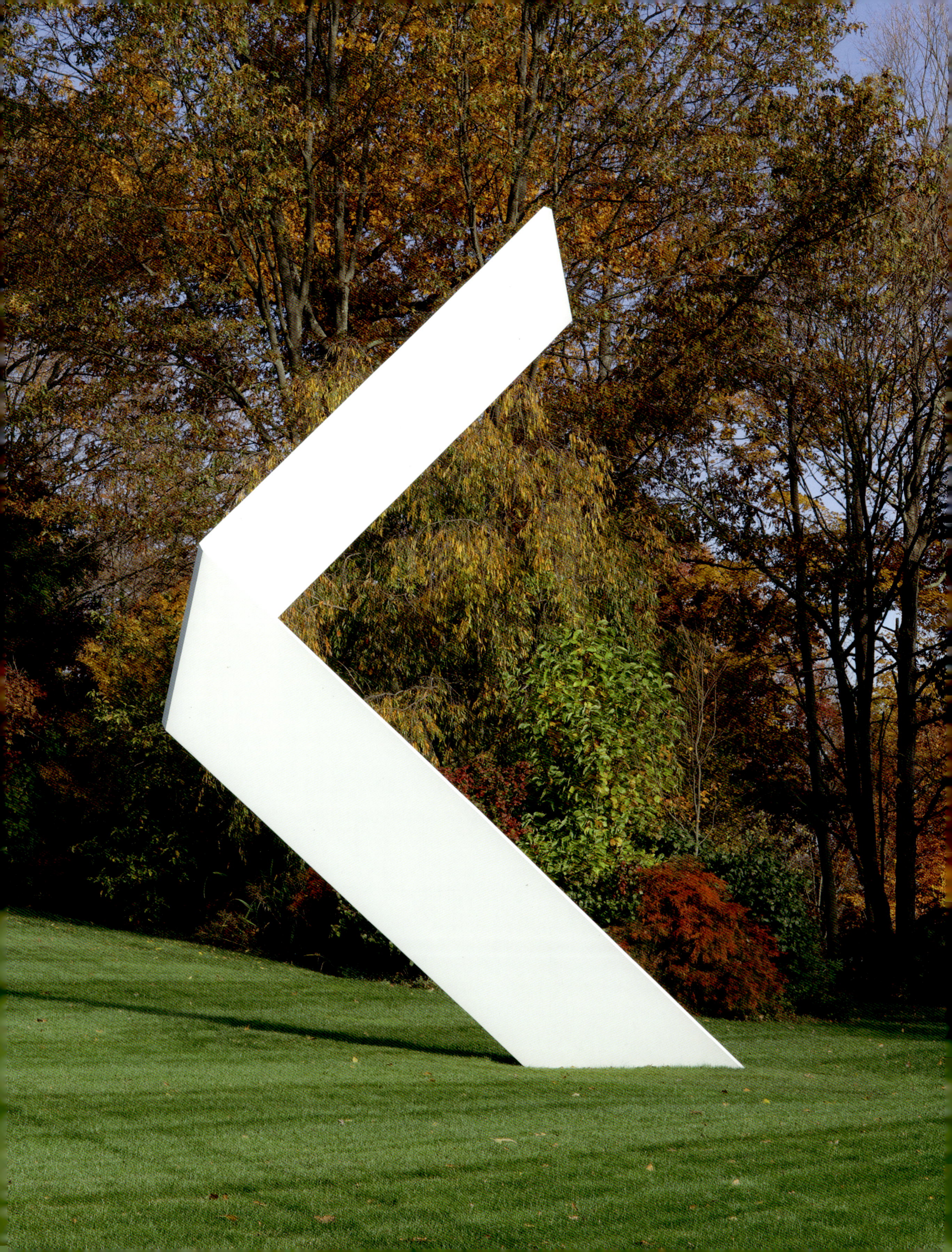

Red White Black Blue, 2014
oil on canvas, 4 joined panels
69½ × 27½ in, 176.5 × 69.9 cm

Red White, 2014
oil on canvas, 4 joined panels
70¼ × 70 in, 178.4 × 177.8 cm

Untitled, 2014
painted aluminum
178¼ × 600 × 162¼ in, 454 × 1524 × 412.1 cm

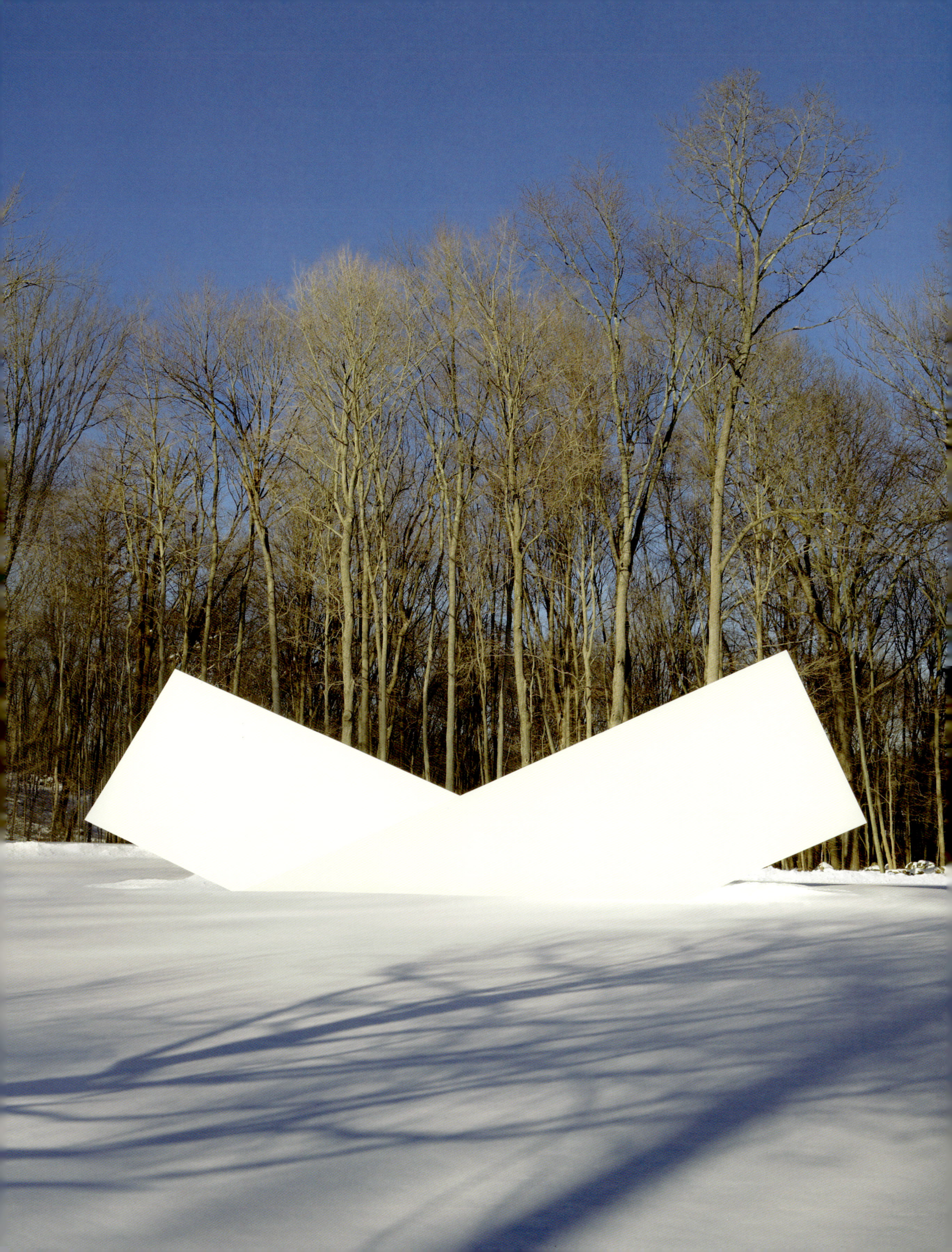

Blue Relief over Yellow, 2014
oil on canvas, 2 joined panels
60 × 65½ × 2½ in, 152.4 × 166.4 × 6.4 cm

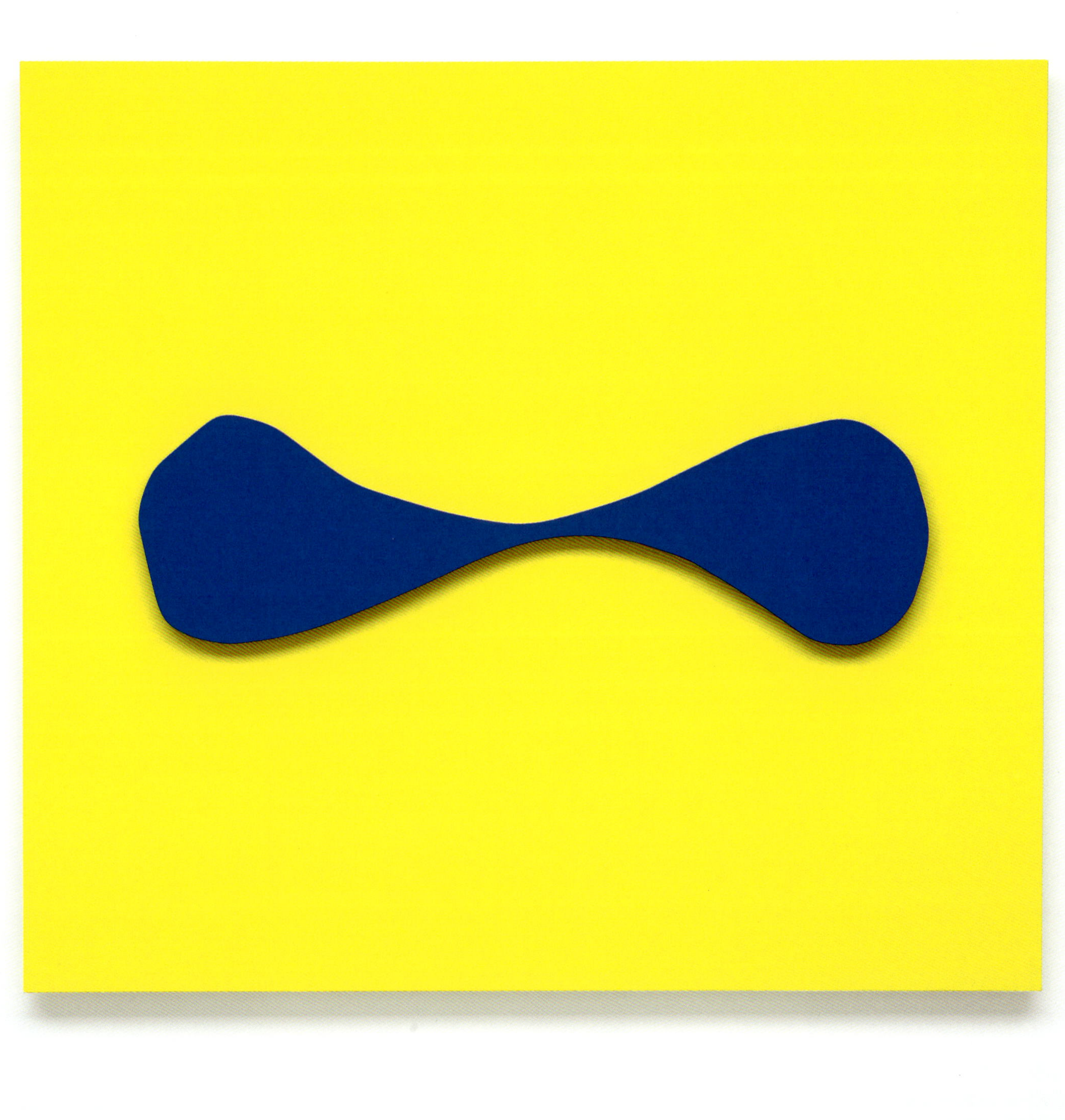

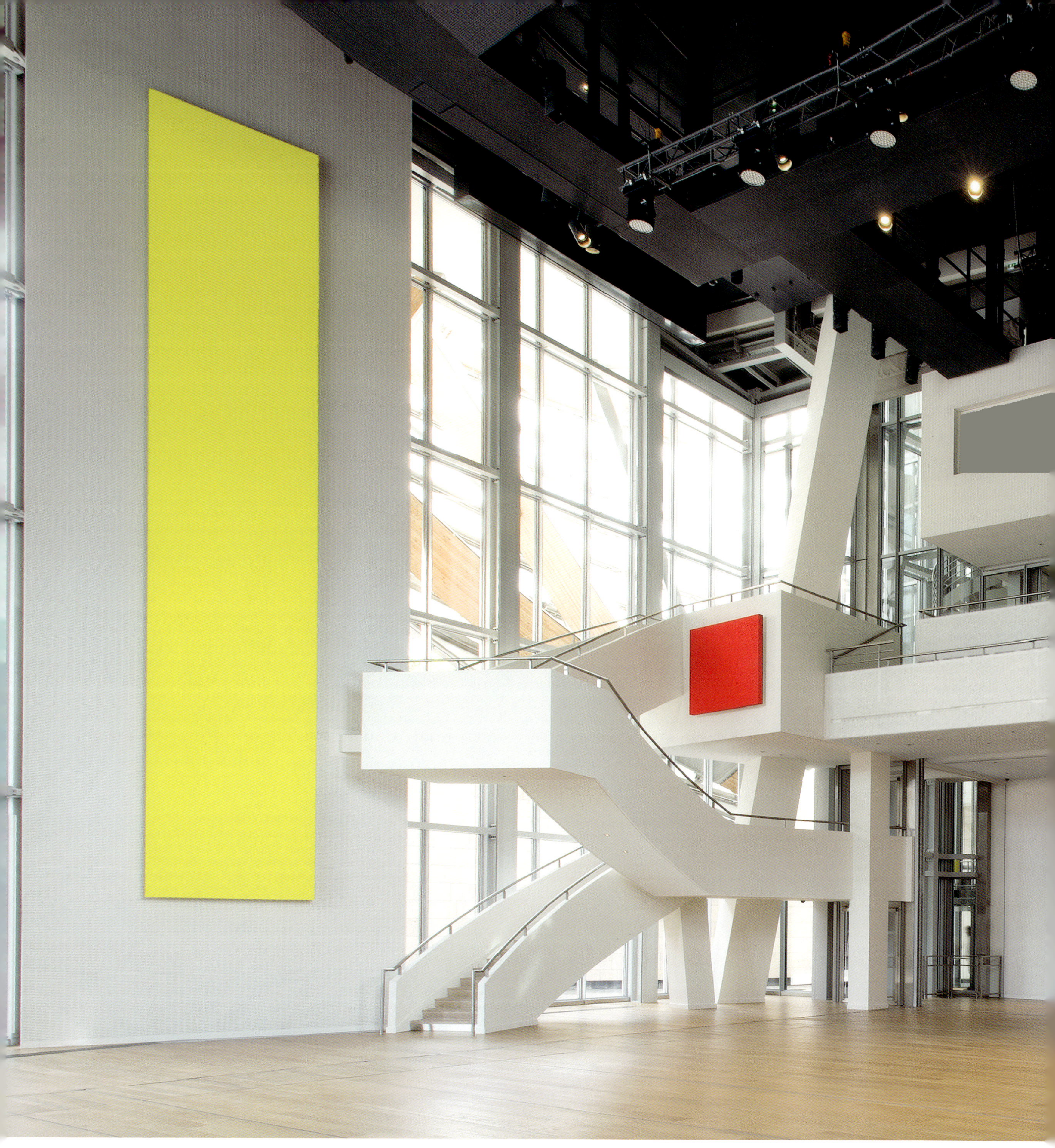

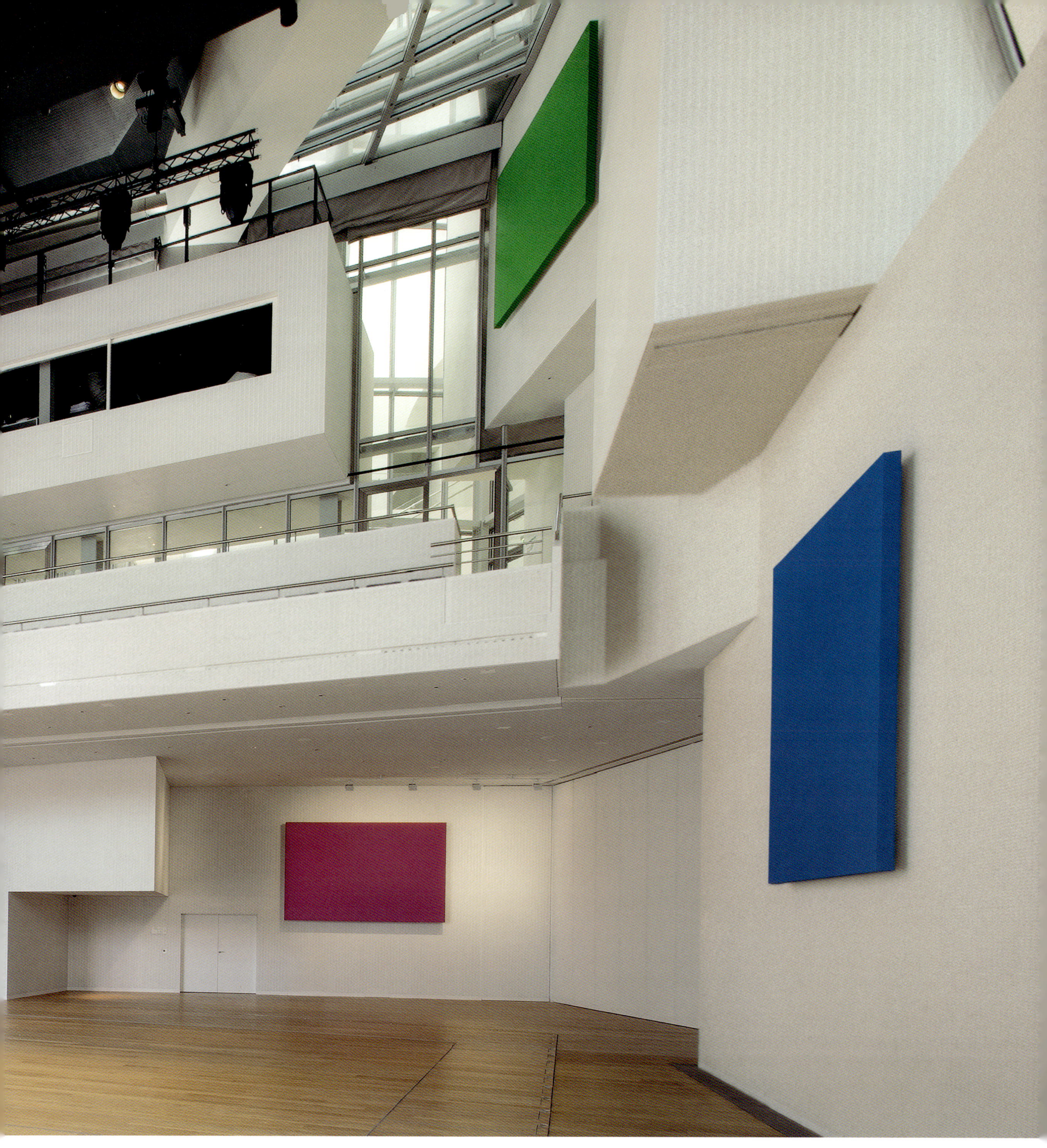

Color Panels (Red Yellow Blue Green Purple), 2014
colored fabric, 5 panels

Painting and Architecture

Gary Garrels

Almost from the beginning of his career, Ellsworth Kelly realized that a painting could be more than a self-contained canvas. A painting for Kelly was as much an object in the world as any other object. At the same time, he also knew that a painting had to be engaged with the architectural ground around it. Thus decisions about a painting's scale, its boundaries, and its placement in relation to a wall or to an architectural setting would be as fundamental to its character as the decisions about how its surface would be treated. The fusion of architecture and the painting as an object established the course of Kelly's work in the late 1940s and distinguished his exceptional inventions for the possibilities of painting in the decades that would follow.

As early as September 1950, Kelly wrote in a letter to John Cage,

> [My] collages are only ideas for things much larger—things to cover walls. In fact all the things I've done I would like to see much larger. I am not interested in painting as it has been accepted for so long—to hang on walls of houses as pictures. To hell with pictures—they should *be* the wall—even better—on the outside wall—of large buildings.[1]

A number of paintings of this period recast architectural elements as the subject for paintings, such as *Window, Museum of Modern Art, Paris* (1949) (p. 53) and *La Combe III* (1951) (fig. 155), but the earliest painting that Kelly expressly considered in terms of its relation to its placement on a wall is *Cité* (1951) (p.63).[2] In the spring of 1951, while teaching at the American School in Paris, Kelly stayed overnight at the Cité Universitaire designed by Le Corbusier and had a dream that his students had painted a mural of black and white stripes. In the morning he made a sketch of his dream, showing a painting covering an entire outside wall of a building (fig. 44). Le Corbusier's Swiss Pavilion at the Cité Universitaire, which included walls between balconies painted bright pastel shades, in part inspired Kelly to consider making works on an architectural scale[3]. He had no means at this time to make a mural, but he did make the painting, eventually titled *Cité*, composed of twenty panels for the wall of his studio. Initially, he had thought that the panels might be continually rearranged to explore the effects of chance, changing patterns, and relationships between the panels. But very quickly he settled on an arrangement that he intuitively felt was right, and then attached the panels together with a support on the back. The support raised the painting off the wall, establishing it in a shallow relief relationship, further enhancing the character of the painting as an object in relation to the wall. Over time, he developed this practice of setting his paintings in shallow relief as a consistent and self-conscious aspect of his work.

In the fall of 1951, Kelly applied to the John Simon Guggenheim Memorial Foundation in New York for a grant to create a book: *Line, Form and Color*.[4] In his application statement, he wrote, "I will create a book which shall be an alphabet of plastic pictorial elements, and which shall aim at establishing a new scale of painting, a closer contact between the artist and the wall, and a new spirit of painting to accompany modern architecture."[5] Harry Cooper summarizes his project as a desire for the "dismounting of painting from the easel, indeed from the gallery or museum wall (from being 'hung on walls'). Only then could painting be reattached to

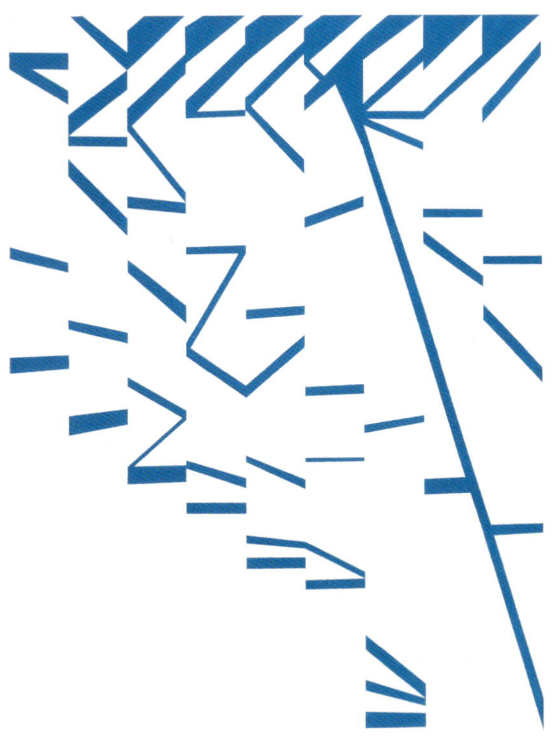

fig. 155: *La Combe III*, 1951, oil on linen, 63½ × 44½ in, 161.3 × 113 cm

the wall—not the gallery wall but the everyday wall, and not as a temporary ornament but as an integral element of appropriate form and scale."[6] Kelly made a trip in 1952 to Marseilles to see Le Corbusier's Unité d'Habitation, an eighteen-storey concrete building that would be completed that year, in which the architect again used different polychrome panels set between balconies.[7] While never meeting Le Corbusier, Kelly did arrange for a friend who knew him to present slides of his paintings to the architect in the hope that he would consider Kelly for a commission, but with no success.[8]

One of the largest paintings that Kelly made during his time in France is *Colors for a Large Wall* (1951) (p. 69), a square measuring almost 8 × 8 feet. He did not have the space or means to make or move a painting on such a scale as a single canvas; it is composed of sixty-four joined panels, in which the colors have been arranged by chance, based on all the leftover squares of colored paper from the series "Spectrum Colors Arranged by Chance" that preceded it. As Roberta Bernstein has noted regarding the title of this painting, "By using the word 'wall' in the title of his largest and most important grid painting, Kelly affirmed the relationship of the painting to the wall as crucial to the direction his art would take from now on ... The wall literally becomes the painting's 'ground,' thereby integrally linking the artwork to its architectural setting."[9] This work sets the foundation for the major public paintings that Kelly would eventually realize in later decades.

Kelly returned to the United States in 1954 and set up a studio in downtown Manhattan. He began developing new ideas for paintings such as *Black Ripe* (1955) (p. 130) and made several paintings based on collages that he had composed in Paris, including *Gaza* (1956) (p. 133). He also continued to seek commissions, and in the summer of 1956 was invited to design a series of brass screens for the restaurant in the new Philadelphia Transportation Building. The success of this work led to a larger and much more significant commission to develop a work for the lobby of the building, completed and installed in 1957—*Sculpture for a Large Wall*.[10] (pp. 140–41) However, attempts to secure other commissions failed, with one exception—a long, thin painting *Eastmore Mural* (1957) (p. 142), for an apartment building on the Upper East Side of Manhattan. By necessity, Kelly focused his attention on works that could be made in his studio, which he did with exceptional inventiveness and rigor. By the time of an interview with Henry Geldzahler in 1963, Kelly declared, "I know that when I was in Europe

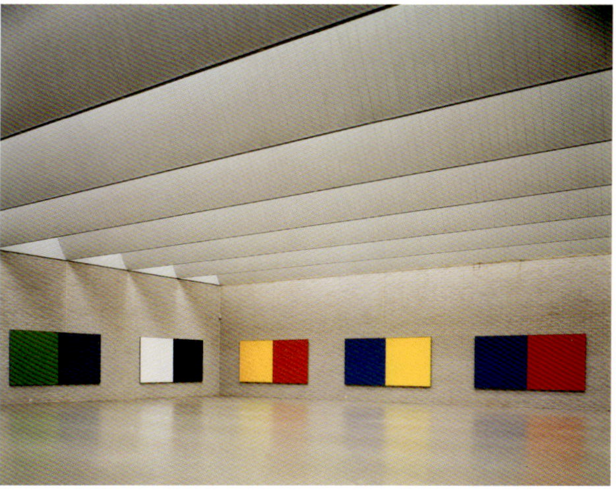

fig. 156: *Series of Five Paintings*, 1966, oil on canvas, 5 panels each comprised of 2 joined panels, each 70 × 140 in, 177.8 × 355.6 cm

I wanted to come back to America and paint huge paintings that covered the outsides of buildings. But now I feel I want to make things in my studio—and let anything bigger grow out of that."[11]

The years 1965 and 1966 were crucial and those in which Kelly reckoned most inventively with his paintings' potential relationships to the wall. In these years, he made two paintings that are among the most unusual works of his career, in which both the wall and the floor are directly engaged: *Red Blue Green Yellow* (1965) and *Blue Red* (1966) (p. 173). Each of these works is composed of two panels of the same size, one mounted on the wall and the other protruding from the wall into the space of the room, so that wall and floor are treated as equals. The panels are set in shallow relief, the vertical panel slightly in front of the wall, and the horizontal panel hovering just above the floor. Although equal in size, the two panels remain oddly different from each other; they cannot be perceptually reconciled. Facing the work directly, the panel on the floor imparts a sense of perspectival recession, while the panel on the wall opposes it as an impenetrable plane. One must move around the work to try to see and understand it, yet the relationship between the two panels is constantly shifting. The end result is a work that is enigmatic, playful, and open-ended —both assertive and vulnerable.[12]

Simultaneously, Kelly began pushing the scale of his paintings to almost mural size in relationship to the walls on which they were installed. He completed a series of four large monochrome canvases, *Green Red Yellow Blue* (1965) (fig. 111), with an overall dimension of 76 inches × 21 feet 3

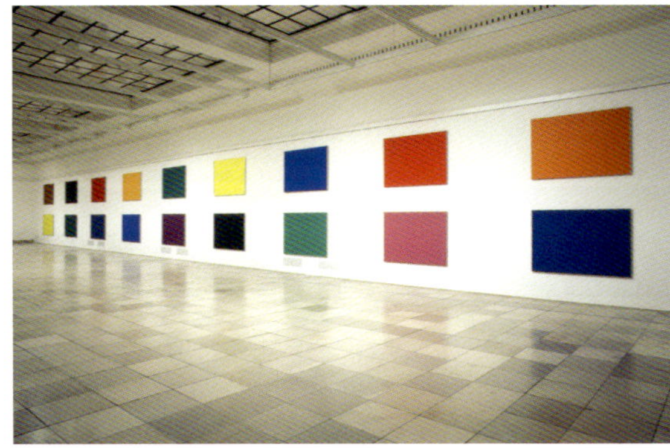

fig. 157: *Color Panels for a Large Wall,* 1978, oil on canvas, 18 panels, 10 × 125 ft, 3.1 × 38.3 m

inches. The work was first presented in an exhibition at the Ferus Gallery in Los Angeles in 1966 and shown there as a "wall installation," with each canvas separated by 9-inch gaps.[13] Also in 1966, Kelly made the monumental work *Series of Five Paintings* (fig. 156), each composed of two canvases of different colors and each measuring 70 inches high × 11 feet 8 inches long. In both these works the tension in relation to the wall is lateral, with the edges of the wall acting as a frame. These works initiated a practice that Kelly has continued through to the present, in which the intervals between single canvases of multi-panel works may be adjusted depending on the overall length of the wall upon which they are presented.

In 1966, Kelly also made his first shaped canvas, a type of painting that he has continued to explore and is now among the types of work most identified with him. *Yellow Piece* (1966) (p. 175) is among his most exemplary works, a single monochrome canvas in which two corners are squared and two are rounded. An illusion that the squared corners extend as points beyond the plane of the canvas is created. In doing this, Kelly intensifies the relationship between the bottom edge of the canvas and the floor, so that the height at which the painting is hung and its relationship on the wall between the floor and ceiling is critical to the perception of the painting. With Kelly's shaped canvases, whether single-panel or composed of two different shaped panels, as well as with his shaped relief sculptures, the height at which the work is hung is crucial; the paintings' relationship to the floor is paramount in order to maintain a tension between the work and the floor. As with every aspect of Kelly's work, there is no system or rationalized set of procedures to determine the height; rather, Kelly makes an intuitive decision about the positioning of the work in relationship to the overall height of a wall, with the most important aspect being the maintenance of the perceptual connection between the painting and the floor. With sculptures set in shallow relief against the wall such as *Diagonal with Curve XIV* (1982) (p. 250), often the lowest corner barely escapes from touching the floor, with the work appearing to be almost floating from that point. With paintings, the distance depends on the shape and the lowest point of the painting as well as color, so that the painting is anchored but maintains a sense of buoyancy and perfect suspended equilibrium.[14] Generally, the viewer is not consciously aware of this carefully considered relationship between the painting, the wall, and the floor but intuitively senses it. To see a Kelly painting sitting directly on the floor or hanging in storage is to see a stranded object waiting to come to life.

The latter part of Kelly's career has seen the full development of his desire to make large paintings as public works in which he has triumphantly fused painting and architecture. What is most astonishing is the variety of approaches he has taken and the specificity of his responses to particular sites. Again, as with all of Kelly's work, there is no formula, no simple solution to the relationship between a painting and a wall or a space. Each work emerges from his intuitive response to the situation, to finding an opening that is unique in the vision of what could be possible. As Kelly has described it, "I don't want my pieces necessarily to be statements. I want them to be fluid, somehow, to relate to all the elements around them. I don't want them to be an end in themselves."[15]

In 1969 Kelly won a commission to make a painting measuring 15 × 15 feet for a wall of the new UNESCO building in Paris.[16] But it was not until 1978 that he was invited to develop his next large-scale public work, *Color Panels for*

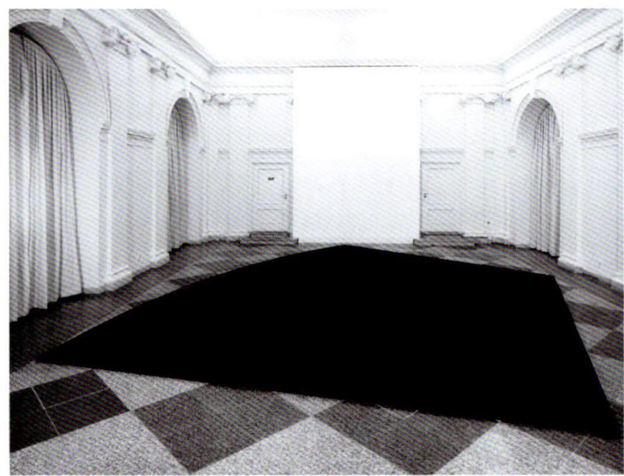

fig. 158: *Black Curve*, 1991, acrylic on canvas on wood, 1 × 343½ × 285¾ in, 2.5 × 872.5 × 725.8 cm

a Large Wall (fig. 157), a suite of eighteen panels, each measuring 48 × 68 inches, installed as a series of nine double panels, with an overall dimension of 10 feet × 125 feet 8 inches. This work directly harks back to *Colors for a Large Wall* (1951) (p. 69), but now at last with the panels set within an architectural frame. Through the 1980s, Kelly was commissioned to make several outdoor sculptures, but only in 1989 was another large public painting *Dallas Panels* (1989) (fig. 143) commissioned, through the initiative of the architect I.M. Pei for his Morton H. Meyerson Symphony Center in Dallas. Here, four tall vertical panels—blue, green, black, and red—each measuring 34 feet high and 4 feet 2 inches wide with an overall width of almost 48 feet—perfectly meshes with a large atrium hall. The proportions of space between the relatively narrow panels and with the outside edges of the wall have been carefully considered by Kelly so that the wall and the panels create one perfectly calibrated composition.

The next decade, the 1990s, brought an increasing number of commissions for both large-scale paintings and sculptures for public sites. But in 1990, in response to a request for a commission from an independent art space called Portikus, in Frankfurt, Germany, Kelly responded with a completely new and idiosyncratic work *Yellow Curve* (1990) (pp. 256–57), set on the floor of the gallery. Portikus consists of a large single room with a high ceiling in which a skylight is set, hovering over almost the entire space. The director Kasper König and assistant director Ulrich Wilmes had expected that Kelly would respond to their invitation to make a work for this space by offering three separate shaped canvases for three walls. Instead, to their surprise, the artist sent a maquette of the gallery with a single work on the floor in bright yellow with two corners touching the

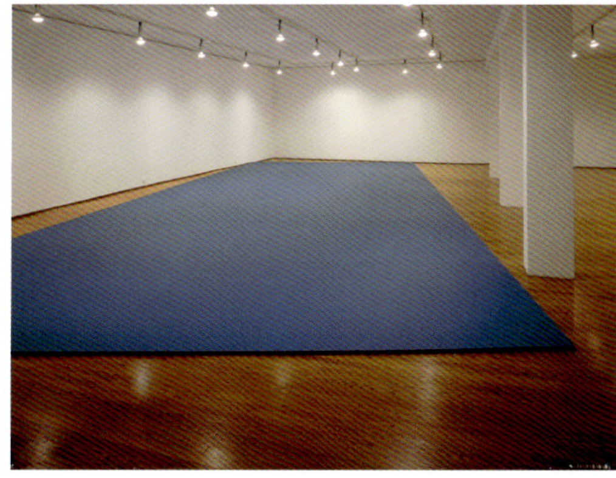

fig. 159: *Blue Floor Panel for Leo*, 1992, acrylic on canvas on wood, 1 × 275 × 576 in, 2.5 × 698.5 × 1463 cm

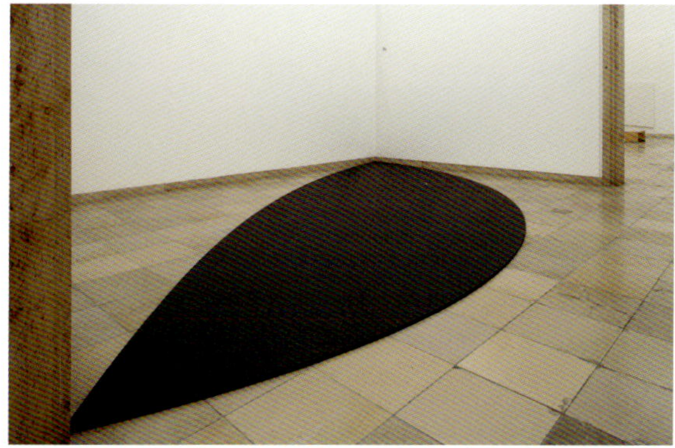

fig. 160: *Black Curves*, 2011, acrylic on canvas on wood, 1 × 250¼ × 368⅞ in, 2.5 × 635.6 × 936.9 cm

lateral walls, impeding passage around the work. It was executed with two centimeters of hardboard laid down directly on the floor to the size and shape specified by Kelly, which was then painted.[17] The architecture of the gallery was completely transformed, with the torque of the shape undermining the plane of the floor and its brilliant yellow reflections partially dissolving the planes of the walls. One could not pass through the space, but the work constituted a visceral invitation to move physically around its perimeters, keeping the architecture in flux and one's perceptions and understanding fluid and unstable. Overall, the experience was an exceptionally dynamic and fresh encounter between a work of art and the space within which it was set. Four other similar works followed: *Black Curve* (1991) (fig. 158), commissioned for the Berlinische Galerie Museum für Moderne Kunst am Schloss Charlottenburg, Berlin; *Red Floor Panel* (1992) (fig. 135), commissioned for the Westfälischer Kunstverein and Landesmuseum, Münster, Germany; *Blue Floor Panel for Leo* (1992) (fig. 159), commissioned for the Leo Castelli Gallery, 420 West Broadway, New York, and *Black Curves* (2011) (fig. 160), commissioned for the Haus der Kunst, Munich. Each of these works responded to the specific architectural character of the space in which they were placed, so that again, the painted object made by Kelly transformed and animated the architecture, fusing art and space into a seamless whole.

Another highly successful commission, *The Boston Panels*, was completed between 1996 and 1998 for the John J. Moakley Federal Courthouse in Boston, designed by Henry Cobb of the architectural firm Pei Cobb Freed & Partners. Here again, Kelly re-engaged ideas generated in *Colors for a Large Wall* (1951) (p. 69). Nine horizontal colored panels, each measuring 10 feet high × 13 feet 9 inches wide, have been set on the curved wall of a towering interior rotunda

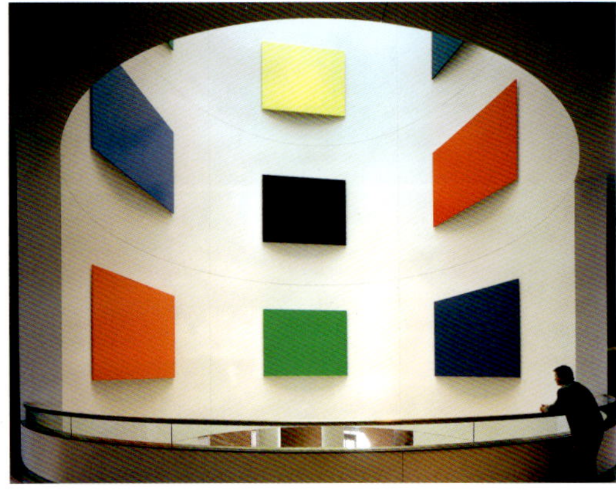

fig. 161: *The Boston Panels*, 1996–98, painted aluminum, each rotunda panel, 132 × 165 × 2½ in, 335.3 × 419.1 × 6.4 cm

(fig. 161), 90 feet tall, with illumination from a large skylight pouring over them. Seen on multiple levels of halls, which themselves are slightly curved and leading to courtrooms and offices, the nine panels constantly shift in their relationships both laterally and vertically, boldly accentuating and activating the curve of the architectural wall. The main courtrooms are distributed down long halls extending from either side of the atrium, and at the end of each of those six halls, Kelly placed a pair of large vertical panels, each of different colors, each measuring 10 feet high but only 7 feet 4 inches in width (fig. 162). Not visible from the main atrium, once in sight these panels pull the visitor down the open corridors and anchor the walls as architectural stopping points.[18] Kelly has stated, "As you walk through the building you are never out of sight of some fragment of color."[19] This work doesn't just engage specific walls or demarcated spaces, but transforms the experience of the entire building, which overall had a bland and officious character, into a stimulating and refreshing architectural encounter.

In contrast to the Boston work, a commission by the Pulitzer Foundation for the Arts in St. Louis for its Tadao Ando-designed building consists of two vertical abutted panels, ***Blue Black*** **(2001)** (p. 275), 28 feet high and 70 and 2½ inches wide. The building is divided into two wings, with a reflecting pool between them. Kelly's work is set at the end of the long gallery in the main wing of the building, hovering over a wide set of stairs descending into lower galleries. Subdued light comes from an overhead skylight and from a partially obscured long lateral window, catching both direct light and light reflected from the pool.[20] The work thus becomes a tranquil, even somewhat somber, icon at the end of what could be described as an austere contemporary chapel. Writing about this work, William J.R. Curtis has observed, "The Wall Sculpture in St. Louis lives in a state of suspension between several worlds. It takes over some of the conventions of pictorial representation, but subverts them. It poses as an architectural element, but insists upon its own status as a work of art."[21] This single work not only engages with the wall on which it is sited but also the entire space of the main section of the building.

Taking on the massive entrance atrium of the East Building of the National Gallery in Washington, DC, designed by Pei, Kelly was asked to reconfigure his *Color Panels for a Large Wall* from 1978, once it had been acquired by the museum. He radically opened the spaces between the panels and aligned them in six tiers of three panels each, achieving an overall size of 54 feet high × 90 feet long when the work was installed in 2003 (fig. 163). Recently, as part of a renovation of the East Building, Kelly has reconsidered the arrangement of the panels, pulling them together more tightly in an ensemble that is more assertive, with a tauter relationship to the wall. The resulting work is grand and eloquent, severely formal and serene, but alert and lively, and at ease in the monumental, asymmetrical architecture of the building.

One of Kelly's most recent and most compelling outdoor works is ***Black Bar for a Wall*** **(2011)** (p. 297), made for the

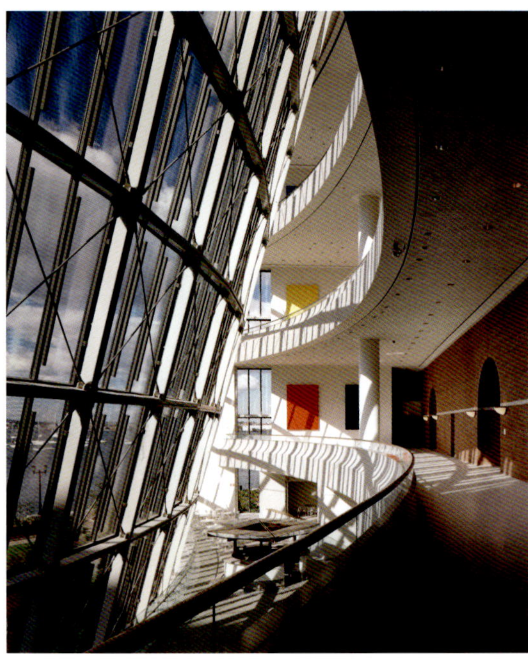

fig. 162: *The Boston Panels* 1996–98, painted aluminum, each east and west wall panel, 132 × 88 × 2½ in, 335.3 × 223.5 × 6.4 cm

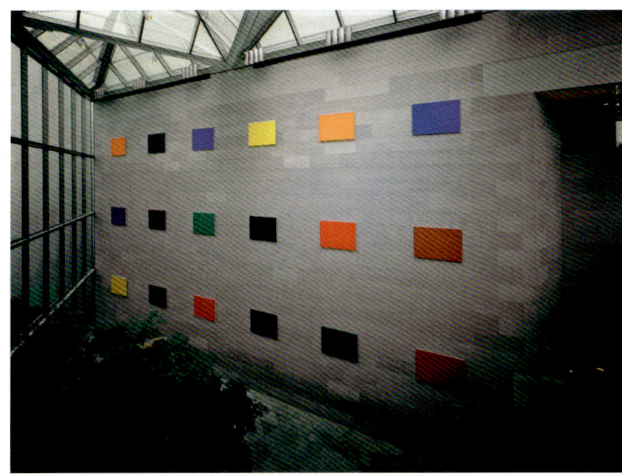

fig. 163: *Color Panels for a Large Wall*, 1978/2003, oil on canvas, 18 panels, 54 × 90 ft, 16.5 × 27.4 m

façade of the Matthew Marks Gallery in Los Angeles. The work finishes off the top of the façade, measuring 8 feet high, extending 39 feet and 4 inches in length across the entire front of the building, and projecting out 10 inches. It recalls two early collages made in Paris, which Kelly translated into full-scale paintings in 1966. But he has said that his immediate inspiration for this work came from noticing on a maquette of the gallery "that the model maker had used a strip of black tape along the inside of the model's roofline to hold it together."[22] As is typical of Kelly's work, the genesis can be traced back to something he has observed, which he then distills into geometric form. He not only introduced the muscular black lintel, but also controlled the entire façade, stripping it back without any articulation except for the door, which he also designed. (A utility pole that had initially been in front of the building was moved.) The result is a reading of the building façade as a single work of art, with a tight but dynamic tension and balance between the white plane of the building and the slightly projecting and floating mass of the black lintel. Where the vertical painting at the Pulitzer Foundation for the Arts accentuated the serene equilibrium of Ando's subtle and sophisticated architecture, this horizontal work gives a muscular kick to what could otherwise have been a somewhat banal commercial façade.

Kelly's most recent commission was for the LVMH Forum Auditorium, a part of a new museum designed by Frank Gehry that opened in Paris in autumn 2014 (pp. 320–21). Here, Kelly has placed six panels, each of a different color and size, on separate discrete walls. The scale of each panel responds to the size of the respective wall on which it is placed. The largest panel is a vertical yellow rectangle measuring 36 feet 8 inches high × 75 inches wide, and the smallest is a red horizontal rectangle measuring 64 inches high × 78 inches wide. Like the building interior itself, the work is fractured and dynamic, fragments or whole panels appear and disappear as one moves through the space. Anchoring the ensemble is a twelve-panel proscenium cover measuring 20 feet 10 inches high × 17 feet 6 inches wide, the largest and most recent of Kelly's spectrum paintings, first initiated with *Spectrum I*, painted in 1953 in Paris.[23]

Finally, Kelly is working to complete his first and only free-standing structure, a non-denominational chapel-like space that will include three sets of colored-glass windows (fig. 164), a cycle of fourteen paintings, and a large sculpture. The building was first developed in response to a commission in 1978 for a ranch in the Santa Maria Valley, near Santa Barbara, California, but will now be realized on the campus of the University of Texas at Austin. The culmination of sixty years focusing on art beyond the traditional, self-contained canvas hung on a wall, *Austin* will be his only work in which

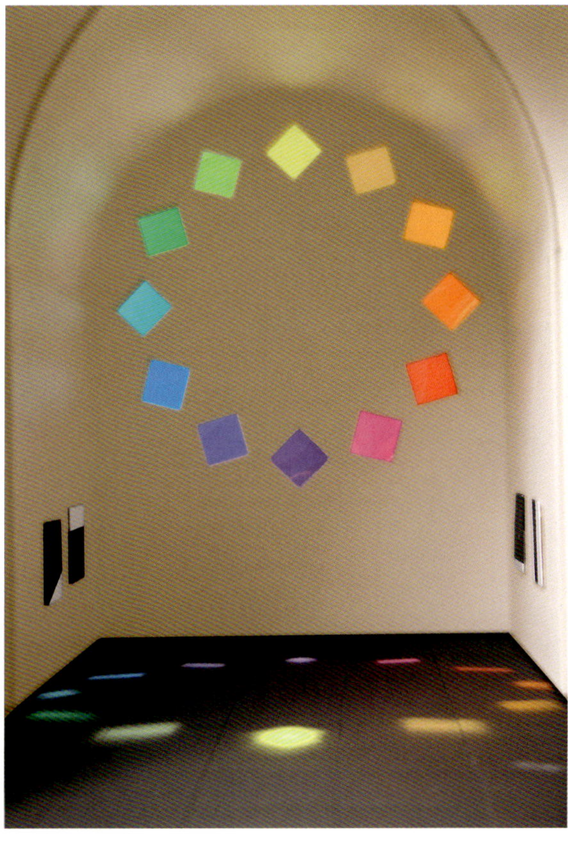

fig. 164: *Austin,* 1986/2015, (scale model) artist-designed building with colored glass windows and interior installation, 28 × 63 × 76 ft, 8.6 × 19.3 × 23.3 m

painting, sculpture, and architecture have been conceived as a single whole.

Kelly has never been assertive about the radical character of his art. He is not an artist who buttresses his work with theory or ideology or who writes manifestos. He has not developed systems that govern the production of his work, and although there is certainly a logic in its development and a set of decisions that inform each other, giving coherence across the decades, it always remains intuitive. Thus his art has remained inventive and fresh, with each work specific to its own set of concerns and circumstances, its own possibilities for invention. He has achieved what he set out to do when a young artist who had only recently arrived in Paris: “We must make our art like the Egyptians, the Chinese and the African and Island primitives—with their relation to life. It should meet the eye—direct.”[24]

1 Quoted in Jack Cowart, "Method and Motif: Ellsworth Kelly's 'Chance' Grids and His Development of Color Panel Paintings, 1948–51," in *Ellsworth Kelly: The Years in France, 1948–1954* (Washington, DC/ Munich: National Gallery of Art/Prestel-Verlag, 1992), p. 41. For an extensive consideration of Kelly's work in relation to mural-scale art, see Michael Plante, "Things to Cover Walls: Ellsworth Kelly's Paris Paintings and the Tradition of Mural Decoration," *American Art*, vol. 9, no. 1 (Spring, 1995), pp. 36–53.

2 The genesis and development of this painting has been described by several authors. See E.C. Goossen, *Ellsworth Kelly* (New York: MoMA, 1973), p. 38; Yve-Alain Bois, "Ellsworth Kelly in France: Anti-Composition in Its Many Guises," in *Ellsworth Kelly: The Years in France*, p. 25; Jack Cowart, ibid., p. 41; Nathalie Brunet, "Chronology, 1943–1954," pp. 189–190; Diane Waldman, "Ellsworth Kelly" and Roberta Bernstein, "Ellsworth Kelly's Multipanel Paintings" in *Ellsworth Kelly: A Retrospective* (New York: The Solomon R. Guggenheim Museum, 1996), pp. 21, 42; James Meyer, "Art for the City: Sculpture for a Large Wall, 1957," in *Ellsworth Kelly: Sculpture for a Large Wall*, 1957 (New York: Matthew Marks Gallery, 1998), pp. 4–8.

3 Goossen 1973, p. 45.

4 This work is discussed in many essays on Kelly, but for the most thorough accounts, see Clare Bell, "At Play with Vision: Ellsworth Kelly's 'Line, Form and Color'," in *Ellsworth Kelly: A Retrospective* (New York: The Solomon R. Guggenheim Museum, 1996), pp. 66–79; and Harry Cooper, "An Intense Detachment: Ellsworth Kelly's *Line Form Color*," in *Ellsworth Kelly: Line Form Color* (Cambridge: Harvard University Art Museums, 1999), pp. 3–23.

5 Quoted in Clare Bell, ibid., p. 66.

6 Cooper, ibid, pp. 13–14.

7 Clare Bell, ibid., p. 69.

8 Goossen 1973, p. 45.

9 Bernstein 1996, p. 43. The genesis and development of this painting have also been discussed by numerous authors. See Goossen 1973, pp. 45–46; Bois 1992, pp. 25–27; Cowart 1992, p. 44; Waldman 1996, p. 24; and Bernstein 1996, pp. 42–44.

10 For the most comprehensive discussions of these commissions, see James Meyer, "Ellsworth Kelly: Sculpture for a Large Wall, 1957," and Judith F. Dolkart, "Meeting the Eye Direct," in *Ellsworth Kelly: Sculpture on the Wall* (Philadelphia: The Barnes Foundation, 2013).

11 Cited in Meyer, ibid., p. 34.

12 The most thorough discussion of these two paintings, as well as of the two closely related sculptures that followed, can be found in an essay by Roberta Bernstein in *Ellsworth Kelly: At Right Angles, 1964–1966* (Los Angeles/San Francisco/New York: Margo Leavin Gallery/John Berggruen Gallery/Paula Cooper Gallery, 1991).

13 Michael Duncan, "Ellworth Kelly's Welcome to L.A.," in *Ellsworth Kelly: Los Angeles* (Los Angeles, Matthew Marks Gallery, 2012).

14 A good figure illustrating this is found in Madeleine Grynsztejn, *Ellsworth Kelly in San Francisco* (Oakland: University of California Press, 2002), p. 16, fig. 12.

15 Hans Ulrich Obrist, *Ellsworth Kelly: Thumbing through the Folder, A Dialogue on Art and Architecture with Hans Ulrich Obrist* (Cologne: Verlag der Buchhandlung Walther Konig, 2009), p. 67.

16 Ibid., pp. 13–14.

17 Information from a conversation between Ulrich Wilmes and the author, November 28, 2014.

18 For a description of this commission, see *Ellsworth Kelly: The Boston Panels, U.S. Courthouse*, brochure produced by U.S. General Services Administration, Public Buildings Service, Historic Buildings & the Arts, 1998 and Obrist 2009, p. 15.

19 Obrist 2009, p. 17.

20 For background on this commission, including a statement by Kelly, see *Abstractions in Space: Tadao Ando, Ellsworth Kelly, Richard Serra* (St. Louis: The Pulitzer Foundation for the Arts, 2001), and Obrist 2009, pp. 20–21.

21 William J.R. Curtis, "Spaces Between," in ibid., p. 27.

22 Duncan 2012, pp. 9–10.

23 Suzanne Pagé and Ann Hindry, *Ellsworth Kelly: Les Cahiers* (Paris: Fondation Louis Vuitton, 2014). For a comprehensive overview of Kelly's "Spectrum" works, see *Ellsworth Kelly Spectrums* (New York: Mitchell-Innes & Nash Gallery in collaboration with Matthew Marks Gallery), 1999.

24 Cowart 1992, p. 41.

Chronology

Chronology, 1923–2015

Compiled by Tricia Y. Paik (with assistance from Eva Huber Walters and Nathan Stobaugh)

This chronology draws from extensive research provided by E.C. Goossen, *Ellsworth Kelly* (1973), and chronologies published in Patterson Sims and Emily Rauh Pulitzer, *Ellsworth Kelly: Sculpture* (1982); Diane Upright, *Ellsworth Kelly: Works on Paper* (1987); and Richard H. Axsom, *The Prints of Ellsworth Kelly: A Catalogue Raisonné, 1949–1985* (1987). Nathalie Brunet's in-depth chronology of the artist's French years published in Yve-Alain Bois, Jack Cowart, and Alfred Pacquement, *Ellsworth Kelly: The Years in France, 1948–1954* (1992) was an exceptional resource as was the detailed chronology featured in Diane Waldman (ed.), *Ellsworth Kelly: A Retrospective* (1996).

To all these sources mentioned above, I am greatly indebted, as I am to Jack Shear, Director of the Ellsworth Kelly Foundation, who shared thoughtful guidance and input, and Eva Walters, Archives Manager, who tended to every detail and provided exhaustive research materials that aided enormously in piecing together this chronology of Kelly's remarkable life and career. Yet most of all, I am indebted to the artist for the willingness and time he dedicated to probing his past during many interviews conducted between 2001 and 2015.

1923–28

Ellsworth Maurice Kelly born on May 31 in Newburgh, NY, to Allan Howe Kelly, who works for the United States Army at West Point, NY, and Florence Githens Kelly, a former schoolteacher, both from Wheeling, WV.

Named after paternal grandfather, Maurice Balmer Kelly, and maternal grandfather, Curran Ellsworth Githens, Ph.D., a professor, mathematician, and educator who served as superintendent of Wheeling public schools around 1900.

Aged six months, moves with parents and older brother Allan, Jr., born 1921, to Pittsburgh, PA. Younger brother David is born there in 1926.

While sick at the age of five, introduced by mother and paternal grandmother Louisa (Rosenlieb) Kelly to bird-watching, a practice that becomes a lifelong hobby.

1929–37

Family moves in 1929 to Oradell, NJ, located approximately 17 miles northwest of New York City, where father works as insurance-company executive. During these years, family moves frequently in and around region of Oradell where Kelly develops bird-watching skills.

At around seven or eight, encounters works of artist and ornithologist John James Audubon at local library. Learns of other bird illustrations by ornithologist Louis Agassiz Fuertes.

Follows sixth-grade teacher Dorothy Opsut's encouraging advice to paint outdoors. Sculpts sphinx figure out of clay and paints watercolors. Attends Oradell Junior High School.

1938–40

Designs covers for his school journal *Chirp*, one featuring daffodils (fig. 165), and listed as "Best Artist" and "Class Giant" in 1938 yearbook.

Spends summer of 1938 painting on Cape Cod, MA.

Begins Dwight Morrow High School, Englewood, NJ, in fall 1938 (fig. 166). Impressed after seeing his first oil painting, art teacher Evelyn Robbins nurtures his talent.

His parents are less enthusiastic about his artistic inclinations, though his mother gives him a copy of 1939 book, *World-Famous Paintings*, edited by Rockwell Kent.

Participates in high school theater club, the Mask and Wig, led by drama teacher Helen Travolta.

His parents agree to financially support his arts education as long as he receives commercial training.

Visits The Metropolitan Museum of Art, New York.

1941–42

Graduates high school.

Moves to Brooklyn, on Gainsborough Street, to attend Pratt Institute where he studies applied arts with Maitland E. Graves.

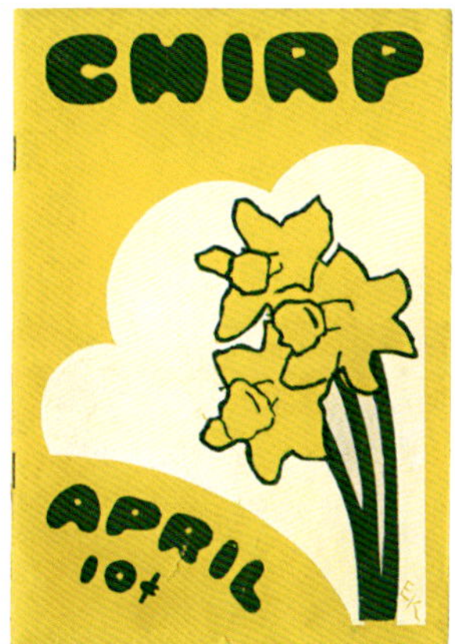

fig. 165: Cover of *Chirp* (Oradell Junior High School journal), 1938

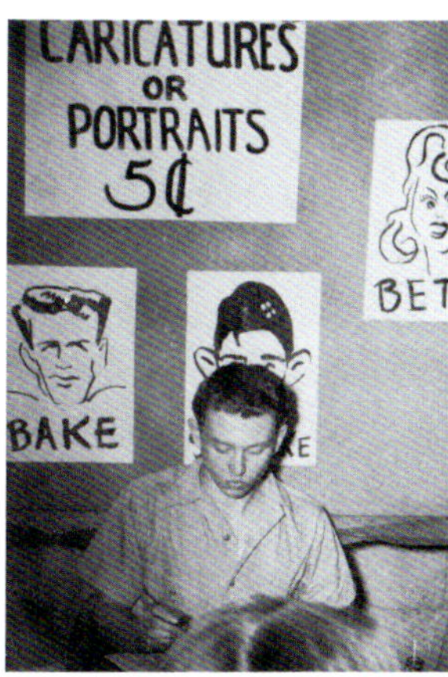

fig. 166: Ellsworth Kelly drawing caricatures and portraits, Dwight Morrow High School, Englewood, NJ, 1941

Completes three semesters as World War II cuts short his schooling.

Volunteers for service, requesting assignment to 603rd Engineers Camouflage Battalion.

1943

Inducted into United States Army at Fort Dix, NJ, on New Year's Day. Sent to Camp Hale, CO, in late January, where he trains with mountain-ski troops.

Transferred in March to 603rd Engineers Camouflage Battalion at Fort Meade, MD, allowing him to regularly visit the National Gallery of Art, Washington, DC.

Meets future fashion designer Bill Blass, a fellow G.I. also assigned to the 603rd.

Executes silkscreen posters, designed by Colonel Homer Saint-Gaudens (son of renowned sculptor Augustus Saint-Gaudens), used to instruct troops in concealment techniques.

1944

In January, his battalion is relocated to Camp Forrest, TN, where it joins the newly formed 23rd Headquarters Special Troops, known today as the "Ghost Army."

Makes drawings and watercolors in sketch-books throughout tour of duty, which takes Kelly to England, France, Belgium, Luxembourg, and Germany (figs 167, 168).

Participates in Allied invasion of Normandy in operation known as "D + 10," ten days after D-Day.

Visits Paris for first time, while stationed in nearby Saint-Germain-en-Laye (fig. 15), though museums are closed due to the war.

1945

His battalion returns to America in May. Discharged with honor on October 23 in Jacksonville, FL.

Unsuccessfully attempts to hitchhike to Black Mountain College, Asheville, NC; decides instead to board a freight plane for New York City, his first time on a plane.

1946–47

In January 1946, enrolls at the School of the Museum of Fine Arts, Boston with tuition and stipend provided via the G.I. Bill of Rights.

Obtains studio and room rent-free in exchange for teaching two evenings a week at the Norfolk House Center (fig. 169), a settlement house in Roxbury, Boston.

At school, draws and paints from female nude in life classes.

Studies with Karl Zerbe, a practitioner of German Expressionism, and Ture Bengtz, who teaches Kelly valuable lessons in contour drawing.

Copies Old Master paintings by Ambrogio Lorenzetti (fig. 24) and Tintoretto on view at the Museum of Fine Arts, Boston, which he regularly visits. There, encounters twelfth-century frescoes from the Catalan Church of Santa Maria de Mur, sparking an appreciation for Romanesque art and architecture. Also develops interest in Byzantine art.

Attends a lecture given by Philip Guston on Piero della Francesca.

Spends time at the Isabella Stewart Gardner Museum as well as museums at Harvard University, Cambridge, MA: the Fogg Museum, the Germanic Museum (now the Busch-Reisinger Museum), and the Peabody Museum of Archaeology and Ethnography where he first sees ancient Native American artifacts. In 1954, will begin to collect carved stone lithics, such as bannerstones and birdstones produced by ancient Mississippian mound-building cultures (fig. 27).

Makes occasional trips to New York to visit The Museum of Modern Art (MoMA) and the Museum of Non-Objective Painting (renamed The Solomon R. Guggenheim Museum in 1952).

Enters *Self-Portrait with Bugle* (1947) (fig. 21) in exhibition at Institute of Modern Art, Boston (which will be renamed the Institute of Contemporary Art the following year), and is awarded scholarship from the Skowhegan School of Painting and Sculpture, allowing him to spend summer of 1947 painting in Maine, in studio provided by the school.

Featured in first gallery exhibition, a group show with figurative painting, *Boy in a Tub* (1947), at Boris Mirski Art Gallery, Boston, where he will show again in 1948 and 1950.

Becomes friends with Ralph Coburn, an artist who works at Boris Mirski.

1948

During spring, attends memorable lectures by two visitors: Max Beckmann, who emphasizes the importance of observing nature, and Herbert Read, British art historian and critic, who declares "easel painting"

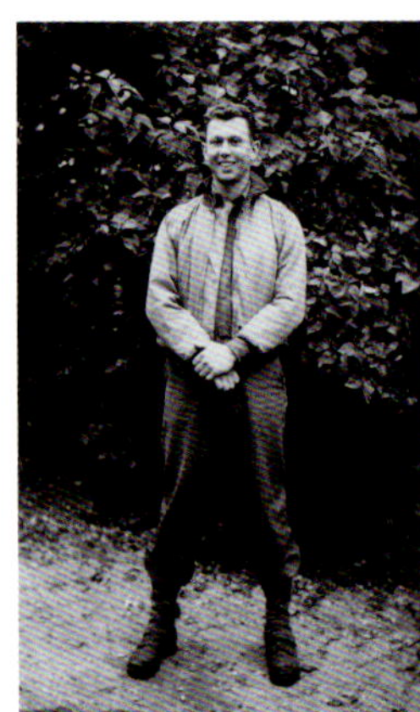

fig. 167: Ellsworth Kelly, Luxembourg, 1944

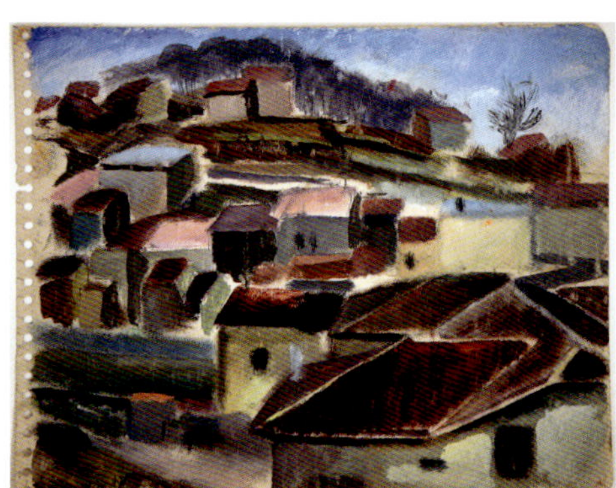

fig. 168: *Briey, France,* 1945, gouache on paper, 7⅞ × 9⅞ in, 20 × 25.1 cm

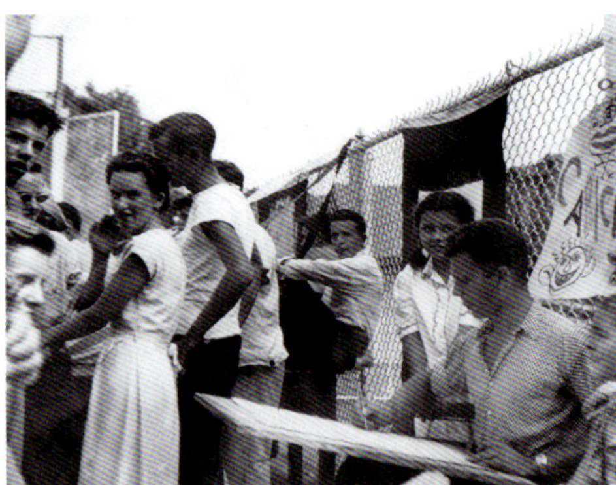

fig. 169: Ellsworth Kelly sketching, Norfolk House Center, Boston, 1947

outdated and calls for collaboration between art and architecture.

Graduates with highest honors from the Boston Museum School (as it was then known) on June 4.

Decides, along with fellow student Onni Saari, to return to Paris and works that summer as a gandy dancer installing wooden railroad ties, earning $200 to pay for ship fare.

Starts journal (fig. 29), keeping meticulously categorized lists, detailing museums, artworks, sites, and collections he wishes to see in Europe.

Arrives in Paris in October. Travels to Colmar, France, to see Matthias Grünewald's *Isenheim Altarpiece* (1512–16) (fig. 46), the subject of a research assignment he had done in Boston.

After a stay at the Hôtel Saint-George, rue Bonaparte, moves to a couple of other Left Bank hotels until spring 1949.

Enrolls in November at the École des Beaux-Arts in order to qualify for tuition and increased stipend of $75 per month provided by the G.I. Bill of Rights.

Becomes friends with Jack Youngerman, one of many other Americans also enrolled at the École on the G.I. Bill. Rarely attends classes, however, and instead regularly visits the Musée de Louvre, the Musée de Cluny (now the Musée national du Moyen Âge), the Musée Guimet, the Musée Cernuschi, as well as the library of the Byzantine Institute, an extension of Harvard University.

Develops his interests in Romanesque and Byzantine art, plus the art of Egypt, Greece, and other ancient cultures, while also becoming increasingly fascinated with the architecture of Paris.

In his paintings, begins to display a move towards abstraction.

Begins making drawings from plants, a practice that will continue throughout his life.

Also visits the Musée de l'Homme, the Muséum national d'Histoire naturelle, and the Musée National d'Art Moderne.

During his years in France, regularly borrows books from the American Library in Paris, often favoring Russian writers, such as Ivan Turgenev, Fyodor Dostoyevsky, Leo Tolstoy, Anton Chekhov, Vladimir Nabokov, as well as French author Stendhal.

1949

Travels to Poitiers, Chauvigny, Saint-Savin-sur-Gartempe, Tavant, Chinon, and Mont-Saint-Michel and draws from frescoes, stonework, and sculptures.

Submits paintings to exhibition at the American Center, but is rejected.

Moves to Hôtel de Bourgogne on Île Saint-Louis (fig. 173), where he stays for almost three years.

Makes his first collage, *Seaweed/Mandorla* (fig. 171) and will continue to rely on collage to explore ideas for painting and sculpture throughout his career.

Coburn arrives from Boston, and together they experiment with Surrealist and chance techniques.

In June, meets John Cage and Merce Cunningham, who happen to be staying at same hotel; Cage visits Kelly's studio and provides encouragement. After their departure, begins correspondence with Cage that lasts during Kelly's time in France.

Travels with Coburn in July to Brittany, meeting French actress Arletty; decides to spend summer on Belle-Île-en-Mer (fig. 172).

With Coburn, calls upon Alice B. Toklas in Paris to see the collection of her late partner, Gertrude Stein.

Sees exhibitions in Paris on Henri Matisse, Wassily Kandinsky, and Paul Gauguin.

Returns to Belle-Île-en-Mer where he makes several paintings, including *Window I* (p. 50) and *Kilometer Marker* (p. 51).

Makes first lithograph using press at the École des Beaux-Arts.

After sketching several drawings based on large windows observed at the Musée National d'Art Moderne, creates *Window, Museum of Modern Art, Paris* (p. 53), using two joined panels for first time.

In December, visits Coburn in Mediterranean town of Sanary-sur-Mer; together they travel to Antibes to visit the Musée Picasso.

1950

Meets French critic Michel Seuphor and early supporter of Piet Mondrian.

Exhibits for first time in Europe at "Premier Salon des Jeunes Peintres," Galerie des Beaux-Arts, Paris, with *Wood Cutout with String III* (1949).

After being introduced to Jean Arp through Seuphor, travels with Coburn and Jack

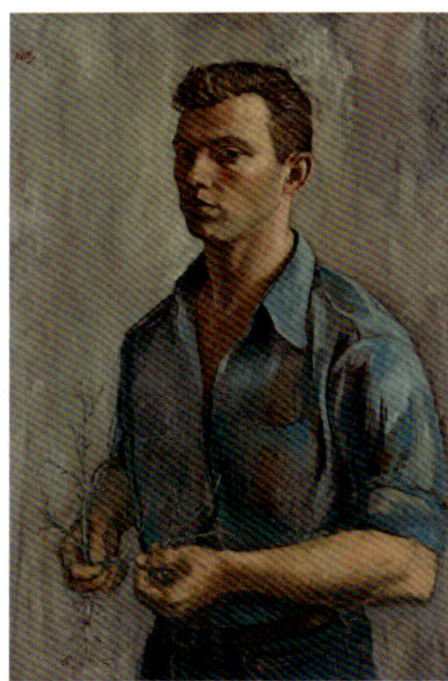

fig. 170: *Self-Portrait with Thorn*, 1947, oil on Masonite, 36 × 24 × 1½ in, 91.4 × 60.9 × 3.8 cm

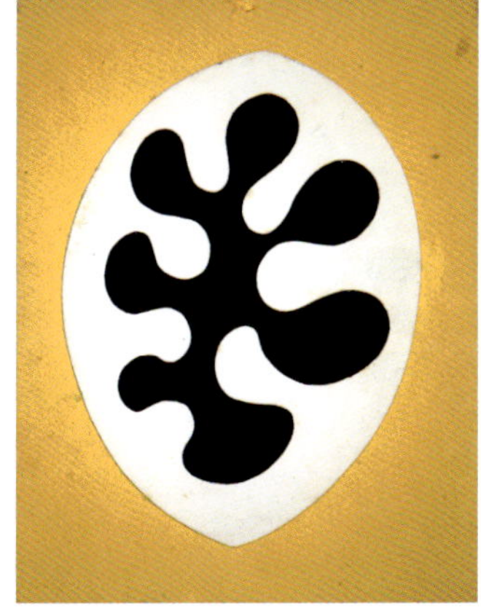

fig. 171: *Seaweed/Mandorla*, 1949, collage on paper, 6¾ × 5⅛ in, 17.1 × 13 cm

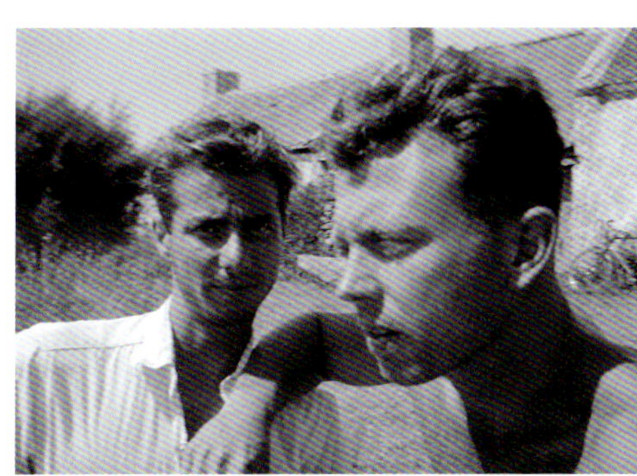

fig. 172: Ellsworth Kelly (right) and Ralph Coburn, Belle-Île-en-Mer, France, 1949

Youngerman in February to Arp's studio outside of Paris in Meudon-Val-Fleury, where he is impressed by the collages of Arp and the late Sophie Taeuber-Arp (fig. 39).

Meets Georges Vantongerloo, Alberto Magnelli, and Francis Picabia.

Invited by Félix Del Marle, secretary general of the Salon des Réalités Nouvelles, to show at their fifth Salon in Paris, where Kelly displays six works, including *Window, Museum of Modern Art, Paris* (p. 53) and *Relief with Blue* (p. 58), their public debut; *White Relief* (p. 59) is rejected based on consensus that it is not art.

Sees Matisse's large-scale cutout *Zulma* (1950) at Salon de Mai, Paris.

Meets Alexander Calder and friendship will continue during his years in New York (fig. 183).

Visits Arp again with Coburn.

In August, stays at La Combe, the villa of Youngerman's in-laws in town of Meschers; earlier that year Youngerman had married French actress Delphine Seyrig, and her father Henri Seyrig, an archaeologist, will make the first purchase of a Kelly work, *Antibes* (1950), in 1951—the only sale Kelly will make during his sojourn in France.

At La Combe, draws shadows of a metal staircase; the motif becomes basis for series of four works, including *La Combe I* (p. 61) and *La Combe II* (p. 60), a folding screen, which is his first work using several joined panels.

By fall, support from G.I. Bill runs out, and he begins teaching art classes to children at the American School. In December, he is invited by Denise René to present his work to her gallery's artists for consideration, but is refused, despite René's support.

1951

Introduced by Eduardo Paolozzi to Louis Clayeux, the director of Galerie Maeght, Paris.

With Youngerman and new friend Georges Koskas, convinces bookstore owners John Koenig and Jean-Robert Arnaud to turn the cellar of their shop into a gallery for young artists as very few Parisian galleries are showing emerging artists.

At the newly named Galerie Arnaud (fig. 175), the first exhibition features Youngerman, the second in April, is Kelly's first solo show, with thirty-one works made since June 1949, including *Window, Museum of Modern Art, Paris* (p. 53), *Gate-Board* (p. 55), *Window V* (p. 57), *White Relief* (p. 59), *Relief with Blue* (p. 58), *La Combe I* (p. 61), *Ormesson* (p. 64), and *La Combe II* (p. 60).

Shows again at the Salon des Réalités Nouvelles with four works, including *Ormesson* (p. 64) and *La Combe II* (p. 60).

His position at the American School in Paris is terminated after the director sees his show at the Galerie Arnaud. Hired as night security guard under auspices of the Marshall Plan, allowing him to paint during the day.

Seeks grant support by writing to Hilla Rebay, director of the Non-Objective Museum of Art, New York (which will be renamed The Solomon R. Guggenheim Museum the following year). In desperate need of money, later in the year, applies for a John Simon Guggenheim Memorial Fellowship proposing a book project titled *Line, Form and Color*. In April of the following year, learns he is rejected.

For its seventy-fifth anniversary, the Boston Museum School mounts exhibition of former students, so Kelly ships *La Combe III* (1951) (fig. 155), the only abstract work in the show. At Kelly's request, Cage picks up the work in March 1952, and the work remains with Cage until Kelly returns to the States in 1954.

With Youngerman and new friend Alain Naudé, visits Paris studio of Constantin Brancusi, forming a lasting impression.

Included in group exhibition, "Tendance," (fig. 176) at Galerie Maeght, Paris, displaying five works, such as *Cité* (p. 63) and *Meschers* (p. 65); the latter is admired by Georges Braque, as well as by Gustav Zumsteg, a Swiss textile manufacturer and art collector, who commissions Kelly to create fabric designs, allowing him to give up his security guard job. Also through Clayeux, meets Joan Miró.

Returns to Sanary in November, spending time with Coburn, Anne Weber, a classmate from the Boston Museum School, and Naudé.

Makes *Colors for a Large Wall* (p. 69), his largest work to date, made of sixty-four joined panels each painted a monochrome color.

1952

Exhibited in group show at a gallery in Nantes, including François Morellet, whom Kelly meets later in Paris.

Remains in Sanary until May and makes *Red Yellow Blue White* (pp. 74–75) and *Painting for a White Wall* (pp. 82–83); the former is made with dyed cotton and marks the first time Kelly separates his panels across the wall, incorporating interstitial spaces in his work. With leftover fabric, designs a dress for Anne Weber (fig. 52).

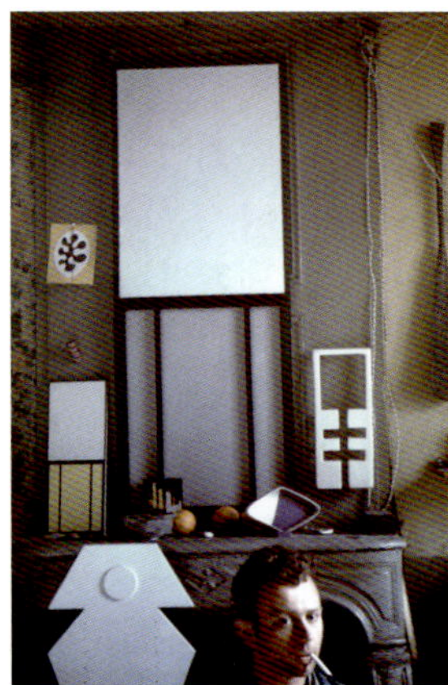

fig. 173: Ellsworth Kelly, Hôtel de Bourgogne studio, Paris, 1950

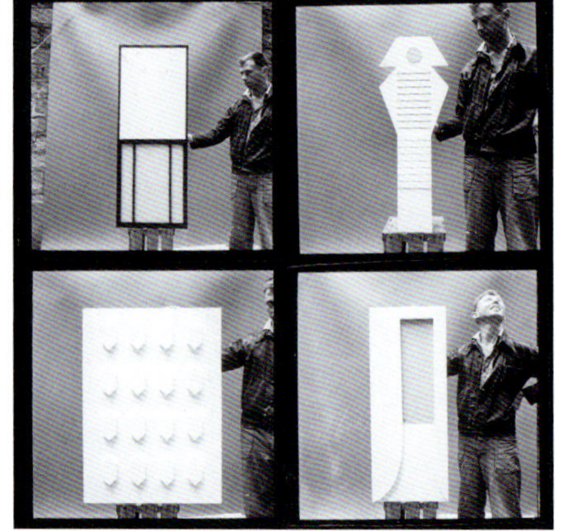

fig. 174: Ellsworth Kelly with reliefs, Paris, 1950

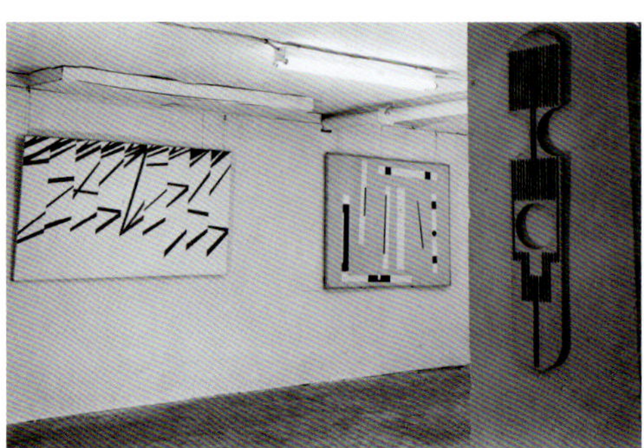

fig. 175: Installation view of "Kelly peintures et reliefs," Galerie Arnaud, Paris, 1951

Travels to Marseilles to see Le Corbusier's Unité d'Habitation, still under construction at the time. Moves to Torcy, a village east of Paris.

Writes to Jean-Pierre Hoschedé, Claude Monet's stepson, who invites him to visit Giverny where he and Naudé see Monet's late "Nymphéas" series paintings haphazardly stored. Inspired by this visit, paints next day at his Torcy studio *Tableau Vert* (p. 76), his first single-canvas monochrome, which he wraps up because he thinks it unsuccessful; will not return to a single-canvas monochrome until 1966 with *Yellow Piece* (p. 175), also his first shaped "cutout" made from canvas.

Featured in two group exhibitions, one in Caracas, and the other at Galerie Maeght, Paris, "Tendance," where he shows four works, including *Colors for a Large Wall* (p. 69), *Méditerranée* (p. 71), and *Fête à Torcy* (p. 72), and where he meets Alberto Giacometti, later visiting the sculptor's studio.

In late September, moves into a studio at Cité des Fleurs, Paris.

1953

Attends premiere of Samuel Beckett's *Waiting for Godot* at the Théâtre de Babylone, Paris, in January.

Shown in group exhibition in Spain at the Museo de Arte Contemporáneo, Santander.

At his Cité des Fleurs studio, creates *Train Landscape* (p. 77), *Red Yellow Blue White and Black II* (pp. 78–79), and *Spectrum I* (p. 87). *White Square* (p. 85) and *Black Square* (p. 84), made with assistance of an *ébéniste*, are Kelly's last paintings completed in Paris.

Hoping for a mural commission, meets Marcel Breuer who is directing the building project of the UNESCO headquarters in Paris.

Evicted from studio at Cité des Fleurs; puts works in storage.

Spends Christmas in Papendrecht, near Rotterdam, at the family home of friend Geert-Jan Visser. With Visser, sees works by Mondrian owned by collector Solomon Slijper and at the Museum Boymans, Rotterdam (now Museum Boijmans van Beuningen).

1954

Hospitalized in Paris for jaundice early in the year and convalesces at Visser home in Papendrecht.

Goes back to Paris with idea of returning to the U.S.

At Brentano's bookstore, reads *ARTnews* review of Ad Reinhardt exhibition at Betty Parsons Gallery, New York, and realizes his work might be better received there.

In mid-June, boards the *Queen Mary*, shipping all his work home on credit, and arrives in New York City on June 22. As suggested by Fred Mitchell, an artist friend from Paris, moves into studio at 109 Broad Street, Lower Manhattan (fig. 177).

Visits Robert Rauschenberg's studio based on Cage's recommendation.

Supports himself with night job sorting mail at main New York City branch of the U.S. Post Office.

Makes his first New York painting, *Black Curves* (p. 129), inspired by curvilinear forms, his so-called "free curves"; new interest in painting figure-ground relationships marks departure from rectilinear panels made in France and will continue over next decade.

Calder pays Kelly visit in late summer at Broad Street studio. Struggling to pay his rent by December, receives letter from Calder with check to cover one month's rent; in letter Calder explains he has written on Kelly's behalf to Alfred H. Barr, Jr., founding director of MoMA, and James Johnson Sweeney, director of The Guggenheim Museum. Sweeney visits Kelly.

Curator Dorothy C. Miller from MoMA visits Kelly's studio and borrows *Window, Museum of Modern Art, Paris* (p. 53); she advises the museum to acquire it, but her suggestion is unsuccessful.

Kelly visits all the major museums in New York. Also visits the New-York Historical Society where he discovers watercolor drawings by Audubon made for his *Birds of America* engravings (fig. 178); learns that Audubon used collage and encourages librarians there to exhibit the drawings, which had never been on public view.

1955

David Herbert, an art dealer who works for Sidney Janis, visits Kelly's Broad Street studio, then encourages Betty Parsons to do the same. Soon afterwards, Parsons offers Kelly a solo exhibition.

Creates *White Plaque: Bridge Arch and Reflection* (p. 131), a shaped work cut from wood, based on a collage made in Paris four years earlier.

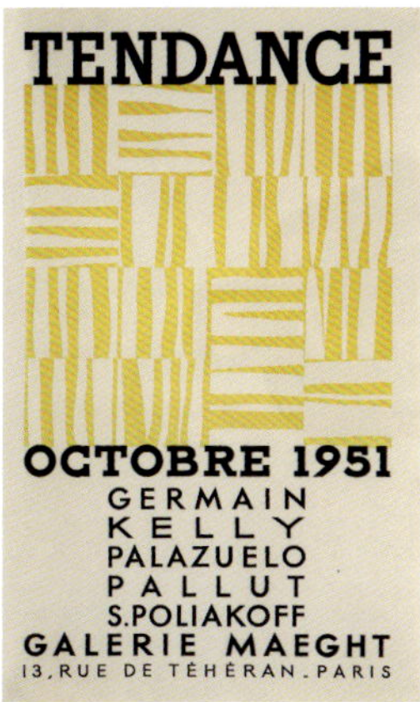

fig. 176: Poster for "Tendance" exhibition, Galerie Maeght, Paris, 1951

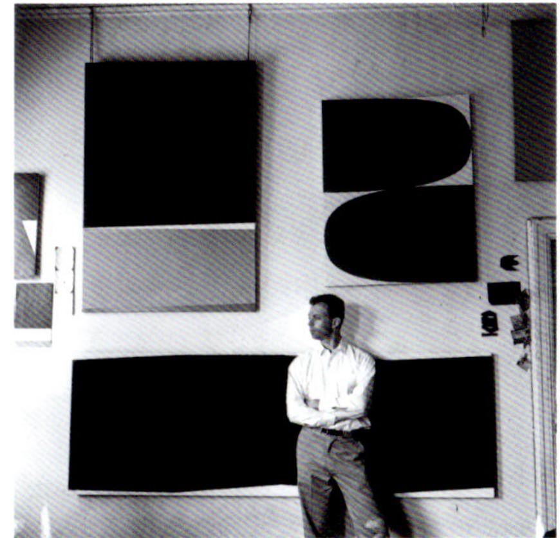

fig. 177: Ellsworth Kelly, Broad Street studio, New York, 1956

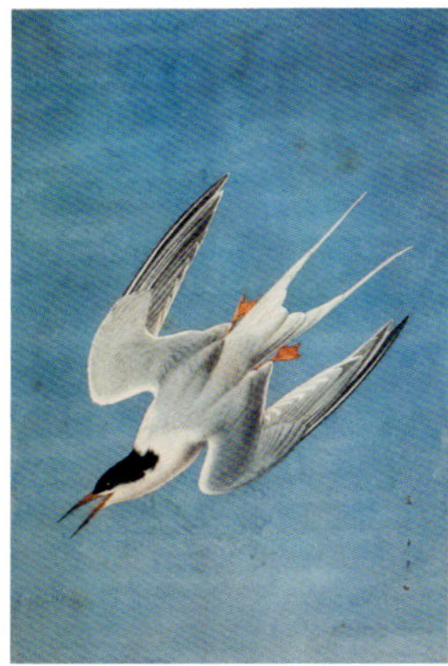

fig. 178: John James Audubon, *Roseate Tern*, 1827–32 (plate 297 from *The Original Water-Color Paintings by John James Audubon for The Birds of America*)

Visits Ad Reinhardt's studio, after seeing his solo show at Parsons; later that evening, through Reinhardt, meets Adolph Gottlieb and Theodore Stamos.

Meets Ray Johnson, whose studio is located at the foot of the Brooklyn Bridge.

1956

Invited to show at his first group exhibition in New York, "Recent Drawings USA," curated by William Lieberman, at MoMA where he shows an ink study for *Black Ripe* (p. 130).

Kelly's first solo exhibition in the U.S. opens in May at Betty Parsons Gallery (fig. 179), New York, where he will show until 1963.

At art supply store on West 57th Street, meets Robert Indiana who is looking for a new studio. Planning to move to Coenties Slip himself, recommends the slip to Indiana, who then relocates to Fred Mitchell's former studio there.

In July, moves a block away from previous studio to a large loft at 3–5 Coenties Slip for $45 a month, where he will remain for the next seven years (figs 180–82).

Through lighting designer Richard Kelly (no relation), is invited to create brass screens for restaurant of the new Transportation Building for Penn Center in Philadelphia, designed by Vincent G. Kling, and then later commissioned to create a large-scale aluminum sculpture spanning 65 feet across for the building's lobby, now known as *Sculpture for a Large Wall* (pp. 140–41); collaborates with fabricator Edison Price, New York, who will help him execute sculptures through 1966. The Philadelphia commissions, his first works in metal, are completed in early 1957.

Makes *Painting in Five Panels* (pp. 134–35), his first using separately hung canvases of varying sizes.

Meets Cy Twombly in Indiana's studio.

1957

"Young America 1957," Kelly's second group museum exhibition, opens at the Whitney Museum of American Art, New York, where he shows *Bar* (p. 132), *Atlantic* (p. 139), and *Painting in Three Panels* (pp. 136–37).

The Whitney purchases *Atlantic*, marking the first museum acquisition of the artist's work.

Featured in "Objects on the Landscape Demanding of the Eye," inaugural exhibition of Ferus Gallery, Los Angeles, co-founded by Walter Hopps and Edward Kienholz.

Includes *Cité* (p. 63) in The Art Institute of Chicago's 17th Annual Contemporary Art Show, the first time shown in Midwest.

Commissioned to create a lobby mural (p. 142) at Eastmore House, an apartment building at East 76th Street and 2nd Avenue in New York.

Opens second solo exhibition featuring eleven works at Betty Parsons in September.

Agnes Martin and Lenore Tawney move to Coenties Slip. Youngerman, Seyrig, and their son Duncan leave France and settle in Coenties Slip.

1958

Painting in Five Panels and *New York* (1957) included in group exhibition, organized by the American Federation of the Arts for the American Pavilion, World's Fair, Brussels.

First solo show presented by Galerie Maeght, Paris; October issue of gallery's *Derrière le Miroir* is published as exhibition catalogue, with essay by critic and curator E.C. Goossen. Lawrence Alloway, director of the Institute of Contemporary Arts, London, sees this show and advises English collector E.J. Power to acquire Kelly's work; among the seven paintings purchased, *Broadway* (p. 144) through Power's 1962 gift to the Tate Gallery, London, becomes the artist's first painting to enter a European museum collection.

Exhibits for first time at the Pittsburgh International Exhibition of Contemporary Painting and Sculpture (renamed the Carnegie International in 1982), Museum of Art, Carnegie Institute, which acquires *Aubade* (1957), Kelly's second museum sale. Through the Carnegie's director, Gordon Bailey Washburn, meets Robert Fraser, who was hired by Washburn to assist with the exhibition. Will be included again in the International in 1961, 1964, 1967 and 1985.

Begins a series of wood reliefs, such as *Concorde Relief I* (p. 143).

Designs costumes and a stage curtain for *Tablet*, an avant-garde ballet choreographed by Paul Taylor, all later used in 1960 at the Festival of Two Worlds in Spoleto, Italy, where Taylor will stage this performance with dancers Pina Bausch and Dan Wagoner (fig. 100).

1959

Invited by Dorothy C. Miller to show in "Sixteen Americans" at MoMA, where Kelly displays *Rebound* (p. 145) and five other works, including *Running White* (1959), which the museum purchases in 1960, acquiring its first Kelly painting. Meets Jasper Johns and Frank Stella, who are also featured in

fig. 179: Poster for "Ellsworth Kelly, Paintings 1951–1956," Betty Parsons Gallery, New York, 1956

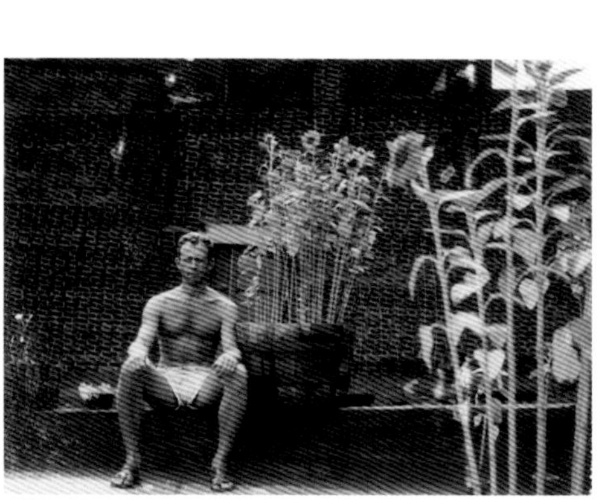

fig. 180: Ellsworth Kelly, Coenties Slip studio roof, New York, 1957

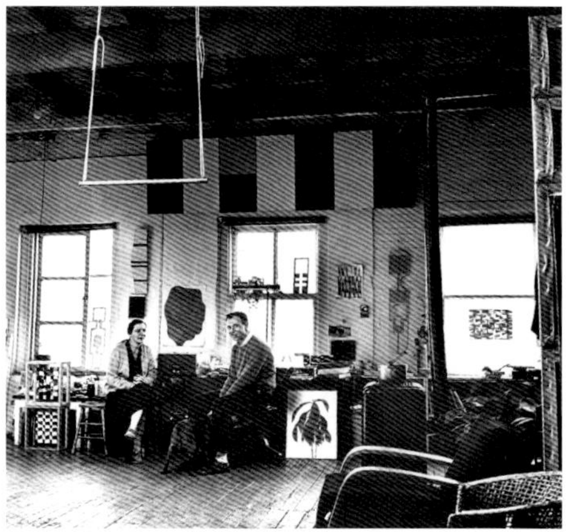

fig. 181: Ellsworth Kelly with Agnes Martin, Coenties Slip studio, New York, 1958

"Sixteen Americans," along with Youngerman and Rauschenberg (whom Kelly had met in 1954).

Through Stella, meets curator Henry Geldzahler at his Coenties Slip studio.

Makes his first freestanding sculptures, *Gate* (p. 150) and *Pony* (p. 148), as well as his first painted metal relief, *Black Venus;* exhibits them at his third show at Parsons in October.

Featured for first time with *East River* (1959) at the Annual Exhibition of Contemporary American Painting (reconceived as the Biennial Exhibition in 1973) at the Whitney. Will be included in the Annual regularly through 1970.

Albright-Knox Art Gallery, Buffalo, NY, becomes third American museum to acquire a Kelly work, *New York* (1957).

1960

Concorde I (1958) featured in group exhibition, "Le Jeune Peinture de la Collection Dotremont," at Stedelijk van Abbemuseum, Eindhoven, The Netherlands.

Spends summer in Springs, East Hampton, NY (fig. 184) where he meets James Rosenquist, who soon moves to Coenties Slip.

Travels to Puerto Rico at Christmas, his first trip to the Caribbean.

1961

Spends second summer in Springs, East Hampton, NY.

Exhibits *Rebound* (p. 145) and *North River* (1959) at "VI Bienal: Estados Unidos 1961" at Museo de Arte Moderna, São Paulo, organized by the International Council of The Museum of Modern Art.

Receives Fourth Painting Prize for *Block Island II* (1960) at his second outing at the Pittsburgh International, Museum of Art, Carnegie Institute.

Train Landscape (p. 77) and *Two Blacks, White and Blue* (1955) included in "Art Abstrait Constructif International," Galerie Denise René, Paris, with catalogue essay by critic Michel Seuphor.

1962

Awarded the Flora Mayer Witkowsky Prize for *Black and White* (p. 152) by The Art Institute of Chicago at its "65th American Exhibition: Some Directions in Contemporary Painting and Sculpture."

Presents *White Blue (formerly Blue White)* (1960) in group exhibition at World's Fair, Seattle, WA.

Solo exhibition of twenty works including *Yellow White* (p. 153) opens in May at Arthur Tooth & Sons, Ltd. (fig. 185), London, with catalogue essay by Lawrence Alloway.

While in London, meets Francis Bacon with Patrick Kinross (Lord Kinross), with whom Kelly had become friends several years earlier when Kinross was visiting New York and writing a travel book about the U.S., *The Innocents at Home*, published in 1959; Kelly is mentioned in the chapter on New York.

Blue White (1961) from the S.C. Johnson Collection included in international touring exhibition, "Art: USA: Now," curated by Lee Nordness and organized by the United States Information Agency (U.S.I.A.), a diplomatic agency established in 1953 by President Dwight D. Eisenhower to promote national interests abroad.

1963

Presents *Green Blue* (1962) at the 28th Biennial Exhibition of Contemporary American Painting, Corcoran Gallery of Art, Washington, DC.

Shows *Gaza* (p. 133) in group exhibition at Green Gallery, New York, by director Richard Bellamy, with artists such as Robert Morris, Larry Poons (who by 1962 lives in Coenties Slip), Kenneth Noland, and Frank Stella.

Receives the Education Minister's Award for *Red White Blue* (1961) at the Seventh International Art Exhibition of Japan, Metropolitan Art Gallery, Tokyo, as well as Brandeis Creative Arts Award from Brandeis University, Waltham, MA; subsequently, the Rose Art Museum at Brandeis acquires *Blue White* (1962).

The Art Institute of Chicago acquires its first Kelly painting, *Black and White* (p. 152).

The Washington Gallery of Modern Art, Washington, DC, hosts Kelly's first solo museum exhibition, "Paintings, Sculpture and Drawings by Ellsworth Kelly," with catalogue featuring artist interview with Henry Geldzahler; show travels to the Institute of Contemporary Art, Boston, in early 1964.

Moves to studio at Hotel des Artistes on Manhattan's Upper West Side, taking his dog, Orange, who once belonged to Youngerman.

The Metropolitan Museum acquires its first Kelly painting, *Blue Green Red* (1963).

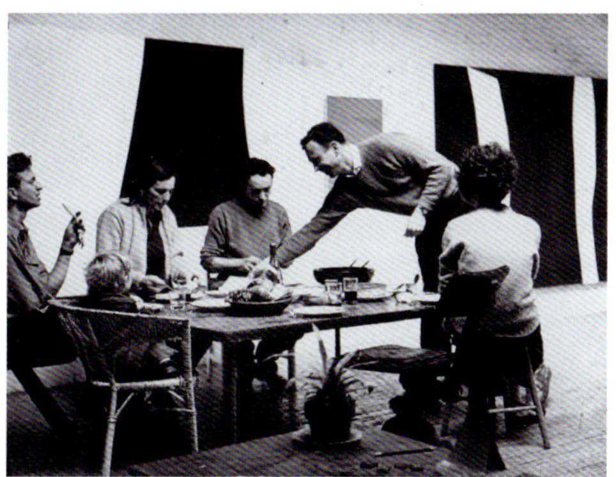

fig. 182: Ellsworth Kelly's Coenties Slip studio, New York, 1958 (Jack Youngerman, Duncan Youngerman, Agnes Martin, Robert Indiana, Ellsworth Kelly, Delphine Seyrig)

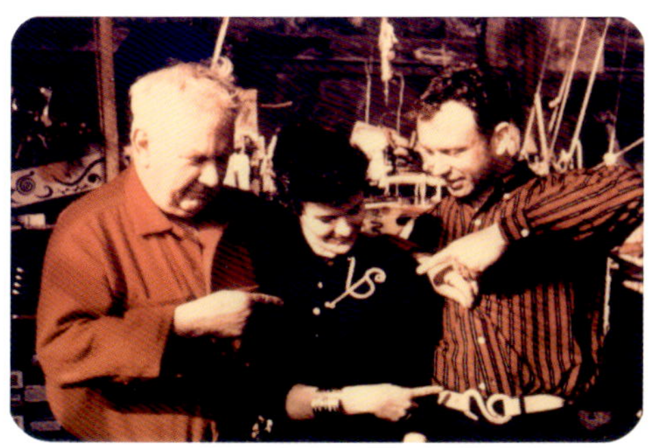

fig. 183: Ellsworth Kelly (right) with Alexander Calder and Delphine Seyrig, Roxbury, CT, 1958

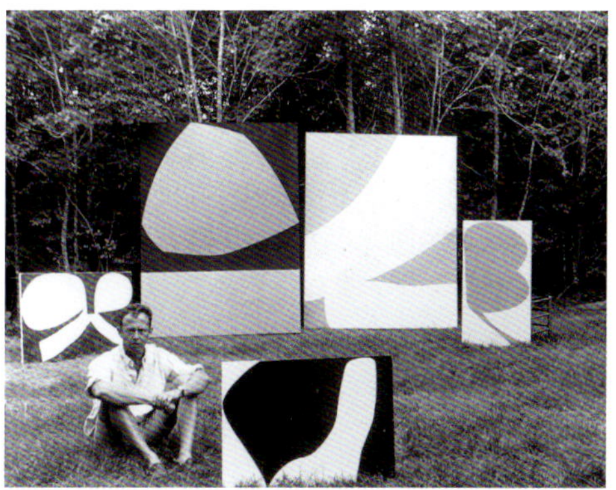

fig. 184: Ellsworth Kelly, Springs, East Hampton, NY, 1960

1964

Yellow Blue (1963) shown in group exhibition, "A View of New York Painting including Major Works by Jasper Johns, Robert Rauschenberg, Andy Warhol, Ellsworth Kelly, Frank Stella, Roy Lichtenstein and Larry Poons," at Ferus Gallery, Los Angeles, now under directorship of Irving Blum.

Invited by critic Clement Greenberg to participate in his exhibition, "Post Painterly Abstraction," Los Angeles County Museum of Art, where Kelly presents three works, including *Blue over Blue* (p. 167).

His large-scale outdoor commission from Philip Johnson, *Two Curves: Blue Red* (p. 165), debuts in April at the Johnson-designed New York State Pavilion at the 1964 World's Fair, Queens, New York, along with other commissioned works by John Chamberlain, Robert Indiana, Roy Lichtenstein, and Rauschenberg; after close of fair, donates work to Harvard University, Cambridge, MA.

The Cleveland Museum of Art acquires *Red Blue* (1962) (fig. 114).

Exhibits *Black Ripe* (p. 130) and *Red Blue Green* (pp. 156–57) at Documenta III, Kassel, curated by Arnold Bode and Werner Haftmann, his first time there.

Receives Painting Prize for *Blue Black Red* (p. 166) during his third appearance at the Pittsburgh International.

Sails for Paris, spending last three months there, where Galerie Maeght presents its second solo exhibition of his work. November issue of *Derrière le Miroir* is published as exhibition catalogue with essay by Dale McConathy, who used to work for Betty Parsons. Also begins work with Maeght Éditeur on *Suite of Twenty-Seven Color Lithographs* (1964–65) and *Suite of Plant Lithographs* (1964–66).

Travels to the south of France, where he meets Marc Chagall; visits Matisse's La Chapelle du Rosaire des Dominicaines de Vence, Saint-Paul-de-Vence in December.

1965

Includes *Blue Green Red* (1964) in "The Responsive Eye," curated by William Seitz, MoMA.

His first solo exhibition at Ferus Gallery, Los Angeles, "An Exhibition of Recent Lithography Executed in France by the Artist Ellsworth Kelly," opens in March. He will show there again a year later, after which it is renamed Irving Blum Gallery.

Sidney Janis Gallery, New York, presents its first solo exhibition of the artist in April including *Red Blue* (1964) (p. 164); Kelly will continue to show there until 1971.

Travels to Paris in May and exhibits *Suite of Twenty-Seven Color Lithographs* (1964–65) at Galerie Maeght, Paris. That summer, visits Belle-Île-en-Mer, Brittany, Dordogne, Normandy, Provence, and Saint-Paul-de-Vence.

Travels to Switzerland for group show at Kunsthalle Basel, including *Blue Green* (p. 155) and *Green Blue Black* (p. 161) among eight works; then travels extensively through Italy, visiting Assisi, Florence, Orvieto, Pompeii, Rome, Torino, Naples, Capua, Milan and Siena.

Makes first of two "wall/floor" paintings, *Red Blue Green Yellow*.

After painting figure-ground compositions for past decade, returns to thorough exploration of multipanel paintings over next several years, with *Red Yellow Blue II* (pp. 168–69), a three-part work separated against the wall, which he shows in a group exhibition at Sidney Janis.

1966

San Francisco Museum of Modern Art (SFMOMA) acquires its first Kelly painting, *Red White* (1962).

With *Blue Disk* (1963) (fig. 112), he is featured in "Primary Structures: Younger American and British Sculptors," curated by Kynaston McShine, at the Jewish Museum, New York.

Represents the United States at the 33rd Venice Biennale, along with Helen Frankenthaler, Roy Lichtenstein, and Jules Olitski, in exhibition curated by Geldzahler (fig. 187); meets Marcel Duchamp while in Venice. Exhibition includes seven works including *Blue Red* (p. 173), his second "wall/floor" piece; *Yellow Piece* (p. 175), his first shaped work using a single monochrome canvas; and *White Angle* (1966), his first of two "angle" sculptures.

After attending the opening in Venice, travels with Geldzahler to Ravenna, viewing mosaics at Mausoleum of Galla Placidia, Basilica of San Vitale, and nearby Basilica Sant'Apollinare in Classe. Travels to Padua to see Giotto's frescoes at Scrovegni Chapel. Also, travels to U.K. and visits Stonehenge.

The Walker Art Center, Minneapolis, MN, acquires its first Kelly, *Red Green Blue* (1964).

Blue Green Yellow Orange Red (pp. 170–71) is shown in "Systemic Painting," curated by Alloway, at The Guggenheim Museum, which acquires the work in 1967, its first Kelly purchase.

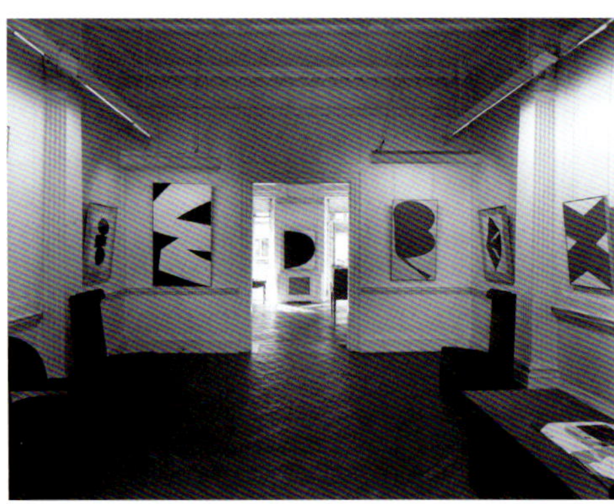

fig. 185: Installation view of "Ellsworth Kelly," Arthur Tooth & Sons, London, 1962

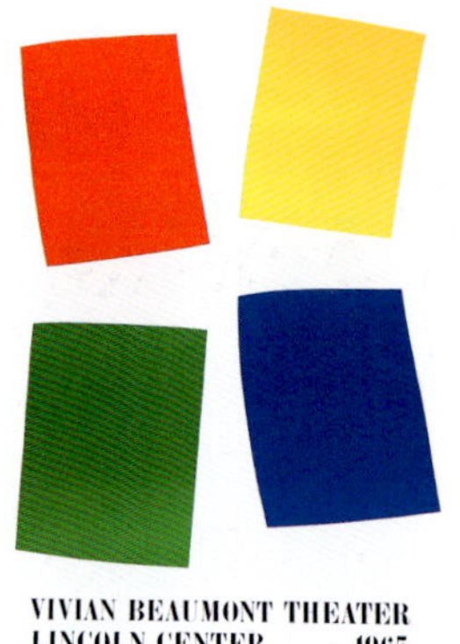

fig. 186: Poster for Vivian Beaumont Theater, Lincoln Center for the Performing Arts, New York, 1965

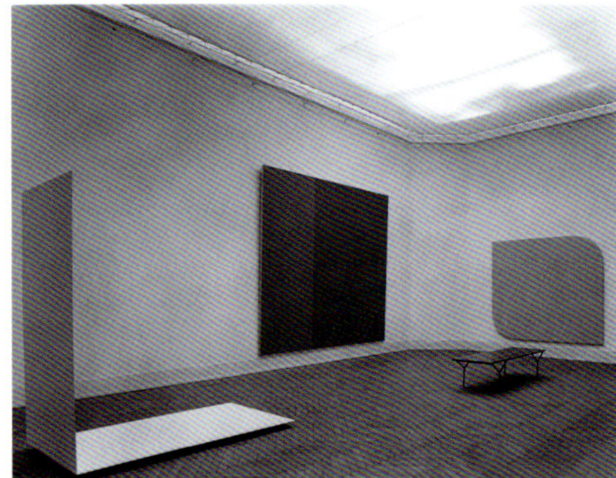

fig. 187: Installation view of Ellsworth Kelly works, U.S. Pavilion, 33rd Venice Biennale, 1966

Henry Persche becomes Kelly's studio assistant.

1967

Saint Louis Art Museum, MO, purchases *Spectrum II* (1966–67) (fig. 110).

Exhibits in "American Sculpture of the Sixties," curated by Maurice Tuchman, Los Angeles County Museum of Art, with *Gate* (p. 150).

Kelly's commission, *White over Blue*, his tallest work to date at 28 feet high, is featured in the United States Pavilion, the geodesic dome designed by Buckminster Fuller, at Expo '67, Montreal.

The Stedelijk Museum, Amsterdam, becomes the first European museum to acquire a work by Kelly, *Blue Green Red I* (1964–65) and later in the year, it acquires *Blue Red Rocker* (p. 160), the first Kelly sculpture to enter a museum collection.

He is given his first solo exhibition at Irving Blum Gallery, Los Angeles, where he will show until 1973.

Travels to Amsterdam, Zurich, and Paris; while in Paris, takes retrospective tour of city with his camera, documenting views (figs 36, 38) that inspired works such as *Window, Museum of Modern Art, Paris* (p. 53), *Ormesson* (p. 64), and *White Plaque: Bridge Arch and Reflection* (p. 131).

Visits Miró in Majorca.

1968

The Whitney purchases *Whites* (1963), his first sculpture to be acquired by an American museum.

Exhibits six works, including *Blue Red* (p. 173), at Documenta 4, Kassel.

Goossen presents Kelly in international traveling exhibition that opens at MoMA, "The Art of the Real: USA 1948–1968," (fig. 188) with six works including *Window, Museum of Modern Art, Paris* (p. 53), *Colors for a Large Wall* (p. 69), *Painting for a White Wall* (pp. 82–83), and *White Plaque: Bridge Arch and Reflection* (p. 131). Exhibition will travel to the Grand Palais, Paris, Kunsthaus Zurich, and the Tate Gallery, London. Kelly will travel that fall to Paris for the installation of the exhibition as well as to Zurich early the next year for the opening where fashion designer Cristóbal Balenciaga compliments Kelly on *Colors for a Large Wall* (p. 69).

Meets curator Diane Waldman, who later visits Kelly at his studio.

Spends summer and the next one in Bridgehampton, NY; while there becomes friends with Lichtenstein (fig. 200) and meets critic Elizabeth C. Baker.

Designs costumes again for Paul Taylor, a dance performance called *Lento*, creating ten leotards of fragmented color inspired by his "Spectrums."

Begins ongoing practice of making uniquely shaped paintings using joined panels each painted a single color.

Starts creating sculptures with Don Lippincott of Lippincott, Inc., New Haven, CT, with whom he will continue working until 1993; one of these first sculptures made with Lippincott, *Green Blue*, an outdoor work, is purchased by MoMA, their first Kelly sculpture acquisition.

Makes *Yellow Blue*, a sculpture commission for Governor Nelson A. Rockefeller Empire State Plaza in Albany, NY.

Shown at "Serial Imagery," curated by John Coplans, Pasadena Art Museum (renamed the Norton Simon Museum in 1975).

1969

Begins making paintings based on his "radial curves." Such curves are fragmented from large circles, an idea to which he returns in 1972, with *Yellow Blue Curve I* (1972) (p. 223) and *Blue Curve III* (1972) (pp. 230–31), and expands further in multiple variations in painting, relief, and sculpture throughout his career.

Receives commission for large-scale painting, *Blue Green* for the UNESCO building, Paris.

Invited by Geldzahler to exhibit in his major survey, "New York Painting and Sculpture: 1940–1970" (fig. 190), which colonizes thirty-five galleries at The Metropolitan Museum; Geldzahler provides Kelly with two galleries, one for seven paintings and five sculptures, such as *Relief with Blue* (p. 58), *Red Yellow Blue I* (p. 163), *White Ring* (p. 159), *Green Rocker* (p. 177), as well as *Spectrum V* (pp. 180–81), which Kelly makes that summer especially for the exhibition; the second gallery displays thirty of his plant drawings for the first time.

William Rubin, recently named chief curator of painting and sculpture at MoMA, begins conversations with Kelly about a mid-career retrospective, which will be held at the museum in 1973.

The Walker purchases its first Kelly sculpture, *Green Rocker* (1968) (p. 177).

He donates his first painting to a museum, *Colors for a Large Wall* (1951) (p. 69) to

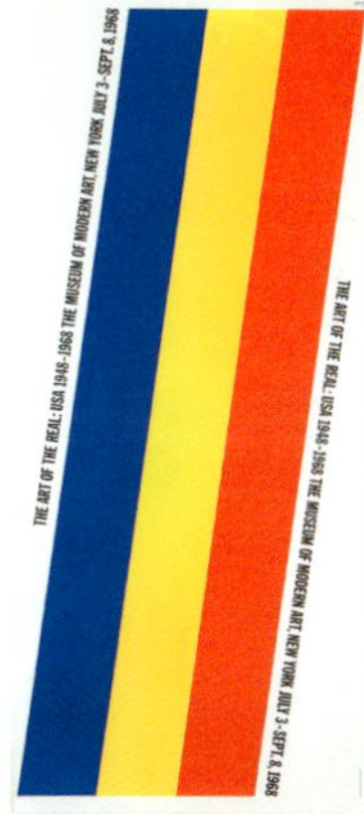

fig. 188: Poster for "The Art of the Real: USA 1948–1968", The Museum of Modern Art, New York, 1968

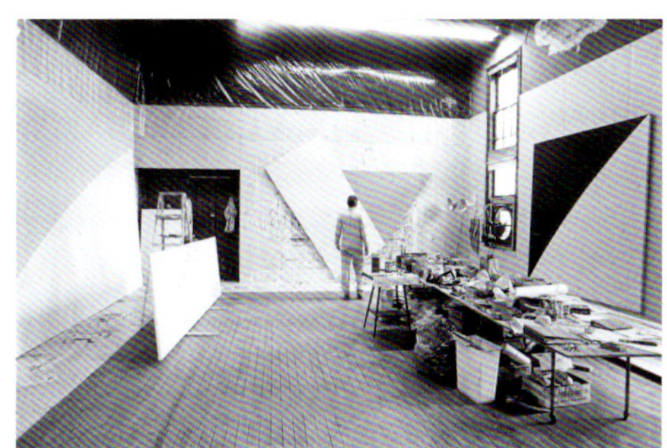

fig. 189: Ellsworth Kelly, Cady's Hall studio, Chatham, NY, 1973

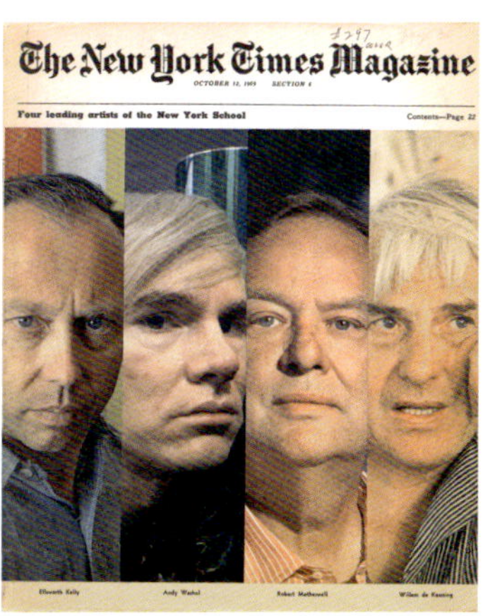

fig. 190: Cover of *The New York Times Magazine* (Ellsworth Kelly, Andy Warhol, Robert Motherwell and Willem de Kooning), October, 12, 1969

MoMA, also the first work from his French years to enter a museum collection. Later that year, Kelly gifts *Spectrum V* (pp. 180–81) to The Metropolitan Museum.

1970

In March, moves upstate to Spencertown, NY, where he buys and renovates an old farmhouse. In nearby town of Chatham, NY, locates and rents a large space in an old theater, Cady's Hall, and transforms it into a studio (fig. 189).

Travels for first time to Saint Martin in the Caribbean, which he will revisit frequently.

Begins first print project with Sidney Felsen, Stanley Grinstein, and Kenneth Tyler of Gemini G.E.L., Los Angeles (Tyler will leave Gemini in 1973), and is featured for first time in solo exhibition there in September, with catalogue essay by Coplans; will continue to produce prints with Gemini G.E.L. and show there to this day.

Red Yellow Blue II (pp. 168–69) and three other works are displayed in group exhibition at the Museum of Contemporary Art, Chicago, "Ellsworth Kelly, Morris Louis, Kenneth Noland, Frank Stella."

Visits George Rickey's studio, who lives nearby in East Chatham, NY.

Makes *Mirrored Concorde*, which is both his first sculpture fabricated by Peter Carlson and first editioned sculpture with Gemini G.E.L.

1971

Coplans and Waldman publish, respectively, the first monographs on Kelly, *Ellsworth Kelly* and *Ellsworth Kelly: Drawings, Collages, Prints*.

Spectrum V (pp. 180–81) and a selection of drawings are shown in "The Structure of Color," curated by Marcia Tucker, at the Whitney.

Solo exhibition presented at Dayton's Gallery 12, Minneapolis, MN, in May, including *Gate* (p. 150) and *Pony* (p. 148).

1972

Galerie Denise René-Hans Meyer, Düsseldorf, mounts solo exhibition of Kelly paintings in July.

Solo exhibition of the fourteen paintings from his "Chatham" series, including *Chatham X: Black Red* (p. 225), presented at Albright-Knox Art Gallery, Buffalo, NY (fig. 191).

1973

Begins making large outdoor sculptures, exploring use of weathering steel, of which *Curve I* (fig. 134), installed flush on the ground, is the first. *Stele I* (p. 233) is his first freestanding outdoor sculpture made of weathering steel.

Featured in the Biennial Exhibition at the Whitney; will be presented again in 1979, 1981, 1991 and 2012.

In April, exhibits *Blue Curve III* (pp. 230–31), along with five other paintings incorporating his "radial curves," in "Ellsworth Kelly: Curved Series," his first solo show at Leo Castelli Gallery, New York, where he will continue to exhibit until 1992.

Los Angeles County Museum of Art purchases *Blue Curve III* (pp. 230–31), its first Kelly work.

He begins exhibiting with Ronald Greenberg at Greenberg Gallery, St. Louis, MO, where he will continue to show until 1993 (including a 1996 solo exhibition at newly named Greenberg Van Doren Gallery, St. Louis).

MoMA presents Kelly's mid-career retrospective, "Ellsworth Kelly," curated by Goossen (fig. 193), which travels to the Pasadena Art Museum, Walker Art Center, Minneapolis, and the Detroit Institute of Arts.

1974

Elected to the National Institute of Arts and Letters (now the American Academy of Arts and Letters).

Begins ongoing series of totem sculptures, created in weathering steel and aluminum such as *Curve X* (p. 236) and *Curve XI* (p. 234).

1975

Receives the Painting Prize from The Art Institute of Chicago.

Chosen as first artist to inaugurate Wadsworth Atheneum's "Matrix" series of solo contemporary exhibitions in Hartford, CT, with 1959 drawings of corn stalks he grew on his roof while living in Coenties Slip.

On his way to California to make prints with Gemini G.E.L. in spring, travels to Colorado. Drives to the Rocky Mountains and then to Pike's Peak (the discoverer of the famed summit, Zebulon Pike, is his distant ancestor); continues to the Meteor Crater in Arizona, then to Sedona, the Grand Canyon, the Mojave Desert, and Death Valley.

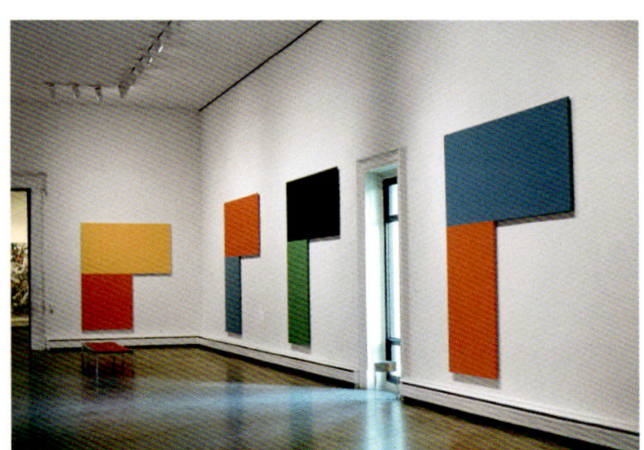

fig. 191: Installation view of "The Chatham Series: Paintings by Ellsworth Kelly," Albright-Knox Art Gallery, Buffalo, NY, 1972

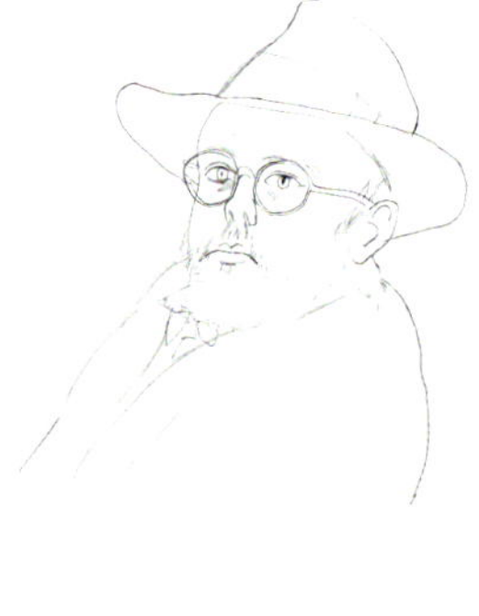

fig. 192: *Henry Geldzahler,* 1983, graphite on paper, 30 × 22 inches, 76.2 × 55.8 cm

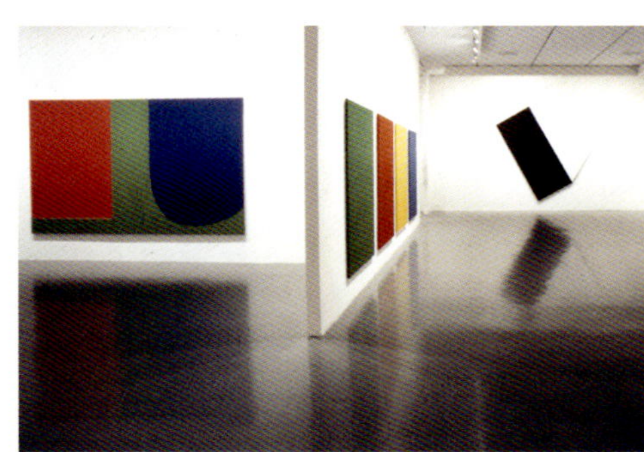

fig. 193: Installation view of "Ellsworth Kelly," The Museum of Modern Art, New York, 1973

In September, first solo show, "Ellsworth Kelly Paintings," held at BlumHelman Gallery, New York, where he will show until 1993.

1976

Included in two traveling exhibitions devoted to drawing, "Twentieth Century American Drawing: Three Avant-Garde Generations," curated by Waldman at The Guggenheim; and "Drawing Now," curated by Bernice Rose, at MoMA.

Completes print series using colored cotton pulp, *Colored Paper Images,* with Kenneth Tyler at Tyler Graphics Ltd, Bedford Village, New York.

Focuses on making black-and-white paintings.

1977

Travels to Spain, Italy, France, Switzerland.

Presented in "Paris-New York," Centre national d'art et de culture Georges Pompidou, Paris, with *Colors for a Large Wall* (p. 69).

Meets curator Alfred Pacquement (fig. 194).

Exhibits selection of drawings at Documenta 6, Kassel.

Meets curator Emily Rauh Pulitzer (fig. 196).

1978

Travels to Barcelona to view Antoni Gaudí's architecture.

Installs *Color Panels for a Large Wall* (fig. 157),a commission from the Central Trust Company, Cincinnati, OH.

Begins to fabricate sculpture with Peter Carlson Enterprises, Sun Valley, CA.

Architects Feibes & Schmitt of Schenectady begin construction on his new studio adjacent to his Spencertown home, replicating his Chatham studio proportions at Cady's Hall. Over time, will buy parcels of land adding to his Spencertown property.

"Colored Paper Images," solo exhibition of prints curated by Riva Castleman, opens at MoMA.

Méditerranée (p. 71) is shown in "Grids: Format and Image in 20th Century Art" at Pace Gallery, New York, with catalogue essay by Rosalind Krauss.

1979

Featured, along with Johns, de Kooning, Lichtenstein and Rauschenberg in the "36th Biennial Exhibition of Contemporary American Painting," organized by Jane Livingston, Corcoran Gallery of Art, Washington, DC.

Curated by Thomas Hess and Lowery Stokes Sims, "Ellsworth Kelly: Recent Paintings and Sculptures" opens at The Metropolitan Museum (fig. 195).

"Ellsworth Kelly: Paintings and Sculptures, 1963–1979," his first major museum exhibition in Europe, originates at the Stedelijk Museum, Amsterdam, under the directorship of Edy de Wilde; the show travels to he Hayward Gallery, London; Centre Georges Pompidou, Musée National d'Art Moderne, Paris; and Staatliche Kunsthalle, Baden-Baden.

1980

Made a Fellow of the Rhode Island School of Design, Providence.

1981

The Pompidou presents five works by Kelly: *Window, Museum of Modern Art, Paris* (p. 53), *White Relief* (p. 59), *Cité* (p. 63), *Fête à Torcy* (p. 72), *Kite II* (pp. 80–81) in "Paris-Paris/Créations en France, 1937–1957."

Completes commission, *Curve XXII*, measuring 36 feet high for Lincoln Park, in Chicago, his tallest to date.

Begins a series of totems made of wood.

Receives sculpture award from the Skowhegan School of Painting and Sculpture, ME.

1982

Meets photographer Jack Shear in Los Angeles (fig. 198), who will become Kelly's partner and collaborator.

"Ellsworth Kelly: Sculpture," a sculpture retrospective curated by Patterson Sims and Emily Rauh Pulitzer, opens at the Whitney and travels to the Saint Louis Art Museum.

Makes *Series of Eleven Wall Panels*, his first multipanel work of uniquely shaped panels separated across the wall, with Carlson and Gemini G.E.L.

1983

Curve XXIX, measuring 20 feet high, is installed on grounds of Farnsworth House, designed by Ludwig Mies van der Rohe, Plano, IL.

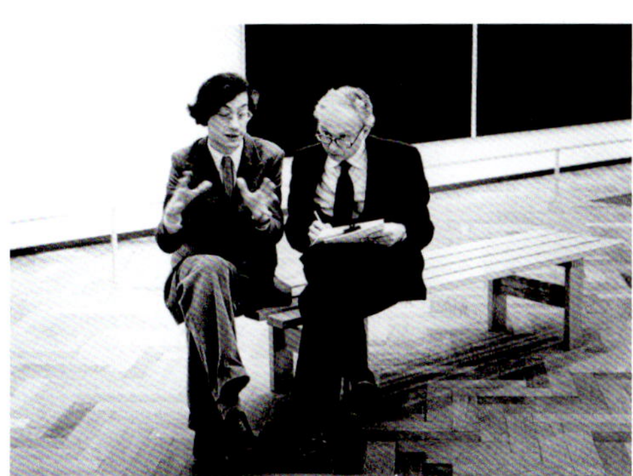

fig. 194: Ellsworth Kelly with Alfred Pacquement at Stedelijk Museum, Amsterdam, 1979

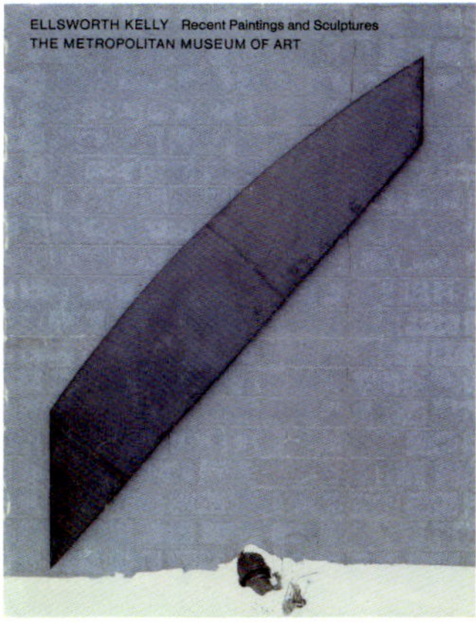

fig. 195: Catalogue for "Ellsworth Kelly: Recent Paintings and Sculptures," The Metropolitan Museum of Art, New York, 1979

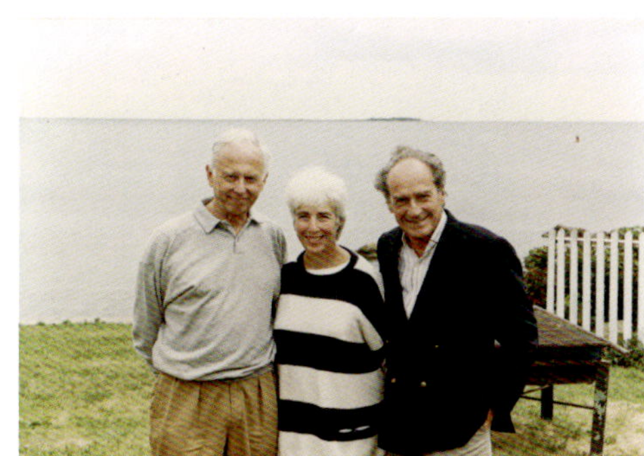

fig. 196: Ellsworth Kelly with Emily Rauh Pulitzer and Joseph Pulitzer, Jr., 1985

Elected to Hall of Fame by Dwight Morrow High School, Englewood, NJ.

1984

Debuts outdoor commission, *Untitled* (1982–83) for reopening of Dallas Museum of Art, redesigned by Edward Larrabee Barnes.

La Combe II (p. 60) is featured in "The Folding Image: Screens by Western Artists of the Nineteenth and Twentieth Centuries," National Gallery of Art, Washington, DC.

A room containing seven paintings including *Window, Museum of Modern Art, Paris* (p. 53), *November Painting* (fig. 40) *and Painting for a White Wall* (pp. 82–83) opens at the National Gallery of Art, Washington, DC.

Meets professor and art historian Richard H. Axsom, who will author the catalogue raisonné of Kelly prints in 1987, with revised and expanded edition in 2012.

Included in "ROSC '84," Art Council, Dublin.

Jack Shear moves from Los Angeles to Spencertown.

Travels to Berlin, Dublin, London, and Paris. Attends opening of "La Grande Parade: Highlights in Painting after 1940" at the Stedelijk Museum in Amsterdam.

1985

Commissioned by city of Barcelona to create two large-scale totems, completed in 1987 (fig. 197); one measuring 49 feet high remains Kelly's tallest sculpture to this day (fig. 140).

Presented in traveling exhibition, "Contrasts of Form: Geometric Abstract Art, 1910-1980," curated by Magdalena Dabrowski at MoMA.

The Aldrich Museum of Contemporary Art, Ridgefield, CT, mounts "A Second Talent: Painters and Sculptors Who Are Also Photographers," where Kelly shows his photographs for first time.

1986

"The Window in Twentieth-Century Art," curated by Suzanne Delehanty, Neuberger Museum, at State University of New York at Purchase, NY, features *Window, Museum of Modern Art, Paris* (p. 53) and two other Kelly works, and travels to Contemporary Arts Museum Houston, TX.

Traveling exhibition curated by Maurice Tuchman, "The Spiritual in Art: Abstract Painting, 1890–1985," opens at the Los Angeles County Museum of Art, featuring three Kelly works including *White Square* (p. 85).

A gallery installation of eight paintings by Kelly is featured in the inaugural exhibition of the new California Plaza building for the Museum of Contemporary Art, Los Angeles.

Creates *Red Curve* for the Raffles City Hotel, designed by I.M. Pei, in Singapore.

Completes commission *Houston Triptych*, for the Lillie and Hugh Roy Cullen Sculpture Garden at the Museum of Fine Arts, Houston, TX.

Designs a chapel, developing a proposed concept through an intricate model, but the project will not be realized until 2015.

1987

The Pompidou acquires *Kite II* (pp. 80–81), the first time a museum purchases a work from Kelly's French years.

Awarded *Chevalier de l'Ordre des Arts et des Lettres* by the French Republic.

"Ellsworth Kelly: Works on Paper," a national traveling retrospective curated by Diane Upright, opens at Fort Worth Art Museum, TX (fig. 199).

Organized by the American Federation of the Arts, "Ellsworth Kelly: A Print Retrospective" originates at the Detroit Institute of Arts, MI, and travels to many venues nationally, with corresponding publication by Axsom, *The Prints of Ellsworth Kelly: A Catalogue Raisonné 1949–1985.*

"Ellsworth Kelly: Seven Paintings (1952–55/1987)," curated by Trevor Fairbrother, is presented at the Museum of Fine Arts, Boston.

Meets professor and art historian Roberta Bernstein, with whom he will regularly birdwatch in upstate New York.

List Visual Arts Center, Massachusetts Institute of Technology, Cambridge, MA, mounts "Ellsworth Kelly: Small Sculpture, 1958–87," curated by Katy Kline.

Meets curator Gary Garrels.

1988

Represented in "Rot Gelb Blau: Die Primärfarben in der Kunst des 20. Jahrhunderts," curated by Bernhard Bürgi, at Kunstmuseum, St Gallen, and then Museum Fridericianum, Kassel, with *Red Yellow Blue II* (1965) (pp. 168–69).

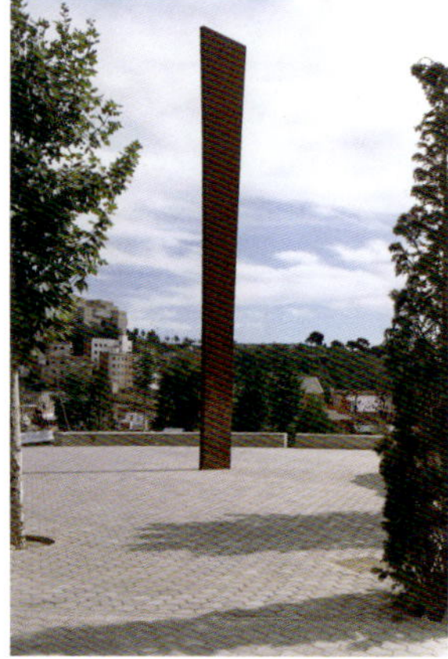

fig. 197: *Creueta del Coll*, 1987, weathering steel, 390 × 57 × 5¼ in, 990.6 × 144.8 × 13.3 cm

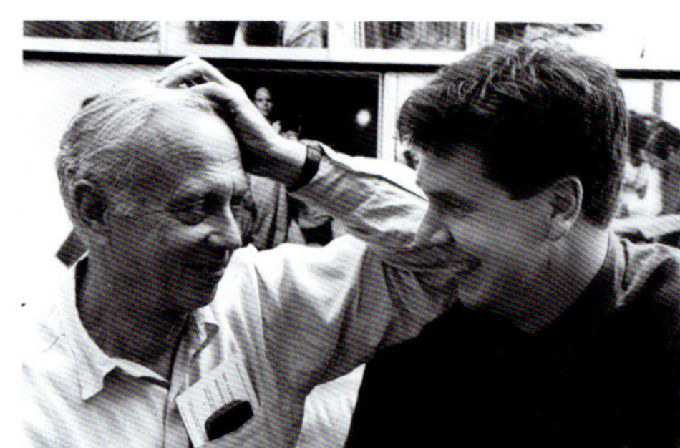

fig. 198: Ellsworth Kelly and Jack Shear, 1988

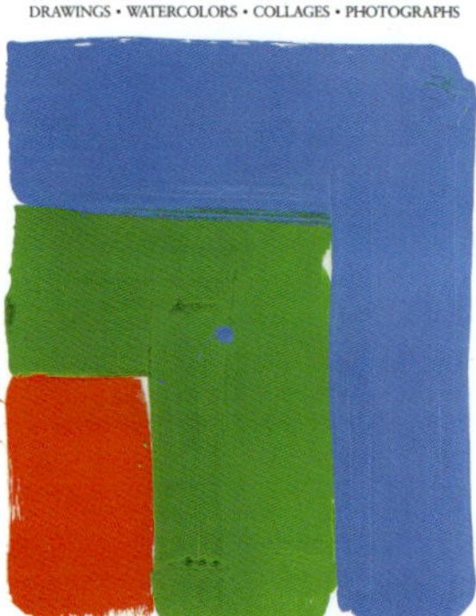

fig. 199: Catalogue for "Ellsworth Kelly: Works on Paper", Fort Worth Art Museum, TX, 1987

Large-scale outdoor commission, *Double Curve* is unveiled at opening of the new Minneapolis Sculpture Garden at the Walker Art Center.

"La Couleur Seule: L'Expérience du Monochrome," curated by Maurice Besset, Musée St Pierre, Lyon, opens with ten Kelly paintings, including *Tableau Vert* (1952) (p. 76) and *Dark Blue Panel* (1985) (p. 251).

BlumHelman Gallery, New York, presents solo exhibition with catalogue essay by curator Robert Storr whom Kelly had met earlier that decade, and who, in the coming years, will write consistently on the artist.

After focusing on single-panel shaped canvases for past several years, returns to making joined-panel paintings, usually duo-paneled.

1989

Museum Overholland, Amsterdam, presents "Ellsworth Kelly: Works on Paper" exhibition.

Long-term courtyard installation of six paintings premieres in the new Daniel F. & Ada Rice Building at The Art Institute of Chicago.

Completes commission for the Morton H. Meyerson Symphony Center, Dallas, TX, (fig. 143) designed by Pei; four fiberglass panels, each measuring 34 feet high, is Kelly's tallest indoor commission to date.

1990

In March, featured in first solo exhibition of prints at Susan Sheehan Gallery, New York, where he will continue to show to this day.

Creates his first floor painting, *Yellow Curve* (pp. 256–57), measuring 25 feet at its widest point, for solo exhibition curated by Ulrich Wilmes and Kasper König for Portikus, Frankfurt, with a catalogue essay by Gottfried Boehm.

Invited by curator Kirk Varnedoe to curate second installment of "Artist's Choice" exhibition series begun the previous year at MoMA and drawn from its collection, "Artist's Choice: Ellsworth Kelly—Fragmentation and the Single Form."

Completes commission, *White Curve, Vevey* for Swiss corporate headquarters of Nestlé SA.

Meets professor and art historian Yve-Alain Bois (fig. 201) who, over the years, will write extensively on the artist, authoring the first volume of the catalogue raisonné of Kelly's paintings, reliefs, and sculptures in 2015.

1991

Included in "Artists' Sketchbooks," inaugural exhibition of Matthew Marks Gallery, New York, on Madison Avenue (fig. 203).

Travels to London to see director Nicholas Serota, whom he had met in the 1980s, to plan the first gallery dedicated to Kelly works at the Tate, in honor of his upcoming 70th birthday. The installation will feature six works, including *Broadway* (p. 144), *Untitled (Mandorla)* (fig. 68), and *Orange Relief with Green* (p. 263).

Two Kelly works, including *Orange Red Relief (for Delphine Seyrig)* (p. 259), among his first overlapping panels, are shown at the Biennial Exhibition at the Whitney.

Featured in solo exhibition, "Ellsworth Kelly: Diagonals and Curved Panels 1970–1990," his first at Gemini G.E.L. at Joni Moisant Weyl, New York, where he will continue to show to this day.

"Ellsworth Kelly: At Right Angles, 1964–1966," with catalogue essay by Bernstein, opens at Margo Leavin Gallery, Los Angeles, and travels to John Berggruen Gallery, San Francisco, and Paula Cooper Gallery, New York.

The Ellsworth Kelly Foundation is established, with the goal of supporting arts conservation, nationally and internationally, as well as supporting the local community where Kelly lives; over the years, the foundation will provide grants to American museums for conservation needs, donations for both international conservation projects and local land conservancies, and support for arts programs in public schools in his county. Shear is named the Foundation's Secretary/ Treasurer and later becomes Director.

1992

Promoted to rank of *Officier de l'Ordre des Arts et des Lettres* by the French Republic.

"Ellsworth Kelly: The Years in France, 1948–1954," curated by Alfred Pacquement and Jack Cowart, opens at Galerie nationale du Jeu de Paume, Paris (fig. 202), with essays by Yve-Alain Bois, Cowart, Pacquement, and chronology by Nathalie Brunet; exhibition travels to Westfälisches Landesmuseum, Münster, where Kelly installs new large-scale work, *Red Floor Panel* (fig. 135), and ends at National Gallery of Art, Washington, DC.

Awarded *Chevalier de Legion d'Honneur* by the French Republic.

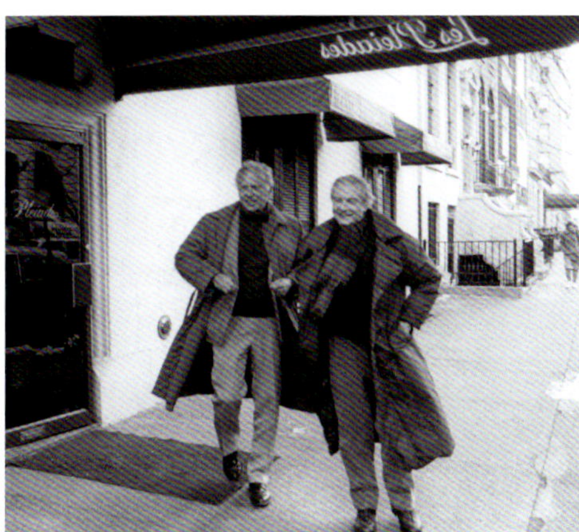

fig. 200: Ellsworth Kelly with Roy Lichtenstein, Upper East Side, New York, 1990

fig. 201: *Yve-Alain Bois,* 1993, ink on paper, 12 × 12 inches, 30.4 × 30.4 cm

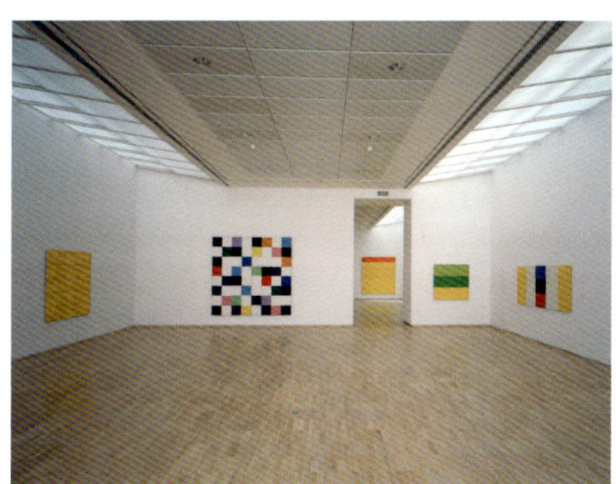

fig. 202: Installation view of "Ellsworth Kelly: The Years in France, 1948–1954", Galerie nationale du Jeu de Paume, Paris, 1992

French journal *Artstudio* devotes spring issue to Kelly, with essays and artist interviews edited by Ann Hindry.

Shown at Documenta IX, Kassel, curated by Jan Hoet, where Kelly presents gallery installation of new paintings, which were introduced earlier that spring at Galerie Daniel Templon, Paris, and subsequently featured at his first solo exhibition at Anthony d'Offay Gallery, London; works are then acquired by Lenbachhaus, Munich.

Meets art historian Éric de Chassey.

Exhibits first solo show at Matthew Marks Gallery in October, "Ellsworth Kelly: Plant Drawings," with catalogue essay by poet John Ashbery, commencing long-time representation by Marks (fig. 203).

Completes *Blue Floor Panel for Leo* (fig. 159), his first floor panel created in U.S. for last exhibition at Leo Castelli Gallery, New York.

Illustrates *Un coup de dés jamais n'abolira le hasard*, the 1870 poem by Stéphane Mallarmé, for an artist's book of eleven lithographs, published by the Limited Edition Club.

Presented with honorary title of *Amic de Barcelona* and medal by mayor of Barcelona.

1993

Pace Gallery mounts "Indiana, Kelly, Martin, Rosenquist, Youngerman at Coenties Slip," curated by Mildred Glimcher, an exhibition that explores specific artistic community in Lower Manhattan where Kelly lived from 1956 to 1963.

United States Holocaust Memorial Museum, designed by James Freed, is dedicated, featuring a commission by Kelly, *Memorial*.

Pratt Institute honors Kelly with Institute Medal and awards him Honorary Doctorate of Fine Arts.

Designed by Norman Foster, Carré d'art, Musée d'art contemporain de Nîmes, is inaugurated with debut of *Gaul*, a 19-foot tall steel sculpture.

Exhibited in "American Art in the Twentieth Century," curated by Norman Rosenthal and Christos M. Joachimides; it originates at Martin Gropius Bau, Berlin, and travels to Royal Academy of Arts, London.

Kelly gifts *Curve X* (p. 236) to the Fogg Art Museum, Harvard University, Cambridge, MA, in memory of Joseph Pulitzer, Jr.

Included in traveling exhibition "The Return of the Cadavre Exquis," curated by Ingrid Schaffner, the Drawing Center, New York.

Nick Walters becomes Kelly's studio manager.

1994

Receives *Médaille du Jubilé* by the French Republic, awarded to American veterans who participated in Battle of Normandy in commemoration of 50th anniversary of D-Day.

Kelly's solo exhibition opens in September at Anthony d'Offay Gallery, London, with catalogue featuring essay by Bois and photographic essay by Shear; it travels to Matthew Marks Gallery, New York, in October, for inaugural opening of gallery on West 22nd Street, Chelsea (fig. 204).

"Ellsworth Kelly: The Process of Seeing," curated by Siri Engberg, opens at the Walker Arts Center, Minneapolis, MN.

Kelly's 1993 illustrated book for Mallarmé's *Un coup de dés* is featured in "A Century of Artists Books," curated by Riva Castleman, at MoMA.

1995

To Hell with the Birds: Looking with Ellsworth Kelly, a documentary by Pierre Aubry and Rachel Stella, is filmed.

1996

Represented in "Abstraction in the Twentieth Century: Total Risk, Freedom, Discipline," curated by Mark Rosenthal, at The Guggenheim, with *Painting for a White Wall* (pp. 82–83), *Train Landscape* (p. 77), *White Square* (p. 85), *Black Ripe* (p. 130), *Broadway* (p. 144), and *Dark Blue Curve* (1995).

Awarded inaugural Medal for Outstanding Achievement in the Arts on 125th anniversary of School of the Museum of Fine Arts, Boston.

Receives Honorary Doctorate of Fine Arts from Bard College, Annandale-on-Hudson, NY.

Elected Fellow of American Academy of Arts and Sciences.

Produces large-scale commission, *The Red and the Black*, for Rafael Viñoly-designed Tokyo International Forum.

Completes *Wright Curve*, a commission for the Peter B. Lewis Theater of the Sackler Center for Arts Education at The Guggenheim.

Focuses over the next few years on making single-panel shaped paintings again.

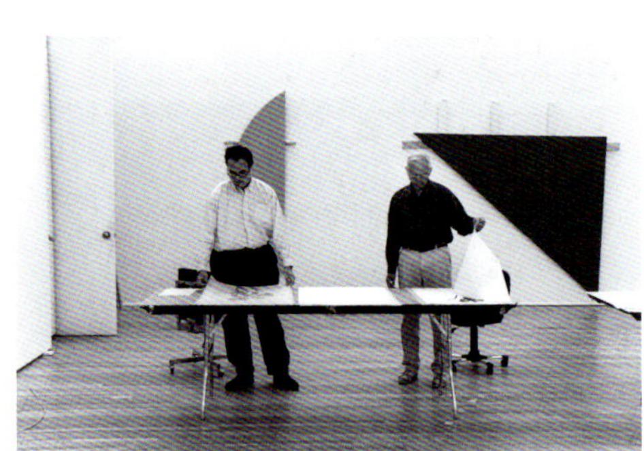

fig. 203: Ellsworth Kelly with Matthew Marks, Spencertown studio, 1991

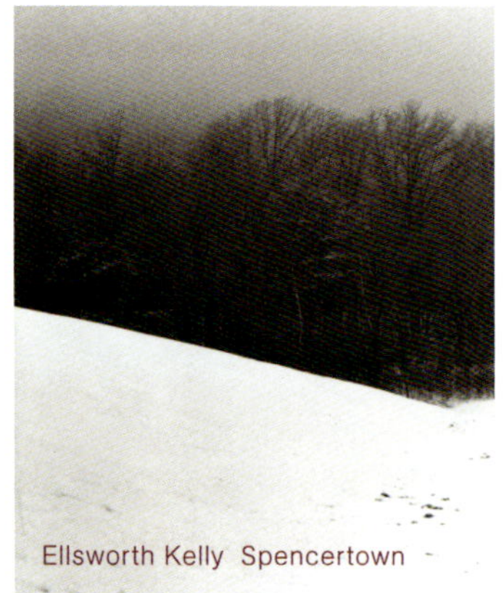

fig. 204: Catalogue for "Ellsworth Kelly, Spencertown," Anthony d'Offay, London, and Matthew Marks Gallery, New York, 1994

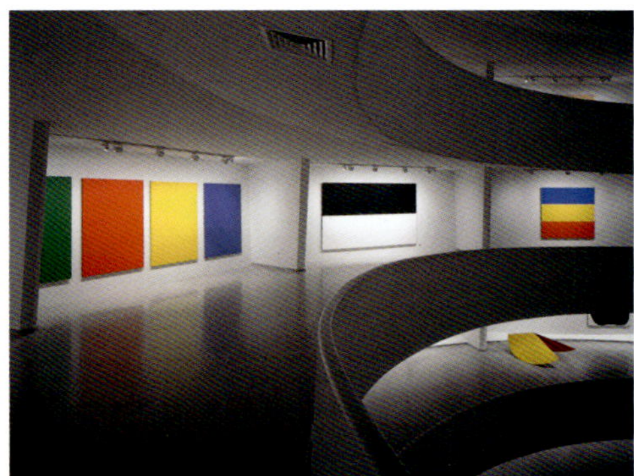

fig. 205: Installation view of "Ellsworth Kelly: A Retrospective," The Solomon R. Guggenheim Museum, New York, 1996

"Ellsworth Kelly: A Retrospective," curated by Waldman, opens at The Guggenheim (fig. 205) and travels to Museum of Contemporary Art, Los Angeles; Tate Gallery, London; and Haus der Kunst, Munich. Kelly will travel to all venues for their installations and respective openings the following year.

1997

Series of Eleven Wall Panels (1983) featured in "Colors and Forms: Ellsworth Kelly," at Indianapolis Museum of Art.

Awarded Honorary Doctorate by Royal College of Art, London.

Represented in "Drawing is Another Kind of Language: Recent American Drawings from a New York Private Collection," Arthur M. Sackler Museum, Harvard University, Cambridge, MA, which travels to national and international venues.

1998

Timed to his seventy-fifth birthday in May, "Ellsworth Kelly on the Roof" (fig. 206), curated by Nan Rosenthal, opens at the Iris and B. Gerald Cantor Roof Garden, The Metropolitan Museum, the inaugural exhibition of contemporary sculpture installations on its rooftop.

Sculpture for a Large Wall (1957) (pp. 140–41), recently removed from original site in Philadelphia, is presented for first time in New York at Matthew Marks Gallery, along with new paintings by Kelly at second Marks gallery location; subsequently, MoMA acquires *Sculpture for a Large Wall*.

Traveling exhibition "Ellsworth Kelly: Recent Prints," curated by Mary Drach McInnes and John Stomberg, opens at Boston University Art Gallery.

Commissioned by the Art in Architecture Program of the U.S. General Services Administration, creates *The Boston Panels*, for new federal courthouse in Boston, designed by Henry N. Cobb (fig. 207).

Presented with New York State Governor's Arts Award, New York State Council on the Arts, at Vivian Beaumont Theater, Lincoln Center for the Performing Arts, New York.

1999

"Ellsworth Kelly: The Early Drawings 1948–1955," the first exhibition exploring Kelly's early drawings, curated by Bois, opens at the Fogg Museum, Harvard University, Cambridge, MA, and travels to the High Museum of Art, Atlanta, and The Art Institute of Chicago. Kelly attends the installations and openings at international venues the following year: Kunstmuseum Winterthur, Switzerland, and Städtische Galerie im Lenbachhaus, Munich. The final presentation for the show is at Kunstmuseum Bonn, Germany.

MoMA displays recent Kelly acquisitions including *Meschers* (p. 65), *Sculpture for a Large Wall* (pp. 140–41), and *Three Panels: Orange, Dark Gray, Green* pp. 252–53), along with selection of drawings.

For first time, four of his "Spectrum" paintings, including *Spectrum I* (p. 87), are shown together in exhibition at Mitchell-Innes and Nash Gallery, New York.

Honored with Edward MacDowell Medal by MacDowell Colony, Peterborough, NH.

Awarded Archives of American Art Medal, Smithsonian Institution, in New York, with small exhibition of archival materials.

Featured in *Parkett* (no. 56) and produces a small lithograph, *Red Curve*, for its Special Edition series.

Installs commission, *The Chicago Panels*, a series of six painted aluminum wall sculptures, in the Rice Building, The Art Institute of Chicago.

2000

Eva Huber Walters becomes Kelly's archivist.

"Correspondences: Isamu Noguchi and Ellsworth Kelly" opens at the Phillip Morris branch of the Whitney.

White Plaque: Bridge Arch and Reflection (p. 131) is displayed in "Making Choices," the second cycle of the MoMA2000 exhibitions presented at MoMA to celebrate the millennium and co-curated by Storr.

Travels through Provence, France; visits Musée Matisse, Nice, and draws vistas of celebrated peak, Mont Sainte-Victoire.

Awarded Praemium Imperiale for Painting by Japan Arts Association and travels to Tokyo for laureate ceremony, including audience with Emperor and Empress of Japan.

Visits Tokyo International Forum and tours a selection of architectural sites and buildings designed by Tadao Ando, including those on Naoshima, Japan's "art island"; also visits Water Temple on island of Awaji and the Emperor's villa in Kyoto.

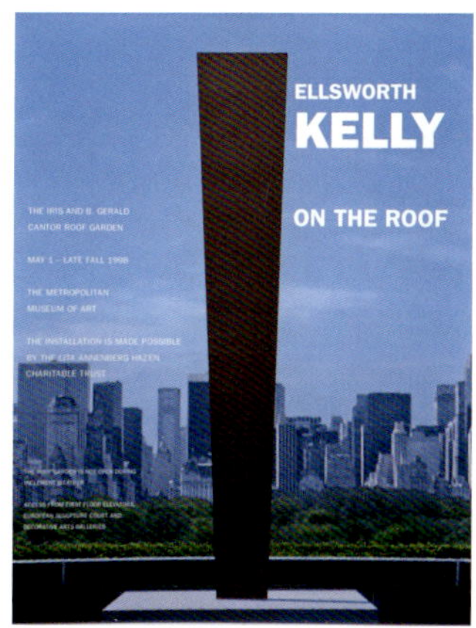

fig. 206: Poster for "Ellsworth Kelly on the Roof," The Metropolitan Museum of Art, New York, 1998

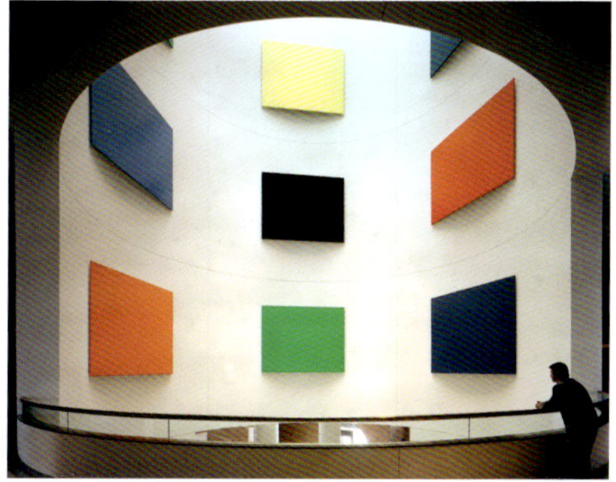

fig. 207: Ellsworth Kelly, *The Boston Panels*, 1996–98, The John J. Moakley Federal Courthouse, Boston

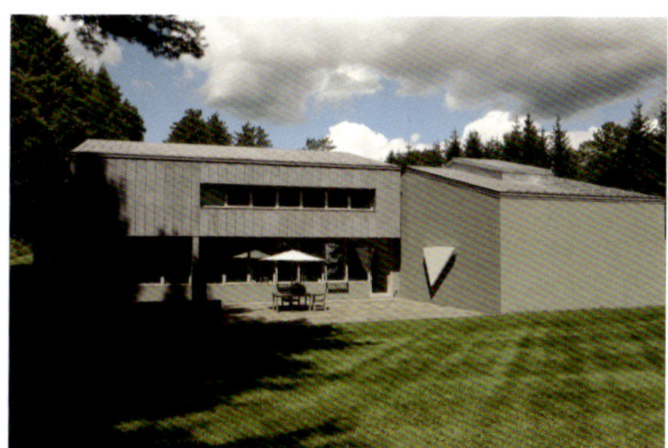

fig. 208: Ellsworth Kelly's studio in Spencertown, NY, 2012

2001

Elevated to top rank, *Commandeur de l'Ordre des Arts et des Lettres* by the French Republic.

Appointed Honorary Royal Academician by Royal Academy of Arts, London.

Commission *Blue Black* (p. 275), measuring 28 feet high, debuts at inaugural opening of Pulitzer Foundation for the Arts, St. Louis, MO, designed by Tadao Ando.

Kelly's monumental lobby commission for the new Bundestag at Paul-Löbe-Haus, the German parliament building in Berlin designed by Stephan Braunfels, is publicly presented.

Reinvestigates joined-panel painting, incorporating overlapping canvases, which will continue in rectilinear formats in relief over next few years.

Completes commission for Fondation Beyeler, Basel, Switzerland, *White Curves* (p. 271), his first outdoor sculpture with a semi-reflective surface.

MoMA acquires original maquettes for Kelly's 1951 proposed artist book, *Line, Form and Color*, and other drawings.

Begins major expansion of Spencertown studio with Richard Gluckman (fig. 208).

2002

Black Square (p. 84) is shown in "Paris: Capital of the Arts, 1900–1968," Royal Academy of Arts, London, and then The Guggenheim Museum, Bilbao.

Visits Paris for opening of "Henri Matisse/Ellsworth Kelly: Plant Drawings," curated by Éric de Chassey and Rémi Labrusse, at the Pompidou.

Participates in symposium on his art at the Pulitzer Foundation for the Arts, St. Louis, coinciding with Pulitzer exhibition, "Selected Works by Ellsworth Kelly from St. Louis Collections," and the Saint Louis Art Museum installation of the Matisse/Kelly exhibition from the Pompidou.

Visits Cahokia Mounds in Collinsville, IL, located about ten miles east of downtown St. Louis, a State Historic Site featuring the remains of ancient mound builders.

The Drawing Center, New York, hosts exhibition curated by Bois, "Ellsworth Kelly: *Tablet* 1949–1973," also to be shown at Musée Cantonal des Beaux-Arts, Lausanne, featuring selections from Kelly's *Tablet,* sheets of collaged drawings, sketches, and mini-collages that he organized during the 1970s.

"Ellsworth Kelly in San Francisco," curated by Madeleine Grynsztejn, opens at SFMOMA to celebrate the museum's significant acquisitions of Kelly's work and those in local private collections.

Travels to Basel for installation of "Ellsworth Kelly: Works 1956–2002" at Fondation Beyeler (fig. 209).

2003

The Museum of Contemporary Art San Diego presents "Ellsworth Kelly: Red Green Blue," curated by Toby Kamps, which travels to the Museum of Fine Arts, Houston, and ends at the Whitney, where Kelly's eightieth birthday is celebrated at the museum's annual gala.

Granted Honorary Doctorate of Arts by Harvard University, Cambridge, MA.

Creates collage *Ground Zero* (fig. 211), his unofficial proposal for the 9/11 memorial, and sends to architectural critic Herbert Muschamp, who publishes it in *The New York Times* on the second anniversary of 9/11; collage is subsequently exhibited at the Whitney, coinciding with exhibition "Ellsworth Kelly: Red Green Blue," and later donated to the museum.

Commissioned by Foundation for Art and Preservation in Embassies (FAPE) to create two major outdoor wall sculptures for United States Embassy in Beijing, to be designed by Craig Hartman of Skidmore, Owings & Merrill; produced by fabricators, Peter Carlson and John Baker of Carlson Arts, *Beijing Panels* (fig. 213), two painted aluminum panels in relief, are installed in 2011.

2004

The Dallas Museum of Art hosts the exhibition "Ellsworth Kelly in Dallas."

Creates his first painting using "free curves" since his New York years, *Two Curves* (p. 281), an idea to which he will return in 2009 and continue to explore.

Begins regular practice of joined-panel painting featuring a shaped canvas set in relief against a rectilinear canvas.

2005

The Menil Collection, Houston, presents "Ellsworth Kelly: *Tablet*" to celebrate recent acquisition of this body of work.

fig. 209: Catalogue for "Ellsworth Kelly: In Between," Fondation Beyeler, Basel, Switzerland, 2002

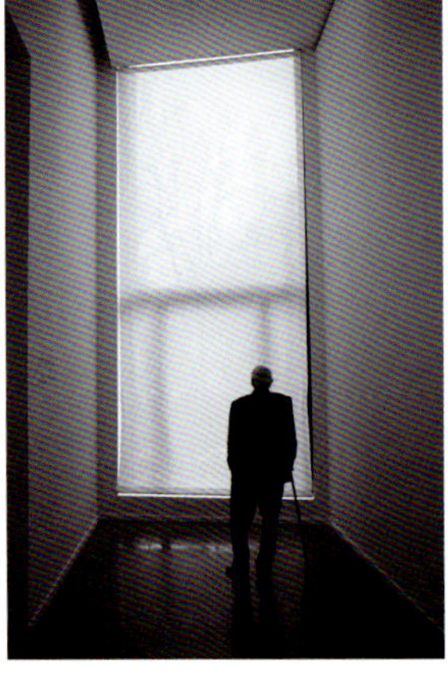

fig. 210: Ellsworth Kelly at the Palais de Tokyo (former location of Musée National d'Art Moderne), Paris, 2006

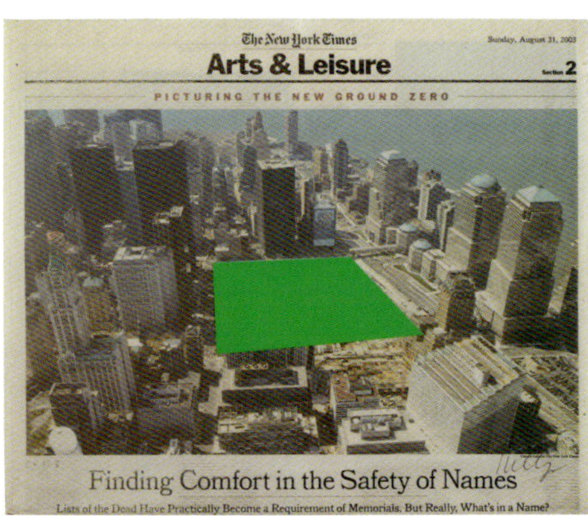

fig. 211: *Ground Zero*, 2003, newsprint collage, 8 × 12¾ in, 20.3 × 32.4 cm

Traveling exhibition, "Drawn from Nature: The Plant Lithographs of Ellsworth Kelly," curated by Axsom, originates at Grand Rapids Art Museum, MI.

Granted Honorary Doctorate of Fine Arts by Williams College, Williamstown, MA.

A documentary about Geldzahler directed by Peter Rosen, *Who Gets to Call It Art?* premieres, featuring a 1969 interview with Kelly.

Travels to London and Nice, France, and returns to Belle-Île-en-Mer, and there draws the "Pyramids" of Port-Coton and the beach at Plage Donnant.

Moves with Shear to new residence near his Spencertown home and studio.

2006

Featured in solo exhibition at Tate St Ives, Cornwall, curated by Christophe Grunenberg.

Travels to London for installation and opening of solo exhibition at Serpentine Gallery, which includes *White Relief over Black* p. 278), *Green Relief over Blue* (p. 280), *Green Orange Yellow* (p. 282), and *White Black Red* (p. 279).

"Ellsworth Kelly: Paris–New York, 1949–1959," curated by Anne d'Harnoncourt, opens at the Philadelphia Museum of Art; becomes long-term revolving installation of early paintings and reliefs, including *Toilette* (fig. 34), *Tennis Court* (p. 54), *Gate-Board* (p. 55), *Window V* (p. 57), *Saint Louis II* (fig. 74) and *Black Curves* (p. 129).

Installs commission for Grand Rapids Art Museum, MI, *Blue White*, measuring over 25 feet tall.

Painting for a White Wall (1952) (pp. 82–83) and five other works, along with a newly commissioned 45-foot stainless steel totem, are acquired and featured in the inaugural exhibition at Glenstone Foundation, Potomac, MD.

Visits Paris (fig. 210) for filming of documentary to be debuted the following year.

Presents drawings from his 1954 "Drawings on a Bus" sketchbook in solo exhibition at Matthew Marks Gallery, and publishes facsimile version of sketchbook with Matthew Marks Gallery and Steidl Publishers.

2007

In May, Checkerboard Film Foundation premieres documentary, *Ellsworth Kelly: Fragments,* directed by Edgar B. Howard and produced by Jo Carole Lauder, at Florence Gould Hall, New York.

Travels to Venice for opening of 52nd Venice Biennale (fig. 212), curated by Storr, who devotes a gallery to Kelly's work, including *Black Relief with White* (p. 289), in Italian Pavilion portion of his exhibition, "Think with the Senses—Feel with the Mind: Art in the Present Tense."

MoMA opens solo exhibition in September, "Focus: Ellsworth Kelly," including *Relief with Blue* (p. 58), *Colors for a Large Wall* (p. 69), and *Three Panels: Orange, Dark Gray, Green* (pp. 252–53).

Travels to Seattle for inauguration of Olympic Sculpture Park which features *Curve XXIV* (1981) from the Virginia and Bagley Wright Collection.

2008

"Color Chart: Reinventing Color, 1950 to Today," curated by Ann Temkin, opens at MoMA, featuring *Colors for a Large Wall* (p. 326) and travels to Tate Liverpool.

Visits Berlin to oversee installation of his second major commission in the city, *Berlin Totem*, a 40-foot tall stainless steel totem commissioned by FAPE for the United States Embassy courtyard.

Designs official award for Leonore and Walter Annenberg Award for Diplomacy through the Arts, established in 2008 by FAPE.

Honored at eighty-fifth birthday celebration jointly hosted by Kathy Fuld, Agnes Gund, Marie-Josée Kravis, and Jo Carole Lauder at the Cloisters, Fort Tryon Park, New York, a site chosen for Kelly's lifelong appreciation for medieval art.

Paired in "Correspondences: Ellsworth Kelly/ Paul Cézanne," curated by Serge Lemoine and Laurence Madeline, Musée d'Orsay, Paris.

2009

Donates *Tableau Vert* (p. 76) to The Art Institute of Chicago.

"Ellsworth Kelly: Drawings 1954–1962," featuring works on paper made during his early New York period, opens at Matthew Marks Gallery in February, with accompanying study by Richard Shiff, published in 2014.

Included in "Cézanne and Beyond," the Philadelphia Museum of Art, with selection of works such as *Meschers* (p. 65), *Train Landscape* (p. 77), *Untitled* (p. 254), and *Lake II* (p. 283).

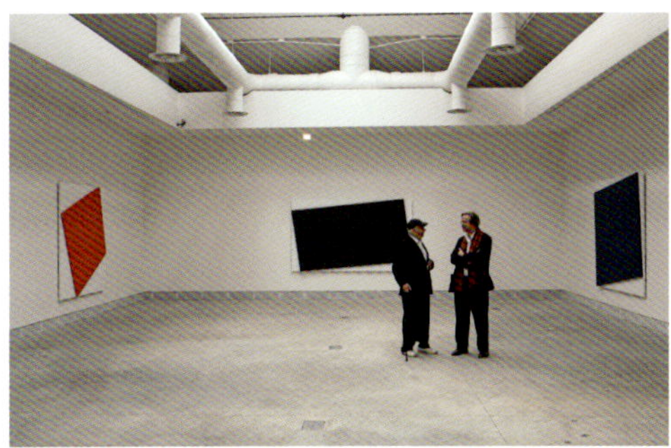

fig. 212: Ellsworth Kelly with Robert Storr, 52nd Venice Biennale, 2007

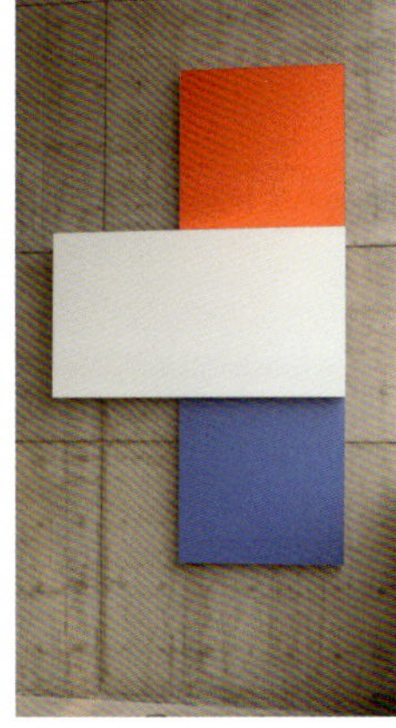

fig. 213: *Beijing Panels* (view of south side), 2011

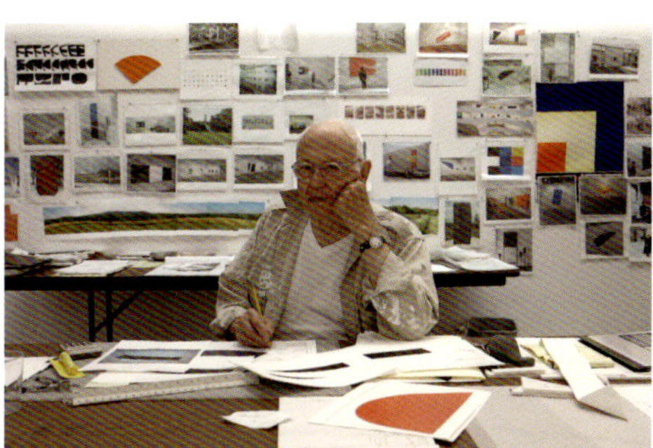

fig. 214: Ellsworth Kelly, Spencertown, NY, 2012

Stele I (p. 233) displayed at inaugural opening of Rooftop Garden at SFMOMA.

The Modern Wing addition designed by Renzo Piano for The Art Institute of Chicago opens, featuring Kelly's second commission for the museum, a work for an outdoor courtyard, *White Curve*, which spans 54 feet.

Advanced to rank of *Officier de la Legion d'Honneur* by the French Republic.

Joseph Yetto becomes Kelly's studio assistant.

2010

Granted Honorary Doctorate of Fine Arts by School of The Art Institute of Chicago.

Attends opening of exhibition curated by Éric de Chassey, "Jean-Auguste-Dominique Ingres/Ellsworth Kelly," at the French Academy in Rome, Villa Medici.

Travels to Madrid visiting the Prado, the Reina Sofia, and the exhibition "Monet y Abstraction" at Museo Thyssen-Bornemisza, which includes *Tableau Vert* (p. 76).

A 1957 portrait drawing of dealer David Herbert (who introduced Kelly's art to Betty Parsons in 1955) is included in "Hide/ Seek: Difference and Desire in American Portraiture," National Portrait Gallery, Smithsonian Institution, Washington, DC, and Brooklyn Museum, New York.

Donates *Red Yellow Blue White* (pp. 74–75) to the Philadelphia Museum of Art, in memory of Anne d'Harnoncourt.

Represented in "On Line: Drawing through the 20th Century," curated by Cornelia H. Butler and Catherine de Zegher, at MoMA, with *Gate-Board* (p. 55) and selection of his drawings.

2011

Ground Zero (2003) (fig. 211) is featured in "September 11," curated by Peter Eleey, MoMA PS1, Long Island City, Queens, NY.

"Ellsworth Kelly: Wood Sculpture," curated by Edward Saywell, opens at the Museum of Fine Arts, Boston.

"Ellsworth Kelly: Plant Drawings" (fig. 216) features the artist's own selection of 100 works and is curated by Michael Semff, Poul Erik Tøjner, and Marla Prather, respectively at Staatliche Graphische Sammlung, Pinakothek der Moderne, Munich; Louisiana Museum of Modern Art, Humlebæk, Denmark, and The Metropolitan Museum of Art, New York.

Haus der Kunst, Munich, presents "Ellsworth Kelly: Black and White," curated by Ulrich Wilmes, which travels to Museum Wiesbaden, where Kelly is awarded the Jawlensky Prize.

Kelly produces *Green Panel (Ground Zero)* (p. 296), a painted aluminum wall sculpture; presented to the Whitney for their new building designed by Renzo Piano.

2012

Presented in solo exhibition in January to inaugurate Matthew Marks Gallery, Los Angeles; exterior of new gallery, designed by Peter Zellner, debuts Kelly wall sculpture that transforms entire façade into large-scale work reminiscent of his 1966 joined-panel painting, *Black over White* (p. 176).

Second edition of *The Prints of Ellsworth Kelly: A Catalogue Raisonné,* by Axsom is published, a two-volume expansion of original 1987 publication.

"Ellsworth Kelly: Prints and Paintings," curated by Stephanie Barron at Los Angeles County Museum of Art, includes *Blue over Blue* (p. 167) and *Blue Curve III* (pp. 230–31).

Kelly print retrospective drawn from the Jordan Schnitzer Collection is held at Portland Art Museum, OR; another exhibition devoted to Kelly prints, curated by Axsom, will take place the following year at Madison Museum of Contemporary Art, WI.

"Ellsworth Kelly Sculpture," curated by Isabelle Derveaux at Morgan Library & Museum, New York, features three monumental totems including *Untitled*, (p. 268) and scale models of four works (pp. 276–77, p. 287, p. 304 and fig. 140).

Barnes Totem (p.304) debuts at opening of the new Barnes Foundation, Philadelphia, designed by Tod Williams and Billie Tsien.

Commission unveiled for the new Black Family Visual Arts Center, Dartmouth College, Hanover, NH, comprising five painted aluminum panels each measuring 22½ feet high (p. 298) and installed on rear façade of the 1962 Hopkins Center designed by Wallace Harrison.

Cahiers d'Art, Paris, exhibits small selection of Kelly works, plus an assortment of ancient Native American artifacts (birdstones and bannerstones) from his personal collection, to coincide with the re-launch of journal *Cahiers d'Art,* featuring image of *Black Form I* (p. 299) on cover, essay by Bois, and statement by artist.

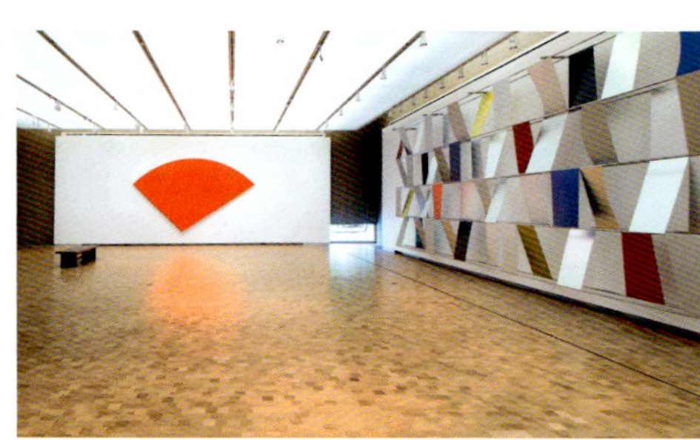

fig. 215: Installation view of "Ellsworth Kelly: Sculpture on the Wall," The Barnes Foundation, Philadelphia, 2013

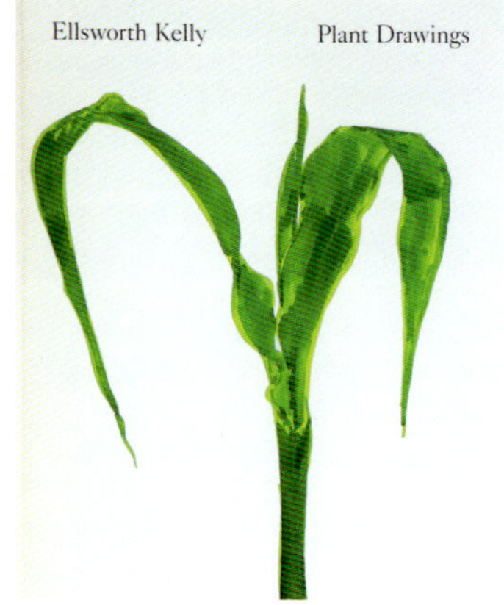

fig. 216: Catalogue for "Ellsworth Kelly Plant Drawings," 2011

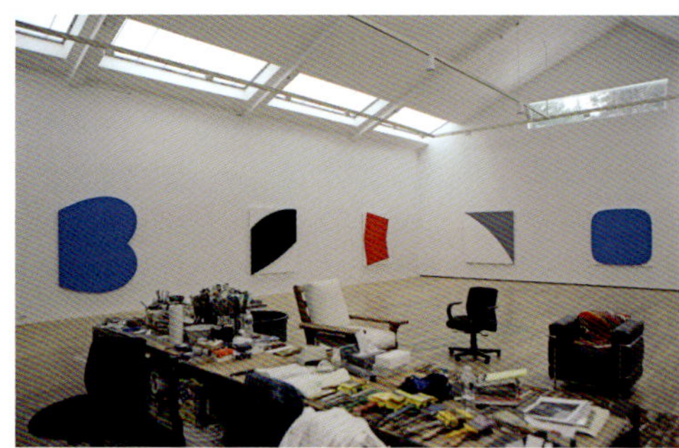

fig. 217: Spencertown studio, 2013

Collaborates with Francisco Costa, women's creative director at Calvin Klein, to create limited edition of the dress Kelly designed in 1952; the new dress will be unveiled the following year at the Calvin Klein flagship store on Madison Avenue, New York, timed to coincide with the artist's ninetieth birthday (fig. 152).

2013

Receives the Distinguished Artist Award for Lifetime Achievement from the College Art Association (CAA).

Mnuchin Gallery, New York, presents in April "Ellsworth Kelly: Singular Forms, 1966–2009," with catalogue essay by Pepe Karmel.

Kelly turns ninety on May 31. Throughout the year, American and European museums host exhibitions and installations in his honor: Pompidou, Paris; SFMOMA; Philadelphia Museum of Art; The Art Institute of Chicago; Tate Modern, London; The Barnes Foundation, Philadelphia ("Ellsworth Kelly: Sculpture on the Wall" (fig. 216), curated by Judith F. Dolkart); MoMA, New York ("Ellsworth Kelly: Chatham Series" (fig. 219), curated by Ann Temkin); Detroit Institute of Arts, and Phillips Collection, Washington, DC. ("Ellsworth Kelly: Panel Paintings, 2004–2009").

Matthew Marks Gallery, Kelly's dealer for over twenty years, mounts the artist's eighteenth solo exhibition at the gallery in May, "Ellsworth Kelly at Ninety," featuring works made in 2012, with catalogue essays by Jean-Pierre Criqui, Robert Storr, Christopher Bedford, and Tricia Y. Paik.

Awarded Honorary Doctorate in Fine Arts by Brandeis University, Waltham, MA.

MoMA's annual Party in the Garden honors Kelly, as well as Cindy Sherman, Mayor Michael R. Bloomberg and the city of New York, in recognition of their support of the museum.

To mark his special birthday, the Ellsworth Kelly Foundation makes donations to public school districts of Columbia County where he lives, in order to continue building permanent endowments for school arts programs.

Attends National Medal of Arts and National Humanities Medal ceremony at White House, Washington, DC, where President Barack Obama awards Kelly with 2012 medal (fig. 218).

2014

Curates exhibition of Matisse drawings selected from the Pierre and Tana Matisse Foundation Collection, accompanied by a small installation of Kelly's plant lithographs, Mount Holyoke College Art Museum, South Hadley, MA.

Honored with Hadrian Award by World Monuments Fund in recognition of his significant contributions to cultural heritage, through donation of his works to FAPE and support of various World Monuments Fund projects around the world.

Fondation Louis Vuitton, Paris, designed by Frank Gehry, opens to public, featuring *Color Panels (Red Yellow Blue Green Purple)* (pp. 320–21) a work of five painted wall panels, and a curtain *Spectrum VIII* (fig. 220), special commissions for its performance space.

Serves as curator for "Monet/Kelly," an exhibition he also conceives and designs, which opens at the new Tadao Ando-designed wing at the Sterling and Francine Clark Art Institute, Williamstown, MA.

2015

Commissioned by the Blanton Museum of Art, the University of Texas at Austin, to realize his chapel design from 1986 as a non-denominational building made of stone and measuring 2,715 square feet. Titled *Austin*, it will function as a space for both spiritual contemplation and appreciation of art: three bays of colored glass windows, a redwood totem, and a series of fourteen black-and-white panels made of marble, all designed by Kelly (figs 147, 148, 164).

Awarded the James Smithson Bicentennial Medal in honor of lifetime achievement in art at Cooper Hewitt, Smithsonian Design Museum, New York.

In May, on occasion of his ninety-second birthday, solo exhibition of new works opens at Matthew Marks Gallery, with catalogue essay by Briony Fer.

First volume of *Ellsworth Kelly: Catalogue Raisonné of Paintings, Reliefs and Sculptures, 1940–1953,* authored by Bois, is published by Cahiers d'Art, Paris.

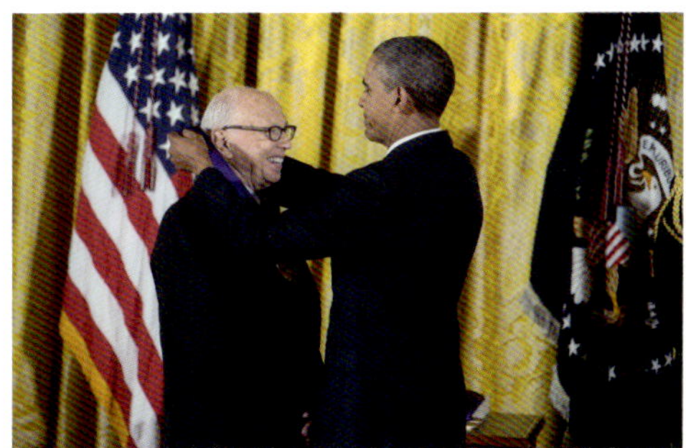

fig. 218: Ellsworth Kelly receiving National Medal of Arts from President Barack Obama, 2013

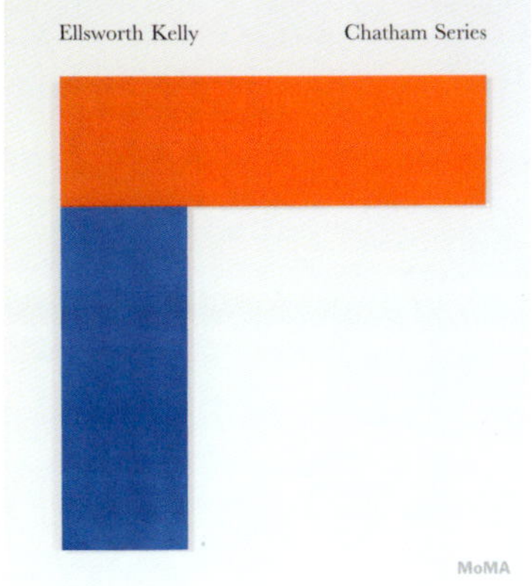

fig. 219: Catalogue for "Ellsworth Kelly Chatham Series," The Museum of Modern Art, New York, 2013

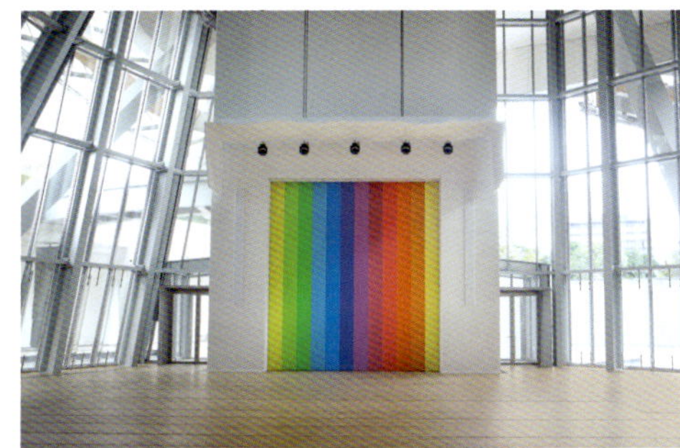

fig. 220: *Spectrum VIII*, 2014, commissioned for Fondation Louis Vuitton, Paris

Selected Bibliography

Solo Exhibition Catalogues

"Ellsworth Kelly." *Derrière le Miroir* [Galerie Maeght, Paris], no. 110 (October 1958). With essay by E.C. Goossen.

Ellsworth Kelly. London: Arthur Tooth & Sons Ltd., 1962. With introduction by Lawrence Alloway.

Paintings, Sculpture and Drawings by Ellsworth Kelly. Washington, DC: Washington Gallery of Modern Art; Boston: Institute of Contemporary Art, 1963. With foreword by Adelyn D. Breeskin and interview with the artist by Henry Geldzahler.

"Ellsworth Kelly." *Derrière le Miroir* [Galerie Maeght, Paris], no. 149 (November 1964). With essay by Dale McConathy.

Ellsworth Kelly: 27 Lithographies. Paris: Galerie Adrien Maeght, 1965. With text by Dale McConathy.

An Exhibition of Recent Paintings by Ellsworth Kelly. New York: Sidney Janis Gallery, 1965.

An Exhibition of New Work by Ellsworth Kelly. New York: Sidney Janis Gallery, 1967.

An Exhibition of Paintings and Sculpture by Ellsworth Kelly. New York: Sidney Janis Gallery, 1968.

Ellsworth Kelly. Los Angeles: Gemini G.E.L., 1970. With text by John Coplans.

Ellsworth Kelly. Minneapolis: Dayton's Gallery 12, 1971.

Recent Paintings by Ellsworth Kelly. New York: Sidney Janis Gallery, 1971.

Goossen, E.C. *Ellsworth Kelly.* New York: The Museum of Modern Art, 1973.

Ellsworth Kelly: Matrix 1. Wadsworth: Wadsworth Atheneum, 1975. Brochure.

Baker, Elizabeth C. *Ellsworth Kelly: Recent Paintings and Sculptures.* New York: The Metropolitan Museum of Art, 1979.

Ellsworth Kelly: Paintings and Sculptures 1963–1979. Amsterdam: Stedelijk Museum, 1979. With essay by Barbara Rose and statement by the artist.

Ellsworth Kelly. New York: Leo Castelli Gallery and BlumHelman Gallery, 1981.

Ellsworth Kelly at Gemini 1979–1982. Los Angeles: Gemini G.E.L., 1982. With text by Carter Ratcliff.

Sims, Patterson, and Emily Rauh Pulitzer. *Ellsworth Kelly: Sculpture.* New York: Whitney Museum of American Art, 1982. With essay, catalogue entries, and chronology.

Ellsworth Kelly: Painted Aluminum Wall Sculpture/ Weathering Steel Wall Sculpture. Los Angeles: Margo Leavin Gallery; New York: Leo Castelli Gallery, 1984. With statement by the artist.

Ellsworth Kelly: Works in Wood. New York: BlumHelman Gallery, 1984.

Ellsworth Kelly at Gemini 1983–1985. Los Angeles: Gemini G.E.L., 1985. With text by Christopher Knight.

Ellsworth Kelly: Paintings and Sculptures, 1986. New York: BlumHelman Gallery, 1986.

Upright, Diane. *Ellsworth Kelly: Works on Paper.* New York: Harry N. Abrams, Inc., in association with The Fort Worth Art Museum, 1987. With introduction by Henry Geldzahler, essay, and chronology.

Fairbrother, Trevor J. *Ellsworth Kelly: Seven Paintings (1952–55/1987).* Boston: Museum of Fine Arts, 1987.

Ellsworth Kelly: Small Sculpture 1958–87. Cambridge, MA: List Visual Arts Center, MIT, 1987. With texts by Katy Kline.

Ellsworth Kelly: New Work. New York: BlumHelman Gallery, 1988. With essay by Robert Storr.

Ellsworth Kelly: Curves/Rectangles. New York: BlumHelman Gallery, 1989. With essay by Barbara Rose.

Portraits at Gemini G.E.L. Los Angeles: Gemini G.E.L., 1990. With essay by Richard H. Axsom.

Ellsworth Kelly: Prints 1949–1989. New York: Susan Sheehan Gallery, 1990. With text by Sheehan.

Ellsworth Kelly: At Right Angles 1964–1966. Los Angeles: Margo Leavin Gallery; San Francisco: John Berggruen Gallery; New York: Paula Cooper Gallery, 1991. With essay by Roberta Bernstein.

Ellsworth Kelly: Yellow Curve. Frankfurt am Main: Portikus and Edition Cantz, 1992. With foreword by Kasper König and essay by Gottfried Boehm.

Bois, Yve-Alain, Jack Cowart, and Alfred Pacquement. *Ellsworth Kelly: The Years in France 1948–1954.* Washington, DC: National Gallery of Art, 1992. With essays by Bois, Cowart, Pacquement, and chronology by Nathalie Brunet.

Ellsworth Kelly: The Paris Prints 1964–1965. New York: Susan Sheehan Gallery, 1992. With essay by Henry Geldzahler and reprint of his 1963 interview with the artist.

Ellsworth Kelly: Plant Drawings. New York: Matthew Marks Gallery, 1992. With essay by John Ashbery.

Ellsworth Kelly. New York: BlumHelman Gallery, 1992. With essay by Klaus Kertess.

Spencertown: Recent Paintings by Ellsworth Kelly. London: Anthony d'Offay Gallery; New York: Matthew Marks Gallery, 1994. With essay by Yve-Alain Bois and photographic essay by Jack Shear.

Ellsworth Kelly: The Process of Seeing. Minneapolis: Walker Art Center, 1994. Brochure. With foreword by Siri Engberg.

Ellsworth Kelly: Colored Paper Images, 1976–77: The Creative Process. New York: Susan Sheehan Gallery, 1995. With introduction by David Kiehl.

Waldman, Diane, ed. *Ellsworth Kelly: A Retrospective.* New York: The Solomon R. Guggenheim Foundation, 1996. With essays by Waldman, Clare Bell, Roberta Bernstein, Carter Ratcliff, Mark Rosenthal, and chronology.

Ellsworth Kelly on the Roof. New York: The Metropolitan Museum of Art, 1998. Brochure. With text by Nan Rosenthal.

Ellsworth Kelly: New Paintings. New York: Matthew Marks Gallery, 1998. With essay by Dave Hickey.

Ellsworth Kelly: Sculpture for a Large Wall, 1957. New York: Matthew Marks Gallery, 1998. With essay by James Meyer.

McInnes, Mary Drach. *Ellsworth Kelly: Recent Prints*. Boston: Boston University Art Gallery; Seattle and London: University of Washington Press, 1998. With essays by McInnes, Richard H. Axsom, and Stuart Steck.

Bois, Yve-Alain. *Ellsworth Kelly: The Early Drawings 1948–1955.* Cambridge, MA: Harvard University Art Museums, 1999. With essay and chronology.

Kelly, Ellsworth. *Line Form Color 1951*. Cambridge, MA: Harvard University Art Museums, 1999. In conjunction with "Ellsworth Kelly: The Early Drawings 1948–1955" (1999). With essay by Harry Cooper.

Ellsworth Kelly: Drawings 1960–1962. New York: Matthew Marks Gallery, 1999. With essay by Linda Nochlin.

Ellsworth Kelly: Spectrums 1953–1972. New York: Mitchell-Innes & Nash, 1999. With essay by David Batchelor.

Ellsworth Kelly: Relief Paintings 1954–2001. New York: Matthew Marks Gallery, 2001. With essay by Sarah K. Rich.

Bois, Yve-Alain. *Ellsworth Kelly: Tablet 1948–1973.* New York: The Drawing Center; Lausanne: Musée Cantonal des Beaux-Arts, 2002.

Grynsztejn, Madeleine, and Julian Myers. *Ellsworth Kelly in San Francisco.* San Francisco: San Francisco Museum of Modern Art, 2002. With foreword by Neal Benezra, essay by Grynsztejn, and texts by Myers.

Ellsworth Kelly: In-Between Spaces. Works 1956–2002. Basel: Fondation Beyeler, 2002. With essays by Gottfried Boehm and Viola Weigel, statement by the artist, and chronology.

Ellsworth Kelly: Red Green Blue. Paintings and Studies 1958–1965. San Diego: Museum of Contemporary Art San Diego, 2002. With essays by Toby Kamps, Roberta Bernstein, Dave Hickey, and Sarah K. Rich.

Ellsworth Kelly: Matrix. New York: Matthew Marks Gallery, 2003. With essay by Benjamin H.D. Buchloh.

Ellsworth Kelly: Self-Portrait Drawings 1944–1992. New York: Matthew Marks Gallery, 2003. With essay by Harry Cooper.

Wylie, Charles. *Ellsworth Kelly in Dallas.* Dallas: Dallas Museum of Art; New Haven and London: Yale University Press, 2004. With essay by Wylie and texts by Yve-Alain Bois, Robert Storr and Wood Roberdeau.

Ellsworth Kelly: Tablet. Houston: The Menil Collection, 2005. Brochure. With text by Susan Braeuer.

Axsom, Richard H. *Drawn from Nature: The Plant Lithographs of Ellsworth Kelly.* New Haven, CT: Yale University Press; Grand Rapids Art Museum, 2005.

Ellsworth Kelly. London: Serpentine Gallery, 2006. With essays by Sarah Whitfield and Rochelle Steiner.

Ellsworth Kelly. London: Tate St. Ives in association with Tate Publishing, 2007. With introduction by Susan Daniel-McElroy and essay by Christoph Grunenberg.

Ellsworth Kelly: The Rivers. New York: Gemini G.E.L. at Joni Moisant Weyl, 2007. Brochure. With essay by Dave Hickey.

Ellsworth Kelly: Drawings on a Bus—Sketchbook 23, 1954. Göttingen: Steidl; New York: Matthew Marks Gallery, 2007.

Ellsworth Kelly: Diagonal. New York: Matthew Marks Gallery, 2009. With essay by Johanna Burton.

Ellsworth Kelly: Reliefs 2009–2010. New York: Matthew Marks Gallery, 2011. With essay by Robert Storr and photographs of the artist by Jack Shear.

Ellsworth Kelly: Wood Sculpture. Boston: Museum of Fine Arts, Boston, 2011. With essay by Brenda Richardson.

Prather, Marla and Michael Semff, eds. *Ellsworth Kelly: Plant Drawings.* Munich: Schirmer/Mosel, 2011. With essay by Semff and interview with the artist by Prather.

Wilmes, Ulrich, ed. *Ellsworth Kelly: Black & White*. Munich: Haus der Kunst; Ostfildern: Hatje Cantz, 2011. With essays by Wilmes, Jörg Daur, Carter E. Foster, and Alexander Klar.

Ellsworth Kelly: Los Angeles. Los Angeles: Matthew Marks Gallery, 2012. With essay by Michael Duncan.

Ellsworth Kelly: Prints and Paintings. Los Angeles: Los Angeles Museum of Art, 2012. Brochure. With text by Richard H. Axsom.

"Ellsworth Kelly." *Cahiers d'Art*, no. 1 (October 2012): 3–71 (cover). In conjunction with journal relaunch. With texts by Yve-Alain Bois, Ann Hindry, Richard F. Townsend, conversation with the artist by Hans Ulrich Obrist, and statement by the artist.

Ellsworth Kelly: Singular Forms, 1966–2009. New York: Mnuchin Gallery, 2013. With essay by Pepe Karmel.

Ellsworth Kelly at Ninety. New York: Matthew Marks Gallery, 2013. With essays by Jean-Pierre Criqui, Robert Storr, Christopher Bedford, and Tricia Y. Paik.

Dolkart, Judith F. *Ellsworth Kelly: Sculpture on the Wall*. Philadelphia: The Barnes Foundation, 2013.

Temkin, Ann. *Ellsworth Kelly: Chatham Series.* New York: The Museum of Modern Art, 2013.

Sretenović, Vesela. *Ellsworth Kelly: Panel Paintings 2004–2009.* Washington, DC: The Phillips Collection, 2013.

Ellsworth Kelly. Paris: Fondation Louis Vuitton/ Manuella Éditions, 2014. With introduction by Suzanne Pagé, conversation with the artist by Robert Storr, essay by Ann Hindry, biographical note by Francesca Pietropaolo.

Ellsworth Kelly: Outside In. New York: Matthew Marks Gallery, 2015. With essay by Briony Fer.

Group Exhibition Catalogues

Premier Salon des jeunes peintres. Paris: Galeries des Beaux-Arts, 1950.

Réalités Nouvelles 5ème Salon. Paris: Palais des Beaux-Arts de la Ville de Paris, 1950.

Réalités Nouvelles 6ème Salon. Paris: Palais des Beaux-Arts de la Ville de Paris, 1951.

"*Tendance.*" *Derrière le Miroir* [Galerie Maeght, Paris], no. 41 (October 1951). With text by Charles Estienne.

"*Tendance.*" *Derrière le Miroir* [Galerie Maeght, Paris], no. 50 (October 1952). With text by Michel Seuphor.

"Recent Drawings U.S.A." In *The Museum of Modern Art Bulletin* 23, no. 4 (1956): 1–32. With foreword by William S. Lieberman.

Young America 1957: Thirty American Painters and Sculptors under Thirty-Five. New York: Whitney Museum of American Art, 1957. With foreword by Lloyd Goodrich.

"Seventeen Contemporary American Painters." In *American Art: Four Exhibitions*, 54–77. Brussels: Universal and International Exhibition, 1958. With text by Grace L. McCann Morley.

The 1958 Pittsburgh Bicentennial International Exhibition of Contemporary Painting and Sculpture. Pittsburgh: Department of Fine Arts, Carnegie Institute, 1958. With introduction by Gordon Bailey Washburn.

1959 Annual Exhibition of Contemporary American Painting. New York: Whitney Museum of American Art, 1959.

Miller, Dorothy C., ed. *Sixteen Americans.* New York: The Museum of Modern Art, 1959. With foreword by Miller and statements by artists [none by Kelly] and others.

Modern Classicism. New York: David Herbert Gallery, 1960. With text by Barbara Butler and reprinted texts by various authors.

Annual Exhibition 1960: Contemporary Sculpture and Drawings. New York: Whitney Museum of American Art, 1960.

American Abstract Painters. London: Arthur Tooth & Sons, Ltd., 1961. With introduction by Lawrence Alloway.

VI Bienal do Museu de Arte Moderna, São Paulo, 1961: Estado Unidos. The Museum of Modern Art, 1961. With foreword by René d'Harnoncourt and texts by Frank O'Hara, Thomas B. Hess, William C. Seitz.

American Abstract Expressionists and Imagists. New York: The Solomon R. Guggenheim Foundation, 1961. With foreword and introduction by H.H. Arnason.

The 1961 Pittsburgh International Exhibition of Contemporary Painting and Sculpture. Pittsburgh: Department of Fine Arts, Carnegie Institute, 1961. With introduction by Gordon Bailey Washburn.

Annual Exhibition 1961: Contemporary American Painting. New York: Whitney Museum of American Art, 1961.

65th American Exhibition: Some Directions in Contemporary Painting and Sculpture. Chicago: The Art Institute of Chicago, 1962. With foreword by A. James Speyer.

Geometric Abstraction in America. New York: Whitney Museum of Art, 1962. With text by John Gordon.

"Art since 1950: American and International." In Norman Davis, *Fine Arts Exhibition: Seattle World's Fair,* 1–63. Seattle, 1962. With foreword by Davis and introduction by Sam Hunter.

Nordness, Lee, ed. *Art: USA: Now.* Lucerne, Switzerland: C. J. Bucher, Ltd., 1962. With introduction by Nordness and text by Allen S. Weller.

Annual Exhibition 1962: Contemporary Sculpture and Drawings. New York: Whitney Museum of American Art, 1962.

Twenty-Eighth Biennial Exhibition of Contemporary American Painting. Washington, DC: The Corcoran Gallery of Art, 1963. With text by Hermann Warner Williams, Jr.

Toward a New Abstraction. New York: The Jewish Museum, 1963. With preface by Alan R. Solomon, introduction by Ben Heller, and texts by authors including Dore Ashton, Michael Fried, Henry Geldzahler, Robert Rosenblum, Irving Sandler, and Leo Steinberg.

Annual Exhibition 1963: Contemporary American Painting. New York: Whitney Museum of American Art, 1963.

Post Painterly Abstraction. Los Angeles: Los Angeles County Museum of Art, 1964. With preface by James Elliott and essay by Clement Greenberg.

Documenta III: Malerei/Skulptur. Cologne: DuMont Schauberg, 1964. With foreword by Karl Branner and texts by Arnold Bode and Werner Haftmann.

American Drawings. New York: The Solomon R. Guggenheim Foundation, 1964. With foreword by Thomas M. Messer and introduction by Lawrence Alloway.

The 1964 Pittsburgh International Exhibition: Contemporary Painting and Sculpture. Pittsburgh: Museum of Art, Carnegie Institute, 1964. With foreword by Gustave von Groschwitz.

Annual Exhibition 1964: Contemporary American Sculpture. New York: Whitney Museum of American Art, 1964.

Seitz, William C. *The Responsive Eye*. New York: The Museum of Modern Art, 1965.

1965 Annual Exhibition: Contemporary American Painting. New York: Whitney Museum of American Art, 1965.

Primary Structures: Younger American and British Sculptors. New York: The Jewish Museum, 1966. With introduction by Kynaston McShine.

XXXIII International Biennial Exhibition of Art Venice 1966 United States. Washington, DC: National Collection of Fine Arts, Smithsonian Institution, 1966. With introduction by Henry Geldzahler and texts by Geldzahler, Clement Greenberg, Robert Rosenblum, and William Rubin.

Systemic Painting. New York: The Solomon R. Guggenheim Foundation, 1966. With introduction by Lawrence Alloway.

Two Decades of American Painting. New York: The Museum of Modern Art, 1966. With preface by Waldo Rasmussen and texts by Lucy R. Lippard, Irving Sandler, and G. R. Swenson.

Annual Exhibition 1966: Contemporary Sculpture and Prints. New York: Whitney Museum of American Art, 1966.

Tuchman, Maurice, ed. *American Sculpture of the Sixties.* Los Angeles: Los Angeles County Museum of Art, 1967. With introduction by Tuchman and essays by Lawrence Alloway, Wayne V. Andersen, Dore Ashton, John Coplans, Clement Greenberg, Max Kozloff, Lucy R. Lippard, James Monte, Barbara Rose, Irving Sandler, and statements by artists [Kelly's statement is excerpted from 1963 published interview with Henry Geldzahler].

American Painting Now [Expo 67, United States Pavilion, Montreal]. Boston: Institute of Contemporary Art, 1967. With essay by Alan Solomon.

Dix Ans d'Art Vivant 1955–1965. Saint-Paul (Alpes-Maritimes): Fondation Maeght, 1967. With preface by François Wehrlin.

Guggenheim International Exhibition 1967: Sculpture from Twenty Nations. New York: The Solomon R. Guggenheim Museum, 1967. With introduction by Edward F. Fry.

1967 Pittsburgh International Exhibition of Contemporary Painting and Sculpture. Pittsburgh: Museum of Art, Carnegie Institute, 1967. With foreword by Gustave von Groschwitz.

1967 Annual Exhibition of Contemporary Painting. New York: Whitney Museum of American Art, 1967.

Cool Art–1967. Ridgefield, CT: The Aldrich Museum of Contemporary Art, 1968. With text by Larry Aldrich.

4. Documenta. Kassel: Druck + Verlag, 1968. With foreword by Karl Branner and texts by Arnold Bode, Max Imdahl, and Jean Leering.

Goossen, E.C. *The Art of the Real: USA 1948–1968.* New York: The Museum of Modern Art, 1968.

Coplans, John. *Serial Imagery.* Pasadena: Pasadena Art Museum and the New York Graphic Society Ltd., 1968.

Geldzahler, Henry. *New York Painting and Sculpture 1940–1970.* New York: The Metropolitan Museum of Art, 1969. With foreword by Thomas P.F. Hoving, essay by Geldzahler and reprinted articles by Michael Fried, Clement Greenberg, Harold Rosenberg, Robert Rosenblum, and William Rubin.

1969 Annual Exhibition: Contemporary American Painting. New York: Whitney Museum of American Art, 1969. With foreword by John I.H. Baur.

Ellsworth Kelly, Morris Louis, Kenneth Noland, Frank Stella. Chicago: The Museum of Contemporary Art, in cooperation with Dayton's Gallery 12, Minneapolis, 1970. Brochure.

Tucker, Marcia. *The Structure of Color.* New York: Whitney Museum of American Art, 1971.

Grids. Philadelphia: Institute of Contemporary Art, University of Pennsylvania, 1972. With text by Lucy R. Lippard.

1973 Biennial Exhibition: Contemporary American Art. New York: Whitney Museum of American Art, 1973. Foreword by John I.H. Baur.

Nine Artists/Coenties Slip. New York: Whitney Museum of American Art, 1974. Brochure.

Twentieth-Century American Drawings: Three Avant-Garde Generations. New York: The Solomon R. Guggenheim Foundation, 1976. With preface by Thomas M. Messer and essay by Diane Waldman.

Rose, Bernice. *Drawing Now*. New York: The Museum of Modern Art, 1976.

Paris—New York. Paris: Centre national d'art et de culture Georges Pompidou, Paris, 1977. With texts by authors including Daniel Abadie, Leo Castelli, Hubert Damisch, Pontus Hulten, Charles Lévi-Strauss, Robert Motherwell, Alfred Pacquement, Harold Rosenberg, Hélène Seckel, Ileana Sonnabend, and chronology.

Documenta 6: Handzeichungen/Utopisches Design/ Bücher. Vol. 3. Kassel: P. Dierichs, 1977. With essay by Wieland Schmied.

Grids: Format and Image in 20th Century Art. New York: The Pace Gallery; Akron: The Akron Art Institute, 1978. With essay by Rosalind Krauss.

1979 Biennial Exhibition. New York: Whitney Museum of American Art, 1979. Preface by Tom Armstrong.

The 36th Biennial Exhibition of Contemporary American Painting. Washington, DC: The Corcoran Gallery of Art, 1979. With text by Jane Livingston.

Americans in Paris: The 50s. Northridge, California: Fine Arts Gallery, California State University, 1979. With introduction by Merle Schipper.

The Fifties: Aspects of Painting in New York. Washington, DC: Hirshhorn Museum and Sculpture Garden, Smithsonian Institution, 1980. With essay by Phyllis Rosenzweig.

1981 Biennial Exhibition. New York: Whitney Museum of American Art, 1981. With foreword by Tom Armstrong.

Paris–Paris/Créations en France 1937–1957. Paris: Musée National d'Art Moderne, Centre Georges Pompidou, Paris, 1981. With preface by Pontus Hulten and essays by various authors.

Komanecky, Michael, and Virginia Fabbri Butera. *The Folding Image: Screens by Western Artists of the Nineteenth and Twentieth Centuries.* New Haven: Yale University Art Gallery; Washington, DC: National Gallery of Art, 1984.

A Second Talent: Painters and Sculptors Who Are Also Photographers. Ridgefield, CT: The Aldrich Museum of Contemporary Art, 1985. With text by Robert Metzger.

Dabrowski, Magdalena. *Contrasts of Form: Geometric Abstract Art 1910–1980.* New York: The Museum of Modern Art, 1985. With introduction by John Elderfield and texts by Dabrowski.

1985 Carnegie International. Pittsburgh: Museum of Art, Carnegie Institute, 1985. With introduction by John R. Lane and John Caldwell, and texts by authors including Benjamin H.D. Buchloh, Germano Celant, Hal Foster, Rudi H. Fuchs, Per Kirkeby, Jannis Kounellis, Hilton Kramer, Donald B. Kuspit, Thomas McEvilley, Mark Rosenthal, Peter Schjeldahl, and Nicholas Serota.

The Window in Twentieth-Century Art. Purchase: Neuberger Museum, State University of New York at Purchase, 1986. With essays by Shirley Neilsen Blum and Suzanne Delehanty.

The Spiritual in Art: Abstract Painting 1890–1985. Los Angeles: Los Angeles County Museum of Art, 1986. With texts by authors including Carel Blotkamp, John E. Bowlt, Donald Kuspit, Rose-Carol Washton Long, Maurice Tuchman, and chronologies by Judi Freeman.

Bürgi, Bernhard, ed. *Rot Gelb Blau: Die Primärfarben in der Kunst des 20. Jahrhunderts.* Stuttgart: Gerd Hatje, 1988. With essays by Bürgi, Felix Thürlemann, and Veit Loers.

La Couleur seule: L'expérience du monochrome. Lyon: Musée Saint Pierre Art Contemporain, Musées de France, 1988. With texts by various authors.

Auping, Michael. *Abstraction, Geometry, Painting: Selected Geometric Abstract Painting in America since 1945.* Buffalo: Albright-Knox Art Gallery, 1989.

Documenta IX. Stuttgart: Edition Cantz; Kassel: Documenta, Museum Fridericianum, 1992. With foreword by Wolfram Bremeier, introduction by Jan Hoet, and essays by various authors.

Indiana, Kelly, Martin, Rosenquist, Youngerman at Coenties Slip. New York: The Pace Gallery, 1993. With essay by Mildred Glimcher.

Copier Créer: de Turner à Picasso: 300 œuvres inspirées par les maîtres du Louvre. Paris: Musée du Louvre, 1993. With texts by various authors.

Joachimides, Christos M., and Norman Rosenthal, eds. *Amerikanische Kunst im 20. Jahrhundert: Malerei und Plastik 1913–1993.* Berlin: Martin-Gropius-Bau, 1993. With essays by authors including David Anfam, Richard Armstrong, Arthur C. Danto, Donald Kuspit, and Carter Ratcliff.

Ferguson, Russell, ed. *Rolywholyover: A Circus*. Los Angeles: The Museum of Contemporary Art, 1993. With texts by various authors.

Philbrick, Jane, ed. *The Return of the Cadavre Exquis.* New York: The Drawing Center, 1993. With texts by Mary Ann Caws, Elizabeth Finch, Ingrid Schaffner, and Charles Simic.

Rosenthal, Mark. *Abstraction in the Twentieth Century: Total Risk, Freedom, Discipline*. New York: The Solomon R. Guggenheim Foundation, 1996.

Rosenthal, Mark, et al. *The Robert and Jane Meyerhoff Collection 1945 to 1995.* Washington, DC: National Gallery of Art, 1996. With texts by Rosenthal, David Anfam, Harry Cooper, Molly Donovan, Ruth E. Fine, Jane Meyerhoff, Marla Prather, Charles Ritchie, and Jeffrey Weiss.

Lee, Pamela and Christine Mehring. *Drawing is Another Kind of Language: Recent American Drawings from a New York Private Collection.* Cambridge, MA: Harvard University Art Museums, 1997.

Rendezvous: Masterpieces from the Centre Georges Pompidou and the Guggenheim Museums. New York: The Solomon R. Guggenheim Foundation; Paris: Éditions du Centre Pompidou, 1998. With essays by Bernard Blistène, Yve-Alain Bois, Stanley Cavell, Jean-Louis Cohen, Lisa Dennison, and Mark C. Taylor.

Correspondences: Isamu Noguchi and Ellsworth Kelly. New York: Whitney Museum of American Art, 2000. Brochure. With text by Beth Venn.

Galassi, Peter, Robert Storr, and Anne Umland. *Making Choices: 1929, 1939, 1948, 1955.* New York: The Museum of Modern Art, 2000.

Garrels, Gary, ed. *Celebrating Modern Art: The Anderson Collection.* San Francisco: San Francisco Museum of Modern Art, 2000. With foreword by David A. Ross, introduction by Garrels, and essays by authors including Michael Auping, Neal Benezra, T.J. Clark, John Elderfield, and Jack Flam.

La Sculpture contemporaine au Jardin des Tuileries. Paris: La domaine national des Tuileries, le Centre des monuments nationaux, 2000. With foreword by Catherine Tasca and texts by Alain Kirili and Robert Storr.

Silver, Kenneth E. *Making Paradise: Art Modernity and the Myth of the French Riviera.* New York: AXA Gallery; Cambridge, MA: MIT Press, 2001.

Stein, Laurie A., ed. *Abstractions in Space: Tadao Ando, Ellsworth Kelly, Richard Serra.* Saint Louis: Pulitzer Foundation for the Arts, 2001. With essay by William J.R. Curtis and photographs by Robert Pettus.

Wilson, Sarah, et al. *Paris: Capital of the Arts 1900–1968*. London: Royal Academy of Arts, 2002. With essays by authors including Éric de Chassey and Kenneth Silver.

Henri Matisse/Ellsworth Kelly: dessins de plantes. Paris: Éditions Gallimard; Centre Pompidou, 2002. With essays by Rémi Labrusse and Éric de Chassey.

McShine, Kynaston and Anne Umland, ed. *To Be Looked At: Painting and Sculpture from the Museum of Modern Art, New York*. New York: The Museum of Modern Art, 2002.

Foster, Carter E., Jeffrey D. Grove, et al. *Drawing Modern: Works from the Agnes Gund Collection*. Seattle: The Cleveland Museum of Art, 2003.

Singular Forms (Sometimes Repeated): Art from 1951 to the Present. New York: The Solomon R. Guggenheim Foundation, 2004. With texts by Nancy Spector and various authors.

Garrels, Gary. *Drawing from the Modern 1945–1975*. Volume 2. New York: The Museum of Modern Art, 2005. With essay by Garrels and texts by various authors.

Houston, Joe. *Optic Nerve: Perceptual Art of the 1960s*. London: Merrell in association with the Columbus Museum of Art, 2007. With introduction by Dave Hickey.

Storr, Robert. *Think with the Senses, Feel with the Mind: Art in the Present Tense. La Biennale di Venezia: 52. Esposizione Internationale d'Arte.* Venice: Fondazione La Biennale di Venezia, 2007. With texts by Storr and various authors.

Rachum, Stephanie, and Yve-Alain Bois. *Glenstone: The Inaugural Exhibition*. Potomac, MD: Glenstone Foundation, 2008.

This Is Not To Be Looked At: Highlights from the Permanent Collection of the Museum of Contemporary Art Los Angeles. Los Angeles: Museum of Contemporary Art, 2008. With essays by Ann Goldstein, Rebecca Morse, and Paul Schimmel.

Temkin, Ann. *Color Chart: Reinventing Color, 1950 to Today*. New York: The Museum of Modern Art, 2008.

Büttner, Philippe, Yve-Alain Bois, et al. *Fernand Léger: Paris—New York*. Basel: Fondation Beyeler, 2008.

Hindry, Ann. *Correspondances: Ellsworth Kelly/ Paul Cézanne*. Paris: Musée d'Orsay, 2008.

Rishel, Joseph and Katherine Sachs. *Cézanne and Beyond.* Philadelphia: Philadelphia Museum of Art; New Haven: Yale University Press, 2009. With essays by authors including Roberta Bernstein, Yve-Alain Bois, John Elderfield, Carolyn Lanchner, Richard Shiff, and Robert Storr.

de Chassey, Éric and Emilie Ovaere. *Ils ont regardé Matisse: Une reception abstraite États-Unis/ Europe 1948–1968*. Le Cateau-Cabrésis: Musée departmental Matisse; Montreuil: Gourcuff Gradenigo, 2009.

Rattemeyer, Christian. *Compass in Hand: Selections from the Judith Rothschild Foundation Contemporary Drawings Collection*. New York: The Museum of Modern Art, 2009.

Malone, Meredith. *Chance Aesthetics*. St. Louis: Mildred Lane Kemper Art Museum, Washington University in St. Louis; Chicago: University of Chicago Press, 2009. With essays by Malone and various authors.

de Chassey, Éric, and Carter Foster. *Jean-Auguste-Dominique Ingres / Ellsworth Kelly.* Rome: French Academy in Rome, Villa Medici, 2010.

Katz, Jonathan D., and David C. Ward. *Hide/Seek: Difference and Desire in American Portraiture.* Washington, DC: Smithsonian Institution, 2010.

Butler, Cornelia H., and Catherine de Zegher. *On Line: Drawing through the Twentieth Century.* New York: The Museum of Modern Art, 2010.

Calder to Warhol: Introducing the Fisher Collection. San Francisco: San Francisco Museum of Modern Art, 2010. With foreword by Neal Benezra and Doris Fisher, essay by Gary Garrels.

Eleey, Peter. *September 11.* Long Island City, NY: MoMA PS1, 2011. With texts by various authors.

Müller-Schareck, Maria, ed. *Fresh Widow: The Window in Art since Matisse and Duchamp.* Düsseldorf: Kunstsammlung Nordrhein-Westfalen; Ostfildern: Hatje-Cantz, 2012.

Franciolli, Marco. *Fenêtres, de la Renaissance à nos jours: Dürer, Monet, Magritte...* Lausanne: Fondation de l'Hermitage; Milan: Skira, 2013.

Cooper, Harry. *Make it New: Abstract Painting from the National Gallery of Art, 1950–1975.* Williamstown, MA: Sterling and Francine Clark Art Institute, 2014.

Monet/Kelly. Williamstown, MA: Sterling and Francine Clark Art Institute; New Haven and London: Yale University Press, 2014. With foreword by Michael Conforti, essays by Sarah Lees and Yve-Alain Bois, and statement by the artist.

Icônes Américaines: Chefs d'Œuvres du SFMOMA et de la collection Fisher. Paris: Galeries nationales du Grand Palais, 2015. With essay by Gary Garrels and texts by various authors.

Monographs, Catalogues Raisonnés, and Theses

Axsom, Richard H. *The Prints of Ellsworth Kelly: A Catalogue Raisonné, 1949–1985*. New York: Hudson Hills Press, 1987. In conjunction with the exhibition "Ellsworth Kelly: A Print Retrospective," Detroit Institute of Arts, 1987. With chronology.

Axsom, Richard H., ed. *Letters to Ellsworth.* Portland: Jordan Schnitzer Family Foundation; Seattle: Marquand Books, Inc., 2011. With introduction by Axsom and texts by various authors.

Axsom, Richard H. *The Prints of Ellsworth Kelly: A Catalogue Raisonné.* Portland: Jordan Schnitzer Family Foundation, 2012.

Bois, Yve-Alain. *Ellsworth Kelly: Catalogue Raisonné of Paintings, Reliefs and Sculptures, 1940–1953.* Vol. 1. Paris: Cahiers d'Art, 2015.

Cade, Carol Beth. "Color in Color Field Painting: Color in the Painting of Ellsworth Kelly, Kenneth Noland, and Frank Stella," Ed.D. thesis (Columbia University, 1973).

Coplans, John. *Ellsworth Kelly.* New York: Harry N. Abrams, 1971.

Ebbighausen, Nina. "Die Tendenz zum Farbobjekt: über Veränderungen der Farbkonzepte und des Bildverständnisses in der zeitgenössischen Malerei unter besonderer Berücksichtigung des Werkes von Ellsworth Kelly," Ph.D. thesis (Universität der Künste, Berlin, 2004).

Di Monte, Maria Giuseppina. *Ellsworth Kelly: La forma è il contenuto.* Rome: De Luca Editori D'Arte, 2010.

Hindry, Ann, ed. *Artstudio: Spécial Ellsworth Kelly*, no. 24 (Spring 1992). Essays by Tiffany Bell, Roberta Bernstein, Ann Hindry, Carter Ratcliff, and Nan Rosenthal; interviews with the artist each by Hindry and Paul Taylor.

Paik, Tricia Y. "A Palpable Vision: Ellsworth Kelly in New York, 1954–1969," Ph.D. thesis (New York University, 2009).

Proctor, Alice Seawright. "Color Confrontations: The Reconstructions of Color Interactions as a New Medium for Visual Semantics," Ph.D. thesis (The University of Texas at Dallas, 1993).

Shiff, Richard. *Ellsworth Kelly: New York Drawings, 1954–1962.* New York: Matthew Marks Gallery; Munich, London, and New York: Prestel, 2014.

Steck, Stuart Y. "Veiling the Subject: Ellsworth Kelly and the Discourses of Modernism," Ph.D. thesis (Boston University, 2008).

Waldman, Diane. *Ellsworth Kelly: Drawings, Collages, Prints.* Greenwich, CT: New York Graphic Society Ltd., 1971.

Statements and Interviews

Unpublished statement for "Line, Form and Color" (November 1951). In Ellsworth Kelly, *Line Form Color,* unpag. Cambridge, MA: Harvard University Art Museums, 1999.

Unpublished statement (1957). In James Meyer, "Art for the City: Sculpture for a Large Wall, 1957," *Ellsworth Kelly: Sculpture for a Large Wall*, 5. New York: Matthew Marks Gallery, 1998.

Geldzahler, Henry. "Interview with Ellsworth Kelly." In *Paintings, Sculpture and Drawings by Ellsworth Kelly*, unpag. Washington, DC: Washington Gallery of Modern Art, 1963. Reprinted in *Art International* 8, no. 1 (February 1964): 47–48; *Ellsworth Kelly: The Paris Prints 1964–1965* (New York: Susan Sheehan Gallery, 1992): unpag.; and Geldzahler, *Making it New: Essays, Interviews, and Talks* (New York: Turtle Point Press, 1994): 68–73.

Lippard, Lucy R. "Homage to the Square." *Art in America* 55, no. 4 (July–August 1967): 50–57.

"Ellsworth Kelly." *Art Now: New York* 1, no. 9 (November 1969): unpag.

Coplans, John. *Ellsworth Kelly,* 20–21, 28–30, 32–33, 36–38. New York: Harry N. Abrams, 1971. [Some of these statements became basis for Kelly's "Notes from 1969," published in 1979.]

Gordon, Leah. "Kelly: 'My Work Is Difficult." *The New York Times*, September 9, 1973, 29, 37.

Halasz, Piri. "He Brightens up the Spectrum of Contemporary Art." *Smithsonian* 4, no. 8 (November 1973): 42–49.

"Notes from 1969." In *Ellsworth Kelly: Paintings and Sculptures 1963–1979*, 30–34. Amsterdam: Stedelijk Museum, 1979. Includes partial revisions of initial statements made in Lippard 1967 and Coplans 1971. Reprinted in *Künstler, Kritisches Lexikon der Gegenwartskunst*, no. 14 (1991): 3–16; and Kristin Stiles and Peter Selz, eds., *Theories and Documents of Contemporary Art: A Source-book of Artists' Writings* (Berkeley and Los Angeles: University of California Press, 1996), 92–93 [slightly revised version by Kelly as "Notes of 1969"].

Brenson, Michael. "In Sculpture, Too, He Is an Artist of Surprises." *The New York Times*, December 12, 1982, section 2, 1, 38.

Raynor, Vivien. "Ellsworth Kelly Keeps His Edge." *ARTnews* 82, no. 3 (March 1983): 52–59 (cover).

Duffy, Robert W. "'It Was the Shape of Things that Came to Matter to Me.'" *St. Louis Post-Dispatch*, March 27, 1983, 5H.

Statement (October 1983). In *Ellsworth Kelly: Painted Aluminum Wall Sculpture/Weathering Steel Wall Sculpture,* unpag. Los Angeles: Margo Leavin Gallery; New York: Leo Castelli Gallery, 1984.

Kutner, Jane. "Inside the Kelly Mystique." *The Dallas Morning News*, September 12, 1987, section C, 1–2.

Dorsey, John. "The World as Color and Shape." *The Baltimore Sun*, May 29, 1988, section P, 1, 3.

Hoffmann, Donald. "Artist Erases the Line Between Object, Image." *The Kansas City Star*, October 23, 1988, section D, 1, 5.

von Ziegesar, Peter. "Ellsworth Kelly." *The Journal of Art* 1, no. 2 (January 1989): 3–6.

von Ziegesar, Peter. "How Chance Operations Guide Work: An Interview with Ellsworth Kelly. *Forum* 14, nos. 2–3 (June/July 1989): 25–27.

Donohue, Marlena. "Interview: Ellsworth Kelly." *The Christian Science Monitor*, July 10, 1989, 16–17.

Statement. In *Artist's Choice: Ellsworth Kelly—Fragmentation and the Single Form*, unpag. New York: The Museum of Modern Art, 1990 [brochure for exhibition curated by the artist].

Hagen, Charles. "The Shape of Seeing: Ellsworth Kelly's Photographs." *Aperture: The Encompassing Eye: Photography as Drawing,* no. 125 (fall 1991): 42–47.

Taylor, Paul. "Ellsworth Kelly: Talking to America's Most Colorful Artist." *Interview* 21, no. 6 (June 1991): 98–103. Reprinted in a revised version in Ann Hindry, ed., *Artstudio: Spécial Ellsworth Kelly*, no. 24 (spring 1992): 154–57.

"Interview: Ellsworth Kelly Talks with Paul Cummings." *Drawing* 13, no. 3 (September/October 1991): 56–61.

Brunet, Nathalie. "Chronology, 1943–1954." In Yve-Alain Bois, Jack Cowart, and Alfred Pacquement. *Ellsworth Kelly: The Years in France, 1948–1954,* 177–194. Washington, DC: National Gallery of Art, 1992.

Götz, Stephan. "Ellsworth Kelly." In Götz, *American Artists in Their New York Studios: Conversations about the Creation of Contemporary Art*, 79–82. Cambridge, MA: Center for Conservation and Technical Studies, Harvard University Art Museums, 1992.

Storr, Robert. "Ellsworth Kelly: rencontres à Paris." *Art Press*, no. 167 (March 1992): 10–18.

Hindry, Ann. "Conversation with Ellsworth Kelly." In Hindry, ed. *Artstudio: Spécial Ellsworth Kelly*, no. 24 (spring 1992): 22–37.

Cembalest, Robin. "Ellsworth Kelly: 'Everything Becomes Abstract.'" *ARTnews* 91, no. 10 (December 1992): 98–103.

"Matisse: A Symposium." *Art in America* 81, no. 5 (May 1993): 74–87.

Diamonstein, Barbaralee. "Ellsworth Kelly." In Diamonstein, *Inside the Art World: Conversations with Barbaralee Diamonstein,* 121–124. New York: Rizzoli, 1994.

Diehl, Carol. "Birds, Beads and Bannerstones." *ARTnews* 95, no. 7 (summer 1996): 76–84.

Cotter, Holland. "A Giant of the New Surveys His Rich Past." *The New York Times*, October 13, 1996, section H, 43.

Ganem, Mark. "Kelly's Peak." *W Magazine* (May 1998): 210–15, 234–35.

"Ellsworth Kelly in conversation with Marla Prather." Audio podcast at the National Gallery of Art, April 21, 1999.

Storr, Robert. "Interview with Ellsworth Kelly." *MoMA* 2, no. 5 (June 1999): 2–7.

"Notes on Sculpture" (May 14, 2002). In *Ellsworth Kelly: In-Between Spaces: Works, 1956–2002*, 46–49. Basel: Fondation Beyeler, 2002.

Gerard, Philip. *Secret Soldiers: The Story of World War II's Heroic Army of Deception*. New York: Dutton, 2002: 62–64, 99, 149–50, 184, 310.

Belcove, Julie L. "In Living Color." *W Magazine* (May 2003): 176–183.

Kastner, Jeffrey. "Ellsworth Kelly's Journey, From All Angles." *The New York Times*, May 4, 2003, section 2, 42.

Homes, A.M. "Art Profile: Ellsworth Kelly." *Vogue Hommes International* (spring/summer 2003): 136–144.

Muschamp, Herbert. "Critic's Notebook: One Vision: A Hill of Green at Ground Zero." *The New York Times*, September 11, 2003, E1, E4.

Bashkoff, Tracey. "Ellsworth Kelly: An Interview." *Guggenheim Magazine* (winter 2004): 14–19.

Ellsworth Kelly: Thumbing through the Folder: A Dialogue on Art and Architecture with Hans Ulrich Obrist. Cologne: Verlag der Buchhandlung Walther König, 2009.

Interview by Gary Garrels et al. Audiofile transcript. San Francisco Museum of Modern Art, May 7, 2009.

Prather, Marla. "Interview with Ellsworth Kelly." In Prather and Michael Semff, eds. *Ellsworth Kelly: Plant Drawings*, 211–224. Munich: Schirmer/Mosel, 2011.

"Ellsworth Kelly by Gwyneth Paltrow." *Interview* 41, no. 8 (October 2011): 122–131.

Loos, Ted. "Seeing the Calligraphy in the Grain." *The New York Times*, November 27, 2011, AR26.

Vogel, Carol. "True to His Abstraction." *The New York Times*, January 20, 2012, AR1.

Homes, A. M. "True to Form." *W Magazine* (July 2012): 74–79. With photographs by Jack Shear.

"Ellsworth Kelly in Conversation with Hans Ulrich Obrist." and statement by Kelly. *Cahiers d'Art*, no.1 (October 2012): 25–28, 52.

Chou, Kimberly. "The Colors Only Get Brighter with Time." *The Wall Street Journal*, May 20, 2013, A24.

"Conversation: Ellsworth Kelly & Robert Storr." In *Ellsworth Kelly,* 11–30. Paris: Fondation Louis Vuitton/Manuella Éditions, 2014.

"Artist's Statement" (12/8/2001). In *Monet/Kelly,* 8–9. Williamstown, MA: Sterling and Francine Clark Art Institute; New Haven and London: Yale University Press, 2014.

Documentaries

To Hell with the Birds: Looking with Ellsworth Kelly (1995). By Pierre Aubry and Rachel Stella.

Ellsworth Kelly: Fragments (2007). By Edgar B. Howard, Checkerboard Film Foundation.

Essays, Articles and Reviews

"About Art and Artists: Lesser Known Figures Give One-Man Shows of Promise at Galleries here." *The New York Times*, May 26, 1956, L41.

Alloway, Lawrence. "Classicism or Hard-Edge." *Art International* 4, nos. 2–3 (1960): 60–61.

Alloway, Lawrence. "Easel Painting at the Guggenheim." *Art International* 5, no. 10 (Christmas 1961): 26–34.

Alloway, Lawrence. "Heraldry and Sculpture." *Art International* 6, no. 3 (April 1962): 52–53.

Alvard, Julien. "Quelques Jeunes Americains de Paris." *Art d'Aujourd'hui*, no. 6 (June 1951): 24–25.

Anderson, Susan Heller. "Paris Hails Ellsworth Kelly, Foster Son, and His Art." *The New York Times*, July 26, 1980, 9.

Anfam, David. "Ellsworth Kelly: London and St. Ives." *The Burlington Magazine* 168, no. 1239 (June 2006): 433–34.

Ashton, Dore. "Kelly's Unique Spatial Experiences." *Studio International* 170, no. 867 (July 1965): 40–43.

Ashton, Dore. "The 'Anti-compositional Attitude' in Sculpture: New York Commentary." *Studio International* 172 (July 1966): 44–47.

Ashton, Dore. "New York Commentary: Ellsworth Kelly at Sidney Janis." *Studio International* 173 (May 1967): 263–64.

Ashton, Dore. "New York Commentary: 'The Art of the Real' at the Museum of Modern Art." *Studio International* 176, no. 903 (September 1968): 92–93.

Axsom, Richard H. "Just the Right Color: Ellsworth Kelly's Red." *Art in Print* 3, no. 3 (September/October 2013): 36–38.

Baker, Elizabeth C. "The Subtleties of Ellsworth Kelly." *ARTnews* 72, no. 9 (November 1973): 30–33.

Baker, Kenneth. "Ellsworth Kelly's 'Rebound'." *Arts Magazine* 51, no. 1 (September 1976): 110–11.

Baker, Kenneth. "Kelly's Timeless Abstracts Hold Up." *San Francisco Chronicle*, January 11, 1992, C7.

Barron, Stephanie. "Giving Art History the Slip." *Art in America* 62, no. 2 (March/April 1974): 80–84.

Bell, Clare. "Ellsworth Kelly and the Legacy of Linear Drawing." *On Paper* 2, no. 1 (September/October 1997): 33–36.

B[urrey], S[uzanne]. "Ellsworth Kelly." *Arts Magazine* 32, no. 1 (October 1957): 56–57.

Bois, Yve-Alain, et al. "Kelly Read: Ellsworth Kelly in Retrospect." *Artforum* 35, no. 2 (October 1996): 86–97, 138–39.

Bouret, Jean. "Le Premier Salon des jeunes peintres." *Arts: Beaux arts, litterature, spectacles*, January 27, 1950, 1, 4.

Butcher, George. "Ellsworth Kelly Exhibition at Tooth's Gallery." *The Guardian*, June 9, 1962, 4.

B[utler], B[arbara]. "In the Galleries: Ellsworth Kelly." *Arts Magazine* 30, no. 4 (June 1956): 52.

Coates, Robert M. "The Art Galleries: Americans, Past and Present." *The New Yorker* (December 19, 1959): 108–111.

Coates, Robert M. "The Art Galleries: The 'Beat' Beat in Art." *The New Yorker* (January 2, 1960): 60–61.

Coplans, John. "Post-Painterly Abstraction: The Long-Awaited Greenberg Exhibition Fails to Make Its Point." *Artforum* 2, no. 11 (summer 1964): 4–9.

Coplans, John. "The Earlier Work of Ellsworth Kelly." *Artforum* 7, no. 10 (summer 1969): 48–55 (cover).

Cotter, Holland. "Ellsworth Kelly: 'At Right Angles, 1964–1966.'" *The New York Times*, March 13, 1992, C28.

Cotter, Holland. "An American in Paris." *Art in America* 80, no. 12 (December 1992): 74–81, 130.

Cotter, Holland. "Where City History Was Made, A 50s Group Made Art History." *The New York Times*, January 5, 1993, C11, C16.

Cotter, Holland. "Following the Paper Trail: Ellsworth Kelly's Adventure." *The New York Times*, April 30, 1999, E40.

Cotter, Holland. "Ellsworth Kelly Reliefs 2009–2010." *The New York Times*, April 8, 2011, C32.

Cotter, Holland. "When an Abstract Artist Falls in Love with Monet." *The New York Times*, February 1, 2015, C1.

Derfner, Phyllis. “Ellsworth Kelly at Castelli Uptown.” *Art in America* 63, no. 4 (July–August 1975): 97–98.

Diehl, Carol. “Kelly Confidential.” *Art in America* 90, no. 12 (December 2002): 78–81.

Douglas, Sarah. “On View: Ellsworth Kelly.” *The New York Observer,* June 3, 2013, B5.

Drolet, Owen. “Ellsworth Kelly: Toward Another Laocoön.” *Flash Art* (January/February 1996): 70–74.

Elderfield, John. “Color and Area: New Paintings by Ellsworth Kelly.” *Artforum* 10, no. 3 (November 1971): 45–49.

Elderfield, John. “Ellsworth Kelly: Drawings, Collages, Prints by Diane Waldman.” *Art in America* 60, no. 6 (November/December 1972): 37.

Fer, Briony. “‘To Hell with Pictures’—Ellsworth Kelly’s Walls.” *Parkett*, no. 56 (September 1999): 32–37.

Fried, Michael. “New York Letter.” *Art International* 7, no. 10 (January 16, 1964): 54–55.

Frigerio, Simone. “Les Expositions à l’étranger: La Documenta III de Kassel.” *Aujourd’hui*, no. 47 (October 1964): 54–55.

G.B. “Kelly.” *Arts: beaux arts, littérature, spectacles*, May 4, 1951.

Geldzahler, Henry. “Frankenthaler, Kelly, Lichtenstein, Olitski: A Preview of the American Selection at the 1966 Venice Biennale.” *Artforum* 4, no. 10 (June 1966): 32–38.

G[enauer], E[mily]. “Art Exhibition Notes: Kelly at Parsons.” *The New York Herald Tribune*, June 2, 1956, section 1, 9.

Genauer, Emily. “U.S. Art Going to Brussels Called Scandal.” *The New York Herald Tribune*, March 17, 1958, 1, 13.

Genauer, Emily. “Show Puts New Light on Our Brussels Art Selections.” *The New York Herald Tribune*, January 4, 1959, section 6, 9, 11.

Genauer, Emily. “Pittsburgh’s Carnegie Institute: Those Olympic Gold Medals in the World of Art.” *The New York Herald Tribune*, October 30, 1964: 23.

Goossen, E.C. “The Paris Years.” *Arts Magazine* 48, no. 2 (November 1973): 32–37.

Goossen, E.C. “Color and Light.” *Arts Magazine* 48, no. 4 (January 1974): 32–41.

Goossen, E.C. “Some Notes on Ellsworth Kelly.” *Forum International* 3, no. 13 (May/August 1992): 54–60.

Greenberg, Clement. “Post-Painterly Abstraction.” *Art International* 8 (summer 1964): 64–65.

Hess, Thomas B. “Sincerely Yours, Ellsworth Kelly.” *New York Magazine* (October 15, 1973): 98–99.

Hindry, Ann. “Ellsworth Kelly: Un Grand Américain à Paris.” *Le Quotidien de l’Art*, May 15, 2012, 1–2.

Hughes, Robert. “Classic Sleeper.” *Time* 102, no. 12 (September 17, 1973): 72.

Janis, Sidney. “Correspondance.” *L’Œil*, no. 155 (November 1967): 64.

Johnson, Philip, [and Donald Judd]. “Young Artists at the Fair and at Lincoln Center.” *Art in America* 52, no. 4 (August 1964): 112–27.

Jouffroy, Alain. “Le Grand Jeu de la Biennale.” *L’Œil* (July/August 1966): 44–51, 61.

Jouffroy, Alain. “Correspondance.” *L’Œil*, no. 155 (November 1967): 64.

Kay, Jane H. “World of Shade and Shape: Kelly’s Colorful, Personal Geometry.” *The Christian Science Monitor*, February 14, 1964, 6.

Kazanjian, Dodie. “In Living Color.” *Vogue* (November 1992): 309–313, 356–358.

“Kelly.” *Combat*, May 8, 1951, 4.

Kellein, Thomas. “An American in Paris.” *Parkett*, no. 56 (September 1999): 24–31.

Kimmelman, Michael. “Ellsworth Kelly’s Coming of Age in Paris.” *The New York Times*, November 1, 1992, section 2, 31.

Kimmelman, Michael “Decades of Doodles Help Illuminate the Creative Process.” *The New York Times*, May 3, 2002, E37.

Kozloff, Max. “Geometric Abstraction in America.” *Art International* 6, nos. 5–6 (summer 1962): 98–103.

Kramer, Hilton. “30 Years of the New York School.” *The New York Times Magazine*, October 12, 1969 (cover).

Kramer, Hilton. “Color Lures the Eye to Kelly’s Paintings.” *The New York Times*, July 26, 1972, 22.

Kramer, Hilton. “Kelly’s ‘Bold Simplicity’ at the Modern Art.” *The New York Times*, September 13, 1973, 62.

Kramer, Hilton. “‘Artist’s Choice’ Show at MoMA: Small, Concentrated and Flawless.” *The New York Observer*, July 16–23, 1990, 1, 27.

Kuspit, Donald. “Ellsworth Kelly: Matthew Marks Gallery.” *Artforum* 33, no. 7 (March 1995): 88–89.

Leider, Philip. “American Sculpture at the Los Angeles County Museum of Art.” *Artforum* 5, no. 10 (June 1967): 6–11.

Levin, Kim. “Ellsworth Kelly.” *ARTnews* 64 (May 1965): 10.

Livingston, Jane. “Ellsworth Kelly.” *Artforum* 6, no. 5 (January 1968): 60–61.

Masheck, Joseph. “Ellsworth Kelly at the Modern.” *Artforum* 12, no. 3 (November 1973): 54–57.

Maurer, Simon. “Forever in the Present.” *Parkett*, no. 56 (September 1999): 58–63.

Millet, Catherine. “Kelly, Noland, Olitski, Poons, Stella: Après l’Expressionisme abstrait.” *Art Press* 7, no. 5 (November/December 1973): 10–15.

Mock, Jean Yves. “Ellsworth Kelly at the Galerie Maeght.” *Apollo* 68, no. 406 (December 1958): 220.

Muschamp, Herbert. “Of Sculpture and the Past: A City’s Portal Revivified.” *The New York Times*, June 17, 1998, E1–2.

Muschamp, Herbert. “Critic’s Notebook: One Vision: A Hill of Green at Ground Zero.” *The New York Times*, September 11, 2003, E1, E4.

Nochlin, Linda. “Kelly: Making Abstraction Anew.” *Art in America* 85, no. 3 (March 1997): 68–78.

Paik, Tricia Y. “A Green Mound for Ground Zero: Ellsworth Kelly’s 9/11 Proposal.” In Elizabeth Pergam (ed.), *Drawing in the 21st Century: The Politics and Poetics of Contemporary Practice*, 101–22. Burlington, VT: Ashgate, 2015.

“Penn Center Transportation Building and Concourse.” *Architectural Record* 121, no. 5 (May 1957): 190–96 (cover).

Perl, Jed. “An American in Paris.” *The New Criterion* 2, no. 5 (January 1993): 46–50.

P[etlin], I[rving] B. “Ellsworth Kelly, Ferus Gallery.” *Artforum* 3, no. 8 (May 1965): 16.

Plagens, Peter. “Beautiful, Quiet and Spare.” *The Wall Street Journal*, October 6, 2011, D5.

Plante, Michael. “‘Things to Cover Walls:’ Ellsworth Kelly’s Paris Paintings and the Tradition of Mural Decoration,” *American Art* 9, no. 1 (spring 1995): 36–53.

Pogrebin, Robin. “Inside Art: Texas Museum to Build Ellsworth Kelly Design.” *The New York Times*, February 6, 2015, C30.

Pollock, Lindsay. “Ellsworth Kelly at Matthew Marks Gallery.” *Art in America* 101, no.5 (May 2013): 5, 37 (cover).

Preston, Stuart. “Art at Opposite Poles: Ellsworth Kelly and Kostas Paniaras Exhibit Nonobjective Extremes.” *The New York Times*, October 21, 1961, L11.

Puvogel, Renata. “Frankfurt: Ellsworth Kelly, Portikus.” *Flash Art* 23, no. 155 (November 1990): 160.

Ragon, Michel. “Kelly annexe Matisse au hard-edge.” *Arts: Lettres, spectacles, musique*, no. 983 (December 2–8, 1964): 25.

Raleigh, Henry P. “New York Painting and Sculpture: 1940–1970. Henry Geldzahler.” *Leonardo* 4, no. 2 (spring 1971): 186.

Ratcliff, Carter. “Mostly Monochrome.” *Art in America* 69 (April 1981): 111–131.

Ratcliff, Carter. "Kelly's Spectrum of Experience." *Art in America* 69, no. 6 (summer 1981): 98–101.

Ratcliff, Carter. "Diary of an Elisionist: Ellsworth Kelly's *Tablet*, 1948–1973."*Art on Paper* 6, no. 6 (July/August 2002): 30–35.

Rimanelli, David. "Why Kelly Now?" *Parkett*, no. 56 (September 1999): 64–67.

"Ripe for Fashion: Tomato Tweed." *Harper's Bazaar* (September 1956): 202–207.

Rose, Barbara. "Beyond Vertigo: Optical Art at the Modern." *Artforum* 3, no. 7 (April 1965): 30–33.

Rose, Barbara. "The Sculpture of Ellsworth Kelly." *Artforum* 5, no. 10 (June 1967): 51–55.

Rosenberg, Harold. "The Art World: École de New York." *The New Yorker* (December 6, 1969): 171–84.

Rosenberg, Harold. "Dogma and Talent." *The New Yorker* (October 15, 1973): 113–19.

Rosenthal, Nan. "New York: Gallery Notes." *Art in America* 53, no. 2 (April 1965): 117–22.

Rubin, William. "From the Exhibition, 'Sixteen Americans' at the Museum of Modern Art, New York." *Art International* 4, no. 1 (January 1960): 24–31.

Rubin, William. "Ellsworth Kelly: The Big Form." *ARTnews* 62 (November 1963): 32–35, 64–65.

Russell, John. "Art: Ellsworth Kelly, A Grand Showing." *The New York Times*, February 18, 1977.

Russell, John. "Ellsworth Kelly: An American in Paris." *The New York Times,* April 5, 1992, 39, 44.

Russell, John. "No Sturm, No Drang, but Poetry in the Simple Shape of Things." *The New York Times*, May 23, 2003, E33.

S[andler], I[rving] H. "Ellsworth Kelly." *ARTnews* 60, no. 7 (November 1961): 13.

Schama, Simon. "Dangerous Curves: Purity and Sensuousness. Understanding the Real Ellsworth Kelly." *The New Yorker* (November 4, 1996): 112–16.

Schjeldahl, Peter. "Taciturn Bliss." *The Village Voice*, November 12, 1996, 95.

Schwabsky, Barry. "Ellsworth Kelly." *Artforum* 31, no. 5 (January 1993): 85.

Schwartz, Ellen. "Ellsworth Kelly." *ARTnews* 76, no. 4 (April 1977): 126.

Siegel, Jeanne. "Ellsworth Kelly." *ARTnews* 72, no. 6 (summer 1973): 99.

Smee, Sebastian. "Kelly's Colors Hold Together, Too." *The Boston Globe*, September 25, 2010, G5.

Smith, Roberta. "Ellsworth Kelly, Leo Castelli Gallery, Uptown." *Artforum* 14, no. 1 (September 1975): 69–71.

Smith, Roberta. "Kelly's Decades of Distillations." *The New York Times*, October 18, 1996, C1, C33.

Smith, Roberta. "At 90, Still Riveting The Mind's Eye." *The New York Times*, June 4, 2013, C1, C2.

Solomon, Deborah. "The Gallery: Ellsworth Kelly." *The Wall Street Journal*, October 21, 1992, A14.

Storr, Robert. *"Quelques heures et encore moins de mots avec Ellsworth Kelly." Art Press*, no. 128 (September 1988): 18–20.

Sylvester, David. "Homage to Venus." *The New Statesmen*, June 8, 1962, 839–40.

T[illim], S[idney]. "New York Exhibitions: In the Galleries: Ellsworth Kelly." *Arts Magazine* (December 1961): 48.

Tillim, Sidney. "Ellsworth Kelly." *Arts Yearbook 3: Paris/New York* (1959): 148–51.

Tuchman, Phyllis. "Ellsworth Kelly's Photographs." *Art in America* 62, no. 1 (January/February 1974): 55–61.

T[yler], P[arker]. "Ellsworth Kelly." *ARTnews* 55, no. 4 (summer 1956): 51.

Tyler, Parker. "Ellsworth Kelly." *ARTnews* 56, no.6 (October 1957): 17–18.

Vogel, Carol. "On the Use of Buildings For Decorative Effect." *The New York Times*, April 28, 1998, E1, E6.

Vogel, Carol. "Galleries Celebrate Ellsworth Kelly at 90." *The New York Times*, April 26, 2013, C26.

Vogel, Carol. "More Kellys at MoMA." *The New York Times*, June 28, 2013, C22.

Vogel, Carol. "Inside Art: Ellsworth Kelly at Work." *The New York Times,* October 17, 2014, C26.

W[aldman], D[iane]. "Ellsworth Kelly." *ARTnews* 66, no. 2 (April 1967): 13.

Waldman, Diane. "Kelly Color." *ARTnews* 67, no. 6 (October 1968): 40–41, 62–64.

Waldman, Diane. "Kelly, Collage and Color." *ARTnews* 70, no. 8 (December 1971): 44–47, 53–55.

List of Illustrated Works

Where no artist is stated in the caption, work illustrated is by Ellsworth Kelly. All measurements are given height before width, and height before width and depth. Works are in private collections unless otherwise indicated.

42nd, 1958
oil on canvas
60½ × 80 in, 153.7 × 203.2 cm
Peggy Guggenheim Collection, Venice. Bequest of Hannelore B. and Rudolf B. Schulhof, 2012
p. 12

Atlantic, 1956
oil on canvas, 2 joined panels
80 × 114 in, 203.2 × 289.6 cm
Whitney Museum of American Art, New York
p. 139

Austin, 1986/2015
artist-designed building with colored glass windows and interior installation
28 × 63 × 76 ft, 8.6 × 19.3 ×23.3 m
Blanton Museum of Art, The University of Texas at Austin. Gift of the artist, with funding generously provided by Jeanne and Michael Klein, Suzanne Deal Booth and David G. Booth, the Scurlock Foundation, Leslie and Jack S. Blanton, Jr., Elizabeth and Peter Wareing, and Kelli and Eddy S. Blanton
pp. 212, 327

Automatic Drawing: Shelled Bunker VI, 1950
graphite on paper
10½ × 13½ in, 26.7 × 34.3 cm
p. 35

Bar, 1955
oil on canvas
32⅝ × 96 in, 82.9 × 243.8 cm
p. 132

Barnes Totem, 2011
stainless steel
40 feet × 80 in × 20 in, 1219.2 × 203.2 × 50.8 cm
The Barnes Foundation, Philadelphia.
Gift of the Neubauer Family Foundation
p. 304

The Barcelona Sculpture at General Moragues Plaza, 1987
stainless steel and weathering steel
two parts: 588 × 86 × 7 in, 14.9 × 2.2 × 0.2 m; 260 × 260 × 227 in, 6.6 × 6.6 × 5.8 m
City of Barcelona, Spain, Artist commission
p. 207

Bay, 1959
oil on canvas
70 × 50 in, 177.8 × 127 cm
p. 183

Beijing Panels, 2003
2 reliefs, painted aluminum
each 225 × 132 × 8 in, 571.5 × 335.3 × 20.3 cm
United States Embassy, Beijing. Gift of the artist, commissioned by the Foundation for Art and Preservation in Embassies
pp. 210, 211, 311

Black and White, 1960–61
oil on canvas
90 × 120 in, 228.6 × 304.8 cm
The Art Institute of Chicago. Restricted gift of Mr. and Mrs. Arnold H. Maremont through the Kate Maremont Foundation
p. 152

Black Bar for a Wall, 2011
painted aluminum
96 × 473 × 6 in, 243.8 × 1201.4 × 15.2 cm
Site-specific installation for Matthew Marks Gallery, Los Angeles. Artist commission
p. 297

Black Blue Red, 1960
oil on canvas
76½ × 66 in, 194.3 × 167.6 cm
p. 151

Black Curve, 1991
acrylic on canvas on wood
1 × 343½ × 285¾ in, 2.5 × 872.5 × 725.8 cm
Site-specific installation for Berlinische Galerie Museum für Moderne Kunst at Schloss Charlottenburg, Berlin
p. 324

Black Curve Diagonal, 2010
oil on canvas, 2 joined panels
40¾ × 120 × 2⅝ in, 103.5 × 305.1 × 6.7 cm
pp. 292–93

Black Curve I, 1970
oil on canvas
41⅞ × 39¼ in, 106.4 × 99.7 cm
p. 239

Black Curves, 1954
oil on canvas
36 × 26 in, 91.4 × 66 cm
p. 129

Black Curves, 1996
oil on canvas
144 × 42½ in, 365.8 × 108 cm
Kunstmuseum Winterthur, Switzerland.
Purchase with funds from the Jubiläumsstiftung
p. 267

Black Curves, 2011
acrylic on canvas on wood
1 × 250¼ × 368⅞ in, 2.5 × 635.6 × 936.9 cm
Site-specific installation for Haus der Kunst, Munich
p. 325

Black Form I, 2011
painted aluminum
80 × 71¾ × 4¼ in, 203.2 × 182.2 × 10.8 cm
p. 299

Black Forms with Red, 1956
collage on paper
6¾ × 12¼ in, 17 × 31.1 cm
p. 213

Black Green, 1970
oil on canvas, 2 joined panels
110 × 84 in, 279.4 × 213.4 cm
p. 219

Black over White, 1966
oil on canvas, 2 joined panels
86 × 80 in, 218.4 × 203.2 cm
p. 176

Black Relief II, 2010
oil on canvas, 2 joined panels
74 × 70 × 2⅝ in, 188 × 177.8 × 6.7 cm
p. 295

Black Relief with White, 2007
oil on canvas, 2 joined panels
65½ × 108 × 2¾ in, 166.4 × 274.3 × 7 cm
p. 289

Black Ripe, 1955
oil on canvas
63¼ × 59⅜ in, 160.7 × 150.8 cm
The Anderson Collection at Stanford University
p. 130

Black Square, 1953
oil on wood
43¼ × 43¼ in, 109.9 × 109.9 cm
p. 84

Black White, 1967
oil on canvas, 2 joined panels
82 × 144 in, 208.3 × 365.8 cm
Marguerite and Robert K. Hoffman Collection. Promised gift to Dallas Museum of Art
p. 228

Black with Red Bar, 1970
oil on canvas, 2 joined panels
68 × 120 in, 172.7 × 304.8 cm
p. 220

Black Yellow-Orange, 1970
oil on canvas
85 × 117 in, 215.9 × 297.2 cm
p. 221

Blue and Orange (Bleu et Orange), 1964–65
lithograph on Rives BFK paper
23⅝ × 35⅜ in, 60 × 90.5 cm
p. 119

Blue Black, 2001
painted aluminum
336 × 70 × 2½ in, 853.4 × 177.8 × 6.4 cm
The Pulitzer Foundation for the Arts.
Artist commission and gift of the artist
p. 275

Blue Black Red, 1964
oil on canvas
91 × 180 in, 231.1 × 457.2 cm
p. 166

Blue Black Red Green, 2000
oil on canvas, 4 panels
100 × 484 in, 254 × 1229.4 cm
Beyeler Collection, Basel, Switzerland
pp. 272–73

Blue Curve, 1994
oil on canvas
86 × 72 in, 218.4 × 182.9 cm
p. 264

Blue Curve III, 1972
oil on canvas
67¾ × 166½ in, 172.1 × 422.9 cm
Los Angeles County Museum of Art. Purchased with funds provided by Paul Rosenberg & Company, Mrs. Lita A. Hazen, and the David E. Bright Bequest
pp. 230–31

Blue Curves, 2009
oil on canvas
80 × 59¾ in, 203.2 × 151.8 cm
p. 294

Blue Disk, 1963
painted aluminum
70 × 72 × ⅛ in, 177.8 × 182.9 × 0.3 cm
p. 126

Blue Floor Panel for Leo, 1992
acrylic on canvas on wood
1 × 275 × 576 in, 2.5 × 698.5 × 1463 cm
Site-specific installation for Leo Castelli Gallery, New York
p. 325

Blue Green, 1962
oil on canvas
86½ × 68 in, 219.7 × 172.7 cm
Jo Carole and Ronald S. Lauder Collection. Promised gift to National Gallery of Art, Washington, DC
p. 155

Blue Green Red II, 1965
oil on canvas
88 × 102, 233.5 × 259.1 cm
Seattle Art Museum. Gift of Virgina and Bagley Wright Collection, in honor of the 75th Anniversary of Seattle Art Museum, 2007
p. 119

Blue Green Yellow Orange Red, 1966
oil on canvas, 5 joined panels
60 × 240 in, 152.4 × 609.6 cm
The Solomon R. Guggenheim Museum, New York
pp. 170–71

Blue over Blue, 1963
painted aluminum
88 × 60 × 7½ in, 223.5 × 152.4 × 19.1 cm
Los Angeles County Museum of Art. Gift of Mr. & Mrs. Frederick R. Weisman in honor of Richard E. Sherwood, Esq.
p. 167

Blue Red, 1965
oil on canvas
65 × 150 in, 165.1 × 381 cm
p. 206

Blue Red, 1966
acrylic on canvas, 2 joined panels
81 × 60 × 81 in, 205.7 × 152.4 × 205.7 cm
San Francisco Museum of Modern Art, the Doris and Donald Fisher Collection at the San Francisco Museum of Modern Art, and the Helen and Charles Schwab Collection
p. 173

Blue Red, 1968
oil on canvas, 2 joined panels
73 × 160 in, 185.4 × 406.4 cm
The Eli & Edythe L. Broad Collection
pp. 178–79

Blue Red Rocker, 1963
painted aluminum
72 × 66½ × 37½ in, 182.9 × 168.9 × 95.3 cm
Stedelijk Museum, Amsterdam
p. 160

Blue Relief over Yellow, 2014
oil on canvas, 2 joined panels
60 × 65½ in, 152.4 × 166.4 cm
p. 319

Blue Relief with Black, 1993
oil on canvas, 2 joined panels
98¼ × 89 x2⅝ in, 249.6 × 226.1 × 6.7 cm
p. 261

Blue Ripe, 1959
oil on canvas
60 × 60 in, 152.4 × 152.4 cm
Caldic Collection
p. 184

Blue-Violet Curve I, 1982
oil on canvas
79¾ × 120¼ in, 202.6 × 305.4 cm
p. 244

Blue White, 1980
oil on linen canvas, 2 joined panels
112¼ × 115 in, 285.1 × 292.1 cm
p. 242

Blue Yellow Red III, 1971
oil on canvas, 3 joined panels
72 × 74 in, 182.9 × 188 cm
p. 227

The Boston Panels, 1996–98
painted aluminum
each east & west wall panel
132 × 88 × 2½ in, 335.3 × 223.5 × 6.4 cm
each rotunda panel
132 × 165 × 2½ in, 335.3 × 419.1 × 6.4 cm
commissioned by the Art in Architecture Program of the US General Services Administration for the John J. Moakley Federal Courthouse, Boston
pp. 326, 347

Briey, France, 1945
gouache on paper
7⅞ × 9⅞ in, 20 × 25.1 cm
p. 334

Broadway, 1958
oil on canvas
78 × 69½ in, 198.1 176.5 cm
Tate, London. Presented by E. J. Power through the Friends of the Tate Gallery
p. 144

Byzantine Head I, 1948
oil on canvas
15 × 15 in, 38.1 × 38.1 cm
p. 29

Chatham X: Black Red, 1971
oil on canvas, 2 joined panels
108 × 95¾ in, 274.3 × 243.2 cm
p. 225

Chimneys, Boulevard de Courcelles, Paris, 1967
gelatin silver print
p. 33

Cité, 1951
oil on wood, 20 joined panels
56¼ × 70¾ × 1¾ in, 142.9 × 179.7 × 4.4 cm
San Francisco Museum of Modern Art, the Doris and Donald Fisher Collection at the San Francisco Museum of Modern Art, and the Helen and Charles Schwab Collection
p. 63

Coenties Slip, 1957
postcard collage
3½ × 5½ in, 9 × 14 cm
p. 113

Color Panels (Red Yellow Blue Green Purple), 2014
colored fabric, 5 panels
Red 64 × 78 in, 162.6 × 198.1 cm
Yellow 440 × 75 in, 1117.6 × 190.5 cm
Blue 120½ x 113 in, 306.1 × 287 cm
Green 90 × 116 in, 228.6 × 294.6 cm
Purple 96 × 144 in, 243.8 × 365.8 cm
Collection Fondation Louis Vuitton. Artist commission
pp. 320–21

Color Panels for a Large Wall, 1978
oil on canvas, 18 panels,
10 × 125 feet, 3.1 × 38.3 m
Artist commission for The Central Trust Company, Cincinnati
p. 324

Color Panels for a Large Wall, 1978/2003
oil on canvas, 18 panels
54 × 90 ft, 16.5 × 27.4 m
National Gallery of Art, Washington, DC, purchased with funds provided and promised by the Glenstone Foundation, Mitchell P. Rales, Founder
p. 327

Colors for a Large Wall, 1951
oil on canvas, 64 joined panels
94½ × 94½ in, 240 × 240 cm
The Museum of Modern Art, New York. Gift of the artist
p. 69

Concorde IV, 1976
oil on canvas, 2 joined panels
96 × 80 in, 243.8 × 203.2 cm
Kunstsammlung Nordrhein-Westfalen, Düsseldorf
p. 238

Concorde Relief I, 1958
elm, 11½ × 7¾ × 1¾ in, 29.2 × 19.7 × 4.4 cm
San Francisco Museum of Modern Art, the Doris and Donald Fisher Collection at the San Francisco Museum of Modern Art, and the Helen and Charles Schwab Collection
p. 143

Costumes and curtain designed by Ellsworth Kelly for Paul Taylor's *Tablet* performed in Italy, 1960
p. 119

Costumes designed by Ellsworth Kelly for Paul Taylor's *Lento*, 1968
p. 120

Creueta del Coll, 1987
weathering steel,
390 × 57 × 5¼ in, 990.6 × 144.8 × 13.3 cm
City of Barcelona, Spain
p. 344

Curve I, 1973
weathering steel
1 × 144 × 118¼ in, 2.5 × 365.8 × 300.4 cm
p. 203

Curve seen from a highway, Austerlitz, NY, 1970
gelatin silver print
p. 199

Curve X, 1974
weathering steel
120 × 20 × ¾ in, 304.8 × 50.8 × 1.9 cm
Harvard Art Museums. Gift of the artist
in memory of Joseph Pulitzer, Jr.
p. 236

Curve XI, 1974
weathering steel
120 × 16 × ¾ in, 304.8 × 40.6 × 1.9 cm
p. 234

Curve XXXIII, 1982
weathering steel
128 × 125½ × 1 in, 325.1 × 318.8 × 2.5 cm
p. 247

Curves on White (Four Panels), 2011
oil on canvas, 4 paintings
each comprised of 2 joined panels
70 × 328 × 2⅝ in, 177.8 × 833.1 × 6.7 cm
pp. 300–01

Cut Up Drawing Rearranged by Chance, 1950
ink and collage on paper
25½ × 19½ in, 64.8 × 49.5 cm
Glenstone
p. 34

Dallas Panels, 1989
fiberglass, 4 panels
408 × 375½ × 2½ in, 103.6 × 95.4 × 0.6 cm
Morton H. Meyerson Symphony Center, Dallas
p. 209

Dark Blue Panel, 1985
oil on canvas
97 × 111 in, 246.4 × 281.9 cm
Musée National d'Art Moderne, Centre Georges
Pompidou, Paris
p. 251

Dartmouth Panels, 2011
painted aluminum, 5 panels
each 264 × 1081 × 3¾ in, 6.7 × 27.5 × 0.1 m
Collection of the Hood Museum of Art, Dartmouth
College. Gift of Debra and Leon Black, Class of 1973
p. 298

Diagonal with Curve XIII, 1980
stainless steel
107½ × 47 × ½ in, 273.1 × 119.4 × 1.3 cm
p. 243

Diagonal with Curve XIV, 1982
weathering steel
67 × 192 × ½ in, 170.2 × 487.7 × 1.3 cm
San Francisco Museum of Modern Art.
Gift of the artist in honor of John Caldwell
p. 250

Diagonal with Curve XV, 1984
red oak, 75⅜ × 86½ × 1¾ in, 191.5 × 219.7 × 4.4 cm
p. 246

Dominican, 1952
oil on canvas and wood
2 joined panels separated by a wood strip
38½ × 25⅝ in, 97.8 × 65.1 cm
p. 100

Dress for Anne Weber, 1952
dyed cotton
approximately 46 × 19 in, 116.8 × 48.3 cm
p. 41

Eastmore Mural, 1957
Micarta
24 × 408 in, 61 × 1036.3 cm
p. 142

Egyptian Woman, 1949
oil canvas
24⅛ × 19¾ in, 61.3 × 50.2 cm
p. 92

Ellsworth Kelly, Hôtel de Bourgogne studio, Paris, 1950
gelatin silver print
p. 336

Fête à Torcy, 1952
oil on canvas and wood
2 panels separated by a wood strip
45½ × 38¼ in, 115.6 × 97.2 cm
Kravis Collection. Promised gift to
The Museum of Modern Art, New York
p. 72

First page of Ellsworth Kelly's journal listing
places to visit in Europe, 1948
p. 29

First Study for *Painting in Five Panels*, 1955
graphite and ink on paper
3 × 9½ in, 7.6 × 24.1 cm
p. 110

Gate, 1959
painted aluminum
67 × 63 × 17 in, 170.2 × 160 × 43.2 cm
Walker Art Center, Minneapolis
Gift of Kate Butler Peterson
p. 150

Gate-Board, 1950
oil on wood with string
26¾ × 35¼ in, 67.9 × 89.5 cm
p. 55

Gauloise Blue with Red Curve, 1954
postcard collage
3¼ × 5½ in, 8.3 × 14 cm
p. 110

Gaza, 1956
oil on canvas, 4 joined panels
89¾ × 79 in, 228 × 200.7 cm
San Francisco Museum of Modern Art, the Doris
and Donald Fisher Collection at the San Francisco
Museum of Modern Art, and the Helen and Charles
Schwab Collection
p. 133

Gironde, 1951
oil and Ripolin on Masonite
45⅝ × 45⅝ in, 116 × 116 cm
p. 99

Gold with Orange Reliefs, 2013
oil on canvas and wood, 3 joined panels
79¼ × 72¾ in, 201.3 × 184.8 cm
Jo Carole and Ronald S. Lauder Collection.
Promised gift to The Museum of Modern Art,
New York
p. 311

Grain Elevator, Oradell, 1940
oil on canvas board
18 × 24 in, 45.7 × 61 cm
p. 13

Gray Panels, 1976
oil on canvas, 4 joined panels
69 × 180 in, 175.3 × 457.2 cm
Staatliche Museen zu Berlin, Nationalgalerie, Berlin
pp. 240–41

Green Black White, 2007
oil on canvas, 3 joined panels
80⅛ × 66 in, 203.5 × 167.6 cm
p. 288

Green Blue Black, 1963
acrylic on canvas
97 × 144 in, 246.4 × 365.8 cm
p. 161

Green Blue Black Red, 2007
oil on canvas, 4 panels
45 × 217 in, 114.3 × 551.2 cm
pp. 290–91

Green Blue Red, 1963
oil on canvas
67½ × 90 in, 171.5 × 228.6 cm
The Eli and Edythe L. Broad Collection
p. 154

Green Curves (from *Line, Form and Color*), 1951
collage on paper
7½ × 8 in, 19.1 × 20.3 cm
The Museum of Modern Art, New York. Gift of the
artist and purchased with funds provided by Jo
Carole and Ronald S. Lauder, Sarah-Ann and Werner
H. Kramarsky, Mr. & Mrs. James R. Hedges, IV,
Kathy and Richard S. Fuld, Jr. and Committee on
Drawings Funds
p. 44

Green Orange, 1970
oil on canvas, 2 joined panels
70 × 107 in, 177.8 × 271.8 cm
Carnegie Museum of Art, Pittsburgh, Gift of Charles
H. Carpenter, Jr. and The Henry L. Hillman Fund
p. 222

Green Orange Yellow, 2004
oil on canvas, 3 joined panels
86¼ × 65¾ in, 219.1 × 167 cm
Glenstone
p. 282

Green Panel (Ground Zero), 2011
painted aluminum
23⅝ × 50 × ½ in, 60 × 127 × 1.3 cm
Whitney Museum of American Art, New York.
Artist commission and gift of the artist
p. 296

Green Red, 1965
oil on canvas
90 × 90 in, 228.6 × 228.6 cm
p. 200

Green Red Yellow Blue, 1965
acrylic on canvas, 4 panels
76 × 255 in, 193 × 647.7 cm
p. 125

Green Relief over Blue, 2004
oil on canvas, 2 joined panels
80 × 74 × 2¾ in, 203.2 × 188 × 7 cm
p. 280

Green Rocker, 1968
painted aluminum
21 × 105 × 112 in, 53.3 × 266.7 × 284.5 cm
Walker Art Center, Minneapolis. Purchase with matching grant from Museum Purchase Plan, National Endowment for the Arts and Art Center Acquisition Fund
p. 177

Ground Zero, 2003
newsprint collage
8 × 12¾ in, 20.3 × 32.4 cm
Whitney Museum of American Art, New York. Gift of the artist and an anonymous donor, 2003
pp. 213, 348

Head with Beard, 1949
newspaper cutout
10¼ × 6¼ in, 26 × 15.9 cm
p. 30

Henry Geldzahler, 1983
graphite on paper
30 × 22 inches, 76.2 × 55.8 cm
p. 342

Horizontal Band (from *Line, Form and Color*), 1951
collage on paper
7½ × 8 in, 19.1 × 20.3 cm
The Museum of Modern Art, New York. Gift of the artist and purchased with funds provided by Jo Carole and Ronald S. Lauder, Sarah-Ann and Werner H. Kramarsky, Mr. & Mrs. James R. Hedges, IV, Kathy and Richard S. Fuld, Jr. and Committee on Drawings Funds
p. 44

Horizontal Curve I, 1996
bronze
13¾ × 240 × 1¼ in, 34.9 × 609.6 × 3.2 cm
p. 269

Horizontal Line (from *Line, Form and Color*), 1951
ink on paper
7½ × 8 in, 19.1 × 20.3 cm
The Museum of Modern Art, New York. Gift of the artist and purchased with funds provided by Jo Carole and Ronald S. Lauder, Sarah-Ann and Werner H. Kramarsky, Mr. & Mrs. James R. Hedges, IV, Kathy and Richard S. Fuld, Jr. and Committee on Drawings Funds, 2000
p. 43

Jack Shear, 1984
graphite on paper
30 × 22 in, 76.2 × 55.9 cm
p. 205

Jersey, 1958
oil on canvas
60 × 72½ in, 152.4 × 184.2 cm
p. 146

Karla–Red Violet and Molly–Orange
(study for Paul Taylor's *Lento*), 1968
graphite and gouache on paper
14 × 17 in, 35.6 × 43.2 cm
p. 120

Kilometer Marker, 1949
oil, gesso, and graphite on plywood
21½ × 18 × 1½ in, 54.6 × 45.7 × 3.8 cm
San Francisco Museum of Modern Art, the Doris and Donald Fisher Collection at the San Francisco Museum of Modern Art, the Helen and Charles Schwab Collection, and the Mimi Haas Collection
p. 51

Kite I, 1952
oil on canvas, 7 joined panels
39⅜ × 91⅝ in, 100 × 232.7 cm
p. 73

Kite II, 1952
oil on canvas, 11 joined panels
31½ × 110¼ in, 80 × 280 cm
Musée National d'Art Moderne, Centre Georges Pompidou, Paris
pp. 80–81

La Combe I, 1950
oil on canvas
38 × 63½ in, 96.5 × 161.3 cm
Whitney Museum of American Art, New York. Gift of the American Contemporary Art Foundation, Inc., Leonard A. Lauder, President
p. 61

La Combe II, 1951
oil on wood, folding screen of 9 hinged panels
39¼ × 44½ × 2⅝ in, 99.7 × 113 × 6.7 cm
p. 60

La Combe III, 1951
oil on linen
63½ × 44½ in, 161.3 × 113 cm
San Francisco Museum of Modern Art, the Doris and Donald Fisher Collection at the San Francisco Museum of Modern Art, and the Helen and Charles Schwab Collection
p. 322

La Combe IV—Collaboration with a 12-year-old Girl, 1951
oil on wood
39½ × 60⅜ in, 100.3 × 153.4 cm
p. 36

Lake II, 2002
oil on canvas
95 × 149⅜ in, 241.3 × 379.4 cm
Beyeler Collection, Basel, Switzerland. Acquisition and partial gift of the artist
p. 283

Loop, 1959
oil on canvas
68¼ × 70½ in, 173.4 × 179.1 cm
p. 147

Marilyn Monroe/Shadows, 1974
postcard collage
3½ × 5½ in, 8.9 × 14 cm
p. 115

Méditerranée, 1952
oil on wood, 9 joined panels, 3 in relief
59¼ × 76¼ × 2¾ in, 150 × 195 × 7 cm
Tate, London
p. 71

Meschers, 1951
oil on canvas
59 × 59 in, 149.9 × 149.9 cm
Collection Jo Carole and Ronald S. Lauder. Fractional and promised gift to The Museum of Modern Art, New York
p. 65

Neuilly, 1950
gesso on cardboard, plywood, and wood
23¼ × 31½ in, 59.1 × 80 cm
p. 96

North River, 1959
oil on canvas, 78 × 70 in, 198.1 × 177.8 cm
p. 118

November Painting, 1950
oil on wood
25½ × 34 in, 64.8 × 86.4 cm
p. 35

Oak, 1964
graphite on paper
28½ × 22½ in, 72.4 × 57.2 cm
p. 124

Orange, 1968
graphite on paper
29⅛ × 23⅛ in, 74 × 58.7 cm
The Metropolitan Museum of Art, New York. Gift of the artist in honor of William S. Lieberman, 1998
p. 13

Orange and Blue over Yellow (Orange et Bleu sur Jaune), 1964–65
lithograph on Rives BFK paper
23⅝ × 35⅝ in, 60 × 90.5 cm
p. 115

Orange Forms on Gold, 1962
collage
8½ × 7⅞ in, 21.6 × 20 cm
p. 89

Orange Red Relief, 1959
oil on canvas, 2 joined panels
60 × 60 × 3 in, 152.4 × 152.4 × 7.6 cm
The Solomon R. Guggenheim Museum, New York
p. 149

Orange Red Relief (for Delphine Seyrig), 1990
oil on canvas, 2 joined panels
120½ × 98½ × 2⅝ in, 305.4 × 250.2 × 6.7 cm
Museo Nacional Centro de Arte Reina Sofia
p. 259

Orange Relief with Blue, 2011
oil on canvas, 2 joined panels
70 × 62¼ × 2⅝ in, 177.8 × 158.1 × 6.7 cm
p. 302

Orange Relief with Green, 1991
oil on canvas, 2 joined panels
93½ × 84¾ × 2⅝ in, 237.5 × 215.3 × 6.7 cm
Tate, London. Presented by the American Fund for the Tate Gallery
p. 263

Original sketch for *Cité*, 1951
ink on paper
1⅞ × 2⅛ in, 4.8 × 5.4 cm
p. 37

Ormesson, 1950
oil on canvas, 3 joined panels
33 × 88¼ in, 83.8 × 224.2 cm
p. 64

Painting for a White Wall, 1952
oil on canvas, 5 joined panels
23½ × 71¼ in, 59.7 × 181 cm
Glenstone
pp. 82–83

Painting in Five Panels, 1955
oil on canvas, 5 panels
36 × 144 in, 91.4 × 365.8 cm
Whitney Museum of American Art, New York. Gift of Charles H. Carpenter, Jr.
pp. 134–35

Painting in Three Panels, 1956
oil on canvas, 3 panels
80 × 139 in, 203.2 × 353.1 cm
pp. 136–37

Pink and Orange (from *Line, Form and Color*), 1951
collage on paper
7½ × 8 in, 19.1 × 20.3 cm
The Museum of Modern Art, New York. Gift of the artist and purchased with funds provided by Jo Carole and Ronald S. Lauder, Sarah-Ann and Werner H. Kramarsky, Mr. & Mrs. James R. Hedges, IV, Kathy and Richard S. Fuld, Jr. and Committee on Drawings Funds
p. 192

Pink Rectangle, 1950
oil on canvas
21¾ × 18⅛ in, 55.2 × 46 cm
p. 98

Plant I, 1949
oil on canvas
14 × 11 in, 35.6 × 27.9 cm
Kröller-Müller Museum, Otterlo, Netherlands. Gift of G.J. Visser, 1987
p. 12

Plant II, 1949
oil on wood
16½ × 13 in, 41.9 × 33 cm
p. 49

Pony, 1959
painted aluminum
31 × 78 × 64 in, 78.7 × 198.1 × 162.6 cm
p. 148

Preliminary study for 1964 World's Fair sculpture *Two Curves: Blue Red*, 1963
cardboard
9 × 7¼ × 3¼ in, 22.9 × 18.4 × 8.3 cm
p. 121

Purple Panel, 1988
oil on canvas
111½ × 111½ in, 283.2 × 283.2 cm
p. 255

Purple Relief over Black, 2002
oil on canvas, 2 joined panels
80 × 77½ × 2⅝ in, 203.2 × 196.9 × 6/7 cm
p. 285

Rebound, 1959
oil on canvas
68¼ × 71½ in, 173.4 × 181.6 cm
p. 145

Red (from *Line, Form and Color*), 1951
collage on paper
7½ × 8 in, 19.1 × 20.3 cm
The Museum of Modern Art, New York. Gift of the artist and purchased with funds provided by Jo Carole and Ronald S. Lauder, Sarah-Ann and Werner H. Kramarsky, Mr. & Mrs. James R. Hedges, IV, Kathy and Richard S. Fuld, Jr. and Committee on Drawings Funds
p. 43

Red Blue, 1964
oil on canvas
90 × 66 in, 228.6 × 167.6 cm
Thomas H. Lee and Ann Tenenbaum Collection. Promised gift to Whitney Museum of American Art, New York
p. 164

Red Blue, 1962
oil on canvas
90 × 69½ in, 228.6 × 176.5 cm
Contemporary Collection of The Cleveland Museum of Art
p. 183

Red Blue Green, 1963
oil on canvas
83⅝ × 135⅞ in, 212.4 × 345.1 cm
Museum of Contemporary Art San Diego. Gift of Dr. and Mrs. Jack M. Farris
pp. 156–57

Red Curve, 1986
oil on canvas, 42⅛ × 205¾ in, 107 × 522.6 cm
pp. 248–49

Red Curve II, 1972
oil on canvas,
45 × 168 in, 114.3 × 426.7 cm
Stedelijk Museum, Amsterdam
p. 202

Red Curves, 1996
oil on canvas
142 × 65½ in, 360.7 × 166.4 cm
The Doris and Donald Fisher Collection at the San Francisco Museum of Modern Art
p. 266

Red Floor Panel, 1992
acrylic on canvas on wood
1 × 316½ × 478¾ in, 2.5 × 803.9 × 1216 cm
p. 203

Red Green Blue, 2002
oil on canvas, 3 joined panels
40 × 181 in, 101.6 × 459.7 cm
Katherine and Keith L. Sachs Collection. Promised gift to the Philadelphia Museum of Art
p. 274

Red Relief over White, 2012
oil on canvas, 2 joined panels
70 × 51¼ × 2⅝ in, 177.8 × 130.2 × 6.7 cm
p. 305

Red White, 2014
oil on canvas, 4 joined panels
70¼ × 70 in, 178.4 × 177.8 cm
p. 315

Red White Black Blue, 2014
oil on canvas, 4 joined panels
69½ × 27½ in, 176.5 × 69.9 cm
p. 314

Red with White Relief, 2002
oil on canvas, 2 joined panels
81 × 63 × 2⅝ in, 205.7 × 160 × 6.7 cm
p. 202

Red, Yellow, Blue (from *Line, Form and Color*), 1951
collage
7½ × 8 in, 19.1 × 20.3 cm
The Museum of Modern Art, New York. Gift of the artist and purchased with funds provided by Jo Carole and Ronald S. Lauder, Sarah-Ann and Werner H. Kramarsky, Mr. & Mrs. James R. Hedges, IV, Kathy and Richard S. Fuld, Jr. and Committee on Drawings Funds
p. 45

Red Yellow Blue I, 1963
acrylic on canvas, 3 joined panels
90 × 90 in, 228.6 × 228.6 cm
Fondation Maeght, Saint-Paul-de-Vence. Gift of Aimé and Marguerite Maeght
p. 163

Red Yellow Blue II, 1965
acrylic on canvas, 3 panels
82 × 189 in, 208.3 × 480.1 cm
Milwaukee Art Museum. Gift of Mrs. Harry Lynde Bradley
pp. 168–69

Red Yellow Blue White, 1952
dyed cotton, 25 panels in 5 parts
60 × 148 in, 152.4 × 375.9 cm
Philadelphia Museum of Art. Gift of the artist in honor of Anne d'Harnoncourt
pp. 74–75

Red Yellow Blue White and Black II, 1953
oil on canvas, 7 joined panels
39 × 138 in, 99 × 350.5 cm
Anstiss and Ronald Krueck Collection. Partial and promised gift to The Art Institute of Chicago
pp. 78–79

Relief with Blue, 1950
oil on wood
44⅞ × 17½ × 1¼ in, 114 × 44.5 × 3.2 cm
Collection Bettina and Donald L. Bryant, Jr. Fractional and promised gift to The Museum of Modern Art, New York in honor of Kirk Varnedoe
p. 58

River II, 2004
2 four-color lithographs on Rives BFK paper mounted on aluminum
80 × 109 in, 203.2 × 276.9 cm
p. 214

Rouleau Bleu, 1950
gesso on unstretched cotton
17½ × 117 in, 44.5 × 297 cm
p. 99

Saint Louis I, 1950
oil and gesso on wood
12½ × 27x 1 in, 31.8 × 68.6 × 2.5 cm
p. 14

Saint Louis II, 1950
oil on cardboard and wood
22 × 39¼ × 1 in, 55.9 × 99.7 × 2.5 cm
p. 97

Sculpture for a Large Wall, 1957
anodyzed aluminum, 104 panels
138 × 785 × 13 in, 3.5 × 19.9 × 0.3 m
The Museum of Modern Art, New York.
Gift of Jo Carole and Ronald S. Lauder
pp. 140–41

Seaweed/Mandorla, 1949
collage on paper
6¾ × 5⅛ in, 17.1 × 13 cm
p. 335

Seine, 1951
oil on wood
16½ × 45¼ in, 41.9 × 114.9 cm
Philadelphia Museum of Art. Purchase with funds in memory of Anne d'Harnoncourt and other Museum funds
p. 66

Self-Portrait, 1947
encaustic on Masonite
20⅛ × 16 in, 51.1 × 40.6 cm
p. 90

Self-Portrait with Bugle, 1947
oil on tar paper mounted on Masonite
65 × 24⅞ in, 165.1 × 63.2 cm
p. 20

Self-Portrait with Thorn, 1947
oil on Masonite
36 × 24 × 1½ in, 91.4 × 60.9 × 3.8 cm
San Francisco Museum of Modern Art.
Gift of the artist
p. 335

Series of Five Paintings, 1966
oil on canvas, 5 panels, each comprised of 2 joined panels, 70 × 140 in, 177.8 × 355.6 cm
Kröller-Müller Museum, Otterlo
p. 323

Shadows on Stairs, Villa La Combe, Meschers, 1950
gelatin silver print
p. 19

Sketches for paintings for a large wall (from sketchbook 15), 1951–52
ink on paper
7 × 5¼ in, 17.8 × 13.3 cm
p. 40

Sketches for white panels (from sketchbook 15), 1951–52
ink on paper
5⅜ × 7½ in, 13.7 × 19.1 cm
pp. 40, 95

Sketches from a train (Paris to Zurich) **(from sketchbook 21), 1953**
ink on paper
6½ × 4⅛ in, 16.5 × 10.5 cm
p. 42

Sluice Gates, 1947
ink on paper
12 × 18 in, 30.5 × 45.7 cm
p. 91

South Ferry, 1956
oil on canvas, 2 joined panels
44 × 38 in, 111.8 × 96.5 cm
p. 138

South of Bastogne (from sketchbook 1), 1944
graphite on paper
5¼ × 8¼ in, 13.3 × 21 cm
p. 18

Spectrum Colors Arranged by Chance, 1951–53
oil on canvas
60 × 60 in, 152.4 × 152.4 cm
San Francisco Museum of Modern Art, the Doris and Donald Fisher Collection at the San Francisco Museum of Modern Art, and the Helen and Charles Schwab Collection
p. 67

Spectrum Colors Arranged by Chance I, 1951
graphite and collage on paper
19½ × 39 in, 49.5 × 99.1 cm
Philadelphia Museum of Art. Purchased with funds contributed by C.K. Williams II (by exchange) 2007
p. 14

Spectrum I, 1953
oil on canvas
60¼ × 60¼ in, 153 × 153 cm
San Francisco Museum of Modern Art, the Doris and Donald Fisher Collection at the San Francisco Museum of Modern Art, and the Helen and Charles Schwab Collection
p. 87

Spectrum II, 1966–67
oil on canvas, 13 joined panels
80 × 273 in, 203.2 × 693.4 cm
Saint Louis Art Museum.
Funds given by the Shoenberg Foundation, Inc.
p. 125

Spectrum V, 1969
oil on canvas, 13 panels
84 × 588 in, 213.4 × 1493.5
The Metropolitan Museum of Art, New York.
Gift of the artist
pp. 180–81

Spectrum VIII, 2014
acrylic on canvas, 12 joined panels
250 × 230 in, 635 × 584.2 cm
Collection Fondation Louis Vuitton, Paris.
Artist commission
p. 14

Stele I, 1973
weathering steel
216 × 120 × 1 in, 548.6 × 304.8 × 2.5 cm
San Francisco Museum of Modern Art, the Doris and Donald Fisher Collection at the San Francisco Museum of Modern Art, and the Helen and Charles Schwab Collection
p. 233

Stele II, 1973
weathering steel
126 × 118⅛ × 1 in, 320 × 300 × 2.5 cm
National Gallery of Art, Washington, DC.
Gift of The Morris and Gwendolyn Cafritz Foundation
p. 235

Study for a sculpture, 1959
metal on paper
11 × 8½ in, 27.9 × 21.6 cm
p. 206

Study for a Yellow and White Sculpture for the Eiffel Tower, 1964
postcard collage
3⅜ × 5⅜ in, 8.6 × 13.7 cm
p. 115

Study for *Atlantic*, 1954
ink on paper
10½ × 15 in, 26.7 × 38.1 cm
p. 114

Study for *Blue White*, 1980
postcard collage
4 × 6 in, 10.2 × 15.3 cm
p. 116

Study for *Chatham XIII*, 1971
collage
7⅝ × 6⅞ in, 19.4 × 17.5 cm
p. 199

Study for *Colors for a Large Wall*, 1951
graphite and collage on paper
7⅞ × 7¾ in, 20 × 19.7 cm
p. 38

Study for *Curve I*, 1968
graphite on paper
10¾ × 14⅛ in, 27.3 × 35.9 cm
p. 203

Study for *Dallas Panels*, 1989
Polaroid collage
4 × 4 in, 10.2 × 10.2 cm
p. 209

Study for *Jersey*, 1957
collage on paper
7 × 8½ in, 17.8 × 21.6 cm
p. 110

Study for *Ormesson*, 1950
collage on paper
22 × 59 in, 55.9 × 149.9 cm
Collection Patricia and William Wilson III.
Fractional and promised gift to San Francisco Museum of Modern Art
p. 33

Study for *Red Yellow Blue White* (from sketchbook 18), 1952
ink on paper, 5¼ × 8¼ in, 13.3 × 21 cm
p. 40

Study for *Seine*, 1951
graphite and ink on paper
4¾ × 15⅞ in, 12.1 × 40.3 cm
Collection Joseph J. Rishel.
Promised Gift to the Philadelphia Museum of Art in memory of Anne d'Harnoncourt
p. 185

Study for *White Plaque: Bridge Arch and Reflection*, 1951
collage
20¼ × 14¼ in, 51.4 × 36.2 cm
The Museum of Modern Art, New York.
Gift of the artist in honor of Emily Rauh Pulitzer and Joseph Pulitzer, Jr.
p. 111

Study for *Window, Museum of Modern Art, Paris*, 1949
ink and graphite on paper
13¾ × 8½ in, 34.9 × 21.6 cm
p. 31

Sumac, 1959
oil on canvas
74 × 63 in, 188 × 160 cm
p. 184

Tableau Vert, 1952
oil on wood
29¼ × 39¼ in, 74.3 × 99.7 cm
The Art Institute of Chicago. Gift of the artist
p. 76

Tablet 34 (Five Sketches), 1950s, 1960s
ink on paper, 15½ × 21 in, 39.4 × 53.3 cm
The Menil Collection, Houston. Gift of Louisa S. Sarofim in honor of James A. Elkins, Jr.
pp. 188, 189

Tablet 94 (Three Sketches), 1960s
ink, graphite, printed papers
15½ × 21 in, 39.4 × 53.3 cm
The Menil Collection, Houston. Gift of Louisa S. Sarofim in honor of James A. Elkins, Jr.
p. 201

Tablet 191 (Three Sketches), 1960s
ink and graphite on paper
15½ × 21 in, 39.4 × 53.3 cm
The Menil Collection, Houston. Gift of Louisa S. Sarofim in honor of James A. Elkins, Jr.
p. 200

Talmont, 1951
oil on canvas
26 × 64¼ in, 66 × 163.2 cm
p. 98

Tennis Court, 1949
oil on canvas,
24 × 19½ in, 61 × 49.5 cm
p. 54

Three Grays, 1975
oil on canvas, 3 joined panels
108 × 108 in, 274.3 × 274.3 cm
p. 237

Three Panels: Orange, Dark Gray, Green, 1986
oil on canvas, 3 panels,
116 × 412½ in, 294.6 × 1047.8 cm
The Museum of Modern Art, New York.
Gift of Douglas S. Cramer Foundation
pp. 252–53

Toilette, 1949
oil on canvas with painted wood frame
24¾ × 18¾ × ½ in, 62.9 × 47.6 × 1.3 cm
p. 31

Totem (for Roy Lichtenstein), 1998
bronze
168 × 28 × 1¼ in, 426.7 × 71.1 × 3.2 cm
Collection Fondation Hubert Looser, Zurich
p. 208

Train Landscape, 1953
oil on canvas, 3 joined panels
44 × 44 in, 111.8 × 111.8 cm
p. 77

Tuileries, 1949
graphite on paper
7¾ × 9⅞ in, 19.7 × 25.1 cm
The Museum of Modern Art, New York.
Gift of the artist
p. 97

Two Curves, 2001
painted aluminum
91 × 452 × 328 in, 231.1 × 1148.1 × 833.1 cm
pp. 276–77

Two Curves, 2004
oil on canvas
82 × 77 in, 208.3 × 195.6 cm
p. 281

Two Curves: Blue Red, 1964
painted aluminum
216 × 216 × 96 in, 548.6 × 548.6 × 243.8
Harvard Art Museums. Commission by Philip Johnson for 1964 World's Fair and gift of the artist
p. 165

Untitled, 1987
bronze
104 × 79 × ¾ in, 264.2 × 200.7 × 1.9 cm
p. 254

Untitled, 1996
redwood
176½ × 25½ × 4½ in, 448.3 × 64.8 × 11.4 cm
p. 268

Untitled, 2004
painted stainless steel and aluminum
314 × 195½ × 78½ in, 797.6 × 496.6 × 199.4 cm
p. 287

Untitled, 2011
painted stainless steel
240 × 34¼ × 3½ in, 609.6 × 89.5 × 8.9 cm
p. 307

Untitled, 2013
painted stainless steel and aluminum
270 × 240 × 129 in, 685.8 × 609.6 × 327.7 cm
p. 313

Untitled, 2014
painted aluminum
178¼ × 600 × 162¼ in, 454 × 1524 × 412.1 cm
p. 317

Untitled (Abstraction), 1946
oil on Masonite
18 × 24 in, 45.7 × 61 cm
p. 19

Untitled (Mandorla), 1988
bronze
101 × 54 × 21½ in, 256.5 × 137.2 × 54.6 cm
San Francisco Museum of Modern Art, The Doris and Donald Fisher Collection at San Francisco Museum of Modern Art, and Helen and Charles Schwab Collection
p. 94

Untitled (Rocker), 1997
weathering steel
114 × 221 × 208 in, 289.6 × 561.3 × 528.3 cm
p. 270

Wall, rue Saint-Louis-en-l'Île, Paris, 1967
gelatin silver print
p. 14

White and Dark Gray Panels I, 1977
oil on canvas, 2 joined panels
106 × 144 in, 269.2 × 365.8 cm
Agnes Gund Collection
p. 245

White Black, 1970
oil on canvas, 2 joined panels
111 × 64 in, 281.9 × 162.6 cm
The Museum of Contemporary Art, Los Angeles.
Gift of Robert H. Halff
p. 218

White Black Red, 2004
oil on canvas, 3 joined panels
81⅜ × 40½ in, 206.7 × 102.9 cm
p. 279

White Curves, 2001
painted aluminum and stainless steel
234 × 131⅞ × 49½ in, 594.4 × 335 × 125.7 cm
Beyeler Collection, Basel, Switzerland
p. 271

White Plaque: Bridge Arch and Reflection, 1955
oil on wood, 2 panels separated by a wood strip
64 × 48 × ½ in, 162.6 × 121.9 × 1.3 cm
The Museum of Modern Art, New York. Promised gift of Emily Rauh Pulitzer; Vincent D'Aquila and Harry Soviak Bequest Fund, and Enid A. Haupt Fund
p. 131

White Relief, 1950
oil on wood
39⅜ × 27⅝ in, 100 × 70.2 cm
San Francisco Museum of Modern Art, the Doris and Donald Fisher Collection at the San Francisco Museum of Modern Art, and the Helen and Charles Schwab Collection
p. 59

White Relief over Black, 2002
oil on canvas, 2 joined panels
80 × 77½ × 2⅝ in, 203.2 × 196.9 × 6.7 cm
p. 278

White Relief over Black, 2012
oil on canvas, 2 joined panels
70 × 70 × 2⅝ in, 177.8 × 177.8 × 6.7 cm
p. 306

White Relief with Black, 2011
oil on canvas, 2 joined panels
54¼ × 90 × 2⅝ in, 137.8 × 228.6 × 6.7 cm
p. 303

White Relief with Black III, 1993
oil on canvas, 2 joined panels
120 × 98 × 2¾ in, 304.8 × 248.9 × 7 cm
Glenstone
p. 265

White Ring, 1963
painted aluminum
70 × 72 × ¼ in, 177.8 × 182.9 × 0.6 cm
p. 159

White Square, 1953
oil on wood
43¼ × 43¼ in, 109.9 × 109.9 cm
p. 85

White, Two Blacks, 1953
oil on canvas, 3 joined panels
23⅝ × 70¾ in, 60 × 179.7 cm
p. 101

Window I, 1949
oil and gesso on wood
25½ × 21 × 1½ in, 64.8 × 53.3 × 3.8 cm
San Francisco Museum of Modern Art, the Doris and Donald Fisher Collection at the San Francisco Museum of Modern Art, the Helen and Charles Schwab Collection, and the Mimi Haas Collection
p. 50

Window V, 1950
oil on wood
27½ × 7¼ in, 69.9 × 18.4 cm
p. 57

Window, Musée National d'Art Moderne, Avenue du Président Wilson, Paris, 1967
gelatin silver print
p. 32

Window, Museum of Modern Art, Paris, 1949
oil on wood and canvas, 2 joined panels
50½ × 19½ in, 128.3 × 49.5 cm
p. 53

Woman with Arm Raised, 1949
oil on canvas
33⅛ × 24 in, 84.1 × 61 cm
p. 93

Yellow Black and White, 1955
oil on canvas
72 × 59¼ in, 182.9 × 150.5 cm
p. 128

Yellow Blue Curve I, 1972
oil on canvas
100 × 100 in, 254 × 254 cm
p. 223

Yellow Curve, 1990
acrylic on canvas on wood
1 × 306 × 292 in, 2.5 × 777.2 × 741.7 cm
Glenstone
pp. 256–57

Yellow Piece, 1966
acrylic on canvas
75 × 75 in, 190.5 × 190.5 cm
The Museum of Modern Art, New York. Gift of the artist and The Riklis Collection of McCrory Corporation (both by exchange)
p. 175

Yellow Relief over Black, 2013
oil on canvas, 2 joined panels
40⅛ × 130 in, 101.9 × 330.2
pp. 308–09

Yellow Relief with Blue, 1991
oil on canvas, 2 joined panels
120 × 52 × 2⅝ in, 304.8 × 132.1 × 6.7 cm
p. 260

Yellow White, 1961
oil on canvas
84¼ × 55¾ in, 214 × 141.6 cm
Beyeler Collection, Basel, Switzerland
p. 153

Yellow with Red Triangle, 1973
oil on canvas, 2 joined panels
119 × 145½ in, 302.3 × 369.6 cm
National Gallery of Art, Washington, DC, Corcoran Collection. Museum Purchase with aid of funds from the Richard King Mellon Foundation
p. 229

Young Soldiers Being Transported to the Front, Remagen, Courtyard, Château de Divonne, France (from sketchbook 2), 1945
ink on paper
5¼ × 8 in, 13.3 × 20.3 cm
p. 18

Yve-Alain Bois, 1993
ink on paper
12 × 12 inches, 30.4 × 30.4 cm
p. 345

We would like to thank all those who gave their kind permission to reproduce the listed material. Every effort has been made to secure all reprint permissions prior to publication. However, in a small number of instances this has not been possible. The editors and publisher apologize for any inadvertent errors or omissions. If notified, the publisher will endeavour to correct these at the earliest opportunity.

All works by Kelly are © Ellsworth Kelly, 2015.

All photographs are courtesy Ellsworth Kelly Archives except where otherwise specified.

Collection Ellsworth Kelly. 94 (fig. 64), 95 (fig. 70); **Courtesy Albright-Knox Art Gallery:** 342 (fig. 191); **Courtesy Beyeler Collection:** 153; **Courtesy Blanton Museum of Art:** 212 (figs 147, 148), 327 (fig. 164); **Courtesy BlumHelman Gallery, New York:** 247; **Courtesy Carlson Arts LLC:** 210, 311; **Courtesy Carnegie Museum of Art:** 222; **Courtesy Corcoran Gallery of Art:** 229; **Courtesy David Zwirner Gallery, New York:** 142; **Courtesy Ellsworth Kelly Archives and MFA Boston:** 268; **Courtesy Fondation Beyeler, Basel:** 271; **Courtesy Fondation Louis Vuitton:** 14 (fig. 11), 320–21; **Courtesy Fondation Maeght, Saint-Paul-de-Vence:** 163; **Courtesy Gagosian Gallery, New York:** 243; **Courtesy Glenstone:** 82–83; **Courtesy Hood Museum of Art, Hanover, NH:** 298; **Courtesy Kröller-Müller Museum** 12 (fig. 3), 323; **Courtesy Marquand:** 115 (fig. 93), 119 (fig. 102), 214; **Courtesy Matthew Marks Gallery** 13 (fig. 5), 34 (fig. 40), 49, 64, 97 (fig. 75), 110 (figs 85, 86), 131, 140–41, 146, 154, 176, 178–79, 184 (fig. 116), 188, 189, 200 (fig. 128), 206 (fig. 138), 216 (fig. 154), 218, 221, 225, 228, 238, 240–41, 244, 245, 264, 266, 276–77, 287, 290–91, 296, 297, 299, 307, 317; **Courtesy Peabody Museum of Archaeology and Ethnology, Cambridge, MA:** 23 (fig. 28); **Courtesy Peggy Guggenheim Collection, Venice:** 12 (fig. 4); **Courtesy the artist:** 17, 31 (fig. 35), 33 (fig. 37), 90 (fig. 61); **Courtesy The Barnes Foundation, Philadelphia:** 350 (fig. 215); **Courtesy the lender:** 65, 139, 147, 242, 134–35; **Courtesy The New York Times:** 341 (fig. 190); **Courtesy Marion Goodman Gallery, Paris:** 300–01; **Courtesy Metropolitan Museum of Art:** 180–81, 235; **Courtesy Milwaukee Art Museum:** 168–69; **Courtesy MoMA, New York** 43 (figs 54, 55), 44 (figs 56, 57); **Courtesy Musée National d'Art Moderne, Paris:** 80–81; **Courtesy Museum Wiesbaden:** 130; **Courtesy Peter Freeman, Inc., New York:** 164; **Courtesy Philadelphia Museum of Art:** 54, 203 (fig. 134), 74–75; **Courtesy President and Fellows of Harvard College:** 165, 236; **Courtesy SFMOMA:** 59, 63, 87, 143, 323, 335 (fig. 170); **Courtesy Stedelijk Museum, Amsterdam:** 160, 202 (fig. 132); **Courtesy Tate:** 71, 144, 263; **Courtesy The Art Institute of Chicago:** 76, 77, 78–79, 152; **Courtesy The Art Institute of Chicago. Helen Birch Bartlett Memorial Collection © 2015. The Art Institute of Chicago/Art Resource/Scala, Florence:** 97 (fig. 76); **Courtesy The Solomon R. Guggenheim Museum, New York:** 149, 170–71, 259, 267, 346 (fig. 205); **Courtesy Walker Art Center:** 150, 177; **Courtesy Walker Art Center and the lender:** 148; **Courtesy Whitney Museum of American Art:** 61, 213 (fig. 149); **Detroit Institute of Arts, USA. Gift of Robert H. Tannahill © 2015. Bridgeman/DACS, London:** 91 (fig. 62); **Gemäldegalerie–Staatliche Museen zu Berlin. Courtesy BPK images:** 90 (fig. 60); **Kröller-Müller Museum, Otterlo, Netherlands © 2014 Bruce Nauman/Artists Rights Society (ARS), New York and DACS, London:** 112; **Louvre Museum, Paris © 2015. White images/Scala, Florence:** 30 (fig. 31); **Musée d'Orsay, Paris. Acquired with the participation of M. Philipe Meyer, through the intermediary of the Fondation Lutèce, 1985 © RMN-Grand Palais (Musée d'Orsay)/Hervé Lewandowski:** 193; **Musée Marmottan Monet, Paris. Courtesy Bridgeman images:** 190 (fig. 122); **© Museum Associates/LACMA:** 167, 230–31; **Museum of Fine Arts, Boston. Charles Potter Kling Fund (39.536):** 22 (fig. 24); **Museum of Fine Arts, Boston. Maria Antoinette Evans Fund (21.1285):** 23 (fig. 26); **Museum of Fine Arts, Boston. Special Fund for the Purchase of Paintings (11.3035):** 22 (fig. 25); **Museum of Fine Arts, Boston. Tompkins Collection–Arthur Gordon Tompkins Fund (24.6):** 21 (fig. 23); **Museum of Fine Arts, Boston. Tompkins Collection–Arthur Gordon Tompkins Fund (RES 32.14) © Succession H. Matisse/DACS, 2015:** 21 (fig. 22); **Museum of Insel Hombroich, Neuss-Holzheim, Germany © DACS, London 2015;** 34 (fig. 38); **Museé Unterlinden, Colmar, France © 2015 Scala, Florence:** 39 (fig. 46); **National Gallery of Art, Washington DC. Andrew W. Mellon Collection (1937.1.44):** 18 (fig. 16); **Private collection © 2015 Morgan Art Foundation Ltd./Artists Rights Society (ARS), New York, DACS, London:** 117 (fig. 98); **Private Collection © 2015 White Images/Scala, Florence:** 92 (fig. 65); **Private Collection © DACS, London 2015:** 96 (fig. 72); **© Succession Picasso/ DACS, London 2015:** 93 (fig. 66); **The Huntington Library, Art Collections and Botanical Gardens, San Merino, CA:** 11 (fig. 2); **The Minneapolis Institute of Arts. The William Hood Dunwoody Fund (49.9). Courtesy Bridgeman Images:** 13 (fig. 6); **The Museum of Modern Art, New York, Fractional gift of Mr. and Mrs. David Rockefeller (69.1991) © 2015. Digital image, The Museum of Modern Art, New York/Scala, Florence:** 190 (fig. 121); **The Museum of Modern Art, Given anonymously (153.1934) © 2014 Artists Rights Society (ARS), New York/ ADAGP, Paris:** 207 (fig. 141); **The Museum of Modern Art, New York. Given anonymously (by exchange) (6.1942.a-c) © 2014 Artists Rights Society (ARS), New York/VG Bild-Kunst, Bonn:** 39 (fig. 46); **The Museum of Modern Art, New York, Nelson A. Rockefeller Bequest, 973.1979 © 2015 Succession Picasso/Artist Rights Society (ARS), New York/ DACS, London:** 31 (fig. 33).

Photographer credits

© David Allison: 213 (fig. 149); **© Ronald Amstutz:** 31 (fig. 34), 36 (fig. 43), 38 (fig. 45), 73, 77 (fig. 77), 92 (fig. 64), 93 (fig. 67), 98 (fig. 77), 227, 242, 296, 313; **© Jörg P. Anders:** 90 (fig. 60); **© Oliver Baker:** 182, 183; **© Ben Blackwell:** 250; **© Niggi Breuning:** 271; **© Emeril Bronson:** 336 (fig. 175); **© Joseph Coscia:** 235; **© Joseph Coscia, Metropolitan Museum of Art, New York:** 208 (fig. 142); **© Louise Dahl-Wolfe:** 108 (fig. 84); **© Marc Domage:** 320–21; **© Katherine Du Tiel:** 59, 87, 322 (fig. 155), 335 (fig. 170); **© Sidney Felsen:** 344 (fig. 198); **© Sante Forlano:** 216 (fig. 153), 336 (fig. 174); **© Marjon Gemmeke, Arnhem:** 112; **© Helga Gilbert:** 119 (fig. 100); **© Stéphan Gladieu:** 14 (fig. 11); **© Gianfranco Gorgoni:** 199 (fig. 126), 189 (fig. 341); **© Glenn Halvorson:** 148, 177; **© David Heald:** 12 (fig. 4), 133, 267, 268; **© Ellsworth Kelly** 14 (fig. 9), 19 (fig. 19), 32, 33 (fig. 38), 199 (fig. 125), 336 (fig. 173); **© Chuck Kennedy, White House Photo Office:** 351 (fig. 218); **© Natalja Kent:** 165, 236; **© Hulya Kolabas:** 53, 58, 67, 72, 84, 85, 100 (fig. 82) 147, 155, 234, 305, 306; **© Museum Associates/ LACMA:** 167, 230–31; **© Robert Laprelle:** 166; **© James Lattanzio:** 215 (fig. 152); **Marcus Leith © Tate:** 71, 144, 263; **© Jack Mitchell:** 204 (fig. 136); **© Hans Namuth:** 117 (fig. 97), 338 (fig. 181), 339 (fig. 18); **© Bill Orcutt:** 64; **© Douglas M. Parker:** 268; **© Richard Payne, FAIA:** 209 (fig. 143); **© Lyle Peterzell:** 327 (fig. 163); **© Robert Pettus:** 275; **© Eric Politzer:** 221, 245; **© Sally Ritts:** 149; **© Stephen Rosenthal:** 326 (fig. 161), 326 (fig. 162), 347 (fig. 207); **© Onni Saari:** 111 (fig. 89), 337 (fig. 177); **© Katrin Schilling, Frankfurt, Germany:** 256–57; **© Jack Shear:** 207 (fig. 140), 304, 344 (fig. 197); 347 (fig. 208), 348 (fig. 210), 349 (fig. 212), 349 (fig. 213), 349 (fig. 214); **© Oren Slor:** 188 (fig. 119), 189 (fig. 120), 200 (fig. 128), 201 (fig. 130); **© Jerry L. Thompson:** 13 (fig. 7), 19 (fig. 20), 20 (fig. 21), 23 (fig. 27), 35 (fig. 41), 49, 50, 51, 55, 57, 60, 66, 90 (fig. 61), 96 (fig. 73), 99 (fig. 80), 100 (fig. 81), 128, 129, 132, 136–37, 139, 145, 151, 159, 161, 173, 175, 219, 233, 237, 239, 246, 248–49, 251, 252–53, 254, 255, 260, 261, 265, 269, 272–73, 274, 278, 279, 280, 281, 282, 283, 285, 288, 289, 292–93, 294, 295, 302, 303, 308–09, 311, 313, 314, 315, 317, 319; **© Joshua White:** 299; **© Lawrence Williams:** 122 (fig. 108); **© Graydon Wood:** 54, 74–75, 97.

Index

Page numbers in italics indicate illustrations

Although numerous solo exhibition catalogues have been published on Ellsworth Kelly, this book is the first major monograph devoted to the artist in almost forty-five years. Capturing the life and career of such a significant and prolific artist as Kelly has thus been an enormous undertaking on the part of many dedicated people.

First and foremost, my profound gratitude goes to Ellsworth Kelly for his generosity, patience, and willingness to share his thoughts and recollections of his extraordinary career. I consider myself incredibly fortunate to have been the beneficiary of such firsthand narratives and in turn, to be able to call him a friend. Furthermore, his careful and methodical selection of works illustrated in the plate sections is a real contribution and a great aid to understanding his art.

Next, I am deeply indebted to all at the Ellsworth Kelly Studio: Jack Shear, Eva Huber Walters, Mary Anne Lee, Nick Walters, Joseph Yetto, Frank Appio, Tierney Risley, and Marilee Sousie. Shear's support has been crucial, stemming back to 1998 when he first suggested that I write my dissertation on Kelly's New York years, a topic then not addressed in the literature. His advice over the years, as well as on this book, warrants a bounty of thanks. Eva Walters contributed substantially to the book through her attention to every detail, her exacting and thorough research materials, and her prompt replies to my queries and to those of the other writers.

Sincere thanks must be extended to Matthew Marks Gallery. Matthew Marks and Jacqueline Tran provided essential counsel and pivotal support while Craig Garrett's thoughtful editorial expertise played an important role. The staff at Phaidon must, of course, be thanked, especially Senior Editor Rebecca Morrill, who provided astute guidance as well as very patient care and attention; Deborah Aaronson, Vice President, Group Publisher; former Commissioning Editor Jacky Klein; and Debra and Leon Black.

Of course, Gavin Delahunty, Gary Garrels, Richard Shiff, and Robert Storr must be acknowledged greatly for their insightful and original essays, contributions that add significant depth and distinctive art historical voices to the publication.

I am grateful to the book's designers Anna Rieger and Adam Michaels, for their hard work from conception to completion of the design, and to Sue Medlicott and Nerissa Vales, The Production Department, for working so closely with the Kelly studio to ensure all the artworks are reproduced in print with the utmost faithfulness to the originals.

I must also acknowledge those who provided both professional and personal support, from the dissertation to this book: Preston Bautista, Brent R. Benjamin, Yve-Alain Bois, Janet Choi, Kate Early, Charlotte Eyerman, Gary Garrels, Fredric Gilde, Claire Gilman, Jodi Hauptman, Cheri Hoffman, Libby Hruska, Barbara Helfgott Hyett, Jennifer Jones, Peter R. Kalb, Lynda Klich, James Kolker, Pilar Korgel, Robert S. Lubar, Sanda M. Lwin, Diana Murphy, Linda Nochlin, Thomas B. Parker, Emily Rauh Pulitzer, Alexandra Schwartz, Mark Sheinkman, Vicki Singer, Caroline Steimle, SaraJane Steinberg, Christopher Stone, Charles L. Venable, Andrew J. Walker, and Edward Yim.

Special thanks go to my two assistants on this book, Molly Moog for her swift and precise research, and Nathan Stobaugh for his thorough and committed work on the chronology. I would also like to thank colleagues who generously answered my research queries on various topics: Ian Alteveer, Lisa Çakmak, Amy Clark, Samantha Friedman, Emily Hamilton, Simon Kelly, Matthew Robb, Richard Townsend, and Jill Ahlberg Yohe. Also, this book would never have been possible if not for Nan Rosenthal, who introduced me to the artist almost twenty years ago and was such a wise and selfless mentor.

Singular and abundant gratitude will always be given to my parents, Hisuh and Jesun Paik, and sister, Felicia Paik Kim, for their unlimited and unwavering support, as well as to the memory of my grandfather, Seung Mann Park.

And once again, I extend a final and heartfelt thanks to Ellsworth Kelly, who, through his art and his words, has taught me how to truly see, as he did many years ago for his lucky students in Paris. It is my hope that this book will allow others to learn from his lessons in looking, to understand what he meant when he said in 1996, "What I've tried to capture is the reality of flux, to keep art an open, incomplete situation, to get at the rapture of seeing."

Tricia Y. Paik

Phaidon Press Limited
Regent's Wharf
All Saints Street
London, N1 9PA

Phaidon Press Inc.
65 Bleecker Street
New York, NY 10012

www.phaidon.com

First published 2015
© 2015 Phaidon Press Limited

ISBN 978 0 7148 6947 6

A CIP catalogue record for this book
is available from the Library of Congress
and the British Library

All rights reserved. No part of this publication may be reproduced, stored in a retrieval system or transmitted, in any form or by any means, electronic, mechanical, photocopying, recording or otherwise, without the written permission of Phaidon Press Limited.

Editor: Rebecca Morrill
Production Controllers: Sue Medlicott and Nerissa Vales, The Production Department
Design: Project Projects

Printed in China

Author Biographies

Tricia Y. Paik is Curator of Contemporary Art at the Indianapolis Museum of Art. She has written about Ellsworth Kelly for publications including *Ellsworth Kelly at Ninety* (Matthew Marks Gallery, New York, 2013) and *Drawing in the 21st Century: The Politics and Poetics of Contemporary Practice* (Ashgate Publishing, London, 2015).

Robert Storr is an artist, curator and critic, and Professor of Painting and Dean of the School of Art at Yale University. He has contributed to numerous books on Ellsworth Kelly and featured the artist's work in his 52nd Venice Biennale, "Think with the Senses, Feel with the Mind: Art in the Present Tense."

Gavin Delahunty is Hoffman Family Senior Curator of Contemporary Art at The Dallas Museum of Art. In 2009 he curated "Ellsworth Kelly Drawings 1954–1962" at the Middlesbrough Institute of Modern Art (mima), UK, which traveled to Dublin City Gallery, The Hugh Lane, in 2010.

Richard Shiff is Effie Marie Cain Regents Chair in Art at The University of Texas at Austin, where he directs the Center for the Study of Modernism. His books include *Ellsworth Kelly: New York Drawings 1954–1962* (Matthew Marks Gallery and Prestel, New York and Munich, 2014).

Gary Garrels is Elise S. Haas Senior Curator of Painting and Sculpture at the San Francisco Museum of Modern Art, where he organized a special survey of paintings to mark the artist's ninetieth birthday and, working closely with Kelly, curated four large galleries dedicated to the artist's work in SFMOMA's new building.